Contents

List of Illustrations

Plates

Medieval Maritime Warfare

Charles D. Stanton

Pen & Sword
MARITIME

First published in Great Britain in 2015
and reprinted in 2020 by
PEN & SWORD MARITIME
An imprint of
Pen & Sword Books Ltd
47 Church Street
Barnsley
South Yorkshire
S70 2AS

ISBN 978-1-52678-219-9

A CIP catalogue record for this book is available from the British Library.

Typeset by Concept, Huddersfield, West Yorkshire, HD4 5JL.
Printed and bound in England by CPI Group (UK) Ltd, Croydon CR0 4YY.

FSC www.fsc.org MIX Paper from responsible sources FSC® C013604

Pen & Sword Books Ltd incorporates the imprints of Pen & Sword Archaeology, Atlas, Aviation, Battleground, Discovery, Family History, History, Maritime, Military, Naval, Politics, Railways, Select, Social History, Transport, True Crime, and Claymore Press, Frontline Books, Leo Cooper, Praetorian Press, Remember When, Seaforth Publishing and Wharncliffe.

For a complete list of Pen & Sword titles please contact
PEN & SWORD BOOKS LIMITED
47 Church Street, Barnsley, South Yorkshire, S70 2AS, England
E-mail: enquiries@pen-and-sword.co.uk
Website: www.pen-and-sword.co.uk

Figures

Maps

Preface

When Rupert Harding, my editor at Pen & Sword Books, first approached me with an idea for a book recounting medieval 'sea battles', I must admit I was a bit intimidated by the vast scope of the project. Maritime warfare is a fascinating and crucial aspect of medieval military history which has yet to be covered in any comprehensive manner, but, in order to give it the proper perspective, the book needed to embrace a time frame from the fall of the Roman Empire to the dawn of the Renaissance (roughly a millennium) and extend geographically from the northern Baltic to the eastern Mediterranean – a daunting task to say the least. That said, I found inspiration, as I have done so often in the past, from my long-time mentor at Cambridge, David Abulafia, whose *The Great Sea: A Human History of the Mediterranean* accomplished an even more prodigious feat in magisterial fashion. I possess neither his perspicacity nor his deftness at prose, but his example convinced me that it was, at least, possible. What follows is my best effort. Accordingly, I have composed a two-part tome with ten chapters, each addressing a readily identifiable conflict in which war at sea was a major component, from around 500 AD (when the Eastern Empire under Justinian began to recover control of the Mediterranean) to 1500 (about the time that the introduction of gunpowder and the cannon fundamentally altered naval combat). Part I contains six conflicts which occurred in the Mediterranean and Black Seas during the period, while Part II deals with four struggles at sea which took place in the English Channel, the Baltic Sea and the North Sea. Appended to each chapter is an in-depth description of an engagement or encounter representative of the contest under discussion. For the sake of context and accessibility, a chronological narrative was employed throughout. While the work was designed as a historical survey for general public consumption, budding scholars and those interested in delving deeper should find the documentation an adequate starting point. Reference to the endnotes is, however, unnecessary for casual readers. All essential factual information is contained in the body of the work. I have also maintained a strong bias towards translated source materials wherever possible, again in the interests of accessibility. In keeping with that theme, the included illustrations were specifically selected to provide the reader with a visual context for many of the maritime concepts presented in the work. The battle scene from the thirteenth-century Vegetius manuscript (Ms Marlay Add I, fol. 86r), depicted on the cover of the book, is particularly emblematic of that effort. Permission to use it was graciously granted by the Fitzwilliam Museum of Cambridge. A special thanks is owed to the great John Pryor, whose groundbreaking work in the maritime history of the medieval Mediterranean I have long admired. The reproduction of his unparalleled drawing of a tenth-century *dromōn* in this book is due to his intellectual generosity. Finally, I must offer heartfelt gratitude to Rupert for suggesting the project in the first place and having the confidence in me to carry it out. And, of course, I would be reprehensively remiss if I did not express indebtedness to my lovely bride Kristy, who provided invaluable technical assistance (not to mention moral support) and turned my masses of squiggly lines into legible maps and line drawings.

Charles Stanton
July 2014

DEDICATION

For my father
Lt. Col. Charles R. Stanton USAF
Tuskegee Airman and Decorated Veteran of
WWII, Korean War, Vietnam

'Master of his Fate, Captain of his Soul.'

Introduction

The Nature of Medieval Maritime Warfare

Western Seas post-*Pax Romana*

When the fleet of Gaius Julius Caesar Augustus (Octavius) crushed that of Cleopatra VII Philopator of Egypt (Cleopatra) and Marcus Antonius (Mark Antony) off a promontory of Epirus called Actium on 2 September 31 BC, the Mediterranean became a Roman lake.[1] The shores which rimmed it were now Roman almost without exception. For the first time, Rome was without major opposition on the Middle Sea. The scourge of piracy had largely been quelled a few decades earlier in 67 BC when Gnaeus Pompeius Magnus (Pompey the Great), backed by the entirety of the Republic's military might, cleared both the Mediterranean and the Black Sea of corsairs in the course of a brilliant three-month campaign.[2] The Mediterranean, the heart of the 'known world', had become the *mare nostrum* ('our sea') of Rome and the *Pax Augustus* (or, as it would later come to be called, the *Pax Romana*) had been established. It would prevail for more than 200 years.[3] Rome maintained fleets at Misenum (near Naples) on the Tyrrhenian and at Ravenna on the Adriatic essentially to keep piracy in check and the sea lanes open, especially for grain shipments from Sicily and Egypt.[4] After Actium there would not be another major naval encounter until 324 AD, when Constantine's 200 *triacontors* (thirty-oared war galleys) and *pentecontors* (fifty-oared warships) prevailed over the 350 triremes (galleys with three files of oarsmen per side) of Valerius Licinianus (Licinius) in the Dardanelles.[5]

As Rome's power waned amid the Germanic invasions of the fifth century, so too its control of the seas receded. The shipyards at Misenum and Ravenna fell into disrepair and the notion of a standing navy became, like the *Pax Romana*, a distant memory. Rome's dominance of the sea had ended long before Odoacer (a German general) snuffed out the last vestiges of imperial authority in 476.[6] And there was no great naval entity to take its place. Without an overarching power to maintain stability, the sea lanes became no safer than Rome's unguarded roads. Piracy, never fully vanquished, returned with a vengeance. The Vandals, an east Germanic people, crossed the Pyrenees in the early fifth century and migrated down the Iberian peninsula to Andalusia, from where they crossed to North Africa. Once there, they advanced eastwards, capturing Carthage in 439. Under their king, Gaiseric, they built a formidable fleet and established a virtual pirate kingdom centred on Carthage, an ancient Phoenician city-state and former maritime power which ironically had once vied with Rome for control of the central Mediterranean (i.e., the three Punic Wars). Numbering 120 warships, their fleet enabled the Vandals eventually to hold sway over Sardinia, Corsica and the Balearics while raiding as far east as Illyria and the Peloponnesos. In 455 Gaiseric even sailed the Vandal fleet up the Tiber and ravaged Rome itself.[7] The Mediterranean was no longer the *mare nostrum* of the 'Eternal City'.

Rome's maritime fortunes suffered a similar reversal in the northern seas at the hands of barbarian pirates. Roman historian Ammianus Marcellinus described a '*barbarica conspiratio*' in which an alliance of Attacotti, Franks, Picts, Scots and Saxons collaborated against Roman rule in Britain in 367. According to John Haywood, an expert on early Anglo-Saxon seafaring, this 'barbarian conspiracy' presaged a scourge of Saxon piracy which plagued both sides of the English Channel in the late fourth century.[8] The raiding became so intense that the string of Roman coastal fortifications along the Channel became known as the *Litus Saxonicum* ('Saxon Shore'). Some modern historians have even referred to this period, which lasted for nearly two centuries, as 'the first Viking Age'. Indeed, Haywood flatly asserts that the Romans 'had effectively lost control of the seas to the Saxons and other pirates by the end of the fourth century'.[9]

To be sure, commerce continued on the waves of the western seas, despite the dangers. Syrian, Coptic, Jewish and Greek merchants persisted in plying their trade in the Mediterranean,[10] while Celts, Franks and Saxons engaged in cabotage commerce along the coasts of Britain, Ireland, Frisia and Brittany.[11] In a world of bandit-besieged byways and great disorder, the sea was increasingly the stage upon which the human struggle of western civilization was played out. The violent competition among the various so-called barbarian tribes to fill the void left by Rome's fall regularly spilled out over its shores and onto its waters. It was the medium upon which commerce was carried and power was projected. And frequently the two activities merged, practised by the same players on the same vessels. Merchants often became combatants and sometimes even corsairs, while merchantmen became men-of-war.[12] Such was the setting from which stemmed medieval maritime warfare.

Maritime Technology

Nautical architecture and navigation remained rudimentary, having hardly changed since classical times. Maritime technology evolved only gradually throughout the medieval era. A Roman mariner of the fourth century would have noticed only a few subtle advancements in the ships of the tenth century. Climatic and cultural variations between northern and southern Europe caused ship construction to develop differently in the two regions, but at the outset of the Middle Ages many parallels persisted. Warships were almost all galley-type vessels characterized by a high length-to-width ratio (as much as 10:1) and a minimal keel, producing a shallow draught and a low freeboard. Propulsion was principally provided by oars, augmented on occasion with one or two sails, while side-mounted steering oars supplied directional control.[13]

A probable prototype was the Roman *liburnian*. Adopted from the Liburni pirates of the Illyrian coast in the first century BC, it became the mainstay of the Roman fleet throughout the Imperial period, according to the late fourth-century Roman strategist Publius Flavius Vegetius Renatus (Vegetius).[14] Measuring just under 20m (about 65ft) in length and a little under 4m (around 13ft) in breadth, it was propelled by fifty oars, a large square sail and a small artemon foresail. Relatively nimble, it could manage about 7 knots in a sprint, but probably averaged less than 3 knots.[15] **(Pl. 1)** It was almost certainly the forerunner of the fifty-oared Byzantine *dromōn* of the sixth century which would eventually evolve into the model for nearly all Mediterranean war galleys until the late eleventh century.[16]

While there is scant evidence that northern shipwrights copied Roman models, the *liburnian*, nonetheless, may even have had some influence on the early warships of northern Europe. Having been used on the Rhine and in the English Channel during the first and second centuries, they appear to have shared some common characteristics with later ships of the Angles and Saxons. The five Roman wrecks from the late fourth century discovered on the Rhine at Mainz seem even more similar. The *naves lusoriae*, as they were called, were light river galleys about 18.3m (60ft) long and nearly 3m (about 10ft) broad, propelled by thirty rowers and a single sail.[17] A representative reconstruction of a *navis lusoria* is currently on display in the *Museum für Antike Schiffahrt* (Museum of Ancient Seafaring) in Mainz. Correspondingly, the fourth-century oak ship (probably Anglian) found at Nydam Moss in Denmark was about 21.3m (70ft) long with 3.6m (12ft) of beam, manned by around thirty oarsmen. And the early seventh-century Sutton Hoo ship of an Anglo-Saxon king unearthed near Woodbridge in Suffolk was 27.13m (89ft) long by 4.27m (14ft) wide with a crew of twenty-eight oarsmen.[18] The narrow, shallow-draught hulls and low freeboards of all these vessels rendered them easily swamped and thus susceptible to the vagaries of weather – particularly in northern climes.

Navigation remained equally primitive. It was primarily celestial and coastal. The compass had not yet been invented and usable maritime charts did not exist in the early Middle Ages. Steering was limited by what could be seen from the deck or mast of a ship. Hence, most vessels sailed within sight of land as much as possible, which meant evading such attendant hazards to maritime traffic as shoals, rocks and reefs. Visibility, therefore, was of paramount concern. This, of course, meant that mariners were, again, at the mercy of the elements. Accordingly, Vegetius devoted four of his six chapters on nautical navigation in the *Epitoma Rei Militaris*, his fourth-century manual of military operations and strategy, to such meteorological phenomena as wind, rain and storms, because 'under their attack the seas, which are naturally tranquil and quiet, rage with boiling waves'. And he insisted that the seas should be scrupulously avoided during the winter months due to 'minimal daylight and long nights, dense cloud-cover, foggy air and violence of winds doubled by rain and snow'.[19] Thus, galley fleets generally got under way only during daylight hours and almost exclusively during the spring and summer months. Even so, contemporary accounts are rife with reports of fleets decimated by tempests.

When conditions permitted vessels to venture out of port, they did so at a snail's pace. Although galleys usually possessed at least one sail, their shallow keels and low freeboard normally prevented its use unless there was a light, following wind. John Guilmartin, an expert on late medieval warships, estimates that '[a] galley could maintain its maximum speed under oars of some 7 knots for no more than twenty minutes and the best sustained speed which it could manage was only about 3 knots or a little more'.[20] In fact, after studying the accounts of dozens of ancient and medieval voyages, maritime scholar Lionel Casson concluded that 'with unfavourable or very light winds, a fleet usually could do no better than 1 to 1½ knots'.[21] These agonizingly slow speeds, combined with limited visibility (probably less than 20km or around 12 miles from a masthead), made interdiction at sea unlikely,[22] prompting Guilmartin to declare the notion of maintaining naval superiority through control of the sea lanes espoused by the great nineteenth-century naval strategist Alfred Thayer Mahan[23] a 'fallacy' in the era of oared vessels.[24] The technology of the time simply would not permit it.

Crew Conditions

Crew conditions fluctuated from merely onerous to utterly appalling. Even under the best of circumstances, rowing was gruelling work, particularly in the Mediterranean where temperatures during the prime sailing season, the summer months, hovered around 35 degrees centigrade (95 degrees Fahrenheit). Much has been learned of the challenges facing galley crews from the sea trials of the *Olympias*, an authentic replica of an Athenian trireme constructed by the Hellenic Navy in 1987. **(Pl. 2)** Dehydration was, by far and away, the most serious danger. Appended to that was the menace of foul air brought on by the lack of ventilation below decks. Reeking with the stench of sweat and urine, this fetid and claustrophobic environment was probably as much of a deleterious factor as the suffocating heat and enervating exertion. It was found that galley crews required enormous quantities of water to function: at least one litre per hour per oarsman.[25] Accordingly, every man could be expected to consume eight litres a day at a minimum, meaning that the standard crew complement of a tenth-century *dromōn*, 108 oarsmen plus officers and marines, needed no less than a metric tonne of water per day.[26]

The standard sustenance for galley crews offered them scant compensation for their labours. It consisted primarily of ship's biscuit.[27] This desiccated concoction of wheat grain, called *panis biscotti* ('twice-baked bread') by the Venetians, had to be ground up with water or some other liquid into a sludge-like stew in order to be rendered palatable.[28] Marino Sanudo Torsello, the fourteenth-century Venetian nobleman who penned a comprehensive plan for the recovery of the Holy Land called the *Liber Secretorum Fidelium Crucis* ('Book of the Secrets of the Faithful of the Cross'), specified that each galley crewman should receive 1.5 pounds (680 grams) of biscuit per day as his basic food ration. He also stipulated that every man should be allocated 1 ounce (28 grams) of cheese per day as well as about 1.6 ounces (45 grams) of salt pork and around 3.5 ounces (100 grams) of beans or 'any other vegetable' (probably dried).[29] And, of course, all these foodstuffs had to be consumed with ample quantities of water.

Water was, thus, the fuel upon which all galley fleets operated. Yet limited cargo space restricted onboard reserves of water to a mere four-days' worth.[30] Constant replenishment was required. Consequently, it was this perpetual prerequisite for mammoth amounts of water which dictated the operating limitations of galley fleets throughout the medieval era. Galley crews had to have ready access to friendly or at least neutral shores in order to obtain the needed water supplies along with victuals, shelter from storms and, of course, the occasional rest from exhausting labour. While under way, oarsmen ate and slept on the rowing benches, rising only occasionally to relieve themselves. Accordingly, galley fleets had to put into shore almost daily. This is why John Pryor, a leading authority on galley warfare, contends, 'Control of the land meant control of the sea, because control of the land carried with it both control of the refuges to which all galley fleets had to have recourse in inclement weather and also control of the water supplies, without which no naval forces could operate for more than a few days.'[31] In other words, whosoever controlled the shorelines also controlled the seas.

Battle Tactics

The low state of medieval maritime technology ensured that battle tactics were just as basic. They had hardly progressed since Roman times. Confrontations at sea remained messy affairs that almost invariably devolved into unpredictable ship-against-ship mêlées. This helps explain why large-scale naval engagements were rare during the Middle Ages. Few naval commanders were willing to risk all in a single battle subject to so many uncontrollable variables. As on land, clashes at sea normally occurred only when one side or both could not avoid it.

The fact that there was no reliable ship-killing weapon compounded the uncertainty surrounding the outcome. The waterline ram or *rostrum* of the classical era was ineffective against the sturdier, frame-first hull construction which began to develop in the Mediterranean as early as the seventh century and found full implementation by the eleventh century.[32] It proved utterly futile against the more robust ship architecture of the northern seas, even in Roman times. In his *Commentarii de Bello Gallico* ('Commentaries on the Gallic War'), Julius Caesar said of the dense oak vessels of the Gauls, 'Our ships could not damage them with the ram (they were so stoutly built).'[33] As a result, no warship in either the north or the south was known to have sported a ram by the seventh century. It was replaced on the Byzantine *dromōn* by a spur, a sort of reinforced bowsprit used to assist in seizing and boarding an enemy ship.[34] The only weapon developed in the medieval period capable of destroying an entire vessel was 'Greek fire', a secret petroleum-based incendiary invented by a Syrian artificer named Kallinikos in the seventh century. Documentary and graphic sources indicate that it was spewed from specially constructed siphon tubes mounted on the bows of *dromōns*.[35] **(Pl. 3)** Unfortunately its utility was extremely restricted. It had limited range and could only be deployed in calm or following winds.[36] The most practical onboard armament of the Middle Ages was the swivel-mounted ballista, a large crossbow contraption which used torsion to fire iron quarrels called 'mice' or 'flies', but none of these was large enough or powerful enough to sink a ship.[37] It was more of an anti-personnel weapon.

Besides, the goal of medieval maritime combatants was not to sink or destroy opposing vessels. Most often it was to capture them as prizes, if at all possible. After all, the chosen vocation or avocation of most seafarers of the age was piracy. The parcelling out of prizes was how crews were often compensated – even merchant crews.[38] Accordingly, combat at sea routinely commenced with exchanges of missiles. Usually these were crossbow bolts, arrows, lances, stones, caltrops, etc., but the chronicles also contain reports of more atypical projectiles, such as clay pots filled with vipers, scorpions, quicklime, naphtha (a highly flammable petroleum distillate) and so on.[39] The idea was to clear the deck of an opposing vessel as much as possible prior to closing. The next phase of the encounter was grappling, followed by boarding. The outcome of the engagement was almost always decided by hand-to-hand combat on the decks of engaged ships.[40] **(Pl. 4)**

This is not to say that strategy was not involved. It often was, at least at the outset of an engagement. Some naval commanders may even have heeded the advice proffered by Vegetius in Book IV of the *Epitoma Rei Militaris*, which covers naval warfare.[41] But if any military manual was consulted at all, it was more likely the early tenth-century *Taktika* of Emperor Leo VI or those of other Byzantine tacticians of the period. First of all, in Constitution XIX of the *Taktika* which concerned naval warfare, the emperor counselled caution: 'Certainly, apart from some urgent necessity forcing you to do so, you should not throw yourself into a pitched battle. For many are the reversals of so-called fortune. What happens in battle is not what one expects.'[42] Along those lines, a ninth-century treatise by a certain Syrianos Magistros (perhaps a naval *strategos* or commander) advised anticipating any encounters with enemy fleets through the deployment of scout ships: 'There should be four of these, two keeping about six miles ahead of the main fleet and the other two in between so that the second group are informed of the disposition of the enemy by the former through certain signals which they will have arranged with each other, and should have done the same with the fleet.'[43]

If, however, it turned out that conflict was unavoidable, it was considered imperative to draw all vessels up into battle formation. (There are multiple contemporary accounts of ships being linked together with chains or cables in order to ensure formation integrity, though the wisdom and practicality of this practice has been questioned.)[44] The favoured formation was what Leo VI called 'crescent-shaped', i.e., a semi-circle line abreast with the flagship in the concave centre and the larger, more formidable ships at the tips of the horns.[45] The objective was to effect an envelopment of the enemy fleet, if possible. The larger or taller ships were selected for the wings, because height mattered in the missile exchanges which ensued. Once ships were engaged with grapples and pikes, caltrops and stones were generally dropped from masthead platforms of one kind or another in an attempt to hole the hull of an opposing vessel.[46] Nonetheless, despite whatever stratagem was initially employed, the clash inevitably degenerated into a chaotic free-for-all on the decks of the conjoined ships, much like in a land battle.

In point of fact, medieval fleets were hardly ever assembled for the purpose of engaging in pitched battle at sea. The intent of almost all medieval naval actions was amphibious assault, logistical support for land operations or the blockade of a hostile port. This is why John Pryor contends, 'Appreciation of the fact that all medieval naval warfare was essentially coastal and amphibious warfare is important since many of the recommended strategies and tactics were devised in that context.'[47] This is particularly true when one takes into account that the primitive state of nautical navigation at the time, the vulnerability of galleys to inclement weather and the need for constant resupply constrained medieval fleets to cling to coastlines anyway.

The Sources

Unfortunately, uncovering the story of medieval maritime warfare has proven challenging for historians because it is mostly contained in a disparate anthology of annals and chronicles written by clerics, ignorant of nautical matters. Theophanes the Confessor, a chronicler of some early Byzantine encounters with the Muslims at sea, is a case in point. An ascetic, orthodox monk who founded his own monastery, Theophanes died in exile in 818 because of his staunch opposition to iconoclasm.[48] His description of how the Byzantines broke the second blockade of Constantinople in 718 is typically bereft of detail and shaped by his spiritual vantage point: 'With God's help, thanks to the intercession of the all-pure Theotokos ["God-bearer" – the Virgin Mary], the enemy were sunk on the spot.'[49]

Worse still, most medieval writers, particularly in the Mediterranean, were trained in the classics and had a tendency to fill in gaps in their knowledge of maritime matters with classical tropes. As a result, the terminology they used to describe vessels and shipboard equipment was often misleading and inaccurate. William of Apulia, an eleventh-century Norman chronicler, described the ships that Robert Guiscard used to defeat the Venetians at Corfu in 1084 as 'triremes', referring to the ancient Hellenic vessel which boasted three banks of oarsmen per side.[50] The trouble is there is no corroborating testimony of any kind that the Normans ever operated triremes in any of their fleets. Guiscard's ships were probably light bireme galleys (i.e., two banks of rowers).[51] (*See* Fig. 1.) To William, trained in the Greek classics, all galleys were triremes. Matthew Paris, an English chronicler and Benedictine monk, suffered from a similar parochial perspective. He portrayed the English vessels at the 1217 Battle of Dover as sporting iron rams ('*galeas ferio rostratas*'),[52] yet there is no physical evidence of any English ship ever being fitted with a ram of any sort. Matthew had obviously imputed his vision of how naval battles were to be fought from classical accounts.[53]

Compounding the problem is the lack of reliable graphic representations of medieval vessels in general and warships in particular. The images found in medieval manuscripts and artwork are rudimentary and fanciful. The sixth-century *Ilias Ambrosiana* manuscript at the Biblioteca Ambrosiana of Milan (Cod. Ambros. F. 205 Inf.) contains some of the earliest known depictions of *dromōns*,

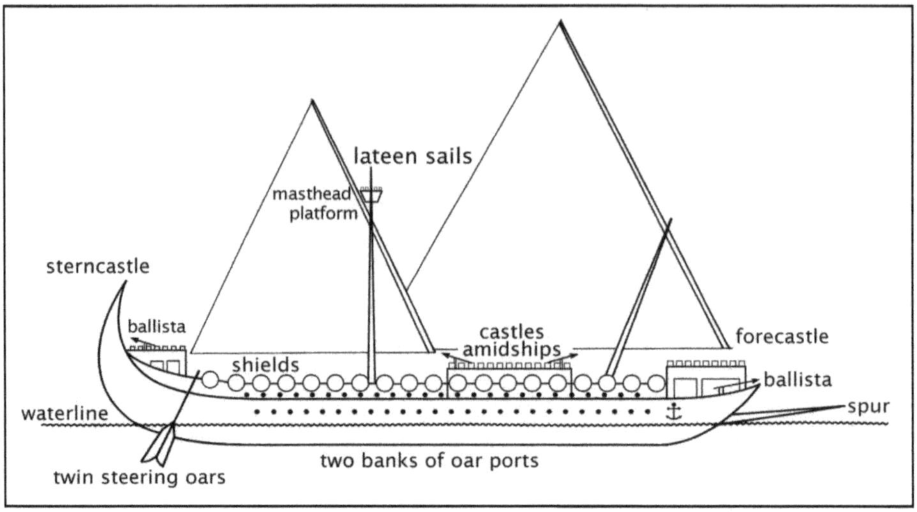

Figure 1. Italo-Norman light bireme galley of the eleventh century. *(C. Stanton with P. Judge with permission of Boydell Press)*

but the images are so unsophisticated and dilapidated that it is difficult to distinguish any detail.[54] The first known illustrations of the twelfth-century Italian *galea* are a set of seven highly stylized, monochrome miniatures placed in the margins of the Paris manuscript of the *Annales Ianuenses* of Genoa (Bibliothèque Nationale, Ms. Suppl. Lat. 773).[55] To the inexpert, they appear to be nothing more than banana-shaped outlines. Nautical archaeology has only been partially productive at filling the void. Few medieval vessels have ever been recovered and discoveries of warships have been rarer still.

That said, marine archaeologists have had some rather spectacular successes of late. In the early 1960s George Bass and Frederick Van Doorninck excavated the seventh-century wreck of a small coastal trader off Yassi Ada Island near Bodrum, Turkey, which appears to show the transition from shell-first ship construction to the stronger skeleton-first style.[56] From 1977 to 1979 the same pair, along with Richard Steffy, salvaged the remains of another small merchant vessel at Serçe Limani, Turkey, this one from the eleventh century. It exhibited no evidence of the mortise-and-tenon joints of the late Roman period: proof that the conversion to frame-first hull construction had been completed.[57] In the north a late fourteenth-century cog, the workhorse of the Hanseatic League, was discovered in the Weser river near Bremen in 1962 and a fifteenth-century version was reclaimed from the Zuiderzee at Almere in the Netherlands in 1986.[58]

Nautical archaeology has made numerous other finds of some significance in the last few decades, but almost all of these have been merchantmen of one kind or another. What has been sorely lacking is some physical evidence of fighting vessels from the medieval period, particularly in the Mediterranean. The most important finds to date have been Viking longships, like the late ninth-century Gokstad ship unearthed at Sandefjord, Norway in 1880 and the eleventh-century

Skuldelev 2 recovered near Roskilde, Denmark in 1962.[59] There have been no comparable discoveries in the Mediterranean – that is, until very recently. In 2004 conservationists working under Sait Başaran in Istanbul uncovered thirty-one shipwrecks in the fourth-century Theodosian Harbour of Constantinople. While excavation is ongoing, four of these appear to be war galleys from the mid-Byzantine era.[60] The project seems quite promising.

Despite the inherent impediments, a number of gifted scholars have been quite successful in interpreting the available evidence. Bernard Bachrach's scrutiny of ship images on the Bayeux Tapestry, for instance, permitted him to make some intriguing observations on the logistical challenges of William the Conqueror's amphibious assault on England in 1066.[61] John Pryor's painstaking examination of vessel illustrations in the Bern manuscript (Codex 120 II) of Peter of Eboli's *Liber ad honorem Augusti sive de rebus Siculis* ('Book to honour the Emperor or concerning the affairs of Sicily') in the Burgerbibliothek allowed him to convincingly identify key characteristics of the twelfth-century Italian *galea*.[62] **(Pl. 5)** And Lawrence Mott's careful reading of the *Capitula pertinentia ad Officium Ammiratae* ('Capitularies pertaining to the Office of Admiral')[63] of Frederick II and the *Capitula officii ammiratiae* ('Capitularies of the office of the Admiral')[64] of Charles of Anjou enabled him to extrapolate critical information concerning fleet command and control.[65] Perhaps the most stimulating recent project has been that of the Dibner Institute for the History of Science and Technology at the Massachusetts Institute of Technology, which sponsored an exhaustive examination of the manuscript of Michael of Rhodes, a Venetian mariner who, in the early fifteenth century, compiled 'the world's first extant treatise on shipbuilding'.[66]

Moreover, maritime historians have learned a great deal about the performance capabilities of medieval vessels from a host of meticulous ship recreations, many of which have undergone extensive sea trials. As mentioned earlier, the reconstructed Athenian trireme *Olympias* has provided modern researchers with a cornucopia of data on real-world galley operations in the medieval Mediterranean.[67] In northern waters scrupulous reproductions of both the Gokstad and Skuldelev Viking ships have been tested.[68] An exact reconstruction of the Gokstad, christened *Viking*, was sailed from Bergen in Norway to the 1893 World's Columbian Exposition in Chicago. No fewer than three full-scale replicas of the Bremen cog have been built with subsequent sea trials held under full sail.[69] Even a half-scale model of the Sutton Hoo ship has been sailed.[70]

All of this is to say that, taken as a whole, there is enough data, despite the challenges, to paint a plausible picture of combat at sea in the Middle Ages. Accordingly, a comprehensive survey of medieval maritime warfare is both possible and desirable. And since distinct environmental and cultural factors shaped the development of naval tradition in northern Europe differently from the south, the picture must be presented in two parts, as was indicated in the Preface. But because both traditions sprang, at least partially, from Roman roots, it is appropriate to begin the story in the south: specifically, in the Mediterranean.

PART I

SOUTHERN EUROPE

The Mediterranean and the Black Sea

Map 1. The Mediterranean and Black Seas. (*Kristy Stanton*)

Medieval sea power in the Mediterranean sprouted from seeds sown by the Roman Empire and those seeds were nurtured in an environment that favoured the galley. John Pryor adroitly sums up that environment in a single sentence: 'For ancient and medieval man, the Mediterranean had a deserved reputation for benevolence.'[1] Tidal effects were minimal, and the winds were more predictable and less blustery, while the temperatures were milder and more consistent across a relatively narrow band of latitudes, engendering fewer storms. These more benign climatic conditions produced comparatively placid sea states, devoid of the giant rollers so prevalent in the North Atlantic. Moreover, the sailing season was longer (March to late October), with relatively clear skies, enabling greater reliance on celestial navigation.[2] The topography of the Mediterranean itself aided navigation: the northern coasts generally boasted lofty profiles with numerous landmarks. Safe havens in the form of bays, inlets and gulfs were abundant, and several large, well watered islands dotted the sea from west to east.[3] All of these attributes promoted the development of the oared warship.

Galleys required relatively calm conditions because their hulls had to be long and narrow in order to bring as many oars to bear as possible and the freeboard (the distance from the waterline to the deck amidships) had to be fairly low so that the oars could enter the water at a nearly flat angle for the sake of efficiency. The downside of these design constraints, of course, was that they made the ship susceptible to being swamped. Simply put, southern shipwrights built these swift but vulnerable vessels because the conditions permitted it. Thus, the environment fostered the evolution of classical oared warships like the Greek trireme.

In antiquity, these vessels were constructed shell-first, by fixing the longitudinal planks of the hull to one another with tenons fastened into mortises with pegs. The shell was then reinforced with interior ribbing. This method made for a light, sturdy hull, but proved labour-intensive, time-consuming and expensive.[4] It also caused the hull to be quite rigid, which made it vulnerable to the ram. Judging by the Athlit ram (the only one ever found), the waterline *rostrum* or *embolos* was specifically designed to defeat this type of hull construction by springing the timbers inwards.[5] Thus, most war galleys of the era were fitted with rams.

As speed and manoeuvrability slowly became prized over size during Rome's reign, ships grew smaller and more agile. Accordingly, the fine-lined *liburnian* emerged from its piratical beginnings to become the principal warship of the late Roman Empire. With just fifty oarsmen, this bireme galley was about half the length (around 20m or just over 65ft) of an ancient Greek trireme, probably a bit faster and certainly more agile.[6] By the early Byzantine period this progression towards supple speed produced the *dromōn* (meaning 'runner'). The *dromōn* appeared in the late fifth century/early sixth century as a cataphract monoreme – that is, a fully decked, single-banked galley.[7] Gradually, as shipbuilding techniques improved, the vessel grew longer and more sophisticated. The mortise-and-tenon technique was phased out from the seventh century to the eleventh century in favour of the more flexible, frame-first hull design, rendering the ram obsolete. By the tenth century the *dromōn* had become a fully decked bireme, roughly 30.5m (100ft) by a little less than 4m (13ft), propelled by a standard *ousia* (crew complement) of 108 rowers augmented as necessary by two lateen sails and directed by twin steering oars mounted on either side of the stern.[8] (*See* Fig. 2) The waterline ram had been replaced by a 'spur', which John Pryor (the prevailing expert on the *dromōn*) says was specifically designed to immobilize an enemy

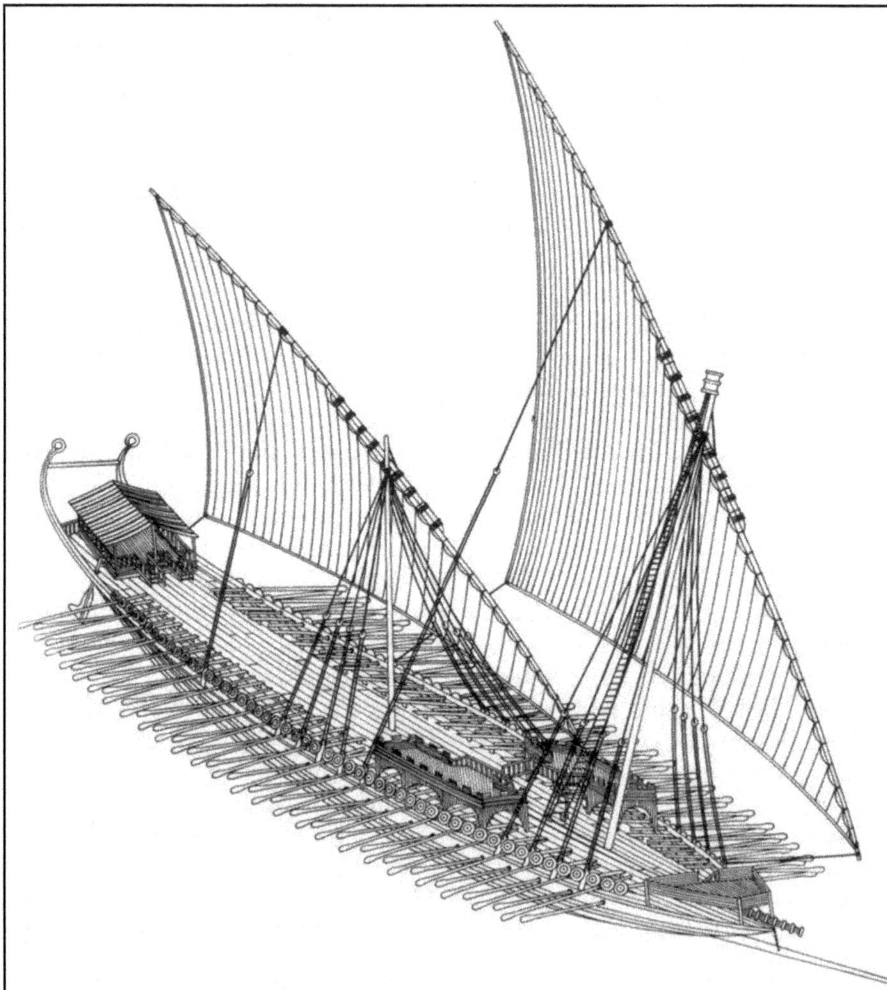

Figure 2. Byzantine *dromōn* of the tenth century. (*John Pryor, copyrighted with all rights reserved*)

galley by riding up over its oars, smashing them.[9] Siphons for spewing 'Greek fire' were eventually mounted on protected platforms at the bow and possibly amidships.[10] The parapeted forecastle (*xylokastron*) housed the main siphon, called the 'raven' (*katakorax*), while the castle amidships was the *kastelloma*. The aftercastle contained the *kravatos*, a structure to shield the *kentarchos* or captain.[11]

The *dromōn* would spawn a host of variants under a welter of names. For instance, there was the *chelandion*. Derived from the classical Greek word *kelēs* (meaning 'courser', as would be applied to a swift riding horse), Pryor believes that '*chelandion* almost certainly originated as a term for horse transports'.[12] The term eventually came to refer to a larger version of a *dromōn*. The late tenth-century German chronicler Thietmar of Merseburg described the *chelandion* as 'a ship of marvellous length and speed, having two banks of oars on each side with space for one hundred and fifty sailors'.[13] In fact, medieval maritime historian Frederick Hocker is convinced the name became synonymous with the largest type of *dromōn*, one which could accommodate as many as 200 oarsmen.[14] Another *dromōn* derivative was the *pamphylos*, apparently a large, oared vessel on the order of a *chelandion*, which was initially configured as a transport but may later have evolved into a warship in the hands of fearsome Mardaite mariners who were settled in the province of *Pamphylia* (on the Gulf of Antalya) by Justinian II.[15] The smallest variation of the vessel was the early *galea* (plural: *galeai*), a monoreme galley with only around fifty oars used primarily for reconnaissance.[16] Most, if not all, of these iterations could presumably be equipped with 'Greek fire' siphons.

The *dromōn* almost certainly served as a prototype for the war galleys of Byzantium's adversaries, the Arabs in particular. Muslims sometimes referred to the vessel using names derived from Greek, like *dromonarios* or *dermin*. Similarly, a *chelandion* was called a *shalandi*. But often they simply used generic Arabic terms for warships, such as *maraqib harbiyya* ('ship of war').[17] Whatever they were called, these warships seemed to have shared the same basic characteristics as their various Greek *dromōn* equivalents: they ranged roughly from 35 to 40m (115 to 130ft) long and up to about 6m (20ft) of beam, while sporting two lateen sails, two stern quarter rudders and around 100 oars.[18] The oared horse transport of the Arabs was normally known as a *tarida*, a name later adopted by Latin mariners for their own horse-carrying galleys. In addition, it is thought, based on some documents of the Cairo Geniza ('storeroom') of the Ben Ezra Synagogue of Fustat, that the Arabs also had some sort of trireme called a *koumbaria*, which was said to be slow and cumbersome. And a Muslim version of the 'fireship' (i.e., one capable of launching some form of 'Greek fire'), called the *harraqa*, made its appearance in the ninth century. It may have lacked Byzantine-style siphons, however, relying instead on catapults and grenades to deploy its incendiary.[19] In the same general timeframe the *dromōn* is also seen to have inspired the principal fighting ship of such emerging Italian maritime powers as the Normans, Pisans, Genoese and Venetians: the *galea*. Enlarged and updated as a speedy bireme galley, its oarsmen rowed *alla sensile* – that is, each man manipulating his own oar in a stand-and-sit stroke fashion from the main deck.[20]

In any event, it was an early version of the *dromōn* which proved so instrumental to Byzantine aspirations of regaining control of the Mediterranean in those first decades following the fall of the Western Empire. They were among the some 600 ships in the fleet of Belisarios, the great Byzantine general whom Emperor Justinian dispatched in 533 to destroy the pirate kingdom of the Vandals. The court scholar Procopius, who accompanied Belisarios on the expedition, wrote in his *History of the Wars*: 'And they also had ships of war prepared as for sea-fighting, to the number of ninety-two, and they were single-banked ships covered by decks, in order that the men rowing them might if possible not be exposed to the bolts of the enemy. Such boats are called "*dromones*" ["runners"] by those of the present time; for they are able to attain a great speed.'[21]

Justinian clearly understood that the best hope of realizing his dream of a revitalized Roman *mare nostrum* was to eliminate the empire's most formidable rival at sea: the Vandals. The fact that the Arian Vandals (who believed that the Son of God was subordinate to God the Father) viciously persecuted the Orthodox clergy of North Africa (who considered the Son as consubstantial with the Father) only added incentive. Accordingly, he sent an envoy with ships and soldiers to the Vandal governor of Sardinia to support the latter's revolt against Gelimer, the Vandal king. The diversion worked. Gelimer dispatched most of his 120-ship fleet with 5,000 men to Sardinia.[22] Thus, when Belisarios' armada disembarked his 15,000-strong army at Caput Vada (modern Chebba, near Mahdiyah, Tunisia), about five days' march south of Carthage, it was unopposed.[23] The Byzantine fleet then shadowed the army as it trooped up the coast. Unable to recall his own fleet in time, Gelimer attempted to ambush Belisarios at Decimum, 16km (10 miles) south of Carthage, but was heavily defeated. As a consequence, Belisarios soon claimed Carthage and captured Gelimer a few months later, destroying the remnants of the Vandal army in the process. Its home-port conquered and its leader in chains, the Vandal fleet eventually dispersed.[24] The Byzantine general completed the campaign by dispatching infantry units to impose Byzantine authority all along the northern shores of Africa as far as Cherchell (Algeria), while sending flotillas to seize Sardinia, Corsica and even the Balearic islands.[25] The Vandal maritime empire was effectively at an end.

With the menace of the Vandal fleet vanquished, Justinian set his sights on Italy, then controlled by the Ostrogoths who were in upheaval following the death of King Theodoric in 526. In 535 the emperor again dispatched Belisarios with a fleet, this time to Sicily, which the general quickly subdued for the Eastern Empire.[26] Belisarios then crossed to Calabria and began working his way up the Italian peninsula, but the expedition stalled after capturing Rome owing to Justinian's reluctance to send reinforcements. Under the inspired leadership of Totila, who ascended to the kingship in 541, the Ostrogoths reversed most of the Byzantine gains in short order. What was worse, Totila managed to assemble a fleet of some 400 warships to counter Imperial naval power. He used it to destroy a pair of Byzantine fleets at Naples in 542, eventually forcing the city's surrender, and again in 546 to starve Rome into submission, despite an attempt by Belisarios to relieve it with 200 fortified *dromōns*. Belisarios' position soon became untenable and he was recalled to Constantinople in 548. Justinian replaced him in 551 with the palace eunuch Narses.[27]

While the latter was marching overland to Italy, two Byzantine generals (John of Salona and Valerian of Ravenna) broke an Ostrogothic blockade of Ancona with an overwhelming naval victory. Fifty East Roman vessels lined up against forty-seven of the East Goths at *Senogallia* (modern Senigallia, 25km or 16 miles north of Ancona). The superior seamanship of the Byzantines carried the day. The Goths apparently could not control their vessels and fight at the same time, while the Greeks could. The Goths lost thirty-six ships in the course of the battle; the remaining eleven escaped only to be burned on the beach afterwards by their own crews. It was a devastating defeat. 'This engagement especially broke the spirit and weakened the power of Totila and the Goths,' wrote Procopius.[28] A few months later, in the summer of 552, Narses thrashed Totila at *Busta Gallorum* (near present-day Gualdo Tadino), terminating Gothic rule in Italy.[29]

Justinian completed his quest to reconquer the Mediterranean for the Eastern Roman Empire in 554 when he dispatched another amphibious expedition that managed to expel the Visigoths from most of Andalusia as well the opposite shores of North Africa. From West to East the *mare nostrum* of Rome had been restored and the Byzantine maritime thalassocracy had begun.[30]

CHAPTER 1

The Byzantine–Muslim Struggle for Supremacy on the Middle Sea

The 'revived Romania' of Justinian did not remain unchallenged for long.[1] Its very nature made it vulnerable to assault. The Byzantine Empire at the time was essentially a maritime one. With the exception of Anatolia (Asia Minor), it was only shoreline deep in most places, buttressed on the landward side by a system of frontier forts. It depended on naval power to hold it together. Instead of the old Roman network of roads, Constantinople relied on sea lanes to communicate with its far-flung provinces and gather nourishment from such grain-producing regions as Egypt.[2] Thus, aside from the main fleet at Constantinople, it maintained smaller flotillas at Cherson on the Black Sea, at Tyre and possibly Acre on the Syrian coast, at Alexandria in Egypt, at Ravenna on the Adriatic, at Syracuse on Sicily, at Carthage and possibly Ceuta in North Africa, and perhaps even a squadron in Andalusia or the Balearics. Byzantium used these fleets to rush its limited land forces to troublespots in order to quell rebellions or staunch invasions.[3]

That is how the empire dealt with simultaneous pressure from the Avars (fierce Turkic nomads who had swept into the Balkans in the sixth century) and the Sassanid Dynasty of Persia. Emperor Maurice, a former general who famously penned a manual of war called *Strategikon*, managed to hold the line for two decades with a firm military mind, but it all began to unravel after his assassination in 602.[4] The very next year the Sassanid monarch Chosroes II launched a massive offensive against Byzantium which Phokas, Maurice's cruel and incompetent successor, was helpless to stem. By 608 Persian forces were at Chalcedon across the Bosporus from Constantinople. Antioch fell to them in 611, Damascus in 613, Jerusalem in 614 and Alexandria in 619.[5] Meanwhile, the Avars had moved into Macedonia and were advancing through Thrace. Heraklios (610–41), Phokas' more reliable replacement, succeeded in forestalling the Avars with a truce in 622 while stymieing the Sassanids with a brilliant Anatolian campaign, but ultimately the two imperial adversaries struck an alliance to besiege the Byzantine capital. In the summer of 626 Sahrvaraz, the great Persian general, mustered his armies at Chalcedon, while the Avars, according to the early ninth-century Byzantine chronicler Theophanes the Confessor, 'filled the gulf of the [Golden] Horn with an immense multitude, beyond all number, whom they had brought from the Danube in carved boats'.[6] Byzantine naval power, however, easily prevailed. The emperor gathered a great fleet of war galleys which had no difficulty dispersing the primitive *monoxyla* (dugouts) of the Avars, and the siege fell apart after a mere ten days. The next year Heraklios used his fleet to support an invasion of the Persian Levant, finally crushing the remnants of Chosroes' armies near Nineveh.[7]

The empire's hold on its Mediterranean domains, nonetheless, remained tenuous and susceptible to large-scale incursions from the interior. And certainly such a security system was never designed to withstand the sort of massive shock-wave that emanated from the Arabian peninsula at the beginning of the seventh century. Ironically, the emperor himself prepared the way for the onslaught. Like his predecessors, and so many of his successors, he dabbled in the religious controversy that would plague the empire until its fall nearly a millennium later. It was Justinian who had begun the practice. Without the restraining influence of the Empress Theodora, who died in June 548, Justinian sought to impose Dyophysite Orthodox dogma (that Christ had two natures: one divine and one human) on the Monophysite churches of Syria and Egypt (which believed that the Son of God had a single divine nature).[8] His successors followed suit with heavy-handed policies designed to enforce state-mandated religious conformity throughout the empire. Heraklios attempted to mend the empire's religious rupture by imposing a ham-fisted compromise between Orthodox Dyophysitism and Monophysitism but it satisfied no one. While conceding that Christ indeed had two natures, one human and one divine, he insisted that the Son of God had only one will and thus one energy (later termed Monothelitism). This view was raucously rejected by both Rome and the Monophysite churches of Syria and Egypt.[9]

To make matters worse, Heraklios declared Greek as the official language of the empire. He then subjected the Monophysite Christians of Syria and the Coptics of Egypt to the punishing persecution of his governors and the fiscal tyranny of his tax collectors. Instead of unifying the empire, Heraklios had hopelessly debilitated it with further philosophical dissonance. This caused a fatal rift which rendered the entire region ripe for invasion. The Semitic peoples on the southern and eastern borders of the empire doubtless had a greater affinity with Muslim monotheism than with the Greek Orthodoxy of Constantinople, in any case. As a consequence, they were more inclined to view the Islamic invaders as liberators to be welcomed openly rather than as potential oppressors to be resisted.[10] The timing could not have been worse.

Sandstorm out of the East: the Rise of Muslim Maritime Might (632–55)

Muhammad died in Medina on 8 June 632. By 634 the storm that was Islam (which means 'submission') was already sweeping into Syria. Damascus fell to the forces of the Rashidun Caliphate of Arabia in September that year. They came by land, of course, in the initial stages, for they had no navy at that point and no need of one. In all fairness to Heraklios, he moved to meet the threat as soon as it had become apparent, but the onslaught was too swift and utterly inexorable. That said, the emperor made a respectable effort to stem the tide, fielding a force of some 80,000 allied soldiers at Antioch under his personal leadership in the spring of 636 against a Rashidun army roughly half its size under the command of Khalid ibn Walid. The two forces faced each other at the Yarmouk river southeast of the Sea of Galilee in August. Theophanes described the denouement of the six-day engagement: 'And as a south wind was blowing in the direction of the Romans, they could not face the enemy on account of the dust and were defeated.'[11] The annihilation of the Byzantines caused the entirety of Syria to devolve to the Arabs.[12]

Metaphorically speaking, the sandstorm continued unabated. Palestine soon suffered the same fate as Syria. Jerusalem was captured in April 637, followed by Caesarea Maritima the next year. By the end of 639 most of Persia, including Ctesiphon and all of Byzantine Armenia and Mesopotamia, was in Muslim hands. At the beginning of 640 the Arabs surged into Egypt behind their brilliant commander Amr ibn al-'As, a contemporary of Muhammad. They seized Heliopolis and Babylon (both near modern Cairo) in July. When Heraklios died of dropsy in February 641, Amr was already marching on Alexandria. It surrendered in September, making the Arabs masters of Egypt.[13]

Still, Byzantium remained a force to be reckoned with on the seas and thus had the means to threaten Arab conquests in the Fertile Crescent. Constans II, Heraklios' heir, dispatched a naval expedition in 645 under an Armenian named Manuel to recover Alexandria. Manuel succeeded with such unexpected ease that it must have alarmed Caliph Uthman ibn Affan. The latter had previously relieved Amr as governor of Egypt, but now hastily reappointed him. The highly effective field commander quickly gathered an army of 15,000 and forced Manuel to withdraw.[14] The experience was a valuable one, nonetheless. It had impressed upon these conquerors from the desert the value of sea power and the vulnerability of their gains to Byzantine fleets. Accordingly, the Rashidun Caliphate became determined to rectify the weakness. First of all, the Egyptian capital was relocated from Alexandria over a hundred miles up the Nile to Fustat in the environs of modern Cairo. Of even greater significance for the future of the Byzantine–Muslim struggle was the decision to develop a naval capability to rival that of Constantinople. Abdullah ibn Sa'ad ibn Abi as-Sarh, a successor to Amr as governor of Egypt, began by building a shipyard on al-Rawdah, an island in the Nile abeam Fustat.[15] It came to be called *dar al-sina'a*, meaning 'house of work', which medieval Italian mariners later adopted as *darsena*, denoting a 'dock', or *arsenale*, referring to a 'dockyard' – and hence the modern term 'arsenal' in the sense of a shipyard.[16]

Little is known about the nautical architecture of these early Arab vessels. No reliable ship descriptions or depictions appear until the thirteenth century. **(Pl. 6)** It is presumed, however, that they were much like their Byzantine counterparts. After all, the shipwrights that the Caliphate relied upon to construct its ships in the newly conquered lands of the Levant were the same Syriac Christians and Coptics that the Byzantines had called upon to build their vessels in these formerly imperial territories. In fact, some of the Arab ships bore names that sounded similar to their Greek equivalents. The *chelandion*, for instance, was sometimes called the *shalandi* in Arabic. John Pryor offers an explanation: 'These terms were used by Greek-speaking functionaries in the chanceries of their Muslim rulers writing directives to fellow Greek-speaking functionaries of other

Muslim officials.'[17] Thus, warships were often referred to as *dromons* in both Arabic and Greek sources.[18] An Arabic translation of the Emperor Leo VI's *Naumachika*, a treatise on naval warfare, is actually contained in the *Al-ahkam al mulukiyya wa'l dawabit al-namusiyya* ('Royal rules and customary regulations for the art of naval warfare') of Muhammad ibn Mankali, a fourteenth-century court official of Mamluk Egypt.[19] Accordingly, Arab fleets were probably composed of ships quite similar to the Byzantine vessels described earlier with the exception that, in the view of medieval maritime specialist Frederick Hocker, 'The main Arab ships were considered to be larger, higher, heavier, and slower than their Byzantine opponents.'[20] The truth is that there is no way of knowing for certain.

Command structure and crew composition also seemed to have shared parallels with their Byzantine counterparts. An *amir* (*emir* = leader) was normally designated a fleet commander and eventually came to be known as an *amir al-rahl*, at least in the West. A ship's captain was a *ra'is*, who was responsible for navigation and anchorage, but direct supervision of the sailors, *nawatiya* (from the classical word *nauta* for 'mariner'), was assigned to the *qa'id al-nawatiya* ('chief of the sailors'). In the early stages the mariners themselves were recruited from local Coptic and Syrian Christian populations, but embarked soldiers or marines were Muslim.[21]

At about the same time as the governor of Egypt was building his fleet at al-Rawdah Island, the governor of Syria, Muawiyah ibn Abi Sufyan, began assembling a fleet at Tyre and Acre.[22] At first, much of the fleet was composed of merchantmen confiscated from Syriac Christians. Muawiyah was clearly quite successful. Theophanes attested that by 649 he was able to launch an armada of some 1,700 ships on a *razzia* (raid) of Cyprus which enabled him to impose a covenant of neutrality on the island's populace.[23] In 652 some 200 Syrian ships swooped in on Sicily and sailed off with a surfeit of spoils, and in 653 Muawiyah's fleet raided Rhodes, supposedly 'casting down the Colossus'.[24] In the same year the great Arab historian Ahmad ibn Yahya ibn Jabir al-Baladhuri insisted that Muawiyah again invaded Cyprus, this time with 500 vessels, in order to chastise the inhabitants for having violated the conditions of their neutrality agreement.[25]

The most telling blow to the notion of Byzantine maritime supremacy, however, came in 655 off the coast of Lycia in south-central Anatolia. Emperor Constans II had learned that Muawiyah was planning an offensive on Constantinople itself, so he gathered an armada of 500 to 1,000 vessels (according to exaggerated contemporary estimates) and proceeded southeastwards along the coast of Asia Minor. Muawiyah was, in fact, leading a land force towards Cappadocia (Central Anatolia) while his Egyptian counterpart, Abdullah ibn Sa'ad, commanded a combined Egyptian–Syrian fleet of perhaps 200 vessels westwards along the south shore of Anatolia. The latter came upon Constans' fleet at Phoinix (present-day Finike).[26] According to Theophanes, the emperor gave the order to engage but 'had taken no measures to draw up his battle line'.[27] The consequences were calamitous. The Arabs maintained formation integrity by linking their ships with chains. They then reportedly used long hooks to cut or tangle the rigging of the Greek vessels.[28] From a distance, the engaged fleets must have appeared as a forest of masts. It was probably for this reason (or perhaps because the area was a source of cypress trees for producing masts – *sawari*) that the Arab sources called the encounter *'Dhat al-Sawari'* ('The Battle of the Masts').[29] 'When the two sides engaged,' reported Theophanes, 'the Romans were defeated and the sea was dyed with Roman blood.' Constans himself barely managed to escape by exchanging clothes with the son of a *boukinator* (trumpeter) and fleeing on a swift ship.[30] As a consequence, the eastern Mediterranean had been laid open to Muslim sea power.

Byzantine Fleet Reorganization (656–71)

Fortunately for Byzantium, the assassination of Caliph Uthman in 656 and the resultant power struggle for the caliphate gave Constans II the breathing space he needed to reorganize his military forces, particularly his navy. Muawiyah, anxious to ensure no interference from Constantinople during the Arab civil war, agreed to a truce in 659, which included a generous tribute: 1,000 *nomismata* (gold coins, each weighing about 4.5 grams), one horse and one slave per day.[31] The respite was a godsend to the emperor who used it to restructure the empire's military establishment into districts called *themata* ('themes'). The closest to the capital, and the most powerful, was the *Opsikion* (Opsician) Theme, composed of the old imperial retinue. Based at Ancyra (present-day Ankara), it covered southern Thrace and northwestern Asia Minor. The *Anatolikon* (Anatoliac) Theme, headquartered at Armorion in western Anatolia, included south-central Asia Minor. The *Armeniakon* (Armeniac) Theme controlled eastern Anatolia from Euchaita (today's Beyozu, Turkey), while the *Thrakesion* (Thracian) Theme guarded the west coast of Asia Minor from Chonae (modern Kona). More significantly for the empire's maritime capability, the emperor created a naval theme called the *Karabisianoi* (Karabisian – derived from *karabis*, meaning 'ship' in Greek) centred on Samos, which protected the Aegean Islands, the southern shores of Asia Minor and the all-important approaches to the Dardanelles.[32]

The army of each theme was commanded by a *strategos* ('general') with the exception of the *Opsikion*, which had a *komes* or 'count' in charge. Beneath these served *tourmarchai*, who led divisions of soldiers called *tourmai*, and, in turn, their subordinates were called *droungarioi*, who headed smaller units of around 1,000 troops known as *droungoi*. Soldiers and sailors were normally recompensed, in part, with plots of land within the geographical confines of the theme.[33]

The *Karabisianoi* and succeeding naval themes seemed to follow the same basic command structure, although naval commanders were customarily considered subordinate in prestige to their land counterparts. None was ever noted at the top of imperial precedence lists. That said, admirals of naval themes were *strategoi* (like their land equivalents) and commanders of subordinate fleets were often given the title *droungarios*. A ship's captain was a *kentarchos* (centurion) and his equivalent of an executive officer was a *bandophoros* (banner-bearer). Serving in the capacity of first mate was the helmsman or *protokarabos* ('first man of the ship'). There were normally two of these. Other key crew members were the *proreus* (bow officer), the *boukinator* (trumpeter) and the *protelatai* ('first oarsmen' or stroke oarsmen) and, from the end of the seventh century, the *siphonatores* (siphon operators for deploying 'Greek fire'). Ordinary oarsmen were called *elatai*. Embarked soldiers were heavily armed and armoured *kataphractoi* or *stratiotai*.[34]

Having arranged a hiatus from Umayyad pressure and seen to the defence of the empire's eastern borders, Constans II looked to the security of his western domains. Since the Levant and Egypt had already been lost to the Arabs, he seemed to realize that imperial control of the entire western Mediterranean was in jeopardy if the central coast of North Africa should also fall to the Arabs. Consequently, sometime around 662 he embarked troops from the *Opsikion* Theme on the ships of the *Karabisianoi* and set sail for Italy. After a brief campaign in Apulia and Calabria to affirm his authority over the local Lombard lords, he settled in Syracuse on Sicily. His intention was evidently to strengthen his hold on the crucial central Mediterranean and, most importantly, the Exarchate of Carthage. Two events, however, conspired against him: first of all, Muawiyah won the dynastic struggle for the Umayyad Caliphate in 661 and resumed his campaign against Byzantium; secondly, Constans himself was assassinated in his bath by a servant in Syracuse in 668.[35]

The First Siege of Constantinople and the Advent of 'Greek Fire' (672–7)

Once Muawiyah had moved his capital to Damascus and consolidated his grip on power, he began preparations for an enormous expedition against Constantinople itself. In 672 he was ready. The caliph unleashed at least two separate fleets on the south coast of Asia Minor. Their activities must have kept the Karabisian fleet fully occupied. Both Crete and Rhodes were raided. One Arab fleet wintered in Cilicia (the southeastern coast of Anatolia) and the other in Lycia (on the south-central coast). Word of these incursions galvanized Constans' son and successor, Constantine IV, into action. According to Theophanes, the emperor 'built large biremes bearing cauldrons of fire and *dromones* equipped with siphons and ordered them to be stationed at the Proclianesian harbour of Caesarius [Constantinople's Theodosian harbour]'.[36] In 673 Muawiyah's fleets surged into the Sea of Marmara and ravaged the Hebdomon district just southwest of Constantinople, then captured Kyzikos on the south shore of the sea. Here they established a base camp for incessant attacks on the city.[37]

Constantinople would endure this maritime assault for the next several years, but the emperor was in possession of a terrible new weapon which would finally – and precipitously – end it. Residing in the city at that time was a Christian refugee from Heliopolis in Syria (modern Baalbek in Lebanon) named Kallinikos. Theophanes described him as an 'architect' or 'artificer' who had 'manufactured a naval fire [or sea fire]' which floated on the surface of the sea and could not be extinguished by water.[38] Its precise ingredients were kept a closely guarded state secret and remain a mystery to this day. This has led to endless speculation through the ages and repeated attempts at replication. A similar Muslim concoction of the twelfth century was said to have included 'dolphin's fat' and 'grease of goat kidneys'. Early scholarly conjecture centred on saltpetre as the main component (as in gunpowder) or some form of quicklime, but recent empirical investigations, particularly by renowned Byzantinist John Haldon, have revealed that its primary ingredient was probably petroleum-based – most likely naphtha or light crude oil. The Byzantines had access to the oil fields of the Caucasus region northeast of the Black Sea where crude seeped to the surface. The theory is that Kallinikos may have distilled this into a paraffin or kerosene, then added wood resins as a thickening agent. The mixture was then heated in an air-tight bronze tank over a brazier and pressured by use of a force pump. The final step was the release of the flammable fluid through a valve for its discharge from a metal-sheathed nozzle, affixed with a flame ignition source. In a 2002 clinical test of this theory, Haldon and his colleagues, Colin Hewes and Andrew Lacey, were able to produce a fire stream in the neighbourhood of 1,000 degrees Celsius that extended at least 15m (49ft).[39]

It was very probably a compound similar to this that Constantine caused to be loaded onto his *dromōns* in the autumn of 677.[40] The fearsome new weapon was unleashed from swivel-mounted siphons in the forecastles with horrific results. Theophanes testified almost matter-of-factly that it 'kindled the ships of the Arabs and burnt them and their crews'.[41] To the Arab victims of his frightful invention, it must have seemed like some early version of 'shock and awe'. The fact that they would have had no idea of how to combat the weapon must have compounded their panic. Water would have been ineffective. At that point they could not have known that the only way to extinguish the 'liquid fire' was with sand, vinegar or urine.[42] The siege soon collapsed. What was left of the Arab armada withdrew, only to be severely mauled by a violent winter storm while passing abeam Syllaem in Pamphylia (on the south coast of Asia Minor between Lycia and Cilicia). Theophanes said, 'It was dashed to pieces and perished entirely.'[43]

The Founding of the *Kibyrrhaeot* fleet and Arab Expansion Westward (678–716)

These events evidently emboldened the Mardaites (Christian marauders who inhabited the Mount Amanus region between Cilicia and Syria) to rebel against their Muslim overlords and migrate south towards Mount Lebanon. They created a path of devastation all the way to the walls of Jerusalem. Believing them to be proxies for the Byzantines, Muawiyah was unnerved enough to seek a peace with Constantinople, which entailed a humiliating annual tribute of 3,000 pounds of gold, fifty slaves and fifty horses.[44] The Mardaites, however, remained a persistent problem for the caliphate. In 689 Abd al-Malik ibn Marwan, one of Muawiyah's successors, was compelled to again petition the *basileus* (the emperor) for relief. He renewed the aforementioned treaty with Constantine's heir Justinian II, with some generous embellishments in return for the relocation of at least 12,000 Mardaites to Byzantine territory.[45]

Most of these Justinian resettled in southern Asia Minor, where they were enlisted into the Karabisian Theme as oarsmen. Around this same time frame the emperor seems to have detached central Greece from the Karabisian Theme to create the *Hellas* Theme based in Corinth. The *Karabisianoi* retained responsibility for the Aegean and the south coast of Asia Minor. Its *strategos* continued to maintain his headquarters at Samos, but his subordinate *droungarios*, accountable for the southern shore of Anatolia, was based at Kibyrrha, home port of what became known as the *Kibyrrhaeot* fleet. Most of the Mardaites served here.[46]

Regrettably, the reign of Justinian II degenerated into sadistic insanity shortly thereafter, ushering in a chaotic period in Constantinople's palace politics, during which no fewer than six different rulers in a score of years would claim the diadem of the Byzantine *basileus*.[47] The Umayyad Caliphate took full advantage to extend its power westwards. Abd al-Malik dispatched an expeditionary force of 40,000 soldiers under Hassan ibn Nu'man al-Ghassani to conquer North Africa.[48] The latter took Carthage in 695, the same year that Justinian II was deposed by Leontios, the *strategos* of the *Hellas* Theme, and banished to Cherson (in southern Crimea).[49] Leontios sent the *Kibyrrhaeot* fleet under *Patrikios* John to recover Carthage in 697. The latter actually accomplished his mission, but only because Hassan ibn Nu'man was distracted by a Berber uprising in the interior. Once the Umayyad general had successfully dealt with the insurrection, he chased the Byzantines off and reclaimed Carthage in 698.[50] The *Kibyrrhaeot* crews, fearing retribution for their failure from the notoriously unforgiving Leontios, murdered *Patrikios* John and named their own *droungarios*, Apsimaros, as emperor. With the help of the *Kibyrrhaeots*, the latter was able to depose Leontios and claim the throne for himself as Tiberios III.[51]

In the meantime, Hassan ibn Nu'man, recognizing the continued vulnerability of Carthage to Constantinople's sea power, elected to move the region's capital slightly inland to Tunis, located on a lake of the same name. Subsequently, Abd al-Aziz, the governor of Egypt and the caliph's brother, appointed Musa ibn Nusayr as governor of Ifriqiyah (north-central Africa) and sent a thousand Coptic shipwrights to construct a fleet. As a consequence, a canal was dug between the Gulf of Tunis and the Lake, permitting a new Arab arsenal to be built at Tunis. By 704 Musa's shipwrights had produced a hundred vessels, which he used to raid Sicily and Sardinia.[52] Worse yet for the Byzantines, Musa's maritime muscle allowed him to continue the Umayyad expansion westwards, exposing all the empire's western provinces to eventual conquest.

And Constantinople was helpless to prevent it. Palace disarray persisted. In 705 Justinian, having struck a marriage alliance with the Bulgar khan Tervel, used the latter's military support to seize the throne once again and executed both Leontios and Tiberios III. His erratic and murderously vindictive behaviour resulted in wholesale purges of key military officers and senseless aggression against his neighbours. When he ungratefully attacked Cherson, his former refuge during his exile, the whole of Crimea revolted and foisted an ousted general named Bardanes onto the throne as Philippikos. Justinian II was executed on 4 November 711.[53] While all this was going on, Musa moved inexorably across the Maghreb ('Land of the Setting Sun'), capturing Ceuta in 711. He then directed his lieutenant, Tariq ibn Zariq, to cross the strait between what the ancients called the 'Pillars of Hercules' (the headlands of modern Morocco and

Iberia) and begin the conquest of Visigothic Spain. Tariq landed with 12,000 troops on a monolithic limestone promontory that became known as *Jabal Tariq* ('Mountain of Tariq', i.e., Gibraltar), and soon extended Musa's control all the way to the Tagus river, establishing the al-Andalus – Muslim Spain.[54] Byzantium's grip on the western Mediterranean was broken forever.

Nonetheless, the Byzantine military establishment remained totally distracted by matters of imperial succession. In June 713 the army of the *Opsikion* Theme deposed Philippikos in favour of a *protosekretis* ('first notary' – head of the chancery) named Artemios, who assumed the title Anastasios II. To his credit, Anastasios became concerned about increasing Arab encroachment and ordered Constantinople's stores to be fully stocked and the city's walls repaired. He also commanded the construction of additional *dromōns* to stave off any intended Arab invasion. Unfortunately Anastasios precipitated his own undoing by ordering the same troops who had placed him on the throne to man these *dromōns* and confront the enemy. When he learned that an Umayyad fleet from Alexandria had landed at Lycia to harvest cypress trees (presumably to build ships), he dispatched a flotilla crewed by soldiers of the *Opsikion* Theme. These soon mutinied, however, and murdered their commander, John the Deacon. The *Opsikions* then conscripted a tax collector from Adramytion (modern Edremit), whom they ensconced in the imperial palace in November 715 as Theodosios III after a six-month siege by land and sea.[55]

The Second Siege of Constantinople and the Fall of the Umayyad Dynasty (717–50)

The continuing turmoil in Constantinople could not have gone unnoticed in Damascus. Earlier that same year Sulayman ibn Abd al-Malik assumed the caliphate and inaugurated his rule by propelling his brother, Maslamah ibn Abd al-Malik, into Asia Minor at the head of 80,000 troops, while a huge armada of reportedly 1,800 vessels made its way around the south coast.[56] Constantinople was about to experience its most dire confrontation with Islam until its final fall over seven centuries later.

The details of the ensuing epic engagement are discussed in a separate section at the end of the chapter as an example of sea combat in the period, but it suffices to say here that it unfolded in a manner similar to the siege of 672–8, with much the same result. As the Arab forces approached Constantinople in the spring of 717, Leo the Isaurian, the *strategos* of the *Anatolikon* Theme, engineered a coup to replace the ill-suited Theodosios III on the throne. Under his inspired leadership as Leo III, the Byzantines then used *dromōns* spewing 'Greek fire' to break up an Umayyad attempt to blockade the Bosporus. The besieging Arab army fared even worse. A particularly harsh winter ravaged it with deprivation and disease. And the following spring offered little relief. Nearly 800 supply ships arrived from Egypt and Ifriqiyah, but their Coptic Christian crews switched sides en masse. Without the precious provisions which these ships carried, Maslama's troops fell easy prey to the Bulgars of Khan Tervel, with whom Leo had formed a propitious alliance. The Bulgars butchered some 22,000 of the Arabs. Umar ibn Abd al-Aziz, the new caliph, had little choice but to recall his forces. It was a battered Umayyad army that retreated across Asia Minor in the autumn of 718 and only five vessels of the once massive Muslim armada managed to run the gauntlet of autumn storms in the Hellespont and Aegean to reach their home port.[57]

It was a disastrous Muslim defeat, which should have put Islam on the defensive for decades to come, but inexplicably Leo chose this time to delve into the religious controversy that was to be the bane of Byzantium. In 726 he inaugurated Iconoclasm (literally, 'the smashing of icons') by ordering the removal of the icon of Christ over the *Chalke* entrance to the imperial palace in Constantinople. In 730 he followed up this action with an imperial decree against all icons. This polemical policy was to rend the fabric of the empire for the next fifty-seven years. It proved particularly unpopular in Italy and the Aegean areas. In early 727 the fleets of the *Hellas* and Karabisian Themes revolted and proclaimed a certain Kosmas as emperor. Leo managed to devastate and disperse these fleets with his own, again using 'Greek fire', the secret of which was apparently restricted to Constantinople at the time.[58]

The episode, nonetheless, prompted the emperor to dissolve the troublesome Karabisian Theme and restructure the provincial fleets in order to dilute their threat to the throne. Leo placed the south coast of Asia Minor, formerly a responsibility of the disbanded Karabisian Theme, under the authority of the more tractable *droungarios* of the *Kibyrrhaeot* fleet, whose headquarters was transferred to Attaleia (present-day Antalya).[59] Land-based themes, like the *Hellas* and *Peloponnesos*, were also allowed to maintain fleets of their own.[60] These modifications to fleet organization were probably intended to help defuse naval power and make it more subservient to the emperor.

Despite their humiliating failure before the walls of Constantinople, the Umayyads took advantage of continued Byzantine upheaval both in the palace and in the Church to nibble away at the edges of the empire. A long period of raid and counter-raid ensued between Damascus and Constantinople, mostly involving either Egypt or Cyprus.[61] But ultimately the Byzantines' advantage in naval organization, possession of 'Greek fire' and virtual monopoly of such critical shipbuilding materials as wood and iron ensured they would prevail, at least in the eastern Mediterranean.[62] The climax of the contest came in 747, when the *Kibyrrhaeot* fleet surprised an enormous armada from Alexandria in a harbour on Cyprus called *Keramaia* (exact location unknown).[63] 'Out of 1,000 *dromōns* it is said only three escaped,' professed Theophanes.[64] This was undoubtedly a chauvinistic exaggeration, but Umayyad naval power was evidently broken by the outcome of the battle and never again posed a serious threat to the Byzantine Empire. The Umayyad Dynasty came to an end just three years later when the Abbasids led by Abu al-Abbas as-Saffah crushed Caliph Marwan II at the Battle of Zab (Mesopotamia) in late January 750. The subsequent Abbasid Caliphate moved its capital from Damascus to Baghdad and focused its initial attention on the East.[65]

Byzantium's Naval Resurgence amid Islamic Dissonance (751–826)

The Abbasid Caliphate's distraction with its eastern provinces allowed Islamic Spain and North Africa to become more autonomous. Constantinople's resurgence at sea only exacerbated the process by obstructing Baghdad's lines of communication with the West. As a result, it was powerless to prevent the establishment of the Umayyad Emirate of Cordoba in 756 by Abd al-Rahman, who had escaped Syria following the Abbasid victory at Zab.[66] By 800 Caliph Harun al-Rashid, lacking any naval capability of his own, was forced to concede the Maghreb (essentially north Africa west of Egypt) to Ibrahim ibn al-Aghlab, who subsequently founded the Aghlabid Dynasty of Kairouan (122km/76 miles south of Tunis).[67]

The fracturing of Islam in the Mediterranean meant that Muslim maritime power became decentralized and regional. Thus the only viable naval force on the Middle Sea in the latter half of the eighth century was that of Byzantium. 'Possessing such islands as Sicily, Crete, Cyprus, Sardinia and perhaps the Balearics, as well as all the most important strategic straits on the East–West trade routes,' comments Lewis, 'Constantinople's naval control could be strict and total, as its ships patrolled hostile coasts and prevented Byzantium's enemies from using the waters of the Mediterranean.'[68] While later historians such as Pryor contend that it was technologically impossible to impose 'strict and total control' of the sea lanes,[69] anecdotal evidence suggests that Byzantium was certainly able to discourage competition. The extent to which Constantinople now commanded the Middle Sea is indicated by the fact that the Muslim capitals of the late eighth century (Baghdad, Fustat, Kairouan and Cordoba) were all located inland. In recounting the events of the Maghreb in the year 752, Ibn al-Athir observed, 'The Rum [Byzantines] had put themselves in a state of readiness everywhere, had built strongholds and places of refuge; each year, their vessels cruised the coasts to ensure their security and more than once had captured Muslim merchant ships who had found themselves in their way.'[70] Moreover, the court of Constantinople effectively curtailed Muslim access to the markets of the Empire, thereby hampering the acquisition of such key shipbuilding materials as timber and iron.[71]

But the revival of Byzantine dominance at sea proved only a brief respite. The situation had begun to deteriorate dramatically by the end of the eighth century. First, there were reverses in Italy. The Lombards under King Aistulf captured Ravenna in 751, only to be supplanted by the Franks of Pepin the Short, who in 756 conferred Rome and the Exarchate of Ravenna upon the Pope. And, in a lasting blow to the prestige of the Eastern Emperor, Pope Leo III crowned Pepin's son Charlemagne as 'Holy Roman Emperor' on Christmas Day 800.[72]

At about the same time the Abbasids, having consolidated their authority in the East, began to exert pressure on the Empire. In 790 their Syrian fleet raided Cyprus, prompting an immediate response from the *Kibyrrhaeot* fleet. The two flotillas encountered each other in the Gulf of Antalya. The Syrians carried the day when they captured the Byzantine *strategos*, a certain Theophilos, whom they subsequently executed.[73] In 806 Theophanes reported that Harun al-Rashid flung a gargantuan force (300,000-strong) against Byzantine Bithynia, just east of the Propontis or Sea of Marmara. The Emperor Nikephoros I eventually bought him off with an annual tribute of 30,000 *nomismata*, but when he subsequently reneged on the deal the Abbasid caliph 'dispatched a fleet to Cyprus, destroyed the churches there, deported the Cypriots, and, by causing much devastation, violated the peace treaty'.[74]

Perceiving a weakened and vulnerable empire, Krum, Khan of the Bulgars, pounced on a Byzantine army at Strymon in Macedonia in 809 and utterly destroyed it.[75] Three years later he ambushed the imperial army led by Nikephoros himself in a mountain pass near Pliska, Bulgaria, and slaughtered it. Krum subsequently had the emperor beheaded.[76] 'After that,' testified Theophanes grimly, 'he bared the skull, riveted it on the outside with silver and, in his pride, made the chieftains of the Sklavinians [Slavic peoples of the Balkans] drink from it.'[77] Krum even attacked the outskirts of Constantinople itself in 813 before dying of a seizure in 814.[78]

Ultimately, however, it was the interminable internal strife that caused Constantinople to relinquish its hold on the seas. And, once again, the usual suspect was religious controversy. The Empress Irene had revoked iconoclasm in 787, but Leo V reinstituted it in 815, essentially to placate the iconoclastic eastern provinces that bore the brunt of Muslim pressure. Leo probably regarded the pronouncement as a pragmatic measure to shore up the empire militarily. Its unintended consequence, however, was to breed dissension and disunity. Most of the western themes remained staunchly iconodule (venerating images), so their loyalty to the court became tenuous at best. Thus when Thomas the Slav, a senior military commander from the *Anatolikon* Theme, took advantage of a murderous palace coup engineered by Michael II 'the Stammerer' to foment a revolt against Constantinople in 820, the Aegean provincial fleets and elements of the *Kibyrrhaeot* fleet quickly joined him.[79]

These fleets coalesced into a single force in the *Helladikon* (Hellas) Theme centred on Corinth, so that when Thomas began the siege of Constantinople in 821, it was readily available to answer his summons. 'Making the voyage, the fleet came quickly and anchored off a place called Berydes [location unknown, but presumably somewhere near the capital], three hundred and fifty warships and supply vessels in all,' reported John Skylitzes, an eleventh-century Byzantine historian. 'When the commanders of the imperial fleet learned of their arrival, they attacked by night while the enemy ships were riding at anchor,' continued Skylitzes, adding grimly, 'So sudden was the attack that they were able to capture several panic-stricken vessels, crews and all, and to burn the other ships with Greek fire.'[80] The rout effectively eviscerated the revolt. In the spring of 823 Michael II, in alliance with the Bulgar Khan Omurtag, scattered the remnants of Thomas the Slav's army and eventually executed him.[81]

The timing of these events could not have been worse for the empire. The destruction of the provincial fleets laid bare Byzantium's Mediterranean interests at a time when the various Islamic fleets were burgeoning in confidence and increasing their activity. Harun al-Rashid's Syrian fleets raided not only Cyprus but Rhodes as well (807).[82] Ibrahim ibn al-Aghlab of the Maghreb had already sent his fleets to plague the Peloponnesos, participating in the Slavic siege of Patras in 805.[83] But it was his son, Abu–l-Abbas Abd Allah who fashioned the Aghlabid navy into the fighting force that tormented the central Mediterranean with raids on Sardinia in 812–13 and again in 816–17 as well as an assault on Sicily in 819.[84] As Lewis ominously observed, 'The provincial fleets, scattered and burnt in the civil war, were badly needed to buttress Constantinople's slipping naval fortunes, as Syrian, North African and other maritime enemies gathered their strength.'[85]

Muslim Dominion in the Mediterranean (827–66)

Inevitably, Constantinople finally lost control of both the central and eastern Mediterranean almost simultaneously. Ironically, the first blow to Byzantine naval supremacy came from neither the Abbasids nor the Aghlabids, but originated in the al-Andalus of Umayyad Spain. In 814 Al-Hakam ibn Hisam ibn Abd-ar-Rahman I (Al-Hakam I), the emir of Cordoba, evicted some 10,000 rebellious *Muladi* (Andalusian Muslims). Many of these took ship under the direction of a corsair leader by the name of Abu Hafs Umar ibn Isa and made their way to Abbasid Egypt, where, in 816, they gained control of Alexandria. The Abbasid Caliph Abu Ja'far Abdullah al-Ma'mun ibn Harun (al-Ma'mun), however, forced them out of Alexandria in 827. From there, they landed on Crete, apparently unopposed. **(Pl. 7)** The destruction of the Aegean provincial fleets during the rebellion of Thomas the Slav had quite probably laid open the way. The Andalusian corsairs soon ensconced themselves in the fortified harbour of *Chandax* (modern Iraklion), from where they began raiding the entire Aegean.[86] Emperor Michael II launched three expeditions to root them out before his death in October 829, but all failed.[87] Many more attempts would be made, but Constantinople would not recover Crete until the middle of the tenth century. In the meantime, its Muslim masters held sway over a huge swathe of the southern Aegean, dominating such islands as Kos, Kythera and Karpathos while raiding the Cyclades at will. They probably even exerted authority over Cyprus and Rhodes.[88] Byzantine suzerainty over the eastern Mediterranean was in tatters.

This turn of events is what most likely prompted another realignment of Byzantine naval themes. In the early to mid-ninth century the court created the *Aigaion Pelagos* (Aegean Theme), which covered the northern Aegean including the Dardanelles and the Sea of Marmara.[89] The southern Aegean, which comprised the Cyclades, the Dodecanese and the Gulf of Kolpos, fell under the new Theme of Samos.[90] In fact, by the mid-ninth century the most powerful fleet by far was the *basilikon ploimon* (Imperial Fleet) commanded by a *droungarios tou ploimou*.[91] Its ships were mostly constructed at the imperial arsenal on the Golden Horn known as the *Neorion* and war galleys were specifically equipped in an adjacent facility called the *exartysis*.[92] Fleet numbers in terms of ships and manpower fluctuated over time depending upon the emperor and the need, but the relative size of the fleets can be estimated from the *De Cerimoniis Aulae Byzantinae*

('Concerning the Ceremonies of the Byzantine Court') of Constantine VII Porphyrogenitos, which described the failed expeditions to recover Crete in 911 and 949.[93] For example, as of 899 the Imperial Fleet was listed as having 19,600 oarsmen and 4,000 marines, compared to only 5,710 oarsmen and 1,000 marines for the *Kibyrrhaeot* fleet. The Aegean and Samos Themes were even smaller. The former numbered 2,600 sailors and 400 marines while the latter had 3,980 mariners plus 600 marines.[94] Initially, this reorganization of Byzantine maritime forces achieved only sporadic and ephemeral success that failed to stem Muslim marauding or provide Constantinople with a clear advantage over its Muslim adversaries at sea.

But if conditions turned challenging in the East, they became abysmal in the West at about the same time. Euphemios, the naval *tourmarches* (commander) of the Sicilian *thema*, gave the Aghlabids of the Maghreb the opportunity for which they had longed. In an acrimonious dispute with Constantine, the Byzantine *strategos* (governor), Euphemios offered to help the Aghlabid emir, Ziyadat Allah I, conquer the island in return for the governorship.[95] So in June 827 an Aghlabid army of around 10,000 infantry and 700 cavalry, transported by some seventy ships, stormed ashore at Mazara. It defeated a Byzantine contingent and drove across the island all the way to the walls of Syracuse.[96] There, pestilence in the Muslim camp and a relief fleet sent by Emperor Michael II in 829 stalled the invasion, but the process had begun and it was inexorable.[97] The Aghlabids, accompanied by a contingent of coreligionists from Andalusia, returned with an armada of nearly 300 ships the next year. They soon subjected Palermo to a suffocating siege, gaining its capitulation in August 831.[98] The capture of Palermo gave the Aghlabids a superb naval base from which they could raid the Calabrian coast of Italy and assault Messina. They took this latter port in 843, winning them control of the strategically vital strait of the same name.[99] 'From then on, the Hagarenes [Aghlabids] became masters not only of Sicily,' bleakly recounted John Skylitzes, 'but of Calabria and the greater part of Italy – where they overran and ravaged everything.'[100]

In actuality, the Muslim conquest of Sicily was a slow, grinding campaign that was not completed until the early years of the tenth century. The port of Cefalù on the north coast did not submit until 858 and the fortress of Castrogiovanni (modern Enna) in the centre of island was only captured in 859.[101] Syracuse endured repeated assaults, notably in 866 and 868, before ultimately succumbing in 878 to a strangling siege inflicted upon it by the island's Aghlabid emir, Ja'far ibn Muhammad.[102] Even then, the Val Demone region in the northeastern corner held on until 902, when Taormina finally fell.[103]

Muslim pirate depredations, however, plagued the Italian peninsula concurrent with the ongoing conquest of Sicily. In 840 a 'Saracen' flotilla captained by an Aghlabid corsair called Saba (Sahib al-Ustul) captured Taranto and converted it into a pirate base for raiding the entire region.[104] A few years later a Berber leader named Kalfun did the same thing with Bari, which officially became an Arab emirate under one of his successors, a man known in Christian chronicles as

Sawdan.[105] These were essentially enclaves of Muslim *ghazi* (raiders) who committed *razzia* (raids) on nearby Christian lands. Plundering expeditions emanating from Bari, a former Byzantine bastion on the Adriatic, became so savage and incessant that Erchempert, a ninth-century monk of Montecassino, was compelled to comment that, 'During that time the Agarenes [North African Muslims] dwelling in Bari began to devastate the land, plundering all of Apulia and Calabria, and started step-by-step to depopulate Salerno as well as Benevento.'[106] Not even Rome itself was spared. In 847 a huge Muslim force of 11,000 men and 500 horses sailed up the Tiber on seventy-three ships and ravaged all the way to the walls of Rome, plundering St Peter's Basilica in the process.[107]

Constantinople made an effort to stem the malevolent tide, only to suffer disheartening results. Emperor Theophilos inveigled the Venetians into sending a sixty-ship flotilla against the Aghlabids of Taranto in 841, but it was vanquished in the Ionian by Saba.[108] In 859 the court dispatched a 300-vessel fleet of its own, presumably to recapture Cefalù on the north coast of Sicily, but it was waylaid by an Aghlabid armada west of Messina and destroyed.[109] A Byzantine fleet successfully relieved Syracuse in 868, but another failed to arrive in time to save the city in 878 due to unfavourable winds.[110] And, of course, there was nothing to stop the Aghlabids of North Africa from making Malta theirs in 870, gaining command of the Sicilian Channel in the process.[111] The problem was that Byzantium could not maintain much of a naval presence in the region. There were just too many distractions. Aside from almost constant pressure from the Abbasids of Syria and Egypt, raids by the Andalusian pirates of Crete continued unabated. And, as if that were not enough, in June 860 the Varangian Rus launched 200 vessels against the capital in the first of a series of assaults which would recur time and again for most of the next two centuries.[112] Thus Constantinople seemed virtually powerless to prevent Muslim pre-eminence on the Middle Sea. No wonder the great fourteenth-century Muslim scholar, Ibn Khaldun, was inspired to proclaim:

> The Christian nations withdrew their fleets to the northeastern side of the Mediterranean, to the coastal regions inhabited by the European Christians and the Slavs, and to the Aegean islands, and did not go beyond them. The Muslim fleet had pounced upon them as eagerly as lions upon their prey. They covered most of the surface of the Mediterranean with their equipment and numbers and travelled its lanes [on missions both] peaceful and warlike. Not a single Christian board floated on it.[113]

Renewed Byzantine Maritime Mastery under Basil the Macedonian (867–86)

Slowly, fitfully, this began to change in 867 with the accession of Basil I, first of the great Macedonian emperors. The loss of the empire's western possessions evidently convinced Basil to bolster Byzantium's naval capability. It was most likely under his administration that several of the more significant refinements to Byzantine fleet organization occurred, particularly in regard to the Imperial

Fleet. For instance, the appointment of a *droungarios tou ploimou* was probably at his behest. He almost certainly recruited the contingent of 4,000 professional marines to serve on the decks of the Imperial Fleet's warships. And Basil is also credited with creating the Samos naval theme to guard the southern Aegean.[114] At the same time Islam began to experience fragmentation. In 868 Ahmad ibn Tulun, a Turkish deputy to the Abbasid governor of Egypt, assumed power from the latter and rapidly extended his authority up the Levant, thus giving rise to the Tulunid Dynasty. The Tulunids maintained fleets in both Egypt and Syria while rebuffing all attempts by Baghdad to bring them to heel until the beginning of the ninth century.[115] It was an unwanted distraction for the Abbasids, who were consequently forced to relax the pressure on the empire's eastern borders. Basil was quick to take advantage.

The emperor began to wield his maritime might almost as soon as he assumed the purple. He dispatched the fleet which successfully relieved the Aghlabid siege of Syracuse in 868, despite having to battle Arab *harraqas* (fireships). That same year Basil sent a second flotilla, numbering a hundred ships under the *droungarios* Niketas Ooryphas, to stave off yet another siege, this one of Ragusa on the Dalmatian coast. Basil then formed the *Thema* of Dalmatia and in 869 ordered naval contingents from Ragusa and the northern Dalmatian coast to assist the German emperor Louis II in the blockade of Muslim-held Bari, which was finally taken in 871.[116] Five years later, when Bari was again imperilled by Muslim marauders, the Eastern Empire occupied the city outright, making it the Byzantine bastion of what would eventually become the Theme of *Longobardia* (Apulia).[117]

Nor did Basil neglect imperial interests in the East. Again he relied on the highly effective *droungarios tou ploimou* of the Imperial Fleet, Niketas Ooryphas, to assert Byzantine authority over eastern waters. When the Arabs of Crete assaulted the Hellespont (Dardanelles) in 873, Niketas caught them off Kardia on the Thracian Chersonese (the Gallipoli peninsula) and, according to John Skylitzes, 'promptly disposed of twenty Cretan ships with "Greek fire", dispatching the barbarians in them with the sword or by fire and water'.[118] Unrepentant, the Cretan raiders returned the following year to ravage the west coast of the Peloponnesos, and once again Niketas was sent out to meet them. When he reached Kenchreai (the port of Corinth on the Aegean side of the isthmus), he learned that the Muslim fleet was entering the Gulf of Corinth from the west. Realizing that he did not have enough time to circumnavigate the Peloponnesian peninsula, the *droungarios* had his seamen portage their ships across the isthmus directly into the gulf. The surprise of the Arabs was total and their defeat absolute. Their commander was executed outright while many of the captured crews were either 'flayed alive' or dunked in 'boiling pitch'.[119]

Niketas' successor, Nasar, picked up where Niketas left off. When Abu Ishaq Ibrahim II ibn Ahmad, the Aghlabid emir of Ifriqiyah, dispatched a fleet in 880 to harry the islands of Cephalonia and Zakynthos in the Ionian, Basil responded by sending Nasar with forty-five warships. Employing the riskiest of tactics, a night attack, the *droungarios* surprised the Aghlabid squadron near Methone (modern

Methoni in the southwestern Peloponnesos) and annihilated it. Sensing an opportunity, he then sailed on to Sicily, raiding the environs of Palermo. On the way back to Constantinople, he hooked up with Prokopios, a *protovestiarios* ('First Servant of the Imperial Wardrobe' – a high-ranking financial official), and Leo Apostypes, the commander of the Thracian and Macedonian themes, in Calabria and helped them reduce several Muslim-held enclaves, winning a naval victory off Punta di Stilo in the process. Leo Apostypes subsequently liberated Taranto from its Muslim masters.[120] A few years later Basil appointed the *Domestikos ton Scholon* ('Domestic of the Schools' – essentially a military commander-in-chief) Nikephoros Phokas as commander of his forces in *Longobardia*. The latter succeeded in reasserting imperial authority in much of Apulia and Calabria.[121]

Byzantine Naval Treatises and the Plague of Muslim Piracy (887–959)

Byzantine fortunes ebbed for a time after Basil's more bookish son, Leo VI (given the sobriquet 'the Philosopher'), inherited the crown of Constantinople in 886. A series of reverses to imperial naval power marked his reign. In the West, an entire Byzantine fleet was vanquished off Milazzo, Sicily in 888 and Reggio was subsequently sacked by the victorious Muslim squadron.[122] The western Mediterranean also saw the formation of fresh Muslim pirate enclaves. Around 890 Andalusian corsairs from Pechina near Almeria captured the mountain fortress of Fraxinetum (modern La Garde-Freinet) above St-Tropez, from where they would torment the northeast Tyrrhenian and control the Alpine passes between Italy and France for decades.[123] A few years earlier (around 882) Aghlabid raiders from North Africa had established a pirate nest at the mouth of the Garigliano river near Gaeta.[124] The Garigliano Arabs not only afflicted the coastal areas of Campania and Latium, but were responsible for one of the worst desecrations of the era: the despoilment of Montecassino in October 883 which left the revered monastery in flames.[125] Lastly, in 902 the Aghlabid emir Ibrahim II ibn Ahmad completed the Muslim conquest of Sicily by taking Taormina amid a display of wanton slaughter. Ibrahim II then crossed the Strait of Messina to reduce Reggio, routing another Byzantine flotilla under Eustathios, the *strategos* of Calabria, in the process.[126]

More serious still were events in the East. A Muslim flotilla operating out of Tarsus in Cilicia under a certain Raghib vanquished a squadron of the *Kibyrrhaeot* fleet in 898 off the south coast of Asia Minor. Many vessels were captured and some 3,000 Byzantine seamen lost their heads.[127] Constantinople's resultant weakness in those waters invited the depredations of Leo of Tripoli, a captured *Kibyrrhaeot* seaman who had converted to Islam. Leo plundered Abydos on the Dardanelles in 904, and then unleashed an awful onslaught on Thessaloniki. During the siege some sixty ships hurled flaming projectiles (presumably pots of 'Greek fire') over the walls. The outcome was devastating. The city was demolished, thousands were slain, and an eyewitness, John Kaminates, claimed 22,000 prisoners were carried off into slavery.[128] **(Pl. 8)**

Lacking the martial mentality of his father, Leo the Philosopher responded in the only way he knew how: intellectually. Around 905 he composed the *Taktika*, the first of a series of treatises on warfare which were to counsel imperial *strategoi* for centuries to come. Constitution XIX of the manual, *Naumachika Leontos Basileos* ('Concerning the naval warfare of the Emperor Leo'), contained comprehensive guidance on the construction, manning and deployment of imperial warships. Included were extensive instructions for the conduct of battle at sea. Formations, weaponry and tactics were all discussed in some detail. Leo himself never led military forces in the field or at sea. His guidelines were derived from ancient manuals and advice offered by experienced military *strategoi*.[129] Nonetheless, the *Naumachika* proved pragmatic and useful enough to spawn similar treatises on the conduct of warfare at sea. For instance, in 960 the *Patrikios* and *Parakoimenos* (Grand Chamberlain) Basil, a bastard son of Emperor Romanos I Lekapenos, commissioned a naval manual which described Byzantine ships and their various components in depth.[130] Towards the end of the tenth century Nikephoros Ouranos, governor of Antioch under Basil II, used Leo's work as a template for his own tome on naval tactics, which focused on various battle formations and stratagems.[131] Leo's son Constantine VII Porphyrogenitos ('Born to the Purple') also contributed to his father's legacy on the conduct of naval warfare: Chapters 44 and 45 of Book II of his *De Cerimoniis Aulae Byzantinae* ('Book of Ceremonies') specifies the ships and equipment supplied for the expeditions to liberate Crete in 911 and 949, as well as a martial mission to *Longobardia* in 935.[132] He also wrote or commissioned the *De Administrando Imperio* ('Concerning Imperial Administration'), which prescribes the outfitting of the imperial galley in Chapter 51.[133] Lastly, Leo VI, Constantine VII and Nikephoros Ouranos all seem to have used as a source the *Naumachiai* ('Naval Battles') of a certain Syrianos Magistros from the ninth century, which delineated the duties of a naval commander.[134]

No one knows how closely these treatises were consulted, but their existence seems to have coincided with yet another revival of Byzantine maritime ascendancy. Most of this activity occurred in the East, although Nikolas Picingli, the *strategos* of *Longobardia*, notably used his fleet to participate in the papal coalition that wiped out the Garigliano pirates' nest in 915.[135] A Byzantine flotilla also assisted Hugh of Provence in destroying much of the Muslim pirate fleet of Fraxinetum in 941.[136] In the eastern Mediterranean, the centre of concern remained the corsairs of Crete. Emperor Leo himself dispatched *Patrikios* Himerios to attack the island in 911, despite the distraction caused by yet another attack of the Kievan Rus on the capital. The emperor bought off the Rus, but Leo of Tripoli ambushed Himerios off Samos with 300 ships in 912 and vanquished his fleet.[137] Retribution, however, would come in the person of Romanos I Lekapenos, a former *droungarios tou ploimou* who took the purple in 920 and seems to have engineered a renaissance of imperial naval prowess. When Leo of Tripoli led his fleet into the Aegean in 923, the *Patrikios* John Rhadenos, *droungarios* of the Imperial Fleet, caught the apostate corsair moored off Lemnos and finally ended his career.[138]

The Rus were back again in 941, this time with a massive armada of some one thousand vessels under the command of Igor, Grand Prince of Kiev, but the

Protovestiarios Theophanes employed a mere fifteen vessels bearing 'Greek fire' to set the Rus fleet ablaze in the Bosporus. The remnants of the Rus ships escaped back to the Black Sea, but were eventually hunted down and destroyed by the Imperial Fleet.[139] Another Byzantine attempt was made on Crete in 949 but ended in a débâcle shortly after coming ashore when the expedition commander, Constantine Gongyles, a palace eunuch appointed by Constantine VII, failed to fortify his camp. The understrength force was all but wiped out by a surprise attack.[140] According to the *Theophanes Continuatus*, a tenth-century series of works continuing the chronicle of Theophanes the Confessor, the path to success was finally cleared in 956 when Basil Hexamilites, the *strategos* of the *Kibyrrhaeot* fleet, won a crushing victory off Lycia over a Muslim flotilla from Tarsus,[141] making it possible for Constantinople to mount yet another undertaking against Crete.

Byzantium Regains its Grip on the Eastern Mediterranean (960–9)

Constantine's son and successor Romanos II took no chances this time. Instead of an incompetent court official, he chose the brilliant field commander Nikephoros Phokas – the new *Domestikos ton Scholon* of the East – to lead the enterprise. Nikephoros and his brother Leo Phokas had already won several key victories in Syria against the great Hamdanid general and emir of Aleppo, Sayf al-Dawla ('Sword of the [Abbasid] Dynasty').[142] And Romanos made certain that Nikephoros would have overwhelming force at his disposal. Estimates vary from 250 warships, some equipped with disembarkation ramps, to well over 3,000 vessels carrying as many as 77,000 men, but there can be little doubt that the amphibious force which landed on Crete in the summer of 960 dwarfed the previous two.[143] Nikephoros deployed it without delay in a strangling siege of *Chandax* (Iraklion), using the ships to form a tight blockade on the seaward side while his soldiers constructed a palisade around the land walls. He subsequently surrounded and slaughtered a huge contingent of some 40,000 Muslim troops sent to surprise his encampment.[144] 'The next day, as soon as the sun rose above the horizon and began to climb towards the vault of heaven,' wrote Leo the Deacon, a tenth-century palace historian, 'Nikephoros ordered his men to impale some barbarian heads on spears and set them up in a row next to the wall he had built, and to hurl others at the town with stone-throwing machines.'[145] The Muslims of *Chandax* held on throughout the winter, nonetheless. While the siege ground on, Sayf al-Dawla attempted to take advantage by invading Cappadocia in Asia Minor, but Nikephoros' brother Leo ambushed him at Adrassos in the Taurus Mountains and annihilated his army. Nikephoros finally brought his undertaking to a close in the spring when his sappers breached the walls of *Chandax* and Byzantine soldiers overran the city amid the customary carnage.[146]

Having ascended the imperial dais upon the unexpected death of Romanos II, Nikephoros followed up his signal success on Crete with an ambitious campaign to reclaim Cilicia, which culminated in the triumphant taking of the strategic port of Tarsus in 965. That same year he dispatched the *Patrikios* Chalkoutzes to return Cyprus to Constantinople's control as well.[147] Nikephoros even saw Antioch restored to the empire in 969.[148] A new era had dawned in the East. As A.R. Lewis cogently observed, 'Byzantium's conquest of Crete, Cyprus, Cilicia and Northern Syria reversed the basic maritime picture in the Mediterranean.'[149]

And once again the Byzantines were aided in their endeavours by dissension within the ranks of their Islamic adversaries. The Fatimids, whose founder Abdullah al-Mahdi Billah claimed descent from Muhammad's daughter Fatimah, had seized power from the Aghlabids in Ifriqiyah in 909 and established Mahdiyah (on the east coast of modern Tunisia) as their capital. In 969 this aggressive Shia caliphate unleashed its great general, Jawhar ibn Abdullah (al-Siqilli – 'the Sicilian'), to conquer Egypt from the Ikhshidids, a dynasty descended from the Turkish slave Muhammad ibn Tughj al-Ikhshid, who had usurped rule of the Nile region from the Abbasids of Baghdad in 935. Jawhar succeeded and founded a new capital at Cairo (from the Arabic *al-Qahira*, meaning 'the Victorious'), from which the Fatimids sought to extend their authority from the Atlantic to the Red Sea and beyond, mostly at the expense of their Muslim coreligionists.[150]

Byzantine Recovery in the West thwarted by Chaos in the East (970–1014)

That said, long supply lines and delayed communication made progress in the West considerably more challenging for Constantinople. When Nikephoros II Phokas set out to win the East back for Romania in 965, he directed his nephew, the *Patrikios* Manuel, to do the same in the West. Specifically, Manuel's mission was the reconquest of Sicily from its 'Saracen' overlords. To accomplish this, John Skylitzes attested the emperor assigned him 'an army and navy of considerable size'.[151] Ibn al-Athir claimed the force included over 40,000 combatants,[152] while Leo the Deacon described the fleet as composed of 'firebearing triremes' and 'large merchantmen'.[153] The *droungarios* of the fleet was a eunuch named Niketas. The expedition went well enough at first. Syracuse, Himera, Taormina and Lentini were all subdued with relative ease, according to Leo the Deacon, but the operation soon turned into a débâcle when the 'hot-headed and self-willed' Manuel led his army into an ambush in the rocky highlands around Rometta (12km/7.5 miles west of Messina).[154] He and most of his land forces were obliterated. Leo the Deacon recounted that his Arab assailants then rushed to the coast where the armada was anchored and captured the lot, including the *droungarios* Niketas,[155] but Arab sources asserted that a Fatimid fleet destroyed the Byzantine armada near Messina in a fierce fight they called the 'Battle of the Strait'.[156] Either way it was an unmitigated disaster for Constantinople.

Moreover, internal and external disruption in the East prevented the court of Constantinople from following up the débâcle in any meaningful way for the remainder of the century. In December 969 one of Nikephoros' best generals, John Tzimiskes, colluded in the emperor's murder and then promptly had the imperial diadem placed upon his own head.[157] John's brief reign was anything but restful. He spent the first several months dealing with the ambitious expansion plans of Prince Svyatoslav of Kiev. After his 'Domestic of the East', Bardas

Skleros, defeated the Rus at Arcadiopolis in the spring of 970, Tzimiskes used the Imperial Fleet to strangle Svyatoslav into submission at Dorostolon (modern Silistra) on the Danube.[158] All this was accomplished while suppressing a revolt in Anatolia fomented by Nikephoros' disaffected relatives.[159] Towards the end of his rule the emperor once again directed his efforts towards the East. The rebellious Shia Qarmatians of Damascus had diverted the attention of both the Abbasids and the Fatimids. Tzimiskes took advantage in order to subject the Emirate of Mosul to tribute and press into southern Syria as far as Tripoli. It was upon his return from this last campaign that he fell ill and died in 976.[160]

His successor, Basil II, was besieged by even more upheaval. He had no sooner assumed the purple than he suffered the first of two revolts that would dominate the initial dozen years or so of his rule. Bardas Skleros declared himself emperor and marched on Constantinople. He even managed to recruit the *Kibyrrhaeot* fleet, which ravaged the Aegean islands and threatened the Dardanelles before the Imperial Fleet decimated it with 'Greek fire' off Phocaea (modern Foça on the west coast of Asia Minor). Skleros was eventually defeated in 979 by another leading general, Bardas Phokas, who in turn also revolted in 987.[161] Aside from personal aspirations of power, both men appear to have been motivated by resentment over the court's attempts to preclude the landed aristocracy of the eastern border areas from gobbling up the small land-owners upon which the imperial army and navy depended. Military duty was tied to the land: each parcel entailed a *strateia* or 'obligation to serve'.[162] The Skleros and Phokas families were two of the wealthiest land-holding dynasties of eastern Anatolia. Basil himself finally suppressed this last insurrection in 989 when he confronted Phokas at Chrysopolis across the Bosporus from Constantinople. The latter died on the battlefield of an apparent seizure and his followers fled.[163]

The turmoil brought about by over a decade of insurgency had, however, severely weakened the empire, making it a tempting target for its enemies. Thousands of its troops had perished in the fighting, its provincial fleets were in tatters and famine ruled the countryside.[164] The Bulgarians seized the initiative even before the last uprising had been quelled. In 986 Samuel, the 'Tsar of the Bulgarian Empire', enticed Basil into battle by capturing Larissa in Thessaly, then trapped him at Trajan's Gate (a mountain pass near Ihtiman, Bulgaria) and massacred most of his army. The emperor escaped, but it was a humiliation he would never forget.[165] Basil struggled sporadically with Samuel's Bulgars for the better part of the next two decades, amid constant distraction, principally from the Fatimids in the East.

In 995 Caliph Abu Mansur Nizar al-Aziz bi-Allah had directed the construction of an immense fleet of some 600 ships at the Misr shipyard near Fustat in order to assert Cairo's control of the Syrian coast. A fire, supposedly set by Byzantine spies, destroyed the arsenal that same year, but the Fatimids were still able to float a force formidable enough to defeat one of Basil's flotillas off Tyre in 998 and supply Tripoli by sea despite an ongoing Byzantine siege.[166] Fatimid strength in the region compelled the emperor to personally command several campaigns to shore up Byzantine holdings in Syria. On one occasion in 995 he even resorted to the extravagant measure of providing two mules to each of his 17,000 troops so that he could move his entire expeditionary force to Aleppo in just sixteen days in order to relieve a Fatimid siege of the city.[167] The struggle soon devolved into a stalemate, however, with the Fatimids maintaining suzerainty over the Syrian shores, thanks to their naval presence.

But for Basil the Bulgarian threat was ever-present and dominant. Samuel's seizure of Durazzo in 1000 even prompted the emperor to give Doge Pietro II Orseolo of Venice a free hand in dealing with the Dalmatian coast, a haven for Croatian pirates. The doge subsequently pacified Dalmatia, rendering it a sort of protectorate under Byzantine suzerainty.[168] Finally exasperated by the interminable conflict with the Bulgars, Basil cornered Samuel at the palisaded pass of Kleidion in the summer of 1014 and butchered his army. Samuel himself eluded capture and made his way to Prilep (in modern Macedonia). But Basil had the 15,000 Bulgar soldiers he had captured in the battle blinded, leaving one out of every hundred with one eye in order to lead the others to Prilep. Samuel reportedly suffered a heart attack at the sight of his mutilated men and died two days later. Basil subsequently bore the title *Bulgaroctonus*, meaning 'Bulgar-Slayer'.[169]

Byzantium's Failure to Recapture Sicily despite Muslim Fragmentation (1015–41)

These protracted struggles in the East meant that the emperor neglected the West. As a consequence, the Kalbites, who had ruled Sicily ever since the Fatimid Caliph had appointed Hassan al-Kalbi as the island's emir in 948, began to raid Byzantine possessions in southern Italy almost incessantly. Some of these incursions were of menacing magnitude. When Constantine VII dispatched *Patrikios* Malakenos with a large fleet to southern Italy in 950, Hassan al-Kalbi responded by seeking the support of the Fatimid Caliph al-Mansur bi-Allah, who sent to Calabria an armada large enough to carry 7,000 cavalry and 3,500 infantry. This force dealt Malakenos a resounding defeat at Gerace in 952.[170] The raiding continued unabated. In the 970s Emir Abu l-Qasim crossed the Strait of Messina on several occasions to wreak havoc in both Calabria and Apulia, assailing such towns as Cosenza, Taranto, Gravina, Oria and Otranto. The German emperor Otto II, considering these depredations as assaults on western imperial territory, led a sizeable force of Bavarians and Swabians into southern Italy to confront the 'Saracens' in the autumn of 981. He found them the next summer near Stilo in Calabria. Abu l-Qasim had once again led his army across the strait on a massive foray. Otto was routed, however, and barely managed to escape on a passing *chelandion*, leaving the flower of German and Lombard nobility on the field of battle.[171]

Nonetheless, the continuing dissolution of the Muslim polity in the Mediterranean gave the Byzantine *basileus* the needed window of opportunity to rectify matters in the West. When the Fatimid Caliph Abu Tamin Ma'add al-Mu'izz li-Din Allah moved his capital to Cairo in 973, he appointed Buluggin ibn Ziri of the Sanhaja Berbers as viceroy for Ifriqiyah. By the early eleventh century the resultant Zirid Dynasty of Kairouan had, to all intents and purposes, become autonomous.[172] In the same general time frame the disintegration of the Caliphate of Cordoba into warring *taifas* (literally 'factions' in Arabic) spelled the demise of Umayyad sea power in the Tyrrhenian.[173] And, concurrently, dynastic discord among the Kalbites resulted in a similar breakdown of authority on Sicily. The island had been rife with rebellion and civil strife ever since Emir Yusuf al-Kalbi suffered a stroke in 998.[174] Basil II saw his chance and in 1025 dispatched his loyal eunuch, the *Protospatharios* ('First Sword-bearer' – a high court dignity) Orestes Kytonitos, with a large fleet and ground force to secure the deliverance of Sicily from the 'Saracens'. The magnitude of the threat was evidently menacing enough to induce Ahmad al-Akhal, the Kalbite emir of Palermo, to seek succour from his Zirid counterpart in Kairouan, al-Mu'izz ibn Badis. The latter answered the appeal with a 400-ship armada, but it was shredded by a storm off the island of Pantelleria. As fate would have it, however, the 67-year-old Byzantine emperor succumbed to illness before he could join the expedition and it soon fell apart.[175]

Hardly a decade later, renewed Kalbite factionalism would give Constantinople another opening to intervene on Sicily. According to John Skylitzes, the court of Michael IV successfully negotiated an alliance with Emir al-Akhal around 1035. His brother Abu Hafs then rebelled and sought the aid of the Zirids of Ifriqiyah. Al-Mu'izz responded by sending his son Abd 'Allah ibn al-Mu'izz at the head of an army which soon defeated the Kalbite emir, prompting the latter to beseech the military support of his Byzantine allies. So Emperor Michael 'the Paphlagonian' ordered the renowned general Giorgios Maniakes, the former governor of Edessa, to prepare an invasion force.[176] At the same time the court took advantage of growing Fatimid dissatisfaction with their Zirid clients to conclude a treaty with the Caliphate of Cairo in which the latter agreed not to interfere.[177] As it happened, al-Akhal was deposed and assassinated in Palermo before Maniakes could come to his aid, but the die was cast.[178] Maniakes came ashore in 1038 at the head of a fearsome expeditionary force, which included Varangians commanded by the redoubtable Harald Hardrada (later king of Norway) and a formidable contingent of 300 Norman knights led by the bellicose Hauteville brothers: William, Drogo and Humphrey. **(Pl. 9)** Maniakes rapidly mastered Messina and rolled over a Muslim army at Rometta to the southwest. He eventually drove on to secure Syracuse, along with several other cities. Reeling, 'Abd Allah sent for additional reinforcements from Ifriqiyah. The two armies clashed on a plain near Troina, west of Mount Etna, in 1040. The result was an overwhelming victory for the Christian coalition, due apparently in no small part to the courageous cavalry charges of the Normans. But it sowed the seeds for the ultimate unravelling of the undertaking.[179]

First of all, Maniakes alienated his highly effective Norman allies with what they perceived was an inequitable distribution of the spoils. The Normans expressed their ardent dissatisfaction by immediately abandoning the enterprise and returning to southern Italy.[180] Secondly, and more seriously, Maniakes, incensed that the admiral of the fleet (Stephen 'the Caulker') had allowed 'Abd

Allah to escape by ship, publicly humiliated the man with verbal and physical abuse. This proved not only intemperate, but also unwise: Stephen was the Emperor Michael's brother-in-law. The vindictive Stephen soon accused Maniakes of conspiracy against the crown. The hot-headed general was recalled to Constantinople and, without his firm leadership, the effort to reconquer the island quickly bogged down. By the end of 1041 it had collapsed altogether, enabling the Muslims to rapidly reclaim all the Christian gains.[181]

Constantinople would never again pose a credible threat to Muslim Sicily – or, for that matter, to any Islamic holdings in the western Mediterranean. Subsequent emperors would allow Byzantine sea power to languish and atrophy. In his *Chronographia*, the Byzantine court historian Michael Psellos wrote that, during the last great Rus assault on Constantinople by sea in 1043, the Emperor Constantine IX Monomachus was forced to assemble 'some hulks of the old fleet' to combat the vessels from Kiev because his own 'naval forces were below strength'.[182] Thus, while imperial warships rotted in the harbour, the empire's maritime defence needs were delegated to such self-interested proxies as the Venetians, who grew wealthy and powerful thanks to generous trade concessions granted them by the court in payment for their services at sea. This did not mean, however, that Islamic sea power would return to pre-eminence or even that Muslim Sicily was safe. Constant internecine warfare among a growing number of competing Muslim dynasties would enervate Islamic naval capability and make it vulnerable to external maritime pressure. And that pressure would come not from the East, but from the West. More specifically in the case of Sicily, it would come from the men of northwestern France – men more accustomed to horses and hauberks than ships and sails. But these men were relentlessly ambitious and extremely adaptable. They had learned much about amphibious assault operations from their erstwhile Byzantine allies during Maniakes' ill-fated invasion of the island, especially in regard to the transportation of their battle-winning mounts by sea. After all, the Normans were descended from Vikings.

* * *

Exemplary Engagement: The Siege of Constantinople (717–18)

The conquest of Constantinople had been a desideratum of Islam from its inception and an obsession of the Umayyad Caliphate of Damascus since the catastrophic failure of its first attempt on the Byzantine capital in 672–8. Byzantium stood in the way of relentless Arab expansion westwards. In the early years of the eighth century Caliph al-Walid ibn al-Malik saw his chance. When troops from the *Opsikion* Theme deposed Emperor Philippikos and replaced him with *Protosekretis* (chief secretary) Artemios as Anastasios II on 3 June 713, it was the fifth violent regime change the empire had endured in just eighteen years.[183] Early in 714 Caliph al-Walid asked his brother Maslamah ibn Abd al-Malik to lay the groundwork for an all-out invasion. That same year the latter led a devastating expedition into Anatolia as far as Galatia (north-central Anatolia) in the *Opsikion* Theme, which was just to the east of the capital.[184] The incursion so alarmed Anastasios that he dispatched *Patrikios* Daniel Sinopites to Damascus to gather intelligence under the guise of negotiating a truce. When Daniel reported back that the caliph was bent on conquest and was amassing a huge invasion force, the emperor initiated defensive preparations without delay. He ordered the city's walls repaired and its towers fortified with catapults and other military machinery designed to repel a siege.[185] He also directed that each inhabitant stock three-years' worth of provisions. And, more crucially as it turns out, he 'appointed overseers and started building dromones, (fire-carrying) biremes (and great triremes)', according to Theophanes the Confessor, the main Greek source for the event.[186]

Caliph al-Walid died unexpectedly on 25 February 715, but his death offered the empire no reprieve. His brother Sulayman ibn Abd al-Malik immediately assumed the reins of power and continued preparations for the conquest. So when Anastasios learned that an Arab fleet from Alexandria had moored at Phoinix in Lycia on the south-central coast of Asia Minor with the apparent intention of harvesting cypress trees for building more ships, the emperor 'chose the swiftest vessels of his own fleet, manned them with soldiers of the *Opsikion* Theme, and ordered that they should all assemble at Rhodes'.[187] His choice of ships' crew, however, proved fateful. Once at Rhodes, the *Opsikions* revolted and scuttled the mission by murdering their commander, *Patrikios* John the Logothete. They then sailed to Adramytion on the west coast of Asia Minor where they found a hapless tax collector named Theodosios and proclaimed him as their leader. After recruiting the rest of the *Opsikion* Theme and many more ships, the rebels managed to depose Anastasios in November 715 after a six-month siege of the capital, placing on the throne in his stead their own man as Theodosios III.[188] Fortunately for the future of the empire, Anastasios had previously appointed as *strategos* of the all-important *Anatolikon* Theme the man who would ultimately save Byzantium: Leo the Isaurian.[189]

The appointment could not have been more propitious. Early in 716 Maslamah began his march on Constantinople at the head of a massive force, estimated to be as many as 120,000 men by some sources. But Leo's *Anatolikon* Theme was right in the path of the invading Arab army. Maslamah sent an advance corps under one of his generals, Sulayman ibn Mu'ad, to clear the way through central Anatolia, while he had another lieutenant, Umar ibn Hubaira, bring an enormous fleet (some 1,800 vessels according to both Theophanes and Nikephoros) along the Cilician coast.[190] In the spring Sulayman arrived at Amorion in central Anatolia and apparently attempted to suborn Leo into some sort of alliance against Theodosios in return for Leo's installation on the throne as the caliphate's puppet. Leo, who was actually not Isaurian but Syrian and thus Arab-speaking, seems to have played along, offering promises of support for the conquest that he had no intention of keeping. Instead, he installed a garrison of 800 men in Amorion, preventing its capture, and escaped to Pisidia (south-central Anatolia). Having been thus duped, Sulayman was forced to retire.[191]

Leo then entered into a union with Artabasdos, the *strategos* of the *Armeniakon* Theme, to whom he promised the hand of his daughter Anna in marriage.[192] Supported by the troops of both the *Anatolikon* and *Armeniakon* Themes, he advanced on Constantinople. At Nicomedia (modern Izmit) Leo chanced upon Theodosios' son with an entourage of court dignitaries. Taking them into his custody, he proceeded to Chrysopolis (modern Üsküdar), across the Bosporus from the capital, and initiated negotiations with Theodosios as well as the Patriarch Germanus and the senate. In the meantime Maslamah rendezvoused with Sulayman in central Anatolia, where he learned of Leo's duplicity. Furious, Maslamah attacked Akroinon (modern Afyon Karahisar) before continuing on to Lydia (the old Roman province of Asia) in southwestern Asia Minor, where he wintered. Umar supposedly wintered the fleet on the coast of Cilicia and it seems likely that Sulayman joined him there.[193]

By the early spring of 717 Leo had managed to convince Theodosios, with the eager consent of the patriarch and the senate, that his and the empire's interests would best be served by his abdication in return for immunity from harm. Accordingly, Leo then entered the city through the Golden Gate and was crowned Emperor Leo III in the Sancta Sophia on 25 March 717. Soon thereafter Artabasdos was married to Anna and rewarded with the rank of *kouropalates* ('caretaker of the palace'), a dignity normally reserved for members of the immediate imperial family.[194] They would not have long to bask in the glory of these newly won honours. At the beginning of the summer Maslamah sacked both Sardis and Pergamum (western Anatolia) before proceeding north to the Hellespont (Dardanelles), which he crossed at Abydos in June. After ravaging several cities in Thrace, he arrived before the land walls of Constantinople on 15 August 717.[195] He then ordered his troops to dig a wide fosse the length of the city walls and construct 'above it a breast-high parapet of dry stone'.[196] The second great siege of Constantinople had begun.

Sulayman, who had assumed command of the fleet from Umar, arrived in the Sea of Marmara two weeks later on 1 September. Initially, he had the vessels moor along the shoreline of the European side between Emperor Valens' old palace of Magnaura in Hebdomon (present-day Bakirköy), about 10km (6 miles) south of the city, and Kyklobion (modern Zeytinburnu) just outside the city walls.[197] This was adjacent to Maslamah's encampment, but the ships were not there simply to support the besieging army in an assault on the city. Taking Constantinople by storm was utterly out of the question. The city stood on a promontory protected on the landward (west) side by not one but three walls. The innermost wall, built by Constantine in the fourth century, was a single bulwark of stone with defensive towers at regular intervals. A little over a kilometre outside that was the Theodosian Wall. Constructed in the fifth century by Theodosios II, it was actually a double wall which stretched about 7km (4.3 miles).[198] The outer barrier was as much as 2m (6ft 7in) thick and 9m (29ft 6in) in height. Just a few metres inside that was the inner bulwark, about 6m (19ft 8in) thick and 12m (39ft 4in) high. Fortified towers, as tall as 20m (65ft 7in) and as wide as 12m (39ft 4in), were built into each wall every 50 to 60m

(164 to 196ft). (Many of these fortifications still stand to this day.) In front of all that was a moat about 20m (65ft 7in) wide and 10m (32ft 10in) deep, with a squat crenellated rampart on the inner embankment. The sea wall which safeguarded the remainder of the promontory was only a single barricade, but it was defended on the north by the Imperial Fleet anchored in the Golden Horn, which was closed by a heavy harbour chain that stretched across the entrance from present-day Sarayburnu (Seraglio Point) on the south side to Galata on the north side. Moreover, the Arabs apparently brought almost no siege machinery. The only practicable way to reduce the city was to starve it into submission by blockade. This meant that the Umayyads had to shut off the city's access not only to the Aegean, but to the Black Sea as well. Cherson (Crimea) and Trebizond (modern Trabzon) had formed links in Constantinople's main trade route with the East ever since the Arab conquest of the Levant and were key sources of resupply.[199]

Accordingly, on 3 September Sulayman took advantage of southerly winds to reposition his fleet. Some vessels sailed to the harbours of Eutripios and Anthemios outside Chalcedon (the present-day Kadiköy district) on the Asian side of the Bosporus. Others sailed up the Bosporus past the city to Galata on the European side and further north to Kleidion (modern Defterdarburnu in the Ortaköy district), also on the west side of the strait. The purpose of this deployment was to effectively control the Bosporus and thus isolate Constantinople from both the Black Sea and Asia Minor. Unfortunately for the Umayyads, the winds becalmed just as a rear-guard of twenty transport vessels, each carrying a hundred armoured soldiers, was transiting the strait. This allowed a northerly current to push them back towards the mouth of the Golden Horn. Leo saw the opportunity and did not hesitate. He immediately launched a squadron of

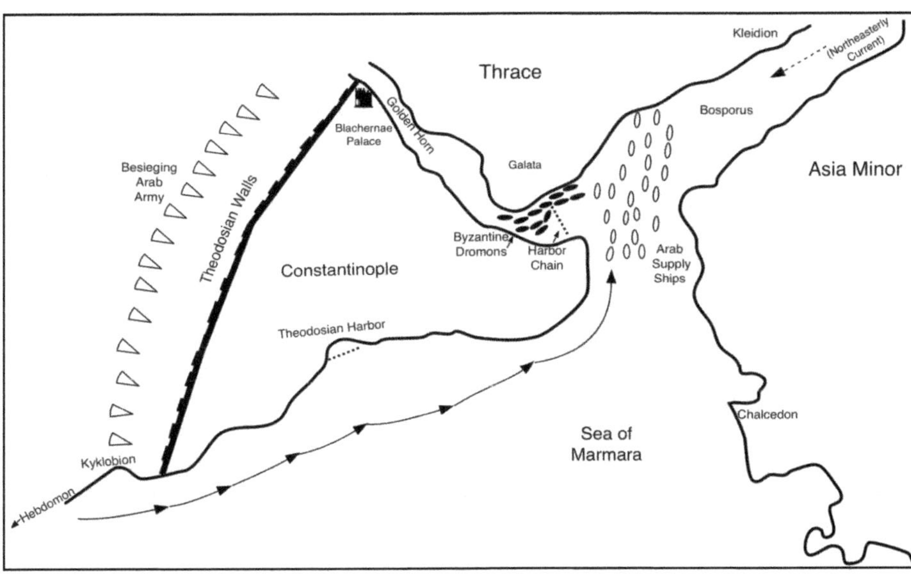

Map 2. Siege of Constantinople, 717–718. *(Kristy Stanton)*

dromōns equipped with 'Greek fire' that soon set alight the lot. (*See* Map 2.) It must have been a stunning spectacle. Some of the 'Saracen' ships sank straightaway with all hands, while others became burning hulks drifting up against the city walls. Still others, all ablaze, were swept as far as the Princes' Islands of Oxiea (modern Sivriada) and Plateia (present-day Yassiada).[200]

Theophanes conjectured that the Arabs 'had intended to beach their ships that evening by the city walls and set their steering paddles upon the battlements'.[201] If, in fact, that had been their plan, it had gone up in flames. Leo even attempted to entice them into the Golden Horn by lowering the chain, but they would have no part of it. Instead, the dispirited Umayyad fleet continued northwards all the way to Sosthenion (modern Istinye) on the extreme northwestern shore of the Bosporus in an effort to avoid any further contact with the Byzantine fleet and its dreadful 'liquid fire'.[202] The Umayyads had clearly abandoned any hope of an effective blockade by sea. It would prove to be their undoing. The siege was doomed from that moment on.

In the weeks ahead the situation grew progressively worse for the Arab expedition. At the end of September Caliph Sulayman ibn Abd al-Malik died suddenly and was succeeded by Umar ibn Abd al-Aziz, Maslamah's inimical and less-supportive cousin. On 8 October rampant disease among the besieging army claimed Sulayman ibn Mu'ad, who was replaced by Umar ibn Hubaira. That winter Thrace was beleaguered by the harshest weather in recent memory. Hard-packed snow remained on the ground for a hundred days.[203] The lightly clothed and relatively exposed besiegers of desert stock must have suffered far more than the well sheltered besieged who had at least three years' worth of provisions to sustain them. The Arabs had surely brought some stores with them, but they could not have lasted long, given the immense size of the force. Moreover, the bleak weather would not have allowed much foraging for food. The mortality from disease and malnutrition must have been staggering. Hundreds of their beasts of burden must have perished as well. Worse still, the frozen ground probably prevented burial of all the corpses, thereby exacerbating the spread of pestilence.

Some relief came in the spring in the form of two huge fleets of supply ships from Muslim North Africa, but that too soon turned to disappointment and tragedy. A fleet of 400 transport vessels 'laden with corn' and an unspecified number of *dromōns* arrived first from Egypt under a commander whom Theophanes called 'Souphiam' (or possibly 'Sufyan') and anchored at Kalos Agros (probably a harbour in the Gulf of Nicomedia, east of Chalcedon). Shortly afterwards, another fleet of 360 transports full of provisions led by one 'Izid' (or perhaps 'Yazid') arrived from Africa and moored at Satyros (present-day Küçükyali), Bryas (modern Maltepe) and Kartalimen (today's Kartal), all on the Asian side of the Bosporus. It seems both fleets were attempting to avoid detection by Leo's 'fire-breathing' *dromōns*. But it was all for naught. Their ships were crewed almost entirely by Coptic Christians, who defected in the ships' skiffs by night to the Byzantines, whom they eagerly informed of the whereabouts of the two Muslim flotillas. The emperor, of course, dispatched his siphon-equipped *dromōns* forthwith to attack the massed Arab fleets. Without their Coptic crews, the Umayyad ships could not manoeuvre and were sitting targets. The Byzantines effortlessly slaughtered the Arab occupants, plundered the provisions and sank the ships.[204]

As a consequence, the city was duly resupplied while the besiegers were, once again, deprived of desperately needed sustenance. Theophanes described the effects in ghastly detail: 'The Arabs, on the other hand, suffered from a severe famine, so that they ate all of their animals, namely horses, asses and camels. It is said that they even cooked in ovens and ate the dead men and their own dung which they leavened.'[205] Such a diet would only have intensified the sickness running rampant through the camp. Adding insult to injury, Leo got wind of a reserve Arab force under a commander named 'Mardasan' that was making its way there by Nicaea (modern Iznik) in northwestern Anatolia, so he ferried some soldiers under a few trusted imperial officers across the Bosporus. These managed to ambush the Arab troops at Libos (Mansio Libum) and Sophon (modern Sapanca) along the Nicaea–Nicomedia road and sent them scurrying back to the frontier. This evidently enabled the Byzantines to fish and forage freely on the Asian side of the Bosporus for a time.[206]

As awful as circumstances were for the Umayyad troops at that point, they only got worse. Leo had previously struck an alliance of convenience with Khan Tervel, whose Bulgars preferred the Christian Byzantines to the Muslims. They now attacked the Arab army camped before the land walls of Constantinople in what must have been something more akin to mass butchery than a battle, given the dangerously debilitated state of the Umayyad soldiery. Around 22,000 were reported to have been massacred.[207] Caliph Umar finally ordered the withdrawal of Umayyad forces and Maslamah complied on 15 August 718.[208] The retreat across Anatolia must have been long and hard, but Maslamah's army was apparently able to do so unmolested. The fleet was not so fortunate. Many vessels were sunk by a freak storm off Prokonnesos (Marmara Island) in the Sea of Marmara, while others met a watery fate in wicked weather off Rhodes. 'The remainder were going through the Aegean when a terrible calamity came over them,' reported Theophanes, 'for a fiery hail fell upon them and brought the sea-water to a boil, and as the pitch of their keels dissolved, their ships sank in the deep, crews and all.'[209] Though surely embellished, the tale may not be as fanciful as might be first supposed. There may well have been significant volcanic activity in the southern Aegean at the time. Only a few years later, in 725, Theophanes recorded a massive eruption emanating from an area between the islands of Thera and Therasia.[220] Just ten vessels managed to elude destruction and, of these, five more were culled out by a passing Byzantine patrol. Only five ships supposedly made it back to Syria.[221]

The impact upon the Umayyads was severe. The extensive losses in ships and soldiers during the siege served to enervate the caliphate, which was supplanted only thirty-two years later by the Abbasids, who then moved the capital from Damascus to Baghdad. Constantinople, on the obverse, would stand as the easternmost bulwark of Christianity for the next seven centuries.

CHAPTER 2

Norman Naval Expansion in the Central Mediterranean

Sicily was the strategic linchpin of the Mediterranean. Situated in the centre of the sea astride the east–west shipping lanes, the island had long been the cornerstone to its dominance. Whosoever held it held the key to movement on the sea. This was due in large measure to the nature of nautical technology at the time. It has been established that the galley fleets which predominated traffic on the sea needed ready access to three things: shelter from storms; large quantities of fresh water; and food, not to mention an occasional rest from exhausting labour.[1] Sicily possessed these things in abundance. Control of it, along with the coasts of Ifriqiyah and southern Italy, meant control of the central Mediterranean. This is why Sicily was at the core of what A.R. Lewis called 'the Islamic Imperium': Muslim domination of the Mediterranean in the ninth and early tenth centuries.[2] Constantinople's failure to recapture Sicily despite numerous ambitious attempts in the late tenth and early eleventh centuries spelled the end of Byzantine hegemony on the Middle Sea forever. The German Empire, backed by a resurgent papacy, proved no more successful in reconquering the region for Christianity. The Muslim stranglehold on the central Mediterranean was finally broken by ragtag bands of disinherited Norman knights led by the predacious progeny of Tancred de Hauteville, a minor noble from the Contentin region of northern France.[3]

Norman Migration into Southern Italy (1016–46)

By the beginning of the eleventh century northern France could no longer contain the Normans. Competition among the nobility for increasingly limited land and the dictates of primogeniture (the first-born's right of inheritance) pushed indigent and dispossessed knights southwards. Some were victims of feuds and power struggles, but many were simply opportunistic soldiers of fortune.[4] Whereas the Normans had temporarily forsaken the maritime traditions of their Scandinavian forebears, they relinquished none of the Viking spirit of adventure and daring. One of their chroniclers, Geoffrey Malaterra, observed that all shared a common trait which he called '*aviditas dominationis*' ('avarice for domination'), a sort of virulent combination of audacity and relentless rapacity which drove them to dominate other men.[5]

The Normans had no thought of establishing a maritime dominion when they first arrived in southern Italy at the turn of the millennium. They came initially as small bands of pilgrims, but their reputation as ruthless warriors soon caused them to be recruited as mercenaries by the local Lombard princes. Amatus of

Montecassino, another Italo-Norman chronicler, told of how forty Norman knights returning from Jerusalem saved Salerno from 'Saracen' attack by sea around the year 1000. They were lavishly rewarded by its prince, who earnestly bade them to return, bringing with them more of their warlike compatriots.[6] Similarly, William of Apulia, yet another Norman historian, described a chance encounter in 1016 at the Sanctuary of St Michael on Monte Gargano (north-eastern Apulia) between Norman pilgrims and the Lombard patriot Melus, in which the latter attempted to enlist their aid in his rebellion against Byzantine rule.[7]

By 1017 hundreds of Norman knights had answered the call – some to muster under the banner of Guaimar III, prince of Salerno, while others joined Melus for his long-planned invasion of Byzantine Apulia. The latter campaign went well at first. The Latin sources register anywhere from three to five victories over the more numerous but hapless Greek forces. Melus and his Norman followers, however, ultimately suffered a catastrophic defeat at the hands of Basil Boiannes, the Byzantine *catepan* (provincial governor), at Cannae in 1018.[8] Those Normans who survived subsequently offered their services to the competing Lombard princes of Campania, changing sides whenever it benefited them. There was no cohesive strategy for subjugating southern Italy in the beginning. The Normans operated in small units under loose leadership and fought with one another as much as they did with the Lombard nobles who paid for their swords. Occasionally they won petty lordships for themselves, but it was more by serendipitous opportunity than any well thought-out purpose. In 1031, for example, Duke Sergius IV of Naples awarded Aversa to Rainulf Drengot, the leader of a Campanian contingent of Norman mercenaries, as a bulwark against his nemesis, Pandulf IV of Capua.[9] There was no master plan and no united front of Norman knights under a strong central command to carry out a conquest of the region.[10]

All that began to change shortly after the arrival of the Hautevilles. Of the twelve sons sired by Tancred de Hauteville, eight would eventually find their way to southern Italy to seek their fortune. The oldest three – William, Drogo and Humphrey – participated in the ill-fated Byzantine invasion of Sicily in 1038, led by the renowned Giorgios Maniakes.[11] Ironically, it was that experience which introduced the Hautevilles to the potential rewards of sea power. As nominal leaders of a 300-knight Norman contingent, the brothers distinguished themselves in the course of the campaign. William, the eldest, killed the *qa'id* (Muslim military governor) of Syracuse in single combat, earning himself the sobriquet 'Iron-Arm'.[12] Outraged at what they viewed as iniquitous treatment by Maniakes, the Normans returned to the mainland in 1041 and established themselves at Melfi (in the Basilicata).[13] They elected William Iron-Arm as their 'count' and soon launched their own campaign of conquest against Byzantine possessions in southern Italy.[14] Under William's leadership, the Normans of Melfi fought several battles with the Byzantines in Apulia, most notably achieving two resounding victories over *Catepan* Michael Dokeianos in 1041: one in March at the river Olivento a few kilometres north of Venosa and another in May at Cannae, avenging the ignominious defeat of 1018.[15] During this time the irrepressible

Normans apportioned several of the towns in the region among twelve of their more prominent nobles, but William seems to have retained overall authority in Apulia.[16] When he succumbed to fever around 1045, Amatus said he 'was succeeded by his brother Drogo who was made count of Apulia'.[17] Within a year came the brother who, more than any other, would make the Norman conquest of southern Italy and Sicily a reality: Robert Guiscard.[18]

Hostile Takeover by the House of Hauteville (1046–59)

Robert's career began inauspiciously as the leader of a band of mounted brigands in the hardscrabble Scribla area of Calabria at the behest of his brother Drogo.[19] His exploits, however, soon earned him his famous sobriquet 'Guiscard', which means 'the cunning' in old French.[20] But it was not until Drogo's murder at Montilaro in Apulia in 1051, in retaliation for Norman ravaging in the region, that Robert's star began to rise.[21] In the wake of Drogo's assassination, his brother Humphrey assumed command of the Apulian Normans and continued the depredations. This elicited the ire of Pope Leo IX, who in 1053 gathered a sizeable army of local Lombards and Italians, augmented by some Swabians from his German homeland, with the intention of ridding the land of the reviled Normans once and for all.[22] In the ensuing encounter at Civitate in the Capitanata of northern Apulia the Normans were heavily outnumbered but won an overwhelming victory,[23] nonetheless, due in no small part to Guiscard's lion-hearted leadership of the Norman left wing.[24] His reputation thus burnished, Robert's fortunes soon soared.

When Humphrey died in 1057, Robert appropriated the lordship of Apulia. At the same time his brother Roger arrived from Normandy.[25] Together the two ruthlessly ambitious brethren immediately embarked upon the conquest of Calabria. With the temporal power of the papacy broken and Byzantium's grip on southern Italy slipping, there was little to oppose them. The Hautevilles quickly claimed Canalea, Maida and Nicastro.[26] Robert was besieging Cariati in 1059 when he received word that Pope Nicholas II was holding a synod at Melfi in the Basilicata.[27] Aware that the Pope, locked in a fierce struggle with papal pretender Benedict X, sorely needed support, Robert seized the moment.[28] At Melfi in August 1059 he swore fealty to the Holy See with an oath that began: 'I, Robert, by the grace of God and St Peter, Duke of Apulia and Calabria, and in the future, with the help of both, of Sicily . . .'[29] Clearly the Hautevilles had conceived a strategy which would culminate in the capture of a major Mediterranean island, necessitating the use of sea power.[30]

An Amphibious Assault on Sicily (1060–4)

Empowered by papal sanction, Robert resumed the implementation of his plan without delay. By late autumn he had completed the siege of Cariati, reduced Rossano, captured Cosenza and gained Gerace.[31] By the early spring of 1060 Reggio was his as well. He and Roger now stood at the Strait of Messina, poised to launch their long-anticipated invasion of Sicily, a land beyond the grasp of Christianity since the early ninth century.[32] They paused only long enough to gather the required maritime assets. Even then, Roger reconnoitred the crossing in the autumn of that same year with only sixty knights.[33] The invasion itself was invited early the next year by an unlikely source: Ibn al-Thumnah, the Muslim Emir of Syracuse and Catania, who was locked in a fierce family feud with his brother-in-law, Ibn al-Hawwas, the Emir of Castrogiovanni (modern Enna), over the former's mistreatment of the latter's sister. The Hautevilles were only too happy to 'help'. That March, Roger led another probe across the strait, this time with 160 knights. The foray nearly ended in disaster when inclement weather delayed their return, but the Normans had gathered valuable intelligence.[34]

By May 1061 they were ready to attempt the crossing in force. The Hautevilles had assembled a fleet by commandeering what vessels they could find in the harbours of Reggio and other conquered ports of Calabria: mostly a motley collection of merchant ships. Whatever they were, they were evidently no match for the twenty-four warships sent by the Emir of Palermo to prevent the Norman invasion.[35] 'For although our fleet was greater in number, theirs was more abundant in bigger and stronger ships,' related Malaterra. 'We had only *germundi* and *galeas* while the Sicilians had not only *catti* and *golafri*, but also *dromundi* and ships of various other constructions.'[36] A daring scouting sortie in what Amatus described as 'two very fast and manoeuvrable galleys' convinced the brothers that subterfuge offered their only chance of success.[37] Accordingly, Roger surreptitiously traversed the strait at night with some 300 knights in thirteen vessels, landing at Tremestieri (a few miles south of Messina).[38] With this small mounted cadre, Roger surprised and took Messina the next morning.[39] Deprived of its safe harbour and source of replenishment, the Muslim fleet returned to Palermo, leaving Robert to negotiate the strait with the rest of his makeshift transport fleet unmolested.[40] The Hautevilles had won their all-important beachhead.

The brothers made two brief forays into the interior of the island as far as Castrogiovanni, but the campaign soon stalled due to a number of factors, not the least of which was a decided lack of manpower.[41] First of all, Guiscard was compelled to return to the mainland in order to solidify his hold on Apulia, leaving Roger with only a small contingent of knights. Roger himself withdrew to Calabria to marry his long-time love-interest, Judith of Évreux.[42] While he was still on the peninsula, a nasty spat broke out between the two brothers over the partitioning of their Calabrian conquests.[43] Worse still, their Muslim ally, Ibn al-Thumnah, was assassinated near Palermo.[44] Once the quarrel with Guiscard was resolved, Roger returned to the island only to be faced with a rebellion of Greek residents in his hilltop headquarters at Troina in the northeast.[45]

Fortunately for the Normans, events were no kinder to their Muslim adversaries. The Zirid Emir of Mahdiyah, Al-Mu'izz Ibn Badis, dispatched a powerful fleet to relieve his coreligionists on Sicily, but it was decimated off Pantelleria by an awful autumn storm. His successor, Tamim, sent his sons Ayub and Ali with another armada in 1062, but these ships moored at Agrigento on the south coast and never entered the fray,[46] not even in 1063 when a sizeable Pisan fleet plundered the harbour of Palermo.[47] Thus, when Roger finally suppressed the revolt at Troina, he was able to bring reinforcements across the Strait of Messina from the mainland at will. This enabled him to inflict a crushing defeat on a combined African–Sicilian army at Cerami (near Castrogiovanni), also in 1063.[48] Still, Roger could do little more than terrorize the island's Muslim population without more troops.

In 1064 Robert was at last able to quell his restive dukedom long enough to assemble an army to continue the conquest. He joined his brother in Calabria and together they crossed the strait with around 500 knights and marched on Palermo. The siege of the city, however, proved to be a humiliating misadventure. While the Normans had the misfortune of bivouacking on a tarantula-infested hill, the Muslim citizens of Palermo received all the replenishment they required through the open port.[49] According to Amatus, it was a lesson not lost on Robert: 'When the most wise duke saw the disposition of Palermo and how provisions were being brought there from neighbouring lands, which would be carried there by sea if anyone denied access by land, he prepared himself to seize other cities in order to gather another fleet of ships with which to encircle Palermo and prevent any aid from reaching it by land or sea.'[50]

Birth of a Norman Navy (1065–76)

Accordingly, Robert resolved to take Bari first. It would supply him the needed ships and sailors with the added benefit that the capture of this last Byzantine bastion in Italy might intimidate the remainder of Apulia into submission. Renewed rebellion among his fractious Norman barony sidetracked the strategy for a few years, but finally, in 1068, he was able to conscript enough vessels from his Calabrian ports to encircle Bari completely.[51] Geoffrey Malaterra described how:

> Because the city of Bari was situated on a certain angle of land that extended out into the sea, Robert used his cavalry to close off, from one shore to the other, that part of the city which opened towards the land. At the same time he used his ships, spread out over the sea and firmly joined to one another with iron chains like a fence, to close off the city from the sea, so that there was no opening anywhere through which anyone could leave the city.[52] (*See* Map 3.)

Even so, it took nearly three years to reduce Bari, due in some degree to continued Norman inexperience on the water, which occasionally allowed the Byzantines to penetrate the blockade. In fact, what finally ended the siege was a Sicilian fleet under his brother's command. In the spring of 1071 Roger, who probably enjoyed greater naval expertise as a result of his efforts to subdue Sicily, was able to intercept a Byzantine relief flotilla of twenty ships led by the Norman renegade Jocelyn of Molfetta. During a rare night engagement the Normans captured nine vessels, including Jocelyn's flagship. The rout of the relief squadron finally caused the city to capitulate.[53] It was the Hautevilles' first victory at sea, prompting William of Apulia to observe that Robert 'foresaw the Normans, henceforth, engaging in naval combat with greater assurance'.[54]

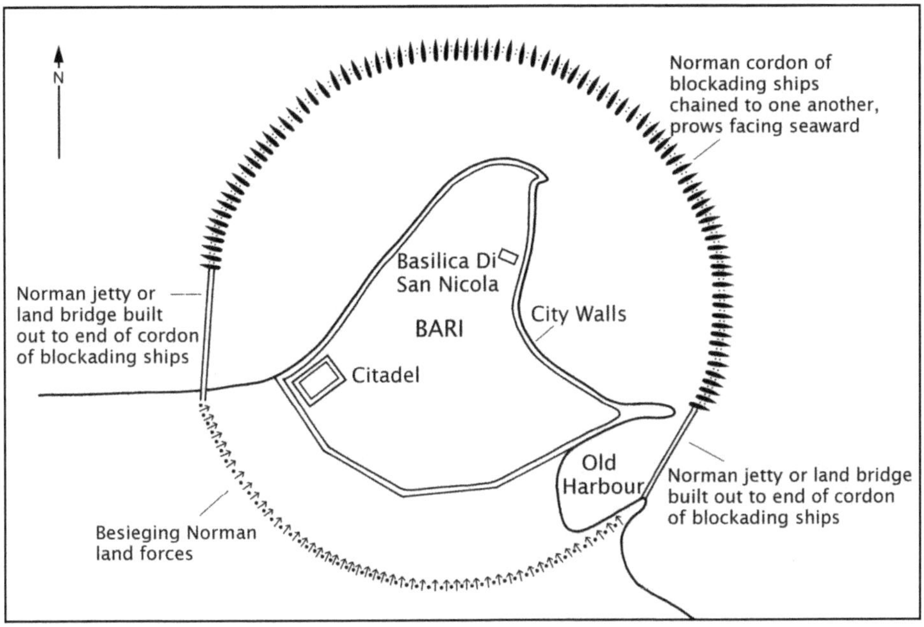

Map 3. Norman blockade of Bari, 1068. (*C. Stanton with P. Judge with permission of Boydell Press*)

Reinforced with ships and sailors from Bari, the Hautevilles promptly pivoted their attention back to Palermo. Roger took command of their land forces, while Robert led a squadron of over fifty ships gathered at Otranto.[55] In the summer of 1071 Guiscard flung his fleet at an African flotilla outside the port of Palermo. It was apparent from the ensuing engagement that the Normans were rapidly adapting to combat at sea. 'They arranged their ships according to all the rules of naval warfare,' recounted William of Apulia, 'and covered them entirely with red felt to repel the blows of the stones and javelins.'[56] The Normans prevailed, chasing the surviving Muslim ships into the harbour and burning several of them.[57] With both the landward and seaward approaches to the city effectively closed off, Robert and Roger triumphantly marched into Palermo in January 1072, after a siege of only a few months.[58] (*See* Map 4.) Guiscard departed the island shortly thereafter, leaving his brother to complete the conquest. He never returned.

Robert next sought to shore up his power on the peninsula. He first took the thriving Apulian port of Trani in early 1073.[59] A second maritime prize, outshining the first, fortuitously dropped into his hands a short time later that same year: Amalfi. The prosperous Campanian port had pleaded for his protection against Gisulf II, prince of Salerno (Robert's brother-in-law). Gisulf had long blamed the Amalfitans for the conspiracy which had taken his father's life in 1052 and was mercilessly harassing Amalfitan shipping.[60] Guiscard accepted the city's submission, but Gisulf's depredations continued, giving the duke the convenient pretext to seize Salerno for himself in 1076.[61] By this time Robert had become

Map 4. Port of Palermo in the eleventh century. (*Vincenzo di Giovanni*)

gruesomely effective in the investment of port cities. 'After four months of siege,' reported William of Apulia, 'such a famine pressed the unfortunate inhabitants of the city that the mob could scarcely sustain themselves on dogs, horses, rats and cadavers of asses.'[62] Salerno surrendered in December 1076, after about six months of siege by land and sea.[63] Robert had successfully used his newfound naval power to consolidate his hold on southern Italy.

The First Balkan Offensive (1077–84)

With southern Italy securely in his grasp, Guiscard fixed his insatiable appetite for acquisition on the Byzantine Empire. The abrogation of a 1074 agreement with the Emperor Michael VII Doukas for the latter's son Constantine to marry Robert's daughter Helena provided the required pretext.[64] When the emperor was overthrown in a palace coup by Nikephoros III Botaniates in 1078, Robert mounted a massive invasion of the empire in 1081 to right the wrong. Contemporary Byzantine historian Anna Comnena (daughter of Alexios, the current emperor) claimed Guiscard's forces included 150 ships, 'each carrying 200 men [30,000 in total] with armour and horses'.[65] While she clearly exaggerated, William of Apulia substantiated that it was an ample armada of at least fifty vessels, which Geoffrey Malaterra maintained was purpose-built: 'Not a single ship but an entire fleet is fitted out.'[66] Moreover, Anna attested that 'wooden towers were constructed in the larger vessels and covered with leather hides; everything essential for a siege was hastily put on board the ships; horses and armed knights embarked on dromons.'[67] Malaterra noted the number of knights at a more realistic 1,300.[68] Assisted by his son Bohemond, Robert took Corfu. Leaving a garrison at the fortress of Kassiopi on a northeastern promontory of the island, he headed northwards up the Adriatic coast of the Balkan peninsula.[69]

Unfortunately, a freak summer storm decimated his fleet off Glossa Point, which enclosed the north end of the present-day Gulf of Vlorë. The deluge soaked the hides covering the siege engines on the larger transports, causing the machines to collapse and sink the ships.[70] Doggedly determined, Robert proceeded on to his objective, Durazzo (modern Durrës), which he immediately besieged. It was there that the Normans would have their first fateful encounter with the Venetians.[71] Alexios Komnenos, lacking a strong fleet of his own, had purchased the aid of Venice with trade concessions so generous that they would enable *La Serenissima* (*La Serenissima Repubblica di Venezia* – 'Most Serene Republic of Venice') to dominate maritime commerce in the eastern Mediterranean for centuries.[72] In point of fact, the Venetians probably needed little incentive. They had no desire to see the grasping Normans control both shores of the southern Adriatic, potentially bottling them up in the north.[73]

Doge Domenico Selvo anchored his fleet off Pallia Point, a few miles north of Durazzo, just as the Normans were setting up their siege. Robert soon dispatched his son Bohemond with a squadron of light galleys in an apparent attempt to inveigle the Venetians into switching sides. (*See* Fig. 1.) What Bohemond found was a floating fortress composed of taller transport vessels lashed together in a semi-circle, forming what Anna Comnena called a 'sea harbour'. The Venetians had built wooden platforms on the mastheads, probably using small boats, upon which fighting men with heavy projectiles had been pre-positioned. Sensing negotiation was out of the question, Bohemond rashly charged the 'sea harbour'. He not only failed to penetrate the waterborne bulwark, but his light galleys offered an easy mark for the stones and large blocks of wood festooned with nails that the Venetians hurled from the mastheads of their vessels. These soon holed Bohemond's own vessel and sank it. Several other Norman ships suffered the same fate, but Bohemond managed to escape on one of the surviving galleys, which fled for the beach, hotly pursued by the Venetians.[74] Malaterra claimed the Venetians even resorted to 'Greek fire', sinking a supply ship with it.[75] Having watched from the walls, the Greek garrison of Durazzo then sortied out to capitalize on the chaos.[76]

Guiscard just managed to avert a total Norman rout, thanks in part to some Ragusan archers firing from the decks of their transports.[77] But he was forced to beach the remainder of his fleet and cede the sea to the Venetians and their Greek allies, who patrolled the coast continuously thereafter.[78] Even so, Robert prevailed in the subsequent land battle with Alexios on a small plain east of Durazzo on 18 October 1081.[79] The city itself fell to him in February of the following year, betrayed, ironically, by a Venetian noble named Domenico.[80] Shortly thereafter, Robert captured Kastoria and seemed on the cusp of marching on Thessaloniki by way of the Via Egnatia (the great Roman road through Illyria and Thrace) when he received word that his Apulian nobles, led by his nephew Abelard, were once again in revolt. Even more worrisome, Henry IV of Germany was approaching Rome with an army, jeopardizing Guiscard's liege lord, Pope Gregory VII. He returned to Italy straightaway, entrusting the Balkan campaign to Bohemond.[81] His son could make little progress, however, because the Venetian and Greek fleets ensured that he could expect no reinforcements from Italy, even if his father could spare any. Bohemond battled valiantly, but could not prevent Norman gains in the Balkans from withering away. By the autumn of 1083 Alexios had recaptured Kastoria and the Venetians had retaken Durazzo. Finally, in the spring of 1084 a noted Greek naval commander named Michael Maurex, at the head of a combined Greco–Venetian fleet, recovered Corfu, aside from the Norman-held citadel at Kassiopi.[82]

The Second Balkan Offensive (1084–5)

By the late summer of 1084, however, the Hautevilles had finally put their house in order. Robert had chastened the Norman rebels at Cannae and chased the German emperor from Rome, thereby fulfilling his obligation to the Pope.[83] He was, at last, ready to resume his Byzantine enterprise. Lupus Protospatarius, an Apulian annalist, reported that Guiscard set about mobilizing an enormous force at Otranto.[84] According to William of Apulia, the fleet alone consisted of 120 warships, along with a number of transport vessels.[85] Sometime in September, this armada sailed from Brindisi with the intention of recapturing Corfu.[86] There, off Kassiopi, Robert's flotilla encountered the Greco–Venetian fleet, and again the Venetians used the now familiar 'sea harbour' formation to defeat the light Norman galleys. Guiscard's ships suffered a second setback three days later in the same manner.[87] After this last loss, the Venetians assumed that Robert wanted no more and settled in at the harbour of Kerkyra on Corfu for the winter. But Guiscard surprised them at anchor and gained the greatest Norman naval triumph to date.[88] (A detailed description of the engagement is provided in the section at the end of this chapter.)

The vagaries of fortune, however, would deny Robert the opportunity to capitalize on his victory. He elected to winter on a river in northern Epirus which chroniclers called the Glykys but was actually known as the Acheron or 'river of woes', like the river of the same name that passed through mythical Hades. There, Robert contracted the 'flux' and, while attempting to capture Cephalonia in the early spring, he fell victim to a few malicious microbes which managed to do what the Byzantine emperor and his Venetian allies could not.[89] On 17 July 1085 the man whose epitaph would be '*terror mundi*' ('the terror of the world') succumbed to fever.[90] Though a propitious development for the Byzantines, it was also a portentous one. Lupus Protospatarius professed that, at the time of his death, Guiscard was 'preparing himself, with the equipping of a great naval force and an innumerable multitude of knights, so that he might direct himself to the royal city [Constantinople] by ship'.[91] The Normans would remain a naval power to be reckoned with for the foreseeable future.

The Conquest of Sicily by Sea Power (1068–91)

While Robert was pursuing his eastern ambitions, his younger brother Roger was constrained to conclude the subjugation of Sicily mostly on his own. Scarce manpower ensured it was a long and arduous process (nearly thirty years from beginning to end), during which the Latin inhabitants of the island never exceeded 1 per cent of the total population.[92] The young count finally gained the upper hand with a land victory at Misilmeri (10km/6 miles east of Palermo) against a combined Zirid–Sicilian army in early 1068 and, of course, there was the previously described capture of Palermo in 1072, but he soon learned that sea power was indispensable to securing an island domain.[93] In 1075 Muslim marauders from Mahdiyah assaulted Mazara with 150 ships. Roger rushed to relieve his garrison there and succeeded in driving the raiders into the sea, but the episode convinced him to shore up his position on the western coast of the island.[94] Accordingly, he assembled an armada which Malaterra effused was the equal of 'the fleet of Alexander the Great' in order to invest Trapani in 1077.[95] His son Jordan quickly obtained the city's surrender by using a few vessels to seize the inhabitants'life-sustaining livestock from a small spit of land jutting out from the sea wall.[96]

Roger employed the fleet again in 1079 to blockade Taormina on the Ionian just as effectively. 'Finally, their bread exhausted, the hungry people are overcome,' recounted Malaterra. 'The count is summoned and he becomes master of the fortress to do with as he wishes.'[97] In the course of the siege, fourteen Muslim *golafri* (warships) from Mahdiyah appeared and offered their services to Roger, indicating that the count had come to terms with Mahdiyah's Zirid emir, Tamim ibn al-Mu'izz ibn Badis. Afterwards, the only major Muslim opposition left in the region was Ibn el-Werd, the emir of Syracuse, and he sealed his fate in 1083 by orchestrating a seaborne assault on Nicotera, not 16km (10 miles) from Roger's Calabrian capital of Mileto. This devastating raid, which included the desecration of the churches of St Nicholas and St George near Reggio as well as the convent of the Virgin Mary at Rocca Asini, so incensed Roger that he vowed to take vengeance on his Muslim adversary.[98] Once again, he outfitted an entire fleet, probably at the arsenal in Messina, and in the spring of 1085 sailed it into Syracuse harbour, where he personally engaged Ibn el-Werd's flagship. The Muslim emir ended up tumbling into the sea mortally wounded. Dispirited, Syracuse itself soon surrendered.[99] Noto, the last 'Saracen' stronghold on the island, submitted unsolicited in 1091 to Roger, who by then had become known as 'the Great Count'.[100]

By this point Roger faced little resistance at sea. His only potential rival was the Zirid fleet at Mahdiyah, which was destroyed in 1087 when the Genoese and Pisans sacked the port.[101] Though invited to participate in that expedition, the count had declined on the basis of a previous peace agreement with Emir Tamim.[102] Roger's final great naval action was the near-bloodless invasion of Malta in 1091. He amassed an armada at Capo Scalambri (southeastern Sicily) so intimidating that it cowed the island's *qa'id* into capitulating with hardly a struggle – just a small cavalry skirmish after landing. Roger's fleet captured Gozo as well and carried the Christian captives of both islands back to Sicily for re-settlement.[103] The Norman conquest of southern Italy and Sicily was, at long last, complete.

Strategy for a Dominion of the Sea

While Roger, the Great Count, deserves credit for establishing a strong Norman naval presence in the central Mediterranean, it was his son Roger II who elevated it to dominance. He transformed his father's legacy of a powerful fiefdom into a virtual maritime empire with Sicily at its core. To accomplish this feat, Roger II employed a highly efficacious naval strategy that enhanced the wealth of his island realm while successfully defending it from a host of covetous competitors, including the German Empire, the Byzantine Empire and his own rebellious barony.[104]

The heart of this strategy was based upon simple geography. Sicily commanded the central Mediterranean. The Strait of Messina separating the island's northeastern corner from the toe of the Italian mainland is barely 3km (2 miles) wide at its narrowest point and the Sicilian Channel from Mazara del Vallo on the southwestern edge to Cape Bon, Tunisia, is not 150km (93 miles) across. Roger knew that if he could command both southern Italy and the Maghreb coast of North Africa, he would be able to control maritime traffic through the centre of the Middle Sea, creating what master of Mediterranean history David Abulafia called 'a naval *cordon sanitaire* around his kingdom'.[105] Hardly a vessel could pass his realm without pulling into his ports or anchoring off his shores, and he knew how to make them pay for the privilege. He very likely realized that he could turn

Sicily into a massive tollgate to the benefit of his coffers.[106] This is why, Abulafia notes, 'Under Norman rule, the island flourished.' He goes on to point out that, 'Messina attracted Latin merchants, acting as a staging post on the trade routes linking Genoa and Pisa to Acre and Alexandria.'[107] Ibn Jubayr, the celebrated pilgrim from Almohad Andalusia, was even more effusive: 'This city is the mart of merchant infidels, the focus of ships from all over the world.'[108]

Nor did Roger overlook political intrigue as a tool to magnify and maintain his power base. He understood that neither the German emperor nor the Byzantine *basileus*, both of whom laid claim to his kingdom, could unseat him from his island throne unless they possessed some sort of sea power. Since the two empires lacked sufficient naval resources at the time, this meant they needed to effect some sort of alliance with the Italian maritime powers of the age: Genoa, Pisa or Venice. Consequently, Roger's diplomacy consisted largely of detaching one or the other of these seafaring city-states from any imperially inspired anti-Norman league.[109] In return for favourable relations, he offered them all a convenient avenue to the markets of the Maghreb, and to the emerging West Italian sea powers he assured easy access to the riches of the East – all at reduced tariffs on trade.[110]

Finally, Roger knew that, in order to implement this shrewd strategy, he would have to develop a formidable fleet. This would enable him to convert his island demesne into an unassailable bastion while keeping his enemies at bay and off balance. Accordingly, he tasked his first minister, who for most of his reign was none other than the gifted George of Antioch, to assemble a worthy armada – mainly from arsenals in Palermo and Messina.[111] George's official title was *amiratus*, a Latinization of the Arabic *emir* or *amir* in the sense of a 'vizier'. It was essentially an administrative position, but George's subsequent success as a naval commander and the performance of several of his successors at sea engendered the etymology for the modern term 'admiral'. When William II of Sicily appointed Walter of Moac to the office in 1177, he bestowed upon him the dignity *regii fortunati stolii amiratus* ('Admiral of the Blessed Royal Fleet').[112]

And the king made certain that his *amiratus* had all the resources necessary to accomplish the task. Roger rendered such crucial ship-building materials as wood, pitch and iron royal monopolies reserved for the use of his fleet.[113] The primary warship of this powerful naval force was the *galea*. The *galea* (plural: *galeae* or *galeas*) was a distinctly Italian descendant of the Byzantine *dromōn*, which John Pryor believes employed the *alla sensile* oarage system. Instead of two or more levels of rowers, stroking from a sitting position, the oarsmen on a Sicilian *galea* sat two per bench on the main deck, each pulling his own oar in a stand-and-sit stroke fashion. This theoretically permitted greater power, which translated into greater speed, while allowing for increased load-carrying capacity – in other words, these galleys were ideal for interdiction at sea and long-range raiding expeditions.[114] Sporting a spur at the prow, two masts and two steering oars at the stern, the *galea* must have appeared quite similar to the *dromōn*, except that its poop was ornamented with a pair of upcurving *ali* or 'wings'.[115] It was such a highly effective ship design that the other Italian maritime powers of the period – Genoa, Pisa and Venice – were thought to have adopted versions of the vessel.

Naval Policy in the Early Years (1101–26)

The unique leadership skills that enabled Roger to develop this strategy he owed not to his father, who died in 1101 when young Roger was less than 6 years old, but to his mother, Adelaide del Vasto, the Great Count's third wife.[116] She initiated the process which would ultimately instil in her son the mindset of an island ruler by moving the comital household from the Great Count's castle at Mileto in Calabria to Sicily shortly after the death of Simon, her eldest son, in September 1105.[117] This served to insulate Roger from the pernicious Norman nobility that pervaded the lower Italian peninsula and exposed him to the more nuanced methods of rule favoured by the Greek and Muslim advisers who held sway on Sicily.[118]

Roger's first adviser was probably the *Amiratus* ('first minister') Christodoulos, a Greek whose name translates as 'servant of Christ'. He seems to have been knowledgeable in both Byzantine and Arab styles of government. Emperor Alexios I conferred upon him the high court dignity of *protonobilissimos* ('first most noble one') and he was known in Arab sources of North Africa as Abd ar-Rahman ('servant of Allah') or Abd Allah an-Nasrani ('servant of the Merciful God').[119] Thus Christodoulos not only schooled his young charge in oriental statecraft, but must also have ensured that Roger was conversant in both the Greek and Arabic languages. But the adviser who would have the most profound and lasting influence on Roger's reign was Christodoulos' replacement, a man known to history as George of Antioch.[120] Though a Greek Melkite,[121] George spoke fluent Arabic and had served as the finance minister for Tamim of Mahdiyah before seeking employment in Roger's court at Palermo in 1108.[122] Therefore, he brought with him an invaluable knowledge of Zirid operating practices and the lucrative opportunities offered by Muslim North Africa. He doubtless also apprised his princely protégé of the Maghreb coast's strategic significance with respect to Sicily.[123]

Barely a decade later and only a half dozen years after his majority in 1112, the young count would send southwards his first expedition: a fleet of twenty-four vessels in support of Rafi ibn Makkan al-Dahmani, the governor of Gabes, who was seeking to break with Mahdiyah. Abu al-Hasan Ali, the Zirid emir of Mahdiyah at the time, rendered the mission a fiasco by sending his own fleet to chase the Sicilian ships back home. Nonetheless, Roger would be dissuaded from neither his African ambitions nor his enmity for Mahdiyah.[124] In 1123 he dispatched both Christodoulos and George of Antioch at the head of a massive 300-ship armada reportedly carrying some 30,000 men and 1,000 horses to take the Zirid capital.[125] The enterprise was, however, an even worse débâcle than the Gabes affair. The two inexperienced bureaucrats failed to take even the most basic military measures. They bivouacked their army on a barren, waterless islet just offshore 16km (10 miles) north of the city and neglected to set a guard. As a consequence, the base camp was overrun at night, compelling the bulk of the force to flee panic-stricken by ship while most of their supplies, horses and the garrison of a small island fortress called Qasr Ad-Dimas were left to the mercy of the Muslims – who showed none.[126]

The Creation of the Kingdom of Sicily (1127–30)

Nonetheless, Roger would likely have pursued his African aspirations straightaway had not peninsular politics intervened. He had already re-established Norman suzerainty on Malta in 1127 when he received word that his cousin, Duke William of Apulia, had died.[127] He immediately proceeded north to Salerno with a seven-ship flotilla to claim the duchy he believed was rightfully his.[128] In an early form of gunboat diplomacy, Roger eventually managed to convince the recalcitrant citizens to accept him as their lord. Benevento, Amalfi and much of the rest of Campania followed suit. Troia, Melfi and the majority of Apulia fell in line next. By the New Year Roger was anointed duke.[129] The young count's claim to the duchy, however, was contested almost immediately. Pope Honorius II considered the investiture of the duke of Apulia a papal prerogative, based upon Guiscard's submission to the Holy See at Melfi in 1059. Thus he fomented a revolt among the mainland barons, principally Count Rainulf of Caiazzo and Robert II of Capua.[130]

It would take Roger another ten years before he could consolidate his hold on the peninsula. During that time his strategy stayed essentially the same. When strife surfaced, he simply withdrew to Sicily and amassed his forces while waiting for the inevitable collapse of whatever coalition had provisionally coalesced against him, and then shipped his 'Saracen' soldiers across the Strait to reclaim any lost territory. Such a scheme was invariably successful. Honorius II, for instance, was forced to recognize Roger as duke of Apulia outside Benevento on 22 August 1128, when the Pope's contentious alliance, held together by feeble feudal obligation, inevitably melted away in the summer sun. All Roger had to do was wait it out.[131] He subsequently ended the baronial revolt by blockading Bari into submission with a fleet of sixty ships.[132] It was a pattern that would repeat itself time and again.

This first brush with a hostile papacy must, however, have convinced Roger of the necessity of an ally in the Lateran Palace. He exploited a schism which occurred in the aftermath of Honorius II's death in 1130 to offer his support to one of the papal pretenders, Anacletus II, in return for recognition as king of Sicily. Anacletus' rival, Innocent II, had acquired the backing of the highly influential Bernard of Clairvaux, who had, in turn, managed to enlist the patronage of most of the monarchs of Europe.[133] Anacletus had little choice but to accede to Roger's demands. Accordingly, he signed a bull proclaiming Roger the sovereign of Sicily, Calabria and Apulia. The latter was subsequently crowned king in Palermo on Christmas Day of 1130.[134] Regrettably, it was this claim of kingship which prompted Lothair III, the powerful German monarch, to throw his full weight behind Innocent II at Liège in 1131 and become the chief challenge to Roger's reign.[135]

Consolidation of Power through Maritime Might (1131–9)

Anticipating the impending onslaught, Roger moved quickly to pre-empt resistance to his rule within his own kingdom. He correctly identified the port cities of Campania as the hotbed of any potential rebellion and in the spring of 1131 dispatched a fleet under George of Antioch, who was '*Maximus Ammiratus*' by this time, northwards to demand the submission of Amalfi. George obtained it by blockading the city's port and reducing nearby Capri, Trivento, Gallo Lungo and Ravello.[136] The action intimidated Naples into acquiescing as well.[137]

Unfortunately, Roger's efforts to permanently suppress any insurgency within his domains did not take. The very next year Rainulf of Caiazzo, the king's brother-in-law, collaborated with Robert of Capua to foment another rebellion, which was soon joined by Sergius, the *magister militum* ('master of soldiers' or, more accurately, 'military commander') of Naples.[138] Roger reacted by blockading Bari and Brindisi into submission.[139] He suffered a setback at the hands of Rainulf at Nocera, but simply retreated to Sicily where he assembled more soldiers and a fleet of some sixty ships which he then used in the spring of 1133 to savagely subjugate all of Apulia. Only Naples, Capua and Benevento continued to resist, but even these finally folded when Roger's sixty-ship fleet set siege to Naples the following spring.[140] Robert of Capua had sought the aid of the Pisans, but none was forthcoming, probably because Roger had bribed their implacable rivals, the Genoese, into making trouble for Pisa in the absence of its fleet.[141]

Chastened, the rebellious Campanian aristocracy feigned loyalty until the next opportunity presented itself. This occurred the succeeding year when Roger contracted a serious illness, perhaps the same one that had consumed his beloved Queen Elvira.[142] While he was disconsolate and thought near death, the king's enemies sought to exploit his malaise. The usual suspects (Robert of Capua, Rainulf of Caiazzo and Sergius of Naples) renewed the revolt, this time finally convincing the Pisans to provide their promised flotilla (twenty galleys) along with some 8,000 combatants.[143] Regaining his health, however, Roger rallied his forces and soon besieged Naples once again with a fleet of some sixty vessels.[144] The Pisans reacted by reinforcing their squadron with another twenty-six warships and making a diversionary assault on Amalfi, which remained loyal to the crown. With Amalfitan warships committed to Roger's siege of Naples, the city was left virtually defenceless. The Pisans mercilessly sacked their long-time maritime rival, along with the allied ports of Atrani, Maiori, Minori and Ravello.[145] As fortune would have it, however, Roger got wind of these depredations just as the Pisans were plundering nearby Fratta. He force-marched his army from Aversa over the Sorrento peninsula and surprised the pillagers while his sixty-ship fleet occupied the Pisan squadron. The defeat was near total: over 1,500 Pisans were killed or captured, including three consuls. The surviving Pisan force soon withdrew and returned home.[146] Bereft of maritime support, the rebels were again at the mercy of the king.

The situation shifted dramatically, however, in 1136. Innocent II, anxious to remove Anacletus and his prime benefactor from power, finally convinced Lothair III to invade Roger's realm.[147] So, in 1137 the Holy Roman Emperor marched inexorably down the Adriatic coast, capturing Trani, along with a squadron of thirty-three Sicilian vessels, and Brindisi, where twenty-five more ships of the crown were seized. Bari later fell to the imperial army after a four-week siege.[148] A Pisan fleet of a hundred warships concomitantly subjected Amalfi to the sword again. Lothair joined the Pisans in July for the siege of Salerno.[149] Meanwhile, Roger, realizing he was badly overmatched, sensibly did what he always did in such circumstances: withdrew to 'fortress' Sicily to await the preordained implosion of the opposition.[150] He knew the odd alliance of German-imperial troops, papal forces, profit-minded Pisans and rebellious Norman nobles would not last long.

And, of course, he was correct. Lothair negotiated a surrender agreement with Sorrento that deprived the Pisans of their expected plunder, propelling them into a deal with Roger for trade concessions. They soon boarded their ships and sailed away.[151] Without naval support, the imperial–papal coalition foundered and fell apart. Lothair headed home, dying of illness along the way. Rainulf won a land victory over Roger at Rignano in Apulia, but suddenly passed away in 1139, leaving Pope Innocent II to contend with Roger on his own.[152] The king cornered the Pope later that same year at Gallucio near San Germano and compelled him to confirm his kingship.[153] Before the year was out Roger obliged Bari to bow to him with a land/sea siege, ending the final challenge to his rule on the mainland.[154] He was, at last, able to redirect his attention back towards his Mediterranean expansion aspirations.

Conquest of the Maghreb Coast (1135–48)

Roger's designs on the Maghreb coast, in particular, were never far from the fore, even in the midst of consolidating his kingdom. For example, in 1135, while still dealing with the rebellions of his peninsular barony, he had sent George of Antioch to subjugate the island of Jerba, a notorious pirate enclave in the Gulf of Gabes.[155] The strategic significance of the North African shoreline with respect to Sicily could not have been lost on the suzerain. After all, it was he who had, as early as 1139, commissioned the great Muslim geographer Muhammad al-Idrisi to produce a detailed textual description of the world (mainly the Mediterranean world), based on eye-witness reports of observers dispatched from Sicily. Entitled the *Kitab Nuzhat al-mushtaq fi-khtiraq al-afaq* ('The Pleasure Excursion of One Who Is Eager to Traverse the Regions of the World'), al-Idrisi later named it simply the *Kitab Rujar* ('Book of Roger') in honour of his benefactor.[156] **(Pl. 10)** Thus, Roger must have known that his island domain's proximity to both the north and south shores of the Middle Sea imbued it with enormous military and economic benefits. As previously noted, the state of maritime technology dictated that ships transiting the central Mediterranean were dependent upon the adjacent shores for navigation, food, shelter and, most vitally, water. Since he had already subjugated southern Italy, Roger knew all that was necessary to complete his plan was to incorporate the North African littoral into his kingdom as well. Once this was accomplished, scarcely a ship would be able to pass east to west or vice versa without permission from the king of Sicily. George of Antioch, his shrewd '*amiratus amiratorum*' ('admiral of admirals'), who had served as tax-collector for the Zirid princes of Ifriqiyah, doubtless knew how to convert that extraordinary advantage into a burgeoning royal fisc.[157]

Now, finally secure in his own domain, Roger dispatched George southwards again in 1142, this time to raid Mahdiyah with a fleet of twenty-five vessels. The admiral seized several ships and burnt others, thereby intimidating Emir al-Hasan into effectively declaring his submission to the Sicilian crown.[158] A year later a modest flotilla carrying a mere 300 knights attempted to take Tripoli. It failed, but sacked defenceless Djidjelli, between Bejaïa and Bona, instead.[159] In 1144 it was the turn of tiny Brashk on the coast of modern Algeria.[160] The following year the Sicilians captured Kerkenna, another island of Muslim marauders opposite Sfax on the Tunisian coast.[161] Then, in 1146, some 200 Sicilian ships under George's personal command capitalized on some factional strife to conquer Tripoli for the Norman throne.[162]

The triumph at Tripoli triggered a domino effect, which rapidly delivered to Roger the remainder of the Maghreb coast from Tripolitania to Tunis. According to the Tunisian chronicler Ibn Abi Dinar, 'the prince of Gabes [a certain Yusuf] wrote to Roger most humbly and servilely, delivering to him the country which he held and being satisfied to become an *amil* [vassal-governor] of the king'.[163] The Zirids of Mahdiyah considered Gabes a client state, so al-Hasan laid siege to the city in early 1148, prompting its citizens to revolt and torture Yusuf to death by gagging him with his own genitalia.[164] The murder of his *amil*, of course, provided Roger with just the pretext he needed to crown his African strategy. The timing could not have been more propitious. Ibn al-Athir testifies that famine and plague had raged through Ifriqiyah since 1142, making it particularly vulnerable.[165] The mere appearance of George of Antioch's 250 galleys on the horizon on the morning of 22 June 1148 was enough to make al-Hasan quit the city without a fight. Mahdiyah simply did not have enough supplies to endure a long siege. The Norman fleet entered the harbour and seized the city unopposed.[166] Susa and Sfax were subdued in rapid succession soon thereafter.[167] This was the summit of Sicilian maritime supremacy in the central Mediterranean. The Norman king now controlled not only the strategically vital Strait of Messina but the Sicilian Channel as well.

Defending a Maritime Empire from Imperial Designs (1135–54)

The Sicilian successes in the central Mediterranean soon raised concerns in the court of Constantinople. It was the emperor's Venetian allies who first alerted him to the growing threat. Following the Norman conquest of Jerba in 1135, piracy apparently continued unabated in the Sicilian Channel – only now it was at the behest of the king of Sicily. The loss of some '4,000 talents'-worth of Venetian merchandise in the vicinity of Jerba prompted *La Serenissima* to propose an anti-Norman alliance to Emperor John II Komnenos. The Venetians found a willing audience.[168] Noted Italo-Norman historian Ferdinand Chalandon explains: 'The attempts of the king of Sicily to command all the great maritime routes could not have been viewed with complacency in the court of Constantinople.'[169] Consequently, the Byzantines joined with the Venetians in seeking an anti-Norman pact with Lothair III at the German imperial court at Merseburg in 1136.[170] Nothing ultimately came of the effort, because Roger evidently succeeded in detaching the Venetians from the coalition by offering them lucrative trading privileges in the kingdom.[171]

Neither imperial court, however, relinquished its antipathy for Roger, whom they felt had usurped longstanding imperial prerogatives in southern Italy. And by 1140 both monarchs were pursuing a marriage alliance for a single purpose, made clear by Frederick Barbarossa's biographer, Otto of Freising: 'They sought to renew the bond of union between the two empires, I mean the western and eastern, because of the insolence of Roger of Sicily.'[172] Years of abortive efforts finally bore fruit in January 1146, when Bertha of Sulzbach, the adopted daughter of Conrad III, married Manuel I Komnenos. Roger must have known then that a combined assault on his kingdom was imminent.[173]

What saved the Norman kingdom of Sicily on this occasion was the Second Crusade. The conquest of Edessa by the Atabeg of Mosul in December 1144 had galvanized the European powers into action.[174] King Louis VII of France announced on Christmas Day 1145 his intention to embark upon a crusade, and Bernard of Clairvaux convinced Conrad to do the same one year later.[175] The invasion of Sicily was off, but Roger knew it was only a reprieve. He was determined to proactively discourage the enterprise and the crusade gave him the desired cover. Manuel Komnenos himself provided the opportunity. Rightfully apprehensive about the hordes of undisciplined crusaders descending upon his capital, the emperor recalled troops from western Greece to protect the environs of Constantinople. This rendered the west coast of the Balkan peninsula and the Peloponnesos susceptible to seaborne attack.[176] Roger pounced.

In April 1147 he launched a sizeable armada against the Adriatic coast of mainland Greece.[177] George of Antioch was believed to have commanded it and the contemporary Norman court chronicler Romuald of Salerno said it was composed of '*galeas et naves plurimas*' ('very many *galeas* and supply ships').[178] Virtually unopposed, George's *galeas* easily captured Corfu and ravaged the Gulf of Corinth, pillaging both Thebes and Corinth in the process.[179] The next year the Byzantines, having purchased the support of the Venetians anew with another generous set of commercial concessions, launched a massive force (over a thousand vessels according to the Byzantine chroniclers) to reclaim Corfu.[180] In order to relieve his garrison there, Roger again dispatched George of Antioch with sixty *galeas* on a diversionary raid. The *amiratus* penetrated the Dardanelles all the way to the Golden Horn, where he ordered flaming arrows to be fired at the Blachernae Palace of the *basileus*.[181] In the same general time frame some of Roger's galleys even managed to succour King Louis VII of France and Queen Eleanor of Aquitaine from a Greek flotilla as they made their way back from the failed Second Crusade on Sicilian ships.[182] The Norman-occupied citadel on Corfu eventually fell,[183] but these diversionary tactics had served their purpose. No imperial assault on Sicily ever took place during Roger's reign.

George of Antioch, Roger's gifted 'admiral of admirals', fell victim to the pedestrian malaise of haemorrhoids and gallstones in 1151.[184] Roger tried to replace him with a Muslim convert named Philip of Mahdiyah, but the latter was burned at the stake as an apostate for displaying excessive leniency towards his former coreligionists following the capture of Bona in 1153.[185] Bereft of his beloved Elvira and his ever-reliable first minister, Roger himself passed away the following year. The great Muslim historian Ibn al-Athir would later pay him this fitting tribute: 'Having organized a large fleet, he made himself lord of the islands which lie between Mahdiyah and Sicily, such as Malta, Pantelleria, Jerba and Kerkenna. And he extended his dominion to the coast of Africa, [where] . . . he did so much pleasing to God.'[186]

Collapse of a Sea Kingdom (1155–94)

Roger became the envy of his world by parlaying Sicily's strategic advantage into enormous wealth and power. It was also the key to the kingdom's survival against a host of adversaries until very nearly the end of the century. As long as his successors adhered to the principle of dominating the central Mediterranean while keeping their enemies off balance and divided, the Norman kingdom flourished. Once they strayed from that fundamental blueprint, they and the naval empire which Roger founded were doomed. Unfortunately, that is exactly what they did. William I, Roger's direct descendant, managed to thwart a Byzantine-led invasion of Apulia by using his fleet to crush a Greek force besieging Brindisi in 1156,[187] but allowed most of the crown's North African holdings to fall prey to a widespread Muslim uprising with hardly a fight.[188] The rest was absorbed by the Almohads under Abd al-Mu'min, who laid siege to Mahdiyah in 1159.[189] The Norman court made a half-hearted effort to relieve its garrison there by diverting a fleet of 150 galleys returning from a raid on the Balearics, but this armada was defeated and chased home by an Almohad flotilla of only seventy ships.[190] No further rescue attempts were made and the city fell in January 1160. Thus, the Kingdom of Sicily lost control of the Sicilian Channel.

Worse yet, William the Bad, as he was later called, failed where his father had repeatedly succeeded: in detaching the other Italian maritime powers of the era from any imperially inspired anti-Norman league. The links between the Venetians and the Byzantine court had been forged long before William assumed the throne, but he stood idly by while the German emperor Frederick I Barbarossa recruited both Pisa and Genoa in 1162 for a planned invasion of the kingdom.[191] Only a falling-out between the two West Italian sea powers over their *fondachi* (trading establishments) in Constantinople that same year prevented their participation in Frederick's expedition, thereby precipitating its postponement.[192] But the recipe for the kingdom's undoing had been written: the collaboration was only dormant, not dead.

While William I had presided over the reduction of the realm and rendered it at risk of ruin, his son and successor William II essentially ensured it, first of all by actively straying from his grandfather's concentration on the central Mediterranean. He was given to large-scale seaborne enterprises that bankrupted the royal treasury and squandered maritime resources which the kingdom could ill-afford. In the summer of 1174, barely four years after attaining his majority, William II launched a massive expedition that included over 200 galleys in an ill-advised assault on Alexandria.[193] William of Tyre described the resulting débâcle: 'During the stay of five or six days made before the city ... [William's] forces sustained great losses by death and capture and were finally obliged to retire in confusion.'[194] Undaunted, William dispatched an armada of 184 galleys, 45 horse transports and 40 supply ships in 1181 to chasten the Almoravid pirates of the Balearic islands.[195] Again, William of Tyre gave a grim assessment of the mission's outcome: 'Driven by unfavourable winds, practically the entire fleet was wrecked in the vicinity of the coastal cities of Savona, Albenga and Ventimiglia, where the tumultuous waves dashed the ships upon the shore.'[196]

However, the worst waste of the realm's maritime muscle occurred in 1185, when William directed some 400 vessels carrying an estimated 85,000 men on an invasion of the Byzantine Empire.[197] Eustathios of Thessaloniki, whose city was savagely sacked by the Sicilians, plausibly pronounced, 'His treasury was emptied and left bare.'[198] The result was a disaster of epic proportions. The land army was ambushed and annihilated near Amphipolis in central Macedonia, while the fleet was soundly rebuffed in the Sea of Marmara and sent staggering back to Sicily. According to the Byzantine court historian Niketas Choniates, few ships made it back to their home port: 'It is said that many ships, men and all, sank in the deep when they encountered tempestuous winds, while famine and disease emptied out the others.'[199]

The most damaging fall-out from the failed enterprise, however, had been prearranged in the planning stage. In order to preclude the possibility of German imperial intervention during his Byzantine campaign, William consented to the betrothal of his aunt Constance, the posthumous daughter of Roger II, to Frederick's son Henry, the heir to the Hohenstaufen crown, and designated Constance as his legal heir should he die childless.[200] It proved a bad bet, because William did indeed pass away unexpectedly without a direct heir in November 1189.[201] Tellingly, his death came just as he was about to mount yet another massive expedition – this one to liberate the Holy Land in the wake of Saladin's victory over the forces of the Latin Kingdom of Jerusalem at the Horns of Hattin in July 1187.[202]

William's ill-advised marriage arrangement proved the death of the dynasty. When his cousin Tancred of Lecce attempted to assume the throne of Sicily, he did so in the face of a competing claim by the German imperial House of Hohenstaufen.[203] This made him a weak monarch whose legitimacy was questioned inside and outside the realm. As a result, he was in no position to resist the excesses of the armies of Richard the Lionheart and Philip II Augustus of France who passed through the kingdom on their way to Palestine during the Third Crusade.[204] An altercation over a loaf of bread between the crusaders and the townspeople of Messina in 1191 reportedly mushroomed into a full-blown battle, during which the royal arsenal and fleet were burned to the waterline.[205] This, of course, rendered the realm virtually defenceless against seaborne assault. And Tancred had few resources with which to rebuild his naval capability. In order to purchase – dearly – the support he needed to remain in power, he had been compelled to draw heavily from a royal treasury already laid low by his predecessor's profligate spending on ill-conceived foreign adventures.[206] On top of all that, Richard and Philip forced him, essentially at sword point, to pay hefty reparations for the Messina fracas.[207] Therefore, when Henry VI Hohenstaufen finally came southwards with his allies, the Pisans and the Genoese, in 1194 to claim the crown he believed was rightfully his by marriage, there was apparently not so much as a single Sicilian ship to contest him.[208] The Norman kingdom of Sicily met its demise in large measure because the great fleet at the core of its power had predeceased it.

Nevertheless, the conquest of Sicily by the Normans and the subsequent establishment of a dominant Latin naval presence in the central Mediterranean at the expense of Islam was to have enormous consequences for European and Near Eastern history for centuries to come. The most important and immediate impact was that it opened up the Middle Sea to the expansion of West Italian sea power, that of Genoa and Pisa in particular, at precisely the moment that, arguably, the most aggressive movement of the Middle Ages exploded eastwards: the Crusades.

* * *

Exemplary Engagement: The Battle of Corfu (November 1084)

By the late summer of 1084 Robert Guiscard must have felt finally ready to resume his Balkan campaign after a three-year hiatus. He had crushed the latest revolt of his Apulian nobles at Cannae,[209] sent the German emperor Henry IV scampering back north of the Alps and rescued his liege lord Pope Gregory VII from Rome, albeit after a savage sacking of the city.[210] The appearance of his son Bohemond in Salerno must, however, have dampened any ephemeral euphoria and disabused him of the notion of an easy expedition.[211] Thanks in large measure to the Greco–Venetian fleet, much of what had been gained before his untimely return to Italy had been lost.

Guiscard's naval capability had never recovered from the defeat it had suffered at the hands of the Venetians off Pallia Point north of Durazzo in July 1081. As a result, his forces had lost freedom of movement on the sea. Anna Comnena explained: 'The Roman and Venetian fleets, tirelessly patrolling the straits [the Strait of Otranto between Apulia and modern Albania], prevented reinforcements crossing from Lombardy [Italy] and delivery of necessary supplies to him [Guiscard] from that area was impeded.'[212] This meant that Bohemond's efforts to continue the Balkan campaign in his father's absence were doomed from the start. He soldiered on nonetheless, defeating Alexios at Ioannina and again near Ochrid. Bohemond then marched into Thessaly where he took Trikkala and laid siege to Larissa. It was there that the young Hauteville, short on supplies and lacking funds to pay his exhausted troops, bogged down. Alexios, at last seeing the futility of head-on encounters with the Norman heavy cavalry, shifted tactics. He suborned many of Bohemond's knights with the compensation Guiscard's son could no longer provide without help from across the Adriatic.[213] The campaign soon crumbled, leaving Bohemond no option but to make his way back to Italy for reinforcement and replenishment.

Meanwhile, the Venetians, urged on by Alexios and supported by the Greek fleet under Michael Maurex, prosecuted the war at sea unchallenged. They recaptured Durazzo in the summer of 1083, then reclaimed all of Corfu, excluding the Norman-held citadel of Kassiopi on the northeastern promontory of the island. By the autumn Alexios had recaptured Kastoria. Aside from Avlona and Kassiopi, almost nothing of Greece remained in Norman hands.[214] And those few Norman forces still loyal to Guiscard had been rendered perilously isolated and susceptible to seaborne attack. Robert must have suffered no illusions: if his Byzantine aspirations were to be realized, he would have to wrench mastery of the lower Adriatic from the Venetians. Preparations for his second Balkan expedition were informed by that knowledge.

Accordingly, Robert amassed at Taranto in the fall of 1084 what Lupus Protospatarius called 'a huge gathering of ships and an innumerable army of men'.[215] There is some controversy about the exact numbers involved. Modern scholars such as Ferdinand Chalandon have estimated that Guiscard's fleet consisted of around 150 ships,[216] but the only contemporary source to offer a precise figure was William of Apulia, who claimed that the armada comprised 120 armed ships ('*armatis centum viginti navibus*') along with an unspecified number of 'transport vessels filled with horses, provisions and arms'.[217] The great Italian maritime historian Camillo Manfroni regards even this estimate as an exaggeration, because the number of galleys alone would have required 12,000 men just to crew them.[218] Nonetheless, given Robert's prior experience with Venetian naval power, the duke probably assembled a fleet of warships much larger than the one he had employed on the initial Balkan expedition three years before.

It was late in the sailing season – perhaps early September – before Robert was ready, so, instead of crossing from Otranto, the port which offered the shortest passage to Corfu, both Lupus Protospatarius and William of Apulia reported that Robert repositioned the fleet to Brindisi because it provided better shelter from autumn storms.[219] He obviously had no wish to repeat the horrendous experience of Glossa Point in 1081, when his fleet was very nearly demolished in its entirety by a terrible tempest. The duke dispatched an advance squadron under his sons Roger Borsa and Guy to secure Avlona once again. Guiscard himself proceeded with sons Bohemond and Robert to Butrinto on the Balkan mainland, just opposite the northeastern coast of Corfu, with the intention of relieving his garrison at Kassiopi. Roger and Guy rendezvoused with him there, but fierce autumn weather forced the entire expedition to hunker down for nearly two months. In the meantime Alexios, having learned of Guiscard's movements, directed the Greco–Venetian fleet to counter the anticipated assault on Corfu. Anna Comnena reported that these ships anchored at the harbour of Passaron, believed to be on the coast of Epirus somewhere to the south of Butrinto.[220] Thus Robert was probably aware of their presence in the vicinity.

Sometime in November, when the weather finally cleared, Guiscard seized the initiative by crossing the Strait of Corfu to Kassiopi with his entire fleet. Soon thereafter the Venetians moved to engage. The two fleets apparently clashed in the harbour of Kassiopi because Anna Comnena says the battle 'took place at close quarters'.[221] In such a battle of limited manoeuvring, the advantage must have been with the taller Venetian vessels, which were able to rain missiles down at will upon Guiscard's galleys with their low freeboard. William of Apulia called them 'triremes', but this was clearly a classicized reference to what were probably bireme *galeas*.[222] 'They [the Venetians] showered arrows from on high on their enemies and threatened them with heavy iron weights,' he recounted. The effect must have been devastating. 'In the ship carrying Roger during this battle scarcely a man could be found unwounded,' added William.[223] The Normans took a terrible beating but survived the encounter only to be attacked again three days later with much the same result.[224]

After this second triumph the Venetians returned to the harbour at Passaron, convinced that Guiscard had been so thoroughly vanquished that he no longer posed a threat. They even went so far as to send their light galleys home for the winter, while relocating their larger vessels to the port of Kerkyra midway down the east coast of Corfu.[225] Such overconfidence was to prove catastrophic. The Venetians had woefully misjudged their adversary. Anna Comnena explained: 'Robert was a determined champion of his own designs and prejudices, absolutely resolved never to give up a decision once taken: in a word indomitable.'[226] Guiscard learned from a defector named Pietro Contarini that the Venetians were, in effect, standing down for the winter, so he hastily prepared his fleet for a surprise attack.[227] He divided the twenty *galeas* that apparently remained to him into four squadrons of five ships each: one each under his sons Roger, Bohemond and Robert, keeping the last one for himself.[228]

When Robert's squadrons suddenly came upon the Venetians in the port of Kerkyra, Anna Comnena said, 'The latter were astounded by the unexpectedness of it, but lost no time in linking their bigger vessels with iron chains in the port of Corfu [Kerkyra], with the smaller ships inside this compact circle [the so-called 'sea harbour'].'[229] While the smaller Venetian galleys had been sent home, the Greek galleys of Maurex apparently remained in support, so Guiscard ordered Roger to separate them from the Venetian flotilla. William of Apulia identified the Greek vessels as *chelandia*. Since Roger's ships were probably *galeas*, which theoretically would have been larger and faster, his squadron would have had the advantage despite the superior number of Greek ships. In any event, the young Hauteville succeeded in chasing them off, leaving the Venetian 'sea harbour', composed of nine large vessels, to face the assault of the other Norman *galeas* on its own.[230]

Anna Comnena describes this 'sea harbour' as a 'compact circle', but in point of fact it was probably what Camillo Manfroni more accurately characterized as a semicircle,[231] i.e., the classic crescent fighting formation prescribed by the Byzantine emperor Leo VI in Constitution XIX of his *Taktika* on naval warfare. Hence, it is likely that Robert would have employed something similar to the tactic Leo VI recommended for combating such a crescent defensive posture: attacking the flanks with two five-ship squadrons while striking the centre with the third.[232] (*See* Map 5.) As fortune would have it, the Venetian floating fortress was especially vulnerable to this sort of assault. According to Anna Comnena, the Venetians had evidently consumed most of the supplies carried by these ships so that the vessels were riding high in the water, making them dangerously top-heavy. Consequently, when the Norman squadrons engaged the ends of the Venetian formation, calamity befell these vessels. Anna described what happened in lurid detail: 'The latter, because they had no cargo, floated on the surface as if buoyed by the waves (the water did not even reach the second line), so that when the men rushed to one side to oppose the enemy, the boats immediately sank.'[233]

Informed conjecture has it then that the ships on the horns of the crescent capsized, quite conceivably dragging down the vessels chained to them, one after the other. Of the nine vessels in the Venetian floating fortress, William of Apulia reported that seven were sunk and the remaining two were effortlessly captured.[234] Most of the Venetian combatants who had the misfortune of tumbling

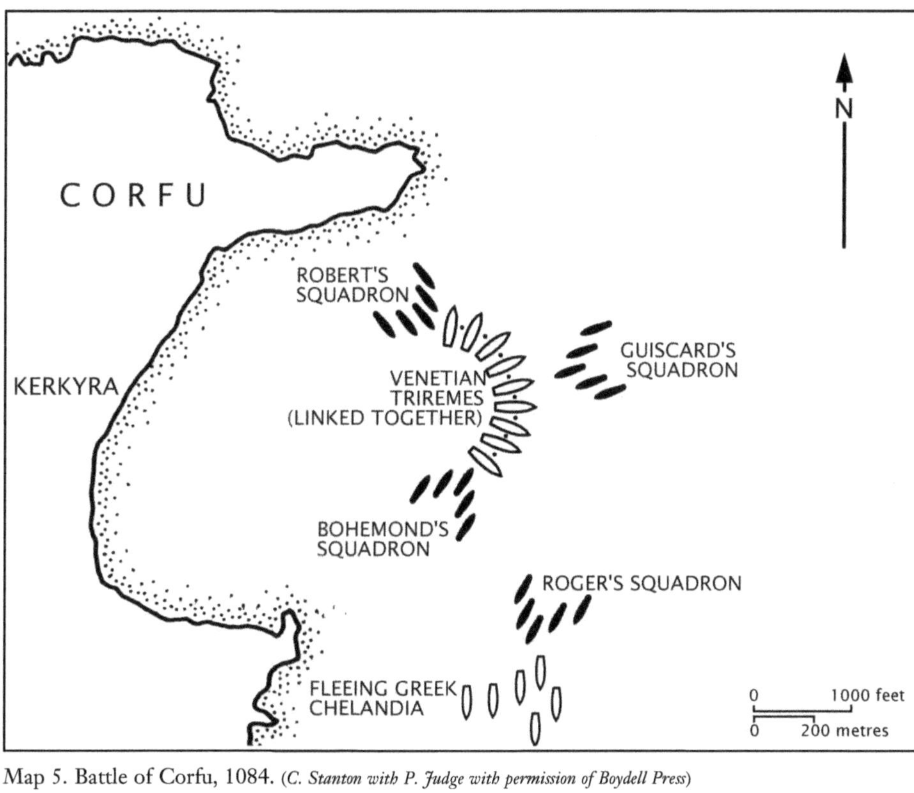

Map 5. Battle of Corfu, 1084. (*C. Stanton with P. Judge with permission of Boydell Press*)

into the sea probably did not survive – it was late November and the water temperature would have made hypothermia a killer. This sort of scenario would account for the appalling loss of life suffered by the Venetians. Anna Comnena lamented that as many as 13,000 were drowned.[235] Lupus Protospatarius claimed a more modest 5,000 mortalities among the Venetians.[236] William of Apulia did not give an estimate of enemy losses, but reported that the Normans took 2,500 captives,[237] whom Anna Comnena insisted fared poorly in Robert's care. 'Many of the prisoners were treated with hideous savagery: some were blinded, others had their noses cut off, others lost hands or feet or both.'[238]

In any case, it is certain that the reverse was one of the worst ever suffered by *La Serenissima*. The Venetian chroniclers hardly spoke of the battle, although it was noted that Domenico Selvo was replaced as doge shortly thereafter. The Venetian historian Andrea Dandolo mentioned a Norman victory over the Venetians near the island of Saseno (modern Sazan Island) off the Albanian coast well to the north of Corfu in 1086, but modern historians regard this as the result of geographic and chronological errors by the Venetian doge, writing two centuries after the fact.[239] Anna Comnena indicated that the Venetians achieved some retribution for the rout at Kerkyra by thrashing the Normans at Butrinto a short time later, but this has also largely been disregarded by modern scholars as wishful revisionism.[240] Robert and his sons wintered on the Glykys (also known as the Acheron), where their main enemies were malnutrition and disease. They continued their campaign the next spring with an invasion of Cephalonia, where Guiscard fell victim to the ravages of dysentery and fever.[241]

Regardless of what occurred in the aftermath, Robert Guiscard had announced the inexorable rise of Norman naval power by orchestrating the disastrous defeat of what would become the greatest Mediterranean maritime power of the era.

CHAPTER 3

The Crusades: The Clash of East and West at Sea

In truth, western sea power was not in the vanguard of the Christian response to Pope Urban II's call for a crusade at the Council of Clermont on 27 November 1095. Credit for that belongs to the armies of knights, infantrymen and peasants who trudged overland by way of Constantinople under the leadership of a handful of middling nobles and clerics. But it is highly improbable that these First Crusaders would have succeeded against all odds in ultimately capturing the Holy Land without some sort of maritime support and all but impossible that they could have held on to it. And that vital support came initially not from the traditional naval powers of eastern Christendom – Venice and Byzantium – but from the emerging maritime city-states of western Italy – Genoa and Pisa. It was by no accident that this propitious expansion of west Italian sea power conterminous with the crusades occurred just as the Normans of southern Italy completed the conquest of Sicily from Islam, opening up the central Mediterranean to western shipping.[1]

Moreover, the role played by sea power in the crusading movement was very different from that of past conflicts. The primary platform for naval operations was not the war galley. To be sure, some variant of the standard bireme galley, mostly the *galea* developed in maritime Italy, served a vital function throughout the era. It was crucial in the initial conquest of the Palestinian coast and indispensable for the defence of its ports. And, of course, the suppression of Muslim sea power which gave the Latins supremacy in Levantine waters for much of the period could not have been achieved without it. But long distances and hostile terrain ensured that the combat component of crusader fleets would, of necessity, take a supporting position to the logistical arm. This meant that the vessels which carried the sinews of war – the men, mounts and materials of crusading armies – would play a leading role in the conquest. And after the Latin Kingdom of Jerusalem had been established by bloody battle, it was such supply ships which brought the pilgrims and provisions that the crusader enclave so desperately needed to survive. In other words, the star of the crusader fleets was the humble transport ship.

Often simply called *naves* (meaning 'ships' in Latin) by chroniclers, these vessels varied from single-decked, coastal sailing ships with one or two masts, like the eleventh-century Serçe Limani wreck (15.66m/51ft 5in long and 5.12m/16ft 10in wide with only 35 metric tonnes of displacement), to the multi-masted, triple-decked transport behemoths of the thirteenth century which measured in excess of 35m (115ft) by 9.5m (31ft) and boasted over 800 metric tonnes of displacement.[2] Perhaps the most specialized and valued support vessels were the horse carriers. Heavy cavalry was at the core of western medieval armies. The knightly nobility which led the crusader movement considered horses an essential element in their campaigns, and getting these highly prized animals to the theatre of combat was crucial. Some horses could, of course, be transported in sailing ships, but large sailing vessels required established port facilities which were often lacking in the Levant. Originally they used shallow-draught oared vessels that could be beached, like the Byzantine *chelandion* which could carry about twelve mounts along the keel, but by the twelfth century crusader expeditions were employing oared horse transports called *uscerii* and *taride* (both apparently derived from Arabic), which could embark and disembark around forty horses each through stern hull ports with landing bridges.[3] A new era in naval warfare had dawned.

The First Crusade (1095–9)

The genesis of the crusading movement was actually a plea for military assistance from the Byzantine emperor Alexios I Komnenos, delivered to Urban II at the Council of Piacenza in March 1095 which, in turn, prompted the Pope to issue his decree at Clermont.[4] The Byzantine Empire had been losing land in Asia Minor to the Seljuk Turks at an alarming rate ever since the catastrophic defeat suffered by Emperor Romanos IV Diogenes at the hands of the Seljuk sultan Arp Arslan at the Battle of Manzikert in Armenia in 1071.[5] So it was only logical that the initial expedition should proceed overland through Byzantine territory. The trouble was that once the crusaders left the nominally hospitable environs of Constantinople and crossed the Bosporus, they found themselves in pitilessly hostile terrain controlled by an implacable enemy. Sustenance was scarce and water more precious still. The only entities in plentiful supply were the harrying hordes of Turks. Consequently, of the three waves of crusader armies who answered Urban's appeal, only one even made it through Asia Minor, much less all the way to Palestine.

The first wave, generally referred to as 'the People's Crusade', comprised a disorganized rabble of around 40,000 men, ostensibly led by a charismatic preacher from Amiens called Peter the Hermit. Mostly composed of peasants, with a few minor knights like Walter Sansavoir interspersed among their ranks, it marched through central Europe in the summer of 1096 in disparate groups which failed to coalesce into a manageable whole. Contingents under Count Emich of Flonheim, a Rhineland monk called Gottschalk and a fanatical Saxon priest named Folkmar were halted in Hungary after numerous excesses, including bloody pogroms against several communities of Rhineland Jews. Peter the Hermit's group, the largest at around 15,000, made it only to the environs of Nicaea before being slaughtered or enslaved by the Seljuks.[6] The third wave, the so-called crusade of 1101, numbered perhaps as many as the first and was commanded by such crusading veterans as Raymond of St Gilles, Hugh of Vermandois and Stephen of

Blois, but it moved as three independent, uncoordinated forces which were individually enveloped and decimated by coalitions of Seljuk princes in Anatolia.[7]

The only wave to succeed was the second and it suffered mightily to do so. Of the estimated 40,000 to 75,000 crusaders who crossed the Bosporus in the spring of 1097, barely 15,000 reached Jerusalem and even that force was vastly diminished.[8] The reason for the high mortality, of course, was that they had to forage and fight their way across some 2,000km (1,200 miles) of unfamiliar and inimical territory in all sorts of weather. The journeys of the disparate contingents of crusaders from their respective regions in western Europe to Constantinople was relatively benign. The brothers Godfrey of Bouillon and Baldwin of Boulogne made their way from Lorraine through southern Germany and Hungary, while Raymond of St Gilles, count of Toulouse, and his entourage trekked across northern Italy and Dalmatia to Thessaloniki and thence to the imperial city. Robert Curthose, Duke of Normandy, Robert of Flanders and Stephen of Blois all travelled by way of Rome to Bari, where they took ship to Durazzo, as did Hugh of Vermandois. And, of course, Bohemond of Taranto, son of the renowned Robert Guiscard, and his Italo-Normans also crossed the Adriatic from Apulia to the Greek mainland and completed the passage by land.[9] It was when they had all gathered on the eastern bank of the Bosporus that the challenge became extreme: they had to march across the arid Anatolian Plateau, stripped bare of sustenance by their Seljuk adversaries, in the scorching heat of summer.

They encountered their first obstacle just 125km (75 miles) to the southeast of Constantinople: Nicaea (the modern Turkish city of Iznik), which the Seljuk sultan Kilij Arslan had claimed as his capital. The crusaders began the siege of the city on 6 May 1097 and finally gained its capitulation on 19 June, largely with the help of a small Byzantine flotilla that Alexios had portaged from Civitot on the Gulf of Astacus (the present-day Gulf of Izmit) some 32km (20 miles) to Lake Askania, which washed the city's western walls.[10] Towards the end of the month the army resumed its march in two large elements: one under Bohemond and Robert Curthose, followed at some distance by the other led by Godfrey, Robert of Flanders and Raymond. At Dorylaeum (modern Karacaşehir, near Eskişehir), about 90km (56 miles) to the southeast of Nicaea, Kilij Arslan and some Danishmend allies ambushed Bohemond's army on 1 July 1097. The anonymous author of the *Gesta Francorum* ('Deeds of the Franks'), probably a vassal of Bohemond, reported that 'the Turks came upon us from all sides, skirmishing, throwing darts and javelins and shooting arrows at an astonishing range'.[11] The second column of crusaders arrived a few hours later and sent the swirling swarm of attacking archers into retreat but the toll had been terrible. As many as 4,000 Christians had fallen.[12] The animals, with no armour to protect them from the black clouds of arrows, must have suffered even more horribly.

The remaining 1,100km (684 miles) from Dorylaeum to Antioch in northern Syria offered no respite. Scholarly conjecture has it that the main army, seeking to avoid an ambush at the Cilician Gates through the Taurus Mountains, traced a circuitous route through Nakoleia (modern Sayitgazi) to ancient Ipsos near today's Afyon, to Philomelion (modern Akşehir), to Ikonion (Konya) to

Herakleia (Ereglia), northeast to Caesarea (Kayseri), southeast again to Mar'ash (modern Kahramanmaraş) and finally more or less due south to Antioch.[13] The searing sun took an appalling tally. Albert of Aachen, a canon of the church of Aachen and chronicler of the crusade, described the effects of single day in August: 'overwhelmed by the anguish of thirst, as many as five hundred people of both sexes gave up the ghost on that same day'. The animals fared no better. 'In addition horses, donkeys, camels, mules, oxen and many animals suffered the same death from extreme thirst.'[14] Nourishment was just as critical a problem. The author of the *Gesta Francorum* claimed that they found only 'prickly plants' to eat: 'On such food we survived wretchedly enough, but we lost most of our horses, so that many of our knights had to go as foot-soldiers, and for the lack of horses we had to use oxen as mounts, and our great need compelled us to use goats, sheep and dogs as beasts of burden.'[15]

Consequently, the combat effectiveness of the crusader force must have been significantly compromised. The core of any Frankish army was its contingent of knights, who, of course, fought on horseback. Noted medieval military historians Bernard Bachrach and John France both estimate that there were around 7,000 knights at the outset of the expedition, and that each would have had at least three mounts: a *destrier* (war-horse), a palfrey (riding mount) and a pack horse.[16] That means there must have been a minimum of 20,000 horses, yet by the time the crusaders arrived at Antioch the tribulations of the journey had winnowed away all but 1,000.[17] In other words, four out of every five knights was horseless. By the siege of Jerusalem fewer than 200 mounts remained.[18] Knights were riding into battle on the backs of asses and mules. The obvious logistical and tactical drawbacks of the overland route would later render sea support indispensable to the crusading movement.

When the main body of crusaders finally arrived at Antioch in northern Syria on 21 October, there were possibly 30,000 of them remaining.[19] Yet, as arduous as the campaign had been up to that point, their travails would continue unabated, for they now faced a gruelling eight-month siege of a heavily fortified, nearly impregnable city. Foraging quickly denuded the surrounding countryside and, once again, malnutrition became more devastating to the crusaders than the enemy. Parties of scavengers were venturing as far as 80km (50 miles) from camp to find food.[20] 'Then the starving people devoured the stalks of beans still growing in the fields,' observed Fulcher of Chartres, the chaplain for Baldwin of Boulogne. 'The poorer people ate even the hides of animals and the seeds of grain found in manure.'[21] But here, at last, they would begin to receive some reinforcement and resupply by sea.

The first to arrive were the Genoese. Urban II had sent two bishops, Hugh Chateauneuf d'Isère of Grenoble and William of Orange, to preach the crusade in Genoa in early 1097 and the commune had responded by dispatching twelve galleys and a *sandanum* (*chelandion* – supply ship) in July. The squadron reached the Port of St Symeon at the mouth of the river Orontes (about 16km or 10 miles from Antioch) around 20 November. The Genoese supplied not only provisions for the siege, but also 600 combatants, including twenty-five horsemen.[22] A small

English fleet and possibly some ships from Venice and Pisa joined the Genoese at St Symeon in March 1098, bringing still more badly needed replenishment.[23] The Genoese contribution, however, was apparently considered crucial. Antioch finally fell on 3 June, thanks to some subterfuge by Bohemond, who on 28 June also orchestrated the stunning defeat of a relief army led by Kerbogha, the Atabeg of Mosul. Bohemond subsequently claimed lordship of the city and amply rewarded his Ligurian allies. On 14 July he conceded to the Genoese a lucrative charter which allotted them a quarter in the city with thirty houses and a market near the church of St John, free from all trade duties. In return, he expected the Genoese to keep open his supply lines to Norman Italy.[24] It would be the first of many such agreements.

Commencing with the investment of Antioch, western maritime support, particularly that of northern Italy, would be an integral component in the crusading movement. The leaders of the First Crusade elected to proceed south from Antioch along the coast specifically so that they could be revictualled by sea. And Genoese, English and Venetian vessels continued to do just that, bringing in goods from Cyprus, Rhodes and other Aegean islands. This proved especially useful during the protracted and ultimately unsuccessful siege of Arqah (a fortress a few kilometres inland from Tripoli) in February 1099.[25] Raymond of Aguilers, chaplain to Raymond of Toulouse, claimed that as many as thirty English ships were initially involved with such resupply operations.[26] Both Albert of Aachen and William, Archbishop of Tyre, described a pirate fleet composed of ships from Antwerp, Tiel, Frisia and Flanders, led by a certain Winemer of Boulogne, who briefly joined Baldwin near Tarsus in the autumn of 1097. They evidently parted company when the latter struck off on his own to assume the lordship of Edessa in March 1098. Winemer then seems to have besieged and temporarily taken Latakia (about 60km or 38 miles south of St Symeon).[27] He and his followers, however, continued to support the Christian cause. William of Tyre noted that their ships were among those shuttling supplies to the crusaders at Arqah in early 1099.[28]

It was the Genoese, however, who managed to contribute directly to the capture of Jerusalem. On 17 June 1099 two vessels of the brothers Guglielmo and Primo Embriaco anchored at Jaffa along with four English ships.[29] Their timing was impeccable. The Franks had already failed several times to breach the walls of the Holy City for lack of siege machinery and famine was once again beginning to dog their efforts.[30] Blockaded in port by a Fatimid flotilla, the Embriaco brothers decided to have their ships disassembled so that the wood could be used to construct siege engines, which were employed in the seizure of the city on 15 July.[31]

The Latin Kingdom of Jerusalem (1099–1125)

The spectacular success of the First Crusaders in capturing Jerusalem in the face of unfathomable hardship owed as much to discord among their Islamic foes and the vagaries of fortune as it did to their own daring and devotion. They would need much more to hold on to it. Jerusalem was an isolated Latin enclave in an unfriendly environment. Both Antioch, ruled by Bohemond, and Edessa, controlled by Baldwin, were too distant from the Holy City and from each other to provide much in the way of effective mutual assistance. The Latin Kingdom would survive only with a massive infusion of aid from the West and clearly, given the horrendous nature of the overland journey there, that support had to come by sea.

The first large-scale naval support came from the Tuscan city-state of Pisa: a huge fleet under the command of Archbishop Daimbert himself. 'He [Daimbert] equipped triremes, dromons and other fast vessels to the number of 900,' effused Anna Comnena with obvious hyperbole, 'and so left for Syria.'[32] The Pisan chronicler Bernardo Maragone offered a more sober assessment: 120 ships.[33] Even so, the fleet was substantial, which helps explain why the expedition took so long to organize. Daimbert had been with Urban II at Clermont when the Pope proclaimed the crusade, and had probably initiated preparations to launch an expedition soon thereafter. Since many of these vessels were thought to be galleys, manning the fleet alone would have required up to 15,000 mariners – a number which must have nearly emptied the city of able-bodied men. Provisioning a fleet of that size must also have been challenging. Both Anna Comnena and Bernardo Maragone reported that it ravaged the Ionian islands of Leucadia and Cephalonia en route, prompting Emperor Alexios to dispatch a Byzantine fleet to intercept it. Daimbert's armada eluded the Byzantines, but, if Venetian chroniclers such as Doge Andrea Dandolo can be believed, there may have been a second Pisan expedition of fifty vessels later that autumn which ran afoul of a Greek-allied Venetian fleet at Rhodes.[34] There is, however, scant confirmation in the sources for the incident.

Daimbert's fleet made landfall in Outremer (meaning 'land beyond the sea' in French), as the Latin Kingdom came to be called, somewhere in the vicinity of Antioch around September 1099. The Pisans soon joined forces with Bohemond to blockade Latakia, a Byzantine port at the time, but the investment was abandoned before the end of November, in part due to the stigma of attacking a Christian city. Daimbert then accompanied Bohemond and Baldwin to Jerusalem to fulfil their crusading vows. They arrived on 21 December 1099, upon which Daimbert demanded forthwith the patriarchate of the city, and Godfrey, as 'Defender of the Holy Sepulchre', had little choice but to accede. He needed the Pisan fleet to help him secure the Palestinian coast – or watch helplessly as his nascent kingdom withered away. As a result, the Pisan prelate was not only chosen to replace Arnulf of Chocques as patriarch, but was also ceded control of most of the Holy City along with the tower of David and a fourth part of Jaffa.[35] In return, the Pisans probably helped Godfrey refurbish and refortify Jaffa's ancient port so that it could serve as a naval base for capturing the other ports of Palestine.[36]

The bulk of Daimbert's fleet departed for home sometime in the spring of 1100,[37] but at least some ships and sailors must have remained. Albert of Aachen reported that Pisans were among the Latin forces which reduced Arsuf in April 1101 and Caesarea in June.[38] Pisan involvement was noted in almost every major coastal investment in Outremer thereafter. Pisan ships reportedly participated in the successful blockades of Jubayl and Acre by Godfrey's successor, Baldwin, in the spring of 1104.[39] And Albert contends that they were also among the ships besieging Sidon in 1107 and Tripoli in 1109.[40] Such accounts are corroborated by numerous commercial concessions subsequently conceded to the Pisans in the Latin Kingdom. 'Thus, in less than a century from the expedition under Daimbert,' concludes English historian William Heywood, 'they [the Pisans] had colonies in Laodicea [Latakia], Antioch, Tripoli, Tyre, Acre, Jaffa, and probably also in Jerusalem and Caesarea.'[41]

The next major naval expedition from the West to reach the Holy Land was probably Venetian. The sources for *La Serenissima* mention an armada of some 200 ships commanded by Enrico Contarini, bishop of Castello, and Giovanni Michiel, the son of Doge Vitale Michiel, which appeared off the coast of Palestine towards the middle of June 1100. It apparently departed Venice in the summer of 1099 and sailed by way of Zara in Dalmatia and Rhodes, where it wintered from the end of October to the following May. If, in fact, a fleet of fifty Pisan ships clashed with Venetian vessels outside the port of Rhodes in the autumn of 1099, as indicated earlier, it was most likely with elements of this armada. In any event, after appropriating the remaining bones of St Nicolas of Myra (the inspiration for Santa Claus) on the south coast of Asia Minor, the Venetians arrived at Jaffa a few weeks before Godfrey's death on 18 July 1100.[42] Godfrey reportedly offered the Venetians a third of any port city captured with their aid (except Tripoli) along with exemption from all duties in return for three months of naval support.[43] The Venetians accepted and, according to Albert of Aachen, assisted in the seizure of Haifa on 20 August.[44]

Much more is known about the Genoese contribution to the Latin Kingdom's coastal expansion thanks to the participation of Caffaro di Caschifellone, the Ligurian city-state's most important chronicler of the period. He was with Guglielmo Embriaco when the latter led yet another expedition to Outremer in the autumn of 1100 – this one composed of twenty-six galleys and four to six supply ships, the largest Genoese crusader fleet to date. Caffaro was almost certainly an eyewitness to many of the subsequent maritime actions which he carefully recorded in either his *Annales Ianuenses* ('Annals of the Genoese') or the *Liber de liberatione civitatum orientis* ('The Book of the liberation of the cities of the East'). The fleet's first order of business was to request confirmation of Bohemond's earlier concessions in Antioch. Bohemond had been captured by the Danishmend Turks a few weeks earlier, but his nephew Tancred, acting as his regent, validated the grants and added a few enticements of his own: a third of the port revenues of St Symeon, half of the revenues of Latakia along with a quarter in that city, a quarter in Jubayl and a quarter in any other city taken with Genoese assistance.[45]

After wintering in the north, the Genoese headed south to Jaffa in April 1101. There, Baldwin, who had assumed the crown of Jerusalem upon his brother's passing, also sought to enlist their services with attractive inducements: a third of the booty of any city captured plus a quarter to hold in perpetuity without crown interference. Arsuf fell to the new partnership within the month, followed a few weeks later by Caesarea.[46] During the latter assault, Fulcher of Chartres recounted how the Genoese demonstrated their resourcefulness by constructing a siege tower of masts and oars, a feat which was doubtless replicated throughout the campaign.[47] Caffaro recorded that Embriaco's fleet returned to Genoa in the autumn of 1101, but the precedent had been set.[48] Genoese participation in the Latin conquest of the Levantine littoral was more or less continuous henceforth.[49] According to Caffaro, 'eight galleys and other oared warships and supply ships' commanded by Mauro de Platea and Paganus de Volta assisted in the taking of Tortosa in April 1102.[50] Forty Genoese vessels were said to have helped Raymond of Toulouse seize Jubayl in March 1104, following an unsuccessful assault on Tripoli.[51] And in May, both Fulcher of Chartres and William of Tyre recounted that 'a fleet of seventy beaked ships' from Genoa enabled Baldwin to win the most strategically significant prize to date after a siege of only twenty days: the port of Acre.[52]

Baldwin clearly regarded Genoese naval support as crucial to the continued existence of the realm, because he paid a premium for it by decreeing that the Genoese be granted: 'in perpetuity a third part of the returns and revenues collected at the port of Acre from sea-borne import and in addition be granted a church in the city and full jurisdiction over one street'.[53] He also conferred upon them similar concessions in Arsuf and Caesarea. Moreover, to ensure lasting Genoese collaboration, he pledged an annual subsidy of 300 *bezants* (Byzantine coins containing about 4.25 grams of gold each), streets in both Jerusalem and Jaffa, as well as a third of any city captured with Genoese assistance in the future, while guaranteeing the inviolability of Genoese persons and property throughout the realm, even after death.[54] The king not only confirmed all these highly profitable privileges in May of the following year, but he also apparently went so far as to have the terms inscribed in gold and placed in the choir of the Holy Sepulchre.[55]

The pay-off persisted for more than a decade after the Latin conquest of Jerusalem. A seventy-ship flotilla under Guglielmo Embriaco and Baldwin joined forces with Bertram of Toulouse, Raymond's son, to finally bring Tripoli to heel in June 1109.[56] The next spring another forty-ship Genoese fleet helped Baldwin besiege Beirut, gaining the city's capitulation the following April.[57] And so, the Genoese had a hand in the capture of nearly every coastal city in the Latin Kingdom in those early years of its existence. There were other contributors, of course, from other maritime regions of western Christendom. The thirteenth-century *Heimskringla* ('Circle of the World'), a saga of the old Norse kings by the Icelandic historian Snorre Sturlason, tells of an expedition of at least sixty ships led by King Sigurd of Norway which reached Palestine in the summer of 1110.[58] And William of Tyre corroborates that the Scandinavians enabled Baldwin to at last seize Sidon in December of that year.[59] By and large, however, it was the northern Italian maritime republics which enabled the embryonic Latin Kingdom of Jerusalem to establish suzerainty over the shores of Syria and Palestine.

And perhaps no single mission by an Italian maritime power did more to ensure Latin supremacy in Levantine waters for decades to come than the one which departed the Venetian Lagoon on 8 August 1122 under the leadership of Doge Domenico Michiel.[60] There would be few expeditions in the history of the crusades that would have greater impact. By the time the doge's armada returned to the Islands of the Rialto in the autumn of 1125, it had won a pivotal naval victory over the Fatimids of Egypt, vanquishing Muslim naval power until the arrival of Saladin, and helped execute the successful siege of the ancient Phoenician port of Tyre, virtually guaranteeing the survival of the Latin Kingdom of Jerusalem for a generation.[61] The benefits accrued to *La Serenissima* by virtue of this enterprise were far-reaching as well. The rich concessions granted to it by the Latin Kingdom in return for its services gave it a virtually autonomous commercial colony in every city of the realm.[62] Furthermore, the ravaging of Byzantine lands en route to and from the Holy Land intimidated the emperor into restoring the trading privileges which had made Venice the dominant economic power in the eastern Mediterranean.[63] The significance of this episode is of such magnitude that it necessitates a special section to delineate just how it came about and why its outcome was so consequential. For now, it suffices to say that it helped perpetuate one of the most influential movements in medieval history and probably played a starring role in the economic resurgence of the West.

As recompense for their participation in the First Crusade and subsequent assistance in the establishment of the Latin Kingdom of Jerusalem, the main Italian maritime powers (Genoa, Pisa and Venice) all won extensive privileges in the new realm, including semi-autonomous merchant enclaves called *fondachi* (*fondaco* in the singular) in all its port cities. The word *fondaco* was derived from the Arabic *funduq* (literally, 'warehouse') and each of these 'warehouse' quarters contained its own market, bath, mill, oven, church and residential edifices that formed a self-sufficient community complete with all the advantages of extraterritoriality.[64] Moreover, having temporarily swept the seas of Muslim competition, the Latin West now enjoyed unhindered access to the bountiful markets of the East. Trade flourished and the Italian commercial colonies in the Latin Levant became, in the aggregate, an enormous engine which powered an economic explosion in western Europe. Hence, David Abulafia was prompted to assert, 'These bases were taps at the end of a long Middle Eastern pipeline bringing spices and drugs and dyes and fabrics from Mesopotamia and beyond to the Frankish settlements, and thence via Messina or Palermo to continental Europe.'[65]

The Second Crusade (1144–8)

On Christmas Eve 1144 miners in the army of Imad al-Din Zangi ibn Aqsunqur, the Atabeg of Mosul, succeeded in collapsing a section of the city walls of Edessa, thereby setting off a chain reaction which would, once again, engulf the region in war.[66] Two bloody days later the city's citadel was in Turkish hands and a psychological tsunami began to crash over all Christendom. According to

William of Tyre, it was as though the Turks were 'laying waste the cities, villas, and fortified places of our people and overrunning the entire East unchecked'.[67] The response from the West was prompt and passionate. Not only was the papacy, in the person of Eugenius III, moved to issue another call to crusade in the form of the *Quantum praedecessores* (a papal bull promising the remission of sins to participants), but the revered Bernard of Clairvaux was tasked with preaching it. And the latter, perhaps the most eloquent ecclesiastic of the era, managed to enlist, for the first time, the participation of kings: Louis VII of France and Conrad III of Germany.[68]

Unfortunately, despite unprecedented enthusiasm, the crusade was doomed from the start by a decision made in the planning stage. At a preparatory conference at Etampes on 16 February 1147, representatives of King Roger II of Sicily offered the use of his magnificent fleet to transport the crusading armies to the Holy Land. Louis, aware of Conrad's enmity for Roger and leery of the latter's motives, elected to take the overland route instead.[69] Conrad, of course, chose to follow suit at his own pre-crusade conference at Frankfurt a month later.[70] The decision would prove disastrous.

Conrad's contingent arrived first at Constantinople in early September 1147 and waited a mere three weeks for its French counterpart before forging ahead alone. Seljuk Turks ambushed the Germans in the vicinity of Dorylaeum and exacted such a heavy toll that Conrad's men were forced to retreat to Nicaea, harried every step of the way by horse-borne archers. Most returned home from there. The French fared little better. Louis reached Constantinople on 4 October, pressing on into Asia Minor shortly thereafter. His forces absorbed the remnants of the German army at Nicaea, but Conrad himself fell ill and was compelled to return to Constantinople to recuperate. By the time the crusaders reached Antalya on the south coast of Asia Minor on 20 January 1148 they were on the brink of starvation and their numbers had been savagely reduced by constant Turkish attacks. Louis took ship from there to Antioch on vessels provided by the Byzantine emperor Manuel Komnenos, but these ships could carry only a fraction of the Frankish forces and almost no horses.[71]

It was a sadly scaled-down French expedition that arrived in Syria in March. Conrad, having recovered, sailed from Constantinople to join Louis in Antioch. Their forces now deemed too small to retrieve Edessa, the two sovereigns made their way down the coast to Acre, where they held a council of war with the leaders of the Latin Kingdom on 24 June. This conclave decided upon Damascus as the objective, probably because it would pose the greater threat to Jerusalem if seized by the aggressive new emir of Aleppo, Nur al-Din Zangi, son of Imad ad-Din. On 24 July the combined army began its assault from the West through orchards watered by the Barada river, but three days later its leaders inexplicably moved their siege operations to the arid east side of the city in hopes of a quick victory. None was to be had and the searing summer sun soon punished the decision to abandon a ready supply of water. Pressed by the imminent arrival of the prince of Aleppo, the crusaders were compelled to begin an ignominious retreat after only a day.[72] Conrad ended up returning to Europe by ship in September and Louis did so the following spring, having achieved nothing at the cost of thousands of lives. It would be the last large-scale crusade launched on behalf of the Latin Kingdom to go almost entirely overland. Ironically, the ships which carried Louis and his bride Eleanor of Aquitaine back to the west were Sicilian, controlled by Roger II, the very same sovereign whose offer of sea support Louis had spurned at the start.[73]

The call to crusade proclaimed by Pope Eugenius III and Bernard of Clairvaux was answered with greater success elsewhere, particularly on the Iberian peninsula. And it was no accident that these triumphs were purchased primarily through the effective use of sea power. The first such expedition, one from northern Europe, was actually headed for the Holy Land and only stopped on the Atlantic coast of Iberia by serendipity. Inspired by the preachings of Bernard, a fleet of around 200 ships manned by Anglo-Normans, Flemings, Frisians and Rhinelanders departed Dartmouth on 19 May 1147 bound for Palestine under the nominal command of Henry of Glanville, Constable of Suffolk. Spring storms forced the ships to seek shelter in the estuary of the Douro river near Oporto, Portugal, on 16 June. There, King Afonso Henriques of the Portuguese convinced the crusaders to help him capture Lisbon from the Moors in return for plunder, ransom, and the partitioning of the conquered territories as fiefs. The siege began on 1 July but did not achieve the city's surrender until 24 October. The vast majority of the crusaders never reached the Holy Land, electing instead to remain in Portugal.[74]

At about the same time, on the Mediterranean side of the Iberian peninsula, the Genoese were assisting King Alfonso VII of Castile and Count Ramon Berenguer IV of Barcelona in the capture of Almeria. Unlike the Portuguese adventure, however, this campaign had been planned well in advance. Caffaro, now a consul and senior statesman, had conducted a Genoese expedition of twenty-two galleys and six smaller ships on a highly remunerative raid of Minorca and Almeria in 1146.[75] While in the region, he had negotiated pacts with Alfonso VII and Ramon Berenguer in September to help them take Almeria and Tortosa the following year in return for a third of each city and exemptions from trade tariffs in the territories of the two sovereigns. The king of Castile had even agreed to contribute 10,000 *marabotini* (Andalusian gold dinars, weighing about 4.25 grams each) for the outfitting of the fleet.[76] Caffaro also claimed that the 'Apostolic See' had specifically called upon the Genoese to send its ships against the 'Saracens of Almeria', giving the expedition the aura of a crusade.

Accordingly, in the summer of 1147 the commune of Genoa launched a formidable fleet of 63 galleys and 163 support ships under the command of no fewer than six consuls. Upon their arrival at Porto Mahon in Minorca, the consuls sent ahead to Almeria a scout squadron of fifteen galleys under Consul Balduino. The latter anchored at Cabo de Gata (about 27km or 17 miles east of the city) and attempted to contact King Alfonso, who was at Baeza. In the meantime the Moors of Almeria sortied out in a fifteen-ship squadron of their own to contest the Genoese, but Balduino apparently held off until the rest of the fleet and their allies could join them. In addition to the Castilians and Catalonians, Provençals and Pisans participated. Ultimately, the Genoese beached their galleys and contributed siege machinery and twelve companies of a thousand combatants each to a conventional land investment which lasted from mid-August to 17 October, when the 'Saracens' finally surrendered the citadel.[77]

After reserving some of the spoils to pay the commune's expenses, the consuls shared out the rest among the ships' crews and sailed north, leaving Ottone de Bonovillano with a thousand men to guard Genoa's third of the city. When they arrived at Barcelona, they beached the entire fleet and wintered there. On 29 June 1148 the Genoese refloated their ships and sailed southwest down the Catalonian coast to the mouth of the Ebro river, which they entered to reach Tortosa around 40km (25 miles) upstream. Again, indications are that they beached their vessels and besieged the city by land. About half the troops took up a position along the river on Tortosa's west side and the other half on the high ground to the east. Once again, their primary weaponry seems to have been siege machinery (i.e., mangonels and towers) and not ships. In fact, the most challenging impediment was a ravine that ran along the east side of the *sueta* or citadel which prevented the positioning of a large siege tower against the ramparts. The besiegers eventually filled in the ravine with rocks and soil, allowing the tower to abut the battlements of the bastion and force its capitulation on 30 December. Upon receiving their promised third of the city plus plunder, the Genoese returned to Liguria in triumph.[78] While their vessels played no direct role in the reduction of either city, the skill of the Genoese mariners in the construction and operation of siege machinery appears to have been crucial to their success. And, of course, the ships provided the logistical underpinning which made the entire campaign feasible.

The Third Crusade (1187–92)

The tripwire for the Third Crusade was provided by a Kurdish general of modest heritage named Yusuf ibn Ayyub. In the scorching heat of early July 1187 he attacked Christian-held Tiberias on the western shores of the Sea of Galilee and thereby lured Guy de Lusignan, the then king of Jerusalem, at the head of the entire army of the Latin Kingdom, onto a parched plateau lorded over by twin volcanic peaks called the Horns of Hattin. There, he used his numerically superior forces (about 30,000) to subject the dangerously dehydrated Frankish army (around 20,000) to a double envelopment which almost entirely annihilated it and captured the king, along with the 'True Cross'. Three months later this brilliant tactician marched triumphant into Jerusalem, cementing his reputation among his people as 'the goodness of the faith' or, in Arabic, 'Salah al-Din'.[79]

Saladin's conquest of Palestine was not without provocation. And a good deal of it had to do with sea power. In truth, much of his motivation was associated with his desire to unify Islam in the Fertile Crescent under his leadership at the expense of the Zangid Dynasty, but as sultan of Egypt he must have felt particularly threatened by the burgeoning naval capability of the Latin East.[80] After all, the menace posed to Egypt by the Latin Kingdom of Jerusalem became evident when King Baldwin III seized Ascalon after a determined eight-month siege in August 1153, thereby denying the Muslims a port in Palestine and clearing the way for an invasion of the land of the Pharaohs.[81] Amalric, Baldwin's younger brother and successor to the throne, would repeatedly endanger Egypt's sovereignty, most notably with an attack on Damietta aided by a large Byzantine fleet in the summer of 1169, just a few months after Saladin became vizier in Cairo.[82] In response, the latter dispatched his nephew Taqi al-Din who successfully dispersed the attempt, but Amalric, undeterred, colluded with King William II of Sicily to assail Alexandria in 1174. According to Ibn al-Athir, the Sicilian monarch mounted a massive expedition: 'The ruler of Sicily equipped a large fleet, numbering two hundred galleys carrying men, thirty-six transports carrying horses, six large ships carrying war materials and forty vessels with provisions.'[83] Only Amalric's premature death due to dysentery averted the city's capture. Stranded before the walls of Alexandria without their expected Frankish allies, the Sicilians fell victim to Saladin's relief forces which swept them and their ships from Egypt's shores. Little wonder that in 1177 Saladin began rebuilding at Alexandria the once-proud Egyptian fleet that the Fatimids had allowed to flag in recent years. Using Coptic mariners and materials from Libya, he enlarged his naval forces to about sixty *shini* (galleys) and twenty *taride* (transport vessels) within just two years.[84]

The most serious incitement, however, may have been psychological. In late 1182 or early 1183 Reynaud of Châtillon, lord of Transjordan (the territory just east of the Dead Sea), ordered five galleys to be constructed in sections at the fortress of Kerak and carried by camel to the Gulf of Aqaba, where they were reassembled and launched in the Red Sea. Two of the galleys assaulted the port of Aqaba, while the other three raided the Egyptian and Saudi shores of the Red Sea, harrying Muslim merchants and pilgrims alike for weeks. Ibn al-Athir was even led to speculate, 'Their plan was to enter the Hijaz, Mecca and Medina (may God Almighty defend them), and to seize the pilgrims and keep them from the Sacred House.' Al-Adil ibn Ayyub, Saladin's brother and the governor of Egypt at the time, eventually portaged his own flotilla from Cairo to the Red Sea, so that it could hunt down the Christian marauders and summarily dispose of them, which it did.[85] The emotional impact remained, nonetheless, resulting in a festering enmity for the Latins in general and Reynaud of Châtillon in particular.

In September 1183 Saladin invaded Galilee and Transjordan, laying siege to Kerak. Achieving little lasting success, he agreed to a truce in 1185 in order to consolidate his position in Syria and Mesopotamia.[86] Reynaud once again wrenched Saladin back into the role of 'Holy Warrior' by attacking a Muslim caravan transiting Transjordan, thereby contravening the aforesaid truce.[87] The end result was the battle at the Horns of Hattin in July 1187. Within a few weeks, Saladin rolled up Acre, Beirut, Sidon, Haifa, Caesarea, Arsuf, Jaffa and Ascalon. By September all the ports of Palestine and most of the Syrian coast were in the sultan's hands. Only Tripoli and Tyre remained to provide a Latin lifeline to the West.[88] Fittingly, Archbishop Jocius of Tyre was dispatched to sound the alarm in western Europe which, in October 1187, prompted Pope Gregory VIII to disseminate the papal encyclical *Audita Tremendi*, proclaiming the Third Crusade.[89]

And, as was the case with the Second Crusade, the principal respondents were kings. The first to act was William II, king of Sicily. In the summer of 1188 he sent his great admiral Margaritus of Brindisi with an armada of fifty to sixty galleys to succour what was left of the beleaguered Latin Levant.[90] The Latin chroniclers of the crusade christened the effort a success. 'Who can doubt that it was a miracle that, with the help of the king's [William's] forces, Antioch was held, Tripoli defended, Tyre saved and the inhabitants of these cities kept secure from famine and the sword?' observed the *Itinerarium Peregrinorum* (a chronicle of the Third Crusade probably composed by Richard de Templo, a canon of Holy Trinity in London), noting, 'Margarit was in command of the royal fleet, a great man of action.'[91] The Sicilian admiral not only dissuaded Saladin from attacking Tripoli and probably Tyre, but he also hounded the sultan's march northwards along the Syrian coast. As Saladin's army passed Maraclea, Margaritus anchored his galleys in a line parallel to the shoreline abeam the Margat, a mammoth Hospitaller fortress perched on a precipice above the beach. Then, in an early example of ship-to-shore battery operations, arbalesters and archers aboard the galleys rendered the narrow passageway almost impassable to the Ayyubid army. Saladin managed to march his men past only after he had them assemble a barricade of mantlets and palisades to deflect the various projectiles.[92] Such tactics helped buy the Latin Kingdom enough time to survive until a campaign could be mounted by the three most powerful sovereigns of western Christendom: Frederick I Barbarossa of Germany, Philip II Augustus of France and Richard I Lionheart of England.

As it was, political circumstances and the logistical challenges of such a massive military undertaking prevented any of the monarchs from reaching the Holy Land until the spring of 1191, nearly four years after Hattin – and one never made it all. Frederick Barbarossa, the Holy Roman Emperor, chose to lead his immense army of 'tens of thousands' overland in the footsteps of so many failed expeditions before him, only to drown in the river Seleph (modern Göksu) in Asia Minor on 10 July 1190.[93] Few of his followers ever arrived in the Levant. Philip and Richard, having elected to come by sea, were more fortunate, but the journey was neither easy nor uneventful. First of all, sea travel in the twelfth century was an enormously expensive proposition and the two monarchs needed time to amass the necessary finances, principally through the collection of the Saladin Tithe (a special tax of 10 per cent on all movable goods).[94] They finally departed Vézelay (central Burgundy) together on 4 July 1190, but parted company at Lyon with the intention of rendezvousing at Messina. Philip took ship at Genoa on rented vessels for his 650 knights and 1300 squires, while Lionheart made his way to Marseilles, where Roger of Howden (an English chronicler and probably a cleric in Richard's entourage) said 'he hired ten large busses [transport ships, each of which could accommodate about forty horses with an equal number of knights and squires] and twenty well armed galleys'.[95] Philip pulled into Messina on 16 September. Richard arrived a week later amid much fanfare. His main fleet, consisting of 108 galleys and an undisclosed number of transport vessels assembled from his lands on both sides of the Channel, had reached Sicily ahead of him.[96] The waning sailing season and the previously mentioned confrontation with the citizens of Messina compelled the two kings to winter on Sicily.

They used the reparations extorted from King Tancred of Sicily over the Messina imbroglio to construct siege machinery and finish refitting their fleets.[97] Richard even exchanged a sword, purported to be the legendary *Excalibur*, for 'four large ships, which they call "ursers" [probably referring to *uissiers*, meaning horse transports], and fifteen galleys'.[98] Philip finally weighed anchor for the Holy Land on 20 March 1191. Richard set sail about three weeks later, with his fiancée Berengaria of Navarre and his sister Queen Joanna of Sicily (wife of the deceased King William II) among his retinue. By that time his fleet had swollen to over 200 ships.[99]

Philip's voyage was apparently prosaic. He arrived in Acre on 20 April, about a month after starting out. The 'Old French Continuation of William of Tyre' characterized Philip's flotilla as 'a great fleet of ships loaded with food and many other supplies',[100] but Saladin's biographer, Baha al-din ibn Shaddad, described it as only a modest squadron of a mere 'six busses'.[101] Lionheart, however, given his more grandiose style, was destined to have a more stimulating passage. Richard made it to Rhodes with most of his armada intact, but around twenty-five of his vessels had become separated from the rest of the fleet during a storm. Three of these, including a buss carrying Berengaria and Joanna, ended up on the south coast of Cyprus, near Limassol. The ruler of the island, a renegade member of the royal family of Constantinople named Isaac Komnenos, had made a pact with Saladin, and thus the crusader ships were received less than graciously. The two women were held offshore on their vessel and refused replenishment. Others who had been shipwrecked were even imprisoned. When word of all this reached Richard on Rhodes on 1 May, he immediately sailed for Cyprus. Five days later he stormed ashore at Limassol with a force of knights in *esneccas* or 'snacks' (Viking-type galleys with around sixty oars, derived from the Scandinavian *snekkjur*, meaning 'snakes') and, after a brief battle, rescued the royal women and freed the captives from Isaac's clutches. He and Berengaria were married at Limassol on 12 May, and shortly thereafter the English king commenced a brilliant conquest of the island.[102] Richard placed the bulk of his land forces under Guy de Lusignan, who had come to the island to consult the king, and directed him to pursue Isaac overland. Richard then assigned half the fleet to Robert of Thornham, whom he commanded to circumnavigate the island one way, capturing castles and towns along the coast, while Richard did the same in the opposite direction with the other half of the ships. The campaign was brought to a triumphant conclusion when Isaac's daughter was captured at Kyrenia, compelling Isaac to capitulate. By 1 June Cyprus belonged to the king of England.[103]

When Richard arrived off Acre a week later at the head of an advance squadron of twenty-five galleys, the siege had already been going on for a long time. The disgraced Guy, released by Saladin in the summer of 1188, had begun the investment with only a handful of troops on 28 August 1189.[104] A steady flow of pilgrim ships, however, had rapidly reinforced Guy's paltry contingent of besiegers. A fleet of fifty Pisan galleys was reported to have joined the effort shortly after

Guy's arrival outside the walls.[105] As Crusades historian Thomas Asbridge astutely puts it, 'At Acre, the Mediterranean acted like a pulsing unstemmable artery, linking Palestine with the West, and while the sultan waited for his armies to assemble, ships began to arrive teeming with Christian troops to bolster the besieging host.'[106] One noteworthy such arrival was a fleet of fifty Danish and Frisian cogs which disengorged 12,000 crusaders on the beaches of Acre in September 1189.[107]

Saladin attempted to staunch the tide of western ships by dispatching a fifty-vessel flotilla of his own to Acre on 31 October.[108] Conrad of Montferrat countered it in March 1190 by bringing down from Tyre a similar-sized fleet, comprised of galleys and *galliots*. A horrendous battle ensued. Both Ambroise and the *Itinerarium Peregrinorum* described it in some detail, but it is the *Itinerarium Peregrinorum* which painted an unusually vivid picture of combat at sea in the era. Here is how it described the types of ships involved:

> A battle fleet, which once charged the enemy with six banks of oars, now rarely exceeds two. What ancients used to call a *liburna* now has a longer waist and modern people call it a galley. Long, slender and low, it had a piece of wood fixed to the prow, commonly known as a 'spur', which rams and holes the enemy's ships. *Galliots* have only one bank of oars, are short and manoeuvrable, more easily steered, run about more nimbly, and are more suited for hurling Greek fire.[109]

It also depicted the pre-engagement deployment of ships:

> As they advanced from both sides into battle our people arranged their ships not into straight lines but curved, so that if the enemy tried to break through they could be surrounded and crushed. They formed crescents like the moon, with the stronger ships at the front, which could inflict a more violent attack while repelling the enemy's assault. Shields were placed closely together all around the upper decks. The rowers sat in the lowest deck, to leave those on the upper deck with more space for fighting.[110]

This is how it recounted the actual engagement:

> As they met, trumpets sounded from both sides, mingling terrible blasts. They opened hostilities by hurling missiles. Our people called on divine aid, worked the oars with all their strength, and drove their prows into the enemy ships. Soon battle was joined: their oars entangled and they fought hand-to-hand. They bound their vessels to each other with grappling irons, and set fire to the decks with the incendiary oil which is popularly called 'Greek fire'.[111]

The *Itinerarium Peregrinorum* even attempted to elucidate the nature of 'Greek fire', a mysterious mixture of resin and naphtha still not positively identified by modern researchers:

> Greek fire has a noxious stench and bluish-grey flames, which burn up flint and iron. It cannot be extinguished with water; but it can be put out by

> shaking sand over it. Pouring vinegar over it brings it under control. What could be more dangerous in a conflict at sea?[112]

The battle itself was inconclusive. The crusaders may have captured a single Muslim man-of-war, but the most significant outcome of the encounter was that Saladin's ships were compelled to seek refuge in Acre's inner harbour, never again to be a factor for the rest of the siege.[113]

Saladin did, however, break the blockade on several occasions. In mid-June 1190 twenty-five relief vessels battled their way into port.[114] In late August a huge round ship from Beirut laden with 400 sacks of grain deceived the crusader cordon by posing as a Frankish vessel.[115] Three more supply ships fought their way into the harbour in mid-September.[116] And on the 29th of that month all but three vessels of a fifteen-ship relief flotilla from Alexandria successfully ran the blockade.[117] But there were failures as well. On New Year's Eve stormy seas smashed seven fully loaded 'Saracen' supply ships on the rocky shoreline outside the harbour.[118] Even Richard was able to contribute to the interdiction effort. On the way from Tyre in early June 1191 his galleys encountered near Sidon a gargantuan transport ship boasting three masts, en route from Beirut with seven emirs, 800 elite troops and huge quantities of provisions. The *Itinerarium Peregrinorum* reported that the vessel even contained 200 poisonous snakes and numerous phials of Greek fire. Divers first immobilized it by tying up its rudders and then Richard's warships assailed it from all sides, eventually forcing the crew to scuttle the ship in order to prevent its capture.[119] Worse still, those ships of Saladin's fleet which managed to gain the sanctuary of Acre's inner harbour, protected by its chain, were never able to venture out again. Consequently, the protracted siege gradually robbed Saladin of his sea power.

On land, the investment of Acre deteriorated into the sort of appalling war of attrition typical of medieval sieges: a stalemate of bloody attack and counter-attack amid debilitating malnourishment and exposure on both sides. The difficulty of resupplying the city became particularly worrisome for Saladin, whose confidence in Acre's ability to hold out continued to decline. At one point he was even reduced to communicating with the city's garrison through the courage of a diver named Isa, who strapped messages and money to his waist and swam beneath the cordon of crusader ships under cover of darkness to reach the port's inner harbour.[120] Fearing that Acre would soon fall, jeopardizing the remaining ports on the southern Palestinian coast, Saladin ordered the fortifications of Caesarea, Arsuf and Jaffa to be demolished to prevent their use by the Franks.[121] The crusaders suffered their share of frustration and doubt as well. They had attempted to breach Acre's defences on several occasions to no avail. One of their more spectacular failures was the stratagem to seize the so-called Tower of Flies, which controlled the entrance to the outer harbour. Pisans constructed a siege tower and two long ladders, all covered with leather, on a pair of galleys which were used to attack the Tower of Flies on 25 September 1190. The Ayyubid defenders, however, promptly incinerated these shipborne contrivances with 'Greek fire'.[122]

Richard's appearance at Acre on 8 June 1191 immediately galvanized the Latin camp and ultimately broke the impasse. He joined forces with Philip to execute a highly aggressive assault on the city walls. They coordinated non-stop catapult bombardments with sapper operations on different sections of the ramparts at once. In early July mines brought down parapets adjoining the so-called Cursed Tower, eventually creating a gap. On 12 July the defenders capitulated in return for their lives.[123] As devastating as the loss of the city and its garrison were to Saladin's prestige, the blow to his military machine was far more shattering. Asbridge explains:

> Saladin's Egyptian fleet, the jewel of his military arsenal, was moored within Acre's sheltered inner harbour. So essential as a lifeline to the city, the bulk of the sultan's navy – some seventy ships in all – had gradually been trapped within the encircled port as the siege progressed. The crusaders now took possession of this armada, vastly augmenting their own naval strength and, in a single blow, ending Saladin's hopes of challenging Christian control of the Mediterranean.[124]

Considering his crusader vows fulfilled, Philip sailed for home at the end of the month, but Richard remained and wasted little time in putting Latin naval superiority to work. He was determined to recover Jerusalem and he thought the best way to achieve that aim was to retake Jaffa, the nearest port to the Holy City. Richard's march of a crusader army numbering as many as 15,000 down the coast of Palestine has long been touted by military historians as a tactical tour de force. And an integral element in this evolution was sea power. On 22 August Richard led his forces south along the shoreline from Acre in three columns: one on the left flank (inland) consisting of infantry and archers, which shielded the centre one composed of cavalry, and one on the right flank made up of more infantry and the baggage train, which marched along the shore shadowed by the Latin fleet, which provided provisions at Haifa, Destroit, Caesarea and Jaffa. In this way the Frankish force was able to beat off Saladin's horse archers while maintaining the integrity of its marching formation all the way to Arsuf. There, the crusaders won a critical victory against Saladin's army – one which would ultimately enable them to take both Jaffa and Ascalon.[125]

But the campaign floundered thereafter. Richard failed to reconquer Jerusalem in the end, largely because it required him to strike inland and forsake his all-important sea support. The expedition was, however, at least partially successful, because the seizure of Ascalon posed a serious threat to Saladin's power base in Egypt. Accordingly, the sultan eventually agreed to a truce on 2 September 1192 which permitted the Christians access to the Holy Sepulchre. Richard, however, did not go himself. He left the Levant on 9 October, frustrated and unfulfilled, only to become the prisoner of Duke Leopold V of Austria.[126] Nevertheless, his achievements during the Third Crusade, substantially aided by naval power, would have an enduring impact on the crusading movement. The conquest of Cyprus and the capture of Acre, along with the coincident confiscation of the Ayyubid fleet, would enable the Latin Kingdom to last another hundred years.

The Fourth Crusade (1198–1204)

The failure to recover Jerusalem and the 'True Cross' upon which Jesus Christ was believed to have been crucified rendered the Third Crusade unfinished business in the minds of men and women of the Christian west. So it was hardly a surprise when a vigorous new Pope, Innocent III, proclaimed yet another crusade barely eight months after his election to the Holy See in January 1198. He began to issue crusading decrees in August of that year and in 1199 recruited the famed French evangelist Fulk of Neuilly to preach it. It took years, however, for his call to be heeded and the response ultimately came not from kings. The costly deprivations of the Third Crusade and domestic concerns precluded the participation of both Richard and Philip, while the German court was in disarray following the death of Henry VI Hohenstaufen in 1197. Instead, it emanated from members of the upper nobility, whose ancestors had partaken in the glory of the First Crusade. Counts Thibald III of Champagne and Louis I of Blois took the cross at a tournament at Écrey (modern Asfeld-la-Ville, north of Reims) in late November 1199. A few months later, on 23 February 1200, Count Baldwin IX of Flanders joined them. The three counts, all related to one another, then selected two delegates each to negotiate sea transportation for an army of crusaders. The maritime power that these six men chose to approach was Venice.[127]

In April 1201 the Frankish envoys successfully reached an agreement with Doge Enrico Dandolo and the Great Council of Venice. Owing to the fact that one of the French delegates was Geoffroy de Villehardouin, the Marshal of Champagne and a chronicler of the crusade, the details of the pact have been preserved: Venice consented to provide passage for 20,000 foot sergeants, 9,000 squires and 4,500 knights along with their horses for a total of 85,000 silver marks of Cologne to be paid in full prior to departure from Venice on 29 June 1202. The Venetians even promised to contribute fifty galleys of their own in return for half of all that was to be acquired.[128] The destination was not Jerusalem but Egypt, the perceived power base of the Ayyubids who ruled the Holy City. The trouble was that these baronial representatives had made commitments on behalf of thousands of crusaders who had no obligation to honour them. Accordingly, by midsummer of 1202 only 13,000 of the projected 33,500 men-at-arms had arrived in the Venetian Lagoon. Even after the expedition's leaders had collected funds from all those present and contributed much of their own wealth, they could provide the Venetians with only 51,000 marks to recompense them for the some 500 ships they had outfitted for the undertaking at their own expense while holding their trading activities in abeyance.[129]

Doge Dandolo, in hopes of salvaging the crusade and attaining for his citizens some return on their investment, proposed that the Republic convert the 34,000-mark shortfall into a loan, if the crusaders would agree to help the Venetians retrieve the rebellious Dalmatian city of Zara (present-day Zadar), absorbed into the kingdom of Hungary in 1186. With little choice, the barons of the crusader army consented, even though Zara was a Christian city under papal protection at the time. Innocent III was outraged by the decision, but later accepted a post-mortem apology for the deviance. By the time the port was finally taken (24 November), the sailing season was over, obliging the Venetians and their armed allies to winter in the city.[130] During this time envoys representing Alexios Angelos, the son of the Byzantine emperor Isaac II Angelos, arrived with a proposal which would provoke yet another dark turn in the crusade. Isaac had been deposed by his brother Alexios III Angelos, and Prince Alexios wanted the crusaders' help in regaining the throne. He offered persuasive inducements to win their support: 200,000 silver marks, provisions for a year, an army of 10,000 Greeks to augment their forces and the promise to maintain 500 knights in Palestine for the rest of his life. For Enrico Dandolo and the Venetians, the opportunity to ensconce a friendly sovereign in the imperial palace must in itself have been simply too great an enticement to resist.[131]

At this juncture there is a back-story of great relevance which must be told. Relations between the Venetians and the emperors of Constantinople had been testy ever since John II Komnenos had, in 1118, unilaterally abrogated the trade treaty bestowed on them by his father Alexios in 1082. And it did not help matters much that the Venetians extorted the restoration of this highly propitious pact in 1126 by ravaging Byzantine lands. John's son and successor Manuel embraced his father's enmity for the sailors of *La Serenissima* when the latter, during an altercation at the joint Byzantine–Venetian siege of the Norman-held citadel of Corfu in 1148, seized the imperial barge and mocked the emperor by placing a dark-skinned Ethiopian slave on its throne.[132] All was forgiven for the sake of the siege at the time, but under the surface Manuel harboured a deep resentment which finally came to a head in 1170. In an attempt to dilute Venetian prominence in the capital, the emperor granted new commercial quarters to Genoa and Pisa. The Venetians reacted by attacking the Genoese quarter, resulting in loss of life and significant property damage. Manuel retaliated by ordering the arrest of every Venetian citizen in the empire and the appropriation of all their property on a single day, 12 March 1171. It amounted to over 20,000 detainees. Doge Vitale II Míchiel reluctantly attempted to compel their release with a fleet of a hundred galleys and twenty transports but a plague contracted on the island of Chios decimated his armada and forced its humiliating retreat. Most of the captives remained incarcerated in Byzantine prisons for the next ten years.[133] Worse yet, in an egregious example of state-sponsored gloating, Emperor Manuel sent Doge Michiel a dispatch:

> For a long time since, your nation has displayed great ignorance regarding what ought to be done. For when you formerly poured into the Romans' state as wanderers really gripped by poverty, you showed extreme disdain towards them. You had great ambition to betray them to their enemies; it is superfluous to enumerate in detail what your present circumstances are. Detected thereby, you were justly expelled from their land. Out of vainglory you decided that a conflict with them would be on equal terms, [you] a nation not even anciently worthy of them, but at length now well known on account of the Romans, yet not comparable [to them] in strength: imagining this, you have incurred much laughter from every hand. How can that be?

> With them [the Byzantines] not even the pick of nations, anywhere whatsoever, could wage war unpunished.[134]

The indignity would not be forgotten.

Enrico Dandolo was in his early nineties at the time of the Fourth Crusade and had been a witness to all of the above-described events. He likely had little hesitation in convincing his fellow citizens to accede to Alexios' wishes. As for the crusaders, their overall commander was Marquis Boniface of Montferrat. He had been selected at Soissons in June 1201 to replace Thibald of Champagne, who had succumbed unexpectedly to an unspecified illness. And Boniface's position on the matter would have been beyond doubt. His wife was Irene Angelos, Prince Alexios' sister.[135] Thus, despite the cloud of papal excommunication hovering over the entire enterprise, a crusader fleet of around 200 ships, including sixty galleys, sailed into the Bosporus on 24 June 1203.[136] It was a formidable force, well equipped for maritime siege warfare. 'The warships, I can assure you,' wrote Geoffroy de Villehardouin, 'carried more than three hundred petraries [stone-throwing machines] and mangonels, as well as a plentiful supply of all such mechanical devices as are of use in taking a city.'[137] This armada anchored at Scuteri (modern Kadiköy) opposite Constantinople.

It did not remain there long. On 6 July the crusaders stormed ashore at Galata on the north side of the Golden Horn and captured the fortified tower controlling the harbour chain which barred the entrance to the inlet. Robert of Clari, an ordinary knight from Picardy, gave a soldier's eye view of an amphibious assault on a defended beach: 'As soon as they had made land, the knights issued forth from the transports on their horses; for the transports were made in such a way that there was a door that could be opened and a bridge thrust out by which the knights could come out on land all mounted.'[138] The Galata tower was quickly taken and the harbour chain was soon severed by the great round ship *Aquila* ('Eagle'), permitting the rest of the Venetian fleet to stream in and seize what Greek ships were in the harbour. At the same time the land forces rapidly marched along the northeast shore of the Horn and rounded it to take up a position before the land walls on the northwest side of the city. On 17 July the two elements orchestrated a coordinated assault: the Frankish ground forces attacked the land walls, while the Venetians assailed the sea wall on the Golden Horn between the Blachernae Palace and the Monastery of Christ Pantocrator along an expanse called the Petrion. Although the walls there were around 9m (30ft) in height, they were more easily surmounted than the sea walls rising precipitously from the waters of the Bosporus and the Sea of Marmara.[139] Robert of Clari describes Dandolo's meticulous preparations:

> Then the doge of Venice had marvellous engines made and very fine, for he had them take spars which carry the sails of the ships, and which were fully thirty *toises* [in reality, probably about 90ft] long and more, and he had them well tied and made fast to the masts with strong ropes, and he had them make good bridges of planks on them and good stakes alongside the ropes [hand rails]. And the bridges were so wide that three knights in armour could

> go side by side. And the doge had the bridges well protected and covered with hides and canvas on the sides, so that those who mounted to the assault need have no fear of the quarrels of crossbows or of arrows.[140]

The Venetians attempted to manoeuvre their transports up against the sea wall so that they could swing the flying bridges from the mastheads to the tops of the battlements, but withering Byzantine missile fire from a host of mangonels in the towers beat them back – that is, until Enrico Dandolo, ancient and blind, heroically stood on the bow of his galley and ordered it beached beneath the walls. This inspired a renewed attack on the walls by the round ships, which enabled the besiegers on the flying bridges to breach the defences of several towers and open the gates for their compatriots on the beach. In this manner the Venetians were able to take around twenty-five towers. A Byzantine sortie in force against the landward army compelled the Venetians to withdraw, but success was achieved, nonetheless. The incursion spooked Alexios III into fleeing in the night. Isaac was released from prison and returned to the palace. His son was crowned co-emperor as Alexios IV on 1 August.[141]

Of course, Alexios could pay the crusaders only a fraction of the exorbitant sum he had promised (roughly half) and his attempts to extort more from his citizenry only turned them against him. In January 1204 both he and his father were turned out in a palace coup led by *Protovestiarios* ('finance minister') Alexios Doukas Mourtzouphlos ('heavy brow'), who then assumed the purple for himself as Alexios V. Exasperation over the continued demands for compensation from the penurious crusaders caused anti-Latin xenophobia among the Byzantines to reach a crescendo by spring. Armed clashes between the crusaders and the citizens soon ignited fires which devastated much of the city.[142] Finally, the Latin leadership decided that their only option was to conquer the Byzantine capital outright. This would be almost entirely a naval action, since all but around 4,000 of the Frankish crusaders had already abandoned the effort for fear of papal anathema, leaving the task mostly to about 27,000 Venetian crewmen.[143] The first assault on 9 April 1204 was repulsed largely because the Venetians could not bring enough force to bear on any single fortified tower. They remedied this problem when they renewed the onslaught three days later with the following solution described by Geoffroy de Villehardouin: 'This time they would have the ships that carried the scaling ladders [about forty round ships] bound together, two by two, so that each pair could make a combined attack on one tower.'[144] A favourable wind pushed one such pair of round ships, the *Pilgrim* and the *Paradise*, up against a tower, allowing a Venetian crewman and a French knight to fight their way in. Others followed, quickly overwhelming the defenders. Gates were soon opened and the remaining ships disengorged their warriors, including knights and their mounts. **(Pl. 11)** Rout rapidly turned to pillage, which lasted for three days.[145]

In the aftermath the booty was divided up as had been agreed by the principal players prior to the assault: three-quarters went to the Venetians. Twelve electors, six of them Venetian, were appointed to choose an emperor who was to be assigned one-quarter of the empire, with the remainder being apportioned equally between the Franks and the Venetians.[146] Baldwin of Flanders was ultimately elected as emperor, but *La Serenissima* ended up with about three-eighths of the empire, including a large quarter in the city adjacent to the harbour and lands along the littorals of both the Adriatic and Aegean Seas.[147] Venice had won for itself a true maritime empire.

The Fifth Crusade (1213–21)

The disastrous diversion of the Fourth Crusade did not dissuade Pope Innocent III from energetically preaching further crusades. He not only continued the movement, but expanded it to include a number of fronts. He declared the Livonian Crusade against the pagans of the Baltic region in October 1199, even before the Fourth Crusade had been launched, and supported it as an ongoing, papally sanctioned campaign throughout the remainder of his pontificate.[148] The murder of Peter of Castelnau, a papal legate to the Languedoc, on 14 January 1208 prompted Innocent to proclaim the Albigensian Crusade against the Cathar heretics of southern France.[149] And in the spring of 1212 he christened as a crusade the campaign of Alfonso VIII of Castile against the Almohads of Andalusia, which ultimately resulted in the watershed victory of Spanish Christianity at Las Navas de Tolosa on 17 July.[150] But from the standpoint of sea power, the most important call to arms of Innocent's later papacy was the one dubbed by historians 'the Fifth Crusade'.

First announced by a papal encyclical called the *Quia Maior* in April 1213, the crusade was directed at the liberation of the Holy Land. The call was refined in late 1215 by the Fourth Lateran Council, which set a departure date of 1 June 1217. Innocent even supported the coronation of Frederick II as king of the Germans at Aachen in 1215 in return for the latter's promise to participate in the great endeavour. The Pope continued to preach the crusade right up to his death on 16 July 1216, after which the summons was taken up by his successor, Honorius III.[151] When the time came for the expedition to commence in the summer of 1217, Frederick was still consolidating his tenuous hold on power, but there appears to have been no shortage of lesser adherents to answer the call. King Andrew of Hungary, Duke Leopold VI of Austria and King Hugh I of Cyprus all assembled in Acre, from where they joined John of Brienne, king of Jerusalem, in a few desultory raids on Ayyubid Syria during the winter of 1217–18.[152] Alas, with the arrival of a fleet of Frisian and Rhenish reinforcements in April 1218, the objective changed to one identified long ago by various leaders of the Latin Kingdom: Egypt. The Lionheart had championed its conquest during the Third Crusade and it was the original goal of the ill-fated Fourth Crusade.[153] Specifically, the destination chosen was the city of Damietta on the Nile Delta, for, according to the German preacher and participant Oliver of Paderborn, 'it was the key to all Egypt'.[154]

The Frankish fleet arrived in the environs of Damietta on 29 May 1218 and established a beachhead 'between the seashore and the [west] bank of the river Nile' about 3 miles above the city, which stood on the opposite bank.[155] Shielded by the Nile on the west and Lake Manzala on the east, Damietta could not be taken by land assault alone. 'In addition to the natural location of the place, by which it is fortified,' testified Oliver of Paderborn, 'this city is surrounded by a triple wall, stoutly protected by many large brick towers.'[156] A waterborne attack by way of the river offered the greatest chance of success, but a stoutly constructed tower on an island abeam the city barred the way. It controlled a heavy iron chain which spanned the river between it and the city walls. The crusaders first had to reduce this 'Chain Tower' in order to bring the full force of their fleet to bear on Damietta's defences.[157] Accordingly, on 24 June, after establishing a fortified encampment opposite the tower, they placed two large ladders on a pair of ships (probably cogs) and built a small castle on the masthead of a third vessel from Frisia. The outcome of the subsequent attempt was calamitous. The two ladders collapsed, carrying many crusaders to their deaths, while the Frisian fortress ship was forced to retire by a hail of javelins and 'Greek fire' hurled from both the city walls and the tower.[158]

It was apparently Oliver of Paderborn himself who devised the solution:

> We joined two ships which we bound together sturdily by means of beams and ropes and so prevented (by their closely connected structure) the danger of drifting. We erected four masts and the same number of sail yards, setting up on the summit a strong fortress joined with poles and a network fortification. We covered it with skins about its circumference, as a protection from the attacks of their machine [some sort of missile-launching device like a catapult], and over its top as a defence against the Greek fire. Under the fortress was made a ladder, hung by very strong ropes and stretching out thirty cubits [about 45ft] beyond the prow [a kind of flying bridge].[159]

This floating siege machine was deployed against the Chain Tower on 24 August and gained its capitulation the next day after a hard-fought battle.[160] **(Pl. 12)**

Before he could react, Sultan al-Adil succumbed to illness on 31 August, but his son al-Kamil soon moved to counter the crusaders' capture of the tower.[161] According to Oliver of Paderborn, his men 'fortified the bank opposite by means of ramparts and a clay-like substance with high wooden defences' and 'all across the river they sank ships and fixed stakes in the eddies'.[162] This blockage prevented the crusaders from bringing supplies and reinforcements up river by ship. 'Seeing this, the Franks turned their attention to a channel there, known as the Blue [Channel], where the main Nile flowed in olden times,' reported Ibn al-Athir, apparently referring to the al-Azraq canal, running between the Mediterranean and the west bank of the Nile. 'They dug and deepened that channel upstream of the ships that had been scuttled in the Nile and they got water to flow in it to the open sea.'[163] This enabled the crusaders to gain control of the river.

Al-Kamil made several concerted attacks on the Frankish encampment but was beaten back each time. As stalemate settled in, the winter proved cruel to besiegers and besieged alike. In late November the Nile overflowed its banks and inundated the crusader encampment.[164] 'The tents floated off, the food supply was destroyed, the fishes of the river and the sea, as though fearing nothing, piled into our sleeping quarters,' reported Oliver, 'and we caught them with our hands, delights nevertheless we were willing to be without.' The Christians soon suffered an outbreak of scurvy as indicated by 'corrupt flesh' which 'covered the gums'.[165] And, of course, the inhabitants of Damietta were distressed by a whole host of malnutrition-related maladies, including 'night blindness'.[166]

Palace intrigue prompted al-Kamil's return to Cairo in early February 1219 and the ensuing chaos among his forces enabled the crusaders to gain a foothold on the east bank, which they rapidly reinforced by building a bridge of boats across the river.[167] That summer they constructed a second bridge using thirty-eight vessels.[168] Still, they lacked the manpower to capitalize on their advantage and the siege dragged dreadfully on.[169] By September conditions had become so desperate inside Damietta that al-Kamil offered to 'restore the kingdom of Jerusalem entirely' except the Transjordanian fortresses of Krak and Montreal, if the crusaders would agree to vacate Egypt. He even promised to hand over the 'True Cross', which had been captured at the Battle of Hattin in July 1187. Astonishingly, the offer was refused, principally through the influence of the papal legate, Cardinal Pelagius of Albano, who had arrived the previous September.[170] Nonetheless, on 5 November 1219, after eighteen unspeakable months, Damietta, 'its streets strewn with the bodies of the dead, wasting away from pestilence and famine', fell to the Frankish forces with hardly a fight.[171] The nearby Ayyubid army retreated to Mansourah, some 60km (37 miles) up the Nile.

The crusade then stalled. For twenty months it remained rooted in Damietta, afflicted by indecisiveness and infighting among its leadership. The discord was chiefly between John of Brienne and Pelagius of Albano, but the entire chain of command had been roiled by the constant comings and goings of various contingents of crusaders. King John himself relinquished his role as overall commander and returned to Palestine, while different fleets of French and English fighters arrived during this period. The excessive delay can, at least in part, be blamed on Frederick II. Upon his coronation as Holy Roman Emperor on 22 November 1220, the Hohenstaufen monarch had sworn to send a force to Egypt the next sailing season.[172] Pelagius, who had assumed overall command of the expedition, was most likely waiting for its arrival. The first imperial elements did, in fact, arrive in May 1221 under the command of Duke Louis I of Bavaria.[173] Frederick also dispatched a flotilla of forty galleys under his new *marini stolii ammiratum* ('admiral of the fleet') Henry Pescatore, the Genoese count of Malta, but it would arrive too late to prevent the fiasco that would mark the crusade's finish.[174]

At the insistence of Pope Honorius III, John of Brienne returned with his men on 7 July 1221 and on 17 July a formidable force of crusaders set out from the environs of Damietta. Oliver of Paderborn estimated 1,200 knights, 4,000 archers, an unspecified number of *Turcopoles* (mounted archers of Christian descent) and countless foot soldiers. These were supported by an enormous fleet, even after taking into account Oliver's evident exaggeration: 'Among the six hundred and thirty larger and smaller ships we clearly counted three hundred casques [small sailing vessels] with eighteen armed galleys, and besides, there were scalanders, tartans, barbots, corsairs and barks [various types of small cargo and scout ships] carrying provisions.'[175] These ships flanked the crusader army as it marched south along the east bank of the river until it reached an angle of land just north of Mansourah between the Nile and its tributary, the Bahr al-Saghir (river Tanis). There, contrary to King John's advice, the force halted on 24 July.[176]

The Ayyubid army was encamped on the south side of the Bahr al-Saghir to the east of the Nile, where the crusaders' long delay at Damietta had allowed it to become thoroughly entrenched. Moreover, the emir of Damascus, al-Ashraf Musa ibn al-Adil, had now joined his brother with an army. That said, al-Kamil, appearing sufficiently intimidated by the crusader force, renewed his offer of a truce on the same generous terms as before. But, in all probability, he was simply playing for time. The annual flooding of the Nile was due to commence in August. In the meantime he directed a portion of his own fleet to enter the Nile behind the crusaders using the al-Mahallah canal from Lake Manzala, cutting off any possible retreat. When the great watercourse began to overflow its banks as expected, al-Kamil had his men open the sluice gates which normally controlled the flooding.[177] By 29 August 1221 the trapped crusaders, slogging through waist-deep water, were forced to sue for peace. Al-Kamil reclaimed Damietta on 8 September, erasing all the crusade's gains.[178]

The Sixth Crusade (1224–9)

There was plenty of blame to go around for the débâcle that was the Fifth Crusade. Pelagius of Albano and John of Brienne received their fair share, but the man most vilified was the newly minted Holy Roman Emperor Frederick II, who had failed to honour his vows in a timely manner.[179] Well aware of the opprobrium he now faced, particularly from the papacy, Frederick was so furious over the failure of his fleet to alter the course of events in Egypt that he imprisoned its admiral, Henry Pescatore, and deprived him of Malta.[180] He also began planning for a new crusade.

As of March 1224, Frederick had renewed his crusading vows to Honorius III and claimed to be constructing a hundred *galeas* and fifty *uscerii* (oared horse transports with stern disembarkation ramps).[181] The promised departure date of 24 June 1225 came and went due to domestic concerns on Sicily, but on 25 July of that year Frederick signed a treaty at San Germano (present-day Cassino) in which he swore under threat of excommunication to commence the crusade on 15 August 1227 by personally commanding a force of fifty *galeas* and a hundred *chelandia* (oared transports) which would carry at least a thousand knights for deployment in the Holy Land for two years at his own expense.[182] The emperor's subsequent marriage to Isabella II, the daughter of John of Brienne and queen of Jerusalem, at Brindisi in November added still more incentive.[183]

Frederick did, indeed, set sail from Brindisi in September 1227 only a few weeks after the prescribed deadline, but a viral illness forced his return to port at Otranto. He sent fifty galleys ahead under the command of Herman von Salza,

Master of the Teutonic Knights, and a transport fleet under Duke Henry of Limberg. Nonetheless, Pope Gregory IX proved even less patient than his predecessor, Honorius III, who had passed away the previous March. The unsympathetic pontiff placed the Holy Roman Emperor under papal anathema before the month was out. Seemingly unfazed, Frederick set out again once he had recovered from his malady in June of the following year.[184]

After a brief interlude on Cyprus to reaffirm imperial suzerainty, Frederick arrived at the port of Acre in early September 1228. Philip of Novara, a lawyer for the Ibelin family whom Frederick had displaced from power on Cyprus, testified that the emperor had with him a fleet of seventy vessels. Forty of these were galleys, while the rest were *taride* and other transport ships.[185] All of these were in addition to the ships Frederick had sent ahead the previous year. Culling clues from a wide variety of sources, medieval maritime expert John Pryor has concluded that Frederick then had at his disposal at least ninety war galleys, probably *galeas*, and a hundred transports, all oared vessels of the *chelandia* type, for a total of 190 ships: a considerable naval complement.[186] What he did with it could best be characterized as a highly efficacious employment of gunboat diplomacy.

The emperor had every reason to believe that the Ayyubid sultan al-Kamil was disposed towards a negotiated settlement. After all, he had twice offered the Christian armies of the Fifth Crusade Jerusalem and much more in exchange for evacuating Egypt. And as early 1226 he had sent a trusted lieutenant, Emir Fakhr al-Din, to seek an alliance with Frederick against his brother al-Mu'azzam, emir of Damascus – again using Jerusalem as an enticement.[187] Al-Kamil's ardour for such a pact had cooled since his brother's death in November 1227, but Frederick was determined to rekindle it. In a show of force reminiscent of Richard the Lionheart's famed march down the coast of Palestine during the Third Crusade, in November 1228 the emperor trooped his army, flanked by his impressive fleet, from Acre down to Jaffa, where he had his men rebuild the fortifications.[188] And it must be emphasized that this was no inconsequential force. Each oared vessel required a crew of 100 to 150 mariners who were all considered combatants. Thus, if the emperor's armada, indeed, numbered 190 oared vessels, his navy alone would have accounted for at least 20,000 fighting men in addition to the knights, squires and foot sergeants that the ships had carried to Outremer.[189]

Apparently the demonstration achieved its intended effect. More concerned with stabilizing his Syrian domains following his brother's demise, al-Kamil agreed to a generous ten-year truce on 18 February 1229.[190] Not only did the sultan surrender Jerusalem, all save the *Haram as-Sharif* (Temple Mount), but he also ceded control of Bethlehem and Nazareth along with a corridor from Jerusalem to the coast. Accordingly, Frederick entered the Holy City on 17 March and the next day in the Church of the Holy Sepulchre placed the crown of the Latin Kingdom on his head with his own hands.[191] He had accomplished what the four previous crusades had failed to achieve, and all without shedding a drop of Christian blood. Yet he was almost universally condemned within Christendom for having done so by treating with the infidel. Not only did he remain excommunicate, but papal armies under Gregory IX attacked his domains in southern Italy. Moreover, his high-handed conduct towards the Latin Kingdom's nobility had done nothing to assuage their antipathy.[192] His claim to the crown of Jerusalem was considered tenuous at best since his wife, Queen Isabella II of Jerusalem, had died shortly after bearing him a son in April the previous year.[193] Philip of Novara, no doubt still bitter over Frederick's overbearing treatment of the Ibelins of Cyprus, described the sovereign's mortifying departure from Acre thusly:

> The emperor arranged for his passage secretly, and on the first day of May at dawn, without letting it be known by anyone, he got into a galley before the street of the butchers. Whence it happened that the butchers and old people of the street, who were most ill-disposed, ran along beside him and pelted him with tripe and bits of meat most scurrilously.[194]

The Seventh Crusade (1244–50)

What was done by Frederick II through protracted negotiation in 1229 was undone almost by happenstance in the summer of 1244 by Khwarezmian mercenaries. The Khwarezmians were fierce Turkic slave warriors of the Seljuk sultans of Central Asia who had founded their own dynasty in the Khwarezm region of Turkistan in the late eleventh century. In the early thirteenth century the Mongols of Genghis Khan pushed them into northern Iraq, where they became swords for hire. A band of 10,000 under Berke Khan were en route to their new employer, Sultan as-Salih Ayyub of Egypt, when on 11 July 1244 they suddenly attacked Jerusalem. By the time the last Latin defenders surrendered the Tower of David on 23 August, the Holy Sepulchre had been so thoroughly desecrated that its marble enclosure had been reduced to rubble. A loose coalition of Latins led by the Military Orders and the Ayyubids of Damascus caught up with the Khwarezmians at La Forbie (Harbiyah) in Gaza on 17 October, but Berke Khan's men routed it with a savage assault in which all but a handful of the Latin Kingdom's remaining knights were slaughtered.[195]

King Louis IX of France, perhaps the most pious Christian sovereign in Europe at the time, took up the cross the following December even as he lay deathly ill. And it was practically preordained that he would spare no expense in the endeavour. He had already acquired, at great cost, from the Latin Empire of Constantinople a fragment of the True Cross, a phial of the Precious Blood and, most prized of all, the Crown of Thorns for which he had begun building the extravagantly exquisite Sainte-Chapelle.[196] His preparations for the Seventh Crusade vastly exceeded those of any previous expedition to the East. He contracted with Genoa and Marseilles for the construction of forty-four state-of-the-art transport ships; renovated the royal port facility at Aigues-Mortes in the Petite Camargue; and stockpiled huge quantities of supplies in Cyprus over a two-year period. John of Joinville, a courtier and chronicler from Champagne who accompanied Louis, claimed that stacks of wine barrels on Cyprus looked like 'barns' from a distance and that heaps of wheat and barley appeared as 'hillocks'.[197] Altogether, these arrangements took four years and cost the crown in excess of

2,000,000 *livres tournois* (gold pounds of Tours) at a time when the royal income was less than 250,000 *livres tournois* per annum.[198]

Louis finally set sail from Aigues-Mortes aboard the royal great ship *Montjoie* on 28 August 1248, arriving in Limassol, Cyprus, on 17 September.[199] Even then, he was in no particular hurry. He over-wintered on the island, mustering his forces and finalizing his strategy. He was determined to proceed deliberately and methodically in the hope of avoiding some of the blunders of past expeditions. It is at this time that he may have decided upon Damietta as the initial objective, following in the footsteps of the Fifth Crusade. He apparently assessed the Ayyubid hold on Egypt under Sultan as-Salih Ayyub to be tenuous.[200]

The problem was that his fleet was dominated by deep-draught round ships, unsuited to operating in the shallow waters of the Nile river estuary.[201] John of Joinville gives the absurdly embellished number of 1,800 vessels,[202] but other participants such as Jean de Beaumont and Guy de Burcey specified 120 *magne naves* ('great ships') and varying numbers of smaller ships. The most important of these *magne naves* were undoubtedly the twenty round ships provided by Marseilles and the twelve round ships from Genoa. (Genoa also supplied twelve *taride*, but these would have been oared horse transports of relatively shallow draught.)[203] The thirty-two round ships were required to carry the core of his force: 2,500–2,800 knights and their mounts.[204] According to the specifications delineated in the construction contracts, they were all two-masted sailing ships, sporting two or three decks. The three-deck variants were over 35m (115ft) long and 9.5m (31ft) maximum beam, producing a displacement in excess of 800 metric tonnes. Each could accommodate around 560 passengers and perhaps as many as a hundred horses below deck.[205] John of Joinville describes the cumbersome embarkation process:

> On the day we embarked the door on the port side of the ship was opened, so that all the horses we wanted to take with us overseas could be put in the hold. As soon as we were inside, the door was closed and carefully caulked, as is done with a cask before plunging it into water, because, once the ship is on the high seas, that door is completely submerged.[206]

Clearly, such craft were designed for disembarkation at established port facilities and not on an enemy beach in the heat of a contested landing. Yet, these were exactly the circumstances which prevailed in the Nile Delta region the following year.

Louis led his armada from Limassol on 13 May 1249 and arrived at the mouth of the Damietta branch of the great river on 4 June.[207] A large reception of Ayyubid warriors, many of them mounted, lined the shoreline under the command of Emir Fakhr al-Din. The king was compelled to anchor his fleet three leagues (about 14.5km or 9 miles) offshore to hold an overnight council of war on the *Montjoie*. Ultimately, fear of adverse winds forced his hand. It was decided that at daybreak the next morning they would execute a highly hazardous amphibious assault. This meant that the crusaders had to transfer at sea as many fighting men as possible into what galleys and other smaller boats of similarly shallow draught they possessed, an awkward evolution fraught with potential catastrophe.[208]

Indeed, at dawn the next day John of Joinville reported that his longboat almost capsized due to overcrowding during the transfer process and he watched one unfortunate knight plunge into the sea and drown. The young noble was in the first wave of boats which drove up onto the beach right in front of an Ayyubid cavalry unit several thousand strong. (The various sources say between 2,000 and 6,000.)[209] When the cavalry charged, John wrote, 'we stuck the sharp ends of our shields into the sand and fixed our lances firmly in the ground with the points towards the enemy'. The tactic worked: the riders 'wheeled round and fled'. Joinville and his men were soon joined by a large galley with 'at least three hundred rowers' commanded by a relative, the count of Jaffa. 'As soon as this galley had been driven into the sand as far as it would go, the count and his knights leapt on shore, well armed and well equipped, and came to take their stand beside us,' reported Joinville.[210] Others were not so fortunate. Some of the boats were simply too deep-draught to reach the beach, compelling some combatants to leap 'fully armed into the sea, some up to their chest, some to their armpits, some deeper, some less so, according to the varying depths of the sea'. These men were subject to lethal missile fire. 'Then our crossbowmen renewed their efforts and shot so thick that it was a wonder to see,' recorded the 'Rothelin Continuation' of William of Tyre's *History*, referring to some 5,000 Frankish archers.[211]

In the end, the landing was successful. The beachhead established, Ayyubid resistance soon melted away. It was an overwhelming Christian victory. 'Few or no Christians were lost in this battle, but the Turks lost up to 500 killed as well as many horses,' reported the 'Rothelin Continuation'.[212] Louis' men entered Damietta the next day unchallenged, the defenders having abandoned the city altogether. **(Pl. 13)** What had taken the men of the Fifth Crusade a year and a half to do, those of the Seventh had accomplished in a mere day and a half.[213] No wonder the Franks became susceptible to the insidious seduction of hubris.

The men of the Seventh Crusade did not commit the errors of arrogance at the outset. Resisting the temptation to launch headlong up the Nile, Louis prudently waited until the river's annual flooding had subsided before beginning the march towards Cairo on 20 November. By then, Sultan as-Salih Ayyub had died of an abscess affliction, leaving Egypt's leadership in temporary upheaval and enhancing the fortunes of the Frankish forces. It was when the crusade reached the precise piece of real estate where the Fifth Crusade had stalled – the triangle of land at the confluence of the Nile and the Bahr al-Saghir tributary (river Tanis) just north of Mansourah – that the enterprise began to unravel. Like his Ayyubid predecessors, Fakhr al-Din had established a new forward base camp on the south bank of the tributary.[214]

At first, Louis tried to construct a covered causeway across the Bahr al-Saghir under cover of protective screens extended from two movable towers called 'cats' and the fire of eighteen catapults, but Fakhr al-Din thwarted this effort with sixteen of his own catapults, hurling incendiaries.[215] John of Joinville described the experience in vivid detail:

> This Greek fire was such that, seen from the front as it darted towards us, it appeared as large as a barrel of verjuice [vinegar substitute], and the tail of fire that streamed behind it was as long as the shaft of a great lance. The noise it made in coming was like that of a thunderbolt falling from the skies; it seemed like a dragon flying through the air.[216]

The king eventually learned of a ford downstream and orchestrated a pre-dawn crossing on 8 February 1250 with his brother Robert of Artois leading a vanguard of some 600 knights. All went stunningly well at first. Robert made the crossing unhindered but, instead of waiting for the main body as ordered, he and his men galloped through the Muslim camp, slaughtering the Ayyubids and their commander, Fakhr al-Din, as they slept. If the impetuous young royal had stopped there, the entire evolution might have turned out very differently. But, as it happened, Robert recklessly spurred his cavalry right into Mansourah, where the mobility of his men's mounts was negated by the crowded confines of the city. Individual horsemen became isolated and vulnerable in the narrow streets. Worse still, billeted within the town was the Bahriyya regiment composed of Mamluks, fierce Turkic slave soldiers recruited from the Kipchak steppes north of the Black and Caspian Seas. They were known as 'the lions of battle' and they cut the crusader cavalry contingent to pieces, including Robert of Artois.[217]

Louis managed to establish a beachhead on the south bank of the Bahr al-Saghir, but he lacked the manpower to exploit it. The offensive stalled there and stalemate set in. The campaign soon degenerated into a waiting game which Louis, beleaguered by long supply lines, could not win. Al-Mu'azzam Turanshah, as-Salih's son and successor, arrived in Mansourah on 25 February.[218] Shortly afterwards, he had fifty galleys sailed down the Bahr Shirbin tributary, which paralleled the Nile a few miles to the west. These vessels were then portaged on camels and carts to the Nile somewhere near Baramun, well north of the crusader encampment at Mansourah. Once again, the crusaders found their supply lines to Damietta severed in a sorry repeat of the Fifth Crusade.[219] 'The fifty galleys on the river captured many of our vessels which were bringing victuals from Damietta to the host,' bemoaned the author of the 'Rothelin Continuation'. In two spectacular reverses the Ayyubids intercepted convoys of 150 or more boats full of 'bread, wine, flour, salt meat and many other things', killing or capturing the crews. The 'Rothelin Continuation' gave a grim accounting of the deleterious impact of this battle of logistics upon the crusader encampment at Mansourah:

> The famine was so severe that even healthy men were too thin and weak to help themselves. They ate the flesh of dead horses, donkeys, mules and other army cattle when they could find them and counted it a luxury. Later, when they could get them, they ate much worse things.[220]

Finally, on 5 April 1250 Louis accepted the inevitable and ordered a retreat to Damietta. All the weak and wounded were placed in what boats remained to the crusaders in the vain hope of running the Ayyubid gauntlet of galleys, while the remainder of the army began the slow, grinding march northwards over open ground, constantly harassed by al-Mu'azzam Turanshah's men. Within a matter of days most of the boats had been burned, their passengers butchered.[221] The land forces fared no better. More than 7,000 crusaders were reported killed and 20,000 captured, most of whom were later executed. Only the upper nobility, including Louis, were spared for ransom.[222]

The Eighth Crusade (1265–70)

Louis IX was ultimately released on 6 May 1250 after the payment of an exorbitant 800,000 gold *bezants*. He took ship for Palestine a few days later and spent the next four years seeing to the defences of such ports as Jaffa, Haifa, Caesarea and, most crucial of all, Acre at enormous personal cost.[223] It would all only be a prelude to the inevitable, for the Seventh Crusade had helped to spawn an inexorable puissance that would eventually bring to an end what remained of the Latin Kingdom of Jerusalem.

The Mamluks, who had played such a significant role in the devastating defeat of the Damietta campaign, overthrew their Ayyubid masters in the immediate aftermath. Then, in September 1260 at Ayn Jalut in Galilee, they took on the seemingly unstoppable Mongol hordes which had already claimed most of Mesopotamia and dealt them a historic thrashing. A few weeks later, on 22 October, one of the commanders responsible for this watershed victory, an exceptionally malevolent young Mamluk named Baybars, managed to murder his way to the sultanate of Egypt by dispatching his main rival, another Mamluk commander called Qutuz.[224] Baybars then turned his attention to what he considered the main regional ally of the Mongol Ilkhanate of Persia: the Latin Kingdom of Jerusalem.

According to Thomas Asbridge, his strategy was 'to wipe the Latin ports from the face of the Holy Land, closing, one by one, the doorways which linked Outremer to the west'.[225] He began by taking Caesarea on 5 March 1265, followed by Arsuf on 30 April.[226] The Mamluk sultan's vicious coastal campaign swiftly engendered acute concern in the West. As early as August 1266 Pope Clement IV was calling for yet another expedition to the East to relieve the Latin Kingdom and, once again, the saintly king of France answered the summons.

Louis IX renewed his crusading vows on 25 March 1267 and immediately began the sort of massive logistical preparations that had preceded his first campaign. The most significant of these arrangements centred on a set of ship contracts made in 1268 with Marseilles, Genoa and Venice, which may have appreciably advanced military maritime technology at the time. From Genoa he leased eight round ships and four *salandria* (oared vessels similar to *taride*). The round-hulled sailing ships in particular were immense by medieval standards. Boasting two decks, they were 37.4m (122ft 8in) long with a beam of 10.04m (32ft 11in) and were purported to carry as many as a hundred horses each. At least some of the fifteen transports promised by Venice were even larger. In the aggregate, they were supposed to hold 4,000 horses and 10,000 crusaders, although John Pryor's research has revealed that the actual capacity must have been somewhat less than that. Three of them were triple-decked *magne naves* ('great ships'), named the *Sancta Maria*, the *Roccafortis* and the *Sanctus Nicolaus*.[227] The largest of these was reported to be the *Roccafortis*, which measured 38.3m (125ft 8in) in length by at least 10.9m (35ft 9in) of beam, with a staggering beam-to-depth ratio of perhaps 1:1.45, meaning it was very deep-draught, indeed. The height amidships had to have been over 9m or 30ft.[228] Frederic Lane, an authority on Venetian ship architecture, notes that the *Roccafortis* had fighting castles in the bow and stern which rose 12m (almost 40ft) above the keel.[229]

Sadly, despite the painstaking and exorbitant preparations, the execution of this expedition was even more haphazard than the last, resulting in another disheartening disaster. For one thing, the planning and organizing took so long that Baybars was able to flatten Jaffa in the early spring of 1268 and reduce Antioch to utter ruination by 18 May.[230] Louis did not set sail from Aigues-Mortes until 2 July 1270, and when he did, he headed not for Palestine, which he had previously declared as his destination, but – incomprehensibly – to Tunis via Sardinia. Apparently on the advice of his brother, Charles of Anjou, who was king of Sicily at the time, he had hoped to inveigle or coerce the city's Hafsid ruler, Abu Abdallah, into a joint invasion of Mamluk Egypt. Instead, on 25 August the future St Louis ended up dying of dysentery under the sizzling North African sun, along with much of his army; the survivors were soon evacuated to Sicily, having achieved nothing.[231]

In a pitiful postscript, the Mamluks took Acre, the most crucial Christian port in Palestine, on 18 May 1291. Within a month the Franks abandoned Tyre, Beirut and Sidon. The few Latins remaining in the Holy Land withdrew to Cyprus.[232] The Latin Levant was no more, never to return. Without ports, western sea power could no longer sustain it. Nonetheless, the maritime legacy of the crusades would endure and the primary beneficiaries would be the west Italian maritime republics of Genoa and Pisa, whose rivalry would reach a crescendo at the end of the thirteenth century.

* * *

Exemplary Engagement: The Venetian Crusade (1122–5)

No great event in history occurs in isolation. There are always causal circumstances, a chain of precipitating incidents. The Venetian Crusade of 1122 was triggered by two seemingly unrelated such occurrences. The first was the death of the Byzantine emperor Alexios I Komnenos on 15 August 1118.[233] This prompted the Venetian Doge Domenico Michiel to dispatch a deputation to Constantinople to request that the emperor's successor, John II Komnenos, confirm the sweeping trade concessions which his father had granted Venice in 1082 to help contain the rising sea power of Norman Italy under Robert Guiscard.[234] But Guiscard was dead and the Norman threat had receded, so John II refused to renew the enormously lucrative privileges.[235] The economic impact on *La Serenissima* must have been devastating, because these concessions were at the core of its commercial empire in the eastern Mediterranean.

The second event took place the following year on 28 June 1119 near Sarmada in northern Syria, midway between Antioch and Aleppo. Roger of Salerno, regent of Antioch, had led an army of around 700 knights and 3,000 infantry to meet an incursion by Il Ghazi ibn Artuq of Mardin, the ruler of Aleppo, who William of Tyre says had 'three divisions of twenty-thousand each'.[236] While the latter estimate was manifestly inflated, Roger's forces appear to have been grossly outnumbered. Furthermore, he made the mistake of setting up camp in a small valley surrounded by the Belus Hills. Ghazi's scouts discovered the encampment and surrounded it during the night. The ensuing battle at dawn the next day was a bloodbath. 'Scarcely a man of the many thousands who followed their lord that day escaped to tell the story,' wrote William of Tyre forlornly.[237] The site soon became known as the *Ager Sanguinis* ('Field of Blood') and it had a traumatic impact on the psyche of the Latin Levant. Never before had a sitting prince of the kingdom perished in combat.[238]

In January 1120 Warmund (Gormond in some texts), the patriarch of Jerusalem, convened a general council at Nablus (just north of the city), attended by King Baldwin II and most of the primary prelates and princes of the kingdom, at which it was decided to seek succour from the West.[239] Emissaries were sent to Rome, of course, in the hope that Pope Calixtus II would issue a renewed call for aid, but delegates were also directed to Venice, for the kingdom's leadership understood by now that the swiftest, most efficacious means of delivering that support would be by sea. The Pope, doubtless guided by the same awareness, dispatched his own messengers to the doge's palace.[240] They found a receptive audience. Domenico Michiel was inured neither to the papal entreaties on spiritual grounds nor to the temporal needs of the Latin Kingdom of Jerusalem for security. After all, he was the son of Giovanni Michiel who had commanded the huge armada of 1099 which had enabled Baldwin I to win Haifa in August 1100. But, perhaps more importantly, Domenico was a shrewd man who saw the appeal as an opportunity for the forceful redress of grievances against the Byzantine Empire for having abrogated its trade treaty with Venice.[241] He had no trouble convincing his fellow citizens to go along.

The result was a massive, state-sponsored enterprise which took over two years to organize. Estimates vary, but all sources indicate that a formidable force was assembled. William of Tyre put the size of the fleet at 72 vessels, composed of 40 galleys, 28 *catti* (huge galleys, possibly *triremes* topped with forecastles and sterncastles) and 4 large transports.[242] Fulcher of Chartres gave the figure of 120, which included 'beaked ships' (probably *galeas*), 'triremes' (possibly *catti*) and 'merchant ships' (most likely sailing vessels), carrying 15,000 'armed men' (presumably not including the crews, who must have numbered at least another 15,000 men) and some 300 horses (probably unprecedented in the crusading era).[243] Venice's own contemporary chronicle, the anonymous *Historia ducum Veneticorum* ('History of the Venetian Doges'), reported that 'between warships and supply ships' there were 200 vessels. When this armada cleared the Lido and sailed out into the Adriatic on 8 August 1122, the doge himself was at the helm and it bore the banner of St Peter, rendering it officially a papally sanctioned crusade.[244]

The Venetians trained this mighty maritime war machine first on the Byzantine Empire. Sometime in September the Venetians arrived at Corfu and laid siege, probably to the citadel at Kassiopi on the northeastern tip of the island. It was a nearly impregnable fortress, which perhaps explains why the investment lasted through the winter despite the fact that the besiegers were apparently well equipped. Fulcher of Chartres noted that in the Venetian vessels 'were loaded very long timbers which, when skilfully made into siege machinery by the carpenters, could be used for scaling and seizing the high walls of cities'.[245] In fact, the Venetians ended up having to abandon the siege in the spring when they learned that King Baldwin II of Jerusalem had been captured at Kharput by Balak ibn Artuq on 18 April 1123.[246]

Given the renewed urgency, the fleet continued on, but even then proceeded at a measured pace with regular stops, including at Modon (Methoni) and Rhodes. Again Fulcher provided the explanation: 'They landed for daily supplies at frequent ports which they found so that they and their horses would not suffer from lack of water.'[247] Upon their arrival at Cyprus the doge ascertained information which interjected even greater urgency: an Egyptian fleet of some seventy to eighty galleys had begun a blockade of Jaffa on 23 May. Viewing the imprisonment of Baldwin as a vulnerability to be exploited, the Fatimid Caliph of Cairo, al-Amir, had ordered a land–sea siege of Jerusalem's nearest port. The Venetians hurried on, reaching Acre at the end of the month only to find that the Fatimid fleet had abandoned the siege of Jaffa. Its land component had been soundly defeated at Ibelin the day before (29 May) by Latin forces led by Eustace Grenier, Constable of the Kingdom. Informed that the Egyptian ships were retiring towards Ascalon, Domenico Michiel immediately set sail in pursuit.[248]

As the Venetians approached Ascalon at daybreak in early June 1123, the doge sent his *catti* ahead, along with the supply ships, all high-profile vessels which would appear as merchantmen from a distance. The remainder of the fleet, the forty fast *galeas*, trailed just beyond the horizon with a following wind. The Fatimid fleet took the bait. In the dim light of dawn the larger Venetian vessels must have seemed like ponderous easy prey for the more numerous and more manoeuvrable Egyptian galleys. It was only after they had already engaged the Venetian vanguard that the full light of morning revealed the trap. By then, it was too late. With the wind at their sterns, the Venetian *galeas* swiftly enveloped the Fatimid fleet.[249] 'The Saracens were confined in such a remarkable manner that neither their ships nor seamen could escape in any direction while the Venetians boarded their ships and cut their men to pieces,' described Fulcher of Chartres.[250] The Venetian victory was total. William of Tyre even claimed that the doge's vessel 'by chance' struck that of the Fatimid commander and nearly capsized it. 'For a circuit of two miles around,' aggrandized the archbishop, 'the adjacent sea became blood red from the bodies thrown therein and from the blood of the slain which flowed from the ships.'[251] Not content with this resounding victory, Domenico directed his fleet to continue south of Ascalon to ensure no elements of the Egyptian fleet had escaped the slaughter. Abeam al-Arish along the north coast of the Sinai their efforts were rewarded with ten fully laden Egyptian merchantmen. With these prizes and an immense haul of plunder, the Venetians returned to Acre unreservedly victorious.[252]

The Muslim naval threat had been virtually eliminated in a single engagement. Supremacy of the eastern seas now belonged to the Christians. The only matter to be determined at that point was what to do with it. Over the next several months Domenico Michiel and the leaders of the Latin Kingdom met in Jerusalem and wrestled with the issue at length. Those from the southern reaches of the realm naturally wished to attack Ascalon and remove its potential as a springboard for future invasions from Egypt, but those in the north favoured taking Tyre since it was the only remaining Muslim stronghold on an otherwise Christian-dominated coastline. William of Tyre tells the fanciful tale whereby an orphan boy was asked to choose between two pieces of parchment placed on the altar (presumably of the Church of the Holy Sepulchre), one bearing the name Tyre, the other Ascalon. Chance supposedly chose Tyre, but in all probability Tyre was the preferred target all along.[253] The well fortified port had been a thriving trading centre since Phoenician times. It was the far richer and strategically more vital prize. A prelate named Odo had been appointed as its prospective archbishop as early as 1122 and Venetian commercial interests were certainly far better served with an enclave in the centrally situated Tyre than in the more isolated Ascalon.[254]

Once the objective had been determined, there was the matter of compensation. Devotional considerations notwithstanding, Venice had heavily invested both manpower and treasure in the expedition and expected commensurate remuneration. Moreover, their celebrated triumph over the Fatimids gave them hefty leverage in the ensuing negotiations, which lasted several weeks. Sometime between 20 January and 16 February 1124 the *Pactum Warmundi* was signed in Acre by the Patriarch Warmund, the other leading clerical figures of the kingdom and the king's constable. Preserved in its entirety by William of Tyre in Book XII, Chapter 25 of his history, the treaty promulgated a sweeping set of concessions to *La Serenissima*, many of which had been promised in advance by the king himself. In summary, this extraordinary document granted the Venetians a third of Tyre, 300 'Saracen besants' annually from the revenues of said city, exemption from all taxes, permission to use their own weights and measures, and the right to adjudicate civil litigation among themselves. Perhaps most remarkable of all was the following clause: 'In every city of the above-mentioned king [Baldwin II], under the rule of his successors also, and in the cities of all his barons, the Venetians shall have a church and one entire street of their own; also a square and a bath and an oven to be held forever by hereditary right, free from all taxation as is the king's own property.'[255] (King Baldwin II, upon his return to Jerusalem

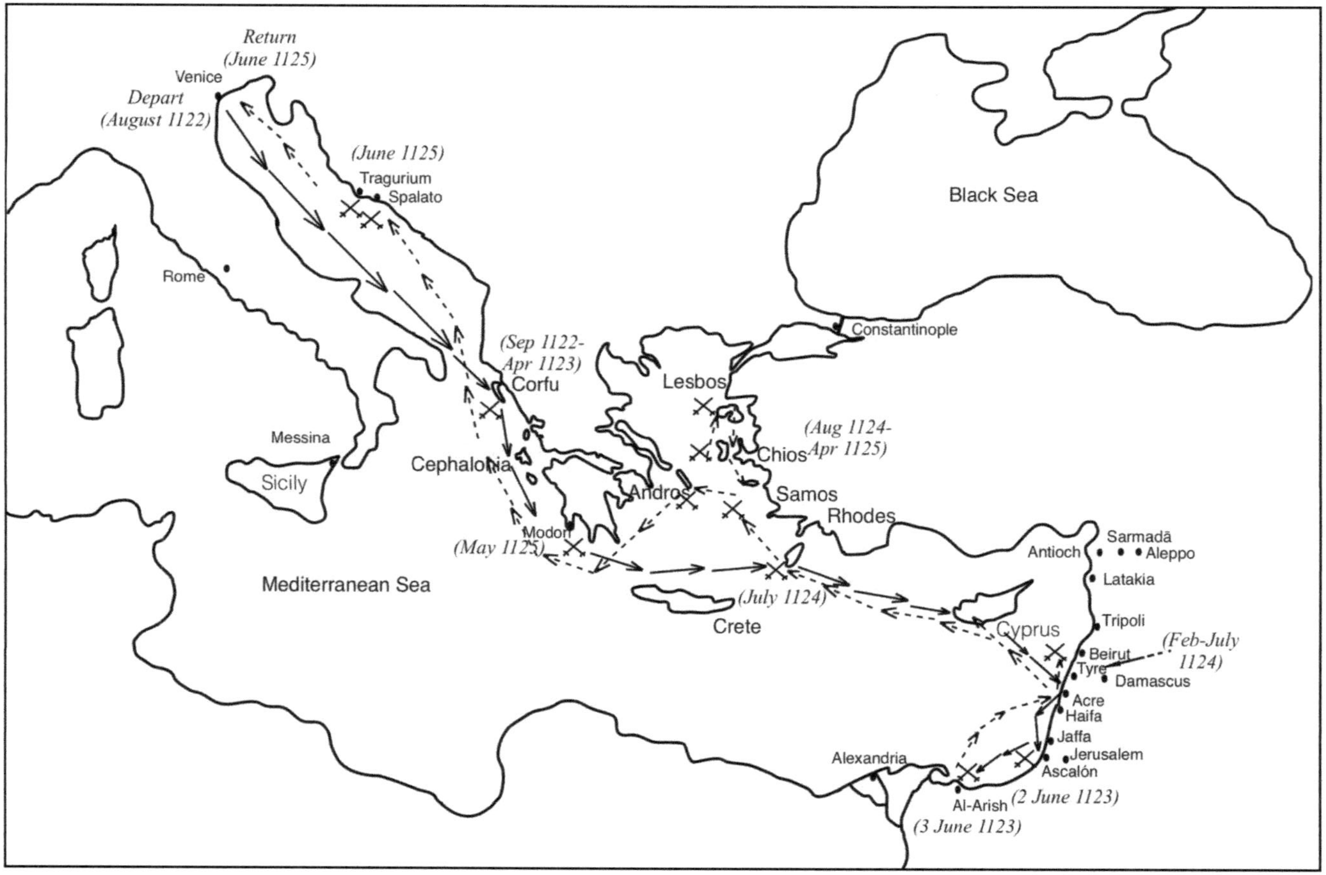

Map 6. Venetian Crusade of 1122–1125. *(Kristy Stanton)*

following his release from captivity, would ratify the treaty with few modifications in May 1125.)[256] With a few strokes of the quill, Venice became one of the largest, most powerful landowners in the Latin Kingdom of Jerusalem.

The deal done, the two parties wasted little time in prosecuting the siege of the city. It began on 16 February 1124 and, although it lasted five months, the outcome was never in doubt. Tyre stood on a stubby promontory connected to the mainland by a narrow isthmus. The besiegers simply took command of the causeway and the aqueduct which ran along it, obviating any possibility of relief by land. As for the seaward approach, the Venetians were so confident that they had completely vanquished Muslim maritime opposition that they beached all their galleys save one, which operated as a waterborne watch.[257] That meant that some 30,000 crew and combatants were available to reinforce the kingdom's army should Tughtigin, the Atabeg of Damascus, attempt to break the siege. The latter, who controlled a third of Tyre, did indeed rally his troops in the hope of doing just that, but, seeing the daunting assemblage of Latin forces arrayed against him, he recognized the hopelessness of the situation and instead negotiated the peaceful surrender of the city on 7 July 1124.[258]

Having satisfied its crusading commitments, the Venetian armada departed the Levant shortly thereafter, but it did not proceed directly home. There was still the quarrel with the Byzantine Empire over the withdrawn trade privileges. The Venetians took out their ire first on Rhodes before venturing into the northern Aegean to winter on the island of Chios. They departed the following spring, taking with them the body of the martyred St Isadore. They ravaged the other Aegean islands of Samos, Lesbos and Andros prior to rounding the Peloponnesos to raid Modon. Not even then did the fleet return to its cherished Lagoon. Apparently, the Hungarians had been encroaching on the Dalmatian domains of *La Serenissima*, so the Venetians used their maritime might to return Spalato (modern-day Split) and Tragurium (Trogir) to the fold. Finally, in June 1125 the triumphant armada of Venice sailed into the Venetian Lagoon laden with loot.[259] The revered Domenico Michiel had but one more mission to round out one of the most successful reigns of any doge. In the spring of 1126 he dispatched a fourteen-ship flotilla to raid the Ionian island of Cephalonia, pilfering the remains of St Donatus in the process.[260] This was apparently the final straw for John II Komnenos, for in August he finally restored, with embellishments, the commercial concessions first granted to the Venetians by his father Alexios.[261] *La Serenissima* was once again the pre-eminent maritime power in the eastern Mediterranean. (*See* Map 6.)

CHAPTER 4

Genoese–Pisan Rivalry for the Western Mediterranean

For more than two hundred years the two great Italian sea powers, Genoa and Pisa, dominated the western Mediterranean. And they spent almost all of that time locked in mortal maritime combat with one another, wielding the *galea* as their chosen weapon of war. Interrupted only by the occasional truce or strategic distraction, hostilities between the two were virtually incessant. From 1066 to 1284 Genoa and Pisa engaged in no fewer than six readily identifiable, multi-year periods of conflict. Four of these were over control of the islands of Corsica and Sardinia alone. Their deadly rivalry was largely a function of geography. Barely 80 nautical miles (148km or 92 miles) apart as the ship sails, there simply was not enough room in the region for both of them. Steven Epstein, an expert on Genoese history, succinctly encapsulated the predicament: 'The Tyrrhenian and Ligurian seas were too small for two major sea powers in the business of overseas trade.'[1] And neither city had any real choice but to seek its fortune upon the sea. Genoa, a port city hemmed in by the Ligurian Apennines, had little arable land upon which to expand inland, while Pisa, a few kilometres from the mouth of the Arno, was the natural port for Tuscany, but powerful Lucca and Florence curtailed its landward ambitions.[2] Thus both ports were compelled by natural circumstance to compete for the same customers on the same seas. It would ultimately become a battle to the death.

Collaboration and Conquest (806–1016)

Ironically, these two west Italian port towns did not initiate their rise to maritime supremacy in the West as implacable adversaries. Their first organized interactions were not for war but for mutual defence, and their objective was not profit or the aggrandizement of power but simple survival. Their shared shoreline on the Ligurian Sea had been subject to 'Saracen' raids since the early ninth century. The naval power of the Byzantines had begun to recede and the Carolingians, lacking any sort of consistent maritime capability, failed to fill the gap. Consequently, the Umayyads of Andalusia in southern Spain and the Aghlabids of the Maghreb in North Africa enjoyed increasingly free rein to terrorize the western seas. Both the French and Italian rivieras from the Rhone to the Tiber were ravaged with regularity between 806 and 815.[3] In 809 and 810 Muslim marauders briefly occupied both Corsica and Sardinia.[4] The invasion of Sicily by the Aghlabids of Kairouan in 827 only made matters worse.[5] By the end of the century conditions along the northwest coastline of the Mediterranean had become so bleak that maritime historian A.R. Lewis was constrained to comment,

'In startling contrast to the humming cities and busy trade of Moslem Spain and North Africa the Christian coastline from Barcelona to the Tiber was all but dead.'[6]

Hardly more than fishing villages at the time, Genoa and Pisa were powerless before the onslaught. They were victimized repeatedly, often by Muslim corsairs operating from bases on Corsica and Sardinia. Around 890 their circumstances actually worsened: pirates from Pechina in the Andalusian province of Almeria established an enclave at Fraxinetum (modern La Garde-Freinet) near St-Tropez in Provence. From there, these freebooters were able to plague the passes of the southwestern Alps and perhaps even threaten the Ligurian littoral.[7] It was, however, the Fatimids of Mahdiyah who nearly dealt Genoa an early demise. In 934 Caliph Abu al-Qasim Muhammad dispatched a fleet of thirty warships under the direction of Ya'qub ibn Ishaq which obliterated the city on 16 August 935.[8] Epstein surmises that the devastation was so complete that 'the site was probably abandoned for a few years'.[9] Both Latin and Arabic sources indicated that the destruction of Genoa was near total. Indeed, the contemporary Lombard historian Bishop Liudprand of Cremona testified that the Fatimids 'massacred everyone except the children and women, and putting on board ship all the treasures belonging to the city and to God's churches sailed back to Africa'.[10]

While there is no record of similar ruin being visited upon Pisa at the time, it is unlikely that the Tuscan port would have escaped the attention of the raiders. Ibn al-Athir noted that the Fatimids preyed on other cities in the region and wreaked havoc on both Corsica and Sardinia.[11] The first direct evidence that Pisa also suffered the ravages of Muslim raiding is provided by the city's first acknowledged historian, Bernardo Maragone, a twelfth-century jurist who was rather cryptic concerning the events of the commune prior to the start of the eleventh century.[12] For the year 1005 (1004 according to the standard Gregorian Calendar), the annalist tersely observed: 'Pisa was captured by the Saracens.'[13] This evidently was a bit of an overstatement, because he noted that the very next year the Pisans attacked Muslim-held Reggio in an apparent retaliation. Maragone documented that the city was again sacked in 1011, this time by a fleet from Spain.[14] What seems to have spurred the two west Italian city-states into concerted action, however, was the dire threat posed by a single common enemy: Mujahid ibn Abd-Allah al-Siqlabi.

Believed to have been born of Christian parents, Mujahid was a slave in the court of Ibn Abi Amir, the great Almansur bi-Allah ('Victorious by God') who had lifted the Umayyad Caliphate of Cordoba to its apogee in the late tenth century. Groomed for leadership and eventually emancipated by his master, Mujahid was well prepared to take advantage of the upheaval which resulted from Almansur's death in 1002. During the civil war in which the caliphate disintegrated into the *taifa* kingdoms, he established himself first at Tortosa, then at Denia on the southeast coast of Iberia, forming his own sham caliphate. Around 1014 he moved to the Balearic Islands, which he converted into a corsair kingdom. It was from this base that, in the summer of 1015, he launched an enormous raiding expedition, consisting of some 120 ships supposedly carrying 1,000 horses to Sardinia. His men ravaged the entire island amid much carnage, beginning with Cagliari.[15] During that same summer, according to contemporary chronicler Bishop Thietmar of Merseburg, Mujahid also devastated Luni and the surrounding coastal border region between Tuscany and Liguria.[16] This was what apparently aroused the collective concerns of Genoa and Pisa.

The implication for the two emerging maritime entrepôts was clear: to allow Sardinia to become a haven for Muslim marauders, free to roam and raid the shores of both the Ligurian and Tyrrhenian Seas, would be tantamount to welcoming their eventual extinction. Accordingly, the towns reacted with dispatch to deal with the shared threat. The combined galley fleets of Genoa and Pisa sailed in force to challenge Mujahid's occupation of the island. The precise size of their joint task force was not delineated, but it must have been substantial, given that its mere appearance offshore induced Mujahid's fleet to flee without a fight. He returned, however, the very next year with reinforcements and once more inflicted cruel repression on the island's inhabitants. Maragone claims that Mujahid coerced the Sardinians into building fortifications, and then had them entombed alive within the walls. In May the Genoese and Pisans arrived again to oust the marauders, only this time they caught the Muslims just as they were embarking and dealt them a resounding defeat. Many of the surviving 'Saracen' ships were supposedly driven ashore by a storm, their crews slaughtered by the Sardinians. Mujahid himself evaded capture, but never attacked the island again.[17]

The First Feud over Sardinia (1066–86)

The spirit of cooperative endeavour between Genoa and Pisa did not, unfortunately, last long. The Spanish 'Saracens' had hardly been evicted from Sardinia before the mariner-merchants of the two port towns began to covet the island's lucrative potential at each other's expense. After all, it was bountiful in livestock, grain, precious metals and, most prized of all, salt.[18] According to Maragone, it was the Genoese who first turned on their erstwhile Tuscan allies in the hope of exploiting the island's wealth for themselves, but it was the Pisans who won the ensuing skirmish, then banished their Ligurian competitors.[19] Regrettably, there is no corroborative testimony for the incident. Caffaro di Caschifellone, the first official historian of Genoa, began his chronicle with the year 1100, making no mention of prior events.[20] In all probability the scuffle on Sardinia was between private companies of merchant-adventurers motivated by greed rather than between citizens of city-states inspired by communal pride.[21] The communal system of government did not even begin until early the next century. That said, it seems from follow-on events that the Pisans did, indeed, gain the upper hand initially.

The success of the Sardinian foray seems to have encouraged the Pisans to extend their activities further afield. In 1034 they sent a fleet to attack the city of Bona (modern Annaba in Algeria). The raid may have been a reprisal: Maragone noted that 'Pisa was burnt' on Christmas Day 1030.[22] But, more than likely, plunder was the objective. That was almost certainly the case for the Pisan assault on Palermo on St Agapitus Day, 20 September 1063. The Norman chronicler Geoffrey Malaterra related that the Pisans had attempted to inveigle Roger de Hauteville into joining the enterprise with his vaunted Norman cavalry, but the latter declined, apparently fearing that the Pisans were 'dedicated more to commercial profits than military exercises'.[23] Undaunted, the Tuscan mariners attacked anyway. They smashed through the harbour chain with the bows of their war galleys and, to the horror of the helpless Muslim inhabitants, culled out six large merchantmen, five of which they burned after relieving them of their cargo. The sixth they retained as a trophy. Even then, they were not finished. The Pisans disembarked near the mouth of the river Oreto, which ran along the southeastern side of the city, and pillaged the environs for several days with apparent impunity. The spoils from the expedition were sufficiently lavish to finance construction of the Santa Maria Assunta, Pisa's opulent Romanesque cathedral. An inscription detailing the exploit adorns the façade of this magnificent edifice (just to the left of the main entrance) to this day.[24]

It may well have been jealousy over Pisa's apparent ascendancy in the Tyrrhenian that prompted Genoa to initiate renewed hostilities with its Tuscan competitor in 1066. A Genoese fleet appeared at the mouth of the Arno with the manifest intent of intimidating Pisan shipping.[25] William Heywood, an authority on Pisa, and Camillo Manfroni, the revered Italian maritime historian, both presume that the action was provoked by commercial competition over Sardinia. No battle was mentioned on this particular occasion, but the Pisan annals suggest that a period of raid and counter-raid between the merchant fleets of the two port cities persisted for roughly the next twenty years.[26] For instance, a Pisan raiding squadron was probably bound for Genoa in 1072 when a storm forced it to seek shelter in the nearby harbour of Portofino. In 1077 Maragone reported that Genoese mariners attacked Vada, a Pisan protectorate, but were promptly repaid with the razing of Rapallo on the Ligurian littoral. The following year a Genoese fleet again presented itself at the mouth of the Arno, only to be driven off by the Pisans.[27] And so it went until 1086, when Pope Victor III managed to mediate a peace between the two warring communities of mariner-merchants.[28] They would celebrate their renewed amity the very next year with their most ambitious collaboration to date: the conquest of Mahdiyah.

The Mahdiyah Campaign of 1087

By the end of the eleventh century the merchant-mariners of Genoa and Pisa had expanded their trading operations to include not only the Tyrrhenian and Ligurian coasts but the ports of Provence, Catalonia and even North Africa. The great nineteenth-century Italian Arabist Michele Amari speculated that the two maritime cities had even concluded a number of trade treaties with the Zirids of the Maghreb between 1070 and 1080.[29] In the same time frame the commercial concourses of the two cities were abuzz with the haggling of merchants from Christian ports ranging from Barcelona to Salerno.[30] Soon the Genoese and Pisans began to look avariciously to the lucrative trade of the East, historically dominated by Venice and Amalfi. Saracen-held Sicily had long been the stumbling block to all west Italian port cities save Amalfi, which had cultivated amicable relations with the Muslims. But the Norman subjugation of Sicily, nearly complete by 1087, had dramatically changed the calculus. The only remaining impediment to trade with the East was now Mahdiyah.

Situated on a small peninsula just south of the Sicilian Channel, the Zirid city had become the bane of Christian coastal communities throughout the central Mediterranean. Ibn al-Athir succinctly explained why: 'The cause was that the Emir Tamim ibn al-Mu'izz ibn Badis, prince of the country, was making frequent maritime raids against the Rum [Latin and Greek Christians], laying waste to the towns and upsetting their populations.'[31] In other words Tamim had made Mahdiyah into a Muslim pirate enclave that routinely pillaged the ports of the Christian west and preyed on its shipping. Thus there can be no doubt that Zirid fleets severely curtailed east–west traffic through the Sicilian Channel. It was a situation that the rising west Italian maritime powers could no longer tolerate. Accordingly, the mariners of Genoa and Pisa, with the blessing of Pope Victor III, combined forces to aggressively address the problem. The *Carmen in Victoria Pisanorum* ('Song about the victory of the Pisans'), an epic poem extolling the exploits of the participants, claimed that they 'collected a thousand ships in only three months'.[32] The Muslim sources noted a more modest but still menacing 300 to 400 vessels, bearing around 30,000 fighting men.[33] Even the Amalfitans, long inveterate allies of the Arabs, joined the expedition in exasperation over the continued harassment stemming from the Zirid capital.[34] Ironically, the Normans of Sicily chose not to participate due to a trade pact that Count Roger maintained with Tamim. But nor did they interfere.[35]

The various Christian naval contingents mustered at Pantelleria, an island roughly halfway between Sicily and Cape Bon of modern Tunisia, quickly subduing its Muslim garrison.[36] When the armada anchored outside Mahdiyah on St Sixtus Day (6 August 1087), an Arab eyewitness said the 'galleys looked like mountains save only that their summits bristled with spears and swords'.[37] Worse yet, the city was virtually undefended: as luck would have it, Tamim was away somewhere inland with the bulk of his land forces repelling a Bedouin incursion. So the west Italians stormed ashore unopposed at Zawilah, the unwalled outskirts of the city (*see* Map 7).[38] 'The enemy assaulted our country in such numbers that they seemed like clouds of locusts or swarms of maggots', bewailed the poet Abu al-Hasan ibn Muhammad al-Haddad.[39] The *Carmen in Victoria Pisanorum* confirmed the bloodbath which ensued: 'All were cut up and killed like cattle.'[40] By the time Tamim received word of the horrific sacking of the city and returned, there was little he could do but seek refuge in the royal citadel. Most of his cavalry mounts had been slaughtered, his arsenal was in flames and his fleet was nothing more than burned out hulks arrayed along the shoreline. Little remained save the citadel. He had no choice but to sue for a humiliating peace.[41]

In addition to paying an enormous tribute (30,000 to 80,000 gold dinars, depending on the source) and liberating all Christian prisoners, Tamim was compelled to swear that he would 'henceforth not impose treacherous attacks on Christians and not levy duties' on their commerce.[42] These concessions,

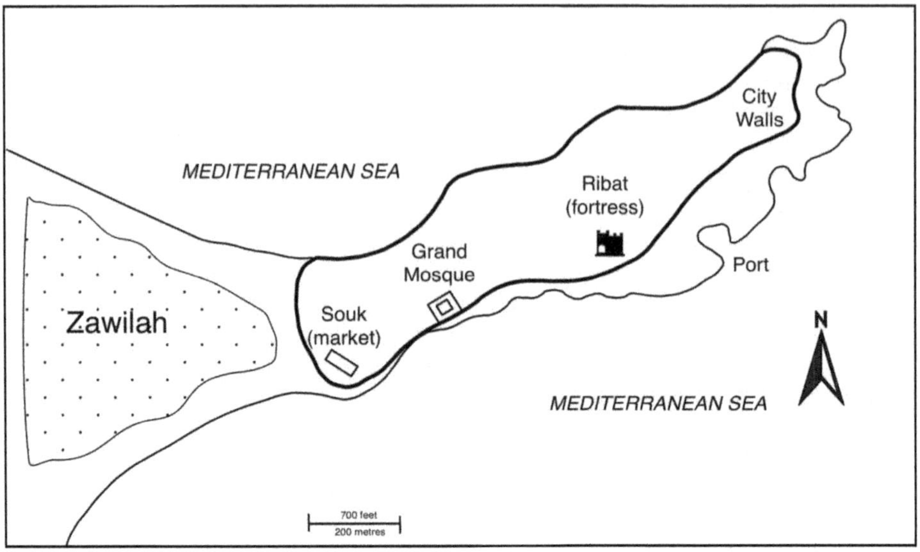

Map 7. Mahdiyah in 1087. *(Kristy Stanton)*

combined with a prodigious plunder in gold, silver and silks, more than compensated the victorious merchant-adventurers for their investment. The Pisans, for example, returned with enough wealth not only to adorn their cathedral with further extravagant embellishment, but also to fund the construction of a church at Cortevecchia dedicated to St Sixtus, on whose day they had triumphed.[43] But by far the most auspicious outcome of the expedition was the destruction of Zirid naval capability.[44] The door to the riches of the East had been flung wide open. And, as it happens, the timing could hardly have been better. Only eight years later, in 1095, Pope Urban II declared at Clermont a movement which would ultimately extend the reach of the two west Italian maritime powers the breadth of the Mediterranean.

The Crusades and Economic Expansion (1097–1110)

The Genoese and Pisan contributions to the Crusades have already been detailed in the preceding chapter, but the consequences of their involvement extended well beyond their military exploits in the East. As has been noted, the two Italian maritime powers were amply rewarded for their roles in establishing the Latin Kingdom of Jerusalem. They both received economic enclaves called *fondachi* ('trading posts') in all the major ports of Christian-held Syria and Palestine. These *fondachi* were privileged, semi-autonomous commercial quarters where Genoese and Pisan merchants purchased from Muslim traders with gold and silver the eastern commodities so highly prized in the West: pepper, cassia, nutmeg, dye pigments, precious stones and pearls. These items they loaded in the holds of their merchantmen for transport back to Genoa and Pisa for distribution throughout the western Mediterranean and northern Europe.[45] At the same time the proliferation of the *commenda* contract, whereby the travelling merchant of a partnership contributed only his services to an enterprise in return for a quarter of the profits, amplified opportunities which, in turn, enlarged the merchant class and greatly expanded the commercial activity of these newly minted maritime powers.[46]

The transfusion of trade transmitted from the East to the West in the round ships of the two west Italian communes was crucial to the revitalization of the European economy. The research of David Abulafia, the leading authority on the medieval Mediterranean, revealed that Provence was the primary conduit for much of this increased commerce from the East. For instance, Genoa handled most of Toulouse's trade with the Latin Levant, while Pisa carried much of the eastern goods that filled the markets of Marseilles.[47] And the twelfth-century Jewish traveller Benjamin of Tudela observed of Montpelier: 'People of all nations are found there doing business through the medium of the Genoese and Pisans.'[48] These exotic spices, rugs and other luxury items then found their way into the great emporia of medieval Europe: the trade fairs of Champagne. The Ligurian and Tuscan mariner-merchants became so successful at supplying these commodities that they were compelled to seek out other markets in Spain as well as southern France. Accordingly, they established *fondachi* not only in Toulouse and Montpelier, but also eventually in Narbonne, Almeria and Tortosa.[49]

Nor was this flurry of renewed economic activity fostered by the Genoese and Pisans limited to Christian markets. The ships of the two mercantile communes could be found in the ports of Muslim North Africa as well.[50] The papers of the Cairo Geniza (a cache of documents discovered in the *geniza* ['storeroom'] of the Ben Ezra synagogue of Fustat [Old Cairo]) are replete with references to Genoese and Pisan traders in the markets of Cairo and Alexandria in the eleventh and twelfth centuries. Moreover, there were several trade treaties with such entrepôts as Tunis and Bougie (Bejaia in Algeria) to attest to the growing west Italian economic interaction with the Maghreb.[51] In fact, the round ships of Genoa and Pisa began to ply the waters of the Mediterranean in such numbers that their merchant fleets became the *de facto* mode of transportation and communication from one end of the sea to the other. The evidence of the Cairo Geniza is clear: by the mid-twelfth century Muslim and Jewish traders usually travelled or corresponded on the vessels of the west Italians.[52]

As the west Italian maritime city-states became more powerful and dominant on the seas, they became less willing to endure disruptions to their growing trade empires, particularly from piracy. As a result, attention inevitably fell upon the Muslim marauders of Majorca.

The Balearic Expedition (1113–15)

Nearly a century after Mujahid had first sailed from the Balearic Islands with a huge armada to assail Sardinia, his descendants still maintained the archipelago as a base from which to beset the entire region. These 'Saracen' pirates no longer challenged the maritime might of Tuscany and Liguria, but they continually savaged the coasts of Catalonia and Provence, crucial markets for the west Italian mariners. The Pisans in particular were incensed by the violent intrusions into what they considered to be their trading territory.[53]

On Easter Sunday 1113 Archbishop Pietro Moriconi of Pisa called for a crusade against the Muslims of Majorca. The response was overwhelming. The leading families of the city immediately voiced their enthusiastic support. Twelve consuls were selected to captain the expedition and all of these joined the archbishop in a delegation to Rome for the purpose of seeking the papal blessing of Pope Paschal II himself.[54] And recruitment extended well beyond the confines of the commune. Volunteers came from Volterra, Pistoia, Siena, Florence, Rome and even arch-enemy Lucca. Notably, the Genoese demurred.[55] Such popular appeal was to prove most propitious, because historians estimate the size of the fleet that was eventually assembled at around 300 vessels. An armada of that magnitude would have required at least 45,000 men to crew it – probably greater than the entire population of Pisa.[56]

The construction of the fleet was apparently a gargantuan undertaking in itself. Pisan shipwrights harvested lumber from as far away as the forests of Luni, Corvara and Corsica in order to build *galeas*, *catti*, *dromōns*, *sagene* (scout galleys), *naves* and *uscieri*.[57] The *uscieri* (also called *uscerii*) were relatively sophisticated horse transports fitted with massive hatches in their sterns which opened outwards to form ramps for easy embarkation. The *naves* were evidently large enough to accommodate a variety of siege machinery: scaling ladders, catapults, battering rams and even siege towers.[58]

A comprehensive account of the expedition is contained in the *Liber Maiolichinus de gestis Pisanorum illustribus* ('The Majorca Book of the deeds of the illustrious Pisans'), a poem written in Homeric hexameters designed to lionize its heroes with a classical flourish. It predictably lacks impartiality, but it contains details only an eyewitness is likely to have known, like the routing. The fleet departed Pisa on 6 August 1113, St Sixtus' Day, in commemoration of the victory at Mahdiyah in 1087, and continued between the islands of Elba and Capraia to the coast of Corsica, which it followed south to the Strait of Bonifacio. It anchored briefly at Porto Torres on the north shore of Sardinia in the Gulf of Asinara before proceeding around Punta Caprara to Capo Caccia near Alghero on the northwest side of the island, where it was joined by a Sardinian contingent.[59] From there, the armada made straight for Majorca. A summer storm, however, intervened and pushed it well north of its course, causing it to make landfall instead at Blanes in Catalonia about 62km (38 miles) northeast of Barcelona.[60]

The misadventure proved providential, because the count of Barcelona, Ramon Berenguer III, endorsed the Pisan enterprise with a treaty of alliance which provided the Pisan merchants with a number of lucrative trade privileges, including exclusion from all imposts within his realm.[61] Many from the surrounding regions followed the count's lead and also joined the expedition, including the count of Montpelier and the viscount of Narbonne, who each contributed a score of ships.[62] The Lucchese, however, not being of sailor stock, had suffered the voyage's storms poorly. They returned home.[63] In hindsight, the decision seems to have been a fortuitous one. An awful autumn tempest smashed sixty of the armada's ships in the harbour at Barcelona.[64] While the main fleet wintered there, a flotilla of thirty vessels was sent back to Pisa for reinforcements.[65] It returned the following June as a fleet of eighty ships.[66]

Shortly afterwards, the fleet of several hundred ships weighed anchor and sailed southwest until abeam the Ebro delta, then straight south past the Columbretes Isles to Ibiza in the Balearics.[67] The island's main town of the same name finally surrendered on 10 August, only to be razed anyway.[68] The expedition soon moved on to Majorca, but its emir, Mubashir ibn Sulayman, had been forewarned. He put up a stout defence of the capital (present-day Palma) which he was able to sustain against a withering assault through the winter and into the succeeding spring. The Christian coalition nearly cracked when the count of Barcelona proposed seeking terms with Mubashir so that he could return home to defend his lands against an intrusion from the Muslims of Denia, but the Pisans would have none of it.[69] Their mission was to eradicate the pirate nest compromising their commerce in the region and they were disinclined to desist until that was accomplished. The outer ramparts finally fell in February 1115, followed the next month by the inner ring of bulwarks. The citadel crumpled on 3 April, accompanied by the horrendous massacre of thousands of Muslim defenders.[70] Paradoxically, most of the plunder consisted of pirate booty previously pillaged from Christian churches and monasteries from Provence to the coast of Aragon.[71]

The Pisans sailed home to the universal adulation of all western Christendom. A scourge of 'Saracen' piracy had been eliminated and thousands of Christian captives had been liberated. Praise poured in, particularly from the papacy and the Holy Roman Emperor. Pisan prestige was at its apex. But, of course, it was all ephemeral. First of all, buccaneering in the Balearics had only been suppressed and not banished. The expedition had been one of punitive conquest rather than colonization. No sooner had the expeditionary forces quit the island than the Almoravids of the Maghreb moved in. Within a few years Majorca was again the haunt of Muslim freebooters. Worse yet for the Pisans, their newfound acclaim garnered them the envy and renewed enmity of their maritime nemesis, the Genoese. In September 1118 Paschal II's successor, Pope Gelasius II, rewarded Pisa by confirming the primacy of its archbishop over the church of Corsica, first proclaimed by Urban II in 1092.[72] This act would ignite a conflict with Genoa over control of Corsica that would endure until 1133.

The First Conflict over Corsica (1119–33)

The Genoese wasted little time in challenging Pisan suzerainty over Corsica. In May 1119 Caffaro recorded that sixteen Genoese galleys captured some fully loaded Pisan merchantmen near the mouth of the Golo river of northeastern Corsica.[73] This corresponds to Maragone's entry for that year: 'War is begun between the Pisans and the Genoese.'[74] Indeed, on 6 August the Pisan chronicler claimed that a Pisan fleet exacted retribution on the Genoese at Porto Venere, a Genoese protectorate.[75] Then, according to Caffaro, the Genoese answered in

1120 by showing up at Porto Pisano (the main seaport of medieval Pisa, just north of modern Livorno) with an immense force, supposedly composed of 22,000 knights and infantrymen carried by no fewer than 80 galleys, 35 *gatti* (*catti* – large triremes), 28 *golabi* (light war galleys) and 4 large transports, bearing 'machines and every manner of instrument necessary for war'.[76] This inflated force allegedly intimidated Pisa into surrendering all Genoese prisoners and its claim to Corsica. Maragone, on the other hand, insisted that only twenty-two Genoese galleys had appeared at the mouth of Arno and that the Pisans summarily defeated these, capturing six vessels in the process.[77] It is impossible to sort through the welter of claims and counter-claims generated by the chroniclers of the two competing communes with any confidence. All that can be deduced with any certainty is that hostilities had broken out and neither city had gained the upper hand.

Therefore, it seems, the Genoese sought to achieve at the Holy See what they could not accomplish on the sea. In the summer of 1120 Caffaro himself journeyed to Rome, well funded to make Genoa's case for Corsica directly to the papal curia. Extant documentary evidence shows that he and his colleague, a certain Barisone, disseminated ample quantities of gold and silver to the Pope's advisors to ensure a favourable hearing on the matter. The money was well spent: on 3 January 1121 Pope Calixtus II issued a bull officially revoking the right of Pisa's archbishop to consecrate Corsican bishops, returning the prerogative to the papacy itself. Pisa protested the ruling, but a papal commission of twelve archbishops and twelve bishops confirmed the pronouncement in April 1123 and Calixtus backed it up with another bull, commanding the Pisans to accept it without further rancour or face excommunication.[78] The Pisans, of course, persisted in their objections and the war of raid and counter-raid continued.

The Pisans persevered in their commerce with both Sardinia and Corsica, often sending their merchant vessels in convoys escorted by war galleys. Caffaro noted that one such convoy of twenty-two *naves* (transport vessels) accompanied by nine Pisan galleys was waylaid in 1123 off the coast of Tuscany near Castagneto di Maremma just south of Vada by seven Genoese galleys, resulting in the capture of all the merchantmen.[79] The Genoese chronicler undoubtedly amplified the magnitude of the Pisan losses, but nonetheless the Pisans returned the favour in 1125 by launching eight galleys into the waters of Provence in order to prey on Genoese merchantmen bound for the markets of Aigues-Mortes and Villeneuve-les-Maguelone. As consul, Caffaro himself captained a squadron of seven galleys sent in pursuit. Unable to find their quarry, the Genoese instead pounced upon defenceless Piombino (a Pisan protectorate) on 15 September, mercilessly sacking the Tuscan town and carrying off the inhabitants as slaves.[80] The Pisans answered by successfully petitioning Pope Calixtus' successor, Honorius II, who reinstated the right of Pisa's archbishop to appoint Corsican suffragans in August 1126.[81] Infuriated, the Genoese perpetrated even greater violence on their Tuscan antagonists. That same year a Genoese fleet arrived at the mouth of the Arno and landed a raiding party which thoroughly ransacked the region. Both Piombino and Vada were pillaged anew. The Ligurian flotilla then crossed the Tyrrhenian and stormed the Pisan-held Castel Sant' Angelo at Cagliari on Corsica.[82] And on went the deadly game of tit-for-tat until finally Innocent II managed to broker a truce between the two exhausted adversaries in August 1130.[83]

There were minor violations, but on the whole the truce held until the Pope could arrange a more lasting peace in March 1133. The papal bull Innocent pronounced at Grosseto was a master stroke of medieval mediation. It designated Genoa as an archbishopric with primacy over the bishoprics of Mariana, Nebbio and San Pietro d'Atto on Corsica, as well as the sees of Bobbio and Brugnato on the mainland. The archbishopric of Pisa retained jurisdiction over the diocese of Ajaccio, Aleria and Salona. The Pisans also received the southern half of the island in fief while the northern half was granted to the Genoese. A second bull issued at the same time provided for a Court of Arbitration composed of four Genoese and four Pisans to deal with any future altercations which may arise between the two communes.[84] The true victor in this settlement was Innocent himself. His desideratum all along had been to arrange a peace between the two great naval powers so that they would be free to commit their fleets to Emperor Lothair III's campaign to conquer the Norman Kingdom of Sicily. This was because Roger II of Sicily was the protector of Innocent's primary competitor for the papal pallium: Anacletus II.

An Uneasy Armistice (1133–62)

For the most part the peace persisted for the next few decades, but this was not due to any concerted effort on the part of the two inimical parties. There were distractions further afield. First of all, the Pisans did, in fact, become embroiled in imperial efforts to absorb the Kingdom of Sicily. As was discussed in Chapter 2, the Pisans sent large fleets to Naples Bay in support of the undertaking both in 1135 and 1137 before coming to a separate accommodation with Roger II. The Genoese appear not to have taken part in the imperial invasion of Roger's realm in any meaningful way. They had enjoyed strong ties with Norman Sicily since 1116, when Roger, then count, had granted the Genoese consul Ogerio Capra and his brother a plot of land near Messina, clearly intended for commercial purposes.[85] From 1127 to 1138 the Genoese instead worked to further trade relations with Provence and Catalonia, acquiring privileges for their merchants in Marseilles, Hyères, Fréjus, Fos and Barcelona.[86] Furthermore, the desire to expand their influence to the eastern shores of the Iberian peninsula was doubtless a major motivating factor for Genoese participation in the sieges of Almeria and Tortosa during the Second Crusade (1146–8). They had a free hand to do so, because during the same basic time period Pisa was immersed in hostilities with its Tuscan arch-rival, Lucca.[87]

For a time it even appeared as though the ongoing imperial quest to seize the Kingdom of Sicily might, once again, unite the fleets of the two maritime powers in a common cause. Requiring naval assistance to subdue the island realm, Frederick I Barbarossa ended up offering both republics enticements so generous that they could hardly refuse. On 6 April 1162 the emperor promised Pisa suzerainty over the shores of the Tyrrhenian from Porto Venere to Civitavecchia. He also conceded the Tuscan city-state half of Palermo, Messina, Salerno and Naples, and all of Gaeta, Mazara and Trapani, as well as a street in each of the remaining cities of the *Regno* (as the Kingdom of Sicily was called), plus a third of the kingdom's royal treasury. He even exempted its merchants from all duties throughout the realm.[88] At Pavia a little over two months later, on 6 June, Frederick conferred a similar privilege on Genoa in return for its naval support. Though not quite as princely as the reward given to Pisa, it was still lavish: control of the Ligurian coast from Monaco to Porto Venere, all of Syracuse, a large fief in the Val de Noto region of Sicily, an enclave in each of the *Regno*'s port cities, a quarter of the kingdom's coffers and exception from imposts.[89]

Only a few days later the promise of profitable cooperation on the seas unravelled in a spate of senseless bloodletting in another empire at the other end of the Mediterranean. Unbridled malice born of age-old antipathy incited a thousand residents of the Pisan quarter of Constantinople to attack the Genoese *fondaco*, killing some of its 300 inhabitants and subjecting the entire enclave to the torch. The incident instantly plunged the two city-states back into the cycle of raid and retribution that predominantly defined their relationship.[90] Upon learning of the assault from the survivors, the Genoese immediately dispatched two letters of indignant protest to the Pisans that arrived at about the same time as a flotilla of twenty-five galleys, which sank three large Pisan merchantmen at anchor at the mouth of the Arno and set three more ablaze at Porto Pisano. The Pisan fortress on the island of Capraia was also razed.[91] Another squadron savaged Pisan ships en route from Corsica and Sardinia, capturing the Pisan consul Bonaccorso in the process. The spark may have been the clash in Constantinople, but Caffaro made it clear that the real cause was underlying bitterness over Sardinia. The letters of outrage which accompanied the Genoese reprisal referred enigmatically to the '*expulsio Sardinie*' ('expulsion of Sardinia'), apparently alluding to the first conflict over the island following the eviction of Mujahid in 1016.[92]

Whatever the reasons, the Pisans needed little urging to join the fray. In July they 'speedily directed ten *galeas* and eleven *sagittias* [small, swift monoremes with around sixteen oars, and often spelt *sagittae* or *sagete*], armed in the manner of galleys, to devastate Capo Corso [northern Corsica]'. This squadron also seized a pair of great ships from the East off the island of Pianosa, 'where sixty-two Genoese died, some beheaded, some killed with the sword'. The combined value of the booty from these ships, along with another from Sicily, was said to have exceeded 20,000 silver pounds. Yet another Pisan fleet of fourteen *sagittae* chased twelve Genoese galleys away from the Tuscan port of Populonia, then captured some more Genoese merchantmen, along with fifty-five prisoners, before returning to port. But what really caused the Genoese concern was a flotilla of twenty-four *galeas* and thirty *sagittae* which the Pisans were preparing for an assault on Porto Venere. This prompted the Ligurians to seek the intercession of the emperor, who imposed a truce at Turin in August 1162.[93] It was doomed, however, by a renewed struggle over Sardinia.

The Second War for Sardinia (1163–75)

What ignited another outbreak of sustained warfare over Sardinia was a succession dispute over one of the four judgeships which traditionally ruled the island. When Costantino of Cagliari passed away in 1163, Barisone II of Arborea invaded in an attempt to add the Cagliaritano to his own domains at the expense of Costantino's heirs. The Pisans, however, apparently intervened in favour of the rightful claimants, causing Barisone to seek the help of the Genoese. The latter, perceiving a golden opportunity, interceded with Frederick Barbarossa in August 1164 on Barisone's behalf and the emperor, still trying to recruit the Genoese for an assault on Sicily, proclaimed Barisone '*regnum Sardinie*' ('king of Sardinia') for the price of 4,000 silver marks over the vociferous objections of the Pisans. Barisone, in return for Genoese political and financial backing, vowed to grant Genoa trade concessions while expelling the Pisans from Sardinia. Pisa responded by paying Barbarossa 13,000 silver pounds to reverse himself, which he did. On 17 April 1165 he annulled Barisone's investiture of Sardinia and instead conferred it upon Pisa.[94] The diplomatic options now exhausted, both sides sought to settle the matter at sea in a struggle that would sputter fitfully along for the next decade.

Like all the previous confrontations, it was a conflict characterized almost entirely by petty, vindictive skirmishes. There were no large-scale pitched battles. In May, for instance, eleven Pisan galleys devastated Sardinia's Porto Torres, which had apparently developed Genoese sympathies.[95] In July Maragone recorded that Pisa sent southwards seven more galleys which took a Genoese *galliot* and some other vessels off Ischia. Three other Pisan galleys were dispatched towards Provence, where they captured a great ship and seven *buthettos* (presumably small sailing vessels).[96] Oberto Nasello Cancelliere ('Chancellor'), a continuator for Caffaro, essentially confirmed the account, saying fourteen Genoese galleys tried to trap the Pisans at St Gilles (a port in Provence on a western branch of the Rhone about 22.5km or 14 miles northeast of Aigues-Mortes), but failed when the Pisan galleys escaped down another small tributary of the Rhone. The Genoese burned some Pisan merchantmen at the wharves of St Gilles out of frustration and returned home.[97] The various annals and chronicles are rife with reports of similar minor episodes of belligerence.

The most serious incident occurred in August 1165: thirty-one Pisan galleys again raided Capo Corso on Corsica, then attacked Albenga (a Genoese protectorate on the Italian Riviera) and reduced it to ashes. The same fleet later captured twenty-eight Genoese merchantmen which were on their way home. Incensed, the Genoese launched forty-five (fifty according to Maragone) of their own galleys in pursuit. The Genoese fleet eventually tracked the Pisan raiders to St Gilles. The Genoese attempted to surprise the Pisans with a night attack while the latter were at anchor, but were instead reminded why night nautical engagements were rare in the era: several of the Genoese galleys ran aground and many more collided with one another. By the time the debris was cleared, it was morning and St Gilles had been alerted to their presence. The townspeople warned the Genoese that an attack on the Pisans in their port would be met with stiff resistance, so the Genoese sought to purchase the aid of Raymond of Toulouse. The Pisans apparently outbid them, however, because in the ensuing battle Raymond's Provençals either joined the Pisans or remained neutral. In any event, the outcome was inconclusive: the Genoese were forced to abandon the engagement when they learned that yet another Pisan flotilla of twenty galleys was heading for Genoa.[98]

Genoa, as it turns out, was spared attack by a providential storm which struck the Pisans just as they were passing the Portofino promontory. Driven southwards, the Pisans ravaged the area around Porto Venere instead and returned home. A second Pisan fleet of twenty-five galleys made another attempt in mid-September, wreaking havoc upon the region around Levanto, but met the same storm-tossed fate as the preceding squadron. When the tempest released its grip, the Pisans again tried to take out their fury on Porto Venere, but were chased off by the Marquis Malaspino, a Genoese ally. Inclement weather also proved the bane of the Pisan fleet returning from Provence. A two-day maelstrom, beginning on 29 October, scattered its ships and wrecked many of them on the shores of Sardinia and Corsica. One was even reportedly captured by Moorish pirates off the coast of North Africa. Only nineteen of the original thirty-one galleys made it back to Porto Pisano.[99]

The remainder of the conflict was a sporadic series of desultory encounters between handfuls of opposing vessels. In June 1166 eight Genoese galleys evaded seventeen Pisan warships near Cagliari and raided Porto Pisano.[100] The next month seven Pisan galleys clashed with an equal number of Genoese galleys off Elba, taking two and capturing over 300 prisoners. In August another Genoese squadron of seven galleys captained by a certain Baldouino Guercio attempted to ensnare seven Pisan galleys from Vada with a feigned flight manoeuvre but was defeated himself with the loss of two vessels and many men.[101] A squadron of eight Genoese galleys destroyed the Pisan fortifications on Pianosa Island in the summer of 1168 and later seized a Pisan galley off Savona.[102] On 15 September 1172 another flotilla of seven Genoese galleys again laid waste the defences of Pianosa. The following month five other Genoese galleys surprised three Pisan galleys near Isola San Pietro off the south coast of Sardinia, capturing them.[103] And in 1174 Pisan privateers made prizes of six fully laden Genoese merchantmen.[104] Neither side really seemed to gain an advantage.

By the autumn of 1175 both sides were weary of a war which had diverted manpower and matériel from the business of profitable maritime commerce. Thus the two antagonists were ready to quietly accept a peace imposed by the emperor on 6 November, which effectively divided Sardinia between them in accordance with existing spheres of influence: the Pisans held sway in the Gallura and Logodura judgeships, while Genoa controlled the Cagliaritano and Arborea. There were occasional flare-ups afterwards, but the peace basically held until the end of the century.[105] Fighting briefly broke out between the two in Sardinia in 1187, only to be snuffed out in February of the following year through the intercession of Pope Clement III in anticipation of the Third Crusade.[106] During said Crusade, Pisans loyal to Guy de Lusignan came to blows with Genoese supporters of

Conrad of Montferrat in the streets of Acre in February 1192, but Richard Lionheart was able to quell the quarrel.[107] And Markward von Anweiler, Emperor Henry VI's seneschal, managed to mediate a cessation of hostilities between the two which had broken out over the spoils of Messina during the imperial conquest of Sicily in the summer of 1194. The Genoese had seized thirteen Pisan ships in the harbour after the Pisans had taken over the Genoese *fondaco*.[108] The final showdown between the two fatally inimical maritime powers would come in the thirteenth century.

A Clash of Corsairs (1202–17)

Maritime enterprise on the medieval Mediterranean was never entirely about the carriage of commerce from one port to another. Piracy, whether state-sponsored or private, was an integral part of the entrepreneurship of the era. It was practised by the mariners of nearly every seagoing city and it formed the core of the conflict between Genoa and Pisa at the start of the thirteenth century. Hostilities began in the waters around Sicily during the minority of Frederick II and soon spread to those in the vicinity of Sardinia. The specific scene of the opening salvos was Syracuse.

In 1202, during the power struggle which followed the death in 1198 of Empress Constance, Queen Regnant of Sicily, the notorious Pisan pirate Ranieri Manente di Segalari seized Syracuse with the consent of his ally, Markward von Anweiler. He soon turned the port into a pirate base from which his galleys preyed on east–west shipping transiting the Sicilian Channel.[109] Inevitably, one of his corsair galleys accosted one belonging to the famed Genoese freebooter Alamanno da Costa, just outside Syracuse harbour in the summer of 1204. Infuriated by the incident, the latter rallied Genoese merchantmen from Syria and Egypt to his banner and assailed Syracuse on 6 August. Joining the attack were galleys of the equally celebrated Genoese privateer Enrico Pescatore di Castello, known to history as Henry of Malta. The city fell after a struggle of only seven days. Luckily for Alamanno, there were four Genoese consuls on those merchantmen from the East. Acting on behalf of the commune, these men endowed the corsair captain with the title 'count of Syracuse'.[110]

And, of course, it was only a matter of time before the mortification of defeat goaded Ranieri Manente into some sort of retribution. The pretext came via a violent encounter the following summer with a Genoese squadron commanded by Guglielmo Porco and Alamanno's son Benvenuto da Costa. Ranieri reacted by laying siege to Syracuse in August 1205 with twelve galleys, ten round ships and a bevy of small boats. Three months later the city was on the verge of capitulating when, once again, Enrico Pescatore stepped in. He armed four of his own galleys on Malta and convinced a number of Genoese merchantmen in the harbour at Messina to join him in a relief operation. With the addition of a ship from Porto Venere and those of Guglielmo Porco, Enrico's squadron swelled to sixteen. In December he led it to the mouth of Syracuse harbour, where he challenged Ranieri to battle. When the day was done, Henry of Malta could claim a hard-won victory in which nearly all the Pisan galleys were vanquished.[111]

The Pisans next sought to even the score through an alliance with the Venetians, from whom Enrico Pescatore was attempting to conquer Crete. On 2 July 1206 the two republics each vowed to supply forty galleys for action against Genoa. But nothing much ever came of the union. Hostilities between the Genoese and Pisans soon shifted to the Tyrrhenian and Venice remained too preoccupied with protecting its possessions in the East to help.[112] So when a small squadron of Genoese privateers blockaded some Pisan merchantmen in the port of Cagliari later that same year, Pisa was on its own. The blockade lasted through the winter, during which both communes prepared fleets to resolve the matter.[113]

Genoese reinforcements were the first to arrive. Ten galleys and ten great ships under the command of Niccolo Doria made Cagliari in May 1207. They immediately attacked the Pisan ships huddled in the harbour, only to be repulsed repeatedly. The Pisans had built some sort of floating palisade around their vessels which the Genoese could not penetrate despite the liberal use of shipboard mangonels, catapults and other petraries. They even attempted to set the Pisan flotilla ablaze with a fireship, but failed. Doria ultimately had to abandon the blockade when a Pisan fleet of seventeen galleys led by Lamberto Galli approached, threatening to trap the Genoese between the two Pisan flotillas.[114]

After this, the Pisans went on the offensive. Together with the remnants of Ranieri Manente's force, they attacked Palermo and took possession of the royal palace. They retreated only after Chancellor Gualtiero Paleario challenged them on behalf of the regency with the backing of Pope Innocent II, who threatened them with excommunication.[115] In the meantime the Genoese could do little to oppose their Tuscan counterparts. Enrico Pescatore was beseeching the commune for help in occupying Crete in the face of vigorous Venetian resistance and, to make matters worse, a storm system had smashed a sizeable Genoese armada on the shores of the Ligurian Riviera near Nervi later in the year. They offered the Pisans a truce, mediated in May 1208 by King Otto IV of Brunswick, claimant to the crown of the Holy Roman Empire.[116]

The lull did not last long. Pisa, sensing it had the upper hand, sought to press the advantage. Raiders issued from the Porto Pisano within days of the accord's enactment. In 1210 Pisan privateers even pounced upon Palmaria and Porto Venere. Genoese colonists beat them back to their ships but the incident caused the commune of Genoa such grave concern that it prepared forty galleys and dispatched a detachment of 2,000 troops expressly for the protection of its southernmost bastion.[117] The two communes eventually agreed to another truce in 1212, but their respective privateer communities continued to prosecute a pirate war against each other until 1217 when Cardinal Ugolino of Ostia (the future Pope Gregory IX) arranged a peace between them at Lerici in anticipation of the Fifth Crusade.[118]

Taking Sides: Guelphs and Ghibellines (1231–56)

It was only a matter of time before the two opposing Italian republics were drawn into the intractable conflict which had dominated the Italian peninsula since the mid-twelfth century: the Guelph–Ghibelline wars. The Guelphs were the papal party named after the Welf (*Guelfo* in Italian) dukes of Bavaria who supported the Pope against the Swabian House of Hohenstaufen, whose castle at Waiblingen (*Ghibellino* in Italian) gave the imperial party its name. The conflict had flared anew and taken on a particularly virulent quality when Pope Gregory IX excommunicated the Holy Roman Emperor Frederick II on the eve of the Sixth Crusade in 1227 and subsequently orchestrated an invasion of his southern Italian domains.[119] In the desperate struggle which followed, both parties of protagonists demanded that the various polities on the peninsula choose sides.

This was not particularly problematic for Pisa. The Tuscan commune had nearly always been a strong supporter of the emperor, especially after Frederick Barbarossa had ultimately favoured Pisa over Genoa in 1165 on the matter of Sardinia.[120] Genoa, on the other hand, was attempting to steer a more neutral course, if for no other reason than the city contained prominent factions representing both parties. Frederick himself forced the issue by declaring at the Diet of Ravenna in 1232 that the exclusion of Lombard officials from city government was a litmus test of loyalty. Inopportunely, Genoa had already selected Pagano de Petrasanta of Milan as its next podestà (chief magistrate). The Genoese petitioned for a dispensation from the policy, but Frederick denied it and ordered an embargo on Genoese trade goods.[121] The matter finally came to a head in 1237 while the emperor was campaigning in Lombardy: Genoa, again, chose a podestà from Milan. The emperor pointedly demanded Genoese fealty. The Genoese not only rejected the imperial ultimatum, but on 30 November 1238 entered into a formal agreement with Venice to support a papal invasion of Sicily.[122] Frederick, for his part, solidified his hold on Pisa by granting his son Enzo the title 'king of Sardinia', while recognizing the island as a protectorate of Pisa. Gregory IX, in turn, excommunicated him again.[123] Thus, the stage was set.

Not content with merely anathematizing Frederick, the Pope called for a general council in Rome in 1241 with the expressed intent of deposing him. The problem was getting the prelates, many of whom were from northern Europe, France in particular, to the Eternal City, given that the emperor controlled most of northern Italy. To resolve the problem, Gregory engaged the Genoese to provide ten galleys and ten *taride* to transport the prelates from Nice to Ostia. He later directed his legate, Cardinal Gregorio di Romagna, to arrange for at least ten more vessels for a total of about thirty. Frederick learned of the contract and directed his new admiral, Ansaldo de Mari, a Genoese with strong Ghibelline sympathies, to arm a squadron to intercept the papal convoy. He also ordered Pisa to prepare a fleet to support the action. The Pisans, for their part, warned the Genoese of their instructions, indicating that they would have no choice but to abrogate the peace between them if the Genoese persisted in transporting the prelates. The admonition was ignored.[124]

In March Genoa dispatched Iacopo Malocello with the thirty vessels to retrieve the French and English prelates from Nice. He then returned to Genoa where he reprovisioned and embarked more prelates from Lombardy. Ghibelline attacks had already begun on Genoese territory and several cities on the Riviera Ponente

(Western Riviera Ligure) under Genoese suzerainty had taken advantage of the situation to rebel. Worse yet, news came that an imperial fleet had marshalled at Civitavecchia.[125] Still the Genoese persevered. The papal convoy, now twenty-seven vessels, departed Genoa on 6 April and made its way down the Riviera Levante (Eastern Riviera Ligure), stopping briefly at Portofino and Levanto before arriving at Porto Venere. Once there, Iacopo Malocello was informed that Ansaldo de Mari had gathered a total of twenty-seven imperial galleys and forty Pisan warships. Malocello was therefore advised to wait for an additional eight galleys, one from each of Genoa's eight *compagnas* (mercantile companies), to reinforce his escort. He was also counselled to alter his route, sailing due west to pass north of Corsica and down its west coast to the Strait of Bonifacio between Corsica and Sardinia and thence to Ostia.[126] He rebuffed all of these recommendations and instead headed straight down the Tuscan littoral. It was a calamitous choice.

On 3 May 1241, at Giglio Island (55km or 34 miles southeast of Elba and less than 16km or 10 miles off the coast), the imperial fleet of twenty-seven galleys commanded by Andreolo de Mari, son of Ansaldo, and the Pisan armada of forty galleys captained by Ugolino Buzzacherino pounced upon the papal convoy. They had probably been lying in wait on the south side of the island. The Genoese fleet found itself swiftly surrounded by vastly superior forces. Moreover, most of its passengers had little training or aptitude for combat at sea. Of the twenty-seven Genoese ships only five escaped. Three were sunk and the rest were captured, along with around 4,000 prisoners.[127]

The Genoese spent the remainder of the conflict on the defensive. Almost all fleet actions occurred along the Ligurian littoral. Frederick ordered a general assault on Genoa soon after the victory at Giglio Island. Oberto Pallavicino, the imperial vicar for the Lunigiana, invaded the Riviera Levante and Marino da Eboli, the imperial vicar for Spoleto, attacked from the north, while the imperial fleet under Ansaldo de Mari hovered outside the harbour. The Genoese, however, managed to neutralize both land threats and deploy a fleet of eighty-three galleys to chase off the imperial fleet. The fighting then focused on rebellious Savona, which Genoa blockaded off and on until the end of the decade. Ansaldo de Mari continually challenged Genoese operations around Savona with an imperial fleet of around sixty galleys, mostly Pisan, but avoided pitched battle in a confrontation which proved prolonged and ultimately inconclusive. Maritime combat from then on devolved to raiding and skirmishing, but the Pisan and imperial fleets generally held sway in the northern Tyrrhenian and Ligurian Seas for the duration. Both Savona and Albenga remained in revolt until the death of Frederick II in December 1250. The fighting fizzled out thereafter. The Tuscan Guelph cities under Florence forced Pisa to sue for peace in 1254 and Genoa ceased hostilities after winning back Lerici in 1256. It failed, however, to expand its toehold on Sardinia.[128] The Genoese had understandably grown more concerned with defending their trading assets in the East. After all, the War of San Sabas between Genoese and Venetian merchants in Acre had just begun.

The Passing of a Great Maritime Power (1282–4)

Genoa and Pisa stood on the precipice of a final climactic confrontation in the war for the West, only to have the denouement delayed by distraction. Genoa, for one, had become locked in a bitter battle for the East with the Venetians. With the aid of a Pisan fleet, Venice's Lorenzo Tiepolo brought the War of San Sabas to a victorious close by crushing Rosso della Turco's Genoese armada outside Acre on 25 June 1258 (to be discussed in greater detail in Chapter 6).[129] The defeat, however, soon proved only a minor setback. In a remarkable stroke of propitious timing, Guglielmo Boccanegra, 'captain of the Genoese people', sent two envoys to negotiate an anti-Venetian pact with Michael VIII Paleologus of Nicaea in the spring of 1261. The emperor ratified the treaty on 28 April and on 25 July his forces regained Constantinople by subterfuge. Within a matter of three months the Genoese had supplanted the Venetians in the Eastern Empire. All the commercial privileges Venice had enjoyed since 1204 were now Genoese, thanks to the treaty with Michael Paleologus. In 1267 he would even award them a huge merchant quarter in Pera (present-day Galata) across the Golden Horn from the imperial city, enabling the Ligurian merchants to effectively control the lucrative Black Sea trade at Venice's expense.[130] *La Serenissima* did not accept the reversal of fortune with quiet resignation. The Venetians contested the Genoese at every turn, winning significant victories over their fleets at Settepozzi in 1263 and Trapani in 1266. Louis IX of France finally arranged a five-year truce between the two in 1269 in anticipation of the Eighth Crusade.[131]

Meanwhile, Pisa remained mired in the Guelph–Ghibelline conflict. When Frederick II's son Manfred usurped the throne of Sicily on 10 August 1258, Pisa quickly announced its support, reigniting Guelph opposition to the Ghibelline cause in Tuscany. The Pisans and their Sienese allies soon gained ascendancy over the Guelphs by routing the Florentines at the battle of Montiperti on 4 September 1260, but Lucca continued to resist until 1265. Worse still, in July 1263 Pope Urban IV backed Charles of Anjou, an ardent Guelph, for the crown of Sicily. The latter validated the title with victories over Manfred at Benevento on 26 February 1266 and over his nephew Conradin at Tagliacozzo on 23 August 1268. Pisa soon found its merchants excluded from the Kingdom of Sicily. Only the intervention of Charles' brother, King Louis, temporarily resolved the matter, for the sake of the Eighth Crusade.[132] Following the failure of Louis' expedition to Tunis, the attention of both Genoa and Pisa was diverted by Charles' aggrandizing actions in the north of Italy. He even invaded the Riviera Ligure in 1273, prompting open warfare with Genoa which lasted until 1276. The menacing Angevin distraction all but evaporated on Easter Monday (30 March) of 1282 in Palermo.[133] The revolt of the Sicilian Vespers absorbed all of Charles' attention and freed the two Italian maritime powers to, once more, focus their animosity on each other. And barely a month later the pretext was once again provided by the political intrigues of Corsica.

In May 1282 the Judge of Cinarca, a certain Sinucello, revolted against his Genoese overlords and attacked the Genoese colony of Bonifacio on the southern tip of Corsica. When repulsed, he fled to Pisa where he declared himself a vassal of the commune. Pisa was apparently receptive, viewing the submission as an opportunity to eject Genoa from its toehold on Corsica.[134] As a result, both republics mobilized. Genoa seemed particularly intent on settling the rivalry once and for all. It appointed a sixteen-member war council called the *Credenza* which immediately set about amassing a fleet of 120 galleys. To that end, it forbade the departure of any merchant vessel after 1 August.[135] By the middle of that month the *Credenza* was able to dispatch twelve galleys belonging to the commune and another twenty-three requisitioned *ad apodixas* (for a limited period of time) from private sources along with twelve *panfili* (smaller light scouting galleys) to Porto Pisano under the command of Niccolino Spinola. They were quickly greeted by thirty-two Pisan galleys commanded by Guicello dei Sismondi and eventually forced to withdraw to Porto Venere. Both sides spent the remainder of the year girding themselves for all-out war.[136]

There were no major engagements the following year, essentially because the Pisans adopted the sensible strategy of avoiding direct confrontations, seeking instead to harry Genoese merchant shipping in the waters around Sardinia, Corsica and Provence. This proved a wise plan of action, since Genoa was able to balloon its war fleet to 199 galleys during the course of 1283 and crew them by conscripting every available able-bodied man on the Riviera Ligure. Thus the Genoese plan of attack was to take the war directly to the Pisans and draw them into battle.[137] They began the year by raiding the Tuscan island of Elba on 3 February and seizing 15,000 pounds' worth of silver.[138] And later, at Piombino, they trapped a Pisan squadron which had barricaded itself behind a line of submerged obstacles and sunken ships. Most of the Pisan vessels made their escape to Porto Pisano when the Genoese were forced to leave station to replenish their water supplies.[139]

Perhaps weary of the toll on its commerce and repeated raids on its territory, Pisa assumed a more aggressive, less cautious stance in 1284. Early in the year the Genoese besieged both Sassari and Porto Torres on Sardinia. They also waylaid a Pisan merchant fleet returning from the East and again blockaded Porto Pisano. Finally, the exasperated Pisan podestà Alberto Morosini allowed himself to be lured out of Porto Pisano on 6 August with nearly the entire Pisan war fleet – seventy-two galleys – to confront the Genoese *Capitano del Popolo* ('Captain of the People') Oberto Doria, who used superior numbers and tactics to decimate Pisan naval capability forever. The course of the battle is detailed in a separate section at the end of the chapter, but it suffices here to point out that Pisa lost more than half its fleet that day. More critically, the numbers of Pisans dead or captured reached almost 15,000. New ships could be built, but these were men that the commune simply did not have the *contado* (surrounding countryside) under its control to replace.[140]

Genoa, on the other hand, could draw amply from the maritime communities which dotted the Ligurian coast to cover its moderate losses. The Riviera Levante alone contributed around 1,500 oarsmen to the Genoese fleet of sixty-five galleys which Oberto Spinola led into Porto Pisano unopposed in 1285 to destroy one of its four towers. Pisa soldiered on until 1288, when it was finally forced to sue for peace.[141] Unhappy with Pisa's adherence to the terms of the subsequent accord, the Genoese returned to Porto Pisano again in 1290 and obliterated the remaining three towers before departing with the harbour chain.[142] Alluvial deposits and silt from the Arno ultimately finished what the Genoese had started. Pisa's status as a premier maritime power in the West was at an end. It would slowly recede into the backwater of history, subordinate even within Tuscany to the growing influence of Florence. In the poetic prose of William Heywood, 'Her sea-power withered away as swiftly and inevitably as a tree withers when its roots are severed.'[143]

* * *

Exemplary Engagement: The Battle of Meloria (August 1284)

Until the spring of 1284 the course of the second Genoese–Pisan war over Corsica consisted largely of Genoa trying to provoke a pivotal encounter and Pisa attempting to avoid one. That all changed in April. Count Donoratico Fazio, the new commanding general for the Pisans in Sardinia, was en route by ship to his post at Castel di Castro in Cagliari when a sudden spring storm separated him from his escort of around twenty-five galleys. The next morning, near the islet of Tavolara off the northeast coast of Sardinia, he found himself enveloped by a Genoese merchant convoy captained by such Ligurian luminaries as Lamba Doria and Benedetto Zaccaria. Accompanying the convoy was a flotilla of about seventeen galleys under Enrico de Mari. This chance convention was soon joined by the Pisan escort commanded by Guido Iacia and Giovanni Cavarca. A fierce fight ensued. Despite roughly equal numbers, the Pisans, apparently fatigued from searching for Fazio's ship during the night, were heavily defeated. Only a handful of Pisan vessels escaped.[144]

The trouncing at Tavolara put Pisa at a serious disadvantage. It no longer possessed the ships and personnel to protect its commercial interests on Corsica and Sardinia. Genoese galleys ravaged Pisan shipping at will in the waters around the two islands and along the Tuscan coast, costing the Pisans still more ships and men. It was a downward spiral that the Pisan podestà Alberto Morosini was desperate to stop and that the Genoese *Capitano del Popolo* Oberto Doria was keen to accelerate. Accordingly, the latter dispatched Benedetto Zaccaria with a squadron of thirty war galleys *ad apodixas* (for a limited deployment) at the end of April to roam the Tuscan archipelago. When Zaccaria received orders in early July to head to Porto Torres on the north shore of Sardinia to aid in the siege of Sassari, Morosini saw his chance to change the course of the war and take the fight to Genoa.[145]

The Pisan podestà ordered the arming of all available galleys as expeditiously as possible. It was all to have been done in secret, but each commune was rife with the spies of the other, so it was impossible to complete such an evolution without the enemy learning of it, especially for an armada of seventy-two galleys.[146] The recruitment of several thousand mariners to man such a fleet alone would have alerted the Genoese. According to one source, all men between the ages of twenty and sixty were required to serve on these ships.[147] Suspecting the worst, Oberto Doria recalled Zaccaria from Sardinia. Morosini must also have had excellent intelligence, because as soon as he became aware of the recall he prepared to set sail with his co-commander Ugolino della Gherardesca. Adverse winds held the fleet at the mouth of the Arno for a few days, but, once they had abated, the armada headed northwest, though not directly to Genoa. Instead, Morosini traced a course towards Albenga (about 70km or 43 miles to the west) with the apparent intention of cutting Zaccaria off.[148]

Oberto Doria did not, however, wait quietly for events to unfold. He hastily equipped all available vessels in port, which amounted to fifty-eight galleys and eight *panfili*. Thus, when Morosini and Gherardesca appeared west of Genoa on 31 July, Doria was able to emerge from the harbour and form a battle line. The latter was evidently hoping that Zaccaria would arrive in time to trap the Pisans between them. And, indeed, Zaccaria came that same day, but, apparently failing to grasp the situation, he slipped into port with his thirty galleys instead of engaging Morosini from the rear. Oberto Doria, now possessing superior forces, attempted to salvage the situation with a ruse. He moved his entire combined armada from Genoa during the night to Sturla, a small cove a few kilometres to the southeast, in the hope of tricking Morosini into attacking the harbour. But the Pisan podestà, his stratagem having nearly ended in disaster, departed the area on the morning of 1 August heading west along the Ligurian coast. Fearing that Morosini intended to raid the Riviera Ponente, Doria followed.[149]

At Porto Maurizio Doria learned that Morosini had indeed been there, but had sailed southeast directly for Capo Corso on the northern tip of Corsica. Doria reached the Corsican headland on 5 August, only to discover he had missed Morosini by just a few hours. The Pisans had replenished their water supplies and made for home. Doria hurried on without delay. He appeared outside Porto Pisano on the afternoon of 6 August, before the Pisan fleet could seek the shelter of the Arno. Utterly determined to force a fight which would bring the conflict to a close, the Genoese *Capitano del Popolo* devised a strategy to inveigle Morosini out of the well protected Porto Pisano.[150]

Located amongst littoral shallows on a rocky span of shoreline just south of the Arno's estuary, the port was protected by sandbars and four fortified towers, two of which had a heavy harbour chain stretched between them barring the entrance.[151] Gaining access would have been difficult, manoeuvring once inside nearly impossible. Thus Doria realized that he had to entice Morosini into battle on the open sea and the only way to do that was to convince the Pisan podestà that he enjoyed numerical superiority. Accordingly, Doria divided his fleet into two squadrons. He retained command of the main body (sixty-three galleys and eight *panfili*), arranging them in a single crescent-shaped line with his flagship at the convex centre. On either side were the ships of Genoa's eight *compagnas* (mercantile companies): Porta, Soziglia, Porta Nuova and Borgo to the left, and Castello, Piazza Lungo, Macagnana and San Lorenzo to the right. Each of these divisions had its own *prontontino* ('vice commander') responsible directly to Doria. The second squadron, Zaccaria's thirty galleys, he held in reserve at some distance behind the main body in a parallel line. Knowing the Pisans would count sails to determine the number of opposing warships, Doria ordered those on his own galleys unfurled while he had Zaccaria strike the sails on his ships so that, at a distance, they might be taken for skiffs or other such small boats.[152]

Morosini took the bait. Late in the afternoon, with the sun in his eyes, he brought his galleys out of the port and formed them up for battle in a single line facing the Genoese main body, which was now abreast of the islet of Meloria (about 5km or 3 miles due west from the modern port of Livorno). Morosini ordered his line to advance and his men rowed robustly ahead. Doria did the same. As the two fleets closed, Morosini must have realized his mistake, but it was too late. The Pisans were committed. To have attempted a retreat at that point would have resulted in disorderly flight and rout. So on they came. The engagement opened with the normal exchange of various sorts of projectiles: rods, bolts, stones and even canisters of hot oil, liquid soap or lye launched from crossbows, mangonels and other petraries.[153]

Once engaged, each side seemed to have its own peculiar set of combat techniques. The 'Templar of Tyre', a secretary and possibly also a knight of Templar Master William of Beaujeu, relayed eyewitness accounts of a sort of whirling iron windlass affixed with long blades, mounted on the prows of the Pisan ships to prevent boarding. He also noted, 'The Pisans were heavily laden with arms [armour], and it was very hot, so that they sweated so much that they became thoroughly soaked.' The Genoese, on the other hand, had spurned heavy armour in favour of agility and endurance. Furthermore, the Cypriot-based chronicler depicted the Pisan ships as being somewhat ponderous: 'The Pisans had their galleys weighed down with rings of defensive iron-work.'[154] He was probably referring to the common practice of mounting shields on the gunnels for extra protection, but the Pisans may have done so to excess, rendering their vessels less manoeuvrable.

Precisely how the battle unfolded is unknown, but it seems probable that Zaccaria, in accordance with previous instructions, swung his ships around one of the Pisan wings in an enveloping manoeuvre (probably the north flank, since Meloria and its shallows were just to the south). In any case, Zaccaria's galley ended up at the stern of Morosini's flagship while it was engaged with Doria's. (*See* Map 8.) Zaccaria had supposedly coupled his ship to another Genoese galley by the use of a chain from one mast to the other, then commanded the two warships to attack Morosini's galley from the rear, one on each side. As the chain raked across the poop, it severed the flagstaff holding the red standard of Pisa.[155] The battle had been bitterly fought up to that moment, but, once Morosini's standard fell, Pisan resistance began to collapse. Seeing his podestà captured, Ugolino Gherardesca took the only sensible course of action: disengage and abscond behind the harbour chain of Porto Pisano with as many vessels as possible – perhaps a couple of dozen.[156]

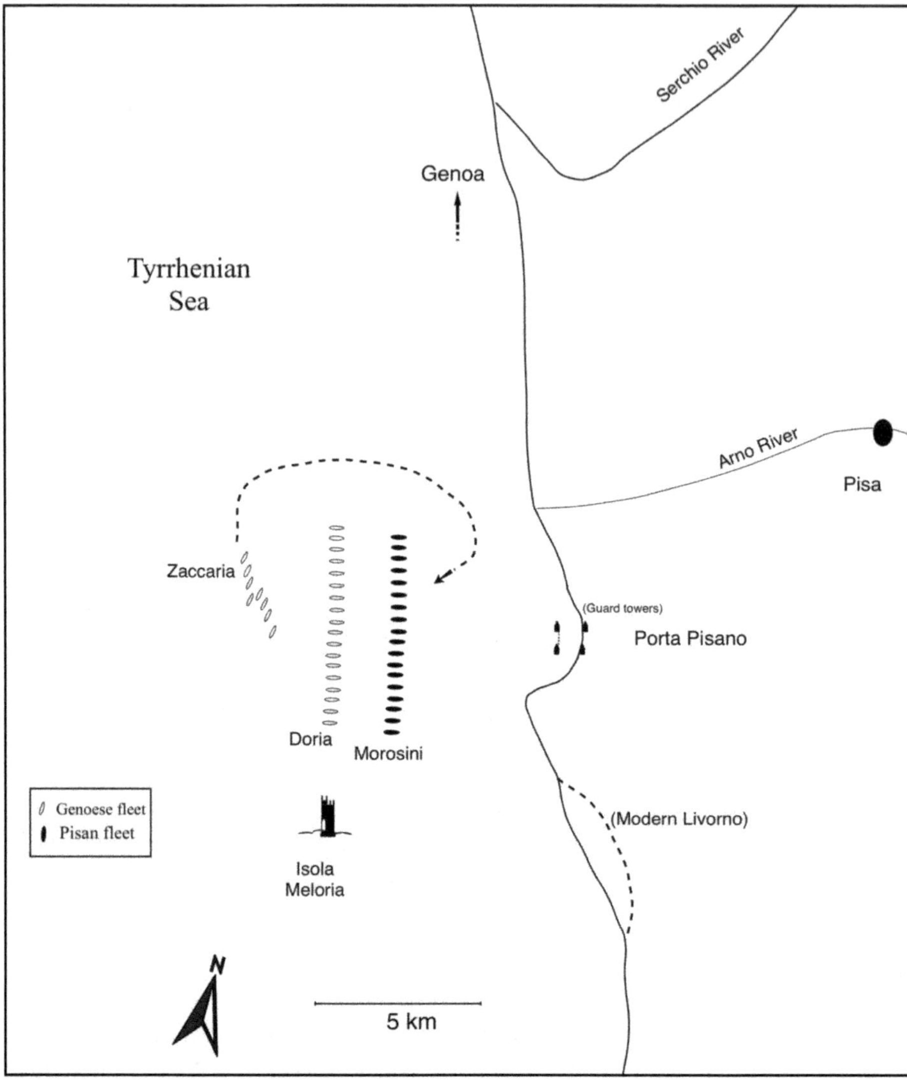

Map 8. Battle of Meloria in 1284. (*Kristy Stanton*)

Genoese losses were characterized as moderate, but the Pisan toll was staggering. 'Of the Pisans,' wrote the Genoese chronicler Iacopo Doria, 'so much slaughter had been made that the sea had been rendered red, covered everywhere with shields, oars and the bodies of the dead.'[157] By Genoese estimates, twenty-nine Pisan ships had been seized and seven sunk. The rest either escaped or ran aground in the attempt. The detriment in manpower was far more dire. Over 5,000 were said to have been killed, while the *Annals Ianuenses* ('Genoese Annals') gave the curiously exact figure of 9,272 Pisan prisoners.[158] The 'Templar of Tyre' estimated the loss was as high as 22,000 men-at-arms.[159] Although this was almost certainly an exaggeration, it is clear that the Tuscan maritime power had suffered a blow that it could ill afford to sustain. Many of these men represented the flower of Pisan nobility. The contemporary north Italian chronicler Salimbene de Adam lamented, 'Also in that year after the battle [Meloria] between the Pisans and the Genoans, many Pisan women – beautiful, noble, rich and powerful ladies – went in groups of thirty and forty, walking on foot from Pisa to Genoa in order to inquire about and to visit captives.'[160] These were men Pisa simply could not replace. Hemmed in by the power of Lucca and Florence, the commune did not control a large enough *cantado* (surrounding countryside) to recruit sufficient men to fill the ships it needed to compete with Genoa, which could draw from all the Ligurian maritime cities of both the Riviera Ponente and the Riviera Levante.[161]

Oberto Doria must certainly have been aware of the Pisan predicament. After the battle he had intended to deliver a *coup de grâce* by destroying the Porto Pisano, but most of his galley crews, weary of battle, withdrew of their own accord to Porto Venere and he had little option but to follow.[162] What he did instead was far more debilitating. He refused to ransom any of the Pisan prisoners. When Marco Polo was captured at the Battle of Curzola in 1298 and imprisoned in Genoa, Rustichello da Pisa, the man who would help him pen his autobiography, had already been there for fourteen years. He was believed to have been captured at Meloria.[163]

The loss of manpower at Meloria was the slow-bleeding wound that Pisa could not staunch. The republic slogged gamely on after the defeat under the able leadership of Ugolino Gherardesca, but its power at sea was forever broken, its fate sealed by the silting of the very river that had been its path to past greatness.[164]

CHAPTER 5

The War of the Sicilian Vespers: Angevin versus Aragonese Sea Power

On Easter Monday, 30 March 1282, just prior to evening prayers (Vespers) at the church of Santo Spirito in Palermo, some inebriated Angevin soldiers accosted a young Sicilian noblewoman. Her husband and a crowd of onlookers took violent exception, slaying the assailants and igniting a general insurrection against the rule of Charles of Anjou which swiftly engulfed the entire island.[1] Within a few weeks nearly every man, woman and child of French descent on Sicily had been slaughtered. The resulting War of the Sicilian Vespers would endure for the next twenty years and would involve almost every part of the Mediterranean in some way. In a conflict characterized by an ever-changing cast of characters, competing objectives and shifting conditions, there were only two discernible constants from a military standpoint: first, that control of Sicily stood at its core, meaning it was fought mostly at sea; and secondly that, in combat at sea, whichever side enjoyed the services of Roger of Lauria was invariably victorious.

Smouldering Embers: Charles of Anjou Asserts Control of Sicily (1250–82)

In truth, the deadly incident at the Santo Spirito in Palermo did not cause the war. It was only the spark. The combustible forces at the core of the conflagration – papal power politics, Angevin and Aragonese ambition and a seething Sicilian desire for self-determination – had been collecting for some time. It all actually began on 13 December 1250 when Emperor Frederick II died of dysentery at the Castel Fiorentino of Torremaggiore in Apulia.[2] His son Conrad IV of Germany was in line to succeed him, but Pope Innocent IV refused to accept the continued rule of the Hohenstaufen family, which the papacy considered 'a brood of vipers'. Doing so would have only perpetuated what it regarded as the imperial encirclement of the Papal States (roughly modern Lazio, Marche, Umbria and Romagna). Thus, the Pope sought an acceptable suitor for the Kingdom of Sicily who would not seek to control the lands to the north of Rome as well as those to the south. He first offered the crown in 1252 to Edmund Crouchback, Earl of Lancaster and the son of King Henry III of England, but the asking price was too high for the English barons to bear. In any event, Conrad IV died unexpectedly of malaria at Lavello on 21 May 1254, leaving the throne temporarily vacant since his son and successor, Conradin ('Little Conrad'), was only two at the time.[3] So Sicilian nobles took matters into their own hands. That same year they elected Frederick's bastard son Manfred as their new monarch. And the latter, seizing on the rumour of Conradin's untimely demise, had himself crowned king of Sicily in Palermo on 10 August 1258.[4]

The papacy was, of course, disinclined to acquiesce to this with equanimity. Innocent IV's successor, Alexander IV, excommunicated Manfred. And Urban IV, who followed in Alexander's footsteps in 1261, renewed in earnest the search for a suitable replacement. Born in Troyes as Jacques Pantaléon, Urban's sympathies were assuredly French, so the choice eventually fell upon Charles of Anjou, the powerful brother of King Louis IX of France. He appeared ideal for the job: not only was he count of Anjou and Maine, but in 1246 he had also obtained Provence by marriage to Beatrice of Provence. This made him wealthy enough to pay the 10,000 ounces in gold demanded by the Holy See annually for the Sicilian crown and, in theory, sufficiently puissant without being tempted to aggrandize more power in northern Italy – also a papal stipulation. In this latter regard the Pope woefully underestimated Charles, but nonetheless the two parties formally ratified the agreement in July 1263.[5]

Urban's successor, Pope Clement IV, subsequently proclaimed Charles as king of Sicily in Rome on 23 May 1265 and very shortly thereafter the latter embarked upon his quest to make the proclamation a reality. Charles met Manfred on the field of battle near Benevento on 26 February the following year and prevailed after a bloody fight in which the Hohenstaufen monarch lost his life, along with those of most of his knights.[6] But by then Manfred had already unwittingly sown the seeds of his vengeance. In June 1262 he had married his daughter Constance to Crown Prince Peter of Aragon, the man who, as King Peter III, would become Charles' nemesis. Worse yet, among the dead in Manfred's knightly entourage was the father of Roger of Lauria, the incomparable future admiral of the Aragonese fleet. Prior to the battle Roger had emigrated to Barcelona with his mother Donna Bella, who was a lady-in-waiting to Constance of Hohenstaufen, the future Queen Consort of Aragon.[7] In victory, Charles had ironically created the instrument of his own destruction or, at the very least, the frustration of his aspirations of empire.

Charles had one last hurdle to clear before he could claim the crown of Sicily outright. Conrad IV's son Conradin had come of age in 1268 and ventured into Italy from southern Germany to take the throne he believed was rightfully his. Those of the realm's nobles who had survived the defeat at Benevento flocked to him, along with the Ghibellines of northern Italy. Charles engaged them at Tagliacozzo in the Abruzzi northeast of Rome on 23 August 1268 and won the day after another bitterly contested confrontation. He had Conradin beheaded in the aftermath, winning him no friends amongst his new subjects. He then proceeded to impose the same ruthlessly efficient Angevin administration that he had implemented in Provence, which had triggered bloody rebellions in 1251 and 1263.[8] In fact, aggressive Angevin tax-collectors had already engendered a full revolt, eagerly abetted by Conradin's agents, on the island of Sicily in the summer of 1267.[9] By the time Charles had dealt with Conradin, only Palermo and Messina remained to him. The insurgency was not fully quelled until the spring of 1270, at which time Charles inflicted a draconian oppression on the populace. The property of all who had taken up arms against him was confiscated.[10] Steven Runciman summed up the end result:

> These repressive measures were all the more intolerable to the easy-going Italians because they were enforced with meticulous care and because the King's agents were almost all of them Frenchmen. They were remarkably effective. Order was soon restored throughout the Kingdom, even in Sicily. But they left a legacy of bitter hatred in the island.[11]

Charles compounded the alienation of his Sicilian subjects by maintaining Naples as the capital of the kingdom instead of Palermo and by using tax revenues from the realm to fuel his ambition of creating a Mediterranean empire which would bring them little benefit. And Charles' grand designs were no secret. As early as 1267 he had claimed Sardinia for his son Philip and then pressured Guelph loyalists in Sassari into having Philip declared king in 1269.[12] There were even rumours that he had advised his brother, King Louis, to divert the Eighth Crusade to Tunis in 1270 so that he could extort a renewal of Hafsid tribute to the Kingdom of Sicily.[13] He allied himself with the Despot of Epiros that same year and seized Durazzo the next, giving him the rationale to proclaim himself 'king of Albania' in 1272.[14] In 1273 he and his Guelph allies in northern Italy invaded the Ligure Levante in open warfare with Genoa which lasted until 1276.[15] In 1274 he purchased the crown of Jerusalem from Maria of Antioch and, as of 1277, called himself 'king of Jerusalem'.[16] Most significantly of all, in July 1281 he reached an accord with Venice and Martin IV, another French Pope, to begin a crusade against Constantinople in April of the following year.[17]

It would never happen. Instead of weighing anchor for Byzantium, the impressive war fleet (fifty to sixty galleys and about thirty support vessels) that Charles had so painstakingly gathered at the royal arsenal in Messina was either burned to the waterline or confiscated when the city fell to Sicilian rebels on 29 April 1282. The War of the Sicilian Vespers had begun.[18]

The Eruption: Peter of Aragon Assumes Suzerainty over Sicily (1282)

The uprising stemming from events at the Santo Spirito in Palermo on Easter Monday probably caught Peter of Aragon as much by surprise as it had Charles of Anjou, but that does not mean he was unprepared for the possibility. After all, as was mentioned earlier, his wife was Constance of Hohenstaufen, whose father, King Manfred, was slain by Charles' forces at Benevento. And on that basis Peter had already voiced his claim to the crown of Sicily as early as 1268. Moreover, Constance was not Peter's only connection to the Hohenstaufen court in Palermo. Giovanni da Procida, who had been doctor to Frederick II and Manfred's chancellor for Sicily, had sought refuge in Barcelona by 1275 and had most certainly won Peter's ear. When Peter became king upon the death of James I in 1276, he chose Giovanni da Procida as his chancellor and put him in charge of Aragon's foreign policy.[19] So there can be little doubt that Peter was open to any opportunity that might manifest itself with regard to the Kingdom of Sicily.

In fact, when the Vespers revolt broke out Peter was assembling a considerable armada – about 150 ships – at Tortosa, ostensibly in preparation for a crusade against the Hafsids of the Maghreb, but timing and geography seem to suggest that he was actually preparing to take advantage of Charles' anticipated departure for Constantinople.[20] King Louis IX's successor, Philip III of France, certainly suspected that was the purpose. The Capetian monarch sent a message to Peter at Port Fangos near Tortosa, threatening the king of Aragon with war if he should direct his fleet against Philip's Uncle Charles in Sicily.[21] When Peter set sail from Port Fangos on 3 June 1282, he did indeed head for the Maghreb after a brief stop in Minorca. His professed intention was to aid the beleaguered ruler of Constantine in the northeast of present-day Algeria, and in point of fact he anchored his fleet at Collo, around 63km or 39 miles north of Constantine.[22] But the chronicles described a desultory, muddled campaign that appeared to go nowhere.[23] Peter was still in Collo when two *llenys* (small, lightly armed galleys about 21.75m/71ft 4in long by 5.18m/17ft wide with forty to eighty oars) arrived in early August with a deputation from Palermo, beseeching him to accept the crown of Sicily.[24]

This was apparently just what Peter had been awaiting. He sailed his entire fleet from Collo to Trapani on 31 August and was proclaimed king of Sicily in Palermo four days later.[25] He had not been the Sicilians' first choice. They had initially sought papal sanction of their right to govern themselves as independent communes much like the city republics of northern Italy, but Pope Martin IV, prior to his election to the Holy See in 1281, had been Simon de Brie – a French prelate responsible for preaching a crusade against Manfred and collecting tithes on behalf of Charles of Anjou.[26] Unsurprisingly, he instead announced his firm support of Charles' right to rule Sicily. At that point the Sicilians had no option. They desperately needed powerful support. Charles had already crossed the Strait on 25 July with an enormous fleet (80 to 160 galleys, depending on the source, plus transport vessels), which he had quickly cobbled together from Calabria, Naples, Provence, Genoa and Pisa in a determined effort to recapture Messina.[27] He had been unsuccessful to date, but the Sicilians knew that it was only a matter of time. They also knew that Peter's armada was conveniently nearby.

The decision paid dividends almost immediately. On 17 September, when Charles learned of Peter's landing on the island, he began an evacuation of his forces from around Messina. But the evacuation was too slow. In late September an advance element of the Aragonese army reached Messina just as the Angevin rear-guard was embarking for Reggio.[28] It was composed of Almugavars, perhaps the finest, most feared light infantry in thirteenth-century Europe. Their name was doubtless derived from the Arabic word *almogàuar*, meaning 'devastator', because they regularly raided 'Saracen' lands. These battle-hardened frontiersmen from the Mudejar (Spanish Muslim) border regions of Aragon and Castile wore only leather tunics, leggings and sandals for protection and carried nothing but a lance, a knife and two javelins as weapons. They relied on speed, agility and toughness to defeat their adversaries, something they rarely failed to do.[29] They were also utterly fearless. Ramon Muntaner, a contemporary Catalan soldier and chronicler, told of an incident in which a hundred Almugavars countered a French cavalry charge by breaking their lances in half and running amongst the horses, gutting them so that they could easily dispatch the dismounted knights.[30] Carrying few provisions and living off the land, the Almugavars moved swiftly and often struck without warning. Accordingly, Peter sent 2,000 of them ahead in the hope of catching the Angevins by surprise. They did. 'Though it is a six days' march to Palermo, they reached it in three,' recorded Muntaner.[31] Dashing in amongst the Frenchmen as they boarded their vessels, the Almugavars managed to massacre at least 500 knights before they could embark.[32] What they did to the Angevin fleet was far more catastrophic, Muntaner contending that 'more than a hundred and fifty galleys and *terides*' were set on fire.[33]

Though this was an obvious embellishment, there can be little doubt that the Angevin armada suffered significant losses. These would be compounded. King Peter himself arrived in Messina on 2 October.[34] Lawrence Mott, an authority on the war, estimates that at the time Charles retained a fleet of twenty-two to twenty-four galleys at Reggio along with thirty to forty supply ships and support vessels.[35] Peter resolved to divest his Angevin adversary of the services of even these, so he dispatched a squadron of fourteen to twenty-two galleys (depending on the source) under Pedro de Queralt and Ramon de Cortada to interdict the remainder of Charles' fleet as it tried to transit the Strait northwards. The Angevin flotilla made it through on its second attempt on 14 October, but the Aragonese squadron caught up with it at Nicotera and dealt Charles' naval capability another devastating defeat. The Angevin fleet lacked unity of command. It included Genoese and Pisan elements which were essentially mercenary with no vested interest in the outcome of the fighting. These attempted to flee at the approach of the Aragonese fleet. There was apparently no thought of mutual support. Thus, although inferior in number, the Aragonese galleys rounded up almost all of the opposing galleys (about twenty-two) and a goodly number of the support vessels.[36]

In a matter of mere months Angevin naval capability had been decimated. Peter took immediate advantage, launching a series of raids across the Strait aimed at Reggio. The most spectacular of these was in January 1283, when Jaime Perez, the king's son and admiral of the fleet, ferried some 2,000 Almugavars in ten galleys from Messina at night to attack the Angevin arsenal at Catona on the outskirts of Reggio. They took the entire garrison by surprise and slaughtered its soldiers, including their commander, Peter I of Alençon, Charles' nephew.[37] Reggio itself finally fell to the Aragonese on 14 February.[38] Peter did not possess the manpower to advance further, but Angevin ally Pope Martin IV validated his victories by excommunicating him. Nevertheless, the king of Aragon remained unfazed and unrepentant.[39] Charles of Anjou had indeed become embroiled in a major military campaign. It was not, however, the one he had envisioned.

Roger of Lauria takes Command of the Seas in the Name of Aragon (1283)

As bad as the situation at sea had become for Charles of Anjou, it was about to get a whole lot worse. His initial reaction to the above-described reverses and the butchery of his nephew was to challenge Peter of Aragon to a duel. The latter picked up the proverbial gauntlet and the two antagonists agreed to meet at

Bordeaux on 1 June 1283 with a hundred knights each, but it was all a sideshow.[40] Neither man had any real intention of deciding their differences in the lists. They cleverly avoided each other while taking more pragmatic measures. Charles, having learned the lesson of Nicotera – that he could not rely on foreign naval support, directed his seneschal in Provence to assemble a flotilla of twenty galleys manned entirely by Frenchmen. As count, he had established Marseilles as a naval base as early as 1257 with a set of administrative reforms known as the *Chapitres de Paix*. As a result, the city had no difficulty in building such a fleet.[41]

The flotilla which Charles caused to be constructed in Provence was probably composed of the same sort of vessels he had assembled for his ill-fated campaign to conquer Constantinople. (*See* Fig. 3.) These were mostly *galeas* – light bireme galleys patterned after a certain 'Red Galley of Provence' specified in a directive issued from Brindisi on 18 February 1275.[42] The document, preserved in the royal *Angevin Registers* for the Kingdom of Naples, delineated precise dimensions: 39.55m (129ft 9in) in overall length, 4.61m (15ft 1in) in beam and 2.04m (6ft 8in) in depth from keel to gunnel amidships. It was to sport a spur at the bow 6.6m (21ft 8in) long and two steering sweeps at the stern (although the sternpost rudder was also in use at this time). Propulsion was provided either by a large lateen sail unfurled from a mast stepped slightly forwards, along with a smaller sail on a shorter mast amidships, or, most often, by 108 oars rowed *alla sensile* fashion from twenty-seven angled thwarts (benches) per side (i.e., two oarsmen per bench).[43] These mandated measurements probably governed the construction of Angevin war galleys throughout much of the war. Another directive dispensed from Brindisi on 10 November 1278 detailed exactly the same specifications.[44] And, if the *Angevin Registers* are any guide, these vessels were well

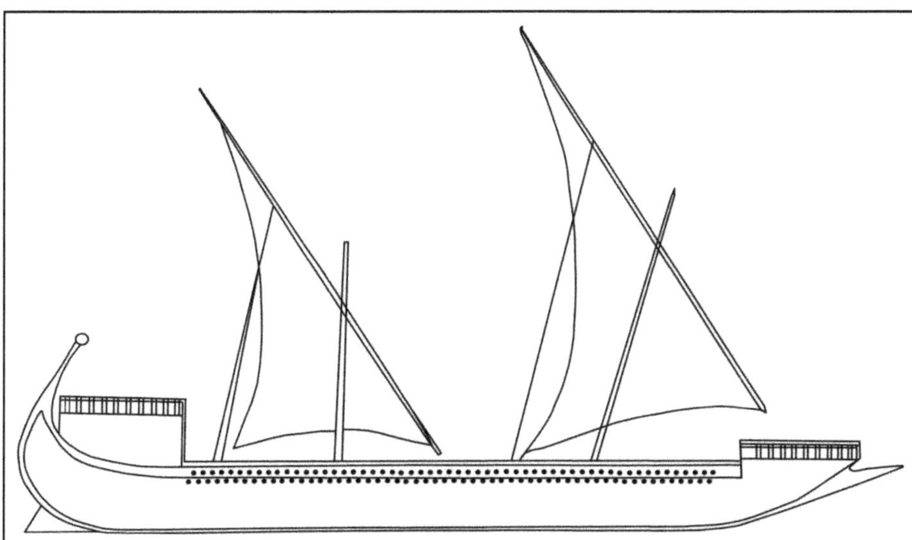

Figure 3. Angevin bireme galley of the late thirteenth century. (*Kristy Stanton*)

armed. In addition to a long sword and a short sword carried by each crewman, there were 35 crossbows, 40 bucklers (small shields), 200 lances, 10 halberds, in excess of 100 pots of quick lime or flammable fluid and an assortment of boarding implements like grapnels, axes and picks.[45]

Although Charles could not have known it at the time, what Peter did in the interim would more than nullify his efforts: on 20 April the king of Aragon appointed Roger of Lauria to replace his own son as Admiral of the Crown of Aragon, Catalonia, Valencia and Sicily.[46] It was a brilliant choice. Peter had already recognized Roger's command capability in October 1278 by naming him governor of Valencia. Lauria had even captained vessels at sea as part of his duties. Furthermore, he was more likely to gain the loyalty of Peter's new south Italian subjects, since he had been born at Scalea in Calabria (*c.*1250). Roger also had a visceral investment in the war. He had been raised in the Hohenstaufen court of King Manfred and, as was mentioned earlier, his father died at the hands of the Angevins at the Battle of Benevento in 1266. Thus he harboured a singular antipathy for the count of Anjou.[47] He would not have to wait long for his first taste of vengeance. By early May 1283 – not a month after his appointment as admiral of the Catalan–Aragonese fleet – the recently assembled Angevin squadron of twenty galleys was on its way south under the command of the Provençal admirals Bartholomé Bonvin and Guillaume de Cornut.[48] Roger was in Sicily, preparing a reception with his own fleet.

The ships Roger commanded were, doubtless, light galleys quite similar to the newly built Angevin vessels, except that they appear to have been heavier and more stoutly constructed. **(Pl. 14)** Muntaner described them in his chronicle as being '*en taula*', meaning they were equipped with fortified, raised platforms. Mott's analysis concluded that these parapeted forecastles and poops were integral to the structure of the ships. This probably made the vessels heavier and a bit more ponderous, but better able to fend off missile barrages while giving crossbowmen a higher firing position. In other words, Catalan shipwrights sacrificed speed and manoeuvrability to provide the vessel's crossbowmen and marines with extra protection.[49] To compensate, they installed space for a *terçol* (*tersol* in Catalan), a third oar per thwart (there were usually only two oarsmen per bench), which could be manned by an available crewman or marine for additional propulsion when closing or fleeing.[50] Moreover, the shipbuilding capability of Barcelona was certainly comparable to that of Marseilles. Its arsenal, built in the mid-thirteenth century and still standing, could accommodate perhaps as many twenty-five galleys in eight covered sheds 150m (492ft) long, 8.4m (27ft 7in) wide and 9m (29ft 6in) high.[51]

The key to Catalan naval superiority was not ship construction, however, but crew composition. When King Peter commissioned Roger, he had mandated:

> Admiral, fit out at once twenty-five galleys, and man them so that each has a Catalan boatswain and one Latin, and four Catalan steersmen and four Latin; and the same for the sailors in the fore-part of the ship, and the rowers shall all be Latins, and the crossbowmen all Catalans. And We wish that,

> henceforth, all fleets you fit out shall be thus ordained and that you, on no account, alter this.[52]

The critical command here was that all crossbowmen should be Catalans. The *balistarii catalani* ('Catalan crossbowmen') were reputed to be the best in Christendom. **(Pl. 15)** Muntaner explained why in no uncertain terms:

> Catalans do not consider anyone a crossbowman unless he knows how to make everything, from beginning to end, of what pertains to a crossbow. And so he carries all his tools in a box, and it is as if he had a workshop. And no other people do this, but the Catalans learn it at their mothers' breasts, and the other people of the world do not. Wherefore the Catalans are the most superior crossbowmen of the world.[53]

And ships' masters knew enough to leave them alone to hone their skills, for the *balistarii* were apparently deadly accurate. 'They did not discharge a shot without killing or disabling the man they attacked,' observed Muntaner darkly.[54] Moreover, the *balistarii* were well equipped. Each possessed an iron cap, a cuirass and a short sword in addition to their primary weapons: one two-foot cocking crossbow and a one-foot cocking crossbow, along with 300 bolts for each.[55] As for the Almugavars, Roger apparently required no comparable guidance on the wisdom of using the vaunted infantrymen as marines. Their agility on the deck of a ship in hand-to-hand combat would have been lethal in the extreme.

Such advantages in ship architecture and crew composition would soon prove their worth. When Bonvin and Cornut arrived in Naples sometime in May, Charles of Salerno, the eldest son of Charles of Anjou, ordered them to relieve the Angevin garrison of the *Castrum Maris* ('Castle of the Sea') in the Grand Harbour of Malta. Roger discovered their plans and surprised them there on 8 June with a similar-sized squadron, handing them a disastrous defeat.[56] The feared *balistarii catalani*, whom the above-described Aragonese ship adaptations were designed to protect, were grimly decisive.[57] Less than a third of the Provençal squadron survived the encounter and over 4,000 irreplaceable crewmen were lost. For Lauria, it was a signature victory which would set the tone for the remainder of the war at sea.[58] As such, it is the subject of the special section scrutinizing an exemplary engagement of the war.

The Battle of Castellammare: Angevin Resurgence at Sea Averted (1284)

Angevin naval capability had been seriously compromised at Malta, but not crippled. Both Charles of Anjou and his son Charles of Salerno reacted with vigour to the setback at Nicotera and the débâcle at Malta. After the abortive duel at Bordeaux, Charles senior proceeded to Provence to raise another fleet. The prince of Salerno, whom Charles had made regent for the kingdom in his absence, did the same in the *Mezzogiorno* (southern Italy). By the spring of 1284 they had amassed fleets that, if allowed to combine into a single armada, could have easily overwhelmed Roger of Lauria's modest Aragonese naval force. Charles had collected at least thirty-four galleys at Marseilles, while his son had assembled a flotilla of thirty at Naples. Another sixty-eight galleys and fifty *taride* had been gathered in the various ports of Apulia. Even more could be garnered from Gaeta, Calabria and the Basilicata. Roger could only muster between thirty-six and forty galleys at the time.[59]

Certainly Lauria must have known the circumstances. The assembly of fleets took too much time and involved too many people to be kept secret. Roger's only recourse was to prevent the various components of the Angevin navy from combining. Accordingly, he set about raiding the coasts of Calabria and Campania in the hope of drawing the fleet under Charles of Salerno, the smallest of the Angevin naval contingents, out of Naples harbour so that he could destroy it before the arrival of his father's fleet from Marseilles. Roger even captured Capri and Ischia to interdict shipping entering or leaving the Gulf of Naples in order to bait the young prince. Of course, Charles of Anjou had anticipated this and had commanded his son that under no circumstances was he to accept the challenge. He was to keep his squadron in port at all events until the arrival of his father. And even though pressure from the maritime merchants of the city must have been unrelenting, the younger Charles successfully resisted the provocation – at least until early June.[60]

Roger, desperate to entice Charles of Salerno into battle, paraded the Aragonese fleet before Baia in the Gulf of Pozzuoli just 16km (10 miles) west of Naples on 4 June. Still, the Angevin prince refused. So Lauria took his fleet out to sea and made as if he were heading back to Sicily, then doubled back to the island of Ponza, with the intention of lying in wait for the Provençal fleet of Charles senior instead.[61] But when it was learned that the latter fleet contained some thirty galleys from Marseilles plus ten from Pisa, Roger and his men decided to make one final attempt to lure out the Neapolitan fleet of Charles junior. By night the Aragonese moved to the islet of Nisida, just off the Capo Posillipo, adjacent to the port of Naples. From there, Roger ordered a *barque* to probe Naples harbour. This alerted the Angevins to their presence. He then took his fleet across the bay to Castellammare, about 24km (15 miles) to the southeast of Naples. Early on the morning of 5 June Lauria again sailed towards the port of Naples, but with only twenty of his galleys. The rest he left in reserve at Castellammare.[62]

The ruse worked. Charles of Salerno, apparently believing that he now had numerical superiority, urged his galley captains to follow him out of the harbour, against their better judgement, in order to engage the Aragonese in battle. At their approach, Roger turned stern and steered back towards Castellammare with the Angevin fleet in pursuit.[63] Once he was within a few kilometres of Castellammare, and too far from Naples for the Angevins to retreat into the safety of its harbour, Roger suddenly swung his squadron around to confront them. He formed his ships up in a tight line abreast with the sun at their sterns, effectively shielding his reserve squadron as it issued from Castellammare. Eighteen of the twenty-eight Angevin galleys were Neapolitan and not directly under the prince's command. These ships turned tail as soon as the trap was sprung, leaving the ten French galleys to deal with the Aragonese on their own. With these, Charles of

Salerno rashly attacked Roger's centre, which was now reinforced with the reserve squadron. He was soon enveloped. All the French galleys were swiftly seized, save Charles' flagship. Crammed with heavily armoured chivalry, it stoutly resisted until Roger sent over a diver with an iron auger to hole its hull. The prince of Salerno had no option but to surrender, giving the Aragonese crown an invaluable captive. Roger consummated his victory by sailing into Naples harbour and obtaining the release of the Lady Beatrice, sister to the Queen Consort of Aragon.[64]

Still, Lauria's triumph was more morale-boosting than strategic. Charles of Anjou arrived three days later with ample ground and naval forces at his disposal. He had only lost ten or so galleys, leaving a fleet still several times the size of Roger's. As a consequence, the Aragonese admiral was forced to withdraw to Messina, leaving Charles to re-establish Angevin authority throughout Campania as well as most of Apulia and Calabria. By late July the Angevin army was at the walls of Reggio. Laying siege to the latter, Charles employed a large Apulian fleet, assembled at Brindisi, to bottle up Lauria's galleys in the harbour of Messina. This enabled him to cross the Strait and capture Catania to the south. It all began to unravel, however, when a summer storm dispersed the Apulian fleet, permitting Roger to slip out of Messina. He then joined forces with a squadron of fourteen Catalan galleys under Ramon Marquet from Barcelona and began raiding the coast of Calabria. They captured several towns, including Nicotera and Castrovillari, which they almost certainly garrisoned with Almugavars. His supply lines effectively cut, Charles was compelled to lift the siege of Reggio and retreat back into Apulia by the end of August. He died unexpectedly at Foggia on 7 January 1285, his kingdom truncated and his dreams of empire forever frustrated.[65] Yet the war was not over: the French Pope Martin IV and the French king Philip III were still to have their final say.

The Aragonese Crusade: Strangulation by Roses (1285)

As early as 13 January 1283 Martin IV had deposed Peter III by papal decree for his invasion of Angevin Sicily and declared the Kingdom of Aragon forfeit in favour of Charles of Valois, the son of Philip III of France. At Angevin urging, the Pope subsequently authorized a crusade against Aragon on 31 March to make it so.[66] King Philip, after considerable bargaining, consented to conduct the crusade in February 1284. Pope Martin passed away on 29 March 1285, but it did not matter. Events had already been set in motion. By May of that year the French monarch had mustered an army of around 8,000 men which he rapidly marched through the Catalan county of Roussillon, thanks to the betrayal of Peter's brother James II of Majorca, and across the Pyrenees to lay siege to Girona on 27 June.[67]

Philip's intention was to take Girona and quickly move on to Barcelona before Peter could seek succour from Sicily. Beset by a recalcitrant barony and the rebellion of his brother James, Peter was woefully overmatched. His best hope was to harass Philip's supply lines through the mountain passes. Philip knew this. That is why he committed nearly a quarter of the total cost of the crusade to naval support. This bought him a gargantuan fleet, which Mott estimates at around 210 ships, including at least 100 galleys. Philip clearly expected that he would have to reprovision his forces by sea. Accordingly, he set up a chain of supply depots along the Catalan coast, the largest and most crucial of which was the port of Rosas ('Roses') about 43km (27 miles) northeast of Girona.[68]

Of course, Peter was well aware that Philip intended to circumvent Aragonese control of the mountain passes by converting his terrestrial supply lines into maritime ones. On 29 May, just as the invasion of his territory was beginning, the king of Aragon wrote from the Col de Panissars Pass in the Pyrenees directly to Roger of Lauria, who was besieging Taranto in Apulia, beseeching him to come posthaste to the Catalan coast with thirty galleys and twelve *taride*. For reasons that are unclear, Roger did not respond immediately. He finally arrived in Barcelona with around thirty galleys on about 23 August, after the siege of Girona was well under way and Rosas had become the linchpin of the Capetian campaign.[69] Roger would, however, reverse the situation in short order.

There were two pivotal naval engagements in the vicinity of Rosas. The first occurred during the night of 1 September in the Gulf of Rosas just outside the harbour. Although Roger was not a participant, the battle would be a prelude to a larger one further south that he would fight a few nights later. Two Catalan captains, Ramon Marquet and Berenguer Mallol, in command of a modest squadron of eleven galleys and two *llenys*, learned from informants that a large flotilla of fifty French galleys had recently departed Rosas, leaving around two dozen galleys in port. When the Catalans went to Rosas to verify the report, they were spotted and the French admiral, Guillaume de Lodève, brought out his twenty-five galleys to confront them. He formed up fifteen of his warships, bridled together in a line abreast, with the remainder held in reserve in the rear.[70]

A night engagement with a French fleet roughly twice the size of their own, and without the element of surprise on their side, was probably not what the Catalan commanders had in mind, but they made the best of it. 'And En Ramon Marquet and En Berenguer Mallol had their galleys lashed together with long ropes,' recounted Muntaner, 'and they made fast all the oars with long ropes, in order that the enemy should not be able to get between them until they wished them to, and until they loosened the oars and came to a hand-to-hand fight.'[71] Even so, the French fleet should have been easily able to envelop and overwhelm the much smaller Catalan squadron. But galley warfare was never about numbers for the Catalan–Aragonese. They rarely had them on their side. Rather it was about the quality of their crews and here they had a decisive advantage.

Based upon a preponderance of evidence, Mott, a widely respected medieval naval historian, has concluded that the losses suffered by the Provençal maritime community at the earlier battles of Nicotera and Malta 'had bled the region of its experienced admirals, marines, rowers, captains and seamen' so that the French fleet was composed mostly of crews with little combat experience led by unseasoned commanders. The Aragonese and Catalan crews, on the other hand, were well trained, highly motivated and superbly supervised.[72] The Catalan crossbowmen proved particularly devastating on this occasion. Ramon Muntaner testified that 'the crossbowmen shot in such a manner that not one dart missed'. Conversely, the chronicler noted, 'And they of the galleys of En Guillem de Lodève remained sword or bordon [a sort of thrusting weapon] in hand, unable to do anything.'[73] Only after they had all but cleared the decks of the French vessels did the Catalans unbridle and begin boarding. In the end it was a massacre. Bernat Desclot, another Catalan chronicler, claimed the French fleet lost half its men and seven galleys, while Muntaner maintained that the Catalans had killed 4,000 of the French crewmen and captured the rest, including Guillaume de Lodève, along with all their galleys. Both chroniclers agree that the Catalans purchased this lopsided victory with the loss of only a hundred or fewer of their own.[74]

Barely two or three nights later Roger delivered the *coup de grâce* to the badly weakened French fleet of war near Islas Formigues ('Ant Islands'), a cluster of rocky islets about 5km (3 miles) northeast of the port of Palamós on today's Costa Brava. There are several conflicting accounts, but it seems likely that Lauria had his forty galleys (thirty Sicilian reinforced by ten Catalan) beached in the vicinity of Castell-Cap Roig just north of Palamós in the early morning hours of 4 September, when a French squadron of twenty-five to thirty galleys was spied making its way south. The French flotilla, commanded by Genoese admirals Enrico de Mari and Giovanni d'Orreo, had apparently been directed from Rosas by Philip to seek out the Catalan squadron under Marquet and Mallol. It may even have been on its way to blockade Barcelona. Whatever the mission, Lauria had been alerted to its approach by other Catalan vessels and may well have been lying in wait.[75]

Lauria lunged to the attack just before dawn amid a terrifying cacophony. 'The men of the galleys of the king of Aragon sounded their trumpets and beat upon drums,' recounted Desclot. 'And they cried out with loud voices "Aragon! Aragon!"'[76] Ramon Muntaner attested that Roger also had multiple lanterns hoisted up to the mastheads, presumably to give the impression of numbers in the hope of engendering a general panic in the French fleet.[77] It worked. Around a dozen Genoese galleys under one of the two admirals, probably Enrico de Mari, fled to the north, abandoning the hopelessly outnumbered Provençal vessels to their own devices.[78] From Desclot's description, Lauria caught these last in a disorganized line and slammed into them from abeam. All the remaining French galleys were either captured or sunk. 'And it was reckoned that in this battle there had been slain or lost five thousand or more of men from Provence or from France,' crowed Desclot.[79]

Realizing that Rosas must now have been lightly defended, Roger swiftly sought to capitalize. Ramon Muntaner contended that he found more than 150 vessels 'between *llenys*, ships and *terides*' in the port. Roger's men wreaked havoc. What they could not take they burned.[80] It was nothing short of a catastrophe for the French campaign. In desperation, Philip dispatched the count of Fois and Ramon Roger to Lauria at Cadaqués to propose a truce, warning that the king of France would launch 300 galleys at him in the coming year. The Aragonese admiral was reported to have responded, 'I do not believe that any galley that he

[King Philip] hath nor any other of his vessels so ever would venture forth upon the sea save only under a safe-conduct from the king of Aragon.'[81]

This was evidently no idle boast. There was no longer a French fleet capable of challenging him. Lauria had dealt the Capetian crusade a grievous blow. Generals Malady and Malnourishment would do the rest. Girona surrendered three days after the Battle of Islas Formigues, but it availed Philip nothing. His lifeline by sea effectively severed, disease and starvation ran rampant through his forces. Philip himself fell victim to the pestilence. In late September he began a slow, agonizing withdrawal, badgered every step of the way by Aragonese guerrilla tactics. Peter permitted Philip and his family safe passage through the Pyrenees, but a force of Almugavars led by Roger of Lauria, among others, fell upon the French at Col de Panissars and massacred many of them. The tattered remnants staggered out of the Pyrenees to Perpignan, where Philip succumbed on 5 October to the dysentery which had already annihilated much of his army.[82]

A little over a month later, on 10 November, at a village called Vilafranca del Panadés about 60km (37 miles) west of Barcelona, King Peter III of Aragon himself fell victim to a dire illness and passed away.[83] Thus, by the end of 1285, the third year of the conflict, all four of the main protagonists were dead. Yet the War of the Sicilian Vespers was not over. It would muddle on through several more iterations for the next seventeen years.

The Battle of the Counts: the Angevin Ability to make War at Sea is ended (1287)

At the beginning of 1286 all the major players had changed: Honorius IV had succeeded Martin IV as Pope in May 1285; Alfonso III had claimed the crown of Aragon upon the death of his father, while his younger brother James had ascended to the throne of Sicily in February; and Philip IV had extended Capetian rule over France with his coronation at Reims on 6 January.[84] But the strategic aims of the war remained the same. Sicily persisted as the prize and the key to controlling it was superiority at sea. To that end, Roger of Lauria strove to maintain the Aragonese advantage by curtailing the Angevin ability to produce fleets of war. In March 1286 he ravaged the French littoral all the way from Cape Leucate in the Languedoc–Roussillon just north of Perpignan to the area of Aigues-Mortes in the Camargue of Provence west of Marseilles. Henceforth, this region ceased to contribute substantially to the Angevin war effort at sea.[85]

While Roger's raiding enhanced the security of Aragon, it was less effective in ensuring the sovereignty of Sicily. James had sought papal sanction for his rule of the island in return for homage, but Honorius IV responded reflexively in the manner of his predecessors: he excommunicated not only James but also Queen Mother Constance and the entire population of Sicily.[86] The Pope then urged a renewed offensive against the Aragonese on Sicily. The Angevins answered the call to arms with vigour. Charles of Salerno, now king of Naples, was still held captive by the Aragonese, but Philip IV had appointed Count Robert of Artois as regent in Charles' absence. Artois initiated an aggressive restoration of Angevin naval capability in the realm. By the spring of 1287 he had accumulated about forty Apulian galleys at Brindisi and another forty-three from Campania at Sorrento.[87]

In contrast, James had allowed Aragonese naval power on Sicily to atrophy. The only recorded activity by Sicilian squadrons in the same time period was a pair of ineffectual raids in the summer of 1286: one conducted by Berengar de Sarriano with a dozen galleys on the islands of Procida and Capri, flanking the Gulf of Naples, and another led by Berengar de Villaragut which swooped in on Brindisi and Corfu with a score of ships. Apparently even the arsenals in Palermo and Messina had fallen into disrepair. It was the renewed Angevin threat that finally caused James to recall Roger of Lauria to rectify the situation. The latter returned to Messina in the spring of 1287 and immediately initiated a feverish effort to expand the fleet.[88]

Lauria's exertions would come none too soon. On 1 May Reynaud III Quarrel, count of Avella, sailed into Augusta Bay just north of Syracuse on the east coast of Sicily with the forty-ship Apulian fleet from Brindisi. On orders from Robert of Artois, he quickly seized both the city of Augusta and its citadel. Roger gathered what galleys he could at Messina and made for Augusta on 13 May, while James marched overland with an army. They arrived only to find that the Angevin fleet had already departed. The Sicilians soon recaptured the town, but it became apparent that the attack on Augusta had been only a feint. Reynaud had taken his armada southwards to avoid the Strait of Messina and rounded the western tip of Sicily into the Tyrrhenian. Roger left James to reduce the citadel on his own and returned to Messina to reinforce his fleet before heading off in search of Quarrel. He reached the Gulf of Naples on 16 June with about forty vessels, but it was too late. What he had long feared had happened. The two Angevin fleets had already combined forces at Castellammare. The Aragonese were outnumbered nearly two to one.[89]

Undismayed, Lauria decided to turn disappointment into opportunity. Angevin naval power had been conveniently concentrated in a single locale so that it could be destroyed once and for all in a single engagement. And numbers had never deterred either Lauria or his Aragonese–Sicilian crews. Accordingly, he did everything he could to inveigle the Angevins into a pitched battle, winner take all. He paraded his fleet before the beached Angevin galleys at Castellammare, firing insults as well as projectiles. He was even reported to have dispatched messengers to formally challenge Robert of Artois to battle.[90]

What finally drew Artois out on 23 June, however, was almost surely the certain knowledge of his numerical superiority. It had also evidently inspired him to arrange his battle line in an unusual formation. Once again, the chroniclers do not concur and provide a confused picture, but it seems the Angevin line consisted of seven squadrons, presumably of nine galleys each, for a total of sixty-three vessels. Aside from Robert of Artois, each squadron was commanded by a count: Reynaud of Avella, Hugh of Brienne, Guy of Montfort, Jean of Joinville, the count of Montpellier and the count of Aquila. Hence it became known as the 'Battle of the Counts'. The exact configuration of these squadrons remains uncertain, but it appears that the ship of each count was fronted by two galleys, trailed by another two and flanked on each side by two more, in a diamond formation. Apparently they were to fight as individual phalanxes once the opposing lines intermeshed. In addition, there were two *taride*, one bearing the banner of the Pope and the other the Angevin crown. The remaining Angevin vessels were apparently held in reserve.[91]

Details on the Aragonese line are even more sketchy, but at least two sources indicate that Lauria feigned flight, causing the Angevin formation to disintegrate in headlong pursuit. When the Aragonese did come about and the ships of the two fleets finally engaged, Lauria had his men endure the initial Angevin missile barrages without responding until the enemy crews were exhausted of both strength and ammunition. Once this occurred, individual Aragonese units targeted the vessels of the counts in accordance with a prearranged plan based on the notion that most of these men were unaccustomed to battle at sea, especially against Almugavars, to whom Roger had reportedly given specific instructions. The fighting was long and hard, but, according to at least two of the chroniclers, the tide turned when the Genoese admiral Enrico de Mari once again fled with his contingent – not an implausible reaction, given Roger's reputation. Whatever the tactics he employed, they were terribly effective. Over forty Angevin galleys and 5,000 prisoners were taken, including most of the nobility.[92] The blow to Angevin naval power was mortal. It would cease to be a factor for the remainder of the war.

Transformation of the War by Treaty (1288–95)

At this point the conflict devolved into a fitful series of failed truces and treaties. Both sides were spent and looking for a way out. Only the papacy seemed to have a vested interest in the war's perpetuation. Roger of Lauria began this new phase himself. Instead of subjecting Naples to the sack for which his Sicilian confederates clamoured, he concluded a two-year truce with Robert of Artois and ransomed back his Angevin captives at an exorbitant cost. Evidence shows that Lauria was acting in consonance with the wishes of Alfonso III. The pay for Roger's crews had been in arrears for several months. The admiral, however, ensured Neapolitan compliance by retaking the islands of Ischia and Capri, which effectively controlled the entrance to the Gulf of Naples.[93]

The month after the Battle of the Counts, King Edward I of England mediated a truce among the protagonists known as the Treaty of Oloron, which called for a cessation of hostilities and the emancipation of Charles II. Nicholas IV, the successor of Pope Honorius IV who died in April, objected because the agreement did not require James to relinquish Sicily. Nevertheless, at Canfrance in October 1288 Edward persuaded Alfonso III to release Charles in return for his three sons as hostages, a healthy indemnity and the promise of his participation in negotiations for a permanent peace. Charles, however, abrogated the deal as soon as he was freed by having himself crowned king of Sicily at Naples in early 1289. James reacted by laying siege to Gaeta with the aid of Lauria's fleet. Robert of Artois then marched up from Naples and besieged the besiegers. The deadlock was broken when Charles II agreed to a two-year truce.[94]

The indefatigable Edward of England again attempted to bring the concerned parties together, resulting in the Treaty of Tarascon on 19 February 1291, whereby Alfonso surrendered his claim to Sicily in exchange for removal of the papal anathema against the crown of Aragon.[95] The document was virtually dead on delivery, however, because James of Sicily was not a signatory. Besides, the death of Alfonso III on 18 June effectively invalidated it anyway.[96] James then ascended to the throne of Aragon and appointed his younger brother Frederick as viceroy of Sicily, which, of course, prompted Nicholas IV to excommunicate the lot of them: King James II, Frederick and all the Sicilians.[97]

Meanwhile, Roger of Lauria kept the Aragonese fleet busy returning much of Calabria to Aragonese control while plundering Apulia at will. In the summer of 1292 he embarked on an extraordinary expedition which attacked Angevin Cephalonia, raided Corfu, ravaged the southern Peloponnesos and even assaulted Angevin possessions in the Greek Cyclades. And, of course, he preyed on Angevin shipping everywhere.[98] The message was a simple one: there was no place in the Mediterranean where Angevin interests were safe from the depredations of Lauria's galleys. At last Charles II grew weary of watching his realm reduced and his coffers slowly drained, so in December 1293 at Figueras he came to terms with James II on a preliminary peace: Charles would pay a substantial remuneration for James to give up his claim to Sicily. The accord was finally formalized by the Treaty of Anagni on 12 June 1295. There were many provisions, but essentially Charles II received Sicily while James II made do with Sardinia, the hand of Charles' daughter in marriage and the lifting of the papal ban on Aragon.[99]

Everyone was satisfied except, of course, James' balky brother Frederick and the Sicilians, who were still adamantly averse to Angevin rule. In open defiance of the Holy See they crowned their Aragonese viceroy as King Frederick III of Sicily in Palermo on 12 December of the same year.[100] And so the war went on in yet another intractable iteration.

The Aragonese–Angevin War on Sicily (1295–1302)

Sicilian obstinacy and the desire for some measure of independence had precipitated a bizarre turn of events which made implacable adversaries into uneasy allies. By treaty obligation, the crown of Aragon was now compelled to support that of Angevin Naples in the recovery of an island which Aragon had ruled for more than a decade. This placed no one in a more difficult position than Roger of Lauria. Born in Calabria and raised in the Hohenstaufen court of King Manfred of Sicily, he had spent much of his military career fighting side-by-side with the Sicilians against whom he was now expected to make war; and yet his loyalties to the house of Aragon, which had provided him refuge as a youth and promoted him to governor of Valencia and admiral of the fleet as an adult, ran deep. In January 1296 James II inevitably forced him to make the only rational choice available: either continue to serve the crown of Aragon or lose everything. And thus Roger left Sicily for good in the entourage of Queen Constance in January 1297 and proceeded to Rome, where King James officially confirmed him as Admiral of the Crown of Aragon and the County of Barcelona on 2 April.[101]

While neither James nor Roger initially demonstrated any great eagerness to join battle against James' brother Frederick, Angevin ground forces pushed into Apulia and Calabria, evicting the Sicilians from the Italian peninsula by the spring of 1299. The invasion of fortress Sicily, however, required strong naval forces. An initial assault was easily rebuffed. Messina, in particular, had proven obdurate.[102] If the island was to be reconquered, Lauria himself would have to bring Aragonese sea power to bear. So, operating under the overall command of King James in the final days of June 1299, Lauria attempted to land a fleet of forty-six Aragonese galleys and a dozen Angevin ones on the northern shore of Sicily at a place called Capo d'Orlando, around 120km (75 miles) east of Palermo and 70km (43 miles) west of Messina. Clearly, the intention was to bypass Messina, where Frederick managed a vigorous defence. When Frederick learned of the expedition, he had his new admiral, Corrado Doria of Genoa, hastily assemble a fleet of forty Sicilian galleys. They arrived at Capo d'Orlando on 3 July, but too late to prevent Lauria's landing. The Aragonese admiral had already beached his galleys stern-first in a strong defensive posture.[103]

Corrado Doria must have realized that he possessed no advantages whatsoever. His opponent had both numerical superiority and a nearly invulnerable position, not to mention the fact that he was the legendary Roger of Lauria – the most feared naval commander of his time. Yet Doria allowed himself to be pressured into action by Frederick, who was understandably anxious to crush the invasion before it could get going. A preliminary assault, with the possible purpose of drawing Lauria off the beach, failed completely. Roger had no intention of relinquishing his tactical edge. At this point Frederick and Doria evidently decided to await the arrival of a few more Sicilian galleys from Cefalù, about 64km (40 miles) to the west. This obliged them to endure a storm-tossed night at sea while Lauria and his men enjoyed the relative comfort of the shore.[104]

As soon as the galleys from Cefalù arrived the next day, 4 July 1299, the Sicilian ships bridled together in a crescent moon formation in preparation for the attack. It was doomed to disaster before it even began. Roger's galleys had also linked themselves together in a tight crescent line, only they had their sterns to the shore with flying bridges extended onto the beach so that the disembarked Angevin–Aragonese army could assist as necessary. When the Sicilians came within missile shot, they were doubtless subjected to fatally accurate fire from the Catalan crossbowmen. One of Frederick's captains, Gombaldus Intenciis, broke free and attempted to engage James' flagship. He was rapidly followed by others. A murderous mêlée ensued, but the issue was never in doubt. Roger signalled six swift galleys that he had evidently hidden around the point to attack from the rear. The Sicilian line and the resolve of its commanders crumbled. Doria and Frederick managed to escape with thirteen to eighteen galleys. The remainder were surrounded and seized.[105]

There were persistent rumours in the aftermath of the battle that James had allowed his brother Frederick to escape. Indeed, his actions in the days that followed seem to lend credence to the allegations. Aragonese forces did not vigorously press their advantage. In September Roger assisted Robert, count of

1. Fresco of Roman *liburnians*, forerunners of medieval war galleys, from the first-century Temple of Isis in Pompeii. *(C. Stanton/Museo Archeologico Nazionale, Naples)*

2. *Olympias*, replica of an Athenian trireme built by the Hellenic Navy in 1987 which subsequently underwent sea trials providing valuable information on the operating capabilities and crew conditions of war galleys. *(Templar52/ Palaio Faliro, Athens)*

3. Miniature showing the shipboard deployment of 'Greek fire' against the rebel fleet of Thomas the Slav in 821 from the twelfth-century *Skylitzes Matritensis* manuscript (Codex Vitr. 26–2, fol. 34v). *(Bridgeman Art Library/Biblioteca Nacionale, Madrid)*

4. Rare miniature of combat at sea between two engaged Byzantine *dromōns* from the eleventh-century *Kynegetika* manuscript of Pseudo-Oppian (Ms. Gr. 479, fol. 23r). (*Bridgeman Art Library/Biblioteca Nazionale Marciana, Venice*)

5. Miniature from the Bern manuscript of Peter of Eboli's *Liber ad honorem Augusti sive rebus Siculis* (Codex 120 II, fol. 119r), containing the best surviving contemporary illustration of a twelfth-century Sicilian *galea*. (*Permission generously granted by Burgerbibliothek Bern ©, with all rights reserved*)

6. Some of the earliest representations of medieval Muslim vessels were those by thirteenth-century Iraqi artist Yahya ibn Mahmud al-Wasiti, but they were highly stylized depictions of transport vessels, not warships – like this one from a manuscript (*c.*1230) of the *Maqamat of al-Hariri* ('The Assemblies of Hariri'). (*The Yorck Project/Institute of Oriental Studies, Russian Academy of Sciences, St Petersburg*)

7. Miniature showing the fleet of Andalusian Muslim freebooter Abu Hafs heading for Crete in 827 from the twelfth-century *Skylitzes Matritensis* manuscript (Codex Vitr. 26–2, fol. 38v). (*Cplakidas/Biblioteca Nacionale, Madrid*)

8. Miniature of the Arab sack of Thessaloniki by Leo of Tripoli in 904 from the twelfth-century *Skylitzes Matritensis* manuscript (Codex Vitr. 26–2, fol. 111v). (*Cplakidas/Biblioteca Nacionale, Madrid*)

9. Miniature of the Byzantine invasion of Saracen Sicily under Giorgios Maniakes in 1038 from the twelfth-century *Skylitzes Matritensis* manuscript (Codex Vitr. 26–2, fol. 212r). (*Wikimedia Commons/Biblioteca Nacionale, Madrid*)

10. Circular world map (oriented south-to-north) of twelfth-century geographer Muhammad al-Idrisi from a copy of his *Kitab Rujar* ('Book of Roger') or *Tabula Rogeriana* produced in Cairo in 1553 (Ms. Pococke 375, fols 3v and 4r). *(Wikimedia Commons/Bodleian Library, Oxford)*

11. Painting of the Venetian-led capture of Constantinople in 1204 during the Fourth Crusade by sixteenth-century artist Iacopo Robusti Tintoretto, prominently featuring the use of masts and spars as siege machinery as well as a large arbalest in the foreground. *(Bridgeman Art Library/Palazzo Ducale, Venice)*

12. Miniature of the crusader assault on the Chain Tower during the 1218 Siege of Damietta of the Fifth Crusade from the thirteenth-century manuscript of the *Chronica Majora* by Matthew Paris (Ms. 16, Roll 178, fol. 59v). *(Arwin7/Parker Library of Corpus Christi College, Cambridge)*

13. Miniature of Saint Louis attacking Damietta in 1249 during the Seventh Crusade from a manuscript of the *Chroniques de Saint-Denis* (Ms. Roy 16 G VI, fol. 409v). *(British Library Catalogue of Illuminated Manuscripts/British Library, London)*

14. Tempera painting on a ceiling beam of a late thirteenth-century Catalan-Aragonese bireme war galley in the Palau Nacional of Barcelona. (*Mary Evans Picture Library/Museu Nacional d'Art de Catalunya, Barcelona*)

15. Thirteenth-century mural of Catalan infantry in the army of King James I in the Palau de Mar (Palacio Real) of Barcelona which appears to show Catalan crossbowmen to the left and lance men, perhaps even Almugavars, to the right. (*Bridgeman Art Library/Museu d'Historia de Catalunya, Barcelona*)

16. *Veduta di Genova nell'anno 1481* ('View of Genoa in the year 1481') by sixteenth-century Genoese painter Cristoforo Grassi, depicting a parade of carracks and galleys in port. *(Bridgeman Art Library/Museo Navale di Pegli, Genoa)*

17. Model of a Venetian trireme commissioned by Admiral Luigi Fincati for the International Geographical Exhibition of Venice in 1881 to demonstrate the *alla sensile* oarage system. (*Myriam Thyles/Museo Storico Navale, Venice*)

18. Ornamented square pillars looted from the Genoese Quarter of Acre in 1258, standing outside the baptistery of Saint Mark's Basilica in Venice. (*Anne Atwell*)

19. Remnants of the Skuldelev 3 ship (a coastal trading vessel) discovered scuttled in a fjord near Skuldelev, Denmark in 1962 along with four other Viking ships, including a longship (the Skuldelev 2). *(Hans Olav Lien/Viking Ship Museum of Roskilde, Denmark)*

20. Remnants of the Bremen cog (*c.*1380), found in the Weser River in 1962, possessing the flat bottom and nearly vertical stem and sternposts typical of this merchant vessel in the later Middle Ages. *(Uwe H. Freise/Deutsches Schiffahrts Museum, Bremerhaven)*

21. Carved dragon post from the early ninth-century Viking ship, the Oseberg. (*Jean-Pierre Dalbéra/ Viking Ship Museum, Oslo*)

22. Hull of the Oseberg ship, a longship of the early ninth century excavated from a burial mound in the Vesfold of Norway in 1904/05. (*Jean-Pierre Dalbéra/Viking Ship Museum, Oslo*)

23. Interior view of the Gokstad ship, a longship of the late ninth century discovered in a burial mound near Sandefjord, Norway in 1880, showing the vessel's rugged construction. (*Concierge2/Viking Ship Museum, Oslo*)

24. Miniature depicting the 'Invasion of the Danes under Hinguar and Hubba' from the twelfth-century (*c.*1130) manuscript of the *Life, Passion and Miracles of St Edmund, King and Martyr* of Bury St Edmunds, England (Ms. 736, fol. 9v). *(Bridgeman Art Library/Pierpoint Morgan Library, New York)*

25. Embroidered scene of the Bayeux Tapestry showing the construction of some of William the Conqueror's ships from scratch. *(Ulrich Harsh/Musée de la Tapisserie in Bayeux, France)*

26. Embroidered scene of the Bayeux Tapestry showing horses being offloaded from Ladby-type ships at Pevensey. *(Ulrich Harsh/Musée de la Tapisserie in Bayeux, France)*

27. Miniature depicting the beheading of Eustace the Monk during the Battle of Dover in a thirteenth-century manuscript of the *Chronica Majora* of Matthew Paris (Ms. 16, Roll 178, fol. 56r). *(Bridgeman Art Library/ Parker Library of Corpus Christi College, Cambridge)*

28. Miniature of two fighting cogs from the *Glossa Ordinaria* of Bernard of Parma (*c.*1340) in the *Decretals of Gregory IX*, known as the 'Smithfield Decretals', (Ms. Roy 10 E IV, fol. 19v). *(British Library Catalogue of Illuminated Manuscripts/British Library, London)*

29. Engraving of a fifteenth-century Flemish carrack (*Kraeck*), the earliest known depiction of this type vessel, probably done in 1468 by goldsmith William A. Gruce for the wedding festivities of Charles the Bold of Burgundy to Margaret of York. *(William A. Gruce/ Ashmolean Museum, Oxford)*

30. Miniature illustrating the 1340 Battle of Sluys from a fifteenth-century manuscript of Jean Froissart's *Chronicles* (Ms. Fr 2643, fol. 82r). (*Mary Evans Picture Library/Bibliothèque Nationale, Paris*)

31. Miniature of the 1372 Battle of La Rochelle from the fourteenth-century manuscript of the *Chroniques de France ou St Denis* (Ms. Roy 20 C VII, fol. 189v). (*British Library Catalogue of Illuminated Manuscripts/British Library, London*)

32. Gold noble (1344) commemorating the victory of Edward III at Sluys in 1340, which portrays the sovereign, sword and shield in hand, aboard the *Cog Thomas*. (*PHGCOM/Cabinet des Médailles of the Bibliothèque Nationale, Paris*)

33. Lübeck town seal of 1280, which symbolizes the creation of the German Hanse by depicting a man wearing the garb of a Westphalian merchant exchanging oaths with a man wearing the hooded *cugel* of a Wendish seaman on a cog-type vessel. (*Wolfgang Sauber*)

34. *Lisa von Lübeck*, a modern reconstruction of a typical Hanseatic caravel of the late fifteenth century, inspired loosely by the giant *Peter von Danzig* of 1462-1475. (*Doris Schütz*)

35. Hans Memling's triptych *The Last Judgement*, commissioned by the Medici and destined for Florence before being pillaged in 1473 from Burgundian galleys off the south coast of England by the *Peter von Danzig*. (*Bridgeman Art Library/Muzeum Narodowe, Gdańsk*)

36. *Rumeli Hisar* ('Fortress of the Romans'), built by Mehmed the Conqueror on the European bank of the Bosporus in the fifteenth century, still stands guard over the strategic strait. (*Radomil Binek*)

37. Dardanelles Gun, an Ottoman bombard caste in 1464 based on the designs of Hungarian engineer Orban for the colossal cannon used by Mehmed II to breach the Theodosian Walls of Constantinople in 1453. (*Gaius Cornelius/British Royal Armouries at Fort Nelson, Portsmouth*)

38. Miniature of the Ottoman siege of Constantinople in 1453 from the fifteenth-century manuscript of *Le Voyage d'Outremer* by Bertrandon de la Broquière (Ms. Fr 9087, fol. 207v), depicting many of the described elements of the evolution: the harbour chain suspended on pontoons, the *Anadolu Hisar*, the *Rumeli Hisar*, the portage of Mehmed's fleet across Galata and Orban's Great Bombard. (*Bridgeman Art Library/ Bibliothèque Nationale, Paris*)

39. Contemporary woodcut of the 1499 Battle of Zonchio, an Ottoman victory over the Venetians in which cannon mounted below deck were first employed with ship-killing effectiveness. *(Wikimedia Commons/British Museum, London)*

40. Depiction of the *Henry Grace à Dieu* or 'Great Harry' (launched 1514), the largest carrack in Henry VIII's fleet (50m/164ft long and up to 1,500 tons), shown bristling with cannon in the *Anthony Roll* of 1546, an illustrated inventory of the Tudor Navy by Anthony Anthony (Surveyor of the Ordnance). *(Jerry Bye/Pepys Library of Magdalene College, Cambridge)*

Calabria and son to Charles II, in the capture of Catania, but attempts to take Messina seemed half-hearted and were easily turned aside. That same month, in fact, James withdrew from the fighting and returned to Aragon with the bulk of his army. This enabled Frederick to annihilate another Angevin invasion attempt. In November Philip of Taranto, another son of Charles II, landed a fleet of forty to fifty galleys at Capo Lilibeo on the western tip of the island near Marsala and marched on Trapani. Frederick confronted him on 1 December on the plain of Falconaria north of Marsala and dealt him a decisive defeat which resulted in his capture.[106] Such successes emboldened Frederick to take the offensive. He directed Corrado Doria to resurrect the Sicilian fleet. By the spring of 1300 the latter had gathered a total of thirty-two galleys, including five Ghibelline ones from his home city of Genoa.[107]

In June Doria sailed north, no doubt on the orders of his overconfident sovereign, and into the Gulf of Naples to confront the Aragonese–Angevin fleet. He found it in the security of Naples harbour, numbering about forty galleys under Lauria's personal command. In what seems in retrospect like a surfeit of hubris, Doria actually challenged Lauria to come out and engage him in battle. And, as at Capo d'Orlando the year before, Lauria refused. Not even when Doria began raiding some of the nearby islands did Lauria pick up the gauntlet. After all, there was no compelling reason why he should. As at Capo d'Orlando, his position was unassailable. What was more, time was on his side. Since he had decimated the Sicilian fleet only the year before, Lauria must have believed that his already outnumbered opponent could expect no auxiliaries, especially so far from his own shores. At the same time Roger knew that a dozen Apulian galleys were headed in his direction, with another seven Guelph galleys coming from Genoa.[108]

Only when these two flotillas had slipped past the plundering Sicilian fleet and added their numbers to his, giving him a near two-to-one advantage, did Roger of Lauria choose to weigh anchor in search of his adversary. He found him near the island of Ponza, 113km (70 miles) west of Naples, on 14 June 1300. While Doria appears to have been a loyal servant of the Sicilian crown, he was no fool. He apparently recoiled at such daunting odds, but, in a council of war with his ships' captains just before the battle, hotter heads prevailed. Little is known about the overall tactics, but the sources say that Doria tried to salvage the situation with a desperate thrust at Lauria's flagship. Roger deftly parried this move and avoided being grappled. In a now familiar pattern, the Ghibellines from Genoa appreciated the hopelessness of the circumstances and abandoned their erstwhile Sicilian allies, who were quickly surrounded. A few got away but around twenty galleys were captured, including Doria's flagship. The Sicilian fleet had effectively been rendered *hors de combat* for the rest of the war.[109]

The Angevins sought to capitalize on the victory with a fresh campaign to seize Sicily. In May 1302 Charles of Valois, cousin to Charles II of Naples, joined the fray by coming ashore with an invasion force at Termini on the north central coast.[110] At the same time Roger of Lauria attacked Palermo, seizing a fortress on the outskirts. But opposition among the Sicilian population to Angevin rule remained staunch and the invaders could make little inroad into the hinterlands. Messina and Palermo remained impervious to Angevin assault. Thus stalemate soon settled in. It became apparent that although Frederick had lost his offensive capability, he could still lead a tenacious defence of the island that would make its conquest extremely arduous, time-consuming and bloody, not to mention costly. Besides, there were now higher priorities elsewhere for the Capetian crown.[111]

So, while engaged in a fruitless siege of Sciacca (on the south coast, east of Mazara) in the scorching summer sun, Charles of Valois exercised the authority delegated to him by his brother, Philip IV of France, to negotiate a settlement.[112] On 31 August 1302 he and Robert of Calabria came to terms with King Frederick III of Sicily at nearby Caltabellotta. Angevin troops were to be withdrawn, giving the Sicilians the measure of independence they had so long sought. Frederick would rule Sicily for the duration of his life with the title 'king of Trinacria' (the ancient Greek name for the island, meaning 'three promontories'), but would renounce his claim to all mainland territories. Upon his death, Sicily was to revert to Angevin rule but Frederick's heirs would be compensated with either Cyprus or Sardinia or 10,000 ounces of gold. Charles II would retain the title 'king of Sicily' but his domains would, paradoxically, not include Sicily until Frederick's passing. Charles betrothed his youngest daughter Eleanora to Frederick to seal the deal. The Treaty of Caltabellotta effectively ended the war, because for the first time it addressed the concerns of all participants.[113]

Angevin and Aragonese adventurism, mixed with Machiavellian papal machinations, had cost all parties in the struggle dearly with one notable exception: Roger of Lauria. From the crown of Aragon, he had won great prestige and bountiful lands in Valencia; from the papacy, the islands of Jerba and Kerkenna as papal fiefs; and from Frederick, in return for homage, the fortress of Aci Castello near Catania.[114] More importantly, he had earned a reputation as an admiral for the ages. He had done so by using his tactical genius to maximize the Aragonese advantages at sea: Almugavar marines, Catalan crossbowmen, sturdier ship construction and excellent crew discipline. Thanks to his inspired leadership, the Aragonese fleet remained dominant throughout the war.[115] Prominent maritime historian John Pryor is unequivocal in his praise: 'As a naval commander, he has no rival in medieval history, not even among the Genoese and the Venetians.'[116]

* * *

Exemplary Engagement: The Battle of Malta (June 1283)

The stage for the Battle of Malta was set by none of the main seaborne protagonists who participated in the resultant naval encounter. Instead, an Aragonese agent by the name of Manfred de Lancia deserves the credit. The Maltese had no more of an affinity for their Angevin masters than did their Sicilian neighbours, so Lancia had no difficulty in fomenting a general insurrection on the island in the autumn of 1282. French troops soon found themselves restricted to the *Castrum Maris*, a citadel (modern Fort St Angelo) which occupied a headland jutting out into the Grand Harbour. As a consequence, the Angevin garrison in the 'Castle of the Sea' had been under siege by indigenous forces for nearly six months by the time the Provençal fleet under Bartholomé Bonvin and Guillaume de Cornut arrived in Naples in May 1283. This was why Charles of Salerno, the eldest son of Charles of Anjou, ordered the admirals to head south immediately: the relief of the garrison on Malta.[117]

The two Provençal admirals set sail from Naples with a total of eighteen galleys (probably *galeas*), eight or nine *barques* (small galleys with about twenty-four oars) and a *panfilus* (a light galley of around a hundred oars). They proceeded by way of the Aeolian chain and Ustica Island north of Sicily, then rounded the west end of the island in order to avoid the Strait of Messina, which was controlled by the Aragonese. As a precaution, Ramon Muntaner related that they had sent three light galleys, probably *sagittae* ('arrows' – small scout ships with around sixteen oars), to the Boca del Faro at the northern entrance to the Strait in order to reconnoitre the Aragonese fleet. If so, this surfeit of caution may have backfired. Roger of Lauria reportedly intercepted these scout vessels and learned of the main Provençal fleet's movements. Even if untrue, it is doubtful the French fleet could have skirted the north coast of Sicily without being observed. Regardless of how, Roger was alerted and the chase was on.[118]

The Provençals probably arrived in the Grand Harbour around 4 June 1283 and beached their galleys in Dockyard Creek on the south side of the *Castrum Maris*. Lauria made Malta a few days later, on 7 June, with an estimated eighteen to twenty-two galleys (mostly *galeas*), but anchored at the nearby island of Gozo under cover of darkness. He then made contact with Lancia to check on the arrangement of Angevin forces on the island and at the same time dispatched a pair of *llenys* with an eight-oared barge to reconnoitre the disposition of the French fleet. The entrance to the Grand Harbour was guarded by two Angevin *llenys*, one moored on each side, but the barge, using muffled oars, was able to slip past them in the darkness and return with its scouting report. Having learned of the enemy's deployment, Lauria surreptitiously moved his entire fleet to the Grand Harbour just before sunrise. (*See* Map 9.) He arrayed his ships in a line abreast across the entrance, bridled together at stem and stern with iron cables called *frenella*. This allowed the galleys to manoeuvre together under oars while maintaining an impenetrable barrier to prevent the Provençal ships from escaping. Lauria then did something so counter-intuitive it confounded the chroniclers: he had his trumpeters announce their presence to the enemy fleet, thereby relinquishing the element of surprise.[119]

What seemed like madness was actually brilliance and demonstrated a nuanced understanding of galley warfare. A beached galley fleet was nearly invincible. Galleys were always beached stern first for ease of relaunching and for defensive purposes. First of all, the bow, with its forecastle and beak or *calcares*, was designed to be the strongest, most defensible part of the ship. Secondly, beached galleys could easily reinforce one another and all crewmen could participate in the fighting since oarsmen were not needed. And thirdly, maintaining formation

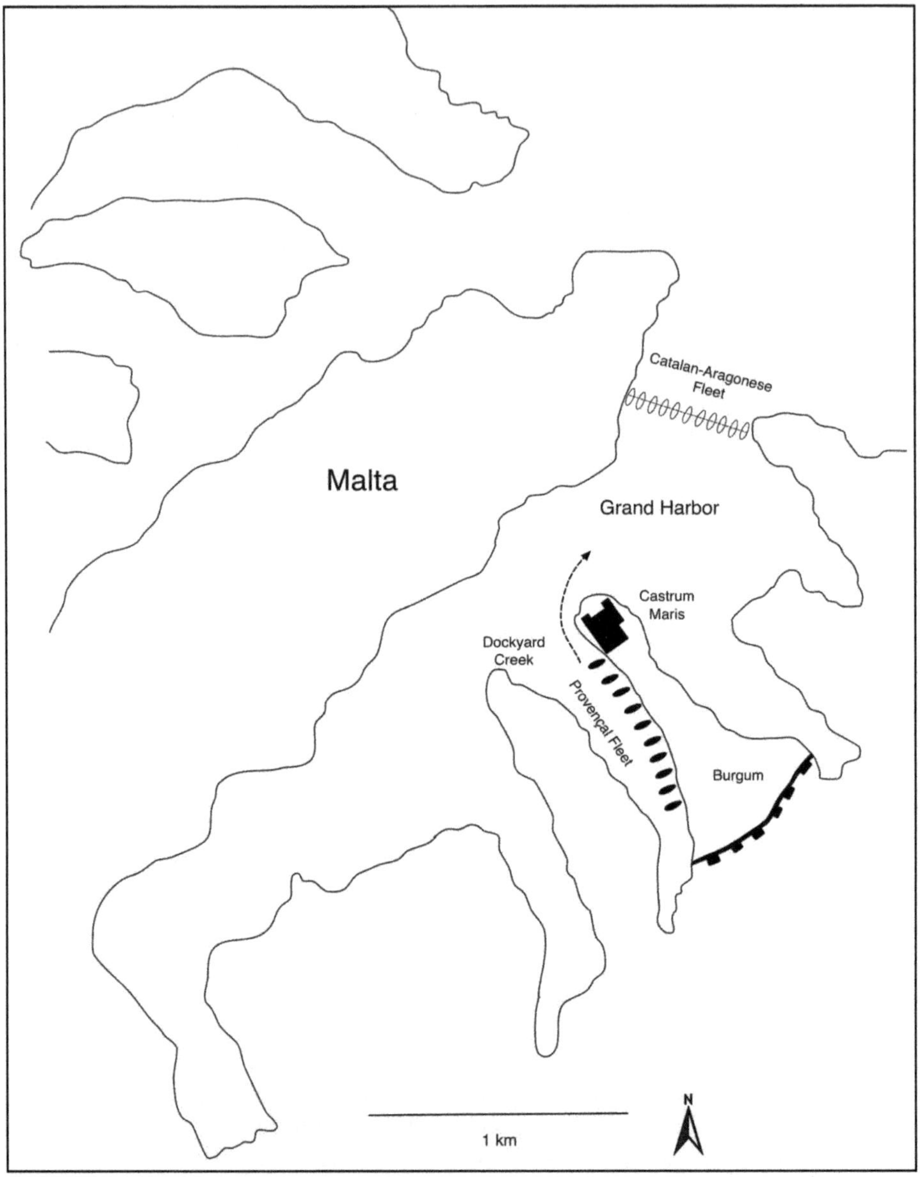

Map 9. Battle of Malta in 1283. (*Kristy Stanton*)

integrity was no problem. In addition, there were factors peculiar to the Grand Harbour which made attacking the beached Angevin fleet imprudent to the point of being suicidal: said beach was located in an inlet only 250m (273 yards) wide in the shadow of a well fortified citadel garrisoned by enemy troops. The Aragonese would have had to attack in a thin column with very little room to manoeuvre and no cover from missile fire from the *Castrum Maris*.[120]

Thus Roger of Lauria summoned his adversaries to battle so that he could deal with them as an integral force in the more open portion of the Grand Harbour. And Bonvin and Cornut had little choice but to comply: all of Malta, aside from the *Castrum Maris* and the adjacent Il Borgo or Burgum (a fortified hamlet), was controlled by inimical forces led by the Aragonese agent Manfred de Lancia. If the Provençals had failed to respond to Lauria's challenge, they would have faced assault from land while trapped in Dockyard Creek with no way to reprovision. So out they came.[121]

Lauria again did something unexpected. Instead of attacking the Provençals while they were in a state of confused disarray, he allowed them to organize into battle formation. Only after they had done so, and the sun had come up, did Roger have his galleys row ahead to meet the French in the centre of the harbour. Most crucially, as the Provençals began launching the anticipated missile volleys, he ordered all his men except the crossbowmen to hold their fire and seek cover behind their bulwarks. This was especially critical for the thinly protected Almugavars. 'This word was sent throughout all the galleys of the Catalans,' reported Bernat de Desclot, another Catalan chronicler, 'so that, thereafter, they hurled no weapons so ever but fought as best they could and suffered the attack of the Provençal galleys wherefrom stones and lances and lime were cast in such deluge that the sight thereof was most fearful to behold.'[122] As horrific as the fusillade may have been, the Catalan crews were evidently sheltered by their sturdier sterncastles and forecastles, according to modern studies.[123] Only at midday, when the enemy had so depleted their ammunition stocks that they were throwing the mortars and pestles for grinding lime, did Lauria unleash the full fury of the Catalan missile barrage.[124] In this he possessed a very special advantage. The skill of the *balistarii catalani* ('Catalan crossbowmen') was reputed to have exceeded even that of the vaunted Genoese.[125] Accordingly, the decks of several of the Provençal ships were soon swept of able-bodied men.

After that, the engagement resembled more of a mopping-up operation than a battle. The Aragonese galleys detached their *frenella* and moved in for the kill. Once they had grappled with the enemy ships, the Almugavars took over. Clad only in leather, lightly armed and agile, they were at home on the pitching deck of a ship.[126] The exhausted, heavily armoured French knights were no match for them. Muntaner contended that 3,500 Provençals lost their lives,[127] one of whom was Guillaume de Cornut, who had personally sworn to Charles of Anjou that he would bring back Roger of Lauria dead or alive. According to Desclot, he perversely met his end in single combat with his quarry. Desclot also indicated that 860 Provençals were taken prisoner, adding 'there was no one in Marseilles that had not lost either his son or his father or his brother or his friend, or some other kinsman'.[128] Larry Mott's analysis indicates that this may have been no empty chest-thumping. The population of Marseilles and its surrounding territory is estimated to have been only about 20,000 at the time. 'The demographic effect on the community of Marseilles must have been staggering,' concludes Mott. 'Not only had the battle cost the lives of Admiral Cornut and his kinsmen, it had effectively stripped Marseilles and the Provençal province of its best naval personnel.'[129]

On the other hand, Roger of Lauria's force suffered only 288 casualties, about 10 per cent. Moreover, he was able to add some ten captured Provençal galleys to his own fleet. Bartholomé Bonvin managed to escape in the midst of the mêlée with about seven galleys, two of which were so heavily damaged they had to be abandoned. The rest were probably either sunk or captured.[130] In sum, Aragonese naval capability was strengthened while Angevin maritime effectiveness was diminished. Mott considers the Battle of Malta 'one of the most important engagements of the War of the Sicilian Vespers', because: 'Not only had it brought to the forefront one of the greatest naval strategists and tacticians of the time, it had inflicted losses on the French fleet from which it would never recover.'[131] Lauria would continue to exploit considerable advantages in both crew composition and warship architecture.

CHAPTER 6

Venetian-Genoese Competition for Control in the East

By the end of the thirteenth century there were just two maritime superpowers remaining in the medieval Mediterranean: Genoa and Venice. Pisa had begun to fade, along with the fortunes of the Hohenstaufen family, when the last great promoter of the Ghibelline cause, Emperor Frederick II, passed away in December 1250. The Tuscan republic would be eclipsed altogether after its disastrous defeat at Meloria in 1284.[1] This cleared the way for one of the great seaborne duels of the Middle Ages. *La Superba* ('The Magnificent One' – Genoa) and *La Serenissima* ('The Most Serene' – Venice) would vie vehemently with one another for a century and a quarter, very nearly vanquishing each other in the process. From 1256 to 1381 they would fight four ruinous wars in competition for a single glittering prize: control over the lucrative trade of the Orient.

While the maritime technology of the era simply did not permit absolute supremacy over so vast an area as the eastern Mediterranean basin, it did allow for the domination of waterborne trade emanating from the East. This is because it was not necessary to hold sway over a large expanse of water – an impossibility due to the limited speed, range and endurance of galley fleets. All that was required was mastery of certain highly frequented routes during certain high traffic times of year. Most oriental trade was channelled through just three entrepôts: Egypt (mainly Alexandria), the Latin Kingdom of Jerusalem (particularly Acre and Tyre) and the Byzantine Empire (especially Constantinople and the Black Sea). Moreover, prevailing winds, sea currents and coastal topography funnelled shipping through just a handful of maritime chokepoints: the Bosporus and the Dardanelles, the passage between Crete and the Peloponnesos, the eastern corridor of the Adriatic and the Strait of Messina. And until the fourteenth century these routes only needed to be monitored in accordance with a sailing schedule that extended from April to October.[2] Thus it was these crucial constrictions and entrepôts that Genoa and Venice fought so savagely to control.

Prelude to War: A Clash over Crete (1206–12)

Once the Crusades had drawn the Genoese eastwards and into contact with the merchants of Venice, it was only a matter of time before the inherent competitiveness of the two rivals flared into open conflict. Ever since May 1082, when Alexios I Komnenos issued a Golden Bull granting the Venetians extraordinary trading privileges throughout the Byzantine Empire in return for naval support against Robert Guiscard, they had considered the eastern Mediterranean basin their exclusive commercial enclave.[3] So when Manuel I Komnenos conceded the Genoese a merchant quarter in the Coparion district of Constantinople adjacent to the Venetian *fondaco* in the summer of 1170, the Venetians reacted by sacking it.[4]

Nor were the Genoese blameless in the progressive souring of relations. A major component of Venetian strategy in the aftermath of the Fourth Crusade was to establish a string of bases to protect their trade routes to and from 'Romania' (Byzantium). Accordingly, outposts were acquired at Negroponte on Euboea, Naxos in the Aegean, Candia on Crete, Modon and Coron in the southwestern Peloponnesos, Corfu in the Ionian, Ragusa and Zara on the Dalmatian coast and Pola in Istria.[5] None was more vital to Venetian interests than Crete. Doge Enrico Dandolo had purchased it for 1,000 silver marks from Boniface of Montferrat following the conquest of Constantinople in 1204.[6] So it must have been with alarmed dismay that the Ducal Palace received news that the Genoese freebooter Enrico Pescatore, otherwise known as Henry of Malta, had led a large fleet into the harbour at Candia in 1206 and captured it. He had subsequently established fourteen strongholds throughout the island with the obvious intention of occupying it. Stirred from its lethargy, *La Serenissima* dispatched Ruggiero Premarino and Ranieri Dandolo, son of the deceased Doge Enrico Dandolo, with thirty-one galleys to regain the island.[7] It was the start of a five-year struggle which would require significant monetary and manpower outlays from both maritime republics.

As it turned out, the initial Venetian expedition to recover Crete did little to dislodge Pescatore and his minions from the island, but it did nonetheless contribute substantially to the Venetian cause. It pushed another Genoese corsair, Leonardo Vetrano, from Corfu at the entrance to the Adriatic and claimed Modon and Coron on the southern tip of the Messenia peninsula.[8] These last two outposts would come to be regarded as the 'two eyes of the Republic', because their strategic location enabled them to monitor traffic to and from the Aegean.[9] Premarino and Dandolo returned with an even larger force in 1207, but again failed to recapture Crete, the latter losing his life in the attempt.[10] Sustained Venetian pressure, however, was beginning to take its toll. Pescatore appealed to Genoa for help in 1208 and was answered with an influx of men, ships and supplies. Determined not to be denied, Venice responded with further reinforcements under commanders Giacomo Longo and Giacomo Tiepolo. Pescatore apparently did not have the resources to keep up the struggle on his own, so he returned to Genoa to seek an additional 20,000 pounds of support. He received 18,000, but the Venetians had made serious inroads on the island in his absence. By 1211 Pescatore had lost most of his fortresses, while vigilant Venetian squadrons had intercepted the majority of his auxiliaries from Genoa. It was hopeless. Pescatore sued for terms while he could still salvage something. As for Genoa itself, the costs had exceeded the benefits. It agreed to a treaty with Venice in July 1212, terminating hostilities.[11]

The War of San Sabas (1256–8)

A peace had been made and it lasted, mostly by distraction, for nearly half a century, but the embers of enmity had not been extinguished. They would rekindle anew with the slightest provocation. Predictably, that provocation occurred in the most probable of places: one of the three main trade entrepôts of the East where the merchants of the two maritime powers lived and worked in close proximity with one another: Acre. In the spring of 1256 a Venetian reportedly beat and killed a Genoese man there, prompting the victim's compatriots to visit violent vengeance on the Venetian quarter.[12] According to the 'Eracles Continuation' of William of Tyre, 'With help from the Pisans, the Genoese defeated the Venetians and took and ransacked their street right up to and in St Marks.'[13] But almost every source concurs that the real objective was a house owned by the Greek Orthodox monastery of San Sabas in the Kidron valley of Judaea east of Jerusalem. The 'Rothelin Continuation' of William of Tyre indicates that this edifice was located in Acre 'by the sea between Genoese and Pisan territory' on land which, if held by the Venetians, could block Genoese access to the harbour.[14] More fundamentally, the Italian maritime historian Camillo Manfroni identified the root cause of the discord as simply 'hatred which stemmed from greed of gain and the desire to monopolize trade'.[15]

The Genoese used the incident to seize the disputed structure by force, along with all the Venetian vessels anchored in the port. The Venetians initially seemed to seek a redress of grievances through diplomacy. They proposed a meeting of emissaries at Bologna. In retrospect, however, they were probably just buying time, because said summit never took place. Instead of sending ambassadors to parlay with their Genoese counterparts, Doge Raniero Zeno directed Lorenzo Tiepolo (the son of former Doge Giacomo Tiepolo) with fourteen well armed galleys to accompany the annual merchant convoy to *Oltremare* (Italian for *Outremer* or 'beyond the sea', i.e., the Latin Kingdom) the next summer.[16] At the same time (14 July 1257) Venetian envoys in Modena negotiated a ten-year alliance with the Pisans, who needed little convincing since the Genoese had attacked their garrison at the Castello di Castro in Cagliari on Sardinia the year before. Tiepolo arrived at Acre with his squadron in September and promptly smashed through the harbour chain with the prow of his flagship. His men quickly subdued the Tower of Flies which guarded the harbour, then put to the torch every Genoese merchant vessel in port. After storming ashore and occupying the house of San Sabas by sword, the Venetians joined forces with their new Pisan allies to besiege the towers of the Genoese quarter.[17] The War of San Sabas had begun in earnest.

The Venetians may have gained the upper hand, but vanquishing the Genoese proved no easy task. The 'Templar of Tyre' (a fourteenth-century historian with the Templars on Cyprus) noted, 'There were in the Genoese quarter about 800 armed men ...'[18] And they controlled one of the most imposing fortified towers in the city. Both sides possessed a daunting arsenal of up to sixty stone-throwing machines from trebuchets to mangonels, ten of which the 'Rothelin Continuation' reported 'could deliver rocks weighing as much as 1,500 pounds weight of Champagne'. The incessant bombardment went on all winter. 'This meant that nearly all the towers and strong houses in Acre were destroyed, except for religious houses,' added the 'Rothelin Continuation'.[19] Even Pope Alexander IV attempted to mediate an end to a war which was clearly counterproductive to the Christian cause, but to no avail.[20]

Genoa responded much as Venice had done, by sending a squadron of galleys. Ten warships under the command of Pasquetto Mallone arrived in Tyre that autumn, joining another seven galleys already in port. Lorenzo Tiepolo soon challenged them, however, with nineteen Venetian galleys. The result was another Genoese setback. The Genoese galleys filed out through the narrow opening of Tyre's harbour one or two at a time, only to be scooped up by the waiting Venetian fleet before the others could help. Tiepolo soon returned to Acre with four captured galleys, including Mallone's flagship.[21] Finally, the Genoese, determined to attenuate the humiliation suffered at the hands of their hated rivals, launched a much larger fleet of twenty-five galleys and four *navi* (large sailing vessels) under the command of Rosso della Turca, a prominent figure in the commune who had previously been chosen to head the Genoese contingent in Louis IX's crusade to Egypt.[22] The stage was set for a climactic naval confrontation outside the port of Acre in June 1258.

The details of this naval engagement divulge much about how the war was prosecuted at sea on both sides, so it is the subject of a special section. It suffices to say here that it went very badly for the Genoese. Despite numerical superiority, their fleet was all but destroyed, precipitating their immediate eviction from Acre altogether. The rest of the war would, therefore, be fought in other venues, but the results in head-to-head clashes with Venetian fleets would be disturbingly similar for the Genoese. Fortunately, they were more successful with other approaches.

Genoa and the *Guerre de Course* (1261–70)

What the Genoese lost with a galley fleet at Acre they more than made up for with a quill at Nymphaion (near modern Izmir in Turkey) on 13 March 1261. In a master stroke of prescient planning, *Capitano del Popolo* Guglielmo Boccanegra had his emissaries negotiate a treaty with Michael VIII Palaiologos, the Emperor of Nicaea, at his winter palace, in which the Ligurian republic promised naval assistance (specifically, fifty armed galleys) to help the emperor retrieve Constantinople from the Venetians in return for special trading status within the empire. Not five months later Michael sent his general, Alexios Strategopulos, to scout the city's defences. On 24 July the latter discovered that the Latin army and the Venetian fleet were elsewhere, so he gained entry with his modest force by subterfuge in the dark of night and assumed control. The Latin emperor, Baldwin II, was forced to flee and the Venetian quarter was torched. Literally overnight, and by virtue of fickle fortune, Genoa had wrenched away Venice's privileged position within the empire without dispatching so much as a single galley.[23]

A year later the Genoese capitalized on their newfound strategic advantage while demonstrating their superiority at another time-honoured form of naval warfare: the *guerre de course* ('war of the chase' – raiding). In 1262 a Genoese flotilla based in Constantinople, in coordination with some Greek galleys, seized a Venetian *nef* (same as a *nave* – a large sailing vessel) and its accompanying three galleys near Abydos in the Dardanelles. The encounter seems relatively insignificant until one considers that the large Venetian merchantman contained an entire year's worth of *La Serenissima*'s Black Sea trade. For Venice, the economic implications of Genoa's control of the Bosporus (and thus access to the Black Sea) were dire indeed.[24]

That said, the performance of Genoese fleets in set-piece engagements with their Venetian counterparts continued to be dismal. In 1263 a Genoese fleet of thirty-eight galleys was conveying provisions to Malvasia (modern Monemvasia on Cape Maleas of the Peloponnesos) at the behest of Emperor Michael when it encountered thirty-two Negroponte-bound Venetian galleys near Settepozzi (the Island of Spetzes at the eastern entrance to the Argolic Gulf). Two of the four Genoese admirals, Lanfranco Spinola and Pietro Advocato, viewed their numerical edge as an opportunity and attacked. Unfortunately for them, only a dozen of the other galleys joined them. The others demurred, according to the *Annales Ianuenses*, on the rationale that the Venetians had claimed exemption from assault due to their supposed status as 'crusaders'.[25] Frederic Lane, however, offers a more plausible explanation: 'Apparently the Genoese fleet had been outfitted in part by contractors and was partly under command of admirals interested in returns to their investors.'[26] Thus, divided, ineffectual command persisted as a problem for Genoese naval operations. The Venetians captured four galleys, including those of Spinola and Advocato, while suffering no losses of their own.[27]

Guerre de course won the Genoese some measure of redemption, however, in the aftermath of the battle. Some of the survivors of Settepozzi ambushed and seized four fully loaded Venetian *taride* (in this case, oared merchantmen) off Malvasia.[28] But the most significant victory for Genoese communal freebooting came the following year, in 1264. It was brought about in large measure by the Venetian *muda* system in which merchant caravans or convoys ran on a set schedule along prescribed routes. These state-supervised convoys left the Lagoon twice a year: in the early spring to return in the autumn and in the late summer to come back in the spring after wintering over. They normally sailed between Crete and the Peloponnesos, splitting after passing Cape Matapan (at the end of the Mani peninsula), one caravan continuing east to *Oltremare* and Alexandria, the other turning north to 'Romania' (Byzantium and the Black Sea). But after Venice's ejection from Constantinople in 1261, most *muda* headed for the Levant.[29] This highly organized but very predictable *modus operandi* proved particularly vulnerable to the type of maritime warfare practised so well by the Genoese: state-sponsored piracy.

The stakes were extremely high. The capture of a single caravan would mean the loss of a whole trading season's worth of revenue for *La Serenissima*, inflicting a devastating impact on its economy while providing Genoa with a commensurate windfall. Both sides were keenly aware of this, so a cat-and-mouse game between Venetian convoy escort vessels and Genoese raiders ensued. In the summer of 1264 rumours reached Venice that Genoa was preparing a fleet of some ninety galleys to intercept the annual caravan to the Levant, so the city's leaders delayed the *muda*'s launch in order to assemble a fleet of fifty war galleys under Andrea Barocio to contend with the Genoese.[30] The Genoese had, in fact, gathered a fleet, but it consisted of a more modest twenty galleys and two large *navi*.[31] The rumours of a larger fleet were probably part of an intentional disinformation campaign prosecuted by its commander, Simone Grillo, to draw out the bulk of Venetian maritime muscle so he could observe its movements through spies and evade it.

In a clever demonstration of *legerdemain*, Simone Grillo ushered his squadron out of Genoa in June 1264 and moved it swiftly down the Tyrrhenian coast of Italy, spreading the word at various ports of call that his destination was the Levant. Andrea Barocio took the bait. He set sail with his fleet and headed for the Strait of Messina, hoping to intercept and destroy the Genoese flotilla. But, instead of turning east once he cleared the Strait, Grillo made directly for Malta, where he waited patiently for his plan to play out. Thus, when Barocio arrived in Sicilian waters he could find only unconfirmed reports that Grillo was already on his way to *Oltremare* to raid Venetian trading interests there. So off to the East he went.[32]

Meanwhile, the Venetian caravan, confident that Barocio's galleys had cleared the way, finally set out from the Lagoon on 1 August with thirteen *taride*, two light galleys, a *saetta* (an oared scout vessel – same as a *sagitta*), a *panzione* (presumably a broad-beamed transport of some sort) and three *navi*, one of which was the giant *Roccafortis* (38.19m/125ft 4in in length, 14.22m/46ft 8in in breadth and 9.35m/30ft 8in in height amidships). Grillo, who seems to have enjoyed an effective network of spies, was obviously aware of these movements, because his timing was more or less perfect. He left Malta only after Barocio had taken his fleet east and the caravan had departed Venice but not yet cleared the Adriatic. He intercepted the latter on 14 August abeam Saseno Island (present-day Sazan) in the Strait of Otranto just south of Durazzo. He had only sixteen galleys with him because he had allowed the two *navi*, escorted by three galleys, to trade in Tunis and had sent one galley to keep an eye on Barocio. But it was more than enough. Only the high-hulled *Roccafortis* escaped.[33] 'Our men captured the *taride*, the *navi* and the galleys, and of them a *nave* was sunk and a *tarida* was burned,' reported the Genoese annals, which went on to claim: 'In that capture, as publicly rumoured, the Venetians suffered damages in excess of 100,000 Genoese lire, and the commune of Genoa earned from the sale of the plunder taken more than 30,000 Genoese lire for its treasury.'[34]

Of course, the Genoese *guerre de course* worked well only as long as their corsair squadrons were able to avoid the Venetian war fleets. Such was not the case off the west coast of Sicily in the spring of 1266. When the Genoese admiral Lanfranco Borbonino departed Bonifacio in Corsica with twenty-seven galleys in early June, he was aware that a Venetian battle fleet was cruising the waters around Sicily. Estimates of thirty or more enemy galleys had reached him. This would explain why he headed for Trapani, instead of the Strait of Messina. In any event, he arrived there on 22 June only to discover that the Venetian fleet was anchored at Marsala, barely 26km (16 miles) to the south. Evasion was no longer an option. The good news was that the Venetian fleet numbered only twenty-four galleys and two *saette*. In a council of war that night Borbonino was advised to stand out to sea for the inevitable confrontation, but instead he chose the more cautious tactic of linking his ships together, sterns to the shore, in a classic defensive posture.[35] In this case it would turn out to be a horrendous blunder.

Normally, it would have been a sensible strategy, but it required reliable, well disciplined crews to carry it out – something which Borbonino did not enjoy. John Dotson, an expert on Venetian maritime warfare, notes that most of Borbonino's mariners were 'hired as substitutes for Genoese citizens who thus evaded their obligation for fleet service'.[36] As a consequence, when Venetian admirals Iacopo Dandolo and Marco Gradenigo showed up at Trapani on 23 June and aggressively advanced amidst strident shouting, the Genoese crewmen panicked. 'The Genoese, having seen that the enemy was coming upon them and having seen that their leader had lost his nerve, composure and reason,' recounted the Genoese annals, 'threw themselves immediately into the sea after having abandoned the galleys, which were all taken without any fight and without defence.'[37] The débâcle was total and unqualified. The Venetians ended up towing away twenty-four Genoese galleys and burning three.

Thereafter stalemate settled in. In an attempt to curtail growing Genoese influence inside the capital, in 1267 Emperor Michael VIII granted them a merchant base across the Golden Horn in Pera (modern Galata), but soon realized his mistake. The colony rapidly grew to dominate commerce in the region. David Abulafia points out that, in time, 'The trade revenues of Genoese Pera dwarfed those of Greek Constantinople, by a ratio of seven to one.'[38] Wary of the mounting mercantile muscle of his erstwhile allies, the emperor reinstated the Venetians in their old quarter within the walls of the city the next year. And in 1269 Louis IX cajoled the two maritime powers into agreeing to a five-year truce, so that both could support his Tunis crusade the following year.[39]

The War of Curzola (1294–9)

The truce of 1269 was renewed several times and a chary coexistence between the two mercantile maritime powers persisted in the eastern Mediterranean for more than twenty years. What finally fractured the peace was precipitated by neither Venice nor Genoa, but by the Mamluks of Egypt. Their conquest of Acre in 1291 contracted the trading environment available to western merchants in the East and sharply elevated competition for what was left. The Venetians, who had lost their substantial quarter in Acre, grew increasingly more resentful of the Genoese presence in the region. An incident in July 1293 amply revealed the *sub rosa* animosity between the two. Near Coron a small Venetian squadron of four galleys by chance came upon seven Genoese merchant galleys returning from 'Romania'. Instead of giving way, the Venetians attacked, resulting in the capture of all their vessels.[40]

The next confrontation would not be by accident. The loss of Acre to Christianity meant that trading posts in Cyprus, especially Famagusta, and in Armenia, specifically the Cilician port of Lajazzo (modern Ayas in Turkey), were all the more vital. And the Venetians wanted these entrepôts for themselves. In 1294 they sent at least fourteen war galleys (possibly as many as twenty-five) under Marco Basegio with the annual caravan to Famagusta and Lajazzo in the apparent hope of duplicating their success in the War of San Sabas thirty-six years earlier. They first raided the Genoese enclave in Limassol, but this served to alert the Genoese of Pera, who quickly armed a flotilla of merchant galleys under the command of Niccolò Spinola. The latter caught the Venetians off Lajazzo with their sails up, ill-prepared for battle, and scored an impressive victory. The Genoese easily outmanoeuvred the Venetian vessels, driving into many of them amidships. They seized nearly all of them.[41]

This last clash signalled all-out war and spurred Genoa to a mammoth mobilization. The Genoese chronicler Iacopo Varagine claimed that the commune's *Credenza* (war council) produced a fleet of 165 galleys, mostly triremes with crews of 220 to 300, amounting to around 45,000 men.[42] Lesser estimates put the total crew complement at about 35,000, which was still, in the words of John Dotson, 'the population equivalent of a substantial medieval city'.[43] In an ostentatious display of logistical execution, the Genoese actually launched this gargantuan task force in August 1295 under Oberto Doria, the hero of Meloria, daring the Venetians to challenge it. They even went so far as to deploy it to Messina to make the meeting easier. However proud of their prowess at sea the Venetians may have been, they were not arrogant fools. They declined the offer, leaving the Genoese to return home, their blood-lust unsated.[44]

Instead, in July of the following year the Venetians charged Ruggiero Morosini (nicknamed 'Malabranca', meaning 'Evil Claw') with conducting an armada of around seventy galleys on a raid of Pera. He not only left the Genoese colony in ashes, but also sank what merchant vessels he could find in the Golden Horn. Morosini later plundered Phocaea, a port on the west coast of Asia Minor owned at the time by the Genoese nobleman Benedetto Zaccaria, famed for his role in the Battle of Meloria. Thereafter, the Venetian admiral detached a squadron under Giovanni Soranzo which then proceeded into the Black Sea to prey on Genoese shipping and ravage the Genoese colony at Caffa (present-day Feodosiya) on the coast of Crimea.[45] Nor did *La Serenissima* neglect *Oltremare*. Nine galleys were also dispatched under Frosio Morosini to pillage Genoese possessions on Cyprus and at Lajazzo.[46] The Venetians had quite evidently learned the value of waging the *guerre de course*.

The Genoese had finally recovered enough from the rigours of amassing Oberto Doria's massive armada of 1295 to attempt some measure of retribution in 1297. They sent a sizeable fleet of eighty war galleys into the Adriatic to wreak havoc on Venetian shipping and coastal properties, but they made the mistake of placing it under the split command of two admirals who reviled each other: Gando de Mari and Tommaso Spinola. They lingered in the area until their *biscotti* ran low, hoping in vain to engage the main Venetian fleet. It was then that the two had their predictable falling-out. Spinola wanted to remain longer; De Mari did not. The latter took fifty galleys and departed for Sardinia; Spinola stayed with the remaining thirty galleys until the Venetian admiral Andrea

Dandolo chased him back to Sicily and beyond with an estimated eighty-two galleys.[47] The Genoese would attempt to penetrate the Adriatic again the next year, but this time it would be under the unified command of Lamba Doria, the younger brother of Oberto Doria, and the results would be very different.

The particulars of the Battle of Curzola remain clouded by a crowd of conflicting accounts, the principal one of which is an epic poem by an anonymous Genoese author whose expressed purpose was to extol the exploits of his compatriots. There are, however, some common elements from which a general picture emerges. Late in the summer of 1298, after a brief stop at Messina, Lamba Doria led his eighty-five or so galleys into the Strait of Otranto. There a fateful storm scattered his armada and he ended up seeking shelter at the port of Antivari (present-day Bar in Montenegro) with about twenty of his ships. Around fifty-seven ships joined him the next day, but at least eight remained unaccounted for. These would later prove crucial, but for the moment Doria decided to proceed north along the Dalmatian coast, pillaging Venetian possessions as he went. By the end of August his fleet of about seventy-seven galleys had made it as far as the island of Curzola (modern Korcûla off the coast of Croatia). There, in an apparent attempt to draw the Venetian fleet out for battle, the Genoese ruthlessly ravaged the Venetian-ruled town of the same name on the east end of the island.[48]

If that was their plan, it worked. When word reached the Rialto, the Venetians hastily collected a fleet, calling on Chioggia and their colonies all along the Dalmatian coast to supply ships. Even Marco Polo, believed to be a native of Curzola, provided a galley on which he personally served as captain. In all, ninety-five galleys and three *navi* were gathered under the overall command of Captain General Andrea Dandolo, the son of the former Doge Giovanni Dandolo. Manning such an armada so quickly proved a daunting challenge and must have resulted in crews below the calibre of those who normally served onboard Venice's vessels. Manfroni went so far as to term them 'a tumultuous collection of improvised crews'. But the size of this fleet made Dandolo overconfident: he ordered Maffeo Quirini, on patrol in the Adriatic with thirteen galleys, to return to Venice because he would not need his ships.[49]

Dandolo's armada found the Genoese on Saturday, 6 September at the east end of the narrow channel between the island of Curzola and the peninsula of Sabbioncello (Pelješac) jutting northwestwards off the Dalmatian mainland. (*See* Map 10.) Lamba Doria immediately ordered his galleys to link together in a line across the strait (about 1,600m or a mile wide abeam the town of Korcûla) and moor with their bows facing northwest towards the Venetians, presumably with the south flank anchored on the town of Curzola, which the Genoese had occupied. But he made no effort to engage. It was sunset and the onset of darkness rendered combat impracticable. So the two fleets sat warily watching each other through the night. Some Venetian sources even reported that Doria, daunted by Dandolo's enormous armada, sought terms, but this has been discounted by most modern historians. If it happened at all, the Genoese naval commander was probably just playing for time in the hope that his straggling galleys would arrive in time. In any event, Dandolo not only rejected the overtures, but dispatched the

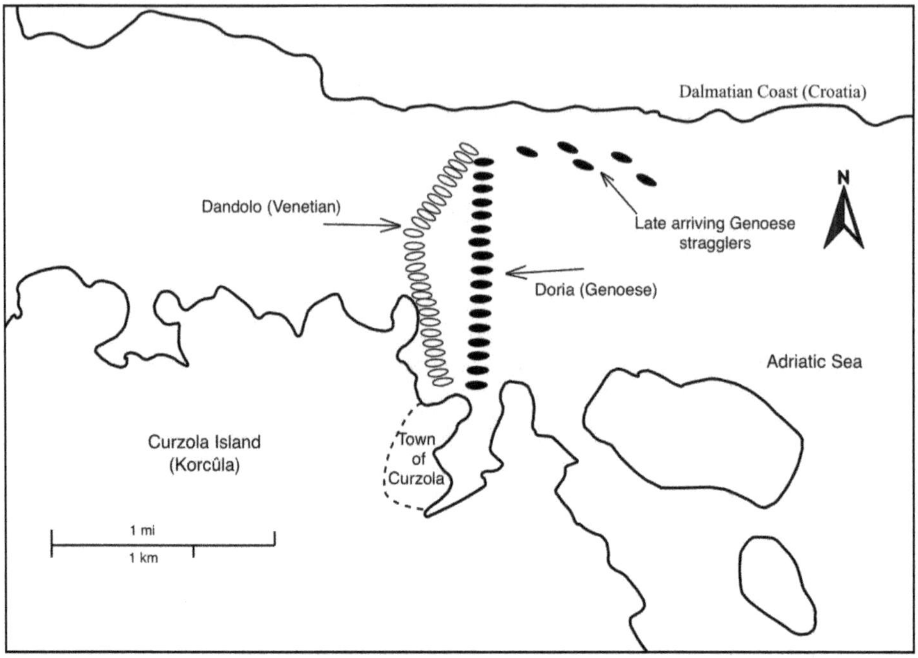

Map 10. Battle of Curzola in 1298. *(Kristy Stanton)*

famed corsair Domenico Schiavo in a *columbet* (a sort of small scout ship) to ensure that the Genoese did not attempt to abscond in the night.[50]

On Sunday morning, 7 September 1298, the Venetians advanced amid the usual missile exchange. Details are scant, but Dandolo was said to have formed his fleet into a semi-circle with the apparent intention of enveloping the smaller Genoese force, particularly the exposed north flank. Doria therefore detached a squadron of eight to ten galleys to counter the encircling wing. It was repulsed, but when the Genoese galleys withdrew back into their line, several Venetian galleys evidently gave chase and the formation's integrity broke down.[51] 'Thus, the Venetians ended up in the midst of the Genoese,' reported the 'Templar of Tyre'.[52] At this point it seems Doria had his ships sever their anchor hawsers and bridling cables in order to manoeuvre at will. The Genoese may have had the advantage here: contemporary reports suggest that their galleys were larger, better equipped and more manoeuvrable. For instance, they were probably employing the highly efficient *terzaruolo* (three oarsmen per bench) rowing system and they almost certainly enjoyed the more responsive sternpost-mounted rudders. Many must have been triremes with crews one and half times the size of the Venetian biremes.[53] In any event, the battle seems to have degenerated into a bloody free-for-all. Doria's own son Octaviano was mortally wounded with a crossbow bolt. Legend has it that Doria had his son's corpse dumped over the side in mid-combat on the premise that there could have been no more fitting interment.[54] The contest was decided at the eleventh hour by the unexpected arrival of the missing eight or so Genoese galleys. These attacked one of the nearly exhausted Venetian flanks, causing its collapse.[55]

It would be the largest battle the Venetians would ever fight against their Ligurian adversaries. It would also be their worst defeat. Of the ninety-six galleys that took part, perhaps only a dozen made it back to Venice, commanded by the resourceful Domenico Schiavo. Over 7,000 men perished. Estimates of those captured range from 8,000 all the way up to 16,000, including Andrea Dandolo himself.[56] Reports of his ultimate fate vary, but the most oft-repeated version is that he killed himself by intentionally bashing his head against the rower's bench to which he had been chained.[57] One man who survived, of course, was Marco Polo, who was transported back to a Genoese gaol, where he would dictate his famous *Travels* to the Pisan, Rustichello. The victory clearly belonged to the Genoese, but it was a Pyrrhic one. Although *La Serenissima* had been rendered virtually defenceless by the annihilation of its armada, Lamba Doria found he was unable to press the advantage. 'It seems that his losses, including deaths and injuries, exceeded those of the Venetians,' surmised Manfroni.[58] Doria instead burned all the captured galleys (presumably because he did not possess the manpower to crew them) and returned to Genoa to a muted homecoming.[59]

Domenico Schiavo attempted to salvage some measure of Venetian pride the next year by leading a raid on Genoa itself. He seized some merchantmen and planted the flag of St Mark on the port's mole (breakwater), but the war had in reality run its course.[60] **(Pl. 16)** Neither power was in any condition to continue. The Venetians had to rebuild their fleet and the Genoese were, once again, afflicted by civil war. Francesco Grimaldi, the head of the Guelph faction, had instigated a rebellion against the Ghibelline rule of the Doria and Spinola families, turning Monaco into a rebel base.[61] Both sides willingly embraced the peace brokered by Matteo Visconti, lord of Milan, in which Venice recognized Genoese supremacy over the Ligurian Riviera and Genoa did the same for Venice in regard to the Adriatic. The pact was signed in Milan under the auspices of Pope Boniface VIII on 15 May 1299.[62] Marco Polo was released, along with many of his compatriots, in August.

The Arsenal of Venice and the Advent of the Great Galley (1294–1335)

The shock of Curzola may well have inspired the largest expansion of the Arsenal of Venice since its founding in 1104. Until the early fourteenth century the state shipyard had covered about 8 acres, enough space to construct and maintain about twenty-four light galleys under the direction of three *patroni*, 'Lords of the Arsenal'. Most of the large war fleets sent out by *La Serenissima* during that time were either conscripted merchantmen or galleys produced in private shipyards. Recent events, however, evidently convinced the Great Council that this system was inadequate for dealing with the city's current threats. Accordingly, it approved two massive enlargements, one in 1303 and another in 1325, which quadrupled the Arsenal's acreage. These additions together were named the New Arsenal.[63] Eventually, the shipyard's operations became so streamlined that it could produce a light galley in less than a day. It built one in an hour for King Henry III of

France in 1574. Constructed ships were stored in covered sheds together with all the necessary components so that they could be swiftly assembled. Lane found that the Arsenal was expected to outfit an entire armada in less than two months: 'Assuming the galleys ready on the docks, all the needed oars, cordage, anchors, sails, masts, spars, deck furnishings, and arms ready and sorted in the warehouses assigned them, the whole fleet of one hundred galleys was to be sent out of the Arsenal fully equipped inside fifty days!'[64]

The creation of the New Arsenal coincided with the advent of a new convoy system and a new ship to serve as its core vessel: the 'great galley'. Until the very end of the thirteenth century Venice had depended upon light bireme galleys (*galie sotil*) about 35–37m (115–121ft) long and 4.5m (14ft 9in) wide to defend commercial caravans of sailing ships (*navi grosse*).[65] In peaceful times the Arsenal normally equipped around ten light galleys called 'galleys of the guard' to police the upper Adriatic and carry out escort duties for caravans. This number increased to twenty or thirty under a 'Captain General of the Sea' in time of war.[66] The destruction of the annual Levantine caravan in 1264 by the Genoese admiral Simone Grillo, who had managed to separate it from its escort by trickery, taught the Great Council that new measures were needed.[67] Thus, in 1294 *La Serenissima*'s Senate instituted production of a galley which could serve as both a warship and a merchantman – i.e., a longer, wider and deeper galley which could accommodate considerable cargo while being crewed by a full complement of fighting oarsmen. The result was the *galea grossa* ('great galley').[68]

The first versions of the vessel were about 40.5m (133ft) long by 5.3m (17ft) wide and 2.5m (8ft) in depth, boasting a cargo capacity of around 140 tons. Later iterations were as long as 46m (151ft) and as wide as 8m (26ft), with 3m (10ft) of depth, capable of carrying 250 tons. All of them were *triremes* which employed the *alla sensile* oarage system *a terzaruolo*. **(Pl. 17)** The rowers all sat on the upper deck, three to a bench, each man pulling his own oar (about 10m/33ft long and weighted at the inboard end) in a stand-and-sit stroke fashion, pivoting through an outrigger. Earlier great galleys contained twenty-five angled benches or thwarts per side for 150 oarsmen while later, larger ones sported thirty per side for at least 180 rowers. (*See* Fig. 4.) The superstructure of these ships was substantial as well. There was a fighting platform on the bow which contained the anchors, a mainmast stepped slightly forward which supported a huge lateen sail and a smaller mast amidships. A multi-level sterncastle, which housed the ship's master and a helmsman who manipulated a sternpost rudder, lorded over it all.[69] The detailed description by a late fifteenth-century pilgrim named Friar Felix Fabri indicated that the Arsenal of Venice invested high construction standards in the vessels, resulting in considerable uniformity:

> Now all galleys of the same size are so much alike in all respects that a man who passes from his own galley on board of another would hardly find out that he was on another, except from the officers and crews being different, for Venetian galleys are as like one to another as swallows' nests. They are built of the stoutest timbers, and fastened together with many bolts, chains, and irons.[70]

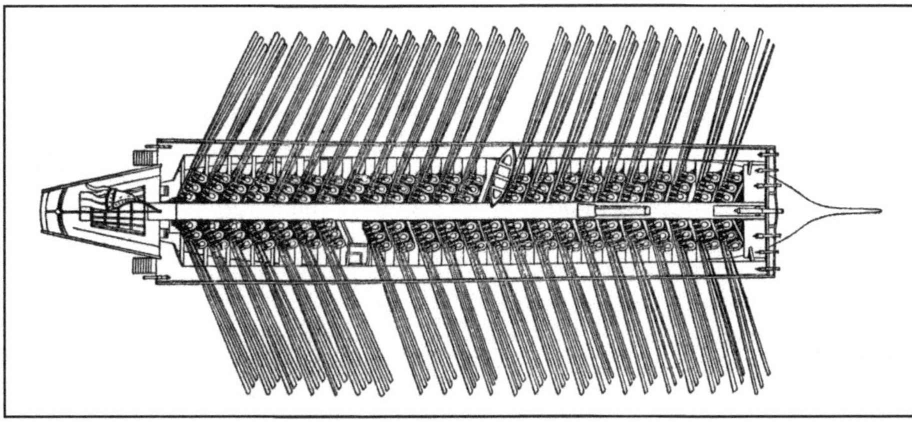

Figure 4. Overhead illustration of a Venetian trireme. (*Luigi Fincati*)

Beginning in 1299, the Senate restructured the caravan system so that all high-value goods such as silks and spices were to be transported on heavily armed vessels like the great galleys.[71] Less dear, bulk commodities were often carried on box-like but cost-effective cogs, which the fourteenth-century Florentine chronicler Giovanni Villani claimed were introduced into the Mediterranean by Bayonnese buccaneers at about the same time (the summer of 1304).[72] The great galleys were all to be built in the Arsenal and rented to merchants by the *Signoria* (government of Venice) for the duration of a caravan or *muda*. This, of course, led to state control of maritime commerce and warfare. Frederic Lane elucidates: 'These state galley fleets were protected from competition of either round ships or privately owned Venetian galleys which might go on the same voyage, and so gradually the state concentrated all galley building in its own hands.'[73] This gave the Venetians a decided advantage in its struggles with Genoa, which did not opt for such rigorous communal control of its maritime assets, although it too eventually adopted a formidable version of a large trireme similar to the great galley.

The War of the Bosporus (1350–5)

The *casus belli* of the Third Genoese–Venetian War was basically the same as the previous spates of open hostility: access to eastern trade. Mamluk domination of the Levant in the late thirteen and early fourteenth centuries had stimulated a shift in the trans-Asian traffic of silks, spices and slaves so that much of it now went through Mongol-controlled territory, namely the Kipchak Khanate of the Golden Horde, which encompassed the Eurasian Steppes north of the Black and Caspian Seas. To tap into this potentially lucrative trade route, Genoa established a base at Caffa (modern Feodosiya) in Crimea on the north shore of the Black Sea, while Venice chose to develop Tana on the Don river estuary as it flows into the Sea of Azov from the northeast.[74] The trouble was that Genoa, by virtue of its presence at Pera on the Bosporus and its colony at Caffa, controlled the sea route to Tana – a matter of considerable frustration to the Venetians. And in the half century since the last conflict between the two, the Genoese had only tightened their grip.[75] In September 1346, for instance, a Genoese fleet under Simone Vignoso won back authority over the key Aegean island of Chios with its alum mines (alum being a naturally occurring chemical compound used as a fixative for dyeing textiles).[76] Venetian patience was running out.

This rising resentment resulted in a renewed *guerre de course* between the two. Maritime historian Susan Rose describes the inevitable progression into full-scale warfare: 'The intermittent, opportunistic taking of vulnerable vessels and their cargos by both sides flared into open conflict when a Venetian fleet of armed galleys sent east under the command of Marco Ruzzini to deal with a quarrel over trading rights at Tana caught about fourteen Genoese galleys in the harbour of Castro near Negroponte and took ten.'[77] Not only did this raid of September 1350 start a new war, but it also backfired. The Venetian fleet consisted of thirty-five galleys and should easily have been able to capture the entire Genoese flotilla. The reason it failed to do so was rooted in a manpower shortage ironically caused by Genoa's Black Sea trade. In the summer of 1347 the Genoese colony at Caffa had been besieged by a Mongol army infected with the bubonic plague. Escaping Genoese ships are believed to have brought the Black Death back to Constantinople, from where the pandemic spread to the rest of western Europe.[78] By 1350 the disease had so decimated the population of Venice that the city could find only enough able-bodied men to crew just twenty-five ships. The rest had to be acquired from Dalmatia and Venice's other colonies. 'But the most serious difficulty', adds Lane, 'was that most of the men drafted in Venice preferred to hire substitutes.' Thus Ruzzini's men were of such poor quality that four of the Genoese galleys were allowed to escape simply through an appalling lack of crew discipline. 'Instead of obeying orders to attack those Genoese galleys which had not yet been subdued,' explains Lane, 'the crews concentrated on plundering the galleys already seized, even jumping into the water and swimming to the surrendered vessels in order to break open the hatches and get at the cargo below.'[79] Ironically, the four Genoese galleys that evaded capture at Castro joined others under Simone Vignoso at Chios and together they sacked the Venetian harbour at Negroponte.[80]

Realizing there would be further retribution, the Venetians sought to address their manpower problems through diplomacy. In January 1351 they negotiated a pact with King Pedro IV of Aragon (Pere III of Catalonia), who was at odds with Genoa over Sardinia, whereby the king would supply eighteen Catalan galleys at his own expense and receive 12,000 ducats (3.5-gram gold coins) per month from Venice to arm an additional twelve warships.[81] They made a similar bargain with the Byzantine emperor John VI Kantakouzenos, promising him the same rate of 1,000 ducats per month for each of eight galleys, if he would arm twelve more from his own coffers.[82] The Catalan and Venetian fleets were to meet at Messina in order to intercept any eastbound Genoese armada, but the Genoese acted before the new allies could arrange their rendezvous. Sometime in the winter or early spring of 1351 Paganino Doria rounded the Peloponnesos into the Aegean at the head of around sixty-four galleys, armed through an extraordinary levy imposed by the communal government.[83]

At the time the only Venetian force operational in the Aegean was a squadron of twenty galleys under the command of Captain General Niccolò Pisani. The latter sought refuge at Negroponte as soon as he learned of the approach of Doria's armada, and even took the precaution of scuttling his ships in order to prevent their capture. Doria laid siege to Negroponte in the summer of 1351, but Pisani and his men managed to hold out.[84] Meanwhile the Aragonese noble Ponç de Santa Pau departed Barcelona with twenty-one galleys in early September to join with the Venetian admiral Pancrazio Giustinian in command of twenty galleys near Messina. Together they relieved Pisani at Negroponte in late October or early November, at which time Doria retired to Pera with the Genoese fleet. Four additional Aragonese galleys captained by Bernat de Ripoll of Valencia also arrived around this time. Pisani then refloated his ships and the allied armada made for Constantinople to link up with the Greek fleet. Heavy north winds and the onset of winter weather, however, compelled them to seek temporary sanctuary at Candia on Crete.[85]

Paganino Doria must have expected that his allied adversaries would await the arrival of calmer spring weather before making their anticipated assault on Pera. If so, he was wrong. Niccolò Pisani and Ponç de Santa Pau were anxious to join the Byzantine flotilla at Constantinople and the invention of the compass late the previous century made it possible despite the darkened clouds of winter.[86] On about 13 February 1352, as the combined Venetian–Catalan armada approached Constantinople, Doria brought his fleet out to prevent its entry into the Golden Horn to unite with the Greek squadron. A strong south wind, however, foiled his efforts.[87] The allies were able to form an amalgamated fleet which, according to the Genoese chronicler Giorgio Stella, consisted of forty-five Venetian galleys, thirty Aragonese and fourteen Greek for a total of eighty-nine warships.[88] Now opposed by a much larger force, John Dotson concludes, 'Doria drew up his sixty [or perhaps sixty-four] galleys in a narrow part of the Bosporus so that their flanks could not be turned by the more numerous allied fleet.'[89]

By all accounts the resulting engagement was a vicious and confused fracas that lasted well into the night. Adding to the horror of a bitter battle in darkness was atrocious winter weather. A violent storm crashed over all, perhaps with attendant flashes of lightning to momentarily illuminate the macabre scene in a frightful freeze-frame. The result was what Frederic Lane described as a 'maniacal slaughter being unchecked by the difficulties of telling friend from foe'.[90] It is certain that neither admiral was able to sustain any semblance of order. 'Because of bad handling by some, and because the battle was disorganized, owing to the weather, for there was a great storm at sea,' wrote Pere III of Catalonia, 'most of the galleys were wrecked and many were lost.'[91] Casualties, consequently, were horrific on both sides. Giorgio Stella plausibly reckoned that 4,000 Venetians and Catalans perished (including Ponç de Santa Pau, who had reportedly initiated the clash with a charge), but less credibly confessed to only 700 Genoese dead.[92] Conversely, Pere III's Catalan chronicle claimed that Genoese losses were 'many more than those of our fleet and that of the Venetians'.[93]

The Genoese, however, were widely considered to have won the encounter simply because Pisani elected to retire the following morning, having assessed his fleet as no longer fit to fight. The Greek galleys had apparently never engaged. In the aftermath of the carnage Emperor John Kantakouzenos chose not to contest the Genoese presence in Pera further. He signed a separate peace with Doria on 6 May.[94] The Aragonese, more concerned about events in the western Mediterranean, withdrew from the theatre. That left the Venetians to uproot the Genoese from the Bosporus alone – a hopeless task, given that the Genoese were allied with the Ottoman sultan Orkhan I, who controlled both banks of the disputed waterway.[95] So the war naturally shifted to the Tyrrhenian.

The Aragonese had bled copiously in the service of Venetian interests in the East and now, as per their pact, they rightfully expected reciprocation from *La Serenissima* in the West. It came at Sardinia in August 1353. The Catalan captain Bernat de Cabrera had assembled a substantial fleet of forty-five galleys, four smaller craft and five large sailing ships at Mahon, Minorca, for the purpose of assaulting Genoese-held Alghero on the northwestern end of Sardinia. Niccolò Pisani waited to join him with twenty Venetian galleys at Cagliari on the southern tip of the island. Cabrera arrived at Alghero on 25 August, immediately disembarking cavalry and Catalan crossbowmen to begin the siege.[96] The Genoese responded with surprising alacrity, quickly gathering sixty galleys under the leadership of Antonio Grimaldi. But the Florentine chronicler Matteo Villani again highlighted the difficulty of arming a sizeable fleet on short notice in the years following the Black Death. He noted that the Genoese could launch only fifty-two of the sixty galleys because they had to cannibalize crewmen from the other eight in order to form complete crews.[97]

When Cabrera learned from scouts that the Genoese fleet was at Asinara, an island about 80km (50 miles) to the north, he called for Riambau de Corbera, the Aragonese governor of Sardinia, to bring the garrison of Sassari (27km or 17 miles northeast) to Alghero. Once Corbera arrived on 27 August with his troops, Cabrera had him assume the siege and then commanded his crews to relaunch their galleys in order to meet the oncoming Genoese fleet. No sooner had they done so than the enemy appeared on the horizon. In a stroke of propitious timing, Niccolò Pisani's squadron of twenty galleys also arrived at that moment. According to Pere III's chronicle, Cabrera wasted no time arranging his ships into battle formation: 'They were all lashed together, that is, one Catalan with one Venetian except for sixteen middle-sized and light galleys, which were behind with five armed ships.'[98] Matteo Villani stated that at least three of these 'armed ships' were actually 'great cogs with castles and four hundred combatants each'.[99] They would come to play a crucial role in the clash ahead.

It was noon by the time the two opposing formations began moving towards one another. The Genoese reportedly had the wind at their backs, but curiously, when they were nearly within crossbow shot of the Catalan line, they 'anchored their galleys by the stern'.[100] Antonio Grimaldi's diffidence is difficult to explain, but he may have been confused by Cabrera's formation or perhaps was concerned that he was outnumbered and thought a defensive posture prudent. He almost certainly saw the high-profile cogs behind the Catalan–Venetian line of galleys. Whatever his reasons, it was a blunder. The allied galleys rowed towards the stationary Genoese line and the usual missile exchange ensued. This went on for two or three hours, and then, late in the afternoon, the wind shifted. The sails of the Catalan cogs filled and the great ships surged forwards into the Genoese line. 'They at once conquered, routed and sank five of the Genoese galleys with all their crews and armament,' recounted Pere III. The battle rapidly devolved into a débâcle from that point.[101]

The chronicle of Pere III claimed that Grimaldi managed to flee with seventeen of his galleys, but Giorgio Stella of Genoa insisted that forty-one galleys were captured.[102] Villani said thirty were seized and nineteen escaped.[103] Regardless of the precise tally, it was an unmitigated disaster for *La Superba*: as many as 8,000 men were reported dead and around 3,200 were taken prisoner. As for the Catalans and Venetians, their losses were comparatively light: 320 dead and a little over 2,000 wounded. One of the latter was Cabrera, who had taken a crossbow bolt to the face, though the wound was not considered life-threatening. The city of Alghero surrendered to him on 30 August.[104]

Both sides were growing weary of a war that had cost their commerce dearly, but there was one final deadly act to play out. The humiliating defeat at Alghero had set off a new round of recriminations in Genoa. The Ghibellines naturally blamed Antonio Grimaldi, a prominent leader of the Guelphs, and a new civil war loomed over the commune. It was only averted by inviting Archbishop Giovanni Visconti, the ruler of Milan, to assume the republic's reins of power in October 1353. Visconti's allegiances were essentially Ghibelline and he was staunchly antithetical towards Venice, which had Guelph leanings. He therefore supported the arming of another twenty-five galleys so that Paganino Doria could renew the *guerre de course* against Venice and its Aragonese allies.[105]

Doria began by raiding the coast of Catalonia the following year (1354), but soon switched operations to the Adriatic. He took several large merchantmen and burned the greater part of the Venetian settlement at Parenzo on Istria (modern Poreč, Croatia).[106] This of course prodded the Venetians into outfitting Niccolò Pisani with a fleet of thirty-five galleys, five castellated sailing vessels and a number of small ships, including *panfili*, *saettie* and *barche*. He eventually hunted Doria down at Chios, but the latter declined battle. Pisani vented his rage on Genoese commerce in the Aegean.[107] In October, with the normal sailing season winding down, Pisani pulled into port at one of the 'two eyes of the Republic' – either Coron or Modon – where he learned that Doria's flotilla had been reinforced with ten more galleys under Visconte Grimaldi. He also received orders to avoid battle, since peace talks had been initiated. Accordingly, Pisani decided to winter his fleet at Porto Longo on Sapienza Island just a few kilometres off Modon on the southwestern tip of the Peloponnesos.[108]

Pisani does not appear to be at fault for what happened next: he seems to have taken all the appropriate precautions. Realizing that a formidable Genoese force remained in the region, he had the five *navi* with castles chained together in the mouth of the harbour and assigned a squadron of fourteen or so galleys under

Nicola Querini to guard the entrance while the rest of the vessels were either moored or beached at the back of the harbour.[109]

In early November local intelligence led Doria to Porto Longo, where he attempted to lure the Venetians out for battle. But it was Pisani's turn to ignore the taunt. Undeterred, Paganino Doria stayed, apparently looking for an opening to exploit. His nephew Giovanni Doria found one. On 4 November, presumably in darkness, he stole past Querini's floating picket in a single galley. When the intrusion went undetected, another dozen Genoese galleys slipped into the harbour. They caught the Venetian vessels near the shore totally unaware and quickly subdued them all. Many of their mariners evidently drowned trying to swim ashore in the chilly winter water. The hapless Venetian guard ships at the entrance were subsequently sandwiched between the two Genoese divisions – Paganino Doria's twenty-two galleys outside the harbour and Giovanni Doria's thirteen inside. Consequently they were soon forced to surrender. Villani described the port area as being littered with the corpses of more than 4,000 Venetians, killed or drowned. Both he and Giorgio Stella noted that over 5,000 prisoners were packed off to Genoa, including Niccolò Pisani – an apparent victim of Querini's incompetence.[110]

Upon his return home, Paganino Doria finally received the victor's triumph he had been denied in the aftermath of the bloody Battle of the Bosporus. He had atoned for the humiliation at Alghero by ensnaring an entire Venetian fleet at the cost of but a few Genoese lives. Nonetheless, the feat ended up buying the commune few advantages. The two mercantile powers were drained by the conflict and wanted peace. Giovanni Visconti of Milan had died on 5 October 1354, leaving his nephews Maffeo, Bernabó and Galeazzo to mediate in June 1355 a treaty which everyone seemed to want. Skilful diplomacy precluded the Venetians from suffering any lasting ill-effects from their crushing defeat at Porto Longo. The peace essentially sanctioned the existing parity between the two protagonists.[111]

The War of Chioggia (1377–81)

The fourth and final Genoese–Venetian war was, for all intents and purposes, a continuation of the third separated by a 22-year truce. The peace of 1355 resolved nothing. 'Basically, the treaty restored peace and established mechanisms for settling future disputes,' aptly encapsulates Steven Epstein, but 'neither side won anything worthy of mention.'[112] The underlying bone of contention remained access to the Black Sea trade. The bitter competition to control that access eventually revealed itself in a rivalry over Tenedos, a little island in the northern Aegean barely 10km (6 miles) by 6.5km (4 miles), i.e., less than 40 square kilometres (15 square miles). Known today as Bozcaada (meaning 'barren island' in Turkish), it is sparsely populated with few fresh water sources. Before the Middle Ages its notoriety resided chiefly in Homeric legend as the place where the Greek fleet hid while the Trojans ushered their deadly gift horse into the city. But in terms of the real-world geopolitics of the late fourteenth century, Frederic Lane succinctly explains its significance: 'Venice and Genoa both sought the island of Tenedos, just south of the Dardanelles [about 24km or 15 miles], for if properly fortified, it could be used to control access to the straits and keep rivals out of the Black Sea altogether.'[113] Tenedos was, then, the gateway to what the ancients called the Hellespont.

This accident of geography was why the Venetians were willing forgive Emperor John V Palaiologos all his debts (about 100,000 *hyperpyra* – 4.5-gram gold coins), return the collateralized crown jewels and pay him the princely sum of 25,000 ducats in the spring of 1370. John accepted, but the deal fell through when his son Andronicos refused to honour it. Andronicos was later half-blinded and imprisoned by his father for attempting to usurp the Byzantine throne. This enabled the Venetians to again offer to buy Tenedos from the penurious emperor in 1376, this time for 30,000 ducats as well as the return of the crown jewels. John again consented, but the Genoese of Galata intervened by freeing Andronicos from the gaol. The latter then succeeded in overthrowing his father and promptly rewarded the Genoese with possession of the coveted island on 23 August. However, the governor, a loyal servant of the father, turned Tenedos over to the Venetians instead. It seems the Genoese remained rather unpopular in the region. The Venetians wasted no time making the most of the situation and immediately dispatched Marco Giustinian with a fleet to take possession. A Venetian soldier of fortune, Carlo Zeno, was sent shortly thereafter with reinforcements. Arone de Struppa arrived from Genoa in November of the following year with ten galleys, but by then the Venetians were too deeply entrenched. They fought him off.[114]

At that point both sides must have understood that all-out war was unavoidable. Renewed animosity had been building for some time. The Venetians could not have been pleased with the invasion and subsequent suppression of Cyprus by Genoa's Pietro Campofregoso at the head of thirty-six galleys in October 1374, because it compromised Venetian commerce with the Levant.[115] They would not suffer being cut off from 'Romania' as well. As for the Genoese, the takeover of Tenedos made them determined to eliminate their Venetian competitors completely. They began lining up allies for the purpose of isolating and curtailing Venice once and for all, just as they had sidelined Pisa at the end of the previous century. The Genoese first detached *La Serenissima*'s strongest confederate in the last war: the king of Aragon. In return for ceding influence in Sardinia, they won from him a promise not to interfere on Venice's behalf. They then made pacts with King Lajos I of Hungary, who had recently conquered Dalmatia from the Venetians, and Francesco da Carrara, the lord of Padua, who wished to claim for himself Venice's *Domini di Terra Ferma* to the west of the Lagoon.[116]

Venice, of course, could count on the support of King Peter II of Cyprus, but there was little help the young monarch could provide. Milan, on the other hand, had designs on incorporating the Ligurian commune in its own sphere of influence and thus made a formidable friend for the beleaguered Venetians. The two city-states signed a four-year pact in November 1377. Not only had Bernabó Visconti of Milan emboldened the marchese of Carretto to seize Albenga with Venice's encouragement, he was raising an army to invade Liguria himself. It was in support of these designs that Vettor Pisani, nephew of Niccolò Pisani, was sent west with fourteen galleys in the spring of 1378. As it happens, Genoa had dispatched Luigi Fieschi with ten galleys towards the Adriatic to bolster the king of Hungary. The small size of the fleets illustrates the deleterious effects that plague and the loss of recruiting territory due to either revolt (the *Riviera Ligure Ponente* for the Genoese) or conquest (Dalmatia for the Venetians) had on fleet manning.[117] In any event, the two flotillas clashed by chance off Anzio, 42km (26 miles) south of Ostia, on 30 May and the Venetians got the better of it. Pisani captured five galleys, including that of Fieschi; one Genoese galley ran into the rocks and four escaped.[118]

In warfare, however, fortune rarely smiles on the same side sequentially. Vettor Pisani retired from the Tyrrhenian and proceeded into the Aegean, where he absorbed a few more galleys into his fleet before re-entering the Adriatic. He asked to return to Venice, but the senate instead commanded him to over-winter at Pola in Istria (modern Pula, Croatia) in order to protect convoys inbound to the Lagoon. He was still there, refitting his ships, when Luciano Doria appeared outside the port on 5 May 1379 with a Genoese fleet. Doria had originally been dispatched at the end of the previous summer with seventeen galleys to harry shipping along the Dalmatian Coast as far as Zara, but he had picked up an additional five along the way to give him a total of twenty-two. Pisani had twenty-one galleys – sixteen *galie sotil* (light galleys) and five *galie grosse* (great galleys) – but some were being careened on the beach, so he initially declined Doria's invitation to fight. However, a council of war with his captains convinced him that eschewing battle would be tantamount to cowardice. After all, only sixteen Genoese galleys could be seen from their vantage point. So out he charged with whatever ships he could make seaworthy. It would prove a terrible mistake.[119]

Initially, Vettor Pisani's verve paid off: Doria's flagship was quickly overwhelmed at the cost of the Genoese admiral's life. But then, just as it appeared victory was in sight, six more Genoese galleys swung around the headland and into the Venetian rear. Triumph rapidly turned to tragedy. Having assessed the hopelessness of the circumstances, Pisani chose to save what he could – six galleys – and bolted for open water. He made good his escape, but he left behind a shambles. All the remaining Venetian vessels were captured, along with more than 2,400 prisoners, including twenty-four nobles. Worse still, the catastrophic defeat had rendered *La Serenissima* nearly defenceless in the face of an emboldened enemy who now possessed the most powerful naval force in the Adriatic. Pisani's reception in Venice reflected the gravity of the situation. Like the Genoese, the Venetians hewed to a rigorous command accountability regimen. They stripped Pisani of command and relegated him to the dungeons – a light sentence actually, considering that the state-mandated punishment for a galley captain who left the scene of an ongoing battle was death.[120]

Just the month before, the Senate of Venice had been so confident in Pisani's ability to protect the home front that they had unleashed Carlo Zeno with five well armed galleys to wage a *guerre de course* on Genoese commerce. Now, after Pisani's pummelling at Pola, the Venetians expanded Zeno's piratical enterprise by sending him an additional six galleys in the hope that his foray into the Tyrrhenian and Ligurian Seas would draw the Genoese fleet out of the Adriatic.[121] Instead, Genoa dispatched reinforcements: fifteen galleys under Pietro Doria, who had been chosen to replace his kinsman as fleet commander. More ships were evidently accumulated along the way, because by the time Doria appeared outside the San Nicolò de Lido entrance to the Lagoon on 6 August 1379 he had with him an estimated forty-seven galleys.[122] Concurrently, the Hungarian forces of King Lajos controlled the roads and rivers to the north and the troops of Francesco da Carrara of Padua pressed Mestre to the west. The situation had not been so dire for *La Serenissima* since Carolingian times.[123]

Seven days later it would get much worse. On 13 August the Genoese fleet, in concert with Francesco da Carrara's 24,000 troops, assaulted the 3,000-man garrison of Chioggia at the southern entrance to the Venetian Lagoon. By 16 August Chioggia was theirs. *La Serenissima*'s enemies not only controlled the surrounding *Terra Ferma* with their land forces and patrolled the northern Adriatic beyond the Lido with their ships, but they now also held a fortified position inside the Lagoon itself. Venice had never been more vulnerable. Panic-stricken, its leaders floated peace overtures.[124] Daniele da Chinazzo, a low-level Venetian city official at the time, famously quoted the response of Pietro Doria, the Genoese Captain of the Sea: 'In the name of God, Lords of Venice, you shall never have peace from either the Lord of Padua or from our Commune of Genoa before we place bridles on those unruly horses of yours which are on the Palace of your Evangelist St Mark.'[125]

The deprecatory reference to the *Triumphal Quadriga*, the four bronze chariot horses looted from Constantinople in 1204 and still housed in St Mark's Basilica, galvanized *La Serenissima*'s leadership into action. The senate imposed a loan on the wealthy based upon a property assessment called the *estimo*, which rapidly produced the sums necessary to hire the *condottiere* Giacomo de Cavalli along with 4,000 cavalry and over 2,000 infantry and crossbowmen.[126] These took responsibility for guarding the various *lidi* (the strands of sandy reef enclosing the Lagoon). The *estimo* also financed the hurried construction of thirty-four to forty galleys in the Arsenal. The problem was manning them. The senate instituted a universal conscription, but most of the able-bodied seamen were either in enemy prisons or on Carlo Zeno's galleys. Those who remained had no interest in serving under the senate's choice for Captain General: Taddeo Giustinian, an arrogant offspring of the old nobility. They preferred the more down-to-earth leadership of the incarcerated Vettor Pisani. After repeated demands for his release, the senate finally relented.[127] 'When at last he was sitting at the bench on the Molo [the current Piazzetta San Marco] to enlist crews,' wrote Frederic Lane, 'the clerks could not write fast enough to enrol all the experienced bowmen, oarsmen, and sailors who crowded around to sign on.'[128]

The Venetians initially expected an imminent attack on their city without walls. The monastery of San Nicolò de Lido was fortified and a defensive stockade complete with towers was constructed along the Lido. Large cogs were sunk in the Lido Inlet and piles marking navigable deep-water channels through the Lagoon were taken up to confuse the potential conquerors. Chinazzo described the lengths that the defenders went to in order to protect the city itself: they closed the western end of the Grand Canal with a reinforced boom and built an ambitious palisade which ran from the San Nicolò de Lido behind San Servolo Island and the Giudecca across the channel leading from Chioggia to the San Martino church by the Arsenal. All of this was guarded by galleys equipped with cannon. An alarm system with the Campanile of San Marco at its core was devised to warn of an impending invasion. Even the San Giorgio Maggiore within sight of the doge's palace was buttressed for battle.[129] It soon became apparent, however, that the Genoese had no intention of attacking Venice itself. Their strategy was to tighten the noose and starve the city into submission. Once Vettor Pisani and Doge Andrea Contarini realized this, they hatched a plan involving the geography and geology of the Lagoon to turn the tables on their besiegers.

From the surface, the Venetian Lagoon appears to be a great open expanse of deep water (about 550 square kilometres or 210 square miles), like a large bay, gulf or inland sea. It is not. Mud flats, tidal shallows and salt marshes comprise almost 80 per cent. Its average depth is less than a metre – about 3ft. At the time most seagoing vessels, particularly those the size of Genoa's triremes, could only navigate it by way of a handful of deep water channels or 'canals'. And all but the shallowest draught ships could access it by just three deep water inlets: the Lido, the Malamocco and the Chioggia. Pisani and Contarini knew that if they could control these access points and the navigable channels within, they would control the Lagoon and any island in its waters – including that of Chioggia.[130]

They set about honing their plan for the remains of the summer and throughout the autumn. They managed to recruit enough shopkeepers, fishermen and craftsmen to crew thirty-four galleys, which they ran back and forth between the Giudecca and the Lido to train their neophyte oarsmen. On the night of 22 December 1379 Pisani and Contarini finally put their plan in motion. Under the cover of darkness, they surreptitiously made their way to the south end of the Lagoon with thirty-three galleys, four large *uscerii* and two great ships. Contarini, who must have been in his seventies, landed south of Chioggia with a large force of infantry and led a dawn assault. It failed, but it was all a diversion. While the Genoese and Paduan garrison was occupied with defensive duties, Pisani and his men were sinking stone-laden hulks in the three deep water channels which connected Chioggia to the mainland and the remainder of the Lagoon. Either at the same time or shortly thereafter, both the Chioggia and Malamocco inlets to the Lagoon were also barred. Within a few hours, the besiegers had become the besieged. Trapped with them was the bulk of the Genoese fleet – at least thirty galleys.[131]

The Genoese and Paduans, of course, fought bitterly to breach the barricaded channels, particularly those waterways leading into the harbour of Brondolo on the south side, but the Venetians, using cannon mounted on the forecastles of their galleys for the first time, managed to hold them off. Both sides grew tired, cold and hungry as a winter war of wills set in. The ageing Contarini steeled the resolve of his compatriots by vowing to remain on the blockade until the Genoese yielded or he died. The tide shifted decisively in favour of the Venetians on

1 January 1380 when Carlo Zeno sailed into the Lagoon after an eight-month absence with fourteen galleys.[132] The concentration of Genoese naval power at Chioggia had allowed him and his crews to ravage Genoese shipping with impunity from one end of the Mediterranean to the other. In Rhodes he had captured the giant cog *Centurione*, reported to be worth a half million ducats, along with three hundred prisoners, many of whom were rich merchants.[133] Now he and his men added fresh vitality to the cordon around Chioggia. A few days later the situation soured still further for the Genoese. Venetian cannon fire brought down a tower in Brandolo on the head of Pietro Doria.[134]

Genoa sent a relief squadron of thirteen galleys under Matteo Maruffo in March. It intercepted a flotilla of twelve Venetian supply ships and four galleys bringing provisions from Apulia under Taddeo Giustinian in April, but ultimately it was of little solace to the Genoese, who were being strangled into submission at Chioggia. Despite repeated attempts and the addition of five more galleys in May, Maruffo's fleet could not break through the Venetian barriers at the Lagoon's inlets. Finally, on 22 June, with food and powder nearly expended, the 4,000 Genoese remaining in Chioggia surrendered, along with nineteen galleys.[135] Vettor Pisani, unfortunately, did not survive the fighting, but Carlo Zeno assumed Pisani's post as Captain of the Sea and gradually cleared the Adriatic of Genoese galleys. The fatigued foes finally agreed to a surprisingly even-handed peace at Turin on 8 August, negotiated through the good offices of Count Amadeus VI of Savoy, in which Genoa retained possession of Tenedos but pledged not to fortify it or impede access to the Black Sea.[136]

Judging from the peace, it almost appears as if Genoa had actually prevailed in its protracted struggle with Venice. It was not so. Venice's more cohesive society and robust political system enabled it to endure despite reverses. It had suffered crushing defeats at Pola and Curzola. 'But events were to prove that Venice,' observed Lane, 'merely by surviving with its spirit, its institutions, and its key colonies intact, had in fact won the long duel with Genoa.'[137] It was an entirely different story for Genoa, which was so rent with internecine conflict that it routinely had to seek recourse to rulers rented from outside the commune. As Steven Epstein noted, 'The city's institutions of government were weak and commanded little respect; perhaps that they survived the war was bad for Genoa.'[138] The Genoese propensity for hiring foreign rulers to do for them what they could not do for themselves inevitably evolved into foreign rule, relegating them to the backwater of history.

Venice's naval organization and its string of bases throughout the eastern Mediterranean gave it advantages, which in the long run Genoa could not overcome, despite such advances in technology as the trireme galley and the *terzaruolo* oarage system. 'The Venetians with their Arsenal and state-owned ships perhaps more nearly approached the modern idea of a navy than did the Genoese combination of state and privately financed fleets,' summarizes John Dotson.[139] Eventually not even that would be enough to stave off the Ottomans who would conquer Constantinople in 1453 and gobble up Venice's colonies one by one.

Exemplary Engagement: The Battle of Acre (June 1258)

The naval engagement which took place off Acre on or about 25 June 1258 clearly illustrates an indisputable maxim endemic to all warfare: battles are usually complicated affairs in which the outcome is often determined by factors other than numerical superiority. When the Genoese admiral Rosso della Turca arrived at Tyre in the spring of 1258 he had with him his original complement of twenty-five galleys and four *navi*, plus eight galleys that the commune had hastily added at the last moment when it learned that Venice had sent reinforcements of its own to *Oltremare*. Waiting for him in the harbour were enough remaining Genoese galleys to give him a total of fifty. In the meanwhile *La Serenissima* had sent Andrea Zeno with another thirteen galleys, followed by Lorenzo Barozzi with about ten more. Three additional Venetian galleys came into Acre from Crete, giving Admiral Lorenzo Tiepolo a fleet of about forty galleys, four large *navi* and perhaps ten smaller vessels.[140] So when the Genoese flotilla showed up outside Acre's breakwater in battle formation in late June, it appeared to enjoy a modest numerical advantage. But, of course, that was not the whole story.

First of all, it seems the Genoese crews were deficient in quality and perhaps even quantity. The *Annales Ianuenses* indicated that Rosso della Turca's fleet was hurriedly scraped together only after the republic's leaders had heard that Venice had already dispatched naval reinforcements to *Oltremare*.[141] This forced them to enlist 'Lombards as soldiers [sailors], men who knew nothing of the sea'.[142] In fact, the last eight Genoese galleys were launched '*sine munitione perfecta*' ('without being fully armed' – meaning without a complete crew complement), 'since in *Oltremare* they lacked galleys more than men'.[143] The obvious implication is that Della Turca was expected to flesh out his crews with inexperienced Genoese colonists upon his arrival in the Latin Kingdom with little or no time to train them. It was a recipe for disaster – fully preparing a green crew for battle would have taken several weeks, if not months.

Furthermore, the Venetians had a vastly superior manpower pool from which to draw. It turns out that the Genoese were singularly unpopular in the Latin Kingdom. The Pisans, the Provençals, the Templars, the Teutonic Knights, most of the inhabitants of Acre and the overwhelming majority of the kingdom's nobility all lined up behind the Venetians, while the Genoese could comfortably count on the support of only the Hospitallers and Philip of Montfort, the lord of Tyre.[144] This was, in part, because the Genoese navigated the convoluted currents of Palestine's politics rather poorly. In February 1258 the very powerful prince of Antioch, Bohemond VI, brought with him to Acre his sister, Queen Plaisance of Cyprus, along with her young son Hugh II, so that they could bid the barony to pay homage to the child 'as the heir and lord of the kingdom of Jerusalem'.[145] Almost all, including the Venetians and Pisans, agreed, but the Genoese, backed by their Hospitaller allies, refused. As a result, 'the queen [Plaisance], on the advice of her brother the prince [Bohemond VI],' recounted the 'Templar of Tyre', 'had all the men of the lordship move to the aid – and into the pay – of the

Pisans and the Venetians, against the Genoese, strictly prohibiting them from taking pay with the Genoese'.[146] Bohemond even went so far as to hire '800 French troops' at his own expense 'to harass' the Hospitallers and Genoese.[147]

More fundamentally, the Genoese in *Oltremare* had apparently acquired the reputation of 'not working and playing well with others', earning the enmity of almost everyone.[148] Thus when the Venetians and Pisans attempted to recruit others to their cause at the handsome rate of 'ten saracenate bezants for the day', there was no shortage of takers. 'As a result,' reported the 'Templar of Tyre', 'they had plenty of men, and they boarded their galleys (forty in number), and equipped other *barques*, *parescalmes* and *panfiles* [various smaller vessels] (of which there were more than seventy), each of which had crossbowmen on board who did the Genoese a great deal of damage and harm.'[149] In an era when missile exchanges and hand-to-hand combat on the decks of engaged vessels were decisive in maritime warfare, a surfeit of so-called *supersalienti* (marines) was a distinct advantage.

Lastly there was the question of leadership. The supervision of the Genoese fleet was manifestly wanting. The commune had placed Rosso della Turca in overall command of the armada, but, according to the Genoese annals, had sent with him his son Mirialdo, 'a staunch and upright man, so that in him, even more than in the father, faith was placed, on account of the old age of the parent'.[150] Clearly, the commune had concerns about the elder Della Turca's continued vigour. He had previously been *Capitano del Popolo* and had been mentioned in the Genoese annals as early as 1214 (forty-four years earlier), meaning he was probably in his late sixties or early seventies. Regrettably, Mirialdo died unexpectedly of unspecified natural causes a few days after the fleet reached Tyre.[151] Thus when Rosso della Turca appeared before Acre with his armada that awful summer morning in June, he was not only still recovering from the rigours of the voyage from Genoa at an advanced age, but was also grieving over the loss of his son.[152] He must have felt very old indeed.

The basic plan of the Genoese and their allies was sound. While the Genoese fleet sailed south from Tyre, Philip of Montfort marched overland with eighty horsemen and thirty archers to a place called *La Vigne-Neuve*, which must have been close enough to Acre to view the oncoming naval engagement. He was to be met there by Brother William of Châteauneuf, Master of the Hospitallers, with as many of his knights and *Turcopoles* as he could muster. Once Rosso della Turca had drawn out the Venetian fleet and destroyed it, Montfort and Châteauneuf were to penetrate the city through the Hospitaller compound and assist their comrades in the Genoese quarter 'seize the two quarters of the Pisans and of the Venetians'.[153] The two bands of confederates did, in fact, join up at *La Vigne-Neuve*, but what they saw happen out at sea was not what they had anticipated.

When the Genoese fleet first appeared offshore, the Venetians and Pisans hesitated 'for fear that the Genoese on land would attack them, and that if they boarded their galleys and the Genoese who were at sea landed, they would lose everything'.[154] They ultimately resolved the quandary by prevailing upon Brother Thomas Bérard, Master of the Templars, to guard their enclaves with his mounted brethren and *Turcopoles*. This accomplished, the Venetians and their allies boarded their vessels and rowed out to confront their Ligurian adversaries.[155] It was then that the best opportunity for a Genoese victory occurred. A 'contrary wind' separated thirteen of the Venetian vessels from the rest as they emerged from the narrow mouth of the harbour.[156]

If Rosso della Turca had positioned his fleet near the point of egress, he would have overwhelmed the divided enemy fleet as surely as his counterpart, Lorenzo Tiepolo, had done to Pasquetto Mallone's flotilla at Tyre the year before. Instead of attacking, however, Della Turca absurdly proceeded to '*prandere*' – that is, 'to take the midday meal'. And, according to the *Annales Ianuenses*, he continued to do so 'between Nones and Vespers' – in other words, from about three in the afternoon to sunset. This gave the Venetian admiral Lorenzo Tiepolo plenty of time to safely egress his entire fleet and arrange it into battle formation with the wind at his back.[157] The consequences for the Genoese fleet during the subsequent battle were nothing short of cataclysmic. Twenty-four of the fifty Genoese galleys were captured and 1,700 of their mariners were either killed or taken prisoner.[158]

Exasperated, Philip of Montfort returned to Tyre. William Châteauneuf, the distraught Master of the Hospitallers, remained in Acre but perished of an undisclosed illness within months afterwards. The consequences for the Genoese colonists of Acre were, perhaps, the most grievous. 'When the Genoese, who were holding their quarter and who had defended it for so long and suffered so much and endured such shortages that an egg could hardly be found for a wounded man to eat, saw that their galleys had been defeated,' wrote the 'Templar of Tyre', 'they abandoned their quarter and took refuge in the Hospital.'[159] They eventually made their way up to Tyre, which then became the main Genoese entrepôt in the Latin Levant. As for the Pisans and Venetians, they dismantled every edifice in the Genoese quarter, including the great fortified tower. Lorenzo Tiepolo personally transported the square pillars from the tower's base back to Venice, where they stand to this day outside the baptistery of St Mark's Basilica.[160] **(Pl. 18)**

PART II

NORTHERN EUROPE

The North Sea, the Baltic Sea and the English Channel

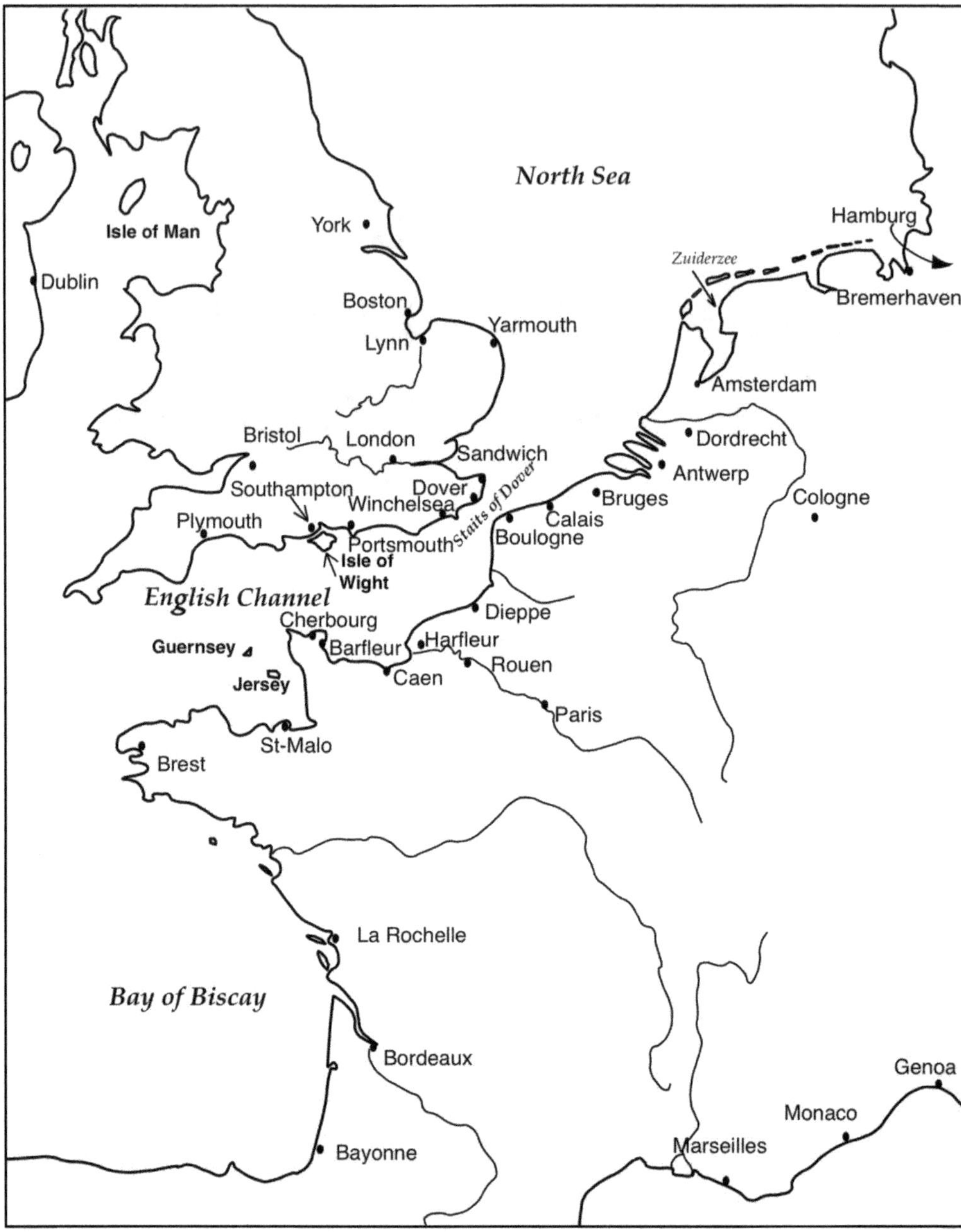

Map 11. The North Sea, English Channel and Bay of Biscay. (*Kristy Stanton*)

Harsher maritime conditions and the dearth of classical models caused nautical architecture and seafaring to evolve uniquely in the northern seas. In comparison to the relatively placid Mediterranean with its consistent climate producing predictable winds and currents, the weather in the North Atlantic and Baltic regions is more tumultuous, characterized by capricious winds and higher sea states. North Sea storms continually pound rocky shorelines. Tides are more pronounced and temperature extremes are more extensive due to the greater breadth of latitude.[1] Moreover, naval traditions inherited from the remnants of Roman rule in the region were threadbare at best. Thus, ship construction techniques were localized and tended to develop mostly in response to environmental factors. Accordingly, the chief criterion was durability. Northern shipwrights constructed hulls using the clinker method, in which overlapping strakes or horizontal planks were nailed together lengthwise in the area of the overlap with iron nails, then braced with crossbeams, as opposed to the carvel construction method prevalent in the Mediterranean, whereby the strakes were fitted edge-to-edge over a prefabricated frame. (*See* Fig. 5.) This theoretically gave northern ships the sturdiness to withstand the rougher northern seas.[2]

Predecessors to early Frankish warships may have been late Roman riverine galleys (*naves lusoriae* – 'playing ships', i.e., light cruising vessels), as represented by the five Rhine shipwrecks (four warships and one transport) discovered at Mainz in 1981–2, but even these were heavily adapted to suit northern conditions. Built of oak over a 'moulding frame' with iron clench nails, then heavily caulked, early medieval maritime specialist John Haywood observed, 'The Mainz warships represent a complete break with the warship types that the Romans used before the third century.'[3] Built in the late fourth century, the Mainz Type A ships (the four war galleys) were about 18.3m (60ft) long and 3m (10ft) broad, with a shallow draught (about half a metre). They were light and manoeuvrable but strong. Crews of thirty could propel them at speeds up to 10 knots, making them well suited for river patrol operations. Though they were designed primarily for rowing, they did include a mast step, indicating a sail. Their construction seems to have been significantly influenced by indigenous Celtic and German shipbuilding traditions.[4] They bear a striking similarity to the mid-fourth-century Anglian oak ship excavated from a bog at Nydam Moss (Denmark) in 1863 which measured about 21.3m (70ft) long by 3.6m (12ft) wide and could also accommodate thirty oarsmen. The parallels end there, however. The Roman Mainz ships were carvel-built, while the Nydam oak ship was clinker-built with iron clench nails, like almost all other northern vessels of the

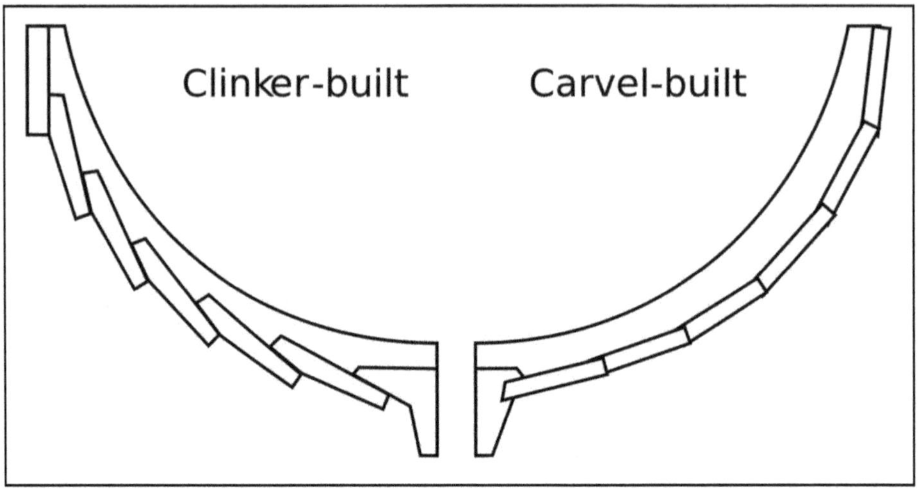

Figure 5. Depiction of clinker and carvel hull construction techniques. (*Willbig*)

period. The famed Sutton Hoo ship buried in East Anglia around 625 was also clinker-built of oak with iron clench nails. Neither it nor the Nydam oak ship contained any visible signs of a mast step.[5] Both were long considered to be purely open rowing barges.[6]

John Haywood, however, does not preclude the possibility that these early Anglian vessels could have been sailed. In fact, nautical researchers Edwin and Joyce Gifford built a half-scale model of the Sutton Hoo ship (13.5m/44ft 4in by 1.1m/3ft 7in), christened the *Sæ Wylfing*, which 'proved to be a highly effective sailing ship, fast, manoeuvrable and, despite its low freeboard, remarkably dry even in choppy seas'.[7] As a matter of fact, Haywood points to a host of physical and literary evidence that suggests Saxons were raiding by sail as early as the fourth century. Sails were in common use among the Angles and the Saxons by the mid-seventh century.[8]

Gillian Hutchinson, an expert in medieval marine architecture, describes a maritime tradition in northern Europe that goes well beyond galley-type vessels and open rowing barges. She identifies three basic ship types unique to the medieval north: the keel, the hulk and the cog.[9] The keel was a ship of Anglo-Saxon or Scandinavian origin, built from the keel up with stem and stern posts scarfed to the ends of the keel and horizontal planking running between the two, giving it a shallow, curved profile like the eleventh-century Skuldelev 3 vessel, one of five Viking ships found scuttled at the entrance to Roskilde Fjord near Skuldelev, Denmark.[10] **(Pl. 19)** The hulk was a crescent or banana-shaped vessel with a rounded hull formed by horizontal planking that terminated in 'collars' or platforms at a high prow and stern. Depictions of it are found on town seals, like that of Shoreham in Sussex, which used to be known as 'Hulksmouth'. No hulk has ever been excavated.[11] The third type, the cog, would later become dominant in the north. It was characterized by an elevated freeboard (high sides), straight stem and stern with a flat keel as represented by the fourteenth-century Bremen cog, discovered in 1962 and preserved at Bremerhaven.[12] **(Pl. 20)** Its high profile made it an ideal missile-launching platform, and thus it was the preferred warship type of the later Middle Ages.[13] All of these vessels, including the galley types, were constructed clinker-style of oak. And, early on, before the Viking invasions, they all sported a single side rudder and a single square sail.[14]

Whatever vessels they used, Anglo-Saxon raiders had little to worry about once Constantine III, claimant to the diadem of the Western Roman Empire, withdrew from Britain with the last Roman troops in 407. The Roman Rhine fleet must have dissolved around the same time.[15] The tactics of the Anglo-Saxons presaged the Vikings: they struck without warning, often in bad weather, using rivers as roads to raid inland, after which they slipped away before local forces could react. This hit-and-run raiding afflicted both sides of the Channel until the middle of the fifth century, when it evolved into the *adventus Saxonum* ('coming of the Saxons') for Britain. The Saxons, already established in Gaul, settled first in eastern Britain between the Humber and the Thames and later in Kent and East Anglia, from where they spread into the Midlands.[16] At the same time Celts, using *curraughs* made of hides stretched over a wooden or wicker frame, established themselves in Brittany, Ireland, Scotland and western Britain.[17] By the end of the seventh century the Saxons had founded the kingdom of Northumbria and extended it to the Irish Sea. The expansion culminated in the invasion of Ireland by King Ecgfrith of Northumbria in 684. Anglo-Saxon raiding disappeared from recorded annals after that date.[18]

While the Saxons were settling in Britain, Frankish naval activity remained muted on the continent. The only Merovingian maritime exploit of any note was the defeat of a large-scale Scandinavian raid on the lower Rhine area in the 520s. Gregory of Tours related that a Danish king (probably from Jutland) named Chlochilaich (called Hygelac in the epic Anglo-Saxon poem *Beowulf*) attacked the coast of northern Gaul and devastated lands ruled by King Theodoric (spelled Theuderic in some sources). The latter responded by dispatching his son Theudebert, who Gregory claimed caught the invaders as they fled with their booty in boats and defeated them in a naval battle. Chlochilaich was apparently killed before he could even embark.[19]

In the eighth century the Frisians who occupied the coastal regions along the North Sea from the present-day Netherlands to western Denmark seemed to take up where the Saxons had left off. Plying the waters between Frankia, Britain and Scandinavia, sometimes raiding and sometimes trading, they were for a short time the most active mariners in the north.[20] That all ended in 734 at the hands of Charles Martel, prince of the Franks and Mayor of the Austrasian Palace, who famously stopped the Umayyad Caliphate of al-Andalus at Tours in 732. He orchestrated perhaps the most successful Frankish naval campaign of the era. Gathering a fleet at Utrecht, where the Vecht river veers from the Rhine, he sailed it down the Vecht to the open sea at Almere, then penetrated Frisia by way of the Middelzee, ravaging the lands on either side, and then moved down the river Boorne deep into the seat of Frisian power. Many historians have theorized that the conquest of Frisia may have removed a potential buffer against an emerging maritime threat from Scandinavia, but in all probability not much could have stemmed that tide.[21] They began coming in the last decade of the century: tall, fearsome men from the north in long, slender ships of shallow draught designed for speed and manoeuvrability – some of which eventually came to be called *drakkar* ('dragon ships').[22] **(Pl. 21)**

CHAPTER 7

The Viking Onslaught

The Anglo-Saxons commonly called them 'Danes' or 'heathens'. To the Franks, they were simply 'the Northmen'.[1] But history knows them as the Vikings, possibly derived from the West Norse word *vikingr*, meaning 'one who fights at sea' or *viking*, 'warfare at sea'.[2] Perhaps it was merely because many of the original Norse raiders of the British Isles came from Viken, the region west of Oslo Fjord. And no one knows for sure why they began their onslaught. There is, of course, no shortage of theories. Some postulate that the cause was population pressure in the rugged north country of Scandinavia, where arable land was at a premium (about 3 per cent in Norway). Others hypothesize that it was political consolidation that pushed the men from the north to seek their fortune in the south. Then again, perhaps it was simply the lure of portable wealth generated by the increased commerce of the more settled south which motivated these seaborne marauders to come.[3] But, whatever the reason, come they did. In the last years of the eighth century Scandinavian men in their longships, driven by the boreal winds, began raiding the British Isles and the west coast of the Carolingian Empire.

At the start they targeted the 'low-hanging fruit' – ill-defended and isolated monasteries near waterways. The first recorded attack was in 793 on St Cuthbert's revered priory at Lindisfarne, a tidal island off the coast of Northumbria. The Peterborough manuscript of the *Anglo-Saxon Chronicle*, like the Canterbury version, notes the event in near-apocalyptic tones:

> Here terrible portents came about over the land of Northumbria, and miserably frightened the people: there were immense flashes of lightning, and fiery dragons were seen flying in the air. A great famine immediately followed these signs; and a little after that in the same year on 8 January [actually 8 June] the raiding of the heathen men miserably devastated God's church in Lindisfarne island by looting and slaughter.[4]

Nor was the Northumbrian monastery which once served as home to the Venerable Bede spared. St Paul's Priory in Jarrow on the Tyne river was plundered the very next year.[5] The year after that St Columba's monastery on the Isle of Iona in the Inner Hebrides of Scotland was sacked. The first known raid on Frankia came four years later in 799. The prey was St Philibert's monastery on Noirmoutier, an island off Aquitaine at the mouth of the Loire.[6] These attacks would win the attention of Charlemagne, but that would matter little in the long run. The raids would increase in frequency and magnitude as the men from the north grew bolder and more confident in their seamanship and fighting skills.

Their quick-strike capability stemmed from ships built svelte and swift. The best preserved examples of these are the Oseberg and the Gokstad ships currently in the Viking Ship Museum of Oslo, which were discovered in burial mounds in the Vestfold of Norway around the turn of the last century. Dating from about 820, the elegant Oseberg ship, at 21.5m (70ft 6in) long by 5.1m (16ft 9in) wide and 1.4m (4ft 7in) deep amidships, was more delicately built and thus suitable only for coastal navigation. **(Pl. 22)** But the Gokstad ship from around 900 was of sturdier construction with a higher freeboard (23m/75ft 6in in length by 5.2m/17ft in beam, and 1.8m/6ft in depth). It was clearly capable of seagoing voyages.[7] **(Pl. 23)** The eleventh-century Skuldelev 2 at the Viking Ship Museum of Roskilde in Denmark, however, is more representative of the warships of the era. Built in Dublin around 1060, it measured 30m (98ft 5in) long and 3.8m (12ft 6in) wide, boasting a length-to-beam ratio of almost 8:1. Propelled by up to sixty oarsmen and augmented by a single square sail, it could achieve speeds of 15 to 20 knots and its shallow draught (less than a metre) enabled it to be easily beached or rowed up-river deep inland. Clinker-built of oak with iron rivets, these vessels were also strong and durable enough to endure transoceanic voyages in all kinds of weather.[8] Before all was said and done, the relentlessly acquisitive and inquisitive adventurers from Scandinavia would use these longships to make their mark from L'Anse aux Meadows at the northern tip of modern Newfoundland to the Varangian Guard of Constantinople. Their descendants would dominate huge swathes of continental Europe and conquer England.

The Nature of the Onslaught from a Naval Perspective

The Viking onslaught was not a single monolithic invasion of the western world by a solitary and homogenous Scandinavian people intent on establishing their own empire. It began as indiscriminate raiding of the richer south by disparate groups of Norwegians, Danes and Svear (Swedes), operating mostly independently of one another, and it only gradually evolved into large-scale incursions which eventually became conquest and settlement. It was mercantile as well as military. The Svear who ventured down the great rivers of the continent such as the Dnieper and the Volga into European Russia and Byzantium were drawn chiefly by the allure of trade, not conquest. And the Norwegians who dared the giant swells of the North Atlantic to reach Iceland, Greenland and Newfoundland did so not to pillage and plunder, but to find new lands upon which to farm and hunt. It was generally only the northern reaches of continental Europe and the British Isles which suffered the brunt of Viking violence. Moreover, what territories the men from the north claimed were won not by battle at sea but by martial means on land. The Scandinavians, famed as seafarers, used their ships principally to transport their warriors for terrestrial combat, not maritime warfare. They faced little opposition at sea. The Vikings were the greatest naval power in the north because they were virtually the only naval power in the north. Neither the Anglo-Saxons nor the Franks could muster fleets to engage them and, in fact, they hardly ever did. There were very few pitched naval battles, and those that did take place were fought almost exclusively between opposing Norse fleets much later in the era. The chief tactical advantages that the Vikings derived from their longships were surprise and mobility.[9]

The Assault on Frankia (799–864)

Charlemagne, of course, must have been aware of and deeply concerned about the attacks on the coasts of his Carolingian Empire. After all, his court at Aachen was home to one of the great scholars of the era, Alcuin of York, who was even more melodramatic than the *Anglo-Saxon Chronicle* about the sacking of Lindisfarne. In a letter to King Æthelred of Northumbria, he wrote:

> We and our fathers have now lived in this fair land for nearly 350 years, and never before has such an atrocity been seen in Britain as we have now suffered at the hands of a pagan people. Such a [sea] voyage was not thought possible. The church of Saint Cuthbert is spattered with the blood of the priests of God, stripped of all its furnishings, exposed to the plundering of pagans – a place more sacred than any in Britain.[10]

Charlemagne apparently got the message. 'Charles' final war was the one taken up against the Northmen who are called Danes,' wrote the Carolingian court scholar Einhard. 'First they operated as pirates, but then they raided the coasts of Gaul and Germany with larger fleets.'[11] In 800, the year after the attack on Noirmoutier, Charlemagne ordered the creation of a Channel fleet (probably based at Boulogne) and personally oversaw the start of its construction. He followed up that action with capitularies in 802 and 808 which added more ships.[12]

A large assault on Frisia in 810 by more than 200 ships at the behest of Godfrid, king of the Danes, convinced Charlemagne that there was still more to be done.[13] The 'heathens' had even begun to ride the rivers into the heartland. So he issued a third capitulary that year which not only called for the construction of still more vessels, but also commanded that they be stationed at the mouths of major rivers like the Rhine, the Loire, the Seine, the Scheldt and the Garonne. In addition, fortifications were built at key ports and a chain of warning beacons was strung along the north shores of the empire.[14] Einhard summed up the system nicely in the *Vita Karoli Magni* ('Life of Charles the Great'):

> He constructed a fleet for use against the Northmen. Ships were built for this purpose near the rivers that flow from Gaul and Germany into the North Sea. Since the Northmen were constantly raiding and ravaging the coasts of Gaul and Germany, fortifications and guards were set up at all the ports and at the mouth of every river that seemed large enough to accommodate ships. With such fortifications he stopped the enemy from being able to come and go freely.[15]

By and large these precautions worked. The Carolingian coastal fleet never actually engaged the raiders, but it was not necessary. 'Charlemagne's decision to concentrate the defences on the river mouths shows complete mastery of the strategic and tactical situation,' adjudged Haywood.[16] It enabled the Franks to effectively discourage access to their hinterlands and hinder escape when penetration was successful. The primary limitation was the difficulty of manning such a system without a large standing army. Recruiting men for tedious guard and garrison duty without the lure of plunder must have been a prodigious challenge, even for Charlemagne. That said, his coastal defence scheme provided enough deterrence to persuade the Northmen to go elsewhere – and go elsewhere they did. They attacked Britain and Ireland instead, leaving the Frankish Empire alone for the most part. There were almost no recorded raids for the remainder of Charlemagne's reign. It was only after his death in 814 that the seaborne marauders from Scandinavia chose to try the Carolingian coast again. A Viking flotilla of thirteen vessels attempted to breach the defences of Frisia in 820 but was rebuffed. It then moved down the coast to the Seine estuary but enjoyed no greater success. It was not until it reached the shores of Aquitaine that it was able to win any booty.[17]

As time wore on, the difficulty of motivating men to maintain the coastal watch system increased. Charlemagne's successor, Louis the Pious, did his best to hold the line, but inevitably it began to break down. Breaches became more frequent and more troubling. Louis' sons (Lothar, Louis the German and Charles the Bald) revolted and briefly deposed him in 833, providing Danish raiders with a golden opportunity. In 834 they rowed up the Rhine and sacked the prosperous Frisian trading town of Dorestad. Louis the Pious regained his throne that same year, but the Danes kept coming. They despoiled Dorestad annually until 837.[18] Louis did not sit idle while all this was happening. He ordered the coastal defences strengthened in 835 and 837, inspecting them himself and ordering a fleet equipped.[19] But the floodgates were finally flung wide open when Louis died in 840. Lothar, Louis the German and Charles the Bald were too distracted by their nasty succession dispute to counter the Viking assault.

In fact, the internecine conflict among the royal brethren encouraged a renewed round of incursions, some abetted by one brother against the others. In 841 Lothar granted the Danish pirate chieftain Harold Klak the island of Welcheren at the mouth of the Scheldt, Rhine and Maas rivers, in effect handing Frisia over to Viking control.[20] Another group of Norse marauders ravaged Rouen and the nearby Abbey of St Wandrille de Fontenelle that same year.[21] The port of Quentovic, just south of Boulogne, was next in 842 and the following year it was the turn of Nantes on the Loire. In each case the raiders spared only those structures they were paid in silver to spare. In the case of Nantes, the attack was timed to coincide with the feast of St John on 24 June so that there would be plenty of rich merchants for ransom.[22] The three warring siblings formally reconciled to a partitioning of the empire a month later in July 843 at Verdun: Louis the German was allotted East Frankia, Lothar the Middle and Charles the Bald the West.[23] But the agreement did little to allay Viking attacks on the empire.

The lands in the West controlled by Charles the Bald bore the brunt of these incursions, which began to take on an ominous permanence. According to the contemporary *Annals of St-Bertin*, the Northmen who looted the Loire in 843 'landed on a certain island [Noirmoutier, no doubt], brought their households over from the mainland, and decided to winter there in something like a permanent settlement'.[24] Viking tactics had obviously evolved from hit-and-run raiding to establishing bases on river islands and wintering over. 'There would be Northmen on the lower Loire until the close of the century and beyond,' observed noted Carolingian scholar Janet Nelson.[25] Moreover, it was no longer primarily just Danes who despoiled Frankia, but Vikings of various Scandinavian origins. Aquitainian sources describe the Northmen who sacked Nantes as *Westfaldingi*, i.e., from west of Oslo Fjord and thus of Norwegian extraction.[26]

It was the Seine, however, which suffered the most serious infestation of Scandinavian invaders. In March 845 a Viking chieftain by the name of Ragnar (believed to be the legendary Ragnar Lodbrok of the Norse sagas and a king of the Danes) led a 120-ship fleet up the Seine all the way to Paris and on Easter Sunday plundered the Ile de la Cité itself. Only the payment of 7,000 pounds of silver from the coffers of Charles the Bald induced the Vikings to withdraw.[27] But eventually not even extorted largesse could get them to leave. By the mid-850s they had set up bases on the islands of Jeufosse and Oissel (between Rouen and Paris) from which they raided even further up the Seine.[28] Paris was sacked in 856 and 857 from Jeufosse, for example.[29] Nor were the Garonne and Dordogne immune from their attentions. In 844 a particularly audacious Viking expedition of around 150 ships sailed up the Garonne all the way to Toulouse. It then backed down the river to attack Asturias (northwestern Spain), before rounding Cape Finisterre to loot the locality of Lisbon. These raiders even had the temerity to row up the Guadalquivir river and ravage the environs of Seville before Abd al-Rahman II, the Umayyad emir of Cordoba, employed a form of 'Greek fire' to crush them in a naval battle at Talayata (adjacent to the city), costing them thirty ships and over a thousand men.[30] Another group besieged Bordeaux in 848 until Charles chased them off and in the same year wasted the township of Melle, home to an imperial mint.[31] Périgueux was pillaged next.[32]

Even the Rhône was raided. 'Danish pirates made a long sea voyage, sailed through the straits between Spain and Africa and then up the Rhône,' reported the *Annals of St-Bertin* for the year 859. 'They ravaged some *civitates* ['towns'] and monasteries and made their base on an island called the Camargue.'[33] This same Viking fleet, consisting of sixty-two ships led by Hasting and Björn Ironside (purportedly the sons of the fabled Ragnar Lodbrok), attacked Arles and ravaged the Rhône as far as Valence the following year. They were even reported to have plundered Pisa and Luna on the Tuscan coast. The entire adventure, extolled in several contemporary accounts – some quite fantastic – was said to have lasted over three years and included attacks on Seville and Algeciras in Andalusia, Cabo de Tres Forcas in Moorish North Africa, Narbonne in Roussillon and Pamplona in Navarre.[34] A monk of Noirmoutier named Ermentarius gave a fairly full account of the calamity inflicted upon the continent up until that time:

> The number of ships grows: the endless stream of Vikings never ceases to increase. Everywhere the Christians are victims of massacres, burnings,

> plunderings: the Vikings conquer all in their path, and no one resists them: they seize Bordeaux, Périgueux, Limoges, Angoulême and Toulouse. Angers, Tours and Orléans are annihilated and an innumerable fleet sails up the Seine and the evil grows in the whole region. Rouen is laid waste, plundered and burned: Paris, Beauvais and Meaux taken, Melun's strong fortress levelled to the ground, Chartres occupied, Evreux and Bayeux plundered, and every town besieged.[35]

Besides basing themselves on river islands, the Vikings employed a number of artifices to achieve their ends. They attacked when least expected: Quentovic was surprised with a dawn raid; Bordeaux was overrun at night; and Tours, like Nantes, was taken during a holy festival. They increased their range and enhanced surprise by using horses: they rode through the night to stun the Abbey of St Denis at dawn on Easter Sunday, 857. They also destroyed bridges and Frankish ships to stymie pursuit.[36] Finally, they intrigued with Viking chieftains supposedly allied with Carolingians in order to have their way in border regions like Frisia. A huge fleet of reportedly some 600 ships sacked Hamburg in 845.[37] Dorestad was devastated in 846, 847, 857 and again in 863.[38]

For his part, Charles the Bald attempted every available stratagem to stem the flow. First of all, he tried to buy them off. In addition to ransoming Paris in 845, he paid the exorbitant sum of 686 pounds of gold and 3,250 pounds of silver to liberate Abbot Louis of St Denis in 858, for instance.[39] Tribute, of course, bought only a temporary respite and only with specific bands of Vikings – other groups of Scandinavian raiders demanded their share as well. So Charles also attempted to employ the sword. In 858 or 859 he besieged a large troop of Danes on Oissel Island in the Seine.[40] When that effort failed, Charles even resorted in 861 to hiring another Viking leader, a certain Weland, who had been operating in the Somme with 200 ships, to renew the siege of the Oissel Island Vikings for 5,000 pounds of silver. After an additional sixty Viking ships joined the siege, the Oissel Danes finally paid 6,000 pounds in gold and silver, so that they would be permitted to sail out to sea.[41] Perhaps his most effective tactic was the fortification of key bridges. When yet another Norse fleet marauded up the Marne in 862, Charles fortified the bridge at Trilbardou (on the Marne east of Paris), trapping the Vikings, and deployed his troops along the banks to prevent them from foraging. The leaders sued for terms and agreed to withdraw. Shortly afterwards, he began the construction of an additional fortified bridge at Pont-de-l'Arch, on the Seine upstream from Rouen, not far from Pîtres.[42] And in July 864 he issued the royal Edict of Pîtres which called for the fortification of bridges over rivers throughout the realm and prohibited the sale of horses to the Northmen under penalty of death.[43] But still the longships and their Viking masters kept coming.

The Assault on Ireland (794–847)

They came mostly from modern Norway by way of the Shetlands and Orkneys. From these archipelagos it was only a short jump to Caithness at the northern tip of Scotland, then either down the east coast to Northumbria and East Anglia or down the west coast through the Hebrides to the Isle of Man and Ireland.[44] They came initially not in great invasion fleets but in small exploratory flotillas of perhaps two or three ships.[45] It is clear from the raid on Lindisfarne off the east coast of Northumbria in 793 and the sack of Iona in the Inner Hebrides in 795 that the Norse raiders probably ravaged the shores of the North and Irish Seas concurrently. Yet aside from the attack on Jarrow in 794, there were no significant recorded assaults on what is known today as England until 835.[46] It was a different story for Ireland, so it is fitting to begin there.

Thanks to the *Annals of Ulster* and other Irish accounts, more is known about the early years of the Viking onslaught on the Emerald Isle than on Britain. In fact, an entry of the *Annals* for the year 794 not only announced the inception of the raids, but also suggested they were part of a wider movement engulfing the whole region: 'Devastation of all the islands of Britain by heathens.'[47] The next year it noted 'the burning of Rechru [referring to monastic foundations on Rathlin Island off the northeast Irish coast] by the heathens'. In the same entry for 795 it added that 'Sci [Isle of Skye] was overwhelmed and laid waste', possibly alluding to the destruction of Iona, also in the Inner Hebrides.[48] Indeed, it seems St Columba's monastery on Iona, being a convenient way-station en route to Ireland, was subject to regular ravishing. It was burned again in 802 and in 806 sixty-eight members of its community were slaughtered, forcing the monks to move the monastery in 807 to Kells in Ireland.[49] The isle of Éire, as it was called in Gaelic, was to prove no safe haven, however. It became a victim of Viking invasions with ever-increasing frequency.

By 798 the Norse marauders had delved into the Irish Sea. That year they plundered Inis Pátraic (the Isle of St Patrick off the Skerries headland just north of modern Dublin) and despoiled the shrine of St Do Chonna. The same entry stated that 'the heathens . . . also made great incursions both in Ireland and in Alba [Scotland]'.[50] As of 807, these bands of Scandinavian sea bandits had begun roaming the western bays. They found the monastery of St Molaise on Innismurray near Sligo and left it in ashes, then raided Roscam in Galway Bay just east of the modern city of the same name.[51] The eastern shores of the island received even more attention. In 821 'the heathens' savaged Howth Head, again north of modern Dublin, and 'carried off a great number of women into captivity'.[52] Growing bolder still, they penetrated deeper into the Irish Sea, rounding the southeastern end of the island at Wexford to hit Cork in 822.[53] And in 824 they reached Skellig off the southwest coast of Kerry, where they abducted the abbot.[54]

Having circumnavigated the entire island, the raiders now seemed to concentrate on the wealthiest, most important monastic institutions. In 824 the Scandinavian freebooters struck the great learning centre at Bangor Abbey on Belfast Lough.[55] More portentous still was the increasing willingness of the Vikings to venture further inland to reach the richest prizes. In 832 the fabulously affluent monastic complex at Armagh, almost 60km (37 miles) from the coast, was plundered 'by the heathens three times in one month'.[56] The following year the revered Lismore Abbey, some 20km (12 miles) from the island's south shore, was burned, its monks massacred.[57] And the renowned monastery of Glendalough, founded by St Kevin in the sixth century on land at least 30km (20 miles) from the east coast, was pillaged in 834 and 836.[58] As many a scholar has pointed out, the Vikings did not target these ecclesiastical establishments because they harboured some heathen abhorrence for Christianity: abbeys were simply where they could find 'the greatest loot'.[59]

The northern freebooters continued their quest for largesse ever more aggressively. According to the *Annals of Ulster*, they were penetrating in force deep inland on the major rivers as early as 837: 'A naval force of the Norsemen sixty ships strong was on the Bóinn [Boyne river], another of sixty ships on the river Life [Liffey].' The *Annals* went on to say, 'Those two forces plundered the plain of Life and the plain of Brega [in modern County Meath], including churches, forts and dwellings.'[60] The local lords fought back, sometimes even winning, but on the raiders came, and in ever greater numbers. The *Annals* signalled a significant change in 841 with the words: 'The heathens were still on Loch nEchach [Lough Neagh – a large freshwater lake in Northern Ireland].' The Vikings had begun wintering over. Then came the *longphoirt*: fortified ship enclosures. That same year the *Annals* reported them at Linn Duachaill (Annagassan) on the central east coast and at a place about 60km (40 miles) to the south called Duiblinn ('Black Pool'), which would eventually become the great Irish capital of Dublin.[61] The Vikings had come to stay.

A few years later, in 845, the Scandinavians sailed their longships up the Shannon and established an encampment under a leader called Turges on Lough Ree in the centre of the island, from which they savaged all Connacht and County Meath.[62] No wonder the *Annals of St-Bertin* made the following grim assessment in 847: 'The Irish, who had been attacked by the Northmen for a number of years, were made into regular tribute-payers. The Northmen also got control of the islands all around Ireland, and stayed there without encountering any resistance from anyone.'[63] As it turns out, this was a bit of an overstatement. The Irish kings soon came together and battled back, often with great success. Once the Vikings surrendered the mobility and quick-strike capability of their ships to fight on land, they did not seem nearly so invincible. They gained no great swathes of territory and their fortunes ebbed and flowed like those of the many competing petty kings of the island. That said, the Vikings would be a significant element in Irish life until the end of the twelfth century.[64]

The Assault on Britain (835–65)

Since the Shetlands, the Orkneys and Caithness in Scotland formed the primary raiding route from Norway to the British Isles, it can be assumed that Scotland was subject to the Norse assault from the beginning. Yet the nature of that assault is obfuscated by the lack of contemporary chronicles and annals covering the region. Nonetheless, occur it did. An entry in the *Annals of Ulster* for the year 839 which refers to a victory of 'the heathens' over the men of Fortrui, a Pictish kingdom in the north of Scotland, has convinced highly regarded Irish scholar

Donnchadh Ó Corráin that 'the Western and Northwestern Isles and the western and northeastern mainland [of Scotland] were already theirs [the Vikings']'.[65] In fact, Ó Corráin believes that the region was the heart of a Norse realm which Irish sources referred to as *Laithlinn*,[66] and archaeological and linguistic evidence strongly supports that conclusion.[67] In all probability, the Viking invasion of Britain followed the pattern already elucidated in Ireland and on the continent: hit-and-run attacks by small squadrons on soft targets on the periphery, followed by incursions in force up rivers into the hinterlands by entire fleets which eventually over-wintered.

The Viking raids on the southern end of the island finally rose to the level of concern in 835 when it merited this terse entry in the *Anglo-Saxon Chronicle*: 'Here heathen men raided across Sheppey.'[68] The incident seems innocuous enough at first glance, but it was a harbinger of the Scandinavian storm surge about to break upon the shores of Britain. For one thing, Sheppey is an island in the Thames estuary, leading into the heart of England. For another, it was merely the first in a long series of raids reported by the *Anglo-Saxon Chronicle*. For the next two centuries hardly a year went by without some mention of the Viking invaders. The Northmen, who must have come from Ireland and the continent as well as Scandinavia, ratcheted up the pressure almost immediately.[69] In 836 Egbert, king of the West Saxons, had to battle a fleet of thirty-five 'Danish' ships at Carhampton on the south coast of the Bristol Channel.[70] Two years later he was fighting 'a great raiding ship-army' in Cornwall.[71] And two years after that, in 840, Ealdorman Wulfheard 'fought at Southampton against thirty-three shiploads', while that same year Ealdorman Æthelhelm dealt with a 'Danish raiding army' on the island of Portland, just south of Dorchester, and lost his life in the process.[72] Another ealdorman, Hereberht, was 'killed by heathen men' along with many others at Romney Marsh on the south coast of Kent the very next year.[73] Rochester, near the north Kentish coast, was next in May 842 along with London itself, where 'there was a great slaughter'.[74] The continental chronicler Nithard, a grandson of Charlemagne, notes that *Hamwic* (Southampton) was also 'ravaged' at this time.[75] And on it went, occasionally with multiple occurrences in the same year, as was the case in 850 when big battles were waged with sizeable Viking contingents in both Somerset and Kent.[76]

It was in 851 that the incursions took a telling turn: 'for the first time the heathen men stayed over the winter'. Perhaps more worrying still, they began coming in greater numbers. 'And that same year 350 ships came into the mouth of the Thames and stormed Canterbury and London,' reported the *Anglo-Saxon Chronicle*, 'and put to flight Beortwulf king of Mercia with his army, and then went over the Thames into Surrey.'[77] In 855 'the heathen men settled in Sheppey over winter'.[78] And ten years later, in 865, it became apparent that the Viking presence had become permanent, as the Northmen increasingly profited from both plunder and tribute: 'Here a heathen raiding-army stayed in Thanet [at the easternmost tip of Kent], and made peace with the inhabitants of Kent; and the inhabitants of Kent promised them money in return for peace.' 'And under cover of that peace and that promise of money,' added the *Anglo-Saxon Chronicle*, 'the raiding-army stole away by night and raided across all eastern Kent.'[79]

The arrival of yet another large Norse force in 865 signalled an even more troubling development in the Viking onslaught on England. The *Anglo-Saxon Chronicle* announced it with the following prosaic entry: 'And the same year a great raiding-army came to the land of the English and took winter quarters in East Anglia and were provided with horses there, and they made peace with them.'[80] It would be the first of many entries in various annals and chronicles referring to the actions of this unusually large Viking war band over the course of the next thirty years or so. And the term 'make peace', in this case, would eventually come to mean more than simple tribute. It would mean the first step in an effort to achieve conquest.

The Operations of the 'Great Army' in Britain (865–79)

The term 'great army', employed by several contemporary sources to describe this unusually large assemblage of Norse raiders, implies a huge horde of perhaps tens of thousands, but it most probably was not. Although no precise figures are given, it is highly doubtful that it numbered more than a few thousand at best.[81] Noted British historian Gwyn Jones estimates that it could have consisted of only 500 to 1,000 warriors.[82] The truth is that its size vacillated as diverse groups under various Viking chieftains came and went. Accordingly, the ship count of its fleet also fluctuated from a few dozen to several hundred. That said, it was a highly effective entity which had a profound impact on early English and French history. It would operate from roughly 865 to 896 on both sides of the English Channel. The resources of entire kingdoms would be mobilized to contend with it and its exploits would ultimately result in the establishment of Scandinavian-dominated territories both in Britain and on the continent for decades: the Danelaw and Normandy.

The 'great army' was essentially a big band of brigands who, in the beginning, operated like a swarm of waterborne locusts. They relied on ships to transport them up navigable rivers to strategic localities deep inland where they either took over old fortifications or built new ones from which they could forage and plunder the land all around, often on horseback.[83] Once they had intimidated the local lords into 'making peace' with them (i.e., the provision of tribute and supplies), they moved on. This arrangement, however, soon evolved into conquest. No one knows for sure what prompted the great army's creation, but legend has it that the original leaders were the brothers Ivar the Boneless, Ubbi and Halfdan, who assembled the host ostensibly to avenge the death of their father, Ragnar Lodbrok, at the hands of Ælla, the king of Northumbria. Ælla allegedly had Ragnar pitched into a pit of vipers.[84] In reality, the motives were probably more mercenary than vengeful. Be that as it may, after the great army 'made peace' with the East Anglians in 865, it moved into Northumbria in 866 and took over York, where 'an immense slaughter was made of the Northumbrians', including Ælla.[85] The latter was supposedly subjected to the quaint Viking custom of 'blood eagling', whereby the victim's ribs were detached from the spine and splayed outwards so that the lungs could be spread over the back like folded wings.[86]

After over-wintering in Northumbria, where it exacted 'a peace' and placed a puppet king on the throne, the 'great army' moved into Mercia in 867 and staged out of Nottingham. King Æthelred of Wessex and his brother Alfred briefly besieged the Northmen there at the behest of King Burhred of Mercia, but ultimately the Mercians also 'made peace' with the invaders.[87] The Viking army returned to Northumbria the next year, but in 869 rode back through Mercia to East Anglia again, this time with no pretence of seeking 'peace'. They took winter quarters at Thetford in 870 and 'conquered all that land', ruthlessly killing King Edmund in the process.[88] Thus, when the great army rode to Reading in Wessex the next year, Æthelred and Alfred must have had few illusions about 'making peace' with it. They attacked the Vikings at Reading in 871. 'And that year there were nine national fights [pitched battles] fought against the raiding army in the kingdom to the south of the Thames,' recounted the *Anglo-Saxon Chronicle*, 'besides those forays which Alfred, the king's brother, and a single ealdorman and king's thegns often rode on, which were never counted.'[89] The Danes apparently won most of these encounters, enabling them to impose a 'peace' of sorts on the West Saxons and take winter quarters in London. But an event occurred that same year which would ensure their ultimate defeat: Æthelred died, leaving the crown to his gifted brother Alfred.[90]

For the next few years the men of the great army concentrated on Mercia. They over-wintered first at Torksey in 872 and then at Repton in 873. Once they had 'conquered all that land', they banished Burhred and placed a certain Ceolwulf on the throne in his stead as their man.[91] Then, in a seminal moment, the great army separated in 874, half following Halfdan back to Northumbria, where it over-wintered on the river Tyne, while the remainder went with chieftains Guthrum, Oscytel and Anund to Cambridge in East Anglia. It was Halfdan who seemed to engineer the transition to settlement which would eventually lead to the establishment of the Danelaw. The next year, in 875, he 'divided up the land of Northumbria' amongst his followers and, according to the *Anglo-Saxon Chronicle*, 'they were ploughing and providing for themselves'.[92] There was a similar sharing out of land in Mercia in 877.[93]

Meanwhile, Guthrum and the others orchestrated a sustained assault on Wessex, over-wintering first at Wareham in 875, then at Exeter in 876. The *Anglo-Saxon Chronicle* reported that the Scandinavian intruders lost a fleet of 120 ships to a storm at Swanage in Dorset, but managed nonetheless to drive Alfred and the remnants of his forces into the Somerset marshlands at Athelney in early 878.[94] The turning point in the struggle, however, came that spring, just a few weeks after Easter. Alfred took the offensive with a reinvigorated force and decisively defeated the Danes at Edington in Wiltshire. He pursued them to Chippenham, where Guthrum was forced to sue for 'peace' on Alfred's terms, which included baptism for him and thirty of his leading men, along with a promise to leave Wessex.[95] The raiding-army then withdrew in 879 via Cirencester into East Anglia, where it 'settled the land, and divided it up'. Soon afterwards Alfred and

Guthrum came to a formal agreement setting the boundaries for what became officially the 'Danelaw'.[96]

The Operations of the Great Army in Frankia (879–92)

That was not, however, the end of the great army. Myth and hyperbolic characterizations by medieval chroniclers have conjured up images of Vikings as fierce warriors impervious to fear who deliberately sought out martial challenges, but the truth is that they were basically waterborne bandits who went where resistance was least. Those members of the great army who had no interest in settling down in the Danelaw simply relocated to the continent, where the pickings were easier. While the bulk of the great army humbled by Alfred moved from Chippenham to Cirencester, a contingent over-wintered at Fulham on the Thames. In 879 the *Anglo-Saxon Chronicle* reported that 'the raiding-army which had settled at Fulham went across the sea to Ghent in the land of the Franks'.[97] Aside from the fact that Alfred had made Wessex inhospitable to incursion, the continent was now a tempting target for Viking invaders because the Frankish Empire had once again fallen into disarray. Louis the German had perished in 876 and Charles the Bald followed him to the sepulchre in 877, leaving Frankia to no fewer than six squabbling monarchs.[98] Wasting little time, the great army group which arrived at Ghent soon sailed up the Scheldt deeper into Flanders in search of fresh plunder.

Having evaded the forces of both West and East Frankia, the Vikings captured the monastery at Corbie and attacked Amiens in early 881. King Louis III of West Frankia managed to slaughter a Viking cavalry contingent at Saucourt near the coast in August, but the incursion progressed nonetheless. The fortress he built at Étrun to prevent the Northmen from moving further up the Scheldt only caused the main body to jump to the Meuse. Once there, the raiders established a stronghold at Asselt, where they anchored their fleet of at least 200 ships.[99] At this point various bands of the great army apparently used the Rhine–Meuse–Scheldt delta complex to infest the entire region like a sort of virulent waterborne plague.[100] The ninth-century *Annals of Fulda* testified that Cambrai, Utrecht, Prüm, Cornelimünster, Stavelot and Malmedy were all ravaged in 881. The Norsemen burnt Bonn and Cologne as well. They even pillaged the royal palace at Aachen, 'where they used the king's chapel as a stable for their horses'.[101] The *Annals of St-Bertin* documented that the Vikings torched Trier, Tongres and Arras in 882. They even menaced Reims and raided Metz. There were small Frankish victories over individual raiding parties, like that of Carloman II (successor to Louis III) over a Viking band at Reims in late 882, but the rapine activities of the great army continued unabated.[102] One war band went up the Scheldt to Condé that same year, while another (probably that of the notorious Danish chieftain Hasting) sailed up the Somme to Amiens the next.[103] The Frankish kings ended up falling back on an old expedient to get rid of the scourge. King Charles the Fat of East Frankia bribed the Viking chieftains Godfrid, Sigfrid and Gorm to abandon Asselt in 882 for 'several thousand pounds of silver and gold'.[104] In 884

Carloman II also resorted to buying them off with a tribute of 12,000 pounds of gold and silver.[105]

The great army then split in two: one part sailed back to Britain to lay siege to Rochester in East Anglia, only to be chased off by Alfred, while the other attempted to besiege Leuven in Flanders with equally unsatisfying results.[106] The various components coalesced again, however, in July 885 at the mouth of the Seine for the most menacing Viking campaign in Frankia to date: the 885–6 siege of Paris. The death of Carloman II of West Frankia in December 884 without an heir had rendered the Seine river valley an open road into the heart of the kingdom for the Scandinavian raiders.[107] Reputed to have involved hundreds of vessels and thousands of Norse warriors over many months, it would be the single most serious Viking incursion on the continent ever. As such, it is the subject of a special, in-depth section. The principal chieftain seems to have been a certain Sigfrid, probably the same man who Charles the Fat had suborned with silver at Asselt in 882 along with Godfrid and Gorm. Godfrid was murdered by Frankish nobles in 884 for reneging on his agreement to protect Frisia, while Gorm was never heard from again.[108] The main source for the siege, an eye-witness account by Abbo of St-Germain-des-Prés, also mentioned a man named Sinric as 'one of the kings of the Danes', but he drowned in the Seine during the fighting.[109] The siege was ultimately unsuccessful, due in large measure to the spirited defence of the city by Count Odo and Bishop Gozlin of Paris. Charles the Fat, now regarded as the Carolingian Emperor ruling over both East and West Frankia, again used silver to induce the Vikings to move on. They did, sailing further up the Seine to Burgundy, which they bedevilled for the next three years (886–9). Verdun, Toul and Troyes all suffered assaults.[110]

The Danes finally grew weary of rifling the region and sailed back down the Seine to Paris, but they were once again rebuffed by Odo, who had assumed the crown of West Frankia from Charles, deposed for his obvious inability to defend the realm. The Viking army continued on, apparently much diminished, to Brittany, but the Bretons were equally inhospitable: they defeated the Danes at St Lô.[111] The remnants of the great army then made its way back to Flanders and established a fortified camp at Leuven by the river Dyle. It was there that Arnulf, king of East Frankia, surprised the Danes in 891, overrunning their camp and killing Sigfrid in the process.[112] This apparently was the final straw: shortly thereafter, in 892, what was left of the great army boarded 250 ships at Boulogne and then 'moved themselves over in a single journey, horses and all' to Britain, sailing up the Rother river to Appledore in Kent. Hasting joined his compatriots in Kent soon afterwards with eighty more ships, settling in at Milton Regis on the Swale river estuary.[113]

The Return of the Great Army to England (892–6)

Alfred, however, was less than welcoming, and he had not been idle in the absence of the 'great army'. In the intervening decade the able king of Wessex had fashioned a highly flexible and effective defensive system which, though it could not make the kingdom impervious to assault, rendered the experience far less rewarding. First of all, he developed a network of some thirty fortified townships (*burhs*), and manned them using the 'Burghal Hidage' system, whereby each *hide* (a measure of land for tax assessment) furnished one man to guard 4ft of rampart. These *burhs* not only provided refuges from raiders, but also housed rapid-reaction forces to run the raiders down.[114] Secondly, the *Anglo-Saxon Chronicle* attested that Alfred arranged for an early form of a standing army: 'The king had separated his army into two, so that there were always half at home and half out, except for those who had hold of the fortresses.'[115] Thirdly, and most pertinent to the subject at hand, the *Chronicle* claimed the king even attempted to counter Viking superiority at sea:

> Then King Alfred ordered long-ships to be built to oppose the 'askrs' [a Norse word for 'warships']; they were well nigh twice as long as others, some had sixty oars, some more; they were both swifter and less flexible, and also more responsive than the others; they were neither of Frisian design nor of Danish, but as it seemed to himself that they might be most useful.[116]

While Alfred's fleet could boast no major engagements with a Scandinavian counterpart, it probably offered a deterrent benefit which, together with the other military measures, made the plunder of his lands unprofitable and imprudent.[117]

The Danes of the Danelaw, of course, aided and abetted their newly returned compatriots in the great army in violation of existing treaties, otherwise Alfred's struggle to suppress this last great incursion would not have lasted as long as it did: basically from 892 to 896.[118] Nonetheless, Alfred's reactive tactics enabled the West Saxons to fight a grinding war of attrition which gradually took its toll on the invaders. He began by dividing his forces to deal with a multi-pronged threat. His son Edward, at the head of one force, confronted a contingent of the great army at Farnham in 893, chasing it onto an islet in the Thames, while Alfred himself rushed with another to the Devon coast to relieve Exeter, which was under assault by a Viking fleet of a hundred vessels.[119] And there were some auspicious triumphs. That same year (893) a large force of Londoners stormed Hasting's headquarters at Benfleet on Hadleigh Ray off the Thames estuary while the Viking chieftain was leading a raid elsewhere. The English not only seized the women, children and an immense quantity of booty, but also 'all the ships they either broke up or burned or brought to London town or to Rochester'.[120]

Meanwhile, other elements of the 'great raiding-army' gathered at Shoebury in Essex. Together with reinforcements from the Danelaw, this large body raided up the Thames and into the Severn. Garrison troops from the *burhs* of central Wessex and Wales under several of Alfred's ealdormen pursued the invaders to Buttington, where they besieged the Vikings with such tenacity that the Northmen were forced to eat some of their own horses to stave off starvation. The siege eventually drove the Danes to fight a pitched battle in which they were badly mauled. The survivors fled, joining what was left of the great army, which then made its way to Chester for the winter. Alfred invested them there, divesting the land all around of livestock and grain. Facing famine, the Viking force had no choice but to winter in Wales instead.[121] The next summer (894) the Vikings evaded Alfred's armies by marching through Northumbria and East Anglia to Mersea Island off the east coast of Essex, where their fleet joined them. Then, before winter, the great army embarked on its ships and rowed up the Thames and the Lea to winter at Hertford about 30km (20 miles) north of London.[122] It was here that Alfred brought the final campaign of the great army to a close. First, he denied it the autumn harvest, and then he built a fortified bridge on the Lea downstream from Hertford, trapping the Danish fleet. The Vikings therefore ended up abandoning their ships and moving by foot to Bridgnorth on the Severn, where they over-wintered, famished and fatigued.[123] The subsequent end to the great army was announced almost prosaically in the *Anglo-Saxon Chronicle*: 'Then the summer after this year [896], the raiding-army went off, some to East Anglia, some to Northumbria, and those who were without money got themselves ships there, and went south across the sea to the Seine.'[124]

Alfred had essentially stifled the great army by robbing it of its mobility – and, like fish unable to swim, it suffocated. Wessex continued to endure sporadic seaborne raids originating from the Danelaw, but Alfred apparently answered them all, no matter how inconsequential. The *Anglo-Saxon Chronicle* described how the king dispatched a nine-ship flotilla in 896 to destroy a Viking squadron of six ships which had been using the Isle of Wight as a base for ravaging the whole south coast. It was a muddled, minor skirmish of little significance, but only one Viking ship survived it.[125] Alfred seemed determined to make every incursion costly.

The Founding of Normandy (911–33)

Those vestiges of the great army that were compelled to migrate back to the continent by Alfred's successful defence of Wessex were no doubt able to link up with other remnants which had remained in West Frankia – like the band led by Rollo. Dudo of St Quentin, a tenth-century Norman panegyrist, claimed a certain Hrolf (Latinized as 'Rollo') had remained to ravage the lower Seine after the 885–6 siege of Paris.[126] While this has been contested by recent scholarship, there can be no doubt that Rollo, who was probably of Norwegian extraction, was active in the area by 905.[127] The Franks eventually defeated him at the battle of Chartres in 911, but Charles the Simple (meaning 'straight-forward', not 'simple-minded'), then king of West Frankia, was looking for a more permanent solution to the problem of Viking attacks on his kingdom by way of the Seine. So he offered Rollo and his companions land centred on Rouen in return for serving as a buffer against future Viking raids up the river. The resultant Treaty of St Clair-sur-Epte of 911 codified the royal land grant which is considered the kernel of what would eventually become *Northmannia*, meaning 'land of the Northmen' – i.e., the dukedom of Normandy.[128]

Additional royal concessions were made in 924 and 933, but most expansion came through martial aggression.[129] At the risk of oversimplification, these 'northmen' (or '*Normanz*' as they were called in old French) were a warrior caste superimposed upon an indigenous population of Frankish peasantry ruled by a divided aristocracy. Vastly outnumbered, they intermarried and quickly adopted the Frankish language and customs which included, most importantly, a form of feudalism.[130] And since additional territorial acquisitions, by necessity, had to be inland, they soon traded their ships for horses, taking on the heavy cavalry tactics of the Franks. Resourceful and highly adaptable, the Normans made these tactics their own and perfected them. The hauberk, kite shield and conical helmet became the distinctive accoutrements of the Norman knights who would ultimately claim England and southern Italy for themselves.[131] Ironically, in order do so, they would, by the middle of the eleventh century, have to rediscover their Scandinavian seafaring roots.

Exploration and Colonization in the North Atlantic (870–1000)

At about the same time that Alfred was beginning his heroic defence of Wessex against the great army (*c.*870), intrepid Norwegian mariners began exploring the 'islands' of the North Atlantic known to the ancients and contemporary historians like Bede as *Thule* – basically the Faroes, Iceland, Greenland and eventually Newfoundland.[132] The first known Icelandic historian, Ari Thorgilsson, wrote in his early twelfth-century *Íslendingabók* ('Book of the Icelanders') that 'Iceland was first settled in the days of Harald the Fine-Haired . . . 870 years after the birth of Christ'.[133] Another Icelandic source, the *Landnámabók* ('Book of Settlements') written around 1100, purported that the motivation for such extreme emigration was the desire to escape the tyrannical rule of Harald Finehair, the first king of a united Norway who reigned from 872 to 930.[134] Tradition has it that Harald won suzerainty over all Norway by defeating a coalition of Viking chieftains from the southwest, principally Rogaland, in the Battle of Hafrsfjord (near Stavanger) in 872. According to Snorre Sturlason, who wrote the *Heimskringla*, a history of the Norse kings, the decisive moment in that encounter came when Harald's longship overwhelmed that of Tore Haklang, 'a mighty berserk'. From then on, Harald imposed his will on the whole land, taxing everyone – a condition considered intolerable by many: hence the great exodus.[135]

In all probability, however, the real reason was much more pragmatic: the sparsely inhabited islands of the North Atlantic offered Norwegian farmer-hunters unexploited lands similar to their own with little or no competition. The soil was virgin and such sought-after fauna as whales, walruses, seals and reindeer were abundant.[136] Hence these Norse adventurers were willing to dare the savage seas of the North Atlantic in ships which provided little shelter. To be sure, they almost certainly disdained the slender, light longships used for raiding in favour of more stoutly built cargo ships designed to carry their livestock and household goods through the high sea states of what Norwegian mariners called the 'North Way'. The most plausible vessel for these kinds of voyage was the ***knarr***, best represented by the Skuldelev 1 ship found at Roskilde. Measuring 16.3m (53ft 6in) long by 4.5m (15ft) wide by 2.1m (7ft) deep, it was of sturdy construction with a relatively broad bow and a high freeboard, giving it a capacity of around 24 tons. Equipped with a few oars, it was primarily designed to be sailed by a crew of only six to eight men. The *Saga Siglar*, a reconstruction of the

Skuldelev 1 ship, reached speeds of up to 10 knots in 'extreme weather conditions'.[137]

The first man to have made the voyage to Iceland was supposedly a Norwegian named Ingólfr who settled at Reykjavík on the island's southwest coast.[138] Ari Thorgilsson stated that 'Iceland was fully settled in sixty years, so that no further settlement was made after that'.[139] This implies that the best plots of land were all taken by 930, about the time the first *Althing*, a general assembly of freemen for legislation and adjudication, was convened at *Thingvellir* ('Thing Plain') just outside Reykjavík – the island's first permanent settlement.[140] A dispute in 962 prompted the partitioning of the island into four well defined territories called 'quarters', each with its own intermediate assembly.[141] Clearly, arable land was becoming a limited commodity, fostering further exploration and emigration. Consequently, Ari related how in around 985 a certain Erik the Red discovered, on a voyage from Iceland, a land to the west which he named 'Greenland' to entice others. The objective was obviously colonization, because the sagas stated that he thoroughly explored it.[142] On his second expedition he led a fleet of twenty-five ships, presumably carrying whole families with all their belongings for settlement. The fact that only fourteen of these vessels actually arrived in Greenland is grim evidence of how perilous such voyages were, even in the summer months with ships built for the purpose.[143]

The foregoing makes the sagas' version of the subsequent discovery of Vinland (North America) all the more credible. Both sagas which described the event, the *Grœnlendinga saga* ('Saga of the Greenlanders') and the *Eiríks saga rauða* ('Saga of Erik the Red'), said that it occurred when ships bound from Iceland or Norway to Greenland around the turn of the millennium veered off course. The former saga gave credit for the discovery to a certain Bjarni Herjólfsson, while the latter claimed Erik's son Leif the Lucky was responsible. Leif was certainly involved in the handful of voyages that followed.[144] The exact location of Vinland remains uncertain, but the only archaeological evidence of these expeditions to date is the small cluster of turf-walled structures located at L'Anse aux Meadows on the northern tip of Newfoundland.[145]

No permanent Viking presence was apparently ever established on Vinland due to an inimical environment populated by a hostile indigenous people. Nor did any of the Norse settlements on Greenland persist into the modern era. Given the state of maritime technology and navigation at the time, both these colonial experiments were simply too isolated to survive in such forbidding surroundings. Iceland, on the other hand, converted to Christianity in 1000 and gradually became reabsorbed into Norway's sphere of influence, beginning with a treaty with King Olaf Haraldsson in 1025 which confirmed the rights of Icelanders in the realm in return for a tariff. Iceland officially accepted the king's authority around 1262.[146]

Expansion Eastwards through Trade (750–989)

Just as the Norwegians led the way westwards, the Svear of what would become modern Sweden spread eastwards along the great rivers of European Russia. The incentive for them was not new farmland, but slaves, furs and Arabian silver – items they acquired by mercantile means, for raiding was not as profitable an option as it was in western Europe. Initially at least, there were few monasteries and wealthy towns along the waterways of eastern Europe to victimize. Moreover, riverine travel was difficult, often requiring the negotiation of rapids and rushing currents in small, light craft (probably *monoxyla*), which occasionally had to be portaged for substantial distances over rough terrain. 'In European Russia, by contrast,' notes Thomas Noonan of the University of Minnesota, 'the Scandinavians had to organize local systems to collect the natural wealth, and then establish trade centres and trading routes to market these goods.'[147]

The first of these trading centres was founded around 750 at Staraja Ladoga near the north end of the Gulf of Finland on the Volkhov river about 13km (8 miles) from where it joins the massive Lake Ladoga. Called *Aldeigjuborg* by its Norse founders, it was the gateway to a set of river routes which flowed across the Eurasian landmass all the way to the rich markets of Byzantium and the Islamic Caliphate.[148] From trading entrepôts such as Birka on Björkö ('Birch Island') in Lake Mälaren of modern Sweden,[149] Scandinavian merchants like the Svear would sail across the Baltic into the Gulf of Finland, then row up the river Neva to Lake Ladoga. At the southern end of the lake they would find the mouth of the Volkhov and a short distance upriver on the left bank lay *Aldeigjuborg*. From there, the Varangians, as they were known to the Greeks and Slavs, had a choice of two basic routes, depending upon their intended destination. Those wishing to reach Constantinople would normally head for the Dnieper river by rowing south along the Volkhov to Novgorod at the north end of Lake Ilmen. From there, they would travel down the Lovat river and the Western Dvina to the headwaters of the Dnieper river, which flowed past Kiev into the Black Sea, and finally, of course, via the Bosporus to Constantinople. Those Varangians journeying to the Caliphate made their way via the mighty Volga. They joined it from Lake Ladoga either by the rivers Sias and Mologa north of Rostov or via the river Svir to Lakes Onega and Beloya to the river Syeksna and finally to the Volga, which flowed into the Caspian Sea at Itil.[150]

The most often travelled, and thus the most lucrative, route seems to have been the Dnieper. Its terminus was the wealthiest city of the western world at the time: Constantinople. The *Annals of St-Bertin* revealed that the Varangians had been journeying there since before 839, when Swedish envoys sent by the Emperor Theophilos arrived in the court of Louis the Pious at Ingelheim.[151] Moreover, the southern end of the Dnieper route could be used to connect to the Volga route.[152] The Varangians naturally sought to control it, particularly the major trading settlements of Novgorod and Kiev. Their desire for domination revealed itself as early as 859, when the *Russian Primary Chronicle* (a twelfth-century history of Kiev) noted, 'The Varangians from beyond the sea imposed tribute upon the Chuds, the Slavs, the Merians, the Ves, and the Krivichians [basically the Finns and East Slavs of northwestern Russia].'[153] But according to the *Russian Primary Chronicle* (also known as *Nestor's Chronicle* or 'The Tale of Bygone Years'), their first opportunity to extend rule over the region came in 862. The Finns and

East Slavs threw off the yoke of their foreign oppressors, but found it difficult to govern themselves, so they invited a group of Varangians led by a certain Riurik and his brothers to rule over them.[154] They called them the 'Rus', a name believed to have been derived from the Finnish word for the Svear, *Ruotsi* (meaning 'rowers'). Hence the realm of the 'Rus', which would eventually give its name to modern Russia, came into being.[155]

Riurik based himself at Novgorod. His two brothers passed away shortly thereafter, leaving him to rule alone. Thus was born the Riurikid dynasty of the Rus. After consolidating his hold on the northwest, Riurik dispatched two of his followers, Askold and Dir, to Kiev, which was ruled by the Khazars at the time. The two eventually assembled enough Varangians to assume control of city and the surrounding territory. Within a few years they felt strong enough to challenge the Byzantine empire itself. In the early 860s they ravaged Greek possessions on the Black Sea with a fleet of 200 ships and even engineered an abortive assault on the environs of Constantinople itself.[156] Riurik died in 879, entrusting the realm to his kinsman Oleg while his own son Igor remained a minor. By 882 Oleg had slain Askold and Dir, setting himself up as the 'prince of Kiev'.[157] At this point the Riurikids ruled what Noonan calls a 'tributary domain from the Polish frontiers to the upper Volga'.[158] The Rus of Kiev then shifted their covetous gaze to the riches of Constantinople.

The Varangians of Kiev soon began to menace the Byzantines. The Rus wanted to increase trade with Constantinople, but the imperial court, wary of Varangian intentions ever since the raid of the early 860s, resisted. Oleg was not to be deterred. He ravaged the environs of the capital in 907 with a huge fleet. (The *Russian Primary Chronicle* gave the extravagant estimate of 2,000 ships.)[159] The assault ultimately failed, but Oleg kept up the pressure until Emperor Leo VI finally agreed to a treaty in 912, granting the Rus access to Constantinople.[160] His successor Igor, having come of age, returned in 941 evidently bent on conquest. The 'Grand Prince of Kiev' was said by both the *Russian Primary Chronicle* and John Skylitzes to have brought a gargantuan armada of some 10,000 vessels with him.[161] Liudprand of Cremona gave the less outlandish figure of 1,000 and indicated that the 'Rusan ships' were quite small so that they could 'move in very shallow water' – like the river Dnieper linking Kiev to the Black Sea.[162]

Whatever the exact number of their fleet, the Varangians soon learned the horrible efficacy of 'Greek fire'. While the Rus ravaged the littorals of the Black Sea, Emperor Romanos I Lekapenos commanded the *Protovestiarios* Theophanes to equip what vessels he could find in the harbour of Constantinople ('fifteen old battered galleys' – probably *dromōns*) with 'fire throwers', i.e., 'Greek fire' siphons. The rest of the Byzantine fleet was elsewhere dealing with the empire's Muslim adversaries. Theophanes met the Rus in calm seas at the northern entrance to the Bosporus.[163] Liudprand of Cremona described what happened next: 'As they lay, surrounded by the enemy, the Greeks began flinging their fire all around; and the Rusi seeing the flames threw themselves in haste from their ships, preferring to be drowned in the water rather than burned alive in the fire.'[164] John Skylitzes confirmed the rout of the Rus: 'Many of their vessels were reduced to cinders with Greek fire while the rest were utterly routed.'[165] And the *Russian Primary Chronicle* gave grim testimony to the profound impact the episode had on the Kievan Rus: 'When they [the Rus survivors] came once more to their native land, where each one recounted to his kinsfolk the course of events and described the fire launched from the ships, they related that the Greeks had in their possession the lightning from heaven and had set them on fire by pouring it forth, so that the Russes could not conquer them.'[166]

Despite some militant posturing by Igor in 944, relations improved appreciably in the aftermath.[167] The Byzantines and the Rus confirmed their commercial ties with a new treaty in 945.[168] Following Igor's death while trying to collect tribute from a tribe of East Slavs called the Derevlians, his widow Olga came to Constantinople and converted to Christianity in 948.[169] Varangians of various sorts began hiring themselves out to the Byzantine court in ever greater numbers. They were probably among the formidable forces that Nikephoros Phokas used to reclaim Crete for the empire in 961.[170] In 988 Grand Prince Vladimir accepted baptism and the hand of the emperor's sister, Anna Porphyrogenita. The following year he sent several thousand Varangians to his new brother-in-law Basil II to aid him in his struggle to suppress the rebellion of Bardas Phokas.[171] Within a decade the famed Varangian Guard had become a well-established institution of the Byzantine court. One of its most renowned members, Harald Sigurdsson (known as Hardrada or 'Hard Ruler'), the future king of Norway, was among the Varangians who accompanied Giorgios Maniakes on the abortive Byzantine invasion of 'Saracen' Sicily in 1038.[172]

The Danish Conquest of England (980–1016)

The final chapter in the Viking saga unfolded as a decades-long competition among kings for control of England amidst a royal rivalry for the north. Though most of the key players were of Scandinavian descent, sea power played only a supporting role. Perhaps because the Northmen still dominated the northern seas, the only naval battles of any significance were fought between Scandinavian adversaries in Scandinavian waters.

The battle for England began with the mysterious murder of King Edward at Corfe Castle in March 978, because this event brought to the throne Æthelred the Unready (or more correctly 'the ill-advised'). Alfred's strong line of successors had dissipated and Æthelred, barely twelve at the time of his accession, was ill-equipped to deal with the renewed Viking assault from the sea. Raids on the south and west coasts of England, taking advantage of the perceived weakness, began coming as early as 980.[173] Initially, the marauders may well have come from Ireland, but soon they began arriving from Scandinavia, due in part to the reduced influx of Arab silver, which had started declining earlier in the century. The raiding parties were small at first and led by minor chieftains, just as they had been at the beginning of the Viking era. Seven ships sacked Southampton in 981 and only three plundered Portland in 982.[174] By the 990s, however, great lords and kings at the head of huge fleets were savaging England's shores. **(Pl. 24)**

Olaf Tryggvason, future king of Norway, ravaged Folkestone in 991 with a fleet of ninety-three ships before moving on to Sandwich, Ipswich and finally Maldon, where he slaughtered Ealdorman Byrhtnoth and his army.[175] Three years later he paired up with Svein Forkbeard of Denmark to attack London with ninety-four ships. Only after exacting a tribute of 16,000 pounds in silver did the two agree to depart. It would be the first of several such payments for peace, later called the *Danegeld* ('Dane tribute').[176] Eventually the crown of England would literally pay enough in tribute to fund its own conquest.[177] Moreover, the payments brought no peace. Fleets of raiders remunerated with English silver were often replaced by others equally as rapacious. Another Danish fleet devastated the southern end of the island all the way from Watchet at the mouth of the Severn in 997 to Rochester in the Thames estuary in 999.[178] The *Anglo-Saxon Chronicle* lamented that Æthelred answered it all with characteristic ineptitude: 'Then the king with his councillors decided that they [the Danish raiders] should be confronted with a ship-army and also with a land army, but when the ships were ready, there was delay from day to day, which distressed the wretched people who lay on the ships.'[179] The Danish fleet finally left for Normandy of its own accord the following summer.[180]

The only respite England received after this last ravaging was when erstwhile allies Olaf Tryggvason and Svein Forkbeard had a falling-out over control of Norway at the turn of the millennium. Olaf exploited the murder of Earl Hakon Sigurdsson, the de facto ruler of Norway, at the hand of a slave in 995 by using his share of the English tribute of 994 to finance his assumption of the Norwegian crown.[181] Svein, however, considered this a provocation, since he regarded himself as overlord of Norway, as had his father and predecessor, Harald Bluetooth. So in September 1000 he arranged with his allies – Earl Erik Hakonsson (Hakon's son) and Olaf Skötkonung, king of the Svear – to ambush Olaf Tryggvason as he sailed home from Wendland on the south shore of the Baltic.[182] Against the allied fleet of seventy-one warships, Tryggvason had only eleven, but one of these was the great *drakkar* ('dragon ship') *Ormrinn Langi* ('Long Serpent'). It was purported to have had thirty-four rowing seats, meaning it was probably about 45m (148ft) long. Moreover, each of these rowing benches was said to have accommodated eight oarsmen for a total of 272 crewmen plus an additional thirty fighters in the bow, giving the vessel a crew complement in excess of 300. And every crew member was specially chosen, most coming from the royal retinue. The *Heimskringla* claimed it was 'the best fitted and most costly ship that was ever built in Norway'.[183] When Olaf Tryggvason saw the enemy host approach at a place in the western Baltic called Svöld (the exact location is uncertain), he ordered all his vessels linked together and made certain that the other two dragon ships, *Short Serpent* and *Crane*, were lashed to his on either side. 'This fight was very sharp and very bloody,' said Snorre Sturlason, the author of the *Heimskringla*. Nonetheless, the outcome of the encounter was never really in doubt. Svein's superior numbers enabled him to attack the ends of Olaf's line and clear each vessel one at a time until reaching the *Long Serpent*. In time, even this great *drakkar* fell and Olaf, his shield over his head, cast himself into the sea to become the stuff of sagas.[184]

None of this, however, made the English less vulnerable to Viking attack. The Danish 'raiding-ship army' which had wintered in Normandy in 1000 came back for more in 1001. Working out of the Isle of Wight, it ravaged the south coast from Devon to Sussex.[185] Æthelred again resorted to bribery in 1002 to get rid of the raiders: 24,000 pounds in silver this time, along with supplies. He then perversely proceeded to expunge any possible benefit from the transaction by ordering the massacre of all Danes in his realm on St Brice's Day, 13 November, that same year.[186] Included among those slain was reportedly the Lady Gunnhild, sister of Svein Forkbeard.[187] This, of course, prompted retribution from the latter the very next year. Exeter, Wilton, Salisbury, Norwich and Thetford all paid the price. The only thing that induced the Danish king to finally quit the kingdom in 1005 was a 'great famine, throughout the English race, such that no one ever remembered one so grim before', according to the *Anglo-Saxon Chronicle*.[188] But Svein was back with his fleet the following year to pick up, very nearly unopposed, where he had left off. By this time, in the year 1007, the realm's ransom had risen to 36,000 pounds of silver plus provisions.[189]

Such ever-increasing tribute payments only seemed to invite further violent extortion. Æthelred attempted to break the cycle of pecuniary appeasement in 1008 by ordering that each 310 hides be responsible for producing one warship, but once more weak leadership doomed the enterprise. At least a hundred ships were actually collected at Sandwich, but in-fighting and treachery caused twenty to be misappropriated and the rest burned.[190] The Danish chieftain Thorkel the Tall arrived at Sandwich in August 1009. His campaign culminated in the capture of Canterbury in 1011. It also cost Archbishop Ælfheah his life in 1012 and Æthelred an additional 48,000 pounds of tribute. To be fair, Æthelred thought he was buying Thorkel's allegiance and getting a fleet of forty-five ships in the deal.[191] It availed him little, however. Svein Forkbeard showed up at Sandwich in July 1013 with a 'numerous fleet' of 'towered ships' so magnificent that a monk of St Omer's monastery in Flanders waxed poetic over it for an entire passage of the *Encomium Emmae Reginae* (an eleventh-century panegyric to Queen Emma of England).[192] Literary embellishment aside, Else Roesdahl is probably right when she says that the ships must have been similar to the Skuldelev 2 and 5 vessels.[193] By the end of the year England was his and Æthelred had taken refuge at the court of Duke Richard II of Normandy, the brother of his wife Emma.[194]

Æthelred's exile was a short one. Svein Forkbeard died on 3 February 1014, mere weeks after winning the kingdom. His forces pledged their allegiance to his son Cnut, barely eighteen years old, but the English nobility recalled Æthelred from Normandy. For a change, the latter acted with some dispatch, disbursing 21,000 pounds in silver to ensure the loyalty of Thorkel's fleet. Facing a united English aristocracy, Cnut was compelled to withdraw to Denmark.[195] But he would not yield so easily what he regarded as his patrimony. With the help of his brother Harald, now king of Denmark, Cnut equipped a powerful new fleet, numbering as many as 200 ships according to the *Encomium Emmae Reginae*.[196] He sailed it back to Sandwich in the summer of 1015 and soon subdued Wessex, prompting the ealdorman Eadric to defect to him with forty of the king's ships.[197] In the spring of 1016 Cnut penetrated the Thames estuary with a fleet of 160. But even before he could reach London, Æthelred gave up his unhappy life on 23 April. 'Then at the Rogation Days [7–9 May] the [Danish] ships came to Greenwich, and immediately turned to London,' recounted the *Anglo-Saxon Chronicle*, 'and dug a ditch on the south side and dragged their ships to the west side of the bridge [London Bridge], and afterwards bedyked the town around so that no one could get in or out.' Æthelred's son Edmund fought gamely on, even relieving London at one point, but at Ashingdon in Essex on 18 October Cnut won his crown. Edmund perished hardly a month later.[198]

The End of the Viking Age (1017–66)

Cnut moved quickly to consolidate his conquest. He had himself formally crowned in London on 6 January 1017 and in July married Æthelred's widow Emma to curry favour with his new subjects.[199] In 1018 he dissolved his great Danish host, save forty ships, with a tribute payment of 10,500 pounds of silver from London alone and 72,000 pounds from the rest of the realm. His brother Harald died that same year, leaving Cnut in control of Denmark.[200] In 1027 Scotland submitted to him and in 1028 he seized Norway from Olaf Haraldsson by parading a magnificent fleet up its coastline unopposed.[201] In the words of Viking scholar Gwyn Jones, 'Yet again a king who had lost command of the sea had lost his kingdom as a consequence, and Knut, who held that command, inherited.'[202] On a pilgrimage to Rome to attend the coronation of Conrad II as Holy Roman Emperor, Cnut penned a letter to the English people proclaiming himself 'king of all England and Denmark and the Norwegians and some of the Swedes'.[203] The Vikings and the Scandinavian inheritors of their legacy had achieved their zenith: they occupied lands as far west as Greenland; Yaroslav the Wise had brought the Varangian Rus to the apex of their power as Grand Prince of Kiev; the Kingdom of Dublin flourished under Sigtrygg Silkbeard; the descendants of the Viking chieftain Rollo ruled over one of the most powerful dukedoms in Christendom; and now the scion of Viking royalty held sway over England and most of Scandinavia.[204]

The very audacity which had helped to create the Viking victory would now contribute to its defeat. Cnut died in Dorset on 12 November 1035, setting in motion a ripple of successions in a short span. Harald Harefoot, his son by his mistress Ælfgifu, inherited the crown of England, while Harthacnut, Cnut's son by Emma, took the throne of Denmark. Magnus, the son of Cnut's erstwhile enemy Olaf Haraldsson, ironically became king of Norway. When Harald Harefoot died in 1040, Harthacnut replaced him as king of England, but he himself passed away in 1042 and was succeeded by Edward, Æthelred's son by Emma.[205] At the same time Magnus assumed suzerainty over Denmark. This was contested by Earl Svein Estridsson, Cnut's nephew, who met Magnus in one of the classic maritime confrontations of the era: the Battle of Aarhus in 1043. The two royal contenders lashed their longships together in opposing lines and the two lines clashed bow-to-bow off the east coast of Jutland around Christmas. As Snorre Sturlason told it, the tide was turned when Magnus sprang from his own shield wall to lead the boarding and subsequent clearing of Svein's flagship.[206] Estridsson himself escaped, however, and in 1045 was joined by Harald Hardrada, Magnus' uncle and rival for control of Norway, who had just returned from service as captain of the Byzantine emperor's Varangian Guard. This caused Magnus to placate Harald by sharing the throne of Norway with him. Magnus' death in 1047 left Harald holding the crown of Norway alone, while Svein Estridsson dominated Denmark. Unwilling to accept this, Harald Hardrada initiated a protracted struggle to absorb Denmark at Svein's expense.[207] The conflict finally came to a climax at the Battle of Nissa off the coast of Halland in the spring of 1062.

According to the *Heimskringla*, Hardrada essentially challenged Svein to a winner-takes-all duel at sea: 'In the winter King Harald sent word south to Denmark to King Svein that the following spring he should come from the south to the Elv [the Göta river in southwestern Sweden just north of Copenhagen] to meet him, and then they should both fight in such a way as to share their lands, and that one of them should have both kingdoms.' Harald gathered a fleet of 150 ships for the purpose, including a great *drakkar* as his flagship. 'Built after the size of the *Long Serpent*', said Snorre Sturlason, it boasted seventy oars between the gilded 'dragon's head' at the bow and the 'dragon's tail' at the stern.[208] Svein, however, failed to show up at the appointed place and time, so Harald harried the coast of Halland (a southwestern province of Sweden) to draw him out. It worked. Svein sought him out with 300 ships and found him at the mouth of the Nissan river (present-day Halmstad) late in the afternoon of 9 August. Both sides lashed all their ships together with the exception of a small squadron under Earl Hakon Ivarsson that Harald allowed to manoeuvre freely. This was decisive. The battle was long and hard-fought, lasting through the night, but eventually Hakon's squadron turned the tide by attacking the flanks of the Danish line and culling out vulnerable vessels so that they could be overwhelmed one at a time. By morning, Svein had fled, along with most of his following, leaving seventy empty ships behind.[209] Notwithstanding the outcome, both kings were weakened by the long war and eventually concluded an even-handed peace in 1064 at the Göta river.[210]

Harald, however, remained determined to increase his holdings. He thought he saw his chance two years later when Edward the Confessor died and his wife's brother, Harold Godwinson, pressed his contested claim to the crown of England. Harald Hardrada's own claim to the throne was a tenuous one based upon an alleged promise Harthacnut made to Harald's nephew Magnus that Magnus would inherit England upon Harthacnut's death without issue. Nonetheless, Harald probably felt his claim was at least as legitimate as that of either Harold Godwinson or William of Normandy. He would not have let the mundane matter of legitimacy dissuade him in any event, since he was clearly confident that he had the military might to back up his contention.

And, indeed, by joining forces with Tostig Godwinson (Harold's rebellious brother) on the Tyne in Scotland, Hardrada was able to assemble a fearsome fleet of 300 ships for his planned invasion. With it, he ravaged the coast of Yorkshire in the summer of 1066 before entering the Humber estuary to finally beach his fleet on the banks of the Ouse near Riccall, 16km (10 miles) south of York. He defeated the combined forces of Edwin of Mercia and Morcar of Northumbria at Gate Fulford on 20 September. York quietly submitted, promising its support in the campaign to conquer England. Harald must have felt supremely self-assured at that point, but hubris would be his undoing. It was at Stamford Bridge, 19km (12 miles) from the Vikings' vaunted longships, that on 25 September Harold Godwinson, after a forced march from the south coast where he had been waiting for William, surprised and defeated the last great army of Viking invaders, fighting beneath a battle banner appropriately named 'Land-waster'.[211]

Snorre Sturlason maintained that before the battle which killed him, Harald Hardrada, this consummate Viking chieftain, was heard to have recited the following Skaldic verse:

> We do not creep into battle
> under the shelter of shields,
> before the crash of weapons;
> this is what the loyal goddess
> of the hawk's land commanded us.
> The bearer of the necklace told me long ago
> to hold the helmet high
> in the din of weapons,
> when the valkyrie's ice
> met the skulls of men.[212]

And so ended the Viking onslaught – not with an encounter at sea, but in an engagement on land, miles from the nearest ships.

* * *

Exemplary Engagement: The Siege of Paris (885–6)

Sometime in the autumn of 885 'seven hundred high-prowed ships and very many smaller ones' snaked up the Seine in a column that 'extended for more than two leagues [10km or 6 miles] down river', according to Abbo of the nearby Abbey of St-Germain-des-Prés, an eyewitness to the event.[213] The young Benedictine monk also insisted that 'the grim ones' who manned those vessels numbered 40,000.[214] And so began what was, perhaps, the most ambitious amphibious assault of the Viking onslaught: the 885–6 siege of Paris.

The Viking force which made its way up the Seine was composed of various elements of the so-called great army forced from England by Alfred's defensive measures, plus other groups of raiders who had been operating in Flanders. The numbers conveyed by the awed Abbo in his epic Latin poem, *Bella parisiacae urbis* ('Wars of the City of Paris') were clearly literary embroidery to enhance the 'divinely inspired' deeds of the 200 or so defenders.[215] Respected medieval military historian Carroll Gillmor has convincingly shown through quantitative methodology that the Viking fleet could have consisted of no more than 200 to 300 ships, probably the size of the Skuldelev 5 vessel (17.3m/57ft long by 2.5m/8ft wide by 0.5m/1ft 8in deep), each carrying a crew of about twenty-six – meaning the whole host was about 5,000 to 8,000 men at most.[216] Actual totals were probably even smaller. That said, this incursion was the largest, most sustained Viking thrust into the heart of West Frankia of the era.

Ironically, the objective of this great Viking armada was not originally Paris itself but the rich upper Seine basin and Burgundy with its as yet unscathed monasteries and towns. When the Northmen rowed up the Seine in November 885 they managed to make it past the fortified bridge built by Charles the Bald at Pont-de-l'Arch, probably because it was inadequately guarded.[217] After all, there was no major population centre in the vicinity. Paris, on the other hand, was a city of perhaps 5,000 inhabitants, located on the Île de la Cité which controlled two fortified bridges blocking the Seine: the Grand Pont extending to the right bank (north side) and the Petit Pont stretching across to the left bank (south side).[218] This was why, according to Abbo, when the Vikings reached Paris in late November, their principal chieftain, Sigfrid, merely asked for passage. Hostilities were precipitated only when the city's leading luminary, Bishop Gozlin, denied permission.[219] (*See* Map 12.)

The Vikings concentrated their initial assault of 26 November on the Grand Pont on the right bank, probably because the tower guarding it remained unfinished. Abbo indicated that the Danes attacked the tower from their ships, but, unfinished or not, its foundation was stoutly constructed of stone and they were repulsed.[220] During the night the defenders topped the tower with a wooden tier half as high again as the original structure. Undeterred, the besiegers battered the bastion the next day with the usual blizzard of 'darts, stones, and javelins … hurled by *ballistae* and slingshots'. They even went at the base of the tower with 'iron picks', but Bishop Gozlin and Odo, count of Paris, had organized an

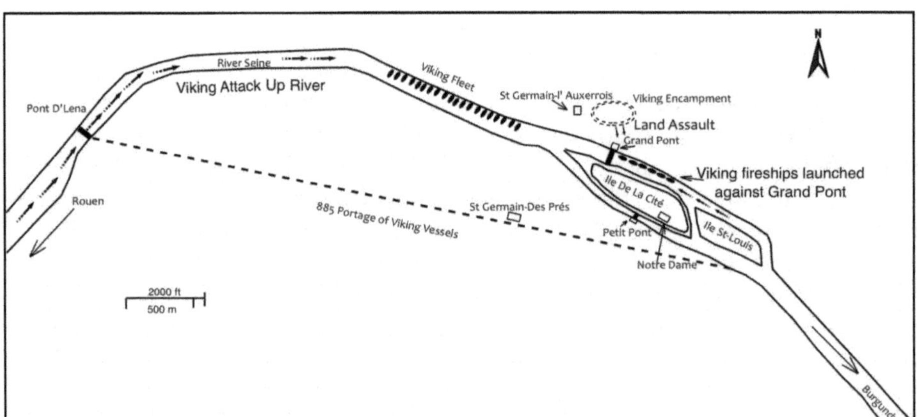

Map 12. Viking Siege of Paris, 885–886. (*Kristy Stanton*)

effective resistance. The defenders showered their attackers with a scalding mixture of oil, wax and pitch 'which burned the hair of the Danes; and made their skulls split open'.[221]

Next, the Danes attempted to set the tower's gate ablaze, but a sortie from the city led by two standard-bearers with banners 'tinted golden with saffron' like some early version of the *Oriflamme* (the royal battle standard of France) drove the attackers off. Odo's brother, Robert the Strong, fell in the course of the battle, but the citizenry remained resolute. The tower was again repaired during the night.[222] Realizing the siege would not be a swift one, the Scandinavians retired to the right bank where they constructed a fortified encampment of stone and earthworks not far from St-German-l'Auxerrois. From there they raided all around in an apparent effort to build up their supplies.[223] Once this was done, they renewed the assault with vigour.

For the next several weeks the Vikings tried every imaginable stratagem. They built several 'roofed' battering rams with 'monstrous wheels'.[224] They made 'a thousand tents, held aloft by upright poles' for deflecting arrows and scorching liquids while attacking the walls.[225] They even fashioned grenades – 'a thousand pots of molten lead' – which they hurled over the city's Roman walls with catapults.[226] At one point the Danes formed three corps, one of which made a diversionary assault on the tower while the other two evidently attempted to ram the bridge in 'painted ships'. None of it worked. The bridge and the tower held fast.[227] Part of the problem was a dyke that the defenders had dug around the tower, preventing the Vikings from moving siege towers into position. Advancing as a *testudo* (a unit of warriors marching in close-order formation using their shields to protect them all around like 'a tortoise'), the Vikings attempted to fill in the ditch with earth and whatever debris they could find, including livestock and the cadavers of dead captives.[228] The results were mixed and ultimately unsuccessful.

According to another contemporary source, Regino of Prüm, the Vikings grew so frustrated that sometime before the end of the year they even considered abandoning the siege altogether. To bypass the fortified bridges, they attempted a complicated portage operation in which they either carried or dragged vessels on rollers (probably logs) from the area of today's Pont d'Iéna through the grounds of St-Germain-des-Prés to a point just east of the Île Saint-Louis – a distance of around 3km (2 miles).[229] The Vikings might have been able to get some of their smaller vessels past the blockage in this manner so that their crews could forage the virginal upper Seine valley, but this solution was clearly impracticable for a fleet of 200 to 300 ships, many the size of the Skuldelev 5 or larger. Consequently, they must have realized that they had no choice but to remove the blockage.

In desperation, the Vikings culled out 'three rowing vessels', dragged them overland on the right bank and refloated them upstream of the city. Once these ships were 'loaded full with forests of branches and mounds of leaves' and set ablaze, the Danes then guided them by rope from the river bank to a position from where the westbound current would carry them into the Grand Pont.[230]

The venture failed spectacularly. The fireships hung up harmlessly on the stone bridgeheads, so that the defenders were able to douse the flames and appropriate the vessels intact.[231] Ironically, nature did to the Petit Pont what the Vikings had repeatedly failed to accomplish on the Grand Pont. On the night of 6 February 886 the Seine, apparently swollen by rain, overflowed its banks, carrying away 'the mid-section' of the span. This, of course, isolated the wooden guard tower on the left bank so that those in the city could no longer reinforce their compatriots in the tower, of whom there were only twelve. In the morning the Vikings were able to complete the encirclement of the wooden tower with their ships. 'And then the Danes brought forward a wagon, piled high with dry hay,' recounted Abbo. 'They set it alight, and pushed it against the wretched tower.' Forced out onto what was left of the bridge, the twelve defenders surrendered, only to be butchered.[232]

The Vikings had evidently invested too much by this time to simply continue upriver, so the siege of the city staggered miserably on. The besiegers persevered at the gates with their battering rams while the besieged fended them off with 'hefty shafts of hard wood, each one pierced at the far end with a keen tooth of iron' and mangonels which launched 'massive stones'.[233] In the spring Charles the Fat (the Carolingian Emperor and king of West Frankia) finally sent help in the form of Heinrich of Saxony, but the latter did little to lift the siege. He was killed when he rode heedlessly into a 3ft-deep stake-filled trench excavated around the Viking encampment.[234] On 16 April plague which had broken out in the city claimed the life of Bishop Gozlin.[235] Sigfrid had also apparently grown sick of the enterprise. It took a mere 60 pounds of silver from the Abbey of St-Germain-des-Prés to convince him and his contingent to depart.[236] Others persisted in the assault, however, so Odo slipped past the Scandinavians to seek succour from the emperor.[237]

That summer the Vikings made one last furious assault. 'The mortal enemies of the city encircled its walls, so that it had to face constant attacks from all directions,' testified Abbo, meaning the Vikings must have surrounded the city with their ships, given that it was located on an island in the middle of the Seine.[238] In any event the effort fell short. Charles the Fat arrived, at long last, in October to relieve the city. His remedy was to ransom it from the Vikings for 700 pounds of silver and free passage to Burgundy, which the remaining Norse raiders then ravaged for the next three years – precisely what the fortified bridges of Paris had been designed to prevent.[239] Such a resolution was widely regarded as spineless and caused Charles to be deposed the following autumn in favour of Count Odo of Paris, an ancestor to the Capetian kings of France.[240]

CHAPTER 8

The Norman Invasion and the Rise of Anglo-French Naval Warfare

The conquest of England in 1066 by Duke William of Normandy, a vassal of the Capetian king of France, virtually ensured that the English Channel and its adjacent waters would be the scene of maritime military operations for centuries to come. Initially this was because, after the Battle of Hastings on 14 October, William and most of his aristocratic entourage came to own lands both in Britain and on the continent, necessitating constant commuting by sea for the maintenance and defence of their territories. Eventually, following the loss of continental possessions to the Capetian crown by William's Norman and Angevin successors, the Channel became a naval combat zone as the English court sought to retrieve lands lost and the French throne threatened invasion to impose its perceived sovereign rights. The technology and tactics of the era dictated that this warfare on the waves took the form of what was essentially a battle over logistics: fleets were used either to transport invasion forces and supplies or to interdict them. Pitched battles were rare and often indecisive.

The Norman Amphibious Assault on England (1066)

Harold Godwinson, king of England, effectively put an end to the centuries-long Viking onslaught with his brilliant victory over the king of Norway, Harald Hardrada, at Stamford Bridge on 25 September 1066. Barely three weeks later another invader of Viking stock, William of Normandy, would end Anglo-Saxon rule in England by defeating Harold at Hastings. It was a close-run confrontation, lasting more than ten hours. The determined English defenders held the high ground on Senlac Hill behind their shield wall and rebuffed repeated Norman cavalry charges with heavy casualties until the very end, when Harold finally fell.[1] William's skilful use of heavy cavalry tactics integrated with archery deserved much of the credit for the victory, but none of it would have been possible without the near-flawless execution of the unopposed amphibious assault which preceded the battle – a logistical tour de force.

William's conquest of England actually began many months earlier when he learned of Harold's accession on 6 January to a throne William believed had been promised to him. Wace, a canon of the cathedral of Bayeux, wrote in his *Roman de Rou* (a history of the dukes of Normandy) that William was informed of Harold's coronation shortly after the event while hunting near Rouen and almost immediately began planning to right what he perceived as a wrong.[2] After all, according to both English and Norman sources, King Edward the Confessor had bequeathed William the crown of England as late as the winter of 1052 in gratitude for the Norman hospitality extended to him during his long exile at the ducal court in Rouen from 1014 to 1041. In fact, Edward had even, just before his death, obliged Harold to swear formally to William in Normandy that he would honour that decision.[3] Consequently, William initiated preparations that winter for an invasion of England.

He began by seeking the benediction of Pope Alexander II for the undertaking, which he subsequently received in the form of a papal banner.[4] He then convened a council of his magnates at Lillebonne (near Le Havre) where, according to William of Malmesbury (the great twelfth-century English historian), 'he encouraged them with lavish promises, and levied a demand on all of them for ships in proportion to their possessions'.[5] 'Then each one said how much he would do for him and how many ships he would bring,' confirmed Wace, adding, 'the duke had everything put in writing and the ships and knights enumerated.'[6] What resulted was a document that has become known as the *Ship List of William the Conqueror*. Based upon data compiled in the months before the conquest, the *Ship List* contains the names of more than a dozen lay and ecclesiastical magnates, along with the numbers of ships each had agreed to furnish for the enterprise. It amounted to 776 vessels, including the flagship *Mora*, which the Duchess Matilda personally provided for her husband.[7] This number dovetails closely with the eyewitness observation of Wace's father, who attested that 'when they [the Normans] set off from St-Valery there were seven hundred ships less four, either ships, boats, or skiffs, carrying weapons and equipment'.[8] The testimony of the *Ship List* is further substantiated by the famed Bayeux Tapestry, which contains an image of William's flagship *Mora* embellished with the figurehead of a gilded youth with a horn to his lips – almost exactly as described in the *Ship List*.[9] While the Conqueror's chaplain, William of Poitiers, put the number of ships at 1,000 and contemporary chronicler William of Jumièges posed the preposterous estimate of 3,000, the size of the armada was probably in the range of 700 vessels.[10]

The Bayeux Tapestry also seems to show William supervising the construction of the fleet at the site of a second conference, Bonneville-sur-Touques, not far from the mouth of the Seine. While the tapestry depicts the ship production process in some detail, from the felling of trees to hull assembly, it is extremely doubtful that the entire fleet was fabricated from scratch.[11] **(Pl. 25)** To have furnished a fleet of some 700 ships thusly within a few months would have denuded the forests of Normandy and required an army of carpenters about the size of the intended invasion force (around 8,400).[12] Most of the armada must have been composed of existing vessels gathered from all over the region. Elizabeth van Houts, the reigning doyenne of Norman scholars, observes, 'All men on the *Ship List* had rights in ports, either on the coast, or on the rivers inland.' She has concluded that they would have had the responsibility of finding and furnishing the ships.[13] Furthermore, William credited his father-in-law Count Baldwin V of Flanders with supplying him with substantial military aid for the enterprise and Flanders was known as a major source of mercenary maritime forces at the time.[14]

A third conference of councillors was held at Caen in June and the armada was ultimately assembled at Dives-sur-Mer by 12 August.[15] The vessels were indubitably of various sorts and represented whatever was available to the duke at the time, but many must have been similar to the Gokstad, Ladby or Skuldelev Viking ships. Most of the troops and provisions were probably transported on seagoing *knarrs* like the Skuldelev 1 described in the preceding chapter and coastal traders like the Skuldelev 3, a small oaken sailing vessel about 14m (46ft) long and 3.3m (10ft 10in) wide with a metre of depth.[16] The transportation of the horses, however, would seem to have required vessels built for the purpose. What those ships might have been can only be imagined. Bernard Bachrach, an authority on medieval logistics, has surmised that the Normans used Byzantine nautical technology transmitted by the Normans of southern Italy to construct them, but the likelihood of that seems remote, given that the Italo-Normans had not adopted such technology themselves by the time of the Conquest.[17] Robert Guiscard was still modifying existing vessels to carry horses when he besieged Palermo in 1072.[18] Moreover, no such specially designed horse transports from the era have ever been found in northern waters. The Normans may simply have 'made do' with extant hull structures. The Bayeux Tapestry shows horses being embarked and disembarked over the gunnels of ships similar to the early tenth-century Ladby, a slender oared vessel 21.6m (71ft) long by 2.85m (9ft 4in) wide, but with only .7m (2ft 4in) of depth, found on Funen Island, Denmark. **(Pl. 26)** An experiment by Danish Boy Scouts in 1967 using a reconstruction of the Ladby demonstrated that it was at least possible.[19] Carol Gilmor believes, however, that the more rugged Gokstad-type vessel (previously described) was the more likely carrier for William's horses.[20] In any event, the amassing of such a large, multi-purpose armada was a staggering achievement in itself.

In fact, the mustering of William's entire invasion force at Dives-sur-Mer only a few months after Lillebonne stands as one of the most auspicious military accomplishments of the Middle Ages. Contemporary observers provide few clues as to its execution. William of Poitiers simply said, 'It would take too long to narrate in detail how under his [William's] prudent direction ships were built and equipped with arms, men, provisions, and the other things necessary for war, and how all Normandy eagerly bent to the task.'[21] Fortunately, Bachrach provides a plausible analysis of the endeavour which illustrates the scale of the achievement.[22] While William of Poitiers and Orderic Vitalis both mention that William had 50,000 men-at-arms and/or knights at his disposal, most scholars estimate that the duke was actually only able to put around 8,000 effectives in the field at Hastings – about the same as Harold.[23] That means that William had to transport at least that number of fully equipped combatants across the Channel. In addition, Bachrach reasons that the duke had to account for 2,000 troops to garrison Pevensey and Hastings, following an amphibious landing on the shores of Sussex. He figured that William also needed some 4,000 mariners to man the fleet. This all means that the duke had to provide for a force of 14,000 men in an encampment at Dives-sur-Mer adjacent to a provisional naval facility capable of accommodating some 700 ships of various sorts.[24]

This task was significantly complicated by the fact that an estimated 2,000 to 3,000 of the effectives were knights, and thus William also had to account for at least that many horses.[25] Sustaining that number of men and mounts for any length of time must have been a monumental undertaking. According to Bachrach, the troops alone would have required 'approximately 28 tons of unmilled wheat grain and 14,000 gallons of clean fresh water per day at a ration of 4 pounds of grain and 1 gallon of water per man.'[26] The mounts would have been highly trained warhorses of the most valuable kind, in the range of 15 to 16 hands and weighing an average of 1,500 pounds each, and they would have consumed a minimum of 14 to 20 tons of grain per day.[27] And William's concerns were not limited to what was consumed – he also had to consider what was evacuated. 'At Dives-sur-Mer William's horses produced a mountain of some 5,000,000 pounds of feces and a river of perhaps some 700,000 gallons of urine,' notes Bachrach.[28] The safe removal of all this waste from men and beasts had to have been a priority for the duke in order to prevent plague from decimating his force before it even embarked.

And William managed to accomplish all this not only throughout the summer as his forces gathered, but for an entire month after all had assembled – from 12 August to 12 September. He did so through the implementation of a centralized command structure by which he personally provided all necessary sustenance at his own expense, according to William of Poitiers. This obviated the need for foraging, which he had forbidden in any case.[29] Consequently, William was able to hold his army and fleet together for as long as he needed without too severely impacting their readiness. It would prove crucial to his ultimate triumph, for Harold was not nearly so successful at preserving the integrity of his forces over time.

Harold's challenge lay in the nature of military recruitment in the kingdom at the time. The troop levy of Anglo-Saxon England was based on the *fyrd*, a sort of army of the realm raised and remunerated by the shires for a limited period of time, normally two months. The naval component also came from the shires, but was called the *scipfyrd* and its ships were apparently funded by a shire tax called the *scipscot*.[30] In addition, Harold could draw upon a pool of mercenary mariners called *butescarls* ('boatmen') in the sources, who were generally based out of what would become the Cinque Ports (Hastings, Romney, Hythe, Dover and Sandwich). The *butescarls*, however, represented only a fraction of the maritime manpower available to the crown. Harold was chiefly reliant on the *scipfyrd* and it was the limited nature of the *scipfyrd*'s military obligation which presented problems for him.

Given the enormity of the Norman enterprise at Dives-sur-Mer, Harold was undoubtedly aware of the looming assault on his kingdom and had always intended to meet it, but the timing of his mobilization may have been fatally altered by his brother Tostig. Late the previous year the younger Godwinson had been ousted as Earl of Northumbria by the county's thegns and exiled with Harold's acquiescence. Tostig reacted by hiring a fleet of some sixty ships in Flanders, which he used to harry the south coast of England from the Isle of Wight all the way to Sandwich in May 1066.[31] This compelled Harold to assemble his forces early in order to deal with the threat. Tostig fled north to the

Humber in Northumbria where Earls Edwin and Morcar humbled him in the field and forced him to take refuge in Scotland. As for Harold, the *Anglo-Saxon Chronicle* recounted how he remained mobilized to counter William's expected invasion: 'And when his fleet was gathered, he went into Wight, and lay there all summer and autumn; and a land-army kept everywhere by the sea, although in the end it was to no avail.'[32]

William, on the other hand, seemed to be in no particular hurry. His army in its entirety was assembled by 12 August and his fleet was fully equipped, yet he waited at Dives-sur-Mer for another entire month. William of Poitiers blamed the delay on 'unfavourable winds', but the late great Norman scholar Marjorie Chibnall begged to differ. The duke had learned from a captured spy that Harold was lying in wait for him at the Isle of Wight with his entire fleet and that his land forces lined the southern littoral. Surely, William must have realized that it behoved him to wait until Harold's forces had exhausted their pay and provisions.[33] And, in fact, that was precisely what occurred. 'Then when it was the Nativity of St Mary [8 September], the men's provisions were gone, and no one could hold them there any longer,' recorded the Abingdon manuscript of the *Anglo-Saxon Chronicle*, adding, 'Then the men were allowed to go home, and the king rode inland, and the ships were sent to London.'[34] William led his armada out of the Gulf of Dives on 12 September.

Even then the destination was not England. Instead, the Norman invasion fleet headed 93km (58 miles) up the coast to St-Valery-sur-Somme, suffering a shipwreck in the course of the two-day voyage. It lingered there an additional two weeks. Again, William of Poitiers suggested that the duke was awaiting a southerly wind and the wind certainly must have been a factor: the Bayeux Tapestry and other physical evidence indicate the Norman fleet was powered mostly by sails, with oars providing auxiliary propulsion only.[35] But there may have been other reasons. First of all, St-Valery-sur-Somme was considerably closer to William's intended point of debarkation: Pevensey and Hastings, which Norman historian R. Allen Brown labelled 'the heartlands of the Godwinson patrimony'.[36] Secondly, William may well have decided to wait there because he was aware of Harald Hardrada's invasion plans. In the words of Viking specialist Gwyn Jones, 'It is difficult to believe that so shrewd a calculator as William knew nothing of Harald's interest, particularly in view of the Scandinavian connection ...'[37] After all, Svein Estridsson, king of Denmark and Hardrada's long-time foe, had sworn his support for William's endeavour and it is rather implausible that Hardrada could have assembled an invasion fleet of around 300 ships without either or both of the monarchs learning of it through their spy networks.[38] In any case, William's timing ended up being suspiciously propitious. He finally set sail for Sussex with a south wind on the evening tide of 27 September, a full week after Hardrada's victory at Fulford and two days after the bloody battle of Stamford Bridge from which Harold emerged triumphant but badly battered.[39]

Maintaining the integrity of a 700-ship fleet during a night crossing was a feat few commanders could have hoped to achieve, yet achieve it William did. He did so through iron discipline and strict control of his maritime assets. Bishop Guy of

Amiens, the author of the *Carmen de Hastingae Proelio* ('Song of the Battle of Hastings'), provided ample illustration of this: 'By a trumpet's call you [William] command all other vessels to leave the shore and make for the deep sea in safety. The ships cast off their moorings and put out to sea in orderly formation.'[40] William of Poitiers added:

> But for fear that they might reach the shore to which they were bound before dawn and run into danger in a hostile and unknown landing place, he has an order proclaimed by a herald that when they reach the open sea they should all rest at anchor for a short watch of the night not far from his ship, until they see a lamp lit at his masthead, and hear the sound of a trumpet as a signal to sail on.[41]

Once the signal was given, Guy of Amiens indicated that formation integrity was maintained during the 97km (60 mile) crossing, despite a moonless and cloudy night, by the use of lanterns hoisted to the topmast of every vessel.[42] And like all accomplished commanders, William demonstrated flexibility and the willingness to adjust the plan as dictated by changing circumstances. The *Mora* was apparently much swifter than the other ships so that William found he had forged well ahead of the main body during the night. Therefore, sometime before dawn he had his flagship heave to and await the remainder of the fleet, which was spotted at dawn by a seaman whom he had ordered to shinny up the mast. The armada landed some time the next morning as a unit, unopposed and without incident, just a few miles from Pevensey.[43]

Even then, William was in no particular rush to march inland. He had his troops reinforce the old Roman fortifications at Pevensey and installed a garrison before moving east along the coast to Hastings, where he had the same done. Both Guy of Amiens and William of Poitiers indicated that the duke also took care to have ramparts built to protect his fleet.[44] He then had his men ravage the region but remain within the immediate environs. William had a number of reasons for lingering in the area. First of all, his invaluable warhorses needed time to get their 'land legs' back after the Channel crossing. And he probably also needed to gather more mounts. Every knight normally needed at least four: the warhorse, palfreys for himself and his squire for everyday riding, and a packhorse. Thus, 3,000 knights would have required around 12,000 horses, considerably more than could be transported by a fleet of 700 ships.[45] Secondly, William and his Normans were now in an inimical environment and it was essential to remain close to his fleet in order to preserve an escape option and keep his supply lines to Normandy open. This was also why he restricted raiding to the local area: to draw Harold into a decisive encounter without penetrating further into hostile territory.[46]

The stratagem could hardly have worked better. While still in York Harold learned of William's landing at Pevensey around 1 October and he immediately headed south. William of Poitiers reported that 'the furious king [Harold] was hastening his march all the more because he had heard the lands near to the Norman camp were being laid waste'.[47] In a mere thirteen days the last Anglo-

Saxon king of England rode 308km (190 miles) from York to London, where he recruited more men, and then force-marched his army through the night to arrive on the morning of 14 October 1066 at Senlac Hill outside Hastings, where William and his Normans, fresh and well rested, outlasted Harold and his Housecarls.[48]

The Decline of English Sea Power under the Norman Kings (1067–1154)

Curiously, no source mentions what became of William's armada in the aftermath of the invasion. Following the Battle of Hastings it virtually disappeared from the public record. The presumption is that the vessels which comprised it went back to their original owners once the Conqueror no longer had use for them. This would, of course, substantiate the supposition that almost all of them had been procured through feudal obligation or some sort of leasing arrangement which lasted only for the duration of the enterprise. Whatever the fate of his fleet, William seems to have retained almost no naval assets in the years subsequent to the conquest. Even more troubling, there is no evidence that he maintained or even adopted the old Anglo-Saxon ship-muster system, the *scipfyrd*. Hardly noted in the sources after 1066, it appears that the Normans let the *scipfyrd* languish so that by 1086, when the Domesday Book was compiled, it had apparently ceased to exist altogether. Worse still, William failed to replace it with a feudal obligation apparatus of the kind implied by the *Ship List*, which had furnished him with his invasion fleet in the first place.[49] The newly minted Norman king of the English had clearly abandoned naval capability as an instrument of policy and a means of defence.

Consequently, England's shores remained vulnerable to seaborne assault. The *Anglo-Saxon Chronicle* reports that in 1068 Harold's sons Godwine and Edmund conducted a 'raiding-ship army' from Ireland to the Avon delta, where they 'raided across all that region' before turning their attention to Bristol and Somerset. They were back again the next year with a fleet of sixty-four ships which they sailed up the Taw river of northern Devon before being battered by land forces under a local earl.[50] The Normans had, in effect, ceded the Irish Sea to the Irish, the Vikings of Dublin and Norwegian freebooters.[51]

The situation was no better on the North Sea side of the island. In the autumn of that same year (1069) Jarl Osborn, brother of King Svein Estridsson of Denmark, along with the king's three sons Harald, Cnut and Bjorn savaged Dover, Sandwich, Ipswich and Norwich with a fleet of 240 to 300 ships before sailing into the Humber to join Edgar the *aetheling* (Anglo-Saxon heir to the crown) and the rebels of Northumbria.[52] Together they demolished the castle of York and slaughtered its Norman garrison, including the commandant, William Malet. King William rushed north to retake the city and chase the *aetheling* back to Scotland, but could do nothing about the Danes.[53] 'And the fleet lay all winter in the Humber, where the king could not come at them,' explained the *Anglo-Saxon Chronicle*.[54] William finally resorted to the age-old Anglo-Saxon practice of paying them off. According to the contemporary English chronicler Florence of Worcester, 'he dispatched messengers to the Danish earl, Osborn, and promised to pay him secretly a large sum of money, and grant him permission for his army to forage freely along the sea coast, on condition that he depart without fighting when the winter was over'.[55] It turned out to be a short-term fix: the *Anglo-Saxon Chronicle* noted that Osborn showed up in the Thames later that summer before eventually making his way back to Denmark.[56]

But it did not stop there. King Svein's son Cnut was back in 1075 with the Jarl Hakon and 200 ships to raid Northumbria again, plundering the York Minster with apparent impunity.[57] More serious still was the latter's planned invasion of England in 1085 as Cnut IV, king of Denmark. Florence of Worcester wrote that the Danish sovereign had 'assembled a powerful fleet for an expedition to England, in which he had the support of his father-in-law, Robert, earl of Flanders.'[58] There is even some charter evidence that Cnut may have imposed on his magnates a ship-levy system called a *leding* (a Scandinavian version of the *scipfyrd*) in order to amass the manpower necessary to crew the fleet.[59] William's response was typical. Instead of amassing his own armada to counter Cnut's, he hired mercenaries – cavalry and infantry – from Normandy, Brittany and France. He stationed them throughout England, presumably in the coastal areas which he ordered to be ravaged in a desperate, self-destructive attempt to deny the invaders provisions as they came ashore.[60] Fortunately for him, they never did. Cnut lost his life in a peasant uprising in Odense the following year.

In all fairness, William did occasionally assemble small flotillas of ships, but only for limited actions which normally did not directly involve combat at sea. When the rebellious Anglo-Saxon earl Morcar and Bishop Æthelwine of Durham sought refuge on the Isle of Ely (which was surrounded by marshy fenlands at the time) in 1071, Florence of Worcester reported, 'The king [William] hearing of this, blocked up every outlet on the eastern side by means of boatmen [*butescarls*], and caused a bridge, two miles long, to be constructed on the western side.'[61] The *Anglo-Saxon Chronicle* corroborated this rather elaborate effort. It proved effective and the English fugitives soon surrendered. The next year William included a 'ship-army' as part of an imposing show of force to convince Malcolm, king of Scotland, to recognize his suzerainty. The *Chronicle* said that the king 'beset the land to seaward with ships' while he brought his 'land-army' over the Forth.[62] Malcolm duly paid homage to William at Abernethy.[63]

William's successors engaged in the same sort of infrequent maritime operations of limited duration. When Bishop Odo of Bayeux rebelled against the Conqueror's heir, William Rufus, in favour of Robert Curthose, Duke of Normandy, William besieged Odo in Pevensey Castle for six weeks in 1088.[64] Resistance finally collapsed after 'the English, who were keeping watch over the sea, overwhelmed and sank a large number' of relief vessels sent by Robert, according to the English historian Henry of Huntingdon.[65] Similarly, King Henry I was also compelled to collect a fleet to counter another invasion attempt by Curthose in 1101. Tellingly, Henry was obliged to call upon a pre-Conquest source to provide the required coastal watch. 'The king, receiving intelligence of this [Robert's intended invasion],' noted Florence of Worcester, 'ordered his *butescarls* to guard the sea, and watch that no one approached the coast of England from Normandy.'

The mercenary nature of these *butescarls* was revealed by the fact that Robert Curthose managed to 'tamper with the fidelity of some' to the extent that 'they deserted to the earl, and became his pilots to England'.[66] Luckily for Henry, hostilities were circumvented by a negotiated settlement. The sources never mention the *butescarls* again.

Naval assets were used sporadically and sparingly for the rest of the century, mostly for transportation. King Stephen had recourse to them in 1136 to oust the rebellious Baldwin de Redvers from the Isle of Wight.[67] Henry II employed a large fleet to transport his army to Dublin in 1171 in support of Rory O'Connor, High King of Ireland, against Richard 'Strongbow' FitzGilbert, the dispossessed Earl of Pembroke. The latter had set up an independent state in Leinster which threatened the interests of both sovereigns. The fleet's composition and origin, however, remain murky.[68] Henry himself is positively known to have owned only one ship, an *esnecca* – a Viking type longship (derived etymologically from *snekkja*, Scandinavian for 'snake') with a crew of fifty-eight oarsmen and a steersman.[69] The greatest naval expedition of the twelfth-century English monarchy, however, was that of Richard the Lionheart to the Holy Land in 1191, already discussed at some length previously. The crown's most routine use of ships at the time was as 'a royal ferry service', according to British naval historian Nicholas Rodger. The kings of England crossed the Channel well over eighty times between the Conquest and the beginning of the thirteenth century.[70] The only dramatic and impactful event this process produced was, of course, the wreck of the *White Ship* on the reef of the Ras de Catteville off Barfleur, Normandy, which resulted in the death of Prince William, heir to Henry I, on 25 November 1120.[71]

The reason why English naval capability contracted under the Norman–Angevin kings was, of course, the fact that they owned both sides of the English Channel, thereby obviating the need for a strong navy. The Capetian kings of France were conspicuously excluded from being a factor by geography, while the Scandinavian sovereigns had become too distracted by their own internecine squabbles to be much of a concern.[72] Thus, without a compelling requirement for maritime military competence, English naval capability atrophied much as Roman maritime might had withered during the *Pax Romana* of the Mediterranean a millennium prior. 'It is a striking paradox that the Norman Conquest, made possible by an impressive fleet, caused the rapid collapse of English sea power,' Rodger appropriately remarked.[73]

The Angevin–Capetian Battle for the Channel (1196–1214)

The English Channel's status as an Anglo-Norman waterway commanded by the kings of England would change radically with the loss of Chateau Gaillard in March 1204 to Philip II Augustus of France. Richard the Lionheart had begun building this imposing fortress overlooking the Seine at Les Andelys, 40km (25 miles) east of Rouen, in 1196 as a bulwark to protect the heartland of Normandy from the aggressive designs of the Capetian crown. The Angevin heir had even taken the additional precaution of having a fleet of seventy light galleys called *cursoria* ('runners') constructed to safeguard the lower Seine valley.[74]

Philip, for his part, was anxious to absorb continental Angevin lands into his own kingdom, particularly Normandy with its access to the Channel.

By 1198 Richard had completed the construction of Chateau Gaillard and had pushed Philip out of Normandy, but he died besieging Chalus Castle the next year, leaving his younger brother John to defend the duchy.[75] The latter proved unequal to the task. The Capetian king built a boat bridge across the Seine at Les Andelys in September 1203 and closely besieged Chateau Gaillard. King John tried to relieve it shortly afterwards with a two-pronged assault: a land force to attack the besiegers directly and a riverine squadron, perhaps comprised of Richard's *cursoria*, to demolish the bridge of boats by which the besiegers received their supplies. Unfortunately, the operation was poorly coordinated. The land contingent under the famed William the Marshal moved first in a night attack and was crushed, enabling the French to concentrate on the riverine element led by Alan Trenchemer ('Plough-the-Sea'), master of the royal *esnecca*, and rout it with a missile bombardment. Chateau Gaillard capitulated in March 1204, followed rapidly by Rouen in June. All of Normandy, Anjou, Maine and Poitou fell to Philip shortly afterwards.[76] Within the span of a few months the Channel had been converted from what was, in effect, an English domestic seaway into a hostile foreign frontier.

The only continental region remaining to the English crown was Gascony (in southwestern France, essentially the Duchy of Aquitaine), a perilous voyage of several hundred nautical miles through a now-contested Channel, round the inimical Cape of Brittany with all its impediments to navigation and finally into the buccaneer-infested Bay of Biscay to reach Bordeaux or Bayonne. In the years immediately following the fall of the Chateau Gaillard, King John's continental concerns seemed mostly to be with maintaining the tenuous sea link with this distant duchy. A rebellion in Poitou (just north of Gascony) in 1206 also returned parts of that province to John's control, adding La Rochelle to the list of ports he felt constrained to service by sea. Accordingly, he hired the notorious pirate leader Eustace 'the Monk', along with other Flemish mercenaries, to assert control over the Channel, particularly the Channel Islands. Based initially at Winchelsea, this cleric-turned-corsair was reported to have claimed the Channel Islands in John's name and ruled them from the Isle of Sark for a time. Eustace was also reputed to have raided upper Normandy as far as Pont-Audemer and even harried Harfleur in the Seine estuary. He served John roughly from 1205 to 1212, at which time he switched sides due to the king's rapprochement with Eustace's arch-enemy, Reynaud of Boulogne.[77]

John's overall strategy for regaining the lost continental possessions involved using Poitou and Flanders as bases to pressure Philip from the north and the south. Many in the Flemish aristocracy favoured England because of the close economic connection vis-à-vis the wool trade. Two of these were Reynaud, count of Boulogne, and Ferrand, count of Flanders. Philip was aware of John's diplomatic machinations and attempted to counter them with his own, not just in the Low Countries but in the Lateran Palace as well. Pope Innocent III had excommunicated King John in the course of a dispute over the right to appoint the

Archbishop of Canterbury in 1209, so Philip was able to win papal encouragement for an invasion of England.[78] Accordingly, he began gathering a great invasion force at Rouen in the spring of 1213. Informants from the continent, which ironically included a papal emissary, warned John:

> Behold, the most potent king of the French is at the mouth of [the] Seine with a countless fleet, and a large army of horse and foot, waiting till he is strengthened with a large force, to come upon you and your kingdom, and to expel you from it by force, as an enemy of the Lord and the supreme pontiff, and afterwards, by authority of the apostolic see to take possession of the kingdom of England forever.[79]

John attempted to parry Philip's plan by formally submitting to Innocent III at the end of April in order to have the anathema and attendant papal sanction for invasion removed. More importantly, he went about assembling a fleet of his own. He issued a warrant to the 'bailiffs of the ports' ordering them to 'make a careful list of all the ships there found capable of carrying six horses or more; and, in our name, you order the masters as well as the owners of those ships, as they regard themselves, and all their property, to have them at Portsmouth at mid-Lent, well equipped with stores, tried seamen, and good soldiers, to enter our service for our deliverance'.[80] For the first time, an English king was collecting a fleet not just for transportation but as an offensive weapon to oppose an enemy invasion armada.[81]

Undeterred by the defection of the Pope, on 10 May Philip mustered his massive fleet at Boulogne, which he had only recently removed from Reynaud on suspicion of disloyalty. It stood just across the Dover Straits from England. His chaplain and biographer, Guillaume Le Breton, wrote in his *Chronique* that Philip's armada numbered 1,700 vessels, a ludicrous figure but indicative of the magnitude of the intended assault. Manned mostly by Normans and Poitevins, it was led by Savari de Mauléon, paradoxically John's seneschal for Poitou, whom Philip had suborned. The Capetian sovereign soon, however, moved the fleet 56km (35 miles) up the coast to Gravelines, because Ferrand of Flanders had promised to meet him there, presumably to join the enterprise. When Ferrand failed to show, Philip apparently decided to reduce Flanders first. His fleet shadowed him along the shoreline while he marched on Ypres, Cassel, Bruges and Ghent, taking each in turn.[82]

Several Flemish nobles, Reynaud of Boulogne among them, sailed to England to advise John on what had transpired. The king's response was swift. He dispatched to Flanders a huge fleet which, in the exaggerated estimation of thirteenth-century chronicler Roger of Wendover, numbered some 500 ships and carried 700 knights, including the dispossessed Flemish nobles. In command was William Longespée ('Longsword'), the illegitimate son of King Henry II and earl of Salisbury, who reportedly was a *custos portuum* ('Keeper of the Ports') for the critical southeast English coast at the time. It departed on 2 June, probably from Dover, and arrived in the Zwyn inlet northwest of Bruges two days later. Created by a monster storm which breached the shoreline in 1134, the Zwyn had become the main artery into Flanders from the North Sea. (It has since silted up.) The ports of Sluys and Damme had been developed to serve the burgeoning influx of traffic bound for the lucrative textile markets of Bruges. It was at Damme that the English, by chance, came upon the entire French fleet with its ships either riding at anchor or beached. Almost all were unattended while their crews pillaged the city. The English anchored their larger ships about 10km (6 miles) from Damme and used their smaller boats (*naves cursoriae*) to attack the French vessels at anchor, capturing as many as they could and burning the others. Most sources estimate that around 400 ships were seized or destroyed. Many that were beached simply could not be reached. Philip ironically burned these when he arrived with his land forces a few days later to chase the English away.[83] He clearly did not trust the Poitevin seamen and, besides, the invasion had effectively been thwarted.

Unfortunately for King John, this unexpected success at sea did not translate into triumph on land. The so-called Flanders War and the issue of the English crown's lost continental domains, particularly Normandy, was decided more or less permanently on 27 July of the following year (1214) at Bouvines when Philip's forces defeated a coalition of Flemish, English and Imperial troops under Otto IV. Longespée, Ferrand and Reynaud were all captured. The reverse would leave King John badly weakened at home and vulnerable to the revolt of his barons (1215–17), inviting further French intervention in the realm's affairs and the next phase of Anglo-French warfare at sea.[84]

The Barons' Revolt and the French Invasion (1215–17)

The failure of King John's campaign to recover Normandy pushed to the breaking point those northern barons who had little vested interest on the continent and even less willingness to pay for John's adventures there. Resistance to his rule grew rapidly and the *Magna Carta*, which resulted from his meeting with the disaffected nobles at Runnymede on 15 June 1215, proved only a temporary palliative.[85] John was only buying time and the rebellious barons knew it. He soon convinced Pope Innocent III to condemn the *Magna Carta* and excommunicate the complicit barons.[86] They in turn initiated the First Barons' War in September by seizing Rochester Castle. By November Rochester was back in John's hands after a seven-week siege, but he knew the rebels would soon seek succour from overseas, namely France.[87] He also realized that sea power was his best means of preventing such assistance from arriving. Early on, he had tried to woo the Cinque Ports to his side but they considered his treatment of them high-handed. They favoured the rebels at first, so John relied mostly on the East Anglian ports. Nonetheless, John failed to block communication with the continent. Philip's son, the Dauphin Louis, received an invitation from the rebels to rule England in John's stead in December 1215.[88]

Despite the threat of anathema from John's new ally Pope Innocent III, Louis had amassed a sizeable invasion fleet at Calais by April 1216. John assembled an even larger one at Dover with the intention of blockading Calais, but an untimely tempest dispersed it. Louis set sail a few days later at the head of an immense armada – somewhere between 300 and 800 vessels, according to the typically overblown estimates of medieval chroniclers. Stormy weather troubled the French fleet as well, but it still managed to seize Sandwich unopposed shortly thereafter. John fled to Winchester. Louis soon marched on London, taking it easily. He then proceeded to neutralize John's ability to interdict his sea supply lines by capturing the principal ports in the southeast. He claimed the Cinque Ports, while his English allies took Dunwich, Lynne and the East Anglian ports. Only Dover, defended by Hubert de Burgh (Justiciar of the Kingdom and earl of Kent), remained loyal but it was under siege. By 19 October John was dead of dysentery, leaving the contested crown in the hands of his nine-year-old son Henry III, while Louis, supported by the dissident barons, held most of the realm.[89]

Paradoxically, it was probably John's demise that turned the tide against Louis and the rebels. First of all, it removed the principal lightning rod of baronial discontent: King John himself. Secondly, it empowered as royal regent the venerated William the Marshal, earl of Pembroke, who immediately embarked upon a regimen of reconciliation. As a result, many of those who had abandoned the royalist cause soon rejoined its ranks. Among them were the Cinque Ports, which had been alienated by the persistent piracy of the dauphin's maritime mercenary, the infamous Eustace the Monk. William had begun to regain their loyalty bit by bit. Realizing that his situation was rapidly unravelling, Louis decided his only option was to return to France to obtain reinforcements. He attempted to do so out of Winchelsea in January 1217, but found himself blockaded there by a fleet based out of Rye commanded by the royalist Philip d'Aubigny, while Willikin of the Weald (a squire of Cassingham) attacked the town from the landward side with Kentish guerrillas. Louis eventually succeeded, but only after the blockade was raised by Eustace, who at one point went to the extent of building a castle on a large ship in order to combat the English vessels.[90]

Louis managed to raise his reinforcements in France, but by the time he was able to return to England in the spring, Willikin had laid waste to his siege works at Dover, forcing the dauphin to fight his way into Sandwich instead. In May, however, Louis resumed the siege of Dover. Meanwhile, his wife, Blanche of Castile (granddaughter to King Henry II of England, ironically), was vigorously recruiting a fresh French army for her husband. The initial instalment sailed as a flotilla of forty ships from Calais in mid-May, but Philip d'Aubigny, at the head of a fleet out of Romney that included twenty large warships, chased it back to Calais, capturing or sinking eight of the French vessels in the process. He then blockaded the French besiegers at Dover. Another French fleet (reportedly numbering 120 ships) later broke through the blockade, but Louis considered the reinforcements it brought inadequate, and by then events elsewhere in England were deciding the fate of his enterprise. On 20 May William the Marshal handed Louis' lieutenant, the compte du Perche, a devastating defeat at Lincoln, killing or capturing many of the remaining rebel barons. Louis, short on supplies and supporters, now found himself in an untenable position. After burning the ships in the harbour, he abandoned the siege of Dover and retreated to London, clinging to the hope that his highly competent wife would be able to send him the help he so desperately needed.[91]

Blanche proved equal to the task. By August a new army had been assembled at Calais, where Eustace the Monk had gathered a flotilla to transport it to England, despite harassment all summer long from English ships. The French relief fleet sailed from Calais on 24 August and made for the Thames estuary. Ships from the Cinque Ports recruited by William the Marshal sailed out to meet them, the principal contingent being a squadron from Dover commanded by Hubert de Burgh. The subsequent encounter which took place in the Downs off Sandwich would not only decide the fate of the Capetian bid to capture the crown of England, but would also be a watershed in the naval history of medieval Europe. For the first time in northern waters a decisive battle of naval tactic and manoeuvre was fought on the open sea. As such, it is the topic of the special section at the end of this chapter. It suffices to say here that the resulting victory for the loyalist naval forces of William the Marshal further isolated Louis in London, compelling him to renounce his claim to the English crown and return to the continent.[92]

Thereafter, maritime hostilities between the two realms shifted from the English Channel to the Atlantic coast of the continent, where the Angevin crown still possessed viable interests, namely in Poitou and Gascony. Philip Augustus passed away on 14 July 1223, leaving the Capetian crown to the dauphin, who became Louis VIII. Denied the throne of England, the latter was determined to consolidate his hold on the continent. He seized La Rochelle and established firm control of Poitou in 1224, furthering imperilling the English sea route to Gascony.[93] Henry III responded with an expedition of some 300 ships to St Malo in Brittany in 1230, but it accomplished little.[94] In 1242 Henry took advantage of yet another revolt of the Poitevin barony to attempt a blockade of La Rochelle, mostly with ships from Bordeaux and Bayonne. It proved a fool's errand, however. Winter weather and incessant harassment by the mariners of Normandy and Brittany eventually forced him to forsake the effort.[95]

The English crown used its sea power chiefly for logistical support in the decades that followed. Meanwhile, hostilities with France reached a hiatus while Henry's successor, Edward I, sought to expand his realm at the expense of Scotland and Wales. Difficult terrain caused King Edward to impress fleets, mainly from the Cinque Ports, in order to transport troops and supplies for his Welsh campaigns in both 1277 and 1282. The same was true of his efforts to subdue Scotland, which began with the invasion of 1296 and continued under his son Edward II. The campaign finally ended in 1328 with the Treaty of Edinburgh–Northampton.[96] Naval activity with France would not resume in earnest until the second quarter of the fourteenth century. That said, the two realms continued to develop the notion of a royal navy in anticipation of renewed conflict across the narrow waterway which separated them.

The Rise of the English and French Royal Navies (1194–1299)

Evidence of a royal naval force began to appear much earlier for England than for its French counterpart, mostly because the Capetian kings of France had little access to northern waters prior to the fall of the Chateau Gaillard in 1204. The first kernel of a royal naval service in post-Conquest England may well have been provided by the realm's first Angevin king, Henry II. As mentioned earlier, Henry was known to have owned at least one *esnecca* under the command of Alan Trenchemer. He used it primarily as a means of moving between the English and continental possessions of what modern historians have called the 'Angevin Empire', referring to the territories ruled by the House of Plantagenet (the dynasty founded by Henry's father, Geoffrey V Plantagenet, count of Anjou). When he needed to transport troops in excess of his household, he apparently hired or impressed the vessels required.[97] Accordingly, around 1155 he issued a royal charter to the Cinque Ports granting the towns of Hastings, Hythe, Romney, Sandwich and Dover special privileges, such as exemption from tolls and a certain degree of self-government, in return for providing the crown with fifty-seven ships for fifteen days each year. The precedent for such annual ship service was apparently derived from an earlier arrangement between the five ports and Edward the Confessor in 1051.[98] The limited duration of the annual service under Henry indicates that it was intended only to provide short-term transportation across the Channel, not to support any large-scale military operations.[99]

Richard I inherited both the royal *esnecca* and its master, Alan Trenchemer, from his father, but soon realized that he would have need of more ships and for a longer period than he could expect from the Cinque Ports in order to deal with Philip II's attacks on his continental properties.[100] So on 2 May 1194, barely three months after his release from captivity in Austria, he issued a royal charter to the city of Portsmouth which essentially established the port as his naval base. He would later build a palace there and, more crucially, port facilities to support royal vessels. In other words, Richard founded Portsmouth as a terminus for cross-channel operations.[101] It was either there or at Rouen that he subsequently caused to be constructed the seventy *cursoria* which he used to defend the lower Seine valley in 1196 – the same *cursoria* that his brother John presumably employed under Alan Trenchemer in his failed bid to break Philip's siege of the Chateau Gaillard in 1203.[102]

John assumed not only Richard's ships and his chief naval officer, but also his naval base at Portsmouth. In May 1212 he had the sheriff of Hampshire add an *exclusa* (walled enclosure) around the port facility and build penthouses to protect royal vessels (probably galleys).[103] At the same time he ordered the sheriff of Southampton to construct a similar perimeter wall around the dockyards of that port city as well. Ship sheds for galleys were also put up at Rye and Winchelsea, the so-called 'ancient towns' associated with the Cinque Ports from the beginning of the thirteenth century.[104] And John seems to have had plenty of ships to preserve. The dorse (back leaf) of the Close Roll (royal chancery record) for 1205 contains a list of fifty-one royal galleys placed under four commands in five general geographic areas: William Marsh was responsible for nine galleys in Ireland, Gloucester and Bristol; Reginald de Cornhille had ten galleys at London and Sandwich; John de la Warr controlled fifteen at Dunwich, Ipswich, Lynn and

Yarmouth; and William de Wrotham commanded seventeen at Exeter, Romney, Rye, Shoreham, Southampton and Winchelsea.[105]

Of the four commanders, William de Wrotham, the archdeacon of Taunton, was the most important by far. Often identified in official correspondence as *custos galliarum* ('Keeper of the King's Galleys') or *custos portuum* ('Keeper of the King's Ports'), he seems to have been John's chief naval administrator and the primary liaison with the Cinque Ports, as well as with many other ports in the southeast of England. From about 1200 to 1215 William de Wrotham was the predominant official responsible for collecting fleets, for which he served as the primary paymaster. Assisted by the so-called 'Barons of the Cinque Ports' (the freemen of the Ports), he supervised the impressment of ships for the king's service in 1207. He even oversaw the construction of new dockyards at Portsmouth in 1212. Perhaps more importantly, he helped organize nearly all of John's continental expeditions, including the disastrous Bouvines campaign of 1214. Unfortunately, the naval administration which William had managed so conscientiously broke down altogether in 1215, when he joined the baronial revolt.[106]

Succeeding sovereigns seem to have depended somewhat more on the Barons of the Cinque Ports, a dubious source of naval support given their pliable loyalty. Henry III sought out their maritime expertise when La Rochelle was lost to Louis VIII in 1224, rendering the English hold on Gascony all the more precarious. And later, in 1225, when he feared a French invasion, Henry prevailed upon the Cinque Ports to help guard the coasts.[107] British naval historian F.W. Brooks went so far as to say, 'All through this period the Cinque Ports seem to have acted as the chief advisors to the Crown in nautical matters.'[108] Henry also relied on the Cinque Ports to defend the southeast coast of England while he was prosecuting his ineffectual blockade of La Rochelle in 1242. Finally, he used the ships of the Cinque Ports on his 1253–4 expedition to quell discontent in Gascony.[109] The Cinque Ports, however, repaid his reliance on them by siding with the rebels in the Second Barons' War led by Simon de Montfort in 1264–7.[110] Yet this did not deter his son Edward I from impressing the vessels of the Cinque Ports for his Welsh campaigns in 1277 and 1282.[111]

Overall, the Cinque Ports revealed themselves to be as much of a liability to the crown as they were an asset. In May 1293 their ships joined others from Gascony to set upon and destroy a Norman fleet off the coast of Brittany, after which they sacked La Rochelle. This resulted in the occupation of Gascony by the troops of King Philip IV of France. England could ill-afford to lose the highly lucrative wine trade which ran through Bordeaux. It had become so crucial to England's maritime commerce that the cargo capacity of its ships came to be measured in 'tuns' – wine barrels each holding the equivalent of around 252 gallons. So Edward devised a plan to fight a holding action in Aquitaine with local forces while he collaborated with his Flemish allies, tied to England by the wool trade, to pressure France from the north. Accordingly, in 1297 Edward assembled a fleet of 273 vessels destined for Flanders, seventy-three of which were from the Cinque Ports. But before the fleet could even reach its destination, the ships of the Cinque Ports torpedoed the expedition by engaging in a pitched sea battle with fifty-nine ships from its arch-rival Yarmouth, which resulted in the destruction of seventeen English vessels.[112]

In the light of the Cinque Ports' lack of loyalty, uncontrollable conduct and penchant for piracy, crown concessions to them through the centuries remain something of a conundrum for modern scholars. They can only be explained within the context of geography. Brooks said it most succinctly: 'They were not the greatest ports of England, they were simply the nearest ports to France.'[113] That sentiment was more recently echoed by Rodger, who observed, 'In all these transactions the Ports do not appear as providers of valuable naval services, but as dangerous troublemakers willing to sell their geographical advantages to the highest bidder.'[114] In any event, their strategic significance was markedly diminished by the fifteenth century due to severe silting of the Kentish coast and to a storm surge that ruptured the shingle bank protecting the shores of Sussex.[115]

French naval capability developed differently from that of England, not only chronologically but geographically. As noted earlier, Louis IX actually initiated the process during the 1240s with the founding of Aigues-Mortes in the Camargue as a royal naval base. It was from there that he launched the Seventh Crusade using ships built for the purpose in Genoa and Marseilles.[116] His brother Charles of Anjou continued the process by upgrading the shipyards of Marseilles in the late 1250s to support his aspirations of empire in the central and eastern Mediterranean.[117] The fleets produced there figured prominently in the War of the Sicilian Vespers which distracted the French court and consumed the crowns of Aragon and Naples for two decades beginning in 1282. No organized royal naval establishment appeared in the north until the last years of the thirteenth century. When it did, it did so at the behest of Philip IV the Fair, using Mediterranean models.

By 1293 he had begun hiring Genoese shipwrights to set up a shipyard on property purchased with royal funds at Rouen in 1295. Apparently patterned after a Castilian naval arsenal constructed on the Guadalquivir river in Seville, the facility they built was composed of a basin equipped with sluice gates to control the water level, surrounded by a fosse and a palisade. It eventually contained as many as thirty covered boat-houses along with storage sheds, an armoury, workshops and barracks for the workers. What these craftsmen constructed there were galleys of Genoese design, i.e., warships – the nucleus of a royal navy. Hence its name became the *Clos des Galées* ('Enclosure of the Galleys'). The small number of ships produced there was probably intended to stiffen the combat effectiveness of an impressed fleet in times of hostilities. And Philip did not stop there. He caused experienced galleymen to be brought up from such Mediterranean ports as Marseilles each spring to man the vessels. He even went to the expense of leasing entire squadrons of galleys, usually from the powerful Grimaldi or Doria families of Genoa. In 1296, for instance, he hired twenty Genoese galleys under the command of Benedetto Zaccaria, a hero of the Battle of Meloria, bestowing on him the title 'admiral general of France'.[118]

Almost immediately these French galley squadrons caused grave concern in the English court. In 1295 one such flotilla raided the Channel Islands and razed a district of Dover before assailing Winchelsea and Hythe.[119] Edward was inspired to respond with his own ship-building programme. In 1294–5 he requisitioned the construction of twenty ships – also galleys (each with 120 oars) – in twenty-six port towns such as Southampton and Ipswich. Only eight were actually known to have been built, but he made an additional order in 1303–4 for Ipswich and Yarmouth, among others.[120] The nascent naval arms race soon receded, however. Edward and Philip concluded a truce in October 1297 which became a permanent peace in June 1299. For the first few decades of the fourteenth century the English crown was consumed with consolidating its hold on Scotland, while the French throne tried to spread its influence into Flanders.[121] The kingdoms of England and France would not clash again at sea in any serious way until the years just preceding the Hundred Years War.

* * *

Exemplary Engagement: The Battle of Dover (also called the Battle of Sandwich) (August 1217)

It was on St Bartholomew's Day, 24 August 1217, that a French fleet of around eighty vessels sailed before southerly winds 'in a formation so tight and orderly' up the Kentish coast towards the Isle of Thanet and the Thames estuary. It was bound for London, held by the Dauphin Louis of France. 'That day was a very fine and clear one and it was possible to see far out to sea,' said the poem dedicated to the deeds of William the Marshal.[122] So there can be little doubt that the French flotilla was observed from the White Cliffs north of Dover – perhaps not by William himself, as the thirteenth-century English chronicler Matthew Paris suggests, but certainly by someone.[123] According to the poem, William had made sure of it as soon as he had learned of the convoy's imminent departure from Calais a few days before, 'for he knew beyond any doubt that, if that French fleet out there was able to put to shore, then the game would have disastrous results and England would be lost'.[124]

The outcome of the First Barons' War and the concomitant invasion of England by Louis, heir to the throne of France, was very much in the balance. While Louis had suffered a devastating setback when his forces lost Lincoln in May, he remained entrenched in London with his army still intact, including 'the majority of the barons'. Moreover, King John's heir, Henry III, was only nine.[125] William, his protector, needed time to garner support and shore up the young king's grip on government – something that significant reinforcements from France would likely curtail. The northern nobility and the so-called 'Barons of the Cinque Ports' had already demonstrated a dismaying propensity to support whichever side seemed to be winning – and, with reinforcements, that could be Louis and the rebel lords. William understood that the best chance for the royalist cause was to preclude the French fleet from ever reaching its destination. To that end, he had beckoned the 'Barons of the Cinque Ports' to Romney on 19 August and bade them face the French fleet in return for the restoration of their privileged status and all the plunder they could win. Although still bitter over King John's overbearing treatment in the past, they agreed, and a watch was set.[126]

That said, when the French armada first appeared, the sailors of the Cinque Ports were daunted. The Dauphin's wife, Blanche of Castile, had gathered a formidable fleet. The *History of William Marshal* estimated it at 300 vessels, but the figure of eighty given by both Roger of Wendover, a contemporary English chronicler, and the anonymous thirteenth-century *Histoire des Ducs de Normandie et des Rois d'Angleterre* ('History of the Dukes of Normandy and of the Kings of England') is probably closer to the truth.[127] Of these, ten were great ships, containing most of the knights (around 125, estimates English historian Henry Cannon) and men-at-arms. The remainder were smaller transports, carrying equipment and provisions.[128] 'Their pilot and commander' was the almost mythical mercenary mariner Eustace the Monk.[129] A former friar at the Benedictine Abbey of St Vulmer at Samer near Boulogne, he had renounced his vows in order to fend for his family when his father was murdered. He served as seneschal for Count Reynaud of Boulogne until false accusations from his father's murderer prompted him to flee, eventually reaching England, where he took up employment with King John. For a number of years, basically between 1205 and 1212, he commanded a small flotilla which ravaged French interests in the English Channel, ultimately setting himself up in the Channel Islands. He switched allegiance to King Philip II Augustus over John's alliance with Reynaud of Boulogne just before the First Barons' War broke out.[130] He then raided the south and east coasts of England, including the Cinque Ports, earning the reputation cited by Roger of Wendover as 'a most disgraceful man and a wicked pirate'.[131] He was also a highly competent commander, for which the sailors of the Cinque Ports realized they had no counterpart – that is, at least until Hubert de Burgh showed up at Sandwich with ships from Dover to stiffen their resolve.[132]

William had wanted to assume command of the English fleet himself, but he must have been nearly seventy at the time and his entourage convinced him that the king would be better served if he remained ashore to direct the overall defence of the realm. Thus, it fell to Hubert de Burgh as Justiciar of the kingdom to command the fleet which comprised 'sixteen well armed ships, not including some small ones which accompanied them to the number of twenty', reported Matthew Paris, to whom Hubert provided an eye-witness account many years later. With him were two prominent knights from the garrison at Dover: Henry de Turville and Richard Suard.[133] They embarked upon what the *History of William Marshal* described as 'a magnificent ship equipped with a fine crew', which must have included sailors from the Cinque Ports. Richard FitzJohn, the bastard son of King John, took charge of another. Philip d'Aubigny apparently assumed command of one as well, while William had his own men-at-arms crew what his *History* specifically called a 'cog', probably fitted with at least a sterncastle. This may, in fact, have been Hubert's ship, but the various accounts are confused in this regard.[134] Both Roger of Wendover and Matthew Paris claim the English also had galleys with 'iron *rostra*' or rams, but this surely was an imaginative invention based upon classical precedents.[135]

The flagship of the French fleet was designated 'the great ship of Bayonne' by William's *History*, which also said that 'it housed the king's treasury'.[136] On board with Eustace were thirty-six highly placed knights; the most exalted was Robert de Courtenay, uncle to the queen of France. He actually held precedence over Eustace. In addition, there were Ralph de la Tourniele and William des Barres, two of Philip's finest. Three other great ships carried the rest of the knights and the remaining six transported most of the men-at-arms.[137] The *History* claims that the vessel from Bayonne was in the van, but this would have been highly unlikely. The *History of William Marshal* itself explained why: 'the monk's ship was greatly overloaded and could only sit so deep down in the waves that the water almost washed over her, the reason being that it carried the siege engine (a trebuchet) and a very heavy load besides, including the fine horses shipped for Louis'.[138] In all probability, Eustace's ship lagged last, a circumstance which would go a long way towards illuminating why the battle unfolded as it did.[139]

As the French fleet streamed northwards with a following wind through the Downs past Sandwich, Hubert de Burgh led his squadron out luffing into the wind, seemingly to intercept it. Instead, he merely feigned an attack and continued due southeast towards Calais, passing astern of the French flagship. Eustace then assumed that Calais was the objective and dismissed it as a foolish assault on a well fortified port.[140] By this time the French fleet, sailing in close order, had covered much of the distance to the Isle of Thanet and Eustace was inclined to simply stay the course.[141] Unfortunately for the French cause, he was not in charge. Robert de Courtenay, believing the outnumbered and outmanned English vessels which had approached so slowly as they close-hauled into the wind were easy prey, ordered the ship to turn and engage.[142] While Eustace's morality and loyalty could be questioned, his seamanship could not. He must surely have sensed that his fate had been sealed the second his ship came about. What Hubert de Burgh was actually doing was acquiring the 'weather gage': the upwind position. Moreover, since it was morning, the sun must have been shining out of the east. Hubert now turned to put both the wind and the sun at his back.[143] The crew of 'the great ship of Bayonne', on the other hand, found themselves in a ponderous, overburdened vessel stalled to windward with the sun in their eyes facing a line of English ships bent upon their destruction. (*See* Map 13.)

The first of the English great ships to reach the slow, barely manoeuvrable French flagship was evidently that of Richard FitzJohn. The French resisted desperately but three other English ships soon joined the fray, one of which was the cog containing William Marshal's men-at-arms. Meanwhile, the rest of the French fleet, pushed by the southerly winds, must have continued on course to the north for some time before realizing that their flagship was engaged. The English cog, lightly loaded and high in the water, quickly turned the tide of

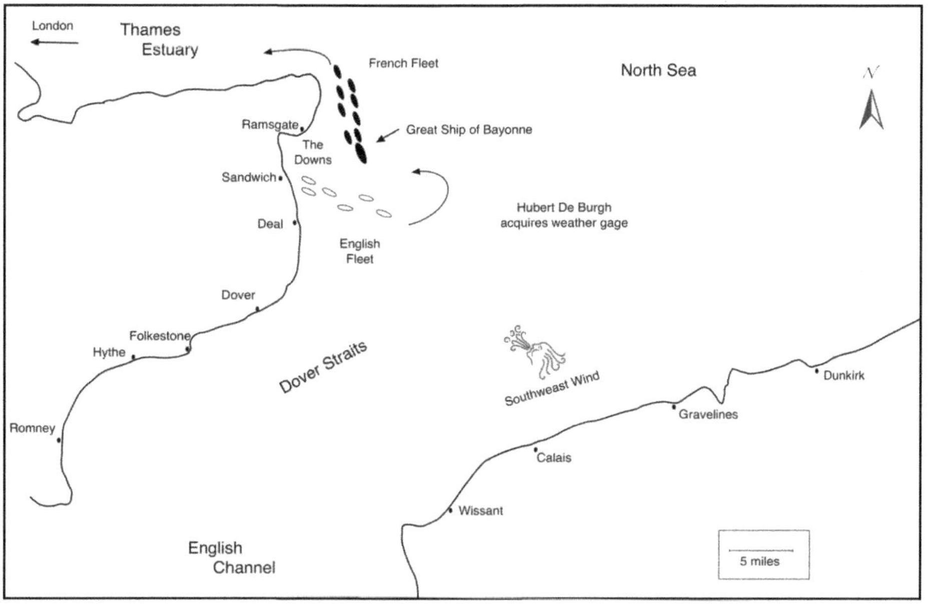

Map 13. Battle of Dover (Sandwich) in 1217. (*Kristy Stanton*)

battle. The usual fusillade of missiles included pots of quicklime hurled from the castle of the cog down onto the deck of 'the great ship of Bayonne'.[144] Several of the contemporary sources testified to the tactic, which makes perfect sense, given the wind and height advantage. Its crew blinded, the French flagship was easily boarded by William's men, who jumped from the cog down onto the deck, scattering the now hapless and helpless French knights. It was probably all over quite quickly. All thirty-six French knights were taken prisoner.[145]

By the time the other great ships of the French fleet were able to come about, it was too late. They merely made themselves easy quarry for the emboldened English mariners. Matthew Paris presented a vivid picture of what followed: 'They [the English] eagerly rushed on the enemy; as soon as they reached the vessels of their adversaries they threw grappling irons and made them fast to their own vessels, and boarding them with their axes, they cut away the rigging supporting the masts and yards, and, the expending sails falling, the French were caught like birds in a net; the English then attacked them and, making prisoners of all of rank amongst them, cut the rest to pieces.'[146]

One 'of rank' who did not survive the bloodletting was 'the wicked pirate Eustace the Monk'. He was found hiding in the bilges of 'the great ship of Bayonne' and dragged on deck, whereupon he was reported to have offered 10,000 marks for his life. A common seaman, a certain Stephen of Winchelsea, took his head instead, according to the *History of William Marshal*.[147] **(Pl. 27)** Roger of Wendover relayed that it was Richard FitzJohn who had the privilege.[148] It probably mattered little to Eustace, who was universally reviled as a traitor by the royalists.

In their bloodlust, the English spared few of the French crewmen aboard the vessels they overtook – 'one or two men, or, sometimes three at most'. Marshal's *History* tallied 4,000 dead, 'not counting those who jumped into the sea and were drowned'.[149] The French sources, namely the *Histoire des Ducs de Normandie*, maintained that nine out of ten of the larger French ships managed to make their way back to Calais, and perhaps as many as fifteen vessels altogether.[150] The rest were almost certainly sunk or seized. Hubert de Burgh was reported to have ensnared two himself.[151] The fact that the spoils were of sufficient quantity to handsomely reward all the participants and still pay for the founding of the Hospital of St Bartholomew's in Sandwich lends credence to the conclusion of English historian F.W. Brooks: 'Most of the French ships were captured and a poor remainder was driven back to Calais.'[152] When 'the great ship of Bayonne' was attacked by multiple vessels of the English fleet, the van of the French formation would have fared far better had it simply considered the flagship a noble sacrifice and continued to run before the wind. Perhaps the assessment of Roger of Wendover should not be dismissed as mere vainglory: 'A severe engagement took place between the fleets, but that of the French, who were not well skilled in naval warfare, was soon defeated.'[153] English mariners had, for the first time in recorded history, employed naval tactics to win a decisive sea battle while under way in open water.[154]

Consequently, the French invasion of England and with it the rebellion of the barons fell apart. Within a few days of the victory off Sandwich, the captured Robert de Courtenay was sent to London to convey to Louis that all was lost and that a negotiated surrender was the only recourse remaining.[155] The result was the Treaty of Kingston (also called the Treaty of Lambeth), ratified in mid-September, by which the dauphin repudiated his quest for the crown of England in return for safe passage back to France. The rebellious nobles were made to contribute 5,000 pounds sterling to hasten the French prince's departure, which occurred at Dover on 28 September.[156] In an ironic postscript, one of the terms of the treaty removed control of the Channel Islands from Eustace's heirs and returned it to England.[157]

CHAPTER 9

The Hundred Years War: Anglo-French Conflict across the Narrow Sea

The Hundred Years War was essentially a continuation of the violent contest for continental European lands between the crowns of England and France created by the Norman Conquest of 1066. The competing claims to these lands stemmed from the king of England's status as vassal to the king of France for those territories adjacent to the Channel and Atlantic coasts of what is modern France, i.e., basically Normandy, Maine, Touraine, Poitou, Anjou and Aquitaine. By 1224 the English sovereign had lost in combat to his Capetian counterpart all but Aquitaine (essentially Gascony) which he still ruled as duke and thus liege to his lord, the king of France. This rather untenable circumstance was confirmed by the October 1259 Treaty of Paris between Henry III of England and Louis IX of France, but in truth the English royal court had never relinquished hope of recovering the lost continental properties, while the French throne remained dedicated not only to retaining them but to acquiring direct control of all Aquitaine as well.[1] As a result, conflict between the two realms remained almost constant through the Napoleonic era. Nineteenth-century historians arbitrarily termed the spate of hostilities which stretched from 1337 to 1453 'the Hundred Years War', though it actually consisted of three relatively distinct stages separated by periods of peace lasting from nine to twenty-six years: the Edwardian Phase (1337–60), the Caroline Phase (1369–89) and the Lancastrian Phase (1415–53). While it was fundamentally a series of land struggles, the fact that England was an island realm ensured that a naval component would be crucial to the conflict.

The Nature of Naval Power in the Hundred Years War

At the beginning of the fourteenth century the kingdoms of both England and France were emerging naval powers of regional significance. As the conflict between them progressed, they developed their naval capability in an ad hoc manner to support substantially dissimilar war strategies dictated by geography.[2] Because the primary theatre of conflict was the continent, it was incumbent upon England to transport its troops and associated military equipment from the island of Britain across the intervening waterways to the west coast of the European continent. Accordingly, the English kings tended to amass fleets composed chiefly of high-capacity cargo vessels, mostly sailing ships like the cog.[3] Conversely, France's challenge was to thwart or, at the very least, hamper such military movements across the Channel and its adjacent waters. And, since, given the nautical technology of the age, interdiction of fleets at sea was as problematic as predicting when and where they would come ashore, the best means of accomplishing said objective was to attack the ports from which such invasion fleets originated. Thus, the French suzerains tended towards fleets full of vessels that could strike quickly and unexpectedly, like the Vikings ships of old, i.e., oared fighting ships – galleys.[4]

British naval historian Nicholas Rodger has quite correctly observed, 'The concept of a navy as a permanent fighting service did not exist in the northern world of the Middle Ages.'[5] So both kingdoms were required to ramp up their naval capabilities as hostilities heightened. England's strategic exigency and long-standing exposure to the sea as an island realm made it more natural for England to do that than for France. After all, the kingdom possessed a ready-made source of the sort of ships it required in its merchant maritime community. Hence the English kings began by simply impressing the vessels they needed, along with their crews. Royal clerks from the Exchequer or Chancery went from port to port within a designated geographic sector, identifying ships suitable for military operations. During the reign of Henry III they were called '*custodes maris*' or '*custodes marinae*' ('Keepers of the Sea'). These clerks then enjoined local officials to see that the ships were appropriately equipped. For instance, some had to be endowed with brows for embarking horses, as well as hurdles for erecting stalls to secure the animals at sea. The larger vessels, like cogs and carracks, were also fitted with fighting castles.[6]

The actual assembly of an impressed armada for a specified maritime expedition often fell to an early version of the English admiral, who was more of an administrator than a fleet commander. Such admirals were normally nobles assigned responsibility for one of three geographic areas or 'admiralties': the Northern Fleet, which extended from the Thames to Berwick on the Scottish border, the Southern Fleet, which included the south coast from the Thames to Bristol, and occasionally a Western Fleet, which guarded the Irish Sea from Bristol to Carlisle. These 'admirals' worked either concurrently or hand-in-hand with royal clerks and sergeants-at-arms to muster mariners as well as vessels at designated ports of embarkation within a specified period of time. They also assumed accountability for the billeting and victualling of troops prior to departure, as well as the modification of the accumulated vessels for war.[7]

The process was complicated and cumbersome. It involved many individuals and multiple layers of execution, impeded by understandably balky shipowners who were seldom compensated for the use of their ships. Expeditions were thus rarely ready expeditiously. Edward III mandated on 28 August 1345 that an armada be martialled for the Crécy campaign at Portsmouth by the middle of October, but preparations were not completed until July of the following year, when the fleet finally sailed for Normandy.[8] The expedition of Edward's son, the Black Prince, to Bordeaux in 1355 also suffered substantial delays. In fact, postponements of three months or more were common. This, of course, increased costs considerably, since those forces awaiting the arrival of ships still needed to be provisioned in the interval.[9] The process was already prohibitively expensive.

In an era when the kingdom's income hovered between 18,000 and 33,000 pounds silver per year, the 1338 expedition of Edward III to the Low Countries, which consisted of 370 ships carrying 8,770 effectives and 4,614 horses, cost 382,000 pounds, according to one estimate. Taxation and direct expenditure from the King's Wardrobe could account for a mere fraction of the total.[10] The only acceptable solution was the acquisition of the required ships through arrestment, despite its obvious detractions.

That said, the impressment system proved relatively effective in amassing the sort of large-scale expeditions sponsored by English sovereigns during the Hundred Years War. Edward III was recorded to have rallied a fleet of 440 vessels for his Brittany campaign of October 1342 and the armada which carried his army to Normandy in the summer of 1346 supposedly numbered 750. Chronicle accounts of the Agincourt campaign in 1415 claimed Henry V commanded a fleet at least twice that size.[11] Even if the estimate was greatly exaggerated, it still would have taken several hundred vessels to convey the campaign's 12,000 combatants, many of whom were mounted, across the Channel.[12] Conversely, the French crown, which relied mainly on hired fleets, was never able to collect a commensurate invasion force at any time during the protracted conflict.

The lack of a standing navy, however, made England vulnerable to the coastal raiding favoured by the French. Impressed fleets simply could not be raised quickly enough to react to such maritime threats in a timely manner. The French monarchs knew this and took full advantage. They sought to degrade England's ability to mount massive invasions of the continent by attacking the ports from which those invasions were mounted. Accordingly, they fashioned fleets which could savage England's thinly protected shores at will. The mainstay of these quick-strike squadrons was the galley, which boasted a shallow draught and oared propulsion, enabling it to operate inshore and up rivers independent of the wind. Most English coastal communities remained unwalled at the time and were thus easy marks for such fleets, which often struck without warning and disappeared before any forces could be assembled to deal with them.[13] Not only did these raids hinder invasion preparations, but they also disrupted commerce and assailed the very legitimacy of the English crown, leading Rodger to assert:

> Failure to protect the kingdom from naval attack in the 1370s and 1380s contributed powerfully to the sense that Edward III in his dotage and Richard II in his youth were failing in that most basic of all obligations of the medieval king, 'good government', of which the core was defence against enemies abroad and the dispensing of equitable justice at home.[14]

Indeed, public outrage over the crown's seeming incapacity to counter the despoilment of the coasts helped cause the Peasants' Revolt of 1381.[15]

The efficacy of this sort of naval warfare was exactly why the French court had the *Clos des Galées* constructed at Rouen in the first place. The arsenal, operated by Genoese shipwrights since the late thirteenth century, continued to produce and preserve Mediterranean-style galleys for military purposes throughout most of the Hundred Years War. The numbers were not great – there were thirteen galleys in Rouen and La Rochelle in 1336, for instance – but not many were required for the hit-and-run raiding primarily practised by French naval forces.[16] The shipyard also served as a key naval support facility where galleys could be hauled out of the water and into covered sheds for repair and refit, not to mention being spared the deleterious effects of winter weather. In fact, the greatest contribution of the *Clos des Galées* to the French war effort may have been from 1338 to 1340, when it was involved in fleet preparations for a planned invasion of England. Around 200 vessels were gathered at Rouen by the winter of 1340 before their fateful encounter with the English fleet at Sluys.[17]

The *Clos des Galées* was never intended, however, to be the sole source of French naval power. Oared vessels were constructed at other places along the northern coasts, such as Caudebec and Dieppe, and galleys were occasionally brought up from French-controlled ports in the Mediterranean, including Aigues-Mortes and Marseilles. Moreover, the king of France could readily raise at least 400 vessels by the same means as the king of England: impressment. This core of French vessels was augmented by squadrons chartered from Castile and Genoa. The Castilian contribution was small – normally fewer than twenty galleys – but they proved instrumental in interrupting English merchant activity with Gascony. Genoa, on the other hand, was a particularly bountiful source of seaborne mercenaries. Its toxic political environment routinely produced outcasts among the competing factions, like the Guelph Grimaldi family who, having been forced out of Genoa, moved with their own galley fleet to Monaco (which they still rule to this day).[18] As early as 1304 a dozen Genoese galleys under the command of Rainier Grimaldi supported a French fleet which fought against a Flemish flotilla for Zierikzee in Zealand.[19] In 1346 Carlo Grimaldi agreed to supply Philip VI with the use of thirty-two galleys.[20] Nor were their arch-rivals, the Ghibelline Doria family, immune to French monetary enticements. They, too, supplied both galleys and commanders to the French cause for a price. Ayton Doria commanded a score of Genoese galleys which joined the French in ravaging England's southern shores in 1338.[21]

Ships and Sailors of the Hundred Years War

The first Genoese galleys that the French court employed in any significant numbers were those leased by Louis IX and his brother Charles of Anjou in the mid-thirteenth century. Already described at some length in Part I, they were basically the same sort of bireme *galeas* that had dominated the Mediterranean since the beginning of the twelfth century. According to the *Angevin Registers* of the Kingdom of Naples, they were generally just under 40m (131ft) long by about 4.5m (15ft) wide and carried at least 108 oarsmen. (*See* Fig. 3.) With officers and marines, the total crew averaged about 150.[22] But by the beginning of the thirteenth century the Genoese had adopted the trireme galley (i.e., three rowers per bench vice only two). It was probably only slightly longer but noticeably broader at the beam (5.3m or 17ft 5in) in order to accommodate the extra oarsmen, like the Venetian 'great galleys' which were introduced at roughly the same time. This increased the crew complement by as much as 50 per cent to perhaps 225, all of whom would have been considered combatants. And since it was probably these triremes that the Genoese contributed to the French war effort in the fourteenth century, a squadron of twenty galleys would have been manned by over 4,500 crewmen – a force which would have easily overwhelmed almost any English coastal community at the time.[23]

To counter the threat, the English also produced galleys, but they were of a distinctly northern design. British nautical historian Ian Friel characterizes them as 'clinker-built vessels with a double-ended hull form, carrying a single square sail'.[24] As a result, Rodger deemed them 'recognizable descendants of the "Viking" type'.[25] The exact dimensions are unknown, as none has been found, but two keel beams bought for the construction of a galley at Newcastle for Edward I around 1295 suggest a vessel about 36.5m (120ft) long. This length is corroborated by two other galleys assembled for Edward at Ipswich and Dunwich that same year, which possessed a hundred oars each. They were all apparently rowed *alla sensile* with two oarsmen sitting side-by-side on the same bench, each working his own oar. Auxiliary power was provided by a single square sail and directional control by a sternpost rudder.

From the late thirteenth century barges were often manufactured alongside galleys. Apparently intended as tenders, they were smaller at first – usually containing around thirty oars – but by the end of the fourteenth century they had become indistinguishable from galleys in contemporary accounts.[26] At the same time references to oared warships called 'balingers' became commonplace. These craft seem to have retained the same basic traits as earlier war galleys and were apparently similar to barges,[27] though they may well have been somewhat swifter, because the name was derived from the Basque whalers that operated in the Bay of Biscay. But that is only conjecture. As in the case of the barges, very little illustrative evidence remains for the balingers.[28] What is certain is that they varied appreciably in size from the hundred-oared *Godegrace* of 1401 to the twenty-oared *Paul* of 1413 and were produced in significant quantities in the late fourteenth and early fifteen centuries.[29]

While fleets of oared warships could not circumvent the savaging of England's south coast, they could and probably did participate in raids of retribution on French shores from the Ile de Ré to Flanders. Boulogne, Harfleur and the Cotentin peninsula were all struck repeatedly throughout the fourteenth century.[30] That said, galley-type vessels only peripherally impacted the course of the Hundred Years War. The mainstay of England's maritime effort from the beginning of the conflict to the end was the cog.

Clinker-built with a high freeboard, a flat bottom and nearly straight stem and sternposts, the cog was basically the same cargo vessel that Frisian merchants had used to ply the North Sea in the early Middle Ages. Of some 1,300 vessels identified during the Edwardian Era of the war (1337–60) nearly 60 per cent were cogs.[31] Several of the king's own ships were cogs which, from 1344 to the end of the Hundred Year's War, fell under the purview of a royal official entitled the 'Clerk of the King's Ships'. Edward III's flagship at the Battle of Sluys in 1340 was the *Cog Thomas*, the finest of the royal fleet.[32] The reasons for this heavy reliance on cogs were manifold and compelling. First of all, from the standpoint of the English kings, these capacious vessels were key to the logistical operations which underpinned their campaigns on the continent. The cog's relatively large load-carrying capacity was ideal for conveying across the Channel the military personnel, equipment and provisions necessary to wage war. The Bremen cog (built around 1380) was 23.3m (76ft 5in) long and 7.6m (25ft) wide with a capacity of around 80 tons, but some, like the *Cog Edward*, reportedly could hold as much as 240 tons. Secondly, they were plentiful. Seaborne commerce to and from England was mostly carried by cogs. They were ideally suited for hauling bulk cargos such as English wool bound for Flanders and sweet Bordeaux wine from Gascony. Propelled by a single square sail and steered by a stern rudder, cogs were also considerably less expensive to construct and crew than galleys. Thus they formed the core of the merchant maritime community which served as a ready source for royal arrestment. Moreover, cogs were easy to convert for combat. Good carpenters and the proper materials were all that was required to install castles fore and aft as well as atop the main mast. Finally, the height of the hull (4.2m or 13ft 9in from keel to gunnel on the Bremen cog) as compared to a galley (around 2m or 6ft 7in) made them excellent fighting platforms from which to rain down projectiles on lower profile enemy vessels.[33] **(Pl. 28)**

Consequently, by the fifteenth century cogs and similar sailing vessels constituted the greater part of English royal fleets. In March 1417 the operational fleet of Henry V included eleven balingers out of twenty-seven vessels, but these oared craft accounted for only 10 per cent of the total tonnage. Under Clerks of the King's Ships William Catton and William Soper, sailing ships had clearly become the principal striking force.[34] One of these was the 540-ton *Trinity Royal*, a high-hulled carrack which boasted multiple masts and towering castles – the first of Henry's 'great ships'.[35] By 1420 he owned three more: the 760-ton *Holyghost*, the 1,000-ton *Jesus* and the 1,400-ton *Gracedieu*, a behemoth in a world where a 500-ton vessel was big. It was reported to have measured 54m (177ft) by 29m (95ft) with the forestage towering 14m (46ft) high. The *Gracedieu*'s remnants remain in the river Hamble near Bursledon, a treasure trove for nautical archaeologists. Unlike their carvel-constructed (skeleton-style) Mediterranean counterparts, all the 'great ships' were clinker-built with a huge rounded hull, upcurving stem and jutting forecastle (which towered over the aftercastle), characteristic of the carrack. **(Pl. 29)** Each bore two masts except the giant *Gracedieu*, which had three.[36]

In addition to the usual assortment of projectile-hurling devices and hand-to-hand combat weapons carried by the crew, their armament included cannons. The *Holyghost* had seven. They were evidently small breech-loaders which fired iron quarrels and lead pellets. Intended strictly as anti-personnel weapons, they were only marginally efficacious. Ship-killing cannon would not appear until the invention of the gun carriage and lidded gunport of the sixteenth century.[37] The deadliest weapons remained projectiles (lances, arrows and iron bolts) cast or shot by individual combatants. To these were added *gads* (oversized iron darts), which were thrown from the topcastle.[38] The preferred projectile-launchers were what they had been for centuries: crossbows and longbows. These tools of the 'God-detested art of slingers and archers' were so lethally effective that their use against Christians had technically been anathematized since the Second Lateran Council of 1139.[39]

Those who commanded and operated these ships in time of war tended to be the same seamen who commanded and operated them in the commission of the other two major maritime activities of the medieval era: commerce and piracy. After all, most maritime merchants of the age were also marauders of opportunity, and the skill-set required for piracy at sea was basically the same as that for warfare at sea. A boarding action in the course of buccaneering was very much like one executed during a sea battle. As a result, notorious corsairs like Eustace the Monk and the Hawleys of Dartmouth served the crown as respected admirals. The only difference was that when they committed their acts of piracy, it was against enemy shipping, for which they were armed with 'letters of marque' from the crown. Nobles like Robert, lord of Morley and John, duke of Bedford (Henry V's brother) were often appointed as overall fleet commanders, but prominent sea captains from the Cinque Ports (like Gervase Alard of Winchelsea) and various other seafaring communities represented a rich reservoir of maritime expertise which the crown could not ignore.[40]

Nonetheless, Susan Rose has observed that under Henry V 'a corps of royal shipmasters had been created, paid by annual grants from the Exchequer'.[41] These shipmasters and the fleet of some thirty to thirty-six warships built or purchased for Henry V between 1410 and 1420 represented an early attempt at a standing royal navy. In retrospect, Henry's purpose seems clear. In addition to dozens of galleys, the French had commissioned the support of Genoese carracks. Henry's 'great ships' were apparently built to counter these. He needed to make the sea safe for the realm's commerce upon which his own revenue relied and the maritime supply lines upon which his continental campaigns depended. Along those lines, Henry also inaugurated maritime patrols in an effort to curb the *guerre de course* which preyed on shipping in the Channel.[42] This went hand-in-hand with the compulsory convoy system implemented by parliamentary policy in the mid-fourteenth century for all commercial traffic with Flanders and Gascony.[43] In other words, the crown was trying to obtain some measure of control over the Channel. The *Libelle of Englyshe Polycye* ('Libel of English Policy'), a polemical poem on naval policy written around 1436, stated the strategy plainly: 'That we bee maysteres of the narowe see.'[44]

The Edwardian Phase Starts with the Savaging of England's Shores (1337–9)

On 24 May 1337 the continuing conflict over continental lands between the crowns of England and France finally erupted into what became known as the Hundred Years War when Philip VI of France declared confiscate Aquitaine, the fief of his nominal vassal, Edward III of England. It had been a long time in coming. The struggle had flared up repeatedly in the decades prior. The ravaging of La Rochelle by seamen of the Cinque Ports and Bayonne had prompted an earlier expropriation of Aquitaine by Philip IV in May 1294. The matter was not resolved until May 1303, when Aquitaine was restored to Edward I in return for homage and the marriage of Edward's heir, the future Edward II, to Philip's daughter Isabella – an event that would later enable what was essentially a territorial contest to masquerade as a dynastic dispute.[45] Hostilities boiled over anew in 1324 when Charles IV of France had a *bastide* (fortified town) built in the Agenais, part of Aquitaine, provoking violent retribution by the English seneschal of Gascony. Once again the French king confiscated Aquitaine and once again the crisis was finally quelled when homage was paid to the French crown in 1325, this time by the prince of Wales (the future Edward III of England). Tensions were heightened yet again to the point of combustion when Charles IV died without an heir in February 1328. Edward III, whose father (Edward II) had been deposed in favour of him in January the previous year, was passed over for the French throne by the French nobility who chose instead the king's cousin Philip of Valois, despite the fact that Edward (as Isabella's son) was the nearest male relative.[46] Edward initially yielded his claim by paying homage to Philip VI, but French support of Scottish resistance to English suzerainty and English intrigues in French Flanders helped bring hostilities to a head. The final spark was Edward's refusal to return the exiled Robert III of Artois to the custody of the French court. Philip answered the affront with an *arrière-ban* ('call to arms') on 30 April 1337.[47]

It was the French who seized the initiative at sea. On 24 March the following year a squadron of French galleys found Portsmouth unprepared and razed it, along with the nearby villages of Portsea and Eastney. It was the opening salvo of French admiral Nicolas Béhuchet's strategy of disrupting English commerce, particularly the trade in wine and salt from the Bay of Biscay. A few days later his galleys attacked the island of Jersey as well. On 8 September his ally Ayton Doria led a flotilla of twenty Genoese galleys on an assault of the other principal Channel Island, Guernsey. The effect of these raids was to hold English shipping in port and thereby curtail crown revenues from trade tariffs.[48]

Such attacks would get much worse and impact the king personally. Earlier, on 16 July, Edward had crossed to Antwerp with a fleet of 346 ships, including the royal flagship *Cog Thomas* and a number of the other king's ships, manned by about 12,000 mariners altogether. He brought with him an army of some 1,400 men-at-arms and 3,000 archers in order to join forces with an alliance of German princes for a push into the Cambrésis region on the border with France.[49] While he was pursuing this objective, French admirals Béhuchet and Hugh Quiéret, at the head of forty-eight galleys and barges, caught the English fleet off-guard at Arnemuiden in the Western Scheldt on 21 September and captured most of it, slaughtering the crews. It was a devastating blow to English royal prestige. Five of the king's ships were seized, including the great *Cog Edward* and the vaunted royal barge *La Christofre* with its three cannon.[50] Worse still, two weeks later, on 5 October, a Franco-Genoese squadron under Quiéret 'sailed into Southampton harbour on Sunday morning when the people were at mass', wrote Jean Froissart, the famed French chronicler from the Hainault. 'The Normans and Genoese entered the town and pillaged and looted it completely.'[51] The archives of St Denys Augustinian Priory reveal that 40 to 50 per cent of the town's structures were razed, and archaeological evidence suggests that this key port city would not recover economically until the fifteenth century.[52]

The attacks abated little in 1339. Ayton Doria assailed Harwich with eighteen Genoese galleys on 23 March, but was driven off.[53] In the same time frame Carlo Grimaldi led a combined French–Genoese flotilla, which included his seventeen galleys, thirty-five Norman barges and the captured *La Christofre*, against Jersey again but was also rebuffed. So after reinforcing the French grip on Guernsey, he made his way to Gascony, where he isolated Bordeaux by taking both Bourg and Blaye in the Gironde estuary in April.[54] Nor was Ayton Doria idle. In May he commanded a fleet of at least twenty galleys and *pinnaces* (small, swift sailing vessels for scouting) which were originally intended to escort a force of 24,000 Normans on an invasion of England's south coast.[55] The promised Norman invasion force never materialized, but Doria descended on Southampton with his fleet on 15 May anyway. The town's defenders had, however, learned the lessons of the previous year. Southampton was heavily fortified with new walls and a well armed militia. The assault was easily repulsed. Doria then took out his frustration on the coasts of Devon, Sussex and Kent. Seven merchantmen were culled out of Plymouth Sound and on 27 May Hastings was put to the torch.[56]

English Retaliation and the Battle of Sluys (1340)

These attacks did not go unanswered, however. In July 1339 Béhuchet's squadron joined those of Grimaldi and Doria to form a fleet which consisted of sixty-seven vessels, thirty-two of them galleys, for a large-scale raid on the Cinque Ports.[57] This time the English defenders were waiting for them. Local militias prevented them from even landing at Sandwich, so the Franco-Genoese fleet tried Rye instead. There, the English admiral Robert Morley nearly trapped them with the Northern Fleet. They escaped but crew morale plummeted. Deprived of plunder and thoroughly exasperated, the Genoese mariners of Doria's squadron subsequently mutinied over remuneration. A delegation sent to seek redress at Philip's court was imprisoned, so many of the mutineers seized their ships and sailed back to Italy, a pair of Grimaldi's galleys joining them. The remainder of the Franco-Genoese fleet withdrew to the Scheldt estuary, leaving the French littoral unprotected. Morley took full, brutal advantage. His fleet demolished Ault and Le Treport on the Channel coast and continued round Brittany to Poitou. Dieppe was raided early the next year, and on 14 January 1340 ships from the Cinque Ports exacted retribution on Boulogne. Under the cover of a foggy night, they swept into the port and reduced eighteen beached French galleys and twenty-four merchantmen to ashes, along with much of the town.[58] The loss of the galleys would be devastating.

Although it may not have been readily apparent to either side at the time, the momentum at sea had shifted. First of all, recent events had curbed French offensive capability. In an unforeseen twist of fate, Doria's mutinous galleymen returned to Genoa to spark the popular Ghibelline insurrection which ousted from power such Guelph nobility as the Doria and Spinola families and installed as the city's first doge, Simone Boccanegra, a leader considered more favourable to the English.[59] (Edward III was allied with the Holy Roman Emperor and king of Italy, Louis IV the Bavarian, who enjoyed Ghibelline sympathies.) Philip's primary source for warships outside of the *Clos des Galées* had temporarily dried up. Worse yet, the eighteen galleys burnt on the beach at Boulogne meant that only four French galleys remained. The English, on the other hand, were emboldened. Edward clearly signalled his intention to take the offensive. On 26 January 1340 at Ghent he proclaimed himself king of France.[60] The following month Edward took ship at Sluys bound for Harwich to prepare an invasion force.

Edward's overall strategy remained the same as his predecessors'. He would attempt to exploit Flemish allies such as his brother-in-law William II, count of Hainault, in order to use Flanders as a springboard for a strike into France. Accordingly, he began assembling a fleet in the Orwell estuary near Harwich to transport his army to the Zwyn inlet. Such a scheme could hardly be kept secret from Philip, who dispatched his *Grand Armée de la Mer* ('Great Army of the Sea'), a substantial force of around 200 vessels (mostly conscripted round ships), to Flanders on 26 May to support his own peremptory incursion into the region. It arrived in the Zwyn on 8 June. Edward, delayed by fleet desertions and dissent among his advisers as to the wisdom of facing the French fleet in Flanders, finally departed from Orwell on 22 June with what ships could be hastily gathered – between 140 and 160. Thus the stage was set for the most pivotal naval confrontation of the entire conflict. As such, it is covered at length in the special section at the end of this chapter.

In short, the battle at Sluys on 24 June 1340 was a spectacular English victory, which established the basis for much of England's success during the Edwardian Phase of the war. **(Pl. 30)** The vast majority of Philip VI's *Grand Armée de la Mer* ended up either at the bottom of the Zwyn or as prizes of war. More dismal still was the egregious loss of maritime manpower. Of the 25,000 or more French casualties suffered at Sluys an estimated 16,000 to 18,000 were reported to have been experienced mariners.[61] These sailors and ships would have been difficult to replace in the short term, leaving the Valois court with little capability to impede English military movements across the Channel. That said, the French still retained some facility for harassing English shipping. Barely a month after Sluys Jean Houdetot gathered what was left of the French fleet (three galleys and seven barges) and joined a squadron of Castilian galleys to waylay an English wool convoy bound for Flanders on 26 July, culling out thirty vessels. The same force attacked the Isle of Wight a few days later, then raided Portland and burned Teignmouth.[62] Moreover, victory at sea was no guarantee of triumph on land. Edward's subsequent siege of Tournai failed and he was forced to accept a truce at Espléchin on 25 September 1340. This was later extended to June 1342, but it did not prevent Edward from pursuing his continental aspirations through war by proxy. The death of Jean III, duke of Brittany, on 30 April 1341 left the succession of the duchy in doubt and gave the English king the opportunity.[63]

The Breton War of Succession and the Crécy Campaign (1341–6)

Historically the dukes of Brittany were also the earls of Richmond, so Edward had a vested interest in the succession struggle. Besides, control of Brittany would have enhanced the security of the vital sea passage between England and Gascony. Thus Edward supported Jean de Montfort, the dead duke's half-brother and designated heir, while Philip fell in line behind Charles of Blois, husband of Jean III's niece and the son of the king's sister. Jean de Montfort was captured early on, but his wife, Joanna of Flanders, soldiered on in the western part of the province. When she became besieged in the castle of Brest by land forces under Charles of Blois and a squadron of fourteen Genoese galleys under Carlo Grimaldi in the summer of 1342, William Bohun, earl of Northampton, came to her rescue. He departed from Portsmouth on 15 August with about 1,350 men in 140 small ships escorted by galleys from Bayonne. As luck would have it, Northampton barely evaded a raid by twenty-one oared warships constructed at the *Clos des Galées* which laid waste to the port. Bohun's subsequent arrival at Brest on 18 August surprised Grimaldi, enabling the English to destroy eleven of the Genoese galleys and lift the siege. This gave the English command of the strategically critical fortress of Brest, which stood at the end of the Breton peninsula.[64] Edward's subsequent siege of Vannes was thwarted, however, and he was again compelled on 19 January 1343 to sign a truce with Philip, which would last until 1346.[65] The so-called War of the Breton Succession would drag on until 1364, but in the meantime the situation soured significantly for the French in the summer of 1346 when Edward embarked on his Crécy campaign.

Edward unilaterally abrogated the latest truce in early 1345 to renew his conflict with the French crown. Philip VI, for his part, understood that an attack was imminent, so he again contracted with Carlo Grimaldi of Monaco to provide as many as thirty-six galleys, each with at least 200 crewmen.[66] The following spring Edward confirmed Philip's fears by amassing the single largest English invasion armada yet assembled: around 750 vessels, manned by an estimated 15,000 mariners.[67] The only problem was that the French king had no clear idea of its target. Edward had managed to keep the fleet's destination a strict secret. Not even when he embarked from Portsmouth on 11 July 1346 did the king let on as to where he was heading. It could have been Gascony, where the expedition of Henry of Grosmont, earl of Lancaster, had enjoyed some success with the capture of Bergerac in August of the previous year, but the threat of blockade by Grimaldi's fleet made that problematic. Brittany was a possibility, but William Bohun's progress had been mixed since the death of Jean de Montfort on 26 September 1345, discouraging further investment by the English court. And while Flanders had been the avenue of previous incursions into France, uncertainty over alliances there made that a less attractive option for Edward as well. In the end he spurned all these previously attempted options for a new one which all but guaranteed the element of surprise.[68]

On 12 July Edward landed the largest English invasion force of the Hundred Years War to date at St-Vaast-la-Hougue on the Cotentin peninsula of Lower Normandy. The operation was virtually unopposed. This was fortunate, because it took five days to disembark the estimated 2,700 men-at-arms, 2,300 Welsh spearmen, 7,000 foot archers and 3,250 mounted archers and hobelars (light cavalry).[69] English naval detachments quickly destroyed Harfleur and Cherbourg. Then, on 18 July, some 200 ships shadowed the army as it marched east along the Cotentin coast towards Caen, savaging French ships and ports as they went. These integrated forces burnt more than a hundred French ships, sixty-one of which were capable of being fitted with fighting castles. Aside from Grimaldi's galleys, still south of La Rochelle, there was little in the way of French sea power left to oppose them. The English took Caen on 19 August, setting aflame several merchantmen in the Oren river in the process.[70]

Edward then executed a ruthless *chevauchée* (a mounted raid) which ravaged the Seine valley all the way to Poissy (within a few miles of Paris) before turning north towards Calais. The manoeuvre finally achieved its main tactical objective on 26 August 1346 at Crécy-en-Ponthieu: forcing Philip into a decisive battle. Edward chose his ground carefully – the summit of a small, gently sloping hill with protected flanks just north of the town. When Philip's forces arrived, Edward used the same lethal advantage that had helped him win an overwhelming victory at Sluys – English longbowmen. They decimated an advance detachment of Genoese crossbowmen. French knights in the commission of an ill-timed cavalry charge finished off the hapless Genoese, only to be slaughtered themselves by the vicious volleys of the English archers. By the time the carnage had run its course, the corpses of over 1,500 of France's chivalry littered the field of battle, along with an untold number of men of lesser rank. For this, Edward paid with the lives of only a few hundred of his own men. It was one of the most lopsided triumphs of the war: a force of around 15,000 had prevailed over one of maybe 25,000. More importantly, it enabled Edward to continue his advance unimpeded towards his ultimate strategic goal: Calais.[71]

The Siege of Calais (1346–7)

Godfrey d'Harcourt, the Norman exile who had urged Edward to invade Normandy in the first place, reportedly advised the king that capturing Calais would be to 'wear the keys to the kingdom of France at [his] belt'.[72] The advantages were clear: it was an excellent port, close to England and thus easily resupplied by sea. It would serve as a superlative beachhead for the conquest of the rest of the kingdom. And, in terms of supremacy at sea, control of Calais would give England near-complete command of the critical Straits of Dover.[73] Edward therefore unstintingly invested the resources of his realm into taking it. Medieval military scholar Clifford Rogers called it 'the largest single military operation undertaken by England until the modern period'. An examination of pay records for the period divulged that in the neighbourhood of 32,000 troops and 900 vessels of various sorts participated in what would be an eleven-month siege, beginning on 3 September 1346.[74]

And Edward evidently suffered no illusions about how arduous the undertaking would be. The city was heavily fortified and virtually unassailable by sea. From land, there were only two approaches, according to Froissart: 'either along the dunes bordering the sea, or over country full of dikes and swamps which could only be crossed by a single bridge at Nieuley'.[75] Moreover, reaching the city after considerable tribulation was only the initial stage in an onerous struggle. Calais was encircled by stout walls, which were themselves surrounded by marshy ground that obviated the use of siege machinery.[76] Accordingly, the English sovereign settled in for the long haul, ordering the construction of a fortified camp he called the Villeneuve-le-Hardi ('Bold New Town'), which Froissart said consisted of 'houses built of heavy planks, thatched with straw and brushwood and set out in properly ordered streets, as though they were to be lived in for a dozen years'.[77] He then enclosed Calais with a wooden wall by land and a cordon of ships by sea. This last measure was crucial because the only feasible means of resupplying the city was through the port. Not content with these measures, Edward also had his naval forces move quickly to interdict Philip's ability to breach the blockade.[78]

As the siege began, the English fleet raided nearby Wissant, Montreuil-sur-Mer, Le Crotoy and even Boulogne in order to forestall any relief attempts by local French naval forces. The French, for their part, endeavoured not only to break the blockade but also to harass English maritime supply lines. Two weeks after the siege started Carlo Grimaldi finally arrived on scene with thirty-two of his galleys and seized twenty-five English supply ships bound for the besiegers. But Grimaldi later left for the winter, while the French struggled to pull together other naval assets for the relief effort: fourteen oared warships, twenty-five sailing ships and sixty smaller boats. In the meantime Philip attempted to draw Edward off by prevailing upon his ally, King David II of Scotland, to invade England from the north. The archbishop of York, however, defeated and captured the Scottish sovereign at Neville's Cross on 17 October.[79]

The following spring the French began to force their way through the blockade. At the end of March fifteen oared warships from Dieppe escorted five transports through the English cordon, and on 1 April another thirty relief vessels made it into port. Edward and his commanders subsequently placed a palisade in the harbour and sank a merchantman at its entrance. Nonetheless, on 25 June a French convoy of twenty-five cargo ships and a barge from Le Crotoy, chaperoned by ten Genoese galleys and twenty-one armed round ships, attempted again to breach the blockade. This effort, however, failed when it ran up against a 120-ship flotilla, bristling with archers, under the command of John Howard, Admiral of the North, and John Montgomery, Admiral of the West. The Genoese galleys quickly deserted their wards, few of which escaped.[80] Meanwhile, another diversion – the siege of La Roche Derrien in Brittany, undertaken by Charles of Blois – ended with the latter's capture by Thomas Dagworth that same month.[81] All other measures having failed, Philip belatedly arrived at Sangatte, on the coast a few miles to the west of Calais, with a relief force of 15,000 to 20,000 men on 27 July, but the English were far too deeply entrenched to be uprooted. Ships full of archers and arbalesters arrayed along the shoreline dissuaded Philip from even approaching the English defensive positions. He departed without giving Edward the decisive battle he so craved, leaving Jean de

Vienne, the military commander of the garrison, little choice but to capitulate on 4 August 1347.[82] The English crown would not relinquish Calais until 8 January 1558.

The Battle of Winchelsea (1349–50)

Weary of war with coffers drained, both sides agreed to a papally mediated truce in September 1347, to last until July of the following year.[83] An apocalyptic event then intervened to ensure the armistice was sustained, at least in the short term: the Black Death. By late 1347 Genoese merchants had introduced the bubonic plague into southern France. By February 1348 the disease raged in Paris.[84] Froissart described it in simple, stark terms: 'People died suddenly and at least a third of all the people in the world died then.'[85] The ceasefire was extended, but in August 1349 Philip broke it by moving against English fortifications in Poitou and Saintonge on the mid-Atlantic coast.[86] Towards the end of the year he contracted with Alfonso XI to have his Castilian mariners, natural competitors of the Gascons, disrupt shipping between Gascony and England. Accordingly, in November a flotilla of around forty-four sailing vessels, carrying Spanish wool to Flanders, raided several small ports on their way north and waylaid ten English merchantmen bearing wine from Bordeaux. The Castilian convoy continued through the Channel, despoiling English shipping as it went, before ultimately sailing into Sluys for the winter.[87]

News of the Castilian fleet's exploits was not well received at the English court. A renewal of the sort of ravaging endured by the English south coast in the 1330s with its attendant impact on the wine trade was feared. So Edward resolved to intercept the Castilian convoy on its return journey south. He issued a summons for the king's ships to muster in Sussex. By late July 1350 around twenty-five royal vessels, including the *Cog Thomas*, *Cog Edward* and the imposing *Jerusalem*, had joined perhaps fifty-five other smaller ships at Winchelsea, where many of the realm's great men had also gathered. Besides William Bohun (Northampton), William Clinton (earl of Huntingdon), Sir Reginald Cobham and Admiral Walter Mauny, were Thomas Beauchamp (earl of Warwick), Richard FitzAlan (earl of Arundel) and Henry Grosmont (duke of Lancaster). Even the Black Prince was present, along with his ten-year-old brother, John of Gaunt, and his brilliant field commander, John Chandos. Such an assembly could hardly have escaped the notice of Carlos de la Cerda, commander of the Castilian fleet at Sluys, especially after Edward had pointedly demanded the Spanish fleet's departure from Flanders. Cerda hired Flemish mercenaries to man his ships' springalds (torsion devices for firing iron bolts) and arbalests (large crossbow-like ballistae).[88]

Edward waited at Winchelsea (apparently amid much merry-making) for nearly two weeks. Finally, at around 4 o'clock in the afternoon on Sunday, 29 August, the masthead lookout on the *Cog Thomas* spied the Spanish ships making their way through the Straits of Dover with a following wind. Edward ordered wine served and prepared for battle.[89] The single column of Castilian carracks was moving too swiftly for any sort of coordinated attack, so the king's ships just made for it the best way they could.[90] In fact, Froissart noted, 'They [the Spanish] were in big ships, well trimmed, with the wind astern, and need never have tangled with the English unless they wanted to.'[91] Evidently in an effort to slow the Spaniards down, Edward pointed at the lead ship and ordered the master of the *Cog Thomas*, William Passelowe: 'Steer at that ship straight ahead of us. I want to have a joust at it.'[92]

Graham Cushway, an expert on Edward's navy, theorizes that Edward may have been quite inebriated at this point. If so, it would go a long way towards explaining why anyone would want to ram a carrack with a cog.[93] The result was predictable. The impact snapped the topcastle off the main mast of the carrack, flinging its occupants to a watery grave, but the Spanish ship was able to sail on, its speed barely diminished. Such was not the case for the *Cog Thomas*. The collision had sprung its seams and it began taking on water so fast that the vessel was in imminent danger of sinking. Faced with drowning, the ship's company grappled onto another passing Castilian carrack.[94] It was not an easy act, as Froissart made all too clear: 'The advantage was by no means with them [the English] for, the Spanish ships being higher than theirs, they were able to shoot down at them and hurl iron bars which did considerable damage.'[95] Nevertheless, Edward's knights fought with the desperation of men in danger of drowning and succeeded in securing the Spaniard.

Several other English vessels endured similar difficulties. *La Bylbauwe*, the Black Prince's ship, was grappled by a large Spanish vessel and 'was holed in several places, through which water came pouring in', recounted Froissart.[96] The ship surely would have sunk along with the Black Prince and his entourage had not the duke of Lancaster intervened with his own ship. Together, the two English crews took the Spaniard. The *Salle du Roi*, which was carrying the king's household under the command of Robert, count of Namur, nearly suffered the same fate when a great Castilian ship grappled it and attempted to tow it away under sail. Disaster was averted when one of Robert's men, a certain Hanekin, leapt aboard the Spaniard and severed several rigging lines, bringing down the mainsail.[97] Aside from such feats of derring-do, what probably tilted the scales in favour of the English was the same advantage that had won them most of the encounters of the war thus far: rapid-fire archery from their longbowmen. Cushway comments, 'The sheer number of English arrows reduced the Castilian arbalesters to sheltering behind tables and hatches and taking pot shots.' 'Enemy archers in the Castilian rigging were cruelly exposed against the sky and shot down,' he adds.[98] Once the missile deluge had been sufficiently suppressed, Edward's armoured and experienced men-at-arms were easily able to deal with the enemy crewmen and their Flemish mercenaries.

By the end of the day the English had captured at least twenty-four of the Spanish ships, all laden with textiles and other merchandise from Flanders. As impressive and profitable as the action may have been, it was also quite costly in terms of casualties. The chroniclers provide no numbers, but the English raconteur Geoffrey le Baker listed a litany of horrendous wounds suffered by the victors, mainly from crossbow bolts.[99] At least two ships were lost and several others were severely damaged. Furthermore, psychological gains were probably blunted by the death of Philip VI on 22 August, which overshadowed news of the victory. Only later was the Battle of Winchelsea, also called *Les Espagnols sur Mer* ('The Spanish on the Sea'), trumpeted as a great triumph by some chroniclers.[100]

The Battle of Poitiers and the End of the Edwardian Phase (1351–60)

'Nevertheless, the 1350s was the most peaceful decade for English shipping in the fourteenth century,' determined Nicholas Rodger.[101] Most events of note took place on the continent. This was due, at least in some modest measure, to a foray out of Calais led by the duke of Lancaster in April 1351. It found in the harbour of Boulogne what appeared to be a French invasion fleet of 120 ships and burned it to the waterline.[102] French maritime undertakings were modest and infrequent thereafter. The Valois court's general apathy towards naval pursuits was most likely generated by English incursions into French territory emanating from both Calais and Gascony. The most serious of these was the operation organized by the Black Prince, who arrived in Bordeaux from Southampton on *La Christofre* in September 1355. The following month he commenced a highly rewarding *chevauchée* with around 2,200 men which extended all the way through the Armagnac lands and the Languedoc to Narbonne and back. Emboldened by such unchallenged success, the prince struck off from Bordeaux again on 6 July 1356 with about 7,000 troops (mostly Gascons). This time he headed north to hook up with the duke of Lancaster, who had landed at St-Vaast-la-Hougue on 18 June, but the planned two-pronged assault on the French heartland failed to materialize when the Black Prince was prevented from crossing the Loire. It was on the return march to Bordeaux that his path was blocked at Poitiers on 19 September by the army of Philip VI's successor, Jean II, which resulted in the latter's defeat and capture.[103]

This, of course, plunged the French court into disarray. The leadership of the Dauphin Charles was soon challenged by Charles II, king of Navarre, a competition which eventually gave rise to the peasant revolt known as the *Jacquerie*. Seeing the opportunity, Edward decided by the autumn of 1359 to seize the French throne for himself by capturing Reims, the city where the kings of France were crowned. In late October he took ship to Calais and by 4 December he was before Reims. The problem was that Edward's army was evidently not suited for siege. Consisting of about 10,000 troops, half men-at-arms and half archers, it seems to have been almost entirely mounted, as for a *chevauchée*. At any rate, the siege failed. Keeping such a large force in the field over the winter months so far from his vital sea link with England proved impossible. Edward's army quit Reims on 11 January and raided towards Paris, eventually surging into Burgundy.[104]

In the meantime, ships from Picardy and Normandy coalesced into a small invasion flotilla at the mouth of the Somme. Its purpose was to make a diversionary assault on Sandwich, the home port of the king's ships, and perhaps even liberate Jean II. Ill-planned and poorly led, with only nominal support from the dauphin, the amphibious force of around 1,500 to 3,000 infantry (including archers) with only a few men-at-arms came ashore on 15 March 1360 at Winchelsea, instead. After slaughtering many of the inhabitants, they put the town to the torch, along with several ships in the harbour, including the giant *La Jerusalem*. They were caught in the course of making their getaway by local militia, suffering several hundred casualties and the loss of two barges. It was a tawdry enterprise which accomplished nothing of value – much like Edward's expedition to Reims.[105] This first phase of the Hundred Years War fizzled out with the Treaty of Brétigny on 8 May. This confirmed Edward's control over Calais, Poitou, Ponthieu and Aquitaine in return for abjuring his claim to the crown of France.[106]

The Castilian Civil War and the Inception of the Caroline Phase (1364–71)
The Treaty of Brétigny, unfortunately, brought no real break in hostilities. The two courts continued the conflict through their respective proxies. Charles of Navarre carried on the civil war in France with some unofficial English backing even after Jean II perished in an English prison on 8 April 1364, enabling the dauphin to assume the throne outright as Charles V. But the French soldier of fortune Bertrand du Guesclin, fighting for the French crown, ended the Navarrese cause at Cocherel on 16 May. The War of the Breton Succession also persisted, but it too was brought to a close in 1364 when, on 29 September, England's John Chandos handed defeat and death to Charles of Blois at Auray, taking Guesclin captive at the same time. The pause did not last long. Two years later the two courts chose sides in the Castilian civil war. In March 1366 Bertrand du Guesclin, recently ransomed by Charles V, joined Enrique of Trastámara in his quest to wrest the crown of Castile from his half-brother Pedro 'the Cruel'. The latter, in turn, petitioned the aid of the English and got it in the person of the Black Prince. At stake was the Castilian galley fleet, which France greatly coveted to rejuvenate its emaciated naval capability. Edward, now prince of Aquitaine, temporarily dashed these hopes with a devastating triumph over Trastámara and his French allies at Nájera on 3 April 1367, capturing Guesclin again in the process.[107]

Fittingly, it was this latest adventure which helped precipitate a renewed outbreak of the Hundred Years War, dubbed the Caroline Phase (after Charles V) by modern scholars. Pedro of Castile was supposed to pay Prince Edward for his participation in the enterprise, but he himself was defeated and dispatched at the Battle of Campo de Montiel in March 1369 by Trastámara before he could honour the obligation. As a result, the penurious Black Prince was compelled to hike taxation in the Aquitaine to such lofty levels that its nobility (particularly Jean d'Armagnac and his nephew Arnaud Amanieu of Albret) sought redress with Charles V, technically Edward's overlord. The assent of the French king to hear such appeals naturally prodded Edward III to resurrect his claim to the French crown in June 1369, which, of course, caused Charles V to yet again confiscate Aquitaine in November. Thus direct war between the two realms was officially reignited with Castile, of course, now firmly in the French camp.[108]

The timing could hardly have been worse for England. Edward had grown elderly and somewhat detached, and governed largely through a coterie of councillors. Equally troubling, the Black Prince's health began to deteriorate to the point that he felt constrained to return to England in January 1371. He would be dead by 8 June 1376 and his father would follow him to the grave a year later.[109] At the same time English naval power was in regression. Much of the naval leadership and many of the assets of earlier years were no longer available. Hardly any of the admirals and ships' masters of Edward's earlier victories remained. Moreover, many of the king's ships were either damaged or in disrepair, while the number of merchantmen available for arrestment had been dramatically decreased by war and piracy.[110] Conversely, French fortunes at sea were on the rise, thanks to the maritime acuity of Jean de Vienne, who reorganized the *Clos des Galées* and the French admiralty beginning in 1373.[111] Furthermore, the French crown now had the support of Castile. Even before ascending to the throne as Enrique II, Trastámara had promised Charles the aid of his galley fleet.[112]

Fears of a French invasion prompted Edward to have the Isle of Thanet fortified, along with Southampton, Portchester and Portsmouth, in June 1369, but these precautions did not prevent Portsmouth from being brutally sacked and burned in September.[113] The French, however, concentrated their efforts where the English were most vulnerable: their continental possessions. The borders of these lands were simply too extensive to protect from the incursions of quick-strike French forces. They had already claimed Ponthieu as of April, raising concerns over Calais. In response, Edward dispatched John of Gaunt as the new lord of Calais in July. The latter ravaged Upper Normandy *chevauchée*-style, assisted by a squadron of barges and perhaps what king's ships were available. But this strategy achieved little lasting advantage against French Fabian tactics, which consisted of fading away from any frontal confrontation with English forces only to attack their rear and flanks. Bertrand du Guesclin, ransomed yet again and appointed constable of France in 1370, practised this ploy to great effect.[114]

The Battle of La Rochelle and the Culmination of the Caroline Phase (1372–89)

Aquitaine, with its enormous expanse, was particularly susceptible to French forays. Furthermore, following the departure of the Black Prince in early 1371 it had only a few hundred men under John of Gaunt to defend it. By the summer of 1372 the situation was dire enough to dispatch John Hastings, earl of Pembroke, with reinforcements.[115] Pembroke took with him only a modest retinue of twenty-four knights, fifty-five squires and eighty archers, but he also carried a horde of 12,000 pounds in gold and silver to hire an army of around 3,000 (500 knights, 1,500 squires and 1,000 archers) upon his arrival in Gascony.[116] His fleet was equally unassuming, being comprised of fourteen to seventeen vessels gathered from the Cinque Ports, of which only three were large enough to accommodate fighting castles.[117]

Pembroke's squadron reached its intended destination, La Rochelle, on 22 June, only to find that a Castilian fleet of twelve galleys and eight carracks under the overall command of the Genoese admiral Ambrosio Boccanegra, supported by the Castilians Fernán Ruiz Cabeza de Vaca and Ruiz Diaz de Rojas, was already at anchor before the port. The young nobleman, doubtless weaned on tales of English victories at Sluys and Winchelsea, pressed the attack without hesitation. **(Pl. 31)** Unlike at Sluys and Winchelsea, however, the English did not have near enough archers to suppress the fire of the Castilian crossbowmen massed on the decks of the carracks. Consequently, Pembroke's men-at-arms were never able to board and engage the enemy. He disengaged at nightfall after losing two of his ships. His intention was to continue the battle in the morning, but as dawn broke he discovered that the tide had receded, leaving the rest of his ships either grounded or wallowing in shallow water. The shallow-draught Castilian galleys then easily manoeuvred among Pembroke's marooned round ships while their Spanish crews lobbed pots filled with oil onto the decks of the hapless English vessels for Castilian crossbowmen to ignite with flaming arrows. Panicking horses trapped in the holds added to the bedlam. Four Poitevin barges from the port attempted to help the English, but it was hopeless. The earl himself was captured along with his treasure when four other Castilian vessels grappled onto his flagship. The entire English fleet was lost and all the surviving men were taken prisoner. It was the worst English setback at sea in a century. Perhaps more significantly, the Castilian blockade of La Rochelle was subsequently reinforced and the city fell to the French a few weeks later in early September.[118]

In the immediate aftermath the débâcle stimulated Edward to refurbish the realm's naval capability. He ordered the building of seventy barges in 1373, but there is little evidence that they were all actually produced; if they were, they were never fused into an effective fighting force.[119] On the other hand, the fortunes of the French at sea soared when Charles V appointed Jean de Vienne 'Admiral of France' that same year. The latter began by reinvigorating the *Clos des Galées*. He reorganized it again in 1377. The result was a refurbished galley squadron which made for a formidable raiding force when paired with that of Genoese commander Rainier Grimaldi. In contrast, when Edward III died on 21 June of that year, only five of his forty or more royal ships remained. Three days after Edward's death Jean de Vienne's fleet began laying waste to Folkestone, Rye, Rottingdean, Lewes, Dartmouth, Portsmouth and Plymouth on the south coast of England. In August he raided the Isle of Wight, then torched Poole and Hastings.[120] The next year Edward's heir, Richard II, ordered the construction of thirty-two balingers for coastal defence. Most of these vessels were built, but they failed to prevent further forays on the southern shores.[121] In 1380 Vienne's fleet, operating in cooperation with a squadron of twenty Castilian galleys, captured Jersey and Guernsey, left Winchelsea and Gravesend in ashes, and even raided up the Thames.[122] As indicated earlier, the crown's failure to protect these coastal communities probably contributed to the Peasants' Revolt of 1381.[123]

The war went no better for England on the continent. The capture of La Réole in 1374 reduced English Gascony to its pre-war borders. The fast-moving campaigns of Bertrand du Guesclin continued to nibble away at England's continental possessions.[124] Hundred Years War historian Charles Allmand reflects that by the time Edward's life ended in 1377 'only Bordeaux, Bayonne, and a coastal strip in that region could be controlled effectively by the English administration'.[125] Calais alone endured in the north. French efforts to evict the English from the continent altogether reached a hiatus in July 1380 when Guesclin died, followed in September by Charles V, leaving his eleven-year-old son (Charles VI) on the throne.[126] But England could not capitalize. By then, it had ceased to send large expeditionary forces to the continent.[127] Instead, the English court attempted to pressure France through its Flemish alliances. The French victory at Roosebeke over pro-English Flemish rebels on 27 November 1382, however, ended those efforts.[128] Then again, the French failed to exploit England's evident debility. Vienne tried to mount several invasions: one which landed in Scotland in 1383, another which gathered 900 to 1,200 ships at Sluys in 1384 and one which was to embark from Harfleur in 1387. All foundered in the initial stages of implementation.[129] In the meantime the English claimed a moral victory at sea when, in March 1387, Richard FitzAlan (earl of Arundel) intercepted a French-Castilian wine convoy in the Straits of Dover and chased it into the Zwyn, where he captured more than seventy prizes.[130] Spent, both sides finally agreed to a short truce on 18 June 1389, followed by another in March 1396 for twenty-eight years.[131]

The Lancastrian Phase and the Loss of the Narrow Sea (1413–53)

There were violations, of course, but the armistice largely held, primarily due to domestic concerns within the respective domains. In England, Richard II (son of the Black Prince) was only ten when he ascended to the throne on 16 July 1377 and, as a result, he endured many challenges to his reign. The most serious of these was from Henry of Bolingbroke, the son of John of Gaunt (the king's uncle). Richard had exiled Henry in 1398, but the latter returned to England after the death of his father in 1399 to depose and murder his rival. As king, Henry IV was too distracted by financial concerns and various petty insurrections to realize any military aspirations on the continent. In France, Charles VI began a descent into insanity by 1393, engendering a power struggle between Jean the Fearless, duke of Burgundy (the king's cousin), and Louis, duke of Orléans (the king's brother). The relative peace between the two realms came to an end when Henry IV died in March 1413. Even before ascending to the throne, his son Henry V recognized the opportunity presented by the political disorder in France.[132]

As prince of Wales, Henry had already dabbled in the French civil war by dispatching Thomas FitzAlan, earl of Arundel, with an army of 800 men-at-arms and 2,000 archers to aid Jean of Burgundy in 1411. An English expedition of 1,000 men-at-arms and 3,000 archers sent by Henry's father the following year in support of the opposing Orléanist faction resulted in the Treaty of Bourges, under which the Orléanists essentially promised to honour the terms of the Brétigny accord with respect to Aquitaine. The pact was disavowed a few months later, however, when the two French factions resolved their differences. Henry V not only refused to accept this repudiation, but, upon his assumption of power in 1413, also demanded the hand of Catherine of Valois, the French sovereign's daughter. When he was rebuffed, he chose to achieve his aims through arms.[133]

On 11 August 1415 the king set sail from Southampton aboard the 540-ton *Trinity Royal* 'in company with about fifteen hundred vessels', according to the contemporary *Gesta Henrici Quinti* ('The Deeds of Henry the Fifth').[134] He arrived in the mouth of the Seine with this massive armada on Tuesday, 13 August and the next day began offloading an army in excess of 12,000 men, three-quarters of whom were archers. Henry soon deployed his soldiers and ships in a siege of Harfleur, for capturing the port was the key to the entire campaign. Pestilence and staunch resistance unexpectedly delayed the city's surrender until 22 September, but Henry's subsequent *chevauchée* through Normandy to Calais with his remaining 9,000 men resulted in the most overwhelming English victory of the war: the Battle of Agincourt on 25 August. Though the French forces under Constable Charles d'Albret were vastly superior (well over 20,000 by the most modest estimates), they suffered thousands of casualties, mostly men-at-arms, compared to only a few hundred English losses at best in another triumph for the English longbow.[135]

The annihilation at Agincourt did not, however, prevent Bernard d'Armagnac from besieging the English garrison at Harfleur by land and sea the next year. Henry dispatched his brother John, duke of Bedford, with a large fleet (perhaps 300 ships) to break the blockade in August 1416. The subsequent engagement in the Seine estuary on 15 August was the most significant naval encounter of the Lancastrian Phase of the war. Though outnumbered, the French boasted eight Genoese carracks carrying at least 600 crossbowmen and an uncertain number of Castilian galleys. (Twelve Genoese galleys had departed just before the battle when their commandant, Gioanni Grimaldi, was killed in a skirmish.) To counter the carracks, Bedford had only four of the king's 'great ships', including the *Holyghost de la Tour*, but he commanded over 7,000 troops, most of whom were archers.[136] In what the *Gesta Henrici Quinti* described as 'an exchange of missiles, iron gads, stones, and other weapons of offence', this was probably decisive.[137] Moreover, his numerous smaller ships were doubtless able to move about the sandbank-strewn Seine estuary more freely than the colossal carracks.

The chroniclers conveyed few details of the clash, aside from the outcome. The account of the *Gesta Henrici Quinti* left little doubt, however, as to who was the victor:

> After a long, drawn-out and most bitter fight of five or six hours, during which, of them [the French] some fifteen hundred souls had been slain and about four hundred made prisoner, and of our men nearly a hundred had been killed under the heavy rain of missiles, and when three great carracks had been captured and one hulk sunk, by God's command victory was yielded to the English, and the remainder of the many ships of the enemy fled to Honfleur, opposite Harfleur on the other side of the river Seine.[138]

A fourth Genoese carrack, which the *Gesta Henrici Quinti* dubbed 'the mother of them all', foundered on a sandbank while fleeing.[139] The three captured carracks were later incorporated into the royal fleet as the *George*, the *Marie Hampton* and the *Marie Sandwich*.

In September 1416 six balingers out of Calais commanded by Richard Beauchamp (earl of Warwick) failed to ensnare yet another carrack, even after pursuing it all the way to Sluys. The size difference in the vessels was simply too great to overcome.[140] John Holland (earl of Huntingdon), however, had more success with a squadron containing a pair of royal 'great ships' (the *Holyghost* and the *Trinity Royal*) on 29 June the following year. According to the Italian chronicler Antonio Morosini, Holland added four more Genoese carracks to the royal naval retinue after a three-hour confrontation in the Channel abeam Harfleur. These later came to be called the *Andrew*, the *Christopher*, the *Peter* and the *Paul*.[141]

Such victories enabled England once again to command both coasts of the Channel and paved the way for Henry's conquest of Normandy. He landed with another invasion force at the mouth of the Touques river on 1 August 1417 and swiftly took Caen and Alençon. Falaise fell to him in February 1418 and Cherbourg on the Cotentin capitulated in September. Rouen surrendered to him in January 1419, after a six-month siege that left the *Clos des Galées* a charred shambles. The subsequent Treaty of Troyes on 21 May 1420 rendered Henry the regent of Charles VI and heir to the throne of France. While still in Troyes, he wedded Catherine of Valois less than a fortnight later on 2 June.[142]

The stunning success that England had realized so quickly on the continent under Henry's stewardship unravelled just as rapidly without it. The king contracted dysentery during the long siege of Meaux, which ended in March 1422. He died on 31 August, leaving as his successor his infant son (Henry VI). This, of course, added further impetus to the Dauphin Charles' claim as the legitimate heir to King Charles VI, who passed away on 21 October of that same year. English forces in alliance with those of Burgundy staved off rising dauphinist resistance with victories at Cravant on 31 July 1423 and Verneuil on 17 August 1424, but the subsequent defection of the duke of Burgundy to the dauphinist cause spelled doom for English interests on the continent. The turning point came in May 1429 when resistance inspired by Joan of Arc broke the siege of Orléans, enabling the coronation of the dauphin as Charles VII at Reims on 17 July. In the summer of 1435 Philip, duke of Burgundy, formally swore his allegiance to Charles. Dieppe and Harfleur fell to the French that autumn. Paris followed suit the next year. Henry VI himself encouraged the final collapse of continental England by secretly ceding Maine in December 1445. Rouen submitted on 29 October 1449 and the subsequent rout of English forces at Formigny in April 1450 forced them out of Normandy altogether. Finally, the French victory at Castillon on 17 July 1453 resulted in the retaking of Bordeaux on 19 October. All that remained to the English crown on the continent was the Pale of Calais.[143]

As for the redoubtable royal fleet which Henry V had so carefully cobbled together to spearhead and sustain the English resurgence on the continent, it virtually disappeared after his death. Almost all of the king's ships were sold off to pay his war debts. Only the four 'great ships' were spared.[144] Of all the medieval English monarchs, Henry came closest to the creation of a standing Royal Navy, inspiring Nicholas Rodger to conclude, 'Henry V can justly be regarded as the first English king since Richard I who understood the use of sea power as a primary weapon of war'.[145] With their continental possessions gone and naval power latent, the English could no longer hope to remain 'masters of the narrow sea'.[146]

Exemplary Engagement: The Battle of Sluys (June 1340)

When Edward III, aboard the royal flagship *Cog Thomas*, came upon the French fleet in the Zwyn inlet on the morning of 24 June 1340, contemporary French chronicler Jean Froissart recounted, 'The King was greatly surprised and asked the commander of his fleet what this could be.'[147] This has led modern naval historians like the highly respected Nicholas Rodger to assert that 'the battle of Sluys was essentially an accident'.[148] It probably was not. Philip VI of France had intentionally positioned his so-called *Grand Armée de la Mer* ('Great Army of the Sea') in the Western Scheldt to block the harbour of Sluys on 8 June, because he had learned from his own spies that Edward was mobilizing a force destined for Flanders, while the English king was well aware of the French fleet's presence because his own chancellor, John of Stratford (archbishop of Canterbury), had been informed of it by English merchants two weeks earlier.[149]

In fact, when Stratford heard that the king intended to challenge the French armada (in excess of 200 ships) with whatever vessels were available (around forty) without delay, he argued strenuously against it, considering such an act rash and foolhardy, if not suicidal. Edward remained adamant, however, believing that if he did not confront the French fleet it would sabotage his plans to attack Tournai and wreck his whole continental strategy. It was also paramount for him that his cross-Channel communications and supply links be kept secure. More gravely, Edward feared that if he failed to deal with Philip's armada straightaway, then it would be used to invade England through Scotland. Accordingly, the king heatedly rejected the Chancellor's counsel, whereupon the latter handed back the Great Seal of his office in a huff. Edward's two principal naval commanders, Robert Morley and the Fleming John Crabbe, ardently agreed with Stratford and only submitted to the king's wishes when he vehemently questioned their courage. They did, however, manage to mollify him enough to wait for favourable winds.[150]

The two-week delay enabled the king to cobble together a fleet of perhaps 120 to 160 ships (depending on the source), personally collecting some from the nearby ports. Edward embarked from Ipswich on 22 June along with over 600 knights and 7,000 archers, according to Edwardian specialist Graham Cushway.[151] These men would prove decisive in the coming clash. Most of the archers carried the lethal English longbow, while many of the men-at-arms were battle-hardened veterans of the Scottish campaigns who had survived such bloody encounters as Halidon Hill and Duplin Moor.[152] The English fleet arrived the next day at Blankenberghe on the Flemish coast, just south of the Zwyn. Scout ships were dispatched to reconnoitre the location of the French fleet, while a small shore detachment was debarked. Among its more illustrious members was Henry Burghersh, bishop of Lincoln, whom Edward had instructed to make for Sluys in order to alert their Flemish allies and hopefully recruit some naval support. The other principal personage in that landing party was the noted banneret (captain of a contingent of knights) Reginald Cobham, who was to confirm from the shore the disposition of enemy forces.[153]

What Cobham and his colleagues found was the French fleet anchored before Sluys, its ships chained together in three 'battles' (lines) stretched across the Zwyn between Cadzand Island and the south shore of the estuary (about 5km or 3 miles wide), facing west. The first 'battle', commanded by Hugh Quiéret, was composed of the larger ships surmounted by heavily reinforced castles, with the captured *La Christofre* at its centre. Behind it was Nicolas Béhuchet's 'battle', followed by the galleys of the Genoese mercenary Egidio Boccanegra, known in Italian sources as Barbanera ('Blackbeard').[154] It must have been a daunting sight. Froissart described the ships of the French fleet as being so numerous 'that their masts resembled a forest'. Altogether, he said, '[it] was made up of close on a hundred and fifty big ships, without counting the barges, and carried a good forty thousand men – Normans, light infantry, Genoese and Picards'.[155] Edward himself observed that 'the number of ships, galleys and great barges of our enemies amounted to 180'.[156] Rodger estimates that there were actually 202 round ships, 6 galleys and 22 Norman barges,[157] while Susan Rose allows that the French fleet could have numbered as many as 250 vessels, based upon some chronicle reports.[158]

But what Edward's scouts could not see was that not all was well within the French ranks. There was much discord at the top echelons of command. Béhuchet, a low-born bureaucrat, detested the aristocratic fleet commander Quiéret, and apparently was not bashful about saying so.[159] Of greater concern, however, were the objections of Barbanera, the experienced Genoese galley master. He had stridently challenged the wisdom of surrendering mobility by 'bridling' the French fleet in the cramped confines of the estuary with all its sandbanks and shallows. He had advocated, instead, engaging the English in the open sea so that the larger French fleet could outmanoeuvre and perhaps envelop its smaller opponent, but he had been overruled.[160] Barbanera was so incensed that his advice had been dismissed that he threatened to withdraw from the fight and – either before or during the battle (the sources are opaque on this point) – he did just that, taking several galleys and barges with him.[161]

In any event, despite the apparent disparity in the size of the opposing fleets, at dawn on 24 June Edward and his admirals arranged their ships for battle just out of view of the French formation.[162] Froissart recorded that they put their 'most powerful ships in the van, placing vessels filled with archers on all sides, and between every two shiploads of archers was one of men-at-arms'.[163] This implies that bowmen thronged the castles and rigging of the larger ships interspersed throughout the line. Morley commanded this first 'battle', which included the *Cog Thomas* carrying the king. Given the confines of the Zwyn, the English probably had to form another line behind the first in order to accommodate the entire fleet. To the rear of this second line, then, was what Froissart portrayed as 'a flanking squadron made up entirely of archers, which was to give support wherever needed to the most heavily engaged'.[164] The commander of this reserve unit seems to have been John Crabbe.[165] (*See* Map 14.)

Once the English fleet had formed up, it sailed into the Zwyn from the North Sea with the west wind. (Rodger contends that the English approached the

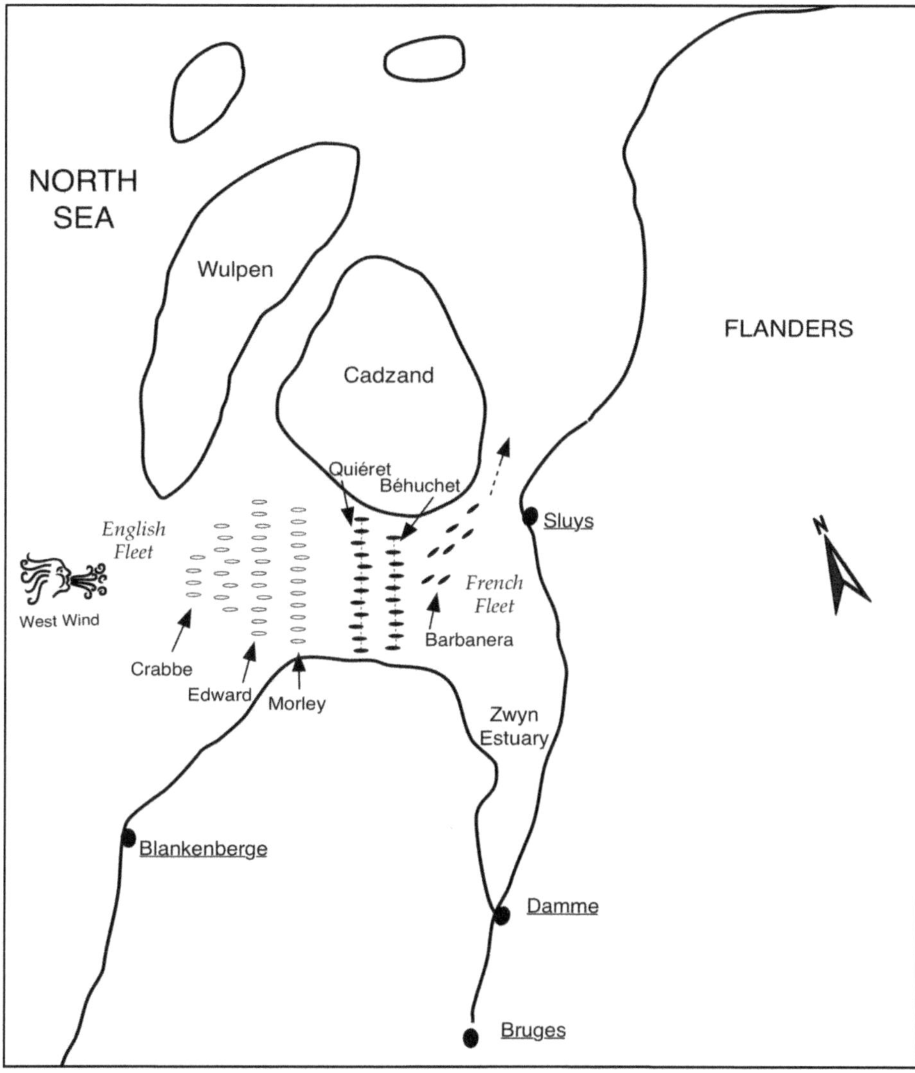

Map 14. Battle of Sluys in 1340. *(Kristy Stanton)*

French formation from the east in order to have the sun at their backs, but he is virtually alone in this.)[166] The attack did not, however, commence immediately. The English ships, instead, dropped anchor and waited. On the counsel of John Crabbe, a former Flemish privateer familiar with the shores about Sluys, they paused until high tide, which occurred at around noon.[167] Then finally, 'well after Nones' (about 3 o'clock in the afternoon) according to Edward, when both the tide and the sun favoured them, they weighed anchor and advanced.[168] Then, just before engaging, Froissart reported that the English vessels veered away. Perceiving it as a loss of nerve, several of the French ships in the front line, including *La Christofre*, unbridled and broke ranks in order to pursue. But the English had apparently only been feigning flight, because they now turned to engage the fragmented French line with the wind once again filling their sails.[169]

The heavy artillery – ballistae firing great bolts and springalds hurling giant stones – must have opened up first, but the preponderance of damage was done by the archers once the adversaries had closed. The English chronicler Geoffrey le Baker characterized the fusillade as 'an iron shower of quarrels from crossbows and arrows from bows'.[170] In this, the English had a decisive advantage. First of all, although the French had more ships, the English seemed to have benefited from a large numerical superiority in combatants. Secondly and perhaps more crucially, the majority of the English archers were apparently longbowmen, while their French and Genoese counterparts were almost certainly crossbowmen. The longbow was said to have had greater range and more power, but the deadly difference here was rate of fire. One modern estimate purports that the English longbow could shoot ten arrows for every two bolts from the crossbow.[171] The few Frenchmen who survived this murderous barrage were constrained to take cover behind bulwarks, unable to shoot back.[172]

Under these circumstances the English ships closed rapidly, suffering little damage and few casualties. Morley's squadron was the first to engage, followed in short order by the ships of William Clinton (earl of Huntingdon), William Bohun (earl of Northampton) and Fleet Admiral Walter Mauny. Screened by the hail of arrows from their archers, the English crews were easily able to grapple with individual French vessels so that their seasoned men-at-arms could clamber aboard and quickly overwhelm the ship's company, mostly lightly armoured mariners.[173] (The records of the *Clos des Galées* reveal there may have been no more than 150 men-at-arms aboard the French ships; the rest were archers and sailors.)[174] Modern military historian Robin Neillands concluded from Froissart's description that 'Edward sent his ships against the enemy in units of three, two ships crammed with archers and one full of men-at-arms.'[175] Using this tactic, the English soon destroyed the broken first French 'battle' in detail. *La Christofre* was one of the first taken and it was swiftly turned against the second French 'battle'.[176]

Even so, it was, in the words of Froissart, 'a bloody and murderous battle'. The integrity of the second French line may well have remained intact, its sailors fighting with the desperation of the doomed into the darkness. 'Sea fights are always fiercer than fights on land, because retreat and flight are not possible,' observed Froissart.[177] The English were forced to go ship-by-ship clearing each one almost to a man. King Edward himself took a crossbow bolt in the thigh. The decks of the French ships were described as being ankle-deep in blood.[178] At some point during the night, panic must have set in. By then, Barbanera had certainly fled with his galleys, leaving the rear of the second French 'battle' open to attack from Flemish maritime auxiliaries recruited by Burghersh. Surviving French sailors leapt into the sea only to be butchered on the beaches by Flemish troops and onlookers.[179]

The carnage continued well into the night and lasted perhaps until dawn of the following morning. In the end it was a sickening massacre. The English victory was total. Of the huge French armada, Edward testified in a letter to his son, Edward of Woodstock (the future Black Prince), only twenty-four vessels escaped. Along with *La Christofre*, all the royal ships taken by the French at Arnemuiden in September 1338 had been repatriated.[180] In addition, the English claimed the largest of the French vessels, like *La George* and the 300-ton *La Denys*, as prizes.[181] Of the 35,000 French and Genoese crewmen and combatants, Edward estimated that barely 5,000 absconded with their lives. The rest, he said, 'lie dead all along the coast of Flanders'.[182] While this may have been hyperbole, most contemporary accounts maintained that at least 25,000 men perished.[183] Among the French fatalities were Quiéret and Béhuchet. The former met his fate in the fighting, while the latter Edward ordered to be hanged from the mast of his own ship in retribution for the slaughter of English crews at Arnemuiden.[184] A passage from Thomas of Burton's *Chronica monasterii de Melsa* exemplifies the exuberant English triumphalism of the moment: 'There was such an infusion of blood that for three days after the battle in all the water of the Zwin all the way to the sea there seemed to be more blood than water. And there were so many dead and drowned French and Normans there that it was said, ridiculing them, that if God had given the fish the power of speech after they had devoured so many of the dead, they would have spoken fluent French.'[185]

Aside from such ghoulish grandstanding, the impact on French maritime capability seems to have been severe. The massive loss of so many skilled seamen undoubtedly left the ports of Normandy and Picardy bereft of much of the maritime expertise France needed to advance its war aims at sea and crippled the commerce of the realm's coastal regions for some time.[186] France was not finished at sea, but it would not be able to mount a large-scale seaborne assault on the British Isles for the remainder of the protracted conflict. The English, on the other hand, suffered relatively few casualties. The highest estimate was 4,000 and the lowest only 400.[187] It was then with some justification that, in the aftermath, Edward claimed 'sovereignty of the seas' and ordered struck a 'noble' (a 9-gram gold coin) emblazoned with his victorious image aboard the *Cog Thomas*.[188] **(Pl. 32)**

CHAPTER 10

The German Hanse: Martial Merchants of the Baltic

The German Hanse, the loose association of German merchants which operated in the Baltic and North Seas from the middle of the twelfth century to the mid-seventeenth, is often referred to in modern historical surveys as the 'Hanseatic League'. It was no such thing. The term 'league' implies a well organized structure which it simply did not possess. It had no charter, no sovereign territory, no corporate treasury and no standing military; it did not even have a permanent governing body. Its only legislative assembly was the Hanse Diet, called the *Hansetag*, which met infrequently amid sparse attendance. It had neither a seal nor even an official title until the mid-thirteenth century, when its members adopted the name *Hansa Teutonicorum, dudesch Hense*.[1] Even the heading 'Hanse' is somewhat amorphous. It was derived from *hansa*, the Latinized version of a word found in the fourth-century Gothic translation of the Bible by the missionary bishop Wulfila, meaning 'troop' as in a 'warrior band'. It eventually came to be applied to groups of travelling German merchants who banded together for mutual protection and increased profit, as in a 'guild'.[2] Aside from ethnicity, the only traits they had in common were language (Middle Low German) and commercial enterprise. The Hanse itself provided perhaps the most precise definition in a 1469 missive to the English Privy Council:

> The *Hansa Theutonica* is . . . a firm *confederatio* [confederation] of many cities, towns and communities for the purpose of ensuring that business enterprises by land and sea should have a desired and favourable outcome and that there should be effective protection against pirates and highwaymen, so that their ambushes should not rob merchants of their goods and valuables.[3]

Accordingly, Philippe Dollinger, the doyen of Hanseatic historians, determined that the German Hanse should more appropriately be labelled the 'Hanseatic Community', a confraternity of German merchants who cooperated in matters of common commercial interest.[4] The venerable French scholar was, however, quick to point out, 'This did not prevent it from replacing the feeble imperial authority and thus becoming a front-rank political power in northern Europe, capable of conducting victorious wars against neighbouring states, though these always served economic objectives.'[5] It has been estimated that by the end of the fifteenth century the Hanse controlled, in the aggregate, a fleet of around a thousand vessels (excluding coastal lighters), boasting some 60,000 tons, making it Europe's leading naval power of the period.[6] It used this power to dominate the Baltic for nearly two centuries.

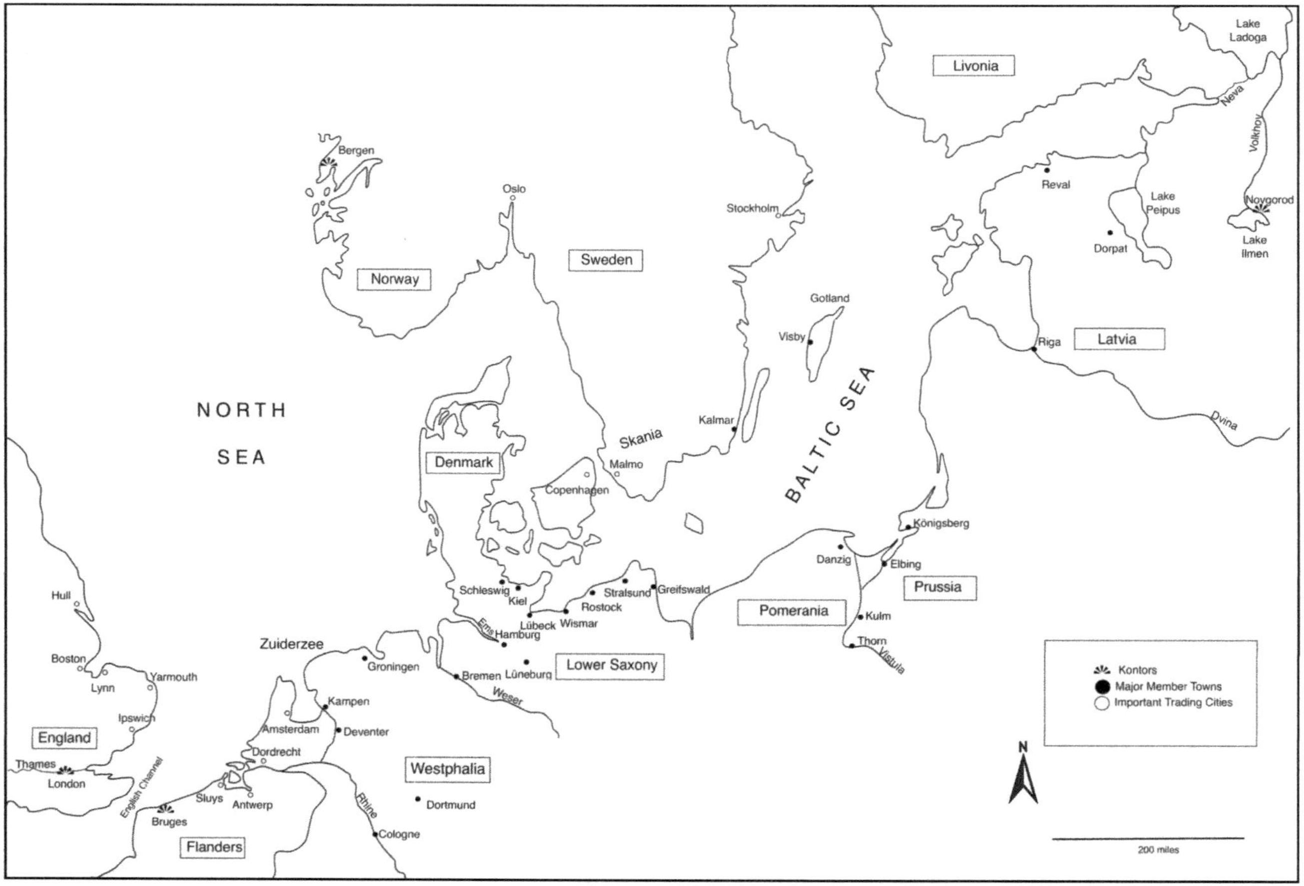

Map 15. World of the Hanse in the fourteenth century. *(Kristy Stanton)*

Foundation and Expansion (1159–1356)

The German Hanse began with the rebirth of Lübeck as a Baltic trading centre in 1159 at the behest of Henry the Lion, duke of Saxony.[7] Its location in the Trave estuary on the southwestern shores of the Baltic made it the perfect port for German merchants to partake in the rich eastern trade which the Frisians and Scandinavians had exploited for centuries. Merchants flocked to Lübeck from Westphalia, Saxony and the Rhineland. Henry the Lion amplified the community's commercial prospects by negotiating a trade agreement with the Scandinavians of Gotland Island in 1161. Gotland, located in the central Baltic, was the gateway to lucrative trade routes through European Russia to the East, so German merchants from Lübeck soon thronged there, setting up their own community at Visby on the island's west coast. These German merchants then travelled with their new-found Gotland trading partners down the Neva river to Novgorod, where in 1189 they won a trade treaty (their first) with Prince Yaroslav III Vladimirovich. This led to the establishment of their own community near the Novgorod market, called *Peterhof*, which Prince Konstantin Vsevolodovich officially recognized around 1206 as the first *Kontor* ('counting house') or merchant quarter of the Hanse.[8] Other major *Kontors* would eventually blossom in Bruges, Bergen and London.

Through the *Peterhof Kontor*, these German merchants acquired coveted commodities such as furs, wax, tar, honey, flax and oriental luxury goods. Moreover, their community in Gotland enabled them to tap into the rich herring fisheries of Skania as well as the copper and iron mines around Falun in eastern Sweden. It also facilitated the establishment of outposts in ancient Livonia on the northeastern shores of the Baltic, where Albert of Buxhoeveden's crusading Brothers of the Sword founded such towns as Riga (in modern Latvia) in 1201, Reval (now Tallinn in Estonia) in 1219 and Dorpat (Tartu, also in Estonia) in 1224. From Livonia the merchants procured timber, amber and resins. The southeastern Baltic was subsequently opened to the Hanse by the Teutonic Knights. In the 1220s Herman von Salza, Grand Master of the Teutonic Order of St Mary's Hospital in Jerusalem (the Teutonic Knights), set about conquering Prussia from the indigenous Slavic pagans at the invitation of Duke Konrad of Masovia (east-central Poland). Operating from Kulm on the east bank of the river Vistula, the Teutonic Knights eventually succeeded with the result that Danzig (modern Gdańsk in Poland) became a vital German port on the Pomeranian coast.[9] It adopted Lübeck law around 1235 and merchants of the Hanse began shipping wheat, rye and barley from its harbour shortly thereafter.

In exchange for all these eastern goods, the merchants of the Hanse imported textiles from Bruges in Flanders, wine from Cologne in the Rhineland and metalworks from Goslar in the Harz Mountains of Lower Saxony.[10] By the second quarter of the thirteenth century the merchants of Lübeck had mastered this lucrative synthesis of land–sea commerce, so aptly symbolized on their 1224 town seal which shows two men on a cog – one a land-based merchant from Westphalia, the other a seafaring trader from Schleswig – swearing an oath to one another.[11] **(Pl. 33)** In 1226 Lübeck became a *freie Reichstadt* ('a free imperial city'), governed by a constitution that catered to its commerce. Called 'Lübeck law', this maritime mercantile code became the template for the charters of Hanseatic towns all along the shores of the Baltic.[12]

As the marriage of land and sea trade routes grew more profitable, the need to protect it from brigands and pirates became more acute. In an age of waning imperial power, the merchants assumed greater responsibility for their own safety through cooperative action. This inevitably led to an alliance of mercantile cities. Lübeck and Hamburg were the first of these. The road between them was one of the most critical commercial arteries in northern Europe. Goods brought from the British Isles and southern Europe by way of the North Sea were transhipped at Hamburg for overland carriage to the Baltic by way of Lübeck. The reverse was true for merchandise from the Baltic bound for the North Sea. This was because the sea passage around the Skaw (Cape Skagen) of the Jutland peninsula through the Skagerrak Strait was notoriously long and treacherous.[13] (Records from the late nineteenth century show that 125 modern ships ran aground on well marked Anholt Island in the adjoining Kattegat in a 23-year period alone.)[14] Accordingly, the citizens of the two cities concluded a pact in 1241 to secure the land route between them. This was the beginning of what Dollinger deemed the 'Hansa of the Towns'.[15]

By 1265 other Wendish cities had joined – most prominently Kiel, Wismar, Rostock and Stralsund.[16] As the Hanse network of towns grew, more opportunities manifested themselves. Hamburg controlled the road to Lüneburg and its saltworks, which the Hanse used to supply the saltfish fairs of Skania. It has been estimated that such herring markets sold 200,000 to 300,000 tons of fish every year at their peak.[17] As demand for saltfish increased, Hanse vessels began bringing additional salt shipments from the Bay of Bourgneuf south of the Breton peninsula. Cargos of wine from Bordeaux naturally followed. Wool came from Yarmouth, Hull, Lynn (King's Lynn), Boston and London in eastern England to feed the textile mills of Flanders by way of Bruges and Ghent, while cod came from Bergen on the southwest coast of Norway to expand the saltfish market. Inevitably, more permanent enclaves were needed in the major market towns to handle the burgeoning volume of merchandise. In 1252 and 1253 Margaret, countess of Flanders, ceded the Hanse a number of commercial privileges which led to the establishment of a *Kontor* in Bruges, integrated into the merchant community. In 1266–7 Henry III of England granted the merchants of Hamburg and Lübeck privileges equal to those of Cologne, who had traded in the realm under royal protection since 1157. By 1281 the traders of the three towns had formed a single German *Hansa* in London with its own *Kontor*. It became known as the *Stalhof* or 'Steelyard'.[18] The last of the four key *Kontors* to be founded was the *Tykebrygge* ('German Quay') of Bergen, the statutes of which were blessed by King Magnus VII Eriksson of Norway in 1343.[19]

As the route structure and volume of commerce expanded, so too did the membership of Hanse towns. By the middle of the thirteenth century the Hanse controlled a highly profitable trade axis extending from Novgorod through Reval, Lübeck, Hamburg and Bruges to London.[20] By the time the association reached its zenith in the mid-fifteenth century some 180 to 200 towns from the English Channel to the Gulf of Finland belonged to it. About seventy to eighty of these were active members or 'towns of the Hansa', who sent delegates to the diets. The rest were considered passive or 'associate towns' (*Beistädte*).[21] Many, particularly the coastal cities, were further linked through the adoption of some form of 'Lübeck law'.[22] They came to be arranged in three basic geographic units called 'thirds': the Wendish–Saxon towns, the Westphalian–Prussian and the Gotland–Livonian. The confederation of Hanse cities was more or less officially consummated in 1356 when it held its first *Hansetag* in Lübeck, which confirmed the subordination of the four principal *Kontors* to the combined will of the Hanseatic towns.[23] By then, corsairs and competitors were already posing serious challenges to the trading alliance.

Cogs, Hulks and Caravels: the Ships of the Hanse

The seafaring tradition of the Hanse began with the launch of its leading city in 1159. 'Lübeck had been founded essentially with seaborne commerce in the Baltic in view,' writes Dollinger, adding, 'Its inhabitants began immediately to build ships, so that its merchants, and also those from the interior, might sail for Gotland and Russia.' And their ship of choice, almost from the start, was the *Kogge* (cog) which they constructed right in the harbour.[24] English economic historian T.H. Lloyd concurs, saying of the city, 'It was settled chiefly by west-German merchants who immediately took to the sea in cogs.'[25] Other coastal communities of the Hanse soon built them as well, often in shipyards along riverbanks called *Lastidie*.[26] After all, cogs were much better suited than their Scandinavian predecessors for hauling the bulk commodities of the Baltic trade. Based on earlier Frisian precedents, the cog was broad at the beam with a flat bottom, which increased cargo capacity.[27] The Bremen cog of the late fourteenth century (discussed in the previous chapter) was 23.3m (76ft 5in) long and 7.6m (25ft) wide with a capacity of around 80 tons. Boasting a high-sided, box-like hull with nearly perpendicular stem- and sternposts, the clinker-built version of the late twelfth and early thirteenth centuries was ideal for the coastal carriage of incipient Hanseatic commerce.[28] As a result cogs were depicted on numerous Hanseatic town seals of the era.[29]

The primitive state of navigation at the time dictated that ships be sailed within sight of land. With no compasses and no charts, the most important navigational tool for the early medieval mariners of the region was the lead-line for determining depth (as illustrated in the 1350 town seal for Elbing), which made it possible to hug the low shorelines of the North Sea as closely as possible without running aground. This was particularly true for the shallow tidal waters of Waddenzee, where maritime historians believe the sea-going cog was first developed.[30] The vessel's low draught and flat bottom allowed it to sail among the sandbars and shoals of this intertidal zone. It could even navigate up coastal rivers like the Eider of Schleswig-Holstein. Since the ninth century, or perhaps even earlier, cogs or similar ships were brought up the Eider and the Treene rivers from the North Sea as far as Hollingstedt and hauled the 16km (10 miles) to Hedeby on the Schlei Inlet leading to the Baltic.[31] Moreover, when the cog reached its destination, which usually lacked sophisticated port facilities like a pier, its nearly level underside permitted it to be beached in shallow waters without heeling over, so that it could be easily offloaded.[32]

The other major advantages the ship offered the merchants of the Hanse were ruggedness and simplicity. Nautical historian Timothy Runyan called the cog 'a durable carrier in the cold and rough waters of the northern seas'.[33] First of all, it was very solidly built. 'The strakes of the Bremen cog are over twice the thickness (5cm or 2in) and three times the width (60cm or 24in) of the strakes on a Viking ship,' notes Runyan.[34] The transverse beams which pierced the hull were a massive 40 × 40cm (about 16 × 16in) and it was all held together with what Kasimiers Slaski of the Poznan History Institute characterizes as 'big, iron, curved end nails'.[35] Its high sides and broad beam enabled it to endure high sea states while the rounded bilge at the edge of the flat bottom gave it an easier ride with better stability. With a square sail on a single mast stepped slightly forwards of amidships, the vessel performed well in a following wind, but could also work to windward if necessary. Initially steered with a side oar attached to the starboard (Old English *steorbord*, meaning 'steering board') side, the cog gained significantly improved handling with the addition of the sternpost rudder sometime before the mid-thirteenth century.[36] The vessel proved not only more seaworthy than its Scandinavian precursors, but also more economical and easier to construct. Planks were sawed rather than split, meaning shipwrights needed less wood and fewer craftsmen to produce a ship.[37] Lastly, all the required materials from timber for the planks to iron for the nails were in ample abundance in the Baltic region.[38]

A critical side benefit of the cog was its ready convertibility from commercial to martial purposes. Their high hulls already made them seem like waterborne fortresses to vessels with lower freeboards, such as galleys and other oared ships.[39] The Hanse enhanced this inherent advantage in the late thirteenth century by adding temporary castles fore and aft, following English precedents. Later, the crenellated castles were made integral to the ship's construction.[40] Thus, ordinary merchantmen could easily be transformed into formidable men-of-war, which the Hanse euphemistically referred to as *vredenschepe* ('peace ships'). All that was necessary was to embark ample men-at-arms along with the appropriate engines of war like arbalests and crossbows.[41] By the fourteenth century it had become common practice for Hanseatic ships transiting the Danish Straits to or from the North Sea to proceed in convoy, escorted by at least two such *vredenschepe* carrying around eighty men-at-arms.[42]

As the fifteenth century opened, commercial traffic had increased to the point that Hanse merchants began seeking a craft with greater cargo capacity. They settled upon an updated version of the hulk shown on the 1295 seal of Shoreham. The Hanseatic hulk of the early fifteenth century (as depicted on the 1400 town seal of Danzig) retained the characteristic banana-shaped hull of clinker construction, but had adopted the keel of the cog, as modified by a curved bottom and rounded bilges. It was broader at the beam with a fuller bow and stern, allowing for larger loads. Also, the crenellated fighting platforms which topped the fore- and aftercastles appear to have been integral to the hull structure. The hulk was still propelled by a single, square sail, but a sternpost rudder had replaced the side oar for directional control. While no hulk has ever been discovered, its design evidently lent itself to enlargement. These vessels grew progressively bigger and more numerous so that by the middle of the century they had almost entirely supplanted the cog.[43]

The final stage in the evolution of Hanse shipping was introduced slightly thereafter. In 1462 a French caravel named the *Saint-Pierre de La Rochelle*, which had apparently carried a cargo of salt from the Bay of Bourgneuf, suffered storm damage in Danzig harbour. Local shipwrights repaired the damage but in the interlude its owner passed away, causing proprietorship to devolve to the city of Danzig. Re-christened the *Peter von Danzig*, the huge ship served as a model for Hanseatic shipwrights for decades to come.[44] **(Pl. 34)** Sometimes called *Das Grosse Kraweel* ('The Great Caravel'), the vessel was immense, measuring 45.2m (148ft) long, 12.2m (40ft) wide with a draught of 5.33m (17ft 6in) giving it a capacity of about 833 tons (though one source estimates as much as 1,225 tons). It owed its size to the skeleton-first, carvel-style of construction in which hull planks were fitted flush to one another and nailed directly onto a prefabricated frame. Contemporary sources considered it a caravel, but its size and rigging (a foremast and a main mast bearing square sails, along with a mizzen mast carrying a lateen sail) suggest a ship more like a carrack. Whatever its precise nomenclature, Hanseatic shipwrights continued to replicate such multi-masted mammoths until the end of the era.[45]

War as an Instrument of Hanse Policy: the Blockade of Norway (1284–5)

The members of the German Hanse involved themselves in hostilities infrequently. Simply put – war was bad for business. It was an expensive, manpower-intensive enterprise which diverted the association's principal capital assets – its ships – from the purpose for which they were intended: profitable commerce. Thus, whenever possible the members preferred economic and diplomatic options for achieving their financial objectives. It was only when these methods failed that they reluctantly resigned themselves to martial means.

A case in point was the perceived harassment of Hanseatic merchants in Bruges in 1280. Envious of the extensive concessions granted to German traders, local merchants insisted that the foreigners could not transact business with one another directly but had to deal through a citizen of the city. The Hansards solved the problem by orchestrating the temporary transfer of the *Kontor* to nearby Aardenburg. Two years later the resultant loss of market revenues caused the townspeople of Bruges not only to recognize previous Hanseatic privileges, but also to add sweeping new ones in order to realize the return of the *Kontor*. The Hansards would use this tactic repeatedly.[46]

In the early 1280s more robust measures were required when Erik II Magnusson of Norway attempted to restrict Hanseatic commerce within his realm. The Hansards were harried, their ships subject to seizure and their merchandise sequestered. The final straw was the confiscation in the spring of 1284 of the

Hanseatic cog carrying a delegation meant to settle the matter. A council of Wendish cities convened at Wismar and concluded that an embargo enforced by naval blockade was necessary. Nearly all the other seagoing coastal towns of the Hanse joined the effort with the notable exception of Bremen, which was temporarily excluded from the alliance for its noncompliance. The participants pledged to prevent the exportation of grain, flour and other foodstuffs to Norway. To accomplish this, they blockaded Norway's ports and stationed cogs in the Danish Straits to circumvent smuggling. Nautical historian Detlev Ellmers notes that this was probably the first incidence of Hanseatic cogs being equipped with English-style fighting castles. Lübeck solidified its status as leader of the league by shouldering almost a quarter of the cost. In any event, these measures proved grimly successful. Contemporary sources claim grain shortages in Norway caused the outbreak of famine. In the summer of 1285 the king of Norway agreed to an armistice brokered by his Swedish counterpart. In the end, all the captured Hanseatic merchants were released, and their ships and merchandise returned to them along with indemnities for any losses they had suffered. Their privileges were not only renewed but expanded.[47]

The War with Denmark (1360–70)

By the end of the thirteenth century the German Hanse had taken firm control over trade on the Baltic. It had virtually excluded English, Flemish and Frisian ships, while transforming the previously international fair of Skania, which sold all sorts of products, into a huge herring market monopolized by the Hanse.[48] Its merchants had managed to steer clear of any hostilities through a mixture of diplomacy, bribes and economic intimidation for the better part of a century, but Scandinavia's monarchs naturally chafed under Hanseatic dominance. Finally, in 1360 Valdemar IV Atterdag of Denmark, in league with his son-in-law Hakon VI of Norway, chose to challenge the Hanse.[49]

In the spring of that year the Danish king seized Skania from the Swedes. There was no indication that he intended to imperil the fish fairs, but it must have made Hanseatic merchants nervous, nevertheless. Late in 1361 Valdemar realized their worst fears by invading Gotland and sacking Visby. It was then clear that the sovereign was bent on establishing a Danish hegemony in the southwestern Baltic at Hanseatic expense. A diet of Wendish and Pomeranian towns convened at Griefswald and decided to impose a blockade financed by a levy upon the ships of all member towns. The effort came to naught when the Prussian ports failed to supply any ships and the Flemish towns of the Zuiderzee continued to conduct commerce as usual with the Danish kingdom. The Wendish towns, led by Lübeck, were left to bear the brunt of the endeavour. In April 1362 the *Bürgermeister* (burgomaster) of Lübeck, Johann Wittenborg, gathered a fleet of twenty-seven cogs and fifteen other vessels to take the war directly to the Danish king. Wittenborg, however, made the cardinal error of dividing his forces. On his way to the Danish capital he directed a squadron to besiege the fortress at Hälsingborg on the Skanian peninsula opposite Copenhagen. This enabled

Valdemar to attack the weakened Wendish fleet, capturing twelve cogs. Wittenborg was forced to accept a humiliating armistice.[50]

The truce held for several years while the Hanse descended into disarray. It was Valdemar himself who brought an end to both the peace and Hanseatic disunity. His policies made no distinction between the Prussian ports and the other Hanseatic towns. In 1366 he seized several Prussian ships in the Sound (the Øresund Strait between Danish Zealand and Swedish Skania) and began mistreating Prussian merchants. This prompted the Grand Master of the Teutonic Order, Winrich von Kniprode, to personally propose to the citizens of Lübeck joint action against the Danish king. Valdemar also alienated the towns of the Zuiderzee by imposing new restrictions on their trade within his realm. They too announced their willingness to participate in a military alliance against Denmark. Delegates of the pertinent parties congregated in Cologne in 1367 to determine a course of action and levy a poundage tariff on commerce to pay for it.[51] The result was the Confederation of Cologne which prescribed precise contributions to be made by each of the members to accomplish Denmark's defeat:

> Firstly, that because of the manifold wrongs and injuries which the kings of Denmark and Norway have inflicted and so still inflict upon the Hanseatic merchants, we have become their enemies and that we shall loyally support one another in the following manner: namely, that the Wendish towns together with the Livonian towns and with those towns which are associated with them, will fit out ten cogs, manned with able men-at-arms, that is, 100 men to each cog; and *Schute* and *Snikke* [light ships] shall accompany each cog. The Prussian towns, that is, the seaports, shall equip five cogs of the like kind ... etc. [22 cogs in all].[52]

The ships from the Zuiderzee towns were to marshal at Marstrand on the west coast of Götaland, Sweden, on Palm Sunday of 1368, while their Hanseatic counterparts were to gather at the Gellen headland at the southern end of Hiddenzee Island in the southwestern Baltic at Easter. The two fleets were to subsequently rendezvous in the Sound.[53] The muster must have been accomplished without difficulty, because the combined force successfully sacked Copenhagen, setting the port ablaze in the process, along with most of the Danish fleet. While Confederation ships continued to ravage the Danish and Norwegian coasts, the Swedes under their new king, Albert of Mecklenburg, surged into Skania. At the same time Count Adolph of Holstein joined the fray by pushing up into Jutland. Norway, once again grievously tormented by a Hanseatic blockade, sued for peace first. The capitulation of Hälsingborg castle on 8 September 1369 finally brought the Danes to their knees.[54]

Valdemar IV was forced from Denmark, leaving his *drost* (a sort of Scandinavian seneschal named Henning Podebusk) to negotiate the Treaty of Stralsund in the spring of 1370 with Jakob Pleskow, the new *Bürgermeister* of Lübeck, and Bertram Wulflam, his counterpart for Stralsund. Signed on 24 May, the accord ensured the German Hanse freedom of trade throughout the Baltic and gave the Confederation of Cologne, for a period of fifteen years, control of the four fortresses that safeguarded the Sound: Hälsingborg, Malmö, Skanör and Falsterbo. More vitally, it conceded to the Confederation veto power over the selection of Valdemar's successor. This explains why Dollinger concludes, 'The Peace of Stralsund marks the emergence in northern Europe of a new power, which here replaced lapsed imperial authority.'[55] It was perhaps the zenith of Hanseatic dominance in the Baltic region.

War on Piracy: Victory over the *Vitalienbrüder* (1375–1400)

Ironically, it was this last empowering clause of the Treaty of Stralsund that spawned the next great test for the German Hanse: a vicious spate of piracy. The death of Valdemar IV on 24 October 1375 triggered the alliance's right to approve Danish succession. The choice was between Valdemar's two surviving offspring: Margaret, married to his erstwhile ally Hakon VI of Norway, and Ingeborg, wife of Henry III of Mecklenburg, who was the son of Duke Albert II of Mecklenburg and the brother of King Albert of Sweden. (Mecklenburg was a large duchy on the Baltic coast of northern Germany which included the Hanseatic cities of Wismar and Rostock.) Fearing the growing power of the Mecklenburg princes, the Hanse decided in favour of Margaret, who then assumed the regency of Denmark. She also became regent of Norway upon Hakon's death in 1380 and by the end of the decade she was accruing power in Sweden at Albert's expense as well. Margaret's growing influence and an increasingly rebellious Swedish nobility soon confined Albert's authority to Stockholm, which was mostly German at the time. The city was eventually besieged. In response, the House of Mecklenburg launched a *Kaperkrieg* or 'privateers' war' against the queen regnant (whom Albert dubbed 'King Trouserless') and called for the provisioning of beleaguered Stockholm by sea. Wismar and Rostock answered the call even though they were technically members of the Hanse. Not only did they equip a relief flotilla, but they also reissued a general summons to the region's freebooters.[56] Detmar, a scribe of Lübeck at the time, described how it all transpired:

> When the ships from Rostock and Wismar were setting sail for Stockholm under Duke Johann, the men from Rostock and Wismar made a proclamation that whosoever wished to try his luck as a freebooter at his own expense, in order to harm the realms of Denmark and Norway, should assemble in the cities of Rostock and Wismar; to be given 'letters of marque', which gave them leave freely to share out, exchange and sell the plundered goods.[57]

This, of course, amounted to a declaration of 'open season' on the ships of Margaret's benefactors – the cities of the Hanse.

'All manner of criminals, journeymen, ruffians and disaffected peasantry' soon collected in the two cities, according to German scholar Dirk Meier. Some of the privateers who responded to the summons were doubtless involved in the relief of Stockholm and thus came to be called *Vitalienbrüder* ('Victualling Brothers'), presumably after the *vitailleurs* of the Hundred Years War who provisioned armies through banditry. Whatever the reason, the name stuck and came to be applied to freebooters of every sort who ravaged the region at the time.[58] Paradoxically, they did the House of Mecklenburg little good. Albert was captured at the Battle of Åasle near Falköping, Sweden, on 24 February 1389 by Margaret's Danish troops and disenchanted Swedish nobility. This did not, however, put an end to either Mecklenburg mischief or the excesses of the *Vitalienbrüder*. The war of attrition on Danish and Hanseatic shipping continued with unabated vigour.[59]

Using Rostock and Wismar as pirate bases, the *Vitalienbrüder* ranged the entirety of the Baltic, visiting such havoc upon maritime commerce that Reimar Kock, a chronicler of Lübeck, claimed that the city's 'entire fleet remained at idle' in 1393. Other reports noted that the herring catch at the time was as little as one-fifth its former level.[60] On 22 April of that year Bergen was brutally pillaged. Malmö, on the southwestern tip of Skania, met the same fate the following year at the hands of an increasingly ruthless *Vitalienbrüder* and their Mecklenburg captains. Most alarmingly, Albrecht von Pecatel, a German captain from Stockholm, led a particularly large band of *Vitalienbrüder* in 1394 on an invasion of Gotland which took Visby. Lübeck and Stralsund battled these seaborne bandits almost alone, but could gain little headway.[61] At one point they attempted to convince their Hanseatic allies to assemble an armada of thirty-six cogs and a few dozen smaller vessels carrying some 3,500 men-at-arms, but the effort fell apart when the Prussian ports demurred, claiming neutrality. Trade on the Baltic ground to a halt.[62]

Matters finally reached a point in 1395 when such unchecked piracy was in no one's best interests except the *Vitalienbrüder*, who had become increasingly indiscriminate and unruly. Lübeck took the lead in mediating a peace among the warring parties. On 25 May the Hanse, Queen Margaret, the Teutonic Knights and the Mecklenburgs consented to the Treaty of Skanör. It called for a cessation of hostilities, the release of Albert from captivity and, most vitally to the Hanse, the departure of the *Vitalienbrüder* from the Baltic. This last provision went unheeded, however. The rampant raiding of shipping continued to beset friend and foe alike. The *Vitalienbrüder* simply selected their own leaders – Klaus Störtebeker and Gödeke Michels were two of the more notorious of these – and began to operate autonomously, basing out of Visby on Gotland instead of Rostock and Wismar.[63] All suffered at their hands. According to one late fourteenth-century Hanseatic *recessi* ('resolution') from the *Kontor* of Bruges, the *Vitalienbrüder* were fond of portraying themselves as 'God's friends and the foes of all the world'.[64] They also took on the sobriquet *Likedeelers* meaning 'equal sharers'. Another *recessi* indicated that it was common practice among these pirates to place their prisoners in empty storage barrels and nail them in with nothing but their heads protruding through the lids until such time as they were either ransomed or dispatched.[65]

By 1398 Grand Master Konrad von Jungingen of the Teutonic Knights had finally had enough. On 17 March he launched from the mouth of the Vistula river a substantial fleet of eighty-four ships bearing 4,000 men-at-arms and 400 horses under the command of Danzig Councilman Konrad Letzkau. Four days later this force came ashore on Gotland and quickly cleared the island of the *Vitalienbrüder*. Those few who survived were soon swept from the Baltic by a reunified Hanse with Lübeck at its head. With no safe haven remaining, the last of the *Vitalienbrüder* followed Störtebeker and Michels to Friesland, from where they afflicted North Sea traffic.[66] This would not be endured for long. In the spring of 1400 a fleet from Lübeck joined another from Hamburg to surprise a nest of the *Vitalienbrüder* in the Ems river estuary, killing at least eighty. Some 300 fled either to Holland with Störtebeker or to Norway with Michels.[67]

Störtebeker, however, made the mistake of re-establishing his band on Heligoland Island, situated about 64km (40 miles) northwest of the entrance to the Elbe – an intolerable circumstance for the Hanse of Hamburg. They equipped a strong fleet that very autumn under Councilmen Nikolaus Schoke and Hermann Lange which attacked the *Vitalienbrüder* at Heligoland with overwhelming force, capturing most of the pirates including Störtebeker. Störtebeker's story is one rife with myths and fanciful anecdotes. (His name, for example, means something like 'Down the beakerful!' in Low German – an apparent reference to his supposed ability to quaff a stein of beer in a single gulp.) All that is known for sure is how the story ended – with his head stacked upon those of his fellow *Vitalienbrüder* in the Grasbrook Meadow of Hamburg. Michels met much the same fate the following year. He was captured with a small squadron in the Weser not far from Bremen and summarily beheaded soon thereafter.[68]

Contending with Castile and Corsairs beyond the Baltic (1402–43)

The successes of the late fourteenth century had won the German Hanse dominance in the Baltic, but they did not quell pressure from corsairs and competitors outside it. Hanseatic expansion into the North Sea and down the Atlantic coasts of France and Spain had engendered envy and enmity, particularly given that Hanseatic traders often enjoyed privileges which exceeded those of indigenous merchants. Such resentment frequently manifested itself as piracy.

At the start of the fifteenth century most of these attacks came from the English. This was due, in part, to the accession of Henry IV in 1399 and England's ongoing hostilities with Scotland and France. The new king made it quite clear that anyone trading with the realm's enemies would be considered *persona non grata* as well. At the same time he abhorred fleet expenditures, so his chosen instrument for punishing maritime offenders was the letter of marque. This meant that Hanseatic shipping in the North Sea and English Channel, especially near French and Scottish shores, was rendered fair game to English ship masters, whether they be privateers or the king's own.[69] For instance, Baron Richard Grey of Codnor, admiral of the king's Northern Fleet, burned two Bremen cogs and captured a ship from Danzig in a Scottish port in May 1402. That same year his men also looted three Prussian ships and another from Stralsund. Other masters with letters of marque ran the total cost to Hanseatic shipping for the year to four ships seized, four destroyed and eight plundered. The next two years were even more damaging to the Hanse. Lloyd estimates that the English captured at least nineteen Hanseatic vessels and wrecked another in 1403, while they took sixteen in 1404 and sank six.[70]

The Hanseatic response was limited to an economic embargo which proved ineffective because not all towns joined the effort. Some Prussian demands for restitution were eventually honoured but complaints from the remainder of the Hanse went unheeded by the English court. The towns of Lübeck, Bremen, Hamburg, Greifswald and Stralsund satisfied themselves with a negotiated return to the peaceful commercial relations of earlier years. Their bargaining position going forward depreciated considerably, however, with the devastating defeat of the Teutonic Order at Tannenberg on 15 July 1410 at the hands of a Polish–Lithuanian coalition. The Grand Master of the Teutonic Knights was the only territorial prince ever granted membership in the Hanse and, as such, represented a key military arm of the alliance. With the Order's power diminished, so too was the power of the Hanse.[71]

Opposition to Hanseatic expansion was, of course, not limited to England. The further its merchants ventured from home waters, the more vulnerable they were to harassment from foreign powers. A case in point was the Kingdom of Castile in 1419. Piqued that traders of the Hanse dared to sell Spanish goods in French ports at the expense of Castilian merchants, Juan II ordered his ships to attack the annual Bay Fleet off La Rochelle. He claimed that it was in retribution for Hanseatic aid rendered to the English during the Franco-Castilian blockade of Harfleur, but the assault was clearly an early example of princely protectionism. Forty German and Flemish vessels were seized and their cargoes confiscated. A war of raid and counter-raid raged for the next twenty-four years with the Hanse at a distinct disadvantage due to the distances involved. The matter was finally resolved in 1443 when the German Hanse consented not to compete with the Castilians either in their own ports or in La Rochelle. The security of the Bay of Biscay was just too important for Hanseatic commerce and capitulation was considered the most cost-effective way of ensuring that.[72]

The Struggle for the Sound (1426–35)

The situation of the Hansards in their own sphere of influence soon soured as well. Relations with Denmark had always been strained, due in no small part to the growing economic dominance of the Hanse. The Treaty of Stralsund (1370) and Hanseatic acquiescence to the unification of the three Scandinavian kingdoms under Margaret I of Denmark at Kalmar castle on 17 June 1397 had mollified the tension, but Margaret's death in 1412 soon roused dormant animosities. At stake was the duchy of Schleswig, a Danish fief at the base of the Jutland peninsula controlled by the German counts of Holstein. Margaret's successor, Erik of Pomerania, wanted Hanseatic support for wresting it away from the House of Schauenburg, the traditional rulers of Holstein. The Hanse, instead, maintained neutrality. The Isthmus of Holstein was much too important for their trade with Hamburg and the North Sea to risk alienating the counts of Holstein. Erik struck back by siding with Poland against the Teutonic Knights and welcoming English and Dutch traders to compete with the Hanse in his domain.

Still, the *Bürgermeister* of Lübeck, Jordan Pleskow, managed to maintain the peace. His death in 1425, however, removed the last restraint to overt belligerence. What ultimately brought this witches' brew of bad feeling bubbling to the surface was Erik's decision in July 1426 to impose a toll on all shipping transiting the Sound.[73]

In September Hamburg and Lüneburg joined the Wendish cities of Lübeck, Wismar, Rostock and Stralsund in declaring war on Denmark. They immediately sought to blockade the Øresund Strait. Unfortunately, this only served to expose the alliance's most persistent and damning detriment: disunity. Once again the Prussian towns declined to go along with it. The Hanseatic towns of the Zuiderzee also refused to support the blockade. As a consequence, the Wendish towns were forced to go it alone, with Lübeck again left to shoulder the bulk of the burden. A flotilla commanded by Pleskow's successor, Tidemann Steen, was overwhelmed in the Sound in the summer of 1427 by a Danish naval force which was subsequently able to capture that year's entire Bay Fleet, some eighty ships loaded with salt from the Bay of Bourgneuf.[74]

Lübeck, however, recovered from the setback. It profited prodigiously from the increased demand for Lüneburg salt to make up for the shortfalls from the Bay of Bourgneuf. The war muddled along for years afterwards as fortune favoured first one side then the other.[75] The Germans even invested Copenhagen for a time in the spring of 1428.[76] But Dutch and English merchantmen routinely broke through the blockade and made serious inroads into Baltic commerce by supplying the Scandinavian realms with the products the Hanse denied them.[77] 'The refusal of the Hanse to open the Sound meant that the Prussians extended a warmer welcome to those English and Dutch merchants who successfully ran the blockade,' writes Lloyd.[78] What finally tipped the scales in the direction of the Hanse were defections among the Swedish nobility. The blockade had interrupted Swedish exports of copper and iron ore, inciting the miners to revolt in 1434. Dissident Swedish nobles then exploited the unrest by pressuring the Danish state council into curtailing the king's powers. Badly weakened, Erik signed the Treaty of Vordingborg in July 1435, which halted hostilities. Besides officially ceding control of the Holstein to Adolph XI of Schauenburg, the treaty confirmed all Hanseatic privileges in the Kalmar kingdoms and exempted the Wendish towns from payment of the Sound toll. The Hanse soon used its improved standing to exclude English and Dutch merchants from the Baltic.[79]

The War with the Dutch (1438–41)

The stranglehold of the Wendish cities on the Sound frustrated the Dutch trading towns (Amsterdam, Leiden, Dordrecht, Deventer, Haarlem, Rotterdam, etc.) that were seeking to expand into the Baltic. They were especially desirous of gaining access to the rich natural resources offered by the Livonian towns, as well as grain from Pomerania. The Wendish cities led by Lübeck would, of course, allow no challenge to their monopoly on such traffic and imposed draconian restrictions on Dutch vessels entering the Baltic.[80] The Dutch reacted by raiding Hanseatic ships in the North Sea. This in turn elicited demands from the Hanse for compensation, which only exacerbated the tension until finally on 7 April 1438 Philip the Good, duke of Burgundy, whose domains included Holland, authorized a privateers' war against Hamburg, Lübeck, Lüneburg, Rostock, Wismar and Stralsund.[81] The very next month Dutch ships seized a dozen Hanseatic ships off Brest carrying salt.[82]

The Wendish cities, for their part, predictably tightened their grip on the Øresund Strait. Erik of Pomerania was deposed as king by the Danish state council in 1439 and the Hanse capitalized by supporting Christopher of Bavaria as his successor in return for additional concessions. One of these privileges was the right to occupy Hälsingborg castle, commanding the Strait. Lübeck took possession of it shortly afterwards. Traffic through the Sound virtually ceased. This, of course, further alienated the eastern Hanseatic cities, particularly those of Prussia, by forcing trade to and from the North Sea to go by way of the Hamburg–Lübeck road.[83] The Dutch countered this rerouting of Baltic merchandise across the Holstein Isthmus by lying in wait at the mouths of the Elbe and Weser rivers to pounce on Hanseatic traffic entering or exiting. They also guarded ingress/egress points to the Baltic. The Dutch were reported to have stationed 104 warships (45 with forecastles) in the approaches to the Sound at the inception of hostilities. These measures proved distressingly efficacious. Nearly two dozen Prussian ships returning from the Bay of Biscay were apprehended at the entrance to the Sound in the first weeks of the war. The Prussians stopped sailing through the Sound thereafter.[84]

The unsustainable stalemate was at long last brought to a conclusion by a combination of factors. The burden of maintaining the blockade became too costly for Lübeck and its allies to bear alone. While the Grand Master of the Teutonic Knights had grudgingly sanctioned the blockade of the Sound by the Wendish cities, the Prussian towns had denied the effort any naval support. At the same time Dutch emissaries were able to procure from Christopher of Denmark trading rights in his realm equal to those of the Hanse. Then, in March 1441, Prussian delegates at a diet in Lübeck pressured their Wendish counterparts into considering peace. This was followed up the next month with preliminary talks in Kampen which led to a formal peace conference in Copenhagen that autumn. The subsequent Treaty of Copenhagen signalled the ultimate decline of the Hanse. By ensuring free trade to both parties, it opened up the East to the Dutch and broke the Baltic monopoly of the German Hanse.[85] The English would soon follow.

The War with the English (1468–74)

Festering antagonism between English and Hanseatic merchants was rooted in the principle of reciprocity. The Hansards enjoyed extensive trading privileges in England, especially at the Steelyard in London, yet they offered their English counterparts no such commercial concessions in their own markets. Hanseatic merchants in England paid a lower tariff on exported woollen cloth than did domestic traders and were also exempted from the poundage excise levied on other merchandise. 'To the fury of English merchants they received no reciprocal benefits of any kind in Hanse towns,' writes Susan Rose, 'rather they faced petty harassment especially in Lübeck, Rostock and the other Wendish ports.'[86] English outrage at this evident inequity occasionally manifested itself in the form of piracy on Hanseatic shipping, for which the Hanse demanded compensation – which, of course, was not forthcoming. A treaty brokered at Arras (in the modern Pas-de-Calais) in 1437 by Heinrich Vorrath, *Bürgermeister* of Danzig, was intended to correct the imbalance, but the leading cities of the Hanse never ratified it.[87] As a result, simmering resentment threatened open warfare throughout much of the fifteenth century. Several particularly egregious events brought the two sides to the brink, only have them step back at the last possible moment for the sake of profit.

On 23 May 1449, for instance, Robert Wenyngton, a former mayor of Dartmouth operating under an indenture from Henry VI to keep the Channel clear of pirates, intercepted a fleet from the Bay of Bourgneuf. Wenyngton himself wrote in a letter to a king's councilman that it was composed 'of a hundred great ships of Prussia, Lübeck, Kampen, Rostock, Holland, Zealand, and Flanders'.[88] Other sources indicated that there were probably between 110 and 130 ships, about half of which were from cities of the German Hanse including sixteen from Lübeck and fourteen from Danzig. Fighting broke out, according to Wenyngton, only when the Bay Fleet failed to acknowledge English suzerainty over the Channel (although plunder seems to have been the actual motive).[89] The English ships, which were apparently smaller and fewer in number, had to endure a deadly volley from '1,000 guns, and quarrels out of number', but Wenyngton said he had 2,000 armed men and the weather gauge. So he was able to cajole the entire Bay Fleet into accompanying his squadron to the Isle of Wight.[90] All except the ships of the Hanse were later released with their cargoes. The Hanseatic vessels and their loads were appropriated, their crews impressed.[91]

'The seizure of the Bay Fleet was one of the two most disastrous and ill-considered episodes in the entire history of Anglo-Hanseatic relations,' concluded Lloyd. The Hanse confiscated all English property in their towns in reprisal and on 18 July the Prussian cities went so far as to arrest all Englishmen and hold them hostage until such time as their merchants were indemnified for their losses. The most punishing stroke, however, was the embargo of English goods in the continental markets of the Hanse. The English clerk of the king's council was dispatched to Bruges as early as September 1449 to negotiate an end to the flare-up, carrying with him a promise to restore some suspended customs concessions to the Hanse. The injured parties were eventually mollified and war was averted.[92]

The second 'ill-considered episode' to disrupt Anglo-Hanseatic relations occurred on 29 July 1458 at the hands of Richard Neville, earl of Warwick, who was Constable of Calais at time. He used his Calais squadron to capture eighteen salt ships bound for their home port of Lübeck, supposedly because their Hanseatic crews had failed to pay proper respects to the royal banner. The matter was adjudicated in the Admiralty court later that same year and Lübeck's mariners were eventually released. Both parties essentially downplayed the gravity of the incident, because neither side benefited from breaking the truce in force at the time.[93] The Wars of the Roses between the Houses of Lancaster and York had just erupted in England and there was no profit in any prolonged dispute for the vast majority of the Hanse, particularly the Prussians.

The next incident would not be so easily overlooked. A bizarre chain of events a decade later led to all-out war between England and the German Hanse. It began in a place on the periphery of Europe's mercantile economy at the time: Iceland, a possession of the Kalmar Union. English merchants had been prohibited from trading in Iceland by the Danish crown since 1426. Nonetheless, fishermen from English ports such as Hull and Bristol ignored the injunction and continued to sail there despite the best efforts of Edward IV to discourage them.[94] Even so, such violations were apparently not a major concern for either monarch – that is, until the murder of Iceland's governor by Englishmen (apparently from Lynn) in 1467 under murky circumstances. Christian I of Denmark responded to the outrage by seizing seven English ships in the Sound in June 1468. Only two were actually from Lynn, so the seizure was taken as an affront to the entire English merchant community, which immediately accused the Hanse of complicity since its vessels often controlled the Sound. Animus was directed especially at Danzig. Consequently, on 28 July the Privy Council ordered the arrest of all Hanseatic merchants and the confiscation of their merchandise. A mob promptly attacked and partially damaged the Steelyard the next day. Its Hansard residents were subsequently incarcerated in London's Ludgate prison.[95]

Caught unprepared and bewildered by the turn of events, the Hanse first sought redress through the adjudication process. Cologne petitioned for an exemption from the retribution which English authorities were only too happy to grant in order to exploit traditional Hanseatic disunity.[96] Positions quickly hardened, however. A diet at Lübeck in the spring of 1469 resulted in a resolution demanding compensation for damages caused by the actions of the English. The escalation continued despite the subsequent release of Hanseatic detainees in London.[97] In the autumn of 1469 the Bruges *Kontor* contracted with Danzig for the equipping of two ships as privateers for operations against the English under command of Paul Beneke and Martin Bardewik. Their first prey was the *Joen* out of Newcastle on New Year's Day 1470. Bardewik, however, was subsequently surprised and defeated by a superior English squadron off the coast of Scotland in May.[98]

Letters of marque were soon issued to other Hanseatic privateers. By the summer of 1470 sixteen to eighteen of them were said to be operating in the North Sea. These were essentially merchantmen manned with additional allocations of marines and perhaps equipped with a few cannon. They were, nevertheless, quite effective.[99] 'English shipping subsequently incurred substantial losses during the summers of 1470 and 1471,' observes English economic scholar John Fudge, 'even though Danzig and Hamburg appeared to be the only major Hanseatic towns interested in an active campaign.'[100] This initial success was due to the fact that the Wars of the Roses still raged and English warships were engaged in the blockade of Lancastrian forces under the earl of Warwick at St-Vaast-la-Hougue, Honfleur and Harfleur from June to September 1470. In fact, vessels from Danzig even helped escort Edward IV back to England from

Flushing on 11 March 1471. Hanseatic privateers also enjoyed the advantage of operating out of Flemish ports with the tacit forbearance of Charles the Bold, duke of Burgundy.[101] Danzig captain Paul Beneke showed himself to be particularly successful. At one point during the summer of 1471 he captured *Le Cygne* of Caen, which was carrying John of Salisbury, the lord mayor of London.[102]

The war, however, dragged on, because Edward IV still refused to restore Hanseatic privileges in England except to Cologne, which the Hanse had expelled in April 1471 for failing to support the struggle.[103] Thus Lübeck was finally forced to contribute to the cause by licensing four privateers of its own for the first time in February 1472 to be ready for action by May. Unfortunately, English naval forces were also reinforced at around the same time. The earl of Warwick's defeat and death at Barnet on 14 April and Edward's victory over the House of Lancaster at Tewkesbury on 4 May enabled the English court to deploy an eighteen-ship flotilla against the Hanse under John Howard by the summer. On 19 July it caught Lübeck's four ships at anchor in the Wielingen channel of the Westerschelde, still licking their wounds after being mangled by a French squadron two weeks before. All four vessels were captured or burned.[104]

It was a sobering setback, but the Hanse soldiered on. Danzig remained particularly determined to continue the *guerre de course* against English shipping. Its council gave command of the mighty caravel *Grosse Kraweel* (officially the *Peter von Danzig*) to the very proficient Paul Beneke in late 1472. After over-wintering in Hamburg, Beneke came upon two merchant galleys from Flanders flying Burgundian colours in the early spring of 1473. Chartered by the Medici, they were bound ultimately for Florence with Hans Memling's *Last Judgement*, but much of the rich cargo (mostly textiles and furs) was owned by English merchants. Moreover, the vessels had been commissioned to offload alum in England and onload consignments of English wool for Italy. Beneke trailed them to the southeastern coast of England, where he finally attacked. One galley reached the shelter of Southampton, but Beneke took the other (the one carrying Memling's altarpiece) after a fierce fight.[105] (The full story of this incident and the fascinating career of the *Grosse Kraweel* are discussed in the special section at the end of this chapter.) While strategically of little value, the encounter had great psychological impact at the time. 'Even other Hanseatic towns were shocked at Beneke's daring,' observes Fudge, who concludes that the exploit 'most certainly expedited a negotiated solution to the strife'.[106]

Even before Beneke's audacious escapade, enthusiasm for the war was waning. The priorities of both parties had shifted. Secure on his throne, Edward was free to focus the realm's maritime might against France. As for the Hanse, Danzig, Hamburg and Lübeck had grown weary of funding the *guerre de course* while other members of the alliance flouted the embargo on English goods. English royal envoys negotiated a truce with Denmark as early as May 1473 and by 14 July the king's secretary, William Hatclyff, had begun talks at Utrecht with a Hanseatic delegation led by Lübeck's *Bürgermeister*, Heinrich Castorp. The Treaty of Utrecht, signed on the last day of February 1474, essentially restored the status quo that had existed prior to the outbreak of hostilities. Hanseatic privileges in England were reinstated in return for vague promises of more even-handed treatment for English traders in Hanse markets.[107] In this case, good relations with Denmark may have been more important for England. Unimpeded access to the Sound would eventually help English and Dutch traders to challenge the German Hanse in its home waters. In the near-term Hanseatic trade resumed as profitably as ever.[108]

Decline and Demise (1494–1669)

Through the prowess of its privateers and diplomats, the Hanse had prevailed in the Anglo-Hanseatic War, but its zenith had passed. Forces were at work that would soon eclipse its mercantile dominance. The Hanse, with its loose political framework and decentralized decision-making process, was simply ill-equipped to compete in an environment of rising royal absolutism and burgeoning nation-states which could generate monolithic trade policies. Too often the various members of the alliance sought separate objectives based upon their own narrow needs. When they chose to act in concert with fellow members, they frequently did so as part of a regional block in opposition to another group within the association, i.e., Wendish towns against Prussian towns, or both against their Rhenish counterparts.[109] As a result, the contending powers of the era gradually eroded the alliance's trade network. Ivan III of Russia closed the Novgorod *Kontor* (*Peterhof*) in 1494. The Bruges *Kontor* languished until 1520, when the Hansards themselves moved it to Antwerp, where it finally withered away by 1546.[110] Queen Elizabeth I shuttered the London Steelyard on 13 January 1598 and evicted the Hanse from England altogether.[111] Only the somewhat isolated Bergen *Kontor* (*Tykebrygge*) survived until the end.[112]

More fundamentally, trading patterns shifted, rendering the Hanseatic commercial route structure, though still viable, less important. The discovery of the Americas at the end of the fifteenth century gradually engendered a transatlantic traffic which favoured the great western ports of England, France, Spain and Portugal. And the Hanse had only a minor, erratic role in expanded Mediterranean commerce.[113] Competition had grown intense everywhere. The Dutch, galvanized by strong manufacturing and a robust shipbuilding industry, began to dominate trade not only in the North Sea but in the Baltic as well. Between 1550 and 1650, Dollinger contends, 'In all the Baltic ports, with the possible exception of Lübeck, Dutch ships were more numerous than German.'[114] Part of the problem may have been a lag in maritime technology. Detlev Ellmers has noted that the Hanse seemed slow to adopt such innovations as the compass, navigation charts, multiple masts and the large-scale, skeleton-first ship architecture needed for long-range voyages. 'All of these medieval advances were introduced by the Hanseatic League on their own ships sometimes considerably after they had come into use in the rest of western Europe,' he writes.[115] Lastly, the disruption and chaos in German lands caused by the Thirty Years' War hastened the dissolution of the Hanse. The last *Hansetag* was convened in July 1669 in Lübeck. Only nine member cities attended. It disbanded without agreement on a single substantive resolution.[116]

Exemplary Engagement: The Strange Voyage of the *Saint-Pierre de La Rochelle* (1462–75)

The career of the caravel *Saint-Pierre de La Rochelle* is, in many ways, emblematic of the Hanseatic era. It is the story of a merchantman claimed as a prize then turned privateer, and it climaxes with the most daring and famous maritime exploit of the German Hanse. The tale began in 1462 in the city of its original namesake: La Rochelle. That year the caravel – actually an 800-ton carrack reputed to be over 45m (148ft) long and 12m (40ft) wide – sailed from La Rochelle with a load of salt (probably from the Bay of Bourgneuf) to Danzig in the Baltic. Unfortunately, while it was anchored in the harbour of the Prussian city its mainmast was struck by lightning. The mast was destroyed and the ship evidently suffered enough structural damage to render it unseaworthy. Danzig's shipwrights were unfamiliar with its skeleton-first, carvel-style of construction, but managed to mend the vessel in due course. In the meantime, the merchant-owner passed away without an heir, causing proprietorship to pass to the French crown. But Louis XI refused to pay the cost of the repairs (around 1,000 silver marks), so the abandoned ship languished for years in the harbour of Danzig.[117]

The carrack was still there when the Anglo-Hanseatic War broke out. Finally, in 1470 the city council of Danzig decided to convert it into a privateer for the *guerre de course* against English shipping. The vessel was overhauled to accommodate 300 men-at-arms and equipped with nineteen cannon, all placed in the fore and aft fighting castles. It was then renamed the *Peter von Danzig*, although it was often called *Das Grosse Kraweel* ('The Great Caravel') in contemporary literature. Councillor Bernt Pawest took command of the great warship the following year and patrolled the Channel as far as Camaret-sur-Mer at the end of the Crozon peninsula of Brittany. Pawest's stewardship was troubled at best, however. The vessel was apparently ponderous in bad weather and even ran aground a few times during the winter of 1471/2.[118] A mutiny finally marooned it in the Zwyn in a state of disrepair, prompting this acerbic assessment from John Fudge: 'Despite all its impressive physical credentials, the *Grosse Kraweel* spent a good part of its early military career immobilized in the Zwin estuary, more a curiosity to visitors than a threat to English shipping.'[119]

That all changed the following year with new ownership and better leadership. Over the winter of 1472/3 Danzig councilmen Johann Sidinghusen, Tydeman Valand and Heinrich Nederhoff purchased the carrack and gave command of it to the very competent Paul Beneke. It would turn out to be a highly propitious and profitable investment.[120] In April 1473 Beneke departed the vicinity of Hamburg, where he had over-wintered, and went hunting. He found, setting out from Flanders, two merchant galleys flying Burgundian colours. Somehow Beneke was able to ascertain that these ships were bound for the Mediterranean by way of England with a rich load of mostly English merchandise – 'furs, gold brocades, tapestries, crimson velvets and satins', according to Hanse scholar Philippe Dollinger.[121] Also onboard was Hans Memling's altarpiece *The Last Judgement*, commissioned for a Florentine church by Agnolo Tani, an agent of the Medici in Bruges. The galleys themselves, chartered by another Medici agent named Tomaso Portinari, also contained a shipment of alum (a fixative for dyeing wool) bound for England, where a consignment of wool was supposed to be onloaded.[122]

Beneke followed the galleys to the southeast English coast despite being warned by Duke Charles of Burgundy that they were off-limits. Then, according to the contemporary chronicle of a Danzig ship-owner named Caspar Weinreich, 'On the second Tuesday after Easter, Paul Beneke in the "Great Caravel" took a galley with a mast twenty-three fathoms [about 138ft] tall and a double forecastle.'[123] This was the galley bearing Memling's masterful triptych. The other galley managed to reach the safety of Southampton. No details of the engagement survive other than the fact that it was hard-fought. Boasting a 'double forecastle', the Burgundian vessel must have been quite large, but it is difficult to conceive how a galley, even one of great size, could have prevailed against a well armed carrack. At any rate, the booty captured was said to have been valued at 60,000 *groschen*, a huge sum at the time.[124] The event caused quite a stir from Danzig to London. In the aftermath Lübeck and Hamburg shunned the *Grosse Kraweel* for fear of further alienating the duke of Burgundy, who briefly detained members of the Hanseatic community in Flanders. The episode, nevertheless, had its desired impact. It would be the last significant engagement of the war.[125] Negotiations for the Treaty of Utrecht, which ended up favouring the Hanse, began that summer. The *Peter von Danzig* ended its existence in 1475 as a shipwreck off the coast of Brittany, not too far from La Rochelle, where the vessel had begun its strange voyage thirteen years before. As for the *Last Judgement* – after having graced St Mary's church in Danzig for centuries, it is currently on display in the Polish National Museum of Gdańsk (Danzig).[126] **(Pl. 35)**

Conclusion
Transition to the Modern Era

In the months preceding the final fall of Constantinople in 1453, the great Ottoman sultan Mehmed (II), the Conqueror, caused to be constructed in less than twenty weeks on the European bank of the Bosporus just north of the city a colossal castle which he called *Baš-kesen*, meaning 'Decapitator' or 'Throat-cutter'. Later called the *Rumeli Hisar* ('Castle of the Roman Lands'), it stood opposite the *Anadolu Hisar* ('Castle of Anatolia'), built in 1394 by his great-grandfather Sultan Bayezit I at the narrowest part of the strait (less than 1km across). It consisted of three main towers and fourteen smaller ones connected by inner and outer curtain walls, covering an area of 31,250 sq. m (almost 7.75 acres). The fortress still stands to this day, glowering down upon passing maritime traffic much as it did when it was completed on 31 August 1452. **(Pl. 36)** The main tower in the middle was 22m (72ft) high and 23.3m (76ft 5in) in diameter, with 6.5m (21ft 4in) thick walls. Named the Halil Pasha after the sultan's vizier who built it, it stood closest to the shoreline.[1] On it, Mehmed had positioned what were described as 'bronze tubes capable of discharging balls weighing over six hundred pounds'.[2] He then gave the citadel's commander, one Firuz Aga, the following explicit instructions:

> Do not allow ships sailing from the Hellespont [Dardanelles] to the Black Sea or from the Black Sea to the Hellespont, no matter under whose flag they may be sailing – Genoese, Venetian, Constantinopolitan, Kaffatinian, Trapezundian, Amisinian, Sinopean, or even under my own flag, and no matter what class they are – triremes, biremes, barques, or skiffs – to sail through without first lowering their sails and paying the customs duties; only after they have done so will you permit them to proceed on their way. Use the cannon to sink the ship that does not comply and submit.[3]

Early the following November two Venetian ships destined for the Dardanelles ignored the injunction and passed through the Bosporus without stopping as ordered. Luckily, they survived the consequent cannonade. A third, carrying grain for Constantinople a short time later, was not so fortunate. The earlier experience had evidently served to provide Firuz Aga's gunners with the proper range. A single stone from one of the cannon 'shattered the ship'. The crew of thirty, including the captain, a certain Antonio Rizzo, were subsequently captured and taken to the sultan in Didymoteichos (in Thrace, about 37km or 23 miles south of Adrianople – modern Edirne). 'He gave orders to behead them all except the captain whose life was to be taken by a stake through the anus,' recorded a fifteenth-century chronicler known only as 'Doukas', who claimed he himself saw Rizzo's rotting corpse only 'a few days later'.[4] The impact on maritime warfare was just as dramatic. The advent of a true ship-killing weapon spelled the end of one age and the beginning of another.

In his watershed study *Gunpowder and Galleys*, early modern military historian John Francis Guilmartin concluded that the one technological innovation most responsible for ushering in a new age of warfare was 'the use of effective heavy cannon'.[5] It was, therefore, fitting that Mehmed II employed perhaps the largest cannon ever built up to that point to vanquish the first great naval power of the passing medieval period. In his campaign to conquer Constantinople, the Ottoman sultan engaged a Hungarian engineer named Orban to produce a sort of supergun which could smash the several-feet thick Theodosian Walls that had protected the capital of the Eastern Roman Empire for a millennium. 'In three months' time a terrifying and extraordinary monster was forged,' testified Doukas.[6] Mehmed's Greek biographer, Michael Kritovoulos, provided precise dimensions: the barrel was cast in bronze some 20cm (8in) thick; it measured about 8m (26ft 8in) long, with a bore at the muzzle of 76cm (30in) in diameter.[7] **(Pl. 37)** In a test, the cannon discharged a 544kg (1,200-pound) stone ball which burrowed itself almost 2m (6ft) into the ground over 1.6km (1 mile) away.[8] Doukas said that thirty wagons pulled by sixty oxen and 200 men were required to haul it from Adrianople to Constantinople where it was positioned to batter the walls south of the Blachernae Palace.[9]

Not content with this ostentatious display of military power, Mehmed then brought to bear the full force of his powerful new fleet. The Byzantines had barred the entrance to the Golden Horn with a giant iron chain suspended on wooden pontoons between two fortified towers, one on each side.[10] (This chain currently resides in the Turkish Naval Museum of Istanbul.) A squadron of ten Greek warships was stationed outside it, while another sixteen from Genoa, Venice and other western maritime cities guarded it from inside. Previous Ottoman assaults on this defensive cordon had failed, so the sultan circumvented it by building a road of greased wooden logs across Galata Hill behind the Genoese colony of Pera on the side of the Golden Horn opposite the city. He then, on 22 April, had seventy to eighty 'biremes on wheeled cradles' hauled over said byway and into the harbour behind the chain.[11] The manoeuvre demoralized the defenders and enabled Mehmed's naval forces to attack the city's sea walls from the Golden Horn at the same time that his army assaulted the land walls. **(Pl. 38)** Inevitably, Constantinople fell on 29 May 1453. Vanquished were the last vestiges of Byzantine imperial power and its maritime thalassocracy remained only as a distant memory.[12]

A great new power had risen in the East and it would soon use its newfound naval prowess to sweep all before it. Not even the Venetians would withstand it. One by one, the Ottomans would claim the naval bases upon which the Venetian fleets depended for refit and replenishment. The loss of Modon and Coron is particularly instructive. The eviction of the Venetians from 'the two eyes of the Republic' was preceded by the Battle of Zonchio near Lepanto in August 1499, which featured, probably for the first time, shipboard cannon with ship-killing capability.[13] In the initial stages of the engagement, which included nearly 400 vessels large and small, three Venetian ships (a carrack, a large galley and a barge) surrounded the Ottoman carrack of Burak Re'is, a *ghazi* captain employed by the Turks. The carrack of Burak Re'is, however, had below deck on each side 'two port holes in which immense guns were placed', according to the contemporary Turkish chronicler Haji Khalifeh (Katib Chelebi in some sources).[14] **(Pl. 39)** Guilmartin estimates these were capable of firing 200-pound balls. In any event, they were big enough to sink the Venetian galley and the barge outright. The cannon played only a minor role for the rest of the encounter, which the Turks won, but war at sea would never be the same again.[15] Heavy cannon mounted below deck on large sailing vessels had proven their efficacy in battle.

The introduction of heavy shipboard cannon was merely the most spectacular innovation amongst a whole host of technological advancements which marked the beginning of a new era in nautical navigation and naval warfare. Ships no longer needed to hug shorelines, cruise during daylight hours only and hazard voyages exclusively in the summer sailing season. Portolan charts and boxed compasses, first used in the early thirteenth century, had become more commonplace, allowing for navigation at night and during the winter months beyond sight of land. Oared propulsion was increasingly giving way to sails. Rigging had become more complex, making use of combinations of lateen and square sails unfurled from multiple masts. As a result, ships were able to sail closer to the wind, decreasing en route times. Shell-first ship architecture had been phased out in favour of skeleton-first, carvel-style construction, enabling the development of larger, more seaworthy vessels. Accordingly, the trireme galley of the late thirteenth and early fourteenth centuries evolved into the 'great galley' of the late fourteenth and early fifteenth centuries. Square-rigged caravels and carracks with high, broad hulls came into common usage.

The emergence of new, centrally administered nation-states like the Ottoman Empire enabled the concept of a standing navy to gain greater acceptance. Such large, powerful polities had the capability of producing purpose-built warships, increasingly differentiated from commercial vessels. Naval architecture was being altered to accommodate such sophisticated weaponry as heavy cannon, mounted below deck for stability, which could fire from specially designed, lidded gunports in the hull with ship-killing capability. **(Pl. 40)** These martial modifications naturally led to changes in battle tactics. Commanders were compelled to take into account such factors as wind and current in manoeuvring their vessels to deadly advantage. Ships were no longer simply platforms for extending land-based combat onto the sea. Engagements, heretofore restricted to bays, inlets, harbours and river estuaries, could now take place in open water. The struggle for superiority at sea was still being fought at times in the same old way – with galleys, crossbows and grappling hooks – particularly in the Mediterranean, but increasingly the upper hand went to the bigger, better-armed sailing vessels, capable of tactical manoeuvre in tune with the elements. The medieval way of waging war at sea was waning; maritime warfare in the modern era had begun.

Beyond technological and organizational transformation, the conquest of Constantinople by the Ottoman Turks underscored a more fundamental transition. The medieval world had long been oriented to the East – towards Byzantium and the Crusader states. Western Europe had fed off the rich markets of the eastern Mediterranean. By the end of the fifteenth century the Latin Kingdom of Jerusalem was a concept of the past, the crusading movement was finished and Byzantium's allure had vanished with the vanquishment of its capital. In any case, western Europe's economy no longer depended on the East. Its new urban markets were flourishing and its orientation was starting to shift westwards towards the Atlantic and beyond to the newly discovered Americas. And that meant seagoing sailing ships with lethal firepower would soon rule the waves.

Notes

Introduction: The Nature of Medieval Maritime Warfare

1. A. Lewis and T. Runyan, *European Naval Maritime History, 300–1500* (Bloomington, 1985), 1–2; W. Rodgers, *Greek and Roman Naval Warfare* (Annapolis, 1937), 538.
2. M. Pitassi, *The Navies of Rome* (Woodbridge, 2009), 156–9.
3. D. Abulafia, *The Great Sea, A Human History of the Mediterranean* (London, 2011), 208–9.
4. Vegetius, *Epitome of Military Science*, trans. N. Miller (Liverpool, 1993), bk IV, ch 31, 132. See also Lewis and Runyan, *European Naval Maritime History*, 2.
5. L. Paine, *The Sea and Civilization: A Maritime History of the World* (New York, 2013), 203; Pitassi, *Navies of Rome*, 197; Rodgers, *Naval Warfare under Oars, 4th to 16th Centuries* (Annapolis, 1940), 3–6.
6. Abulafia, *Great Sea*, 226–33.
7. Lewis and Runyan, *European Naval Maritime History*, 10–11; Paine, *Sea and Civilization*, 204; Pitassi, *Navies of Rome*, 309; Rodgers, *Naval Warfare under Oars*, 6–7.
8. J. Haywood, *Dark Age Naval Power* (Norfolk, 1999), 67–70.
9. Ibid., 77–81.
10. Lewis, *Naval Power and Trade in the Mediterranean, A.D. 500–1100* (Princeton, 1951), 10–17.
11. Lewis and Runyan, *European Naval Maritime History*, 86–7.
12. S. Rose, *Medieval Naval Warfare, 1000–1500* (London, 2002), 1.
13. F. Hocker, 'Late Roman, Byzantine, and Islamic Galleys and Fleets', in *Age of the Galley, Mediterranean Oared Vessels since Pre-Classical Times*, eds R. Gardiner and J. Morrison (London, 1995), 86–100, esp. 94–7.
14. Vegetius, *Epitome of Military Science*, bk IV, ch 33, 133.
15. J. Morrison, *Greek and Roman Oared Warships 399–30 B.C.* (Oxford, 1996), 316–17.
16. Hocker, 'Late Roman, Byzantine, and Islamic Galleys', 94–5; J. Pryor and E. Jeffreys, *The Age of ΔΡΟΜΩΝ (Dromōn), The Byzantine Navy ca 500–1204* (Leiden, 2006), 123–8.
17. Haywood, *Dark Age Naval Power*, 70–6; O. Höckmann, 'Late Roman Rhine vessels from Mainz, Germany', *International Journal of Nautical Archaeology – IJNA*, 22 (May 1993), 125–35.
18. Haywood, *Dark Age Naval Power*, 93–100.
19. Vegetius, *Epitome of Military Science*, bk IV, chs 38–41, 136–40.
20. J. Guilmartin, *Gunpowder & Galleys* (Cambridge, 2003), 77.
21. L. Casson, *Ships and Seamanship in the Ancient World* (Baltimore, 1995), 296.
22. Pryor and Jeffreys, *Dromōn*, 388–9.
23. A. Mahan, *The Influence of Sea Power upon History, 1660–1783* (London, 1890), 219.
24. Guilmartin, *Gunpowder & Galleys*, 31–55.
25. J. Coates, J. Morrison, and N. Rankov, *The Athenian Trireme* (Cambridge, 2000), 238.
26. Pryor and Jeffreys, *Dromōn*, 357.
27. Guilmartin, *Gunpowder and Galleys*, note 26 on 54 and 115.
28. C. Stanton, *Norman Naval Operations in the Mediterranean* (Woodbridge, 2011), 5.
29. Marino Sanudo Torsello, *The Book of the Secrets of the Faithful of the Cross*, trans. P. Lock (Surrey, 2011), bk 2, ch 10, 108–9.
30. Pryor, 'A view from a masthead: the First Crusade from the Sea', *Crusades*, VII (2008), 87–152, esp. 104.
31. Pryor, 'Byzantium and the Sea: Byzantine Fleets and the History of the Empire in the Age of the Macedonian Emperors, c.900–1025 CE', in *War at Sea in the Middle Ages and the Renaissance*, eds Hattendorf and Unger (Woodbridge, 2003), 83–104, esp. 99.

32. Pryor and Jeffreys, *Dromōn*, 143–7.
33. Julius Caesar, *The Gallic War*, trans. H. Edwards (Cambridge, Mass., 1917), bk III, 157.
34. Pryor and Jeffreys, *Dromōn*, 143–4.
35. Ibid., App 6, 607–31.
36. Liudprand of Cremona, *Antapodosis*, in *The Works of Liudprand of Cremona*, trans. F. Wright (London, 1930), bk V, ch 15, 186. See also Pryor and Jeffreys, *Dromōn*, 383–5.
37. Stanton, *Norman Naval Operations*, App. A, 230–1.
38. M. Bennett, J. Bradbury, K. Devries, I. Dickie and P. Jestice, *Fighting Techniques of the Medieval World, AD 500–AD 1500* (New York, 2005), 212–13; Rose, *Medieval Naval Warfare*, 43, 71–3; Pryor, *Geography, technology, and war: Studies in the maritime history of the Mediterranean 649–1571* (Cambridge, 1988), 39.
39. Leo VI, *The Taktika of Leo VI*, trans. G. Dennis (Washington DC, 2010), Constitution 19, par 60, 527.
40. Stanton, *Norman Naval Operations*, App A, 231.
41. Vegetius, *Epitome of Military Science*, bk IV, chs 38–46, 132–42.
42. Leo VI, *Taktika*, Constitution 19, par 36, 517.
43. Syrianos Magistros, *Naval Battles of Syrianos Magistros*, trans. Jeffreys, *Dromōn*, App. 1, par 3, 460–1.
44. Rose, *Medieval Naval Warfare*, 46–7.
45. Leo VI, *Taktika*, Constitution 19, par 36, 523.
46. Bennett et al., *Fighting Techniques of the Medieval World*, 226.
47. Pryor and Jeffreys, *Dromōn*, 391.
48. H. Turtledove, 'Introduction', *The Chronicle of Theophanes* (Philadelphia, 1982), viii–ix.
49. Theophanes the Confessor, *The Chronicle of Theophanes Confessor*, trans. C. Mango and R. Scott (New York, 1997), *anno* 6209, 546.
50. William of Apulia, *La Geste de Robert Guiscard*, trans. M. Mathieu (Palermo, 1961), bk V, vv 156–9, 244–5.
51. Stanton, *Norman Naval Operations*, App. A, 231, fig. 8.
52. Matthew Paris, *Historia Anglorum*, ed. F. Madden (3 vols, Roll Series 44, London, 1866), II, 219–20.
53. Rose, *Medieval Naval Warfare*, 30.
54. Pryor and Jeffreys, *Dromōn*, 139–42.
55. Ibid., 424–6.
56. G. Bass and F. Van Doorninck, *Yassi Ada: A Seventh-Century Byzantine Shipwreck* (College Station, 1982), 69, 84–6.
57. Bass, S. Matthews, J. Steffy and Van Doorninck, *Serçe Limani: An Eleventh-Century Byzantine Shipwreck* (College Station, 2004), 153–87.
58. Hocker, 'A 15th-Century Cog in the Zuiderzee: Almere, Netherlands', in *Beneath the Seven Seas*, ed. Bass (New York, 2005), 134–5; G. Hutchinson, *Medieval Ships and Shipping* (London, 1994), 15–20.
59. J. Bill, 'Ships and Seamanship', in *The Oxford Illustrated History of the Vikings*, ed. P. Sawyer (Oxford, 1997), 182–201, esp. 188–93.
60. U. Kocabaş, ed., *The 'Old Ships' of the 'New Gate', Yenikapi Shipwrecks, Vol. I* (Istanbul, 2008), 176–83.
61. B. Bachrach, 'On the Origins of William the Conqueror's Horse Transports', *Technology and Culture*, XXVI (1985), 505–31, esp. 506–10.
62. Pryor and Jeffreys, *Dromōn*, 429–31.
63. J. Huillard-Bréholles, ed., *Historia Diplomatica Friderici Secundi* (6 vols, Paris, 1852–61), V, Pt 1, 577–83.
64. C. Riccio, *De' grandi officiali del regno de Sicilia* (Naples, 1872), 17–19.
65. L. Mott, *Sea Power in the Medieval Mediterranean* (Gainesville, 2003), 64–9, 77–81.
66. Michael of Rhodes, *The Book of Michael of Rhodes: A Fifteenth-Century Maritime Manuscript*, eds D. McGee, P. Long and A. Stahl (3 vols, Cambridge, Mass., 2009), I, vii.

67. Coates, Morrison, and Rankov, *Athenian Trireme*, 231–75; Rankov, 'The Trireme', in *Sailing into the Past: Learning from Replica Ships*, ed. J. Bennett (Barnsley, 2009), 34–51, esp. 44–50.
68. Bill, 'Ships and Seamanship', 188–96; R. Johansen, 'The Viking Ships of Skuldelev', in *Sailing into the Past*, 52–69, esp. 62–9.
69. W. Hoheisel, 'The Hanseatic Cog', in *Sailing into the Past*, 68–83, esp. 78–80; Hutchinson, *Medieval Ships*, 59–60.
70. Haywood, *Dark Age Naval Power*, 101–3.

Part 1. Southern Europe (The Mediterranean and the Black Sea)

1. Pryor, *Geography, technology, and war*, 12.
2. F. Fernandez-Armesto, 'Naval Warfare after the Viking Age, c.1100–1500', in *Medieval Warfare*, ed. M. Keen (Oxford, 1999), 230–52, esp. 231; Pryor, *Geography, technology, and war*, 12.
3. Pryor, *Geography, technology, and war*, 21 and 24.
4. L. Casson, *Ships and Seamanship in the Ancient World* (Princeton, 1995), 201–13; Morrison, *Greek and Roman Oared Warships*, 327–9.
5. Casson and Steffy, eds, *The Athlit Ram* (College Station, 1991), 38.
6. Morrison, *Greek and Roman Oared Warships*, 316–17, 330.
7. Pryor and Jeffreys, *Dromōn*, 127–8.
8. Pryor, 'From Dromōn to Galea: Mediterranean bireme galleys AD 500–1300', in *Age of the Galley*, 101–16, esp. 103–5.
9. Pryor and Jeffreys, *Dromōn*, 143–4.
10. Leo VI, *The Taktika of Leo VI*, trans. G. Dennis (Washington DC, 2010), Constitution 19, par. 8, 505–7; Nikephoros Ouranos, *On fighting at sea*, trans. Jeffreys, *Dromōn*, App 5, par 7, 574–7.
11. Hocker, 'Late Roman, Byzantine, and Islamic Galleys', 86–100, esp. 96.
12. Pryor and Jeffreys, *Dromōn*, 167.
13. Thietmar of Merseburg, *Ottonian Germany: The Chronicon of Thietmar of Merseburg*, trans. D. Warner (Manchester, 2001), bk 3, ch 23, 145–6.
14. Hocker, 'Late Roman, Byzantine, and Islamic Galleys and Fleets', 94.
15. Pryor and Jeffreys, *Dromōn*, 191–2.
16. Hocker, 'Late Roman, Byzantine, and Islamic Galleys', 95; Pryor, 'From Dromōn to Galea', 105.
17. Pryor, 'From Dromōn to Galea', 107.
18. Hocker, 'Late Roman, Byzantine, and Islamic Galleys', 95.
19. D. Haldane, 'The Fire-ship of al-Sālih Ayyūb and Muslim use of "Greek Fire"', in *The Circle of War in the Middle Ages*, eds D. Kagay and L. Villalon (Woodbridge, 1999), 137–44, esp. 138–42; Pryor and Jeffreys, *Dromōn*, App 6, 609–12; Pryor, 'From Dromōn to Galea', 107–9.
20. Pryor and Jeffreys, *Dromōn*, 423–31.
21. Procopius, *History of the Wars*, trans. H. Dewing (4 vols, London, 1916), II, bk III, ch 11, 104–5.
22. Ibid., II, bk III, chs 10-1, 99–107.
23. Ibid., II, bk III, ch 16, 130–1.
24. Rodgers, *Naval Warfare under Oars*, 12–14; W. Treadgold, *A History of the Byzantine State and Society* (Stanford, 1997), 184–5.
25. Procopius, *History of the Wars*, II, bk IV, ch 5, 247–9.
26. Ibid., III, bk V, ch 5, 43–9.
27. Pryor and Jeffreys, *Dromōn*, 15–18.
28. Procopius, *History of the Wars*, V, bk VIII, ch 23, 296–303.
29. Ibid., V, bk VIII, chs 29–32, 353–85.
30. Lewis, *Naval Power and Trade*, 24–5.

Chapter 1. The Byzantine–Muslim Struggle for Supremacy on the Middle Sea

1. Lewis and Runyan, *European Naval and Maritime History*, 19–24.
2. Hocker, 'Late Roman, Byzantine, and Islamic Galleys', 91; Lewis, *Naval Power and Trade*, 26–30.
3. Lewis and Runyan, *European Naval and Maritime History*, 19–22.

4. Treadgold, *History of the Byzantine State*, 227–36.
5. Nikephoros, Patriarch of Constantinople, *Short History (Breviarium)*, trans. C. Mango (Washington DC, 1990), ch 6, 44–5. See also Treadgold, *History of the Byzantine State*, 287–93.
6. Theophanes, *Chronicle*, *anno* 6117, 446–7.
7. Nikephoros, *Short History*, chs 12–15, 54–63. See also Hocker, 'Late Roman, Byzantine, and Islamic Galleys', 91; Lewis, *Naval Power and Trade*, 51; Treadgold, *History of the Byzantine State*, 294–9.
8. Lewis, *Naval Power and Trade*, 49.
9. Theophanes, *Chronicle*, *anno* 6121, 460–2.
10. Abulafia, *Great Sea*, 244–5; Lewis, *Naval Power and Trade*, 52–3.
11. Theophanes, *Chronicle*, *anno* 6121, 470.
12. Treadgold, *History of the Byzantine State*, 301–3.
13. Ibid., 304–6.
14. Ibid., 311–12.
15. A. Fahmy, *Muslim Sea-Power in the Eastern Mediterranean from the Seventh to the Tenth Century A.D.* (London, 1950), 35–42; Pryor and Jeffreys, *Dromōn*, 24–5.
16. Fahmy, *Muslim Sea-Power*, 23.
17. Pryor, 'From Dromōn to Galea', 106–7.
18. Hocker, 'Late Roman, Byzantine, and Islamic Galleys', 91.
19. Muhammad ibn Mankali, *Al-ahkam al mulukiyya wa'l dawabit al-namusiyya*, trans. A. Shboul, in App. 8, Pryor and Jeffreys, *Dromōn*, 645–66, esp. 656–66; Pryor, 'From Dromōn to Galea', 106.
20. Hocker, 'Late Roman, Byzantine, and Islamic Galleys', 95.
21. Fahmy, *Muslim Sea-Power*, 138–40; Hocker, 'Late Roman, Byzantine, and Islamic Galleys', 97–8.
22. Fahmy, *Muslim Sea-Power*, 51–2.
23. Al-Baladhuri, *The Origins of the Islamic State*, trans. P. Hitti (New York, 1916), 235–6; Theophanes, *Chronicle*, *anno* 6140, 478. See also Pryor and Jeffreys, *Dromōn*, 25.
24. Al-Baladhuri, *Origins of the Islamic State*, 375–6; Theophanes, *Chronicle*, *anno* 6145, 481. See also M. Amari, *Storia dei Musulmani di Sicilia*, ed. C. Nallino (3 vols, Catania, 1935–9), I, 195–6.
25. Al-Baladhuri, *Origins of the Islamic State*, 236.
26. Pryor and Jeffreys, *Dromōn*, 25; Rodgers, *Naval Warfare under Oars*, 35.
27. Theophanes, *Chronicle*, *anno* 6146, 482.
28. Lewis, *Naval Power and Trade*, 57.
29. P. Hitti, *History of the Arabs* (New York, 2002), 200 and note 6; Pryor and Jeffreys, *Dromōn*, 25.
30. Theophanes, *Chronicle*, *anno* 6146, 482.
31. Theophanes, *Chronicle*, *anno* 6150, 484. See also Treadgold, *History of the Byzantine State*, 315.
32. Treadgold, *History of the Byzantine State*, 315.
33. Ibid., 316.
34. Hocker, 'Late Roman, Byzantine, and Islamic Galleys', 97–8; Pryor and Jeffreys, *Dromōn*, 268–75.
35. Lewis, *Naval Power and Trade*, 60–1; Treadgold, *History of the Byzantine State*, 318–22.
36. Theophanes, *Chronicle*, *anno* 6164, 493. See also Lewis, *Naval Power and Trade*, 60–1; Pryor and Jeffreys, *Dromōn*, 26–7; Treadgold, *History of the Byzantine State*, 325.
37. Nikephoros, *Short History*, ch 34, 84–5; Theophanes, *Chronicle*, *anno* 6165, 493–4.
38. Theophanes, *Chronicle*, *anno* 6165, 494. See also Pryor and Jeffreys, *Dromōn*, App. 6, 608, 617.
39. J. Haldon, 'Greek fire revisited: recent and current research', in *Byzantine Style and Civilization*, ed. Jeffreys (Cambridge, 2006), 290–325, esp. 297–315; Pryor and Jeffreys, *Dromōn*, App. 6, 607–31.
40. Pryor and Jeffreys, *Dromōn*, App. 6, 624.
41. Theophanes, *Chronicle*, *anno* 6165, 494.
42. Pryor and Jeffreys, *Dromōn*, App. 6, 617.
43. Nikephoros, *Short History*, ch 34, 86–7; Theophanes, *Chronicle*, *anno* 6165, 494. See also Treadgold, *History of the Byzantine State*, 326–7.
44. Nikephoros, *Short History*, ch 34, 86–7; Theophanes, *Chronicle*, *anno* 6169, 496.
45. Theophanes, *Chronicle*, *anno* 6178, 506.

46. Treadgold, *Byzantium and its Army, 284–1081* (Stanford, 1995), 26; *History of the Byzantine State*, 332.
47. Pryor and Jeffreys, *Dromōn*, 31.
48. Al-Baladhuri, *Origins of the Islamic State*, 360. See also Lewis, *Naval Power and Trade*, 63–4.
49. Theophanes, *Chronicle*, *anno* 6187, 514–15.
50. Al-Baladhuri, *Origins of the Islamic State*, 360; Nikephoros, *Short History*, ch 41, 98–101; Theophanes, *Chronicle*, *anno* 6190, 516.
51. Nikephoros, *Short History*, ch 41, 98–101; Theophanes, *Chronicle*, *anno* 6190, 517. See also Treadgold, *History of the Byzantine State*, 337–8.
52. Lewis, *Naval Power and Trade*, 64–5; Pryor and Jeffreys, *Dromōn*, 28.
53. Nikephoros, *Short History*, chs 42–5, 100–13; Theophanes, *Chronicle*, *anni* 6197–203, 522–9. See also Treadgold, *History of the Byzantine State*, 340–2.
54. Paine, *Sea and Civilization*, 207; Pryor and Jeffreys, *Dromōn*, 29.
55. Nikephoros, *Short History*, chs 48–51, 114–19; Theophanes, *Chronicle*, *anni* 6205–7, 533–6. See also Pryor and Jeffreys, *Dromōn*, 31.
56. Nikephoros, *Short History*, ch 52, 121–2; Theophanes, *Chronicle*, *anni* 6208–9, 538–45. See also Rodgers, *Naval Warfare under Oars*, 37; Treadgold, *History of the Byzantine State*, 346.
57. Nikephoros, *Short History*, chs 54–6, 122–7; Theophanes, *Chronicle*, *anni mundi* 6209–10, 545–50. See also Lewis, *Naval Power and Trade*, 66–7; Pryor and Jeffreys, *Dromōn*, 31–2; Rodgers, *Naval Warfare under Oars*, 38–9; Treadgold, *History of the Byzantine State*, 347–8.
58. Nikephoros, *Short History*, ch 60, 128–31; Theophanes, *Chronicle*, *anno* 6218, 559–60. See also Lewis, *Naval Power and Trade*, 67; Pryor and Jeffreys, *Dromōn*, 32; Treadgold, *History of the Byzantine State*, 352.
59. H. Ahrweiler, *Byzance et la mer: la marine de guerre* (Paris, 1966), 81–5; Pryor and Jeffreys, *Dromōn*, 32; Treadgold, *History of the Byzantine State*, 352.
60. Ahrweiller, *Byzance et la mer*, 83–5.
61. Lewis, *Naval Power and Trade*, 68–9.
62. Ibid., 71–3.
63. Nikephoros, *Short History*, ch 68, 140–1.
64. Theophanes, *Chronicle*, *anno* 6238, 586. See also Pryor and Jeffreys, *Dromōn*, 33.
65. Hitti, *History of the Arabs*, 285–9.
66. Hitti, *History of the Arabs*, 505–7; Pryor and Jeffreys, *Dromōn*, 34.
67. J. Abun-Nasr, *A History of the Maghrib in the Islamic Period* (Cambridge, 1987), 53–4.
68. Lewis, *Naval Power and Trade*, 99.
69. Pryor and Jeffreys, *Dromōn*, 388–9.
70. Ibn al-Athir, *Annales du Maghreb et de l'Espagne, 22–603 de l'Hegire/642–1207 ap. J.-C.*, trans. E. Fagnan (Algiers, 2007), ch 28, 78. See also Lewis, *Naval Power and Trade*, 99.
71. Lewis and Runyan, *European Naval and Maritime History*, 29.
72. H. Pirenne, *Mohammed and Charlemagne*, trans. B. Miall (New York, 1992), 224–35.
73. Theophanes, *Chronicle*, *anno* 6282, 639. See also Pryor and Jeffreys, *Dromōn*, 41.
74. Theophanes, *Chronicle*, *anno* 6298, 661–2. See also Treadgold, *History of the Byzantine State*, 427.
75. Theophanes, *Chronicle*, *anno* 6301, 665–6.
76. Treadgold, *History of the Byzantine State*, 427–9.
77. Theophanes, *Chronicle*, *anno* 6303, 673–4.
78. Treadgold, *History of the Byzantine State*, 431–2.
79. Ibid., 432–4.
80. John Skylitzes, *Synopsis of Byzantine History*, trans. J. Wortley (Cambridge, 2010), 'Michael II', ch 10, 40.
81. John Skylitzes, *Synopsis*, 'Michael II', chs 5–13, 32–43. See also Treadgold, *History of the Byzantine State*, 433–5.
82. Theophanes, *Chronicle*, *anno* 6300, 663.
83. Constantine VII Porphyrogenitus, *De Administrando Imperio*, ed. G. Moravcsik, trans. R. Jenkins (2nd edn, Washington DC, 1967), ch 49, 228–9.

84. *Annales Cavenses*, ed. G. Pertz (Monumenta Germaniae Historica – MGH, SS, III, Hanover, 1839), *anno* 819, 188; Ibn al-Athir, *Biblioteca Arabo-Sicula (BAS)*, ed. Amari (2 vols, Turin, 1880–1), I, 364. See also A. Ahmad, *A History of Islamic Sicily* (Edinburgh, 1975), 5; Stanton, *Norman Naval Operations*, 9–10.
85. Lewis, *Naval Power and Trade*, 107–8.
86. Constantine VII Porphyrogenitus, *De Administrando Imperio*, ch 49, 94–7; John Skylitzes, *Synopsis*, 'Michael II', ch 16, 44–7. See also V. Christides, *The Conquest of Crete by the Arabs (ca.824)* (Athens, 1984), 81–5; Lewis, *Naval Power and Trade*, 104, 108; D. Tsounkarakes, *Byzantine Crete from the 5th century to the Venetian Conquest* (Athens, 1988), 30–4.
87. John Skylitzes, *Synopsis*, 'Michael II', chs 16–19, 44–8. See also Pryor and Jeffreys, *Dromōn*, 46.
88. John Skylitzes, *Synopsis*, 'Michael III', ch 18, 108. See also Pryor and Jeffreys, *Dromōn*, 46–7.
89. Ahrweiller, *Byzance et la mer*, 76–9; Pryor and Jeffreys, *Dromōn*, 47.
90. Ahrweiller, *Byzance et la mer*, 79–81; Pryor and Jeffreys, *Dromōn*, 47.
91. Ahrweiller, *Byzance et la mer*, 73–4.
92. Ahrweiller, *Byzance et la mer*, 430–3; Paine, *Sea and Civilization*, 215.
93. Constantine VII Porphyrogenitus, *De Cerimoniis Aulae Byzantinae*, Chapters 44 and 45 of Book II, trans. Haldon in 'Theory and Practice in Tenth-Century Military Administration', *Travaux et Memoires*, XIII (2000), 201–352, esp. 203–33; Jeffreys, *Dromōn*, App. 4, 547–70.
94. Treadgold, *Byzantium and its Army*, Table 2, 67.
95. Ibn al-Athir, *BAS*, I, 364–5; John Skylitzes, *Synopsis*, 'Michael II', ch 20, 48–9. See also Stanton, *Norman Naval Operations*, 10.
96. Ibn Idhari (Al-Bayan), *BAS*, II, 5; Ibn al-Athir, *BAS*, I, 365–7. See also L. Chiarelli, *A History of Muslim Sicily* (Malta, 2011), 23–9.
97. Ibn al-Athir, *BAS*, I, 367–8; John the Deacon, *Gesta Episcoporum Neapolitanorum*, ed. G. Waitz (MGH, SRLI, VI–IX, Hanover, 1878), ch 54, 29–30; Al-Nuwayri, *BAS*, II, 117–19. See also Pryor and Jeffreys, *Dromōn*, 48; Stanton, *Norman Naval Operations*, 10; Treadgold, *History of the Byzantine State*, 436.
98. *Cambridge Chronicle*, *BAS*, I, 278; Ibn al-Athir, *BAS*, I, 368–9.
99. Ibn al-Athir, *BAS*, I, 374.
100. John Skylitzes, *Synopsis*, 'Michael II', ch 21, 50.
101. Ibn Idhari, *BAS*, II, 12.
102. *Cambridge Chronicle*, *BAS*, I, 278; Ibn al-Athir, *BAS*, I, 388, 396; Ibn Khaldun, *BAS*, II, 183–4.
103. Ibn al-Athir, *BAS*, I, 393–4; Al-Nuwayri, *BAS*, II, 151–2; John Skylitzes, *Synopsis*, 'Leo VI', ch 21, 65.
104. *Chronicon Salernitanum*, ed. U. Westerbergh (Stockholm, 1956), ch 81, 79. See also G. Musca, *L'Emirato di Bari, 847–871* (Bari, 1964), 17–18.
105. Al-Baladhuri, *BAS*, I, 269–70.
106. Erchempert, *Historia Langobardorum*, ed. Waitz (MGH, SRLI, VI–IX, Hanover, 1878), ch 20, 242.
107. John the Deacon, *Gesta*, ch 60, 432–3; *Liber Pontificalis*, ed. L. Duchesne (3 vols, Bibliothèque des Écoles Françaises d'Athènes et de Rome – BEFAR 2, series 3, Paris, 1886–1957), II, 'Vita Sergius II', 99–100.
108. *Chronicon Venetum*, in *Cronache veneziane antichissime*, ed. G. Monticolo (Fonti per la storia d'Italia – FSI, XIX, Rome, 1890), 113–14. See also Musca, *Emirato di Bari*, 18–19.
109. Ibn al-Athir, *BAS*, I, 380–1. See also Ahmad, *History of Islamic Sicily*, 13.
110. Ibn al-Athir, *BAS*, I, 385; John Skylitzes, *Synopsis*, 'Basil I', ch 37, 152–3.
111. *Cambridge Chronicle*, *BAS*, I, 279; Ibn al-Athir, *BAS*, I, 370–1, 387.
112. John Skylitzes, *Synopsis*, 'Michael III', ch 18, 107–8; Photios, *Homilies of Photios, Patriarch of Constantinople*, trans. Mango (Cambridge, 1958), III–IV, 74–110. See also Pryor and Jeffreys, *Dromōn*, 60.
113. Ibn Khaldun, *The Muqaddimah, An Introduction to History*, trans. F. Rosenthal (Princeton, 1967), 210.
114. Ahrweiller, *Byzance et la mer*, 97–9; Treadgold, *History of the Byzantine State*, 456–8.
115. Fahmy, *Muslim Sea-Power*, 42–5; Pryor and Jeffreys, *Dromōn*, 50.

116. Constantine VII Porphyrogenitus, *De Administrando Imperio*, ch 29, 126–9; Ibn al-Athir, *BAS*, I, 385; John Skylitzes, *Synopsis*, 'Basil I', ch 26, 142–3. See also Treadgold, *History of the Byzantine State*, 456.
117. Treadgold, *History of the Byzantine State*, 458.
118. John Skylitzes, *Synopsis*, 'Basil I', ch 30, 147–8. See also Treadgold, *History of the Byzantine State*, 457.
119. John Skylitzes, *Synopsis*, 'Basil I', ch 31, 148–9. See also Treadgold, *History of the Byzantine State*, 457.
120. John Skylitzes, *Synopsis*, 'Basil I', chs 32–4, 149–51. See also Pryor and Jeffreys, *Dromōn*, 65–6.
121. John Skylitzes, *Synopsis*, 'Basil I', ch 38, 154. See also Pryor and Jeffreys, *Dromōn*, 66.
122. *Cambridge Chronicle*, *BAS*, I, 279; Erchempert, *Historia Langobardorum*, ch 81, 264.
123. Liudprand of Cremona, *Antapodosis* in *The Works of Liudprand of Cremona*, trans. F. Wright (London, 1930), bk I, chs 2–4, 33–4. See also Pryor and Jeffreys, *Dromōn*, 69.
124. Erchempert, *Historia Langobardorum*, ch 51, 256; Liudprand of Cremona, *Antapodosis*, bk II, ch 44, 90–1. See also Stanton, *Norman Naval Operations*, 9.
125. *Chronica Monasterii Casinensis*, ed. H. Hoffmann (MGH, SS, XXXIV, Hanover, 1980), bk I, ch 44, 11–15.
126. Ibn al-Athir, *BAS*, I, 393–4; Al-Nuwayri, *BAS*, II, 151–2; John Skylitzes, *Synopsis*, 'Leo VI', ch 21, 175. See also Stanton, *Norman Naval Operations*, 11–12.
127. Pryor and Jeffreys, *Dromōn*, 62.
128. John Kaminiates, *The Capture of Thessaloniki*, trans. D. Frendo and A. Foitiou (Perth, 2000), ch 73, 121–2; John Skylitzes, *Synopsis*, 'Leo VI', ch 23, 176–7. See also Pryor and Jeffreys, *Dromōn*, 62–3.
129. Leo VI, *Taktika*, Constitution 19, 502–35. See also Pryor and Jeffreys, *Dromōn*, 176–7.
130. Anonymous, *Naval warfare, commissioned by Basil, the patrikios and parakoimomenos*, trans. Jeffreys, *Dromōn*, App. 3, 521–45. See also Pryor and Jeffreys, *Dromōn*, 183.
131. Nikephoros Ouranos, *On fighting at sea*, trans. Jeffreys, *Dromōn*, App. 5, 571–605. See also Pryor and Jeffreys, *Dromōn*, 181–2.
132. Constantine VII Porphyrogenitus, *De Cerimoniis Aulae Byzantinae*, trans. Haldon in 'Tenth-Century Military Administration', bk II, chs 44 and 45, 201–352. See also Pryor and Jeffreys, *Dromōn*, 186–7.
133. Constantine VII Porphyrogenitus, *De Administrando Imperio*, ch 51, 246–57.
134. Syrianos Magistros, *Naval battles of Syrianos Magistros*, trans. Jeffreys, *Dromōn*, App. 1, 455–81. See also Pryor and Jeffreys, *Dromōn*, 178–81.
135. *Annales Beneventani*, ed. Pertz (MGH, SS, III, Hanover, 1839), *anno* 916, 175; *Chronica Monasterii Casinensis*, bk I, ch 52, 133–4; Liudprand of Cremona, *Antapodosis*, bk II, chs 51–4, 94–6; Lupus Protospatarius, *Annales*, ed. Pertz (MGH, SS, V, Hanover, 1844), *anno* 916, 53.
136. Liudprand of Cremona, *Antapodosis*, bk V, ch 16, 86–7. Fraxinetum was not cleared of Muslim corsairs until 972, when William, Count of Arles, and Arduin, Marquess of Turin, combined land forces to do so, according to Rodulfus Glaber, *Historiarum Libri Quinque*, trans. J. France (Oxford, 1989), bk I, ch 9, 19–23.
137. John Skylitzes, *Synopsis*, 'Leo VI', chs 29 and 33, 29, 185–6. See also Pryor and Jeffreys, *Dromōn*, 63.
138. John Skylitzes, *Synopsis*, 'Romanos I Lekapenos', ch 11, 211. See also Pryor and Jeffreys, *Dromōn*, 64.
139. John Skylitzes, *Synopsis*, 'Romanos I Lekapenos', ch 31, 221–2; Liudprand of Cremona, *Antapodosis*, bk V, ch 15, 185–6. John Skylitzes' claim of 10,000 Rus vessels is clearly an exaggeration; Liudprand's estimate of 1,000 ships seems more accurate. See also Treadgold, *History of the Byzantine State*, 484.
140. John Skylitzes, *Synopsis*, 'Constantine VII', ch 15, 236–7; Leo the Deacon, *The History of Leo the Deacon*, trans. D. Sullivan and A. Talbot (Washington DC, 2005), bk I, ch 2, 58–60. See also Pryor and Jeffreys, *Dromōn*, 71; Treadgold, *History of the Byzantine State*, 489.

141. *Theophanes continuatus*, ed. I. Bekker (3 vols, Bonn, 1838), I, ch 29, 453. See also Pryor, 'Byzantium and the Sea: Byzantine Fleets in the Age of the Macedonian Emperors, C.900–1025 CE', in *War at Sea in the Middle Ages*, 84–104, esp. 100; Treadgold, *History of the Byzantine State*, 492.
142. John Skylitzes, *Synopsis*, 'Romanos II', ch 4, 240; Leo the Deacon, *History*, bk I, ch 3, 60. See also Treadgold, *History of the Byzantine State*, 483, 492–5.
143. *Theophanes continuatus*, I, chs 7–12, 473–8. See also Tsounkarakes, *Byzantine Crete*, 62–3. *Theophanes continuatus* notes 2,000 ships with 'Greek fire', 1,000 *dromōns* and 307 supply ships, but such an armada would have required 300,000 men to crew it. Tsounkarakes more realistically estimates about 250 warships.
144. Leo the Deacon, *History*, bk I, chs 3–7, 60–7.
145. Ibid., bk I, ch 8, 67.
146. John Skylitzes, *Synopsis*, 'Romanos II', ch 4, 240–1; Leo the Deacon, *History*, bk II, chs 6–7, 76–9. See also Lewis, *Naval Power and Trade*, 184–6; Treadgold, *History of the Byzantine State*, 494–5.
147. John Skylitzes, *Synopsis*, 'Nikephoros II Phokas', chs 11–15, 257–9; Leo the Deacon, *History*, bk III, chs 10–11, 101–3; Bk IV, chs 1–4, 104–9.
148. John Skylitzes, *Synopsis*, 'Nikephoros II Phokas', ch 17, 260–2; Leo the Deacon, *History*, bk IV, chs 10–11, 119–25; bk V, ch 4, 132–4.
149. Lewis, *Naval Power and Trade*, 203.
150. Pryor and Jeffreys, *Dromōn*, 50–1.
151. John Skylitzes, *Synopsis*, 'Nikephoros II Phokas', ch 3, 251–2.
152. Ibn al-Athir, *BAS*, I, 425.
153. Leo the Deacon, *History*, bk IV, ch 7, 115.
154. Ibid., bk IV, ch 7, 115–16.
155. Leo the Deacon, *History*, bk IV, ch 8, 116–17; John Skylitzes, *Synopsis*, 'Nikephoros II Phokas', ch 9, 256.
156. *Cambridge Chronicle*, *BAS*, I, 293; Ibn al-Athir, *BAS*, I, 425–9. See also Stanton, *Norman Naval Operations*, 27–8.
157. John Skylitzes, *Synopsis*, 'Nikephoros II Phokas', ch 22, 268–9; 'John Tzimiskes', ch 1, 12, 271–2; Leo the Deacon, *History*, bk V, chs 6–8, 136–9; bk VI, ch 1, 143–4. See Treadgold, *History of the Byzantine State*, 505.
158. John Skylitzes, *Synopsis*, 'John Tzimiskes', ch 5, 275–7; ch 12, 286–8; Leo the Deacon, *History*, bk VI, chs 11–13, 157–61; bk IX, chs 1–11, 186–200. See also Pryor and Jeffreys, *Dromōn*, 73.
159. John Skylitzes, *Synopsis*, 'John Tzimiskes', ch 7, 278–81; Leo the Deacon, *History*, VII, chs 1–8, 162–73.
160. John Skylitzes, *Synopsis*, 'John Tzimiskes', chs 21–2, 295–6; Leo the Deacon, *History*, bk X, chs 4–6, 207–12. See also Lewis, *Naval Power and Trade*, 187–9.
161. John Skylitzes, *Synopsis*, 'Basil II', chs 2–10, 300–11; Leo the Deacon, *History*, bk X, ch 7, 212–13.
162. Haldon, *Warfare, State and Society in the Byzantine World, 565–1204* (London, 1999), 266–7.
163. John Skylitzes, *Synopsis*, 'Basil II', chs 14–18, 314–20; Leo the Deacon, *History*, bk X, ch 9, 215–17. See also Treadgold, *History of the Byzantine State*, 513–18.
164. Treadgold, *History of the Byzantine State*, 514–16.
165. John Skylitzes, *Synopsis*, 'Basil II', chs 11–12, 311–13; Leo the Deacon, *History*, bk X, ch 8, 213–15. See also Treadgold, *History of the Byzantine State*, 517.
166. Fahmy, *Muslim Sea-Power*, 48–50, 130; Lewis, *Naval Power and Trade*, 91.
167. J. Norwich, *Byzantium, Apogee* (London, 1991), 250–1; Treadgold, *History of the Byzantine State*, 520–1.
168. John Skylitzes, *Synopsis*, 'Basil II', chs 24–5, 324–5. See also Lewis, *Naval Power and Trade*, 199; Norwich, *Apogee*, 257; Treadgold, *History of the Byzantine State*, 523.
169. John Skylitzes, *Synopsis*, 'Basil II', ch 35, 330–1. See Treadgold, *History of the Byzantine State*, 525–6.
170. Ibn al-Athir, *BAS*, I, 419–21; Lupus Protospatarius, *Annales*, *anno* 951, 54; John Skylitzes, *Synopsis*, 'Nikephoros II Phokas', ch 7, 255. See also Ahmad, *Islamic Sicily*, 30–4; Chiarelli, *Muslim Sicily*, 95–9.

171. *Annales Beneventani*, *anno* 982, 176; *Chronica Monasterii Casinensis*, bk II, ch 9, 186–7; Ibn al-Athir, *BAS*, I, 431–2; Lupus Protospatarius, *Annales*, *anni* 976–977, 981, 55; Thietmar of Merseburg, *Ottonian Germany: The Chronicon of Thietmar of Merseburg*, trans. D. Warner (Manchester, 2001), bk 3, chs 20–1, 143–4. See also Stanton, *Norman Naval Operations*, 21.
172. Ahmad, *Islamic Sicily*, 31; Chiarelli, *Muslim Sicily*, 120; Pryor and Jeffreys, *Dromōn*, 51.
173. S. Barton, 'Spain in the eleventh century', *The New Cambridge Medieval History, IV, c.1024–c.1198, Part II*, eds D. Luscombe and J. Riley-Smith (Cambridge, 2004), 154–90, esp. 155–7.
174. Ibn al-Athir, *BAS*, I, 442–4. See also Ahmad, *Islamic Sicily*, 32; Chiarelli, *Muslim Sicily*, 119–21.
175. *Annales Barenses*, ed. Pertz (MGH, SS, V, Hanover, 1844) *anno* 929, 53; Ibn al-Athir, *BAS*, I, 440; John Skylitzes, *Synopsis*, 'Basil II', ch 47, 348. See also Stanton, *Norman Naval Operations*, 28.
176. Ibn al-Athir, *BAS*, I, 444–5; John Skylitzes, *Synopsis*, 'Michael IV', chs 8–11, 375–8.
177. Lewis, *Naval Power and Trade*, 195.
178. Ibn Abi Dinar, *BAS*, II, 286. See also Ahmad, *Islamic Sicily*, 33; Chiarelli, *Muslim Sicily*, 122–5.
179. Amatus of Montecassino, *The History of the Normans*, trans. P. Dunbar (Woodbridge, 2004), bk II, chs 8–9, 66–7; Geoffrey Malaterra, *Deeds of Count Roger of Calabria and Sicily and of his brother Duke Robert Guiscard*, trans. K. Wolf (Ann Arbor, 2005), bk 1, chs 7–8, 55–7; John Skylitzes, *Synopsis*, 'Michael IV', ch 16, 380. See also F. Chalandon, *Histoire de la Domination Normande en Italie et en Sicile* (2 vols, Paris, 1907), I, 90–3; G. Loud, *The Age of Robert Guiscard, Southern Italy and the Norman Conquest* (Harlow, 2000), 78–9; Stanton, *Norman Naval Operations*, 28–9; Treadgold, *History of the Byzantine State*, 587–8.
180. Malaterra, *Deeds of Count Roger*, bk 1, ch 8, 56–7; William of Apulia, *Geste de Robert Guiscard*, bk I, vv 196–221, 108–11.
181. John Skylitzes, *Synopsis*, 'Michael IV', ch 20, 381–3. See also Chalandon, *Histoire de la Domination Normande*, I, 94–5.
182. Michael Psellos, *Fourteen Byzantine Rulers*, trans. E. Sewter (Baltimore, 1966), bk VI, 93.
183. Nikephoros, *Short History*, ch 48, 115–17; Theophanes, *Chronicle*, *anno* 6205, 533.
184. Theophanes, *Chronicle*, *anno* 6206, 534. See also Treadgold, *History of the Byzantine State*, 343–4.
185. Nikephoros, *Short History*, ch 49, 116–17; Theophanes, *Chronicle*, *anno* 6206, 534.
186. Theophanes, *Chronicle*, *anno* 6206, 534.
187. Ibid., *anno* 6207, 535.
188. Nikephoros, *Short History*, chs 50–1, 16–19; Theophanes, *Chronicle*, *anno* 6207, 535–6.
189. Theophanes, *Chronicle*, *anno* 6209, 544.
190. Nikephoros, *Short History*, ch 52, 120–1; Theophanes, *Chronicle*, *anni* 6208–9, 538, 545. See also Rodgers, *Naval Warfare under Oars*, 37; Treadgold, *History of the Byzantine State*, 345–6.
191. Theophanes, *Chronicle*, *anno* 6208, 538–9.
192. Ibid., *anno* 6207, 536.
193. Nikephoros, *Short History*, ch 52, 120–1; Theophanes, *Chronicle*, *anno* 6208, 540.
194. Nikephoros, *Short History*, ch 52, 120–1; Theophanes, *Chronicle*, *anno* 6209, 545.
195. Nikephoros, *Short History*, chs 52–3, 120–3; Theophanes, *Chronicle*, *anni* 6208–9, 541, 545.
196. Theophanes, *Chronicle*, *anno* 6209, 545.
197. Ibid., *anno* 6209, 545.
198. J. Fuller, *A Military History of the Western World* (3 vols, New York, 1954), I, 336.
199. Lewis, *Naval Power and Trade*, 84–5, 93–5, 112–13.
200. Nikephoros, *Short History*, ch 54, 123–4; Theophanes, *Chronicle*, *anno* 6209, 545.
201. Theophanes, *Chronicle*, *anno* 6209, 545.
202. Nikephoros, *Short History*, ch 54, 123–4; Theophanes, *Chronicle*, *anno* 6209, 545.
203. Nikephoros, *Short History*, ch 54, 123–4; Theophanes, *Chronicle*, *anno* 6209, 546.
204. Nikephoros, *Short History*, ch 54, 122–5; Theophanes, *Chronicle*, *anno* 6209, 546.
205. Theophanes, *Chronicle*, *anno* 6209, 546.
206. Ibid.
207. Theophanes, *Chronicle*, *anno* 6209, 546. See also Pryor and Jeffreys, *Dromōn*, 32.
208. Nikephoros, *Short History*, ch 56, 124–7; Theophanes, *Chronicle*, *anno* 6210, 550.
209. Theophanes, *Chronicle*, *anno* 6210, 550.

210. Ibid., *anno* 6218, 559.
211. Nikephoros, *Short History*, ch 56, 124–7; Theophanes, *Chronicle*, *anno* 6210, 550.

Chapter 2. Norman Naval Expansion in the Central Mediterranean

1. Pryor, 'Byzantium and the Sea', 99.
2. Lewis, *Naval Power and Trade*, 132.
3. Stanton, *Norman Naval Operations*, 1–8.
4. R. Brown, *The Normans* (Woodbridge, 1984), 79; M. Chibnall, *The Normans* (Oxford, 2000), 75.
5. Malaterra, *Deeds of Count Roger*, bk 1, ch 3, 52. See also Wolf, *Making History: The Normans and their Historians in Eleventh-century Italy* (Philadelphia, 1995), 149–53. See also E. Joranson, 'The inception of the career of the Normans in Italy – legend and history', *Speculum*, XXIII (1948), 353–96; France, 'The occasion of the coming of the Normans to Italy', *Journal of Medieval History*, XVII (1991), 185–205.
6. Amatus, *History of the Normans*, bk I, chs 17–19, 49–50.
7. William of Apulia, *Geste de Robert Guiscard*, bk I, vv 11–27, 98–101.
8. *Chronica Monasterii Casinensis*, bk 2, ch 37, 239–40; Lupus Protospatarius, *Annales*, *anno* 1019, 57; William of Apulia, *Geste de Robert Guiscard*, bk I, vv 91–4, 104–5.
9. Amatus, *History of the Normans*, bk I, ch 42, 60; William of Apulia, *Geste de Robert Guiscard*, bk I, vv 170–4, 108–9. See also Loud, *Age of Robert Guiscard*, 74–5.
10. Stanton, *Norman Naval Operations*, 27.
11. Amatus, *History of the Normans*, bk II, ch 8, 66; Malaterra, *Deeds of Count Roger*, bk 1, ch 7, 55–6.
12. Malaterra, *Deeds of Count Roger*, bk 1, ch 7, 56.
13. Amatus, *History of the Normans*, bk II, chs 15–19, 69–70; Malaterra, *Deeds of Count Roger*, bk 1, chs 8–9, 56–7; William of Apulia, *Geste de Robert Guiscard*, bk I, vv 196–245, 108–13.
14. Amatus, *History of the Normans*, bk II, ch 29, 76; Lupus Protospatarius, *Annales*, *anno* 1042, 58.
15. Amatus, *History of the Normans*, bk II, chs 21–3, 71–3; Lupus Protospatarius, *Annales*, *anno* 1041, 58; Malaterra, *Deeds of Count Roger*, bk 1, chs 9–10, 57–9; William of Apulia, *Geste de Robert Guiscard*, bk I, vv 254–304, 112–15; John Skylitzes, *Synopsis*, 'Constantine IX Monomachus', ch 4, 400–1.
16. Amatus, *History of the Normans*, bk II, ch 31, 77; William of Apulia, *Geste de Robert Guiscard*, bk I, vv 232–9, 110–13.
17. Amatus, *History of the Normans*, bk II, ch 35, 79.
18. Ibid., bk II, ch 46, 85.
19. Amatus, *History of the Normans*, bk III, chs 7–9, 88–9; Malaterra, *Deeds of Count Roger*, bk 1, ch 12, 60.
20. Amatus, *History of the Normans*, bk III, ch 11, 89; Malaterra, *Deeds of Count Roger*, bk 1, chs 16–17, 62–5; William of Apulia, *Geste de Robert Guiscard*, bk II, vv 127–30, 138–9.
21. Amatus, *History of the Normans*, bk III, ch 22, 93–4; Malaterra, *Deeds of Count Roger*, bk 1, ch 13, 60–1; William of Apulia, *Geste de Robert Guiscard*, bk II, vv 75–80, 136–7.
22. Malaterra, *Deeds of Count Roger*, bk 1, ch 14, 61; William of Apulia, *Geste de Robert Guiscard*, bk II, vv 80–4, 136–7.
23. Amatus, *History of the Normans*, bk III, chs 39–40, 100–1; Malaterra, *Deeds of Count Roger*, bk 1, ch 14, 61–2; William of Apulia, *Geste de Robert Guiscard*, bk II, vv 80–286, 136–49.
24. Amatus, *History of the Normans*, bk III, chs 39–40, 100; Malaterra, *Deeds of Count Roger*, bk 1, ch 14, 61–2; William of Apulia, *Geste de Robert Guiscard*, bk II, vv 82–257, 136–47.
25. Amatus, *History of the Normans*, bk III, ch 43, 100; bk IV, ch 2, 111; Malaterra, *Deeds of Count Roger*, bk 1, chs 18–19, 66; William of Apulia, *Geste de Robert Guiscard*, bk II, vv 358–80, 150–3.
26. Malaterra, *Deeds of Count Roger*, bk 1, chs 18–19, 66–7.
27. William of Apulia, *Geste de Robert Guiscard*, bk II, vv 389–406, 152–3.
28. H. Cowdrey, *The Age of Abbot Desiderius* (Oxford, 1983), 112–13.
29. *Le Liber Censuum de l'Eglise Romaine*, eds P. Fabre and L. Duchesne (3 vols, BEFAR 2, série 6, Paris, 1889–1952), I, 421–2. See also Loud, *Age of Robert Guiscard*, 130.
30. Stanton, *Norman Naval Operations*, 33–4.

31. William of Apulia, *Geste de Robert Guiscard*, bk II, vv 407–15, 154–5. See also Chalandon, *Histoire de la Domination Normande*, I, 173.
32. Amatus, *History of the Normans*, bk IV, ch 3, 112; Malaterra, *Deeds of Count Roger*, bk 1, ch 34, 74.
33. Malaterra, *Deeds of Count Roger*, bk 2, ch 1, 86.
34. Malaterra, *Deeds of Count Roger*, bk 2, chs 4–7, 87–9. See Loud, *Age of Robert Guiscard*, 148–9.
35. Amatus, *History of the Normans*, bk V, ch 13, 138.
36. Malaterra, *Deeds of Count Roger*, bk 2, ch 8, 90. Amari, *Storia dei Musulmani di Sicilia* (III, 68) considers '*germundos*' a Latinized distortion of the Arabic word '*dermudos*' for *dromōns*. Gardiner and Morrison, *Age of the Galley*, (249) define the '*galea*' of late Roman times as a 'light, fast, single banked scouting vessel'. They identify '*cattos*' (248) as large Muslim galleys, perhaps *triremes* with castles. Pryor, *Dromōn*, surmises that '*golafros*' was a Latin term for galleys derived from the Arabic '*ghurāb*', 'war galley'.
37. Amatus, *History of the Normans*, bk V, ch 14, 138.
38. Amatus, *History of the Normans*, bk V, ch 15, 138; Malaterra, *Deeds of Count Roger*, bk 2, ch 10, 90–1.
39. Amatus, *History of the Normans*, bk V, ch 15–18, 138–9; Malaterra, *Deeds of Count Roger*, bk 2, ch 10, 91.
40. Amatus, *History of the Normans*, bk V, ch 18, 139; Malaterra, *Deeds of Count Roger*, bk 2, ch 12, 91.
41. Amatus, *History of the Normans*, bk V, chs 20–3, 140–1; Malaterra, *Deeds of Count Roger*, bk 2, chs 13–17, 92–4.
42. Malaterra, *Deeds of Count Roger*, bk 2, ch 19, 95. (Judith was the half-sister of Robert de Grandmesnil, the Norman abbot of St Eufemia in Calabria.)
43. Ibid., bk 2, chs 21–8, 96–102.
44. Ibid., bk 2, ch 22, 96–7.
45. Ibid., bk 2, chs 29–30, 102–5.
46. Ibn Al-Athir, *BAS*, I, 448.
47. Bernardo Maragone, *Gli annales Pisani di Bernardo Maragone*, ed. M. Gentile (Rerum Italicarum Scriptores – RIS, vol. VI, part II, Bologna, 1936), 5–6. See also W. Heywood, *A History of Pisa, Eleventh and Twelfth Centuries* (Cambridge, 1921), 26–9.
48. Malaterra, *Deeds of Count Roger*, bk 2, ch 33, 107–11.
49. Lupus Protospatarius, *Annales*, *anno* 1065, 59; Malaterra, *Deeds of Count Roger*, bk 2, ch 36, 114.
50. Amatus, *History of the Normans*, bk V, ch 26, 143.
51. Lupus Protospatarius, *Annales*, *anno* 1068, 59; William of Apulia, *Geste de Robert Guiscard*, bk II, vv 445–78, 156–9.
52. Malaterra, *Deeds of Count Roger*, bk 2, ch 40, 117.
53. Amatus, *History of the Normans*, bk V, ch 27, 145; Malaterra, *Deeds of Count Roger*, bk 2, ch 43, 120–2; William of Apulia, *Geste de Robert Guiscard*, bk III, vv 112–31, 170–1.
54. William of Apulia, *Geste de Robert Guiscard*, bk III, vv 137–8, 17.
55. Amatus, *History of the Normans*, bk VI, ch 14, 156; Lupus Protospatarius, *Annales*, *anno* 1071, 60; Malaterra, *Deeds of Count Roger*, bk 2, ch 43, 122.
56. William of Apulia, *Geste de Robert Guiscard*, bk III, vv 229–33, 176–7.
57. Ibid., bk III, vv 225–54,176–9.
58. Amatus, *History of the Normans*, bk VI, chs 13–19, 155–8; Malaterra, *Deeds of Count Roger*, bk 2, ch 45, 124–5; William of Apulia, *Geste de Robert Guiscard*, bk III, vv 187–337, 174–83.
59. Lupus Protospatarius, *Annales*, *anno* 1073, 60.
60. Amatus, *History of the Normans*, bk VIII, chs 6–7, 191; William of Apulia, *Geste de Robert Guiscard*, bk III, vv 413–19, 186–7.
61. Amatus, *History of the Normans*, bk VIII, ch 14, 194; William of Apulia, *Geste de Robert Guiscard*, bk III, vv 424–45, 186–9.
62. William of Apulia, *Geste de Robert Guiscard*, bk III, vv 427–30, 186.
63. Amatus, *History of the Normans*, bk VIII, ch 24, 199–200; Lupus Protospatarius, *Annales*, *anno* 1077, 60; William of Apulia, *Geste de Robert Guiscard*, bk III, vv 442–6, 188–9.
64. Anna Comnena, *The Alexiad of Anna Comnena*, trans. Sewter (London, 1969), 57–8.
65. Ibid., 69.

66. Malaterra, *Deeds of Count Roger*, bk 3, ch 14, 145; William of Apulia, *Geste de Robert Guiscard*, bk IV, vv 200–1, 214–15.
67. Anna Comnena, *Alexiad*, 131.
68. Malaterra, *Deeds of Count Roger*, bk 3, ch 24, 154.
69. Lupus Protospatarius, *Annales*, *anno* 1081, 60; Malaterra, *Deeds of Count Roger*, bk 3, ch 24, 153–4.
70. Anna Comnena, *Alexiad*, 132.
71. Anna Comnena, *Alexiad*, 131–5; Lupus Protospatarius, *Annales*, *anno* 1081, 60–1; William of Apulia, *Geste de Robert Guiscard*, bk IV, vv 200–34, 214–17.
72. C. Manfroni, *Storia della Marina italiana* (3 vols, Livorno, 1899), I, 121–5. *La Serenissima* is a diminutive of *La Serenissima Repubblica di Venezia*, meaning 'Most Serene Republic of Venice'.
73. Stanton, *Norman Naval Operations*, 48.
74. Anna Comnena, *Alexiad*, 137–8. See also M. Bennett, 'Amphibious Operations from the Norman Conquest to the Crusades of Saint Louis, c.1050–c.1250', *Amphibious Warfare 1000–1700: Commerce, State Formation and European Expansion*, eds D. Trim and M. Fissel (Leiden, 2011), 51–68, esp. 56–7.
75. Malaterra, *Deeds of Count Roger*, bk 3, ch 26, 156.
76. Anna Comnena, *Alexiad*, 138.
77. William of Apulia, *Geste de Robert Guiscard*, bk IV, vv 300–6, 220–1.
78. Anna Comnena, *Alexiad*, 138–9.
79. Anna Comnena, *Alexiad*, 146–8; Malaterra, *Deeds of Count Roger*, bk 3, ch 27, 157–8; William of Apulia, *Geste de Robert Guiscard*, bk IV, vv 367–424, 224–7.
80. Lupus Protospatarius, *Annales*, *anno* 1082, 61; Malaterra, *Deeds of Count Roger*, bk 3, ch 28, 158–9; William of Apulia, *Geste de Robert Guiscard*, bk IV, vv 450–504, 229–31.
81. Anna Comnena, *Alexiad*, 161–2; Malaterra, *Deeds of Count Roger*, bk 3, chs 33–4, 163–4; William of Apulia, *Geste de Robert Guiscard*, bk IV, vv 506–45, 231–5.
82. William of Apulia, *Geste de Robert Guiscard*, bk V, vv 80–105, 240–3. See also Loud, *Age of Robert Guiscard*, 219.
83. Lupus Protospatarius, *Annales*, *anno* 1084, 61; Malaterra, *Deeds of Count Roger*, bk 3, chs 34–7, 164–8; William of Apulia, *Geste de Robert Guiscard*, bk IV, vv 524–71, 233–5.
84. Lupus Protospatarius, *Annales*, *anno* 1085, 61.
85. William of Apulia, *Geste de Robert Guiscard*, bk V, vv 146–50, 244–5.
86. Ibid., bk V, vv 130–56, 242–5.
87. Anna Comnena, *Alexiad*, 189.
88. Anna Comnena, *Alexiad*, 190; William of Apulia, *Geste de Robert Guiscard*, bk V, vv 187–201, 246–7.
89. Anna Comnena, *Alexiad*, 191–2; Lupus Protospatarius, *Annales*, *anno* 1085, 61–2; William of Apulia, *Geste de Robert Guiscard*, bk V, vv 202–54 and 292–338, 248–55.
90. William of Malmesbury, *Gesta Regum Anglorum*, trans. R. Mynors, R. Thomson and M. Winterbottom (Oxford, 1998), 484–5. See also Loud, *Age of Robert Guiscard*, 223.
91. Lupus Protospatarius, *Annales*, *anno* 1085, 62.
92. Abulafia, *Great Sea*, 281–2.
93. Malaterra, *Deeds of Count Roger*, bk 2, ch 41, 119.
94. Lupus Protospatarius, *Annales*, *anno* 1076, 60; Malaterra, *Deeds of Count Roger*, bk 3, ch 9, 138–9.
95. Malaterra, *Deeds of Count Roger*, bk 3, ch 11, 140.
96. Ibid., bk 3, ch 11, 140–2.
97. Ibid., bk 3, chs 15–18, 146–9.
98. Ibid., bk 4, ch 1, 177.
99. Lupus Protospatarius, *Annales*, *anno* 1088, 62; Malaterra, *Deeds of Count Roger*, bk 4, ch 2, 177–9.
100. Malaterra, *Deeds of Count Roger*, bk 4, ch 15, 190.
101. *Carmen in victoriam Pisanorum*, ed. Cowdrey in 'The Mahdia campaign of 1087', *English Historical Review*, CCCLXII (1977), 1–29, esp. 9, 24–9; Ibn al-Athir in *BAS*, I, 440–2.
102. Ibn al-Athir in *BAS*, I, 451; Malaterra, *Deeds of Count Roger*, bk 4, ch 3, 193–4.
103. Malaterra, *Deeds of Count Roger*, bk 4, ch 16, 192–4.

104. Abulafia, *Great Sea*, 320–1; Stanton, *Norman Naval Operations*, 67.
105. Abulafia, *Great Sea*, 321.
106. Stanton, *Norman Naval Operations*, 114.
107. Abulafia, *Great Sea*, 318.
108. Ibn Jubayr, *The Travels of Ibn Jubayr*, trans. R. Broadhurst (London, 1952), 338.
109. Stanton, 'The Naval Strategy of Roger II, King of Sicily', *New Interpretations in Naval History: Selected Papers from the Fifteenth Naval History Symposium*, ed. M. Yu (Annapolis, 2009), 14–27, esp. 22–7.
110. Abulafia, *Great Sea*, 322–3; Stanton, *Norman Naval Operations*, 117–19.
111. L.-R. Ménager, *Amiratus: L'Émirat et les origines de l'amirauté, XIe–XIIIe siècles* (Paris, 1960), 44–54.
112. Abulafia, *Great Sea*, 321–2; Ménager, *Amiratus*, 51–2; Stanton, *Norman Naval Operations*, 260–1.
113. Abulafia, 'The Crown and the economy under Roger II and his successors', *Dumbarton Oaks Papers*, 37 (1983), 1–14, esp. 6–7; *Great Sea*, 318; Stanton, *Norman Naval Operations*, 118–19.
114. Pryor and Jeffreys, *Dromōn*, 423–44. (The proper plural of *galea* is *galeae*, but '*galeas*' is often used in the sources, so '*galeas*' will be used throughout for the sake of consistency.)
115. Pryor, 'From Dromōn to Galea', 110–11.
116. Al-Idrisi, *La première géographie de l'Occident*, eds H. Bresc and A. Nef (Paris, 1999), IV, 2, 306; Romuald of Salerno, *Romualdi Salernitani Chronicon*, ed. C. Garufi (RIS, 2nd edn, vol. VII, Citta di Castello, 1935), 202–3, 236. See also Loud, *Roger II and the Creation of the Kingdom of Sicily* (Manchester, 2012), 357.
117. E. Caspar, *Roger II (1101–1154) und die Gründung der Normannisch-sicilischen Monarchie* (Innsbruck, 1904), Reg 4–19, 483–7. See also Chalandon, *Histoire de la Domination Normande*, I, 357–9; H. Houben, *Roger II of Sicily, A Ruler between East and West*, trans. Loud and D. Milburn (Cambridge, 1992), 26–7.
118. Stanton, *Norman Naval Operations*, 68.
119. At-Tijani, *BAS*, II, 66. See also Ménager, *Amiratus*, 28–9, 36, App. II, no. 5, 171–2; H. Takayama, *The Administration of the Norman Kingdom of Sicily* (Leiden, 1993), 44–5.
120. Stanton, *Norman Naval Operations*, 68–9.
121. A Melkite is a Christian who abides by Greek Orthodox liturgy, but recognizes the authority of the Pope.
122. Al-Maqrizi, trans. J. Johns, *Arabic Administration in Norman Sicily: The royal dīwān* (Cambridge, 2002), 80–2; At-Tijani, *BAS*, II, 65–6; Ibn Khaldun, *BAS*, II, 206.
123. Stanton, *Norman Naval Operations*, 70.
124. Al-Nuwayri, *BAS*, II, 154; At-Tijani, *BAS*, II, 51–5; Ibn abi Dinar, *BAS*, II, 289–90; Ibn al-Athir; *The Chronicle of Ibn al-Athir for the Crusading Period, Part I*, trans. D. Richards (Aldershot, 2006), 185–6.
125. At-Tijani, *BAS*, II, 71.
126. Ibn Idhari, *BAS*, II, 34–6; At-Tijani, *BAS*, II, 68–74; Ibn abi Dinar, *BAS*, II, 290; Ibn al-Athir, *Chronicle of Ibn al-Athir, Part I*, 245–6.
127. Alexander of Telese, *The History of the Most Serene Roger, First King of Sicily*, trans. Loud in *Roger II*, bk I, ch 4, 66; Falco of Benevento, *Chronicle*, in *Roger II*, 174; Romuald of Salerno, *Chronicon sive Annales*, in *Roger II*, 250–1.
128. Alexander of Telese, *History of King Roger of Sicily*, trans. Loud in *Roger II*, bk I, chs 4–5, 66–7; Falco of Benevento, *Chronicle*, in *Roger II*, 173–4.
129. Alexander of Telese, *History of King Roger of Sicily*, trans. Loud in *Roger II*, bk I, chs 6–7, 67–8; Falco of Benevento, *Chronicle*, in *Roger II*, 175.
130. Alexander of Telese, *History of King Roger of Sicily*, trans. Loud in *Roger II*, bk I, chs 8–11, 68–9.
131. Alexander of Telese, *History of King Roger of Sicily*, trans. Loud in *Roger II*, bk I, ch 14, 71; Falco of Benevento, *Chronicle*, in *Roger II*, 180–1; Romuald of Salerno, *Chronicon sive Annales*, in *Roger II*, 252–3.
132. Romuald of Salerno, *Chronicon sive Annales*, trans. Loud in *Roger II*, 253–4 and note 8.

133. Bernard of Clairvaux, *The Letters of St Bernard of Clairvaux*, trans. B. James (London, 1953), no. 127, 188–9. See also I. Robinson, *The Papacy 1073–1198, Continuity and Innovation* (Cambridge, 1990), 69–77.
134. Alexander of Telese, *History of King Roger of Sicily*, trans. Loud in *Roger II*, bk II, chs 3–6, 78–9; Falco of Benevento, *Chronicon*, in *Roger II*, 184; Romuald of Salerno, *Chronicon sive Annales*, in *Roger II*, 252–3.
135. Robinson, *Papacy 1073–1198*, 442–6.
136. Alexander of Telese, *History of King Roger of Sicily*, trans. Loud in *Roger II*, bk II, chs 8–11, 80–1; Falco of Benevento, *Chronicle*, in *Roger II*, 185; Romuald of Salerno, *Chronicon sive Annales*, in *Roger II*, 254.
137. Alexander of Telese, *History of King Roger of Sicily*, trans. Loud in *Roger II*, bk II, ch 12, 81–2.
138. Alexander of Telese, *History of King Roger of Sicily*, trans. Loud in *Roger II*, bk II, chs 81–4; Falco of Benevento, *Chronicle*, in *Roger II*, 190.
139. Alexander of Telese, *History of King Roger of Sicily*, trans. Loud in *Roger II*, bk II, chs 18–21, 84–5; Falco of Benevento, *Chronicle*, in *Roger II*, 190–1; Romuald of Salerno, *Chronicon sive Annales*, in *Roger II*, 254.
140. Alexander of Telese, *History of King Roger of Sicily*, trans. Loud in *Roger II*, bk II, chs 29–52, 87–96; Falco of Benevento, *Chronicle*, in *Roger II*, 196–208; Romuald of Salerno, *Chronicon sive Annales*, in *Roger II*, 255.
141. Alexander of Telese, *History of King Roger of Sicily*, trans. Loud in *Roger II*, bk II, chs 37 and 56, 91 and 98; Falco of Benevento, *Chronicon*, in *Roger II*, 208–9, 212. See also Caspar, *Roger II*, 142–5; Chalandon, *Histoire de la Domination Normande*, II, 34–5; Heywood, *History of Pisa*, 83.
142. Alexander of Telese, *History of King Roger of Sicily*, trans. Loud in *Roger II*, bk III, ch 1, 104.
143. Alexander of Telese, *History of King Roger of Sicily*, trans. Loud in *Roger II*, bk III, chs 1–2 and 7, 104–5, 107; Falco of Benevento, *Chronicle*, in *Roger II*, 215.
144. Alexander of Telese, *History of King Roger of Sicily*, trans. Loud in *Roger II*, bk III, chs 9 and 19, 108, 112; Bernardo Maragone, *Annales Pisani*, 10; Falco of Benevento, *Chronicon*, in *Roger II*, 215.
145. Alexander of Telese, *History of King Roger of Sicily*, trans. Loud in *Roger II*, bk III, chs 24–5, 114; Falco of Benevento, *Chronicle*, in *Roger II*, 215; Bernardo Maragone, *Annales Pisani*, 9–10; Romuald of Salerno, *Chronicon sive Annales*, in *Roger II*, 255.
146. Alexander of Telese, *History of King Roger of Sicily*, trans. Loud in *Roger II*, bk III, ch 26, 114–5; Bernardo Maragone, *Annales Pisani*, 10; Romuald of Salerno, *Chronicon sive Annales*, in *Roger II*, 255.
147. Falco of Benevento, *Chronicle*, trans. Loud in *Roger II*, 215–16.
148. *Annalista Saxo*, ed. K. Nass (MGH, SS, XXXVII, Hanover, 2006), 605–10; Falco of Benevento, *Chronicle*, trans. Loud in *Roger II*, 220–1.
149. Bernardo Maragone, *Annales Pisani*, 11; Falco of Benevento, *Chronicle*, trans. Loud in *Roger II*, 221–2.
150. Romuald of Salerno, *Chronicon sive Annales*, trans. Loud in *Roger II*, 256.
151. Falco of Benevento, *Chronicle*, trans. Loud in *Roger II*, 222; Bernardo Maragone, *Annales Pisani*, 11; Romuald of Salerno, *Chronicon sive Annales*, in *Roger II*, 257.
152. *Annalisto Saxo*, 610–11; Falco of Benevento, *Chronicle*, trans. Loud, *Roger II*, 222–3, 225; Romuald of Salerno, *Chronicon sive Annales*, in *Roger II*, 257.
153. Falco of Benevento, *Chronicle*, trans. Loud in *Roger II*, 236–9; Romuald of Salerno, *Chronicon sive Annales*, in *Roger II*, 259.
154. Falco of Benevento, *Chronicle*, trans. Loud in *Roger II*, 241–3; Romuald of Salerno, *Chronicon sive Annales*, in *Roger II*, 259.
155. Al-Nuwayri, *BAS*, II, 156–7; At-Tijani, *BAS*, II, 55; Ibn abi Dinar, *BAS*, II, 291–2; Ibn al-Athir, *Chronicle of Ibn al-Athir, Part I*, 321–2; Ibn Idhari, *BAS*, II, 37; Ibn Khaldun, *BAS*, II, 220–2.
156. Ibn Khaldun, *BAS*, II, 203. See also Houben, *Roger II of Sicily*, 102–4.
157. C. Brühl, *Rogerii II. Regis Diplomata Latina* (Cologne, 1987), no. 24, 66–8. See also Stanton, *Norman Naval Power*, 114.
158. Ibn Idari, *BAS*, II, 37; At-Tijani, *BAS*, II, 75–6; Ibn al-Athir, *BAS*, *Chronicle of Ibn al-Athir, Part I*, 365.

159. *Chronica ignoti monachi S. Mariae de Ferraria*, ed. A. Gaudenzi (Naples, 1888), *anno* 1143, 27; Al-Idrisi, *La première géographie*, 173; Ibn al-Athir, *Chronicle of Ibn al-Athir, Part I*, 366–7; Ibn Khaldun, *BAS*, II, 223.
160. Al-Idrisi, *La première géographie*, 163; Ibn al-Athir, *Chronicle of Ibn al-Athir, Part I*, 375.
161. Ibn abi Dinar, *BAS*, II, 293; Ibn al-Athir, *Chronicle of Ibn al-Athir, Part I*, 378.
162. Abulfeda, *BAS*, II, 100; Al-Nuwayri, *BAS*, II, 157–8; At-Tijani, *BAS*, II, 60; *Chronica de Ferraria*, *anno* 1147, 28; Ibn abi Dinar, *BAS*, II, 293; Ibn al-Athir, *Chronicle of Ibn al-Athir, Part I*, 380.
163. Ibn abi Dinar, *BAS*, II, 293.
164. Ibn al-Athir, *Chronicle of Ibn al-Athir, Part 2*, trans. Richards (Aldershot, 2007), 14.
165. Ibid., 16–17.
166. Abulfeda, *BAS*, II, 101; Ibn al-Athir, *Chronicle of Ibn al-Athir, Part 2*, 18–19; Ibn Khaldun, *BAS*, II, 226; Al-Maqrizi, trans. Johns, *Arabic Administration in Norman Sicily*, 82; At-Tijani, *BAS*, II, 76.
167. Ibn abi Dinar, *BAS*, II, 295; Ibn al-Athir, *Chronicle of Ibn al-Athir, Part 2*, 20; Ibn Khaldun, *BAS*, II, 227–8.
168. *Annales Erphesfurtenses*, ed. Pertz (MGH, SS, VI, Hanover, 1844), *anno* 1135, 540. See also Loud, *Roger II*, 269. In ancient Greece a *talent* was equivalent to around 25.8 kilos of silver.
169. Chalandon, *Histoire de la Domination Normande*, II, 124–5.
170. *Annales Erphesfurtenses*, *anno* 1135, 540; *Annalista Saxo*, 610. See also Loud, *Roger II*, 269–71.
171. Manfroni, *Storia della Marina italiana*, I, 189–90.
172. Otto of Freising, *The Deeds of Frederick Barbarossa*, trans. C. Mierow (New York, 1953), bk I, ch 24, 54.
173. John Kinnamos, *Deeds of John and Manuel Comnenus*, trans. C. Brand (New York, 1976), bk II, ch 4, 36.
174. Ibn al-Athir, *Chronicle of Ibn al-Athir, Part I*, 372–3.
175. Odo of Deuil, *De Profectione Ludovici VII in Orientem*, trans. V. Berry (New York, 1948), bk I, 6–7; Otto of Freising, *Deeds of Frederick Barbarossa*, bk I, ch 40, 74–5.
176. John Kinnamos, *John and Manuel Comnenus*, bk II, chs 12–13, 58–61, bk III, ch 2, 76; Niketas Choniates, *O City of Byzantium! Annals of Niketas Choniates*, trans. H. Magoulias (Detroit, 1984), 36. See also Chalandon, *Histoire de la Domination Normande*, II, 135.
177. *Chronica de Ferraria*, *anno* 1147, 28.
178. Romuald of Salerno, *Chronicon sive Annales*, trans. Loud in *Roger II*, 260 and note 22.
179. Niketas Choniates, *City of Byzantium*, 43–5.
180. John Kinnamos, *John and Manuel Comnenus*, bk III, ch 2, 76; Niketas Choniates, *City of Byzantium*, 45.
181. Andrea Dandolo, *Chronica Per Extensum Descripta*, ed. E. Pastorello (RIS, vol. XII, Bologna, 1942), 243.
182. John Kinnamos, *John and Manuel Comnenus*, bk II, ch 19, 72.
183. Niketas Choniates, *City of Byzantium*, 51–2.
184. Ibn al-Athir, *Chronicle of Ibn al-Athir, Part 2*, 32.
185. Ibn al-Athir, *Chronicle of Ibn al-Athir, Part 2*, 62–3; Ibn Khaldun, *BAS*, II, 229; Romuald of Salerno, *Chronicon sive Annales*, trans. Loud in *Roger II*, 266–8.
186. Ibn al-Athir, *BAS*, I, 450.
187. *Chronica de Ferraria*, *anno* 1156, 29; 'Hugo Falcandus', *The History of the Tyrants of Sicily, 1154–1169*, trans. Loud and T. Wiedemann (Manchester, 1998), 73; John Kinnamos, *John and Manuel Comnenus*, bk IV, ch 13, 128–9; Romuald of Salerno, *Romualdi Salernitani Chronicon*, 239–40; William of Tyre, *A History of Deeds Done beyond the Sea*, trans. E. Babcock and A. Krey (2 vols, New York, 1943), II, bk 18, ch 8, 250.
188. Ibn al-Athir, *Chronicle of Ibn al-Athir, Part 2*, 76–77; At-Tijani, *BAS*, II, 50–1, 60.
189. *Annales Casinenses*, ed. Pertz (MGH, SS, XIX, Hanover, 1866), *anno* 1160, 311; Ibn al-Athir, *Chronicle of Ibn al-Athir, Part 2*, 106; Ibn Khaldun, *BAS*, II, 233–4.
190. 'Hugo Falcandus', *History of the Tyrants of Sicily*, 78–80; Ibn al-Athir, *Chronicle of Ibn al-Athir, Part 2*, 105; Ibn Khaldun, *BAS*, II, 233; At-Tijani, *BAS*, II, 80.

191. Caffaro, *Annales Ianuenses*, in *Annali genovesi di Caffaro e de'suoi continuatori dal MXCIX al MCCXCIII*, eds L. Belgrano and C. Imperiale di Sant'Angelo (5 vols, FSI, Genoa, 1890–1929), I, 65–6; *Friderici I. Diplomata (1158–1167)*, ed. H. Appelt (MGH, Diplomata Regum et Imperatorem Germaniae, X, II, Hanover, 1979), no. 356, 198–203 and no. 367, 220–5. See also Abulafia, *The Two Italies, Economic relations between the Norman Kingdom of Sicily and the Northern Communes* (Cambridge, 1977), 90–6, 124–5.
192. Caffaro, *Annales Ianuenses*, I, 67–71.
193. Ibn al-Athir, *Chronicle of Ibn al-Athir, Part 2*, 229; William of Tyre, *History of Deeds Done beyond the Sea*, II, bk 21, ch 3, 399.
194. William of Tyre, *History of Deeds Done beyond the Sea*, II, bk 21, ch 3, 399–400.
195. Salem Maragone, *Annales Pisani*, 72.
196. William of Tyre, *History of Deeds Done beyond the Sea*, II, bk 22, ch 8, 458.
197. Eustathios of Thessaloniki, *The Capture of Thessaloniki*, trans. J. Melville Jones (Canberra, 1988), ch 138, 151; Ibn Jubayr, *Travels*, 354.
198. Eustathios of Thessaloniki, *Capture of Thessaloniki*, ch 51, 62–3.
199. Niketas Choniates, *City of Byzantium*, 198–201.
200. *Annales Casinenses*, *anno* 1185, 312. See also Chalandon, *Histoire de la Domination Normande*, II, 386–7.
201. *Chronica de Ferraria*, *anno* 1189, 31; Richard of San Germano, *Ryccardi de Sancto Germano Notarii Chronica*, ed. Garufi (RIS, 2nd edn, VIIb, Bologna, 1938), *Explicit Prologus*, 4–6.
202. Ambroise, *History of the Holy War*, trans. M. Ailes (2 vols, Woodbridge, 2003), II, vv 2526–73, 68–9; Baha al-Din ibn Shaddad, *The Rare and Excellent History of Saladin*, trans. Richards (Aldershot, 2002), 72–5; *Itinerarium Peregrinorum*, trans. H. Nicholson in *Chronicle of the Third Crusade* (Aldershot, 1997), bk 1, ch 5, 32–3; Ibn al-Athir, *Chronicle of Ibn al-Athir, Part 2*, 322–4; 'The old French Continuation of William of Tyre, 1184–1197', trans. P. Edbury in *The Conquest of Jerusalem and the Third Crusade* (Aldershot, 1996), chs 40–2, 45–7; Roger of Howden, *Annals of Roger de Hoveden*, trans. H. Riley (2 vols, London, 1853), II, 64–5.
203. Roger of Howden, *Annals*, II, 101–2.
204. *Itinerarium Peregrinorum*, bk 2, ch 9, 151.
205. Ambroise, *History of the Holy War*, II, 714–817, 41–2; *Itinerarium Peregrinorum*, bk 2, chs 15–16, 159–63.
206. Richard of San Germano, *Notarii Chronica*, *anno* 1190, 9.
207. Ambroise, *History of the Holy War*, II, vv 866–73, 43; *Itinerarium Peregrinorum*, bk 2, ch 18, 164–5; Roger of Howden, *Annals*, II, 163.
208. *Chronica de Ferraria*, *anno* 1194, 32; Richard of San Germano, *Notarii Chronica*, *anno* 1194, 16. See also Stanton, *Norman Naval Operations*, 172–3.
209. Lupus Protospatarius, *Annales*, *anno* 1083, 61; William of Apulia, *Geste de Robert Guiscard*, bk IV, vv 528–31, 232–3.
210. Lupus Protospatarius, *Annales*, *anno* 1084, 61; Malaterra, *Deeds of Count Roger*, bk 3, chs 34–7, 164–8; William of Apulia, *Geste de Robert Guiscard*, bk IV, vv 524–71, 233–5.
211. Anna Comnena, *Alexiad*, 188.
212. Ibid., 139.
213. Anna Comnena, *Alexiad*, 163–73; William of Apulia, *Geste de Robert Guiscard*, bk V, vv 1–79, 237–41. See also Loud, *Age of Robert Guiscard*, 219.
214. Anna Comnena, *Alexiad*, 181–3; William of Apulia, *Geste de Robert Guiscard*, bk V, vv 80–105, 241–3.
215. Lupus Protospatarius, *Annales*, *anno* 1085, 61; William of Apulia, *Geste de Robert Guiscard*, bk V, vv 140–5, 242–3.
216. Chalandon, *Histoire de la Domination Normande*, I, 282.
217. William of Apulia, *Geste de Robert Guiscard*, bk V, vv 146–50, 244–5.
218. Manfroni, *Storia della Marina italiana*, I, 129.
219. Lupus Protospatarius, *Annales*, *anno* 1085, 61; William of Apulia, *Geste de Robert Guiscard*, bk V, vv 130–40, 242–3.
220. Anna Comnena, *Alexiad*, 189; William of Apulia, *Geste de Robert Guiscard*, bk V, vv 153–6, 244–5.

221. Anna Comnena, *Alexiad*, 189.
222. William of Apulia, *Geste de Robert Guiscard*, bk V, vv 156–8, 244–5.
223. Ibid., bk V, vv 163–70, 244–5.
224. Anna Comnena, *Alexiad*, 189.
225. Ibid., 189–90.
226. Ibid., 188.
227. Ibid., 189.
228. William of Apulia, *Geste de Robert Guiscard*, bk V, vv 157–60, 244–5.
229. Anna Comnena, *Alexiad*, 190; William of Apulia, *Geste de Robert Guiscard*, bk V, vv 162–73, 244–5.
230. William of Apulia, *Geste de Robert Guiscard*, bk V, vv 174–84, 244–6.
231. Manfroni, *Storia della Marina italiana*, I, 130.
232. Leo VI, *Taktika*, Constitution 19, paras 50 and 52, 523–5.
233. Anna Comnena, *Alexiad*, 190.
234. William of Apulia, *Geste de Robert Guiscard*, bk V, vv 187–98, 246–7.
235. Anna Comnena, *Alexiad*, 190.
236. Lupus Protospatarius, *Annales*, *anno* 1085, 61.
237. William of Apulia, *Geste de Robert Guiscard*, bk V, vv 198–201, 246–7.
238. Anna Comnena, *Alexiad*, 190.
239. Andrea Dandolo, *Chronica Per Extensum Descripta*, 217–18. See also Manfroni, *Storia della Marina italiana*, I, 131–3.
240. Anna Comnena, *Alexiad*, 190–1.
241. Anna Comnena, *Alexiad*, 191–2; Lupus Protospatarius, *Annales*, *anno* 1085, 61–2; William of Apulia, *Geste de Robert Guiscard*, bk V, vv 292–338, 252–5.

Chapter 3. The Crusades: The Clash of East and West at Sea

1. Stanton, *Norman Naval Operations*, 189.
2. Bass et al., *Serçe Limani*, 153–87; Pryor, 'The Naval Architecture of Crusader Transport Ships', *Mariner's Mirror*, LXX (1984), 171–219, 275–92, 363–86, esp. 202–13; 'Mediterranean Round Ship', in *Cogs, Caravels and Galleons, The Sailing Ship 1000–1650*, eds Gardiner and Unger (London, 1994), 59–76, esp. 64.
3. Pryor, 'Transportation of horses by sea during the era of the Crusades', *The Mariner's Mirror*, LXVIII (1982), 9–27, 103–25, esp. 12–13.
4. Fulcher of Chartres, *A History of the Expedition to Jerusalem, 1095–1127*, trans. F. Ryan (New York, 1969), bk I, chs 2–3, 61–7. See also T. Asbridge, *The Crusades* (New York, 2010), 34.
5. Treadgold, *History of the Byzantine State*, 602–6.
6. Asbridge, *Crusades*, 41; Riley-Smith, *The Crusades, A History* (London, 2005), 18, 26–9.
7. Asbridge, *Crusades*, 107; Riley-Smith, *Crusades*, 44–6.
8. Asbridge, *Crusades*, 52, 94; Bachrach, 'Crusader logistics: from victory at Nicaea to resupply at Dorylaion', in *Logistics of Warfare in the Age of the Crusades*, ed. Pryor (Aldershot, 2006), 43–62, esp. 49.
9. Riley-Smith, *Crusades*, 29–32.
10. Albert of Aachen, *Historia Ierosolimitana, History of the Journey to Jerusalem*, trans. S. Edgington (Oxford, 2007), bk II, chs 32–3, 114–17; Anna Comnena, *Alexiad*, 336–7; *Gesta Francorum, The Deeds of the Franks and the other Pilgrims to Jerusalem*, trans. R. Hill (Oxford, 1962), bk II, 16–17.
11. *Gesta Francorum*, bk III, 19.
12. Albert of Aachen, *Historia Ierosolimitana*, bk II, chs 39–41, 130–3. See also Asbridge, *Crusades*, 59.
13. Bachrach, 'The Crusader March from Dorylaion to Herakleia, 4 July–ca.2 September 1097', in *Shipping, Trade and Crusade in the Medieval Mediterranean*, eds R. Gertwagen and Jeffreys (Farnham, 2012), 231–54; Riley-Smith, *Crusades*, 35–7.
14. Albert of Aachen, *Historia Ierosolimitana*, bk III, ch 1, 138–9.
15. *Gesta Francorum*, bk IV, 23.

16. Bachrach, 'Crusader March from Dorylaion', 233–4; France, *Victory in the East, A military history of the First Crusade* (Cambridge, 1994), 126; M. Bennett and N. Hooper, *Cambridge Illustrated Atlas, Warfare, the Middle Ages, 768–1487* (Cambridge, 1996), 155.
17. Albert of Aachen, *Historia Ierosolimitana*, bk III, ch 60, 232–3; *Gesta Francorum*, bk VI, 34.
18. France, *Victory in the East*, 282; Riley-Smith, *Crusades*, 37.
19. *Gesta Francorum*, bk V, 28. See also Riley-Smith, *Crusades*, 37.
20. Fulcher of Chartres, *History of the Expedition to Jerusalem*, bk I, ch 15, 94–5.
21. Ibid., bk I, ch 16, 96.
22. Caffaro, *Liberatio Orientis* in *Annali genovesi*, I, 101–3; Raymond of Aguilers, *Historia Francorum qui ceperunt Iherusalem*, trans. J. and L. Hill (Philadelphia, 1968), ch 4, 32.
23. Gilo of Paris, *Historia Vie Hierosolimitane*, eds C. Grocock and J. Siberry (Oxford, 1997), bk V, 112–13; William of Tyre, *History of Deeds Done beyond the Sea*, I, bk 5, ch 4, 229.
24. *Codice Diplomatico della Repubblica di Genova*, ed. Imperiale di Sant'Angelo (3 vols, Rome, 1936–42), I, no. 7, 11–12; *Regesta regni Hierosolymitani 1097–1291*, ed. R. Röhricht (Innsbruch, 1893), no. 12, 2.
25. Raymond of Aguilers, *Historia Francorum*, ch 11, 85–8; William of Tyre, *History of Deeds Done beyond the Sea*, I, bk VII, ch 21, 330.
26. Raymond of Aguilers, *Historia Francorum*, ch 13, 113.
27. Albert of Aachen, *Historia Ierosolimitana*, bk III, ch 59, 230–1; bk VI, ch 55, 476–9; William of Tyre, *History of Deeds Done beyond the Sea*, I, bk III, ch 23, 183–4; bk VII, chs 16, 21, 321, 330.
28. William of Tyre, *History of Deeds Done beyond the Sea*, I, bk VII, ch 21, 330.
29. Caffaro, *Liberatio Orientis*, 110.
30. Peter Tudebode, *Historia de Hierosolymitano Itinere*, trans. J. and L. Hill (Philadelphia, 1974), ch 11, 113; Raymond of Aguilers, *Historia Francorum*, ch 14, 117.
31. Caffaro, *Liberatio Orientis*, 110–11.
32. Anna Comnena, *Alexiad*, 360.
33. Bernardo Maragone, *Annales Pisani*, 7.
34. Andrea Dandolo, *Chronica Per Extensum Descripta*, 221. See also Heywood, *History of Pisa*, 51; Pryor, 'A View from a Masthead: The First Crusade from the Sea', *Crusades*, Vol. 7 (2007), 87–152, esp. 99–101.
35. Albert of Aachen, *Historia Ierosolimitana*, bk VII, ch 7, 496–7; William of Tyre, *History of Deeds Done beyond the Sea*, I, bk 9, chs 15–16, 402–4.
36. Albert of Aachen, *Historia Ierosolimitana*, bk VII, ch 12, 502–3. See also S. Runciman, *A History of the Crusades* (3 vols, Cambridge, 1951), I, 308.
37. Heywood, *History of Pisa*, 52; Pryor, 'View from a Masthead', 98–9.
38. Albert of Aachen, *Historia Ierosolimitana*, bk VII, chs 54–5, 562–5.
39. Ibid., bk IX, chs 26–8, 670–5.
40. Albert of Aachen, *Historia Ierosolimitana*, bk X, ch 46, 760–1; bk XI, chs 13–15, 782–7.
41. Heywood, *History of Pisa*, 115.
42. *Monachi anonymi Littorensis historia de translatione sanctorum Magni Nicolai...*, *Recueil des historiens des croisades, Historiens occidentaux*, ed. Académie des Inscriptions et Belles Letters (5 vols, Paris, 1844–95), V, 253–82; Andrea Dandolo, *Chronica Per Extensum Descripta*, 221–3. See also Pryor, 'View from a Masthead', 98–101. (Mariners from Bari had previously robbed most of the saint's remains from Myra in 1087.)
43. Röhricht, *Regesta regni Hierosolymitani*, no. 31, 4.
44. Albert of Aachen, *Historia Ierosolimitana*, bk VII, chs 18–20, 510–15.
45. *Codice Diplomatico di Genova*, I, no. 12, 16–18; Röhricht, *Regesta regni Hierosolymitani*, no. 35, 5.
46. Albert of Aachen, *Historia Ierosolimitana*, bk VII, chs 54–5, 562–5; Caffaro, *Annales Ianuenses*, I, 9–12; Ibn al-Qalanisi, *The Damascus Chronicle of the Crusades*, trans. H. Gibb (London, 1932), 51; William of Tyre, *History of Deeds Done beyond the Sea*, I, bk 10, chs 14–16, 433–7.
47. Fulcher of Chartres, *Expedition to Jerusalem*, bk II, ch 9, 153–4.
48. Caffaro, *Annales Ianuenses*, I, 13.
49. S. Epstein, *Genoa and the Genoese, 958–1528* (Chapel Hill, 1996), 31.
50. Caffaro, *Liberatio Orientis*, 118–19; Fulcher of Chartres, *Expedition to Jerusalem*, bk II, ch 17, 166.

51. Albert of Aachen, *Historia Ierosolimitana*, bk IX, ch 26, 670–1; Caffaro, *Annales Ianuenses*, I, 13–14; *Liberatio Orientis*, 120–1.
52. Fulcher of Chartres, *Expedition to Jerusalem*, bk II, ch 25, 176; William of Tyre, *History of Deeds Done beyond the Sea*, I, bk 10, ch 28, 454–5. Ibn al-Qalanisi claimed there were over ninety Genoese vessels in the *Damascus Chronicle* (61) while Caffaro gives the number forty in the *Liberatio Orientis* (121).
53. William of Tyre, *History of Deeds Done beyond the Sea*, I, bk 10, ch 28, 455–6.
54. *Codice Diplomatico di Genova*, I, no. 15, 20; Röhricht, *Regesta regni Hierosolymitani*, no. 43, 8.
55. Caffaro, *Liberatio Orientis*, 118–19; *Codice Diplomatico di Genova*, I, no. 16, 21–2; Röhricht, *Regesta regni Hierosolymitani*, nos 45–6, 8–9. See also B. Kedar, 'Genoa's Golden Inscription in the Church of the Holy Sepulchre', *I Comuni Italiani nel Regno Crociato di Gerusalemme* (Genoa, 1986), 318–35.
56. Albert of Aachen, *Historia Ierosolimitana*, bk XI, chs 13–15, 782–7; Caffaro, *Annales Ianuenses*, I, 14; *Liberatio Orientis*, 123–4; Fulcher of Chartres, *Expedition to Jerusalem*, bk II, ch 41, 195; Ibn al-Qalanisi, *Damascus Chronicle*, 88–90; William of Tyre, *History of Deeds Done beyond the Sea*, I, bk 11, chs 9–10, 475–8.
57. Caffaro, *Annales Ianuenses*, I, 15; Fulcher of Chartres, *Expedition to Jerusalem*, bk II, ch 42, 196–7; Ibn al-Qalanisi, *Damascus Chronicle*, 99–100; William of Tyre, *History of Deeds Done beyond the Sea*, I, bk 11, ch 13, 484–6.
58. Snorre Sturlason, *Heimskringla or The Lives of the Norse Kings*, trans. E. Monsen and A. Smith (Cambridge, 1932), 611–12.
59. William of Tyre, *History of Deeds Done beyond the Sea*, I, bk 11, ch 14, 486–8.
60. Fulcher of Chartres, *History of the Expedition to Jerusalem*, bk III, chs 14–15, 238–9; *Historia ducum Veneticorum*, ed. H. Simonsfeld (MGH, SS, XIV, Hanover, 1883), 73.
61. F. Lane, *Venice, A Maritime Republic* (Baltimore, 1973), 34.
62. William of Tyre, *History of Deeds Done beyond the Sea*, I, bk 12, ch 25, 552–6. See also Abulafia, *Great Sea*, 293.
63. G. Tafel and G. Thomas, *Urkunden zur älteren Handels-und Staatsgeschichte der Republik Venedig* (2 vols, Vienna, 1856), I, no. XLIII, 95–8. See also Riley-Smith, 'The Venetian Crusade of 1122–1124', *I Comuni Italiani nel Regno Crociato di Gerusalemme*, 338–50.
64. W. Heyd, *Histoire du commerce du Levant au moyan âge* (2 vols, Leipzig, 1885), I, 153–4; J. Prawer, *The Crusaders' Kingdom: European Colonialism in the Middle Ages* (New York, 1972), 489–90.
65. Abulafia, *Two Italies* (Cambridge, 1977), 53.
66. Ibn al-Athir, *Chronicle of Ibn al-Athir, Part I*, 372–3; William of Tyre, *History of Deeds Done beyond the Sea*, I, bk 16, ch 5, 143.
67. William of Tyre, *History of Deeds Done beyond the Sea*, II, bk 16, ch 18, 163–4.
68. Odo of Deuil, *Ludovici VII in Orientem*, bk I, 6–9; Otto of Freising, *Deeds of Frederick Barbarossa*, bk I, ch 40, 74–5. See also Riley-Smith, *Crusades*, 122–3.
69. Odo of Deuil, *Ludovici VII in Orientem*, bk I, 10–15.
70. Otto of Freising, *Deeds of Frederick Barbarossa*, bk I, ch 40, 74–5.
71. William of Tyre, *History of Deeds Done beyond the Sea*, II, bk 16, chs 20–6, 167–79. See also Asbridge, *Crusades*, 220–1; Riley-Smith, *Crusades*, 126–8.
72. Ibn al-Athir, *Chronicle of Ibn al-Athir, Part 2*, 21–2; William of Tyre, *History of Deeds Done beyond the Sea*, II, bk 17, chs 1–6, 184–92. See also Asbridge, *Crusades*, 233–5; Riley-Smith, *Crusades*, 129.
73. William of Tyre, *History of Deeds Done beyond the Sea*, II, bk 17, ch 8, 195–6. See also Riley-Smith, *Crusades*, 129–30; Runciman, *History of the Crusades*, II, 285–6; Stanton, *Norman Naval Operations*, 101.
74. Raol Osbernus, *De expugnatione Lyxbonensi*, trans. C. David (New York, 1936). See also Runciman, *History of the Crusades*, II, 258.
75. Caffaro, *Annales Ianuenses*, I, 33–5. See also Epstein, *Genoa and the Genoese*, 49.
76. *Codice diplomatico di Genova*, I, nos 166–9, 204–17.
77. Caffaro, 'The Genoese Capture of Almeria (1147)', trans. Loud in *Medieval Italy, Texts in Translation*, eds K. Jansen, J. Drell and F. Andrews (Philadelphia, 2009), 117–21. See Epstein, *Genoa and the Genoese*, 50.

78. Caffaro, '*Ystoria Captionis Almerie et Turtuose*', in *Annali genovesi*, I, Pt. II, 79–89. See also Epstein, *Genoa and the Genoese*, 49–53.
79. Baha al-Din ibn Shaddad, *History of Saladin*, 72–5; Ibn al-Athir, *Chronicle of Ibn al-Athir, Part 2*, 320–4, 330–5; 'Old French Continuation of William of Tyre, 1184–1197', chs 40–3, 45–8.
80. Asbridge, *Crusades*, 285–99.
81. Ibn al-Athir, *Chronicle of Ibn al-Athir, Part 2*, 64–5; William of Tyre, *History of Deeds Done beyond the Sea*, II, chs 23–9, 220–31.
82. Ibn al-Athir, *Chronicle of Ibn al-Athir, Part 2*, 183–4.
83. Ibid., 229.
84. A. Ehrenkreutz, 'The Place of Saladin in the Naval History of the Mediterranean in the Middle Ages', *Journal of the American Oriental Society*, vol. 75, no. 2 (Apr–Jun 1955), 100–16, esp. 105–6.
85. Ibn al-Athir, *Chronicle of Ibn al-Athir, Part 2*, 289–90.
86. Ibn al-Athir, *Chronicle of Ibn al-Athir, Part 2*, 300–1. See also Asbridge, *Crusades*, 326–9, 332–3.
87. Ibn al-Athir, *Chronicle of Ibn al-Athir, Part 2*, 316–17. See also Asbridge, *Crusades*, 343.
88. Ibn al-Athir, *Chronicle of Ibn al-Athir, Part 2*, 324–38. See also Asbridge, *Crusades*, 354–5.
89. *Itinerarium Peregrinorum*, bk 1, ch 17, 47; 'Old French Continuation of William of Tyre', ch 74, 75; Roger of Howden, *Annals*, II, 70–4. See also Asbridge, *Crusades*, 367–71; Riley-Smith, *Crusades*, 137–8.
90. *Itinerarium Peregrinorum*, bk 1, ch 14, 43; Ibn al-Athir, *Chronicle of Ibn al-Athir, Part 2*, 345; 'Old French Continuation of William of Tyre', chs 72–3, 73–4. See also Asbridge, *Crusades*, 343.
91. *Itinerarium Peregrinorum*, bk 1, ch 14, 43–4.
92. Ibn al-Athir, *Chronicle of Ibn al-Athir, Part 2*, 345.
93. *Itinerarium Peregrinorum*, bk 1, ch 24, 64–5; 'Old French Continuation of William of Tyre', ch 94, 87–8. See also Asbridge, *Crusades*, 382, 421.
94. Roger of Howden, *Annals*, II, 79. See also Asbridge, *Crusades*, 385–6; Riley-Smith, *Crusades*, 138.
95. Roger of Howden, *Annals*, II, 143. See also Asbridge, *Crusades*, 388–9; Bennett, 'Amphibious Operations', 55; J. Gillingham, *Richard the Lionheart* (New York, 1978), 145–6.
96. *Itinerarium Peregrinorum*, bk 2, ch 7, 149.
97. Roger of Howden, *Annals*, II, 173–4.
98. Roger of Howden, *Annals*, II, 94. See also Gillingham, *Richard the Lionheart*, 159.
99. Roger of Howden, *Annals*, II, 200.
100. 'Old French Continuation of William of Tyre', ch 107, 98.
101. Baha al-Din ibn Shaddad, *History of Saladin*, 145. See also Asbridge, *Crusades*, 431.
102. Ambroise, *History of the Holy War*, II, vv 1194–1761, 48–56; *Itinerarium Peregrinorum*, bk 2, chs 27–41, 175–95; 'Old French Continuation of William of Tyre', chs 111–19, 100–4. On the *esneccas*, see also I. Dear and P. Kemp, eds, *The Oxford Companion to Ships and the Sea* (Oxford, 2005), 193; N. Rodger, *The Safeguard of the Sea, A Naval History of Britain 660–1649* (London, 1997), 47.
103. Ambroise, *History of the Holy War*, II, vv 1762–2061, 56–60; Roger of Howden, *Annals*, II, 200–5. See also Gillingham, *Richard the Lionheart*, 63–7.
104. *Itinerarium Peregrinorum*, bk 1, chs 25–6, 68–9; 'Old French Continuation of William of Tyre', chs 78–81, 79–80. See also Asbridge, *Crusades*, 400.
105. *Itinerarium Peregrinorum*, bk 1, ch 26, 70. See also Heywood, *History of Pisa*, 217; Pryor, 'Naval History, 1100–1249', *The Crusades, an Encyclopedia*, ed. A. Murray (4 vols, Santa Barbara, 2006), III, 869–76.
106. Asbridge, *Crusades*, 403.
107. *Itinerarium Peregrinorum*, bk 1, ch 27, 73; 'Old French Continuation of William of Tyre', ch 84, 81–2.
108. *Itinerarium Peregrinorum*, bk 1, ch 33, 85.
109. Ibid., bk 1, ch 34, 88.
110. Ibid.
111. Ibid.
112. Ibid.

113. Ambroise, *History of the Holy War*, II, vv 3228–427, 78–80; *Itinerarium Peregrinorum*, bk 1, ch 34, 86–8. See also Asbridge, *Crusades*, 412–15.
114. *Itinerarium Peregrinorum*, bk 1, ch 39, 94; Baha al-Din ibn Shaddad, *History of Saladin*, 112–13.
115. Baha al-Din ibn Shaddad, *History of Saladin*, 123–4.
116. Baha al-Din ibn Shaddad, *History of Saladin*, 26–7. See also Asbridge, *Crusades*, 414.
117. Ambroise, *History of the Holy War*, II, vv 3903–54, 86–7; *Itinerarium Peregrinorum*, bk 1, ch 60, 117.
118. Baha al-Din ibn Shaddad, *History of Saladin*, 141–2. See also Asbridge, *Crusades*, 425.
119. Ambroise, *History of the Holy War*, II, vv 2062–294, 60–5; Baha al-Din ibn Shaddad, *History of Saladin*, 151; *Itinerarium Peregrinorum*, bk 2, ch 42, 196–9; 'Old French Continuation of William of Tyre', ch 120, 104; Roger of Howden, *Annals*, II, 206–7. See also Asbridge, *Crusades*, 432–3.
120. Baha al-Din ibn Shaddad, *History of Saladin*, 124.
121. Asbridge, *Crusades*, 423.
122. Ambroise, *History of the Holy War*, II, vv 3765–812, 84–5; Baha al-Din ibn Shaddad, *History of Saladin*, 127–8; *Itinerarium Peregrinorum*, bk 1, ch 58, 113–14. See also Asbridge, *Crusades*, 414.
123. *Itinerarium Peregrinorum*, bk 3, chs 7–17, 208–19. See also Asbridge, *Crusades*, 437–44.
124. Asbridge, *Crusades*, 445.
125. Ambroise, *History of the Holy War*, II, vv 5714–6031, 111–14; Baha al-Din ibn Shaddad, *History of Saladin*, 165–73; *Itinerarium Peregrinorum*, bk 4, chs 10–19, 236–57; Roger of Howden, *Annals*, II, 220. See also Gillingham, *Richard the Lionheart*, 184–94; Riley-Smith, ed., *Atlas of the Crusades* (New York, 1991), 64.
126. Riley-Smith, *Crusades*, 145–6.
127. Geoffroy de Villehardouin, *Conquest of Constantinople*, in *Chronicles of the Crusades*, trans. M. Shaw (London, 1963), 27–160, esp. 29–31; Robert of Clari, *Conquest of Constantinople*, trans. E. McNeal (New York, 1936), 31–7. See also Asbridge, *Crusades*, 521–7; T. Madden, *Venice, A New History* (New York, 2012), 114–17.
128. Geoffroy de Villehardouin, *Conquest of Constantinople*, 33–5.
129. Geoffroy de Villehardouin, *Conquest of Constantinople*, 42–3. See also Madden, *Venice*, 125–8; Riley-Smith, *Crusades*, 154.
130. Geoffroy de Villehardouin, *Conquest of Constantinople*, 43–8; Robert of Clari, *Conquest of Constantinople*, 41–5.
131. Geoffroy de Villehardouin, *Conquest of Constantinople*, 50.
132. John Kinnamos, *John and Manuel Comnenus*, bk III, ch 5, 80; Niketas Choniates, *City of Byzantium*, 50–1.
133. Madden, *Venice*, 85–90; Treadgold, *History of the Byzantine State*, 648.
134. John Kinnamos, *John and Manuel Comnenus*, bk VI, ch 10, 213.
135. Riley-Smith, *Crusades*, 152–3.
136. Madden, *Venice*, 138–40; Riley-Smith, *Crusades*, 155.
137. Geoffroy de Villehardouin, *Conquest of Constantinople*, 46.
138. Robert of Clari, *Conquest of Constantinople*, 68.
139. Bennett et al., *Fighting Techniques of the Medieval World*, 227–9; 'Amphibious Operations', 59–60.
140. Robert of Clari, *Conquest of Constantinople*, 70–1.
141. Geoffroy de Villehardouin, *Conquest of Constantinople*, 67–73. See also Riley-Smith, *Crusades*, 156–8.
142. Geoffroy de Villehardouin, *Conquest of Constantinople*, 82–6. See also Madden, *Venice*, 143–4; Riley-Smith, *Crusades*, 156–7; Treadgold, *History of the Byzantine State*, 665–6.
143. Riley-Smith, *Crusades*, 159.
144. Geoffroy de Villehardouin, *Conquest of Constantinople*, 90.
145. Geoffroy de Villehardouin, *Conquest of Constantinople*, 91. See Bennett, 'Amphibious Operations', 61–2.
146. Geoffroy de Villehardouin, *Conquest of Constantinople*, 88.
147. Geoffroy de Villehardouin, *Conquest of Constantinople*, 94–7. See also Madden, *Venice*, 147–9; Riley-Smith, *Crusades*, 217–18.

148. Riley-Smith, *Crusades*, 161–2.
149. Ibid., 166.
150. Ibid., 169–70.
151. Asbridge, *Crusades*, 551–2; Riley-Smith, *Crusades*, 173–6.
152. Oliver of Paderborn, *The Capture of Damietta*, trans. J. Gavigan in *Christian Society and the Crusades, 1198–1229* (Philadelphia, 1948), 49–139, esp. ch 1, 51–2.
153. Oliver of Paderborn, *Capture of Damietta*, ch 10, 61; Roger of Wendover, *Flowers of History, The History of England from the Descent of of the Saxons to A.D. 1235*, trans. J. Giles (2 vols, London, 1849), II, 404–6. See also Asbridge, *Crusades*, 551–2.
154. Oliver of Paderborn, *Capture of Damietta*, ch 32, 88.
155. Ibid., ch 10, 62.
156. Ibid., ch 32, 88.
157. Ibn al-Athir, *Chronicle of Ibn al-Athir. Part 3*, trans. Richards (Aldershot, 2008), 176.
158. Oliver of Paderborn, *Capture of Damietta*, ch 11, 63–4; Roger of Wendover, *Flowers of History*, II, 406–7. See also Bennett, 'Amphibious Operations', 63.
159. Oliver of Paderborn, *Capture of Damietta*, ch 12, 65.
160. Oliver of Paderborn, *Capture of Damietta*, chs 13–14, 65–8; Roger of Wendover, *Flowers of History*, II, 407–10. See also Asbridge, *Crusades*, 552–3.
161. Roger of Wendover, *Flowers of History*, II, 410–11.
162. Oliver of Paderborn, *Capture of Damietta*, ch 22, 73–4.
163. Ibn al-Athir, *Chronicle of Ibn al-Athir. Part 3*, 176–7.
164. Roger of Wendover, *Flowers of History*, II, 412–13. See also Riley-Smith, *Atlas of the Crusades*, 94–5; *Crusades*, 178; Hooper and Bennett, *Cambridge Illustrated Atlas*, 111–12.
165. Oliver of Paderborn, *Capture of Damietta*, ch 19, 71–2.
166. Ibid., ch 31, 85.
167. Ibn al-Athir, *Chronicle of Ibn al-Athir. Part 3*, 177; Oliver of Paderborn, *Capture of Damietta*, ch 22, 74–5; Roger of Wendover, *Flowers of History*, II, 414–16.
168. Riley-Smith, *Crusades*, 179.
169. Roger of Wendover, *Flowers of History*, II, 416–20.
170. Oliver of Paderborn, *Capture of Damietta*, ch 31, 85–6; Roger of Wendover, *Flowers of History*, II, 422–3. See also Asbridge, *Crusades*, 557; Riley-Smith, *Crusades*, 179.
171. Oliver of Paderborn, *Capture of Damietta*, ch 32, 88; Roger of Wendover, *Flowers of History*, II, 423.
172. Asbridge, *Crusades*, 559; Riley-Smith, *Crusades*, 179.
173. Asbridge, *Crusades*, 560.
174. Marchiso Scriba, *Annales Ianuenses*, II, 178; Richard of San Germano, *Notarii Chronica, anno* 1221, 95. See also Abulafia, 'Henry Count of Malta and his Mediterranean Activities, 1203–1230, in *Medieval Malta: Studies on Malta before the Knights*, ed. A. Luttrell (Rome, 1975), 104–25, esp. 119–22.
175. Oliver of Paderborn, *Capture of Damietta*, ch 57, 114. See also Asbridge, *Crusades*, 560.
176. Oliver of Paderborn, *Capture of Damietta*, chs 57–9, 114–16. See also *Crusades*, Riley-Smith, 180.
177. Ibn al-Athir, *Chronicle of Ibn al-Athir, Part 3*, 178–81. See also Asbridge, *Crusades*, 560–1; Hooper and Bennet, *Cambridge Illustrated Atlas*, 111–12; Riley-Smith, *Atlas of the Crusades*, 94–5.
178. Oliver of Paderborn, *Capture of Damietta*, chs 75–8, 128–30; Roger of Wendover, *Flowers of History*, II, 435–8. See also Asbridge, *Crusades*, 561–2.
179. Asbridge, *Crusades*, 562.
180. Richard of San Germano, *Notarii Chronica, anno* 1221, 100. See also Abulafia, 'Henry Count of Malta', 121.
181. Huillard-Bréholles, ed., *Historia Diplomatica Friderici Secundi*, II, Pt. I, 410.
182. Huillard-Bréholles, *Historia Diplomatica Friderici Secundi*, II, pt 1, 501–3; Roger of Wendover, *Flowers of History*, II, 501. See also Riley-Smith, *Crusades*, 180–1.
183. Asbridge, *Crusades*, 565; Riley-Smith, *Crusades*, 181.

184. Richard of San Germano, *Notarii Chronica*, *anno* 1227, 148. See also Abulafia, *Frederick II, A Medieval Emperor* (Oxford, 1988), 164–74; Pryor, 'The Crusade of Emperor Frederick II, 1220–29: The Implications of the Maritime Evidence', *American Neptune*, 52 (1992), 113–32, esp. 127.
185. Philip of Novara, *The Wars of Frederick II against the Ibelins in Syria and Cyprus*, trans. J. La Monte (New York, 1936), ch 18, 73 and ch 40, 88. See also Pryor, 'Crusade of Emperor Frederick II', 127.
186. Pryor, 'Crusade of Emperor Frederick II', 127–8.
187. Abulafia, *Frederick II*, 170–1; Asbridge, *Crusades*, 565–6; Riley-Smith, *Crusades*, 181.
188. Philip of Novara, *Wars of Frederick II*, ch 40, 88–9; Roger of Wendover, *Flowers of History*, II, 511–12. See also Abulafia, *Frederick II*, 180–2; Asbridge, *Crusades*, 568–9; Riley-Smith, *Crusades*, 181.
189. Pryor, 'Crusade of Emperor Frederick II', 127–8, 131–2.
190. Ibn Wasil, in *Arab Historians of the Crusades*, trans. F. Gabrieli (London, 1969), 269–70.
191. Frederick II, 'Letter from Frederick II to Henry III of England, the Imperial Achievement', in Roger of Wendover, *Flowers of History*, II, 522–4; Huillard-Bréholles, *Historia Diplomatica Friderici Secundi*, III, 93–9, esp. 97; *L'estoire de Eracles empereur et la conqueste de la terre d'Outremer*, *Recueil des historiens des croisades*, *Historiens occidentaux*, II, 375. See also Abulafia, *Frederick II*, 183–7.
192. Abulafia, *Frederick II*, 189–95.
193. Ibid., 172.
194. Philip of Novara, *Wars of Frederick II*, ch 43, 91.
195. 'Rothelin Continuation of the History of William of Tyre', trans. J. Shirley in *Crusader Syria in the Thirteenth Century* (Aldershot, 1999), 13–120, esp. 63–5.
196. Asbridge, *Crusades*, 578–80; Riley-Smith, *Crusades*, 190–1.
197. John of Joinville, *The Life of Saint Louis*, in *Chronicles of the Crusades*, 161–353, esp. 197. See also Asbridge, *Crusades*, 580–1; Riley-Smith, *Crusades*, 193.
198. Asbridge, *Crusades*, 580–2; Riley-Smith, *Crusades*, 193.
199. John of Joinville, *Life of Saint Louis*, 196–7; 'Rothelin Continuation', 67.
200. Asbridge, *Crusades*, 584–5.
201. Pryor, 'Transportation of horses by sea', 103.
202. John of Joinville, *Life of Saint Louis*, 201. See also P. Jackson, ed. and trans., *The Seventh Crusade, 1244–1254: Sources and Documents* (Farnham, 2009), 63–4.
203. Pryor, 'Transportation of horses by sea', 105.
204. John of Joinville, *Life of Saint Louis*, 201, 269; 'Rothelin Continuation', 69.
205. Pryor, 'Mediterranean Round Ship', 63–4.
206. John of Joinville, *Life of Saint Louis*, 196.
207. 'Rothelin Continuation', 67–9.
208. John of Joinville, *Life of Saint Louis*, 201–2; 'Rothelin Continuation', 85.
209. John of Joinville, *Life of Saint Louis*, 202–3; 'Rothelin Continuation', 86.
210. John of Joinville, *Life of Saint Louis*, 203–4.
211. 'Rothelin Continuation', 69, 86.
212. Ibid., 86.
213. Ibn Wasil, in *Arab Historians of the Crusades*, 284–5.
214. John of Joinville, *Life of Saint Louis*, 211–13; 'Rothelin Continuation', 91. See Asbridge, *Crusades*, 592–3.
215. John of Joinville, *Life of Saint Louis*, 213–16; 'Rothelin Continuation', 92–3. See also Asbridge, *Crusades*, 594–5; Bennett, 'Amphibious Operations', 65.
216. John of Joinville, *Life of Saint Louis*, 216.
217. Ibn Walid, in *Arab Historians of the Crusades*, 291–2; John of Joinville, *Life of Saint Louis*, 216–19; 'Rothelin Continuation', 94–6. See also Asbridge, *Crusades*, 596–7; Bennett, 'Amphibious Operations', 66.
218. 'Rothelin Continuation', 96–8.

219. Ibn Walid, in *Arab Historians of the Crusades*, 292; John of Joinville, *Life of Saint Louis*, 237; 'Rothelin Continuation', 99. See also Hooper and Bennett, *Cambridge Illustrated Atlas*, 112–13.
220. 'Rothelin Continuation', 99.
221. John of Joinville, *Life of Saint Louis*, 240–2; 'Rothelin Continuation', 100–3.
222. Jackson, *Seventh Crusade*, 160.
223. John of Joinville, *Life of Saint Louis*, 253–318; 'Rothelin Continuation', 104–6, 112–13.
224. Asbridge, *Crusades*, 615–20; P. Thorau, *The Lion of Egypt: Sultan Baybars I and the Near East in the Thirteenth Century*, trans. P. Holt (London, 1992), 77–82.
225. Asbridge, *Crusades*, 633.
226. Thorau, *Lion of Egypt*, 158–62.
227. Pryor, 'Transportation of horses by sea', 107–8.
228. M. Balard, 'Coastal Shipping and Navigation in the Mediterranean', in *Cogs, Caravels and Galleons*, 131–8, esp. 135; Pryor, 'Naval Architecture of Crusader Transport Ships', 175–85, 208–9.
229. Lane, *Venetian Ships and Shipbuilders of the Renaissance* (Baltimore, 1934), 36.
230. Ibn 'Abd Az-Zahir, in *Arab Historians of the Crusades*, 307–12. See also Asbridge, *Crusades*, 635–7.
231. Al-Maqrizi, in *Arab Historians of the Crusades*, 303–4; John of Joinville, *Life of Saint Louis*, 345–50. See also Asbridge, *Crusades*, 640–1; Riley-Smith, *Crusades*, 210–11.
232. Abu l-Fida, in *Arab Historians of the Crusades*, 344–6. See also Asbridge, *Crusades*, 652–4.
233. John Kinnamos, *John and Manuel Comnenus*, bk I, ch 2, 14.
234. Tafel and Thomas, *Urkunden der Republik Venedig*, I, no. XXIII, 43–54.
235. Andrea Dandolo, *Chronica Per Extensum Descripta*, 232; *Historia ducum Veneticorum*, 73. See also Treadgold, *History of the Byzantine State*, 629–30.
236. William of Tyre, *History of Deeds Done beyond the Sea*, I, bk 12, ch 9, 529.
237. Ibid., I, bk 12, ch 10, 531.
238. Andrea Dandolo, *Chronica Per Extensum Descripta*, 232; Fulcher of Chartres, *History of the Expedition to Jerusalem*, bk III, ch 3, 227, note 4; Ibn al-Qalanisi, *Damascus Chronicle*, 159–61; Ibn al-Athir, *Chronicle of Ibn al-Athir, Part I*, 203–5; William of Tyre, *History of Deeds Done beyond the Sea*, I, bk 12, chs 9–10, 528–31.
239. Andrea Dandolo, *Chronica Per Extensum Descripta*, 232; William of Tyre, *History of Deeds Done beyond the Sea*, I, bk 12, ch 13, 535–6. See also Asbridge, *Crusades*, 179.
240. Andrea Dandolo, *Chronica Per Extensum Descripta*, 232; *Historia ducum Veneticorum*, 73; Röhricht, *Regesta regni Hierosolymitani*, no. 102, 23.
241. Andrea Dandolo, *Chronica Per Extensum Descripta*, 232; Fulcher of Chartres, *History of the Expedition to Jerusalem*, bk III, ch 14, 238 and note 2; *Historia ducum Veneticorum*, 73; William of Tyre, *History of Deeds Done beyond the Sea*, I, bk 12, ch 22, 548 and note 66.
242. William of Tyre, *History of Deeds Done beyond the Sea*, I, bk 12, ch 22, 548.
243. Fulcher of Chartres, *History of the Expedition to Jerusalem*, bk III, chs 14–15, 238–9.
244. *Historia ducum Veneticorum*, 73.
245. Fulcher of Chartres, *History of the Expedition to Jerusalem*, bk III, ch 14, 238–9.
246. Fulcher of Chartres, *History of the Expedion to Jersualem*, bk III, ch 16, 239–40, note 1; *Historia ducum Veneticorum*, 73; William of Tyre, *History of Deeds Done beyond the Sea*, I, bk 12, ch 17, 539–41, note 57.
247. Fulcher of Chartres, *History of the Expedition to Jerusalem*, bk III, ch 16, 239.
248. Andrea Dandolo, *Chronica Per Extensum Descripta*, 233; Fulcher of Chartres, *History of the Expedition to Jerusalem*, bk III, chs 17–20, 240–3; William of Tyre, *History of Deeds Done beyond the Sea*, I, bk 12, chs 21–2, 545–8.
249. Andrea Dandolo, *Chronica Per Extensum Descripta*, 233; Fulcher of Chartres, *History of the Expedition to Jerusalem*, bk III, ch 20, 243–5; William of Tyre, *History of Deeds Done beyond the Sea*, I, bk 12, chs 22–3, 548–9.
250. Fulcher of Chartres, *History of the Expedition to Jerusalem*, bk III, ch 20, 244.
251. William of Tyre, *History of Deeds Done beyond the Sea*, I, bk 12, ch 23, 549–50.
252. Fulcher of Chartres, *History of the Expedition to Jerusalem*, bk III, ch 20, 244–5.
253. William of Tyre, *History of Deeds Done beyond the Sea*, I, bk 12, ch 24, 550–2.

254. Fulcher of Chartres, *History of the Expedition to Jerusalem*, bk III, ch 11, 235.
255. William of Tyre, *History of Deeds Done beyond the Sea*, I, bk 12, ch 25, 552–6.
256. Röhricht, *Regesta regni Hierosolymitani*, no. 105, 25; Tafel and Thomas, *Urkunden der Republik Venedig*, I, no. XLI, 90–4.
257. Fulcher of Chartres, *History of the Expedition to Jerusalem*, bk III, chs 27–28, 255–6; *Historia ducum Veneticorum*, 74; William of Tyre, *History of Deeds Done beyond the Sea*, II, bk 13, chs 6–7, 10–12.
258. Fulcher of Chartres, *History of the Expedition to Jerusalem*, bk III, ch 24, 266; Ibn al-Athir, *Chronicle of Ibn al-Athir*, 251–3; Ibn al-Qalanisi, *Damascus Chronicle*, 170–2; William of Tyre, *History of Deeds Done beyond the Sea*, II, bk 13, chs 9 and 13, 13–15 and 18–19.
259. Andrea Dandolo, *Chronica Per Extensum Descripta*, 234–5; Fulcher of Chartres, *History of the Expedition to Jerusalem*, bk III, ch 41, 276; *Historia ducum Veneticorum*, 74.
260. Andrea Dandolo, *Chronica Per Extensum Descripta*, 236.
261. Tafel and Thomas, *Urkunden der Republik Venedig*, I, no. XLIII, 95–8. See also Riley-Smith, 'The Venetian Crusade of 1122–1124', *I Comuni Italiani nel Regno Crociato di Gerusalemme* (Genoa, 1986), 338–50.

Chapter 4. Genoese–Pisan Rivalry for the Western Mediterranean

1. Epstein, *Genoa and the Genoese*, 140.
2. Epstein, *Genoa and the Genoese*, 26; Heywood, *History of Pisa*, 70–1.
3. Lewis, *Naval Power and Trade*, 103.
4. Pirenne, *Mohammed and Charlemagne*, 160.
5. Ibn al-Athir, *BAS*, I, 365–7.
6. Lewis, *Naval Power and Trade*, 177.
7. Liudprand of Cremona, *Antapodosis*, bk I, chs 2–4, 33–4. See also Pryor and Jeffreys, *Dromōn*, 69.
8. Ibn al-Athir, *BAS*, I, 412. See also Amari, *Storia dei Musulmani di Sicilia*, I, 211–13.
9. Epstein, *Genoa and the Genoese*, 14.
10. Liudprand of Cremona, *Antapodosis*, bk IV, ch 5, 144.
11. Ibn al-Athir, *BAS*, I, 412.
12. P. Classen, '*Res Gestae*, Universal History', *Renaissance and Renewal in the Twelfth Century*, eds R. Benson, G. Constable and C. Lanham (Cambridge, Mass., 1982), 387–417, esp. 395–6.
13. Bernardo Maragone, *Annales Pisani*, 4. (Medieval Pisa used the *calculus Pisanus* for dating, meaning its calendar started on 25 March and thus was about nine months ahead on most dates.)
14. Ibid.
15. Ibn al-Athir, *BAS*, I, 436. See also Heywood, *History of Pisa*, 19–20.
16. Thietmar of Merseburg, *Chronicon*, bk 7, ch 45, 338–9.
17. Bernardo Maragone, *Annales Pisani*, 4; Ibn al-Athir, *BAS*, I, 436–7; *Liber maiolichinus de gestis Pisanorum illustribus*, ed. C. Calisse (Rome, 1904), vv 930–41, 41. See also Epstein, *Genoa and the Genoese*, 22–3; Heywood, *History of Pisa*, 20–2.
18. Abulafia, *Great Sea*, 174–5.
19. Bernardo Maragone, *Annales Pisani*, 4–5.
20. Classen, '*Res Gestae*', 396–7.
21. Heywood, *History of Pisa*, 20–2.
22. Bernardo Maragone, *Annales Pisani*, 5.
23. Geoffrey Malaterra, *Deeds of Count Roger*, bk 2, ch 34, 111–12.
24. Bernardo Maragone, *Annales Pisani*, 5–6. See also Heywood, *History of Pisa*, 23.
25. Bernardo Maragone, *Annales Pisani*, 6.
26. Heywood, *History of Pisa*, 30–1; Manfroni, *Storia della Marina italiana*, I, 167.
27. Bernardo Maragone, *Annales Pisani*, 6.
28. Heywood, *History of Pisa*, 31; Manfroni, *Storia della Marina italiana*, I, 168.
29. Amari, *I Diplomi Arabi del R. Archivio Fiorentino* (Florence, 1863), *Introduzione storica*; Heywood, *History of Pisa*, 31; Manfroni, *Storia della Marina italiana*, I, 99.
30. G. Luzzatto, *An Economic History of Italy*, trans. P. Jones (London, 1961), 55.
31. Ibn al-Athir, *BAS*, I, 440.

32. *Carmen in Victoria Pisanorum*, ed. Cowdrey in 'The Mahdia campaign of 1087', *English Historical Review*, CCCLXII (1977), 1–29, esp. 24, par. 10.
33. Ibn abi Dinar, *BAS*, II, 283; At-Tijani, *BAS*, II, 62; Ibn al-Athir, *BAS*, I, 441.
34. *Carmen in Victoria Pisanorum*, 25, par. 11–13.
35. Ibn al-Athir, *BAS*, I, 451; Malaterra, *Deeds of Count Roger*, bk 4, ch 3, 193–4.
36. *Carmen in Victoria Pisanorum*, 25, par. 15; Ibn al-Athir, *BAS*, I, 441; Al-Nuwayri, *BAS*, II, 153.
37. At-Tijani, *BAS*, II, 65.
38. Bernardo Maragone, *Annales Pisani*, 6.
39. At-Tijani, *BAS*, II, 64.
40. *Carmen in Victoria Pisanorum*, 26, par. 37.
41. Ibid., 26, par. 52–4.
42. Al-Nuwayri, *BAS*, II, 153; *Carmen in Victoria Pisanorum*, 28, par. 58; Ibn al-Athir, *BAS*, I, 441.
43. Bernardo Maragone, *Annales Pisani*, 7.
44. Heywood, *History of Pisa*, 43.
45. H. Krueger, 'The Wares of Exchange in the Genoese–African Traffic of the Twelfth Century', *Speculum*, XII, (1937), 57–71, esp. 65 and 71; R. Lopez, 'Market Expansion: The Case of Genoa', *Journal of Economic History*, XXIV (1964), 445–64, esp. 450; Prawer, *Crusaders' Kingdom*, 496–7; Riley-Smith, 'Government in Latin Syria and the commercial privileges of foreign merchants', in *Relations between East and West in the Middle Ages*, ed. D. Baker (Edinburgh, 1973), 109–32, esp. 115–22.
46. Abulafia, *Great Sea*, 278.
47. Abulafia, *Two Italies*, 95–6.
48. Benjamin of Tudela, *The Itinerary of Bejamin of Tudela*, trans. M. Adler (London, 1907), 2.
49. E. Byrne, 'Genoese Colonies in Syria', in *The Crusades and other Historical Essays presented to Dana C. Munro by his former students*, ed. L. Paetow (New York, 1928), 139–82, esp. 143.
50. Krueger, 'Wares of Exchange in Genoese–African Traffic', 59–61, 70–1; Prawer, *Crusaders' Kingdom*, 496.
51. Abulafia, *Great Sea*, 258–70; S. Goitein, *A Mediterranean Society* (6 vols, Berkeley, 1967), I, 310.
52. Goitein, *Mediterranean Society*, I, 40, 59 and 211; 'Glimpses from the Cairo Geniza on naval warfare in the Mediterranean', *Studi Orientalistici in onore di Giorgio Levi della Vita* (Rome, 1956), 393–408, esp. 397.
53. Heywood, *History of Pisa*, 58.
54. *Liber maiolichinus*, vv 39–75, 7–8. See also Heywood, *History of Pisa*, 59–60.
55. *Liber maiolichinus*, vv 133–6, 11–12.
56. Bernardo Maragone, *Annales Pisani*, 8; *Liber maiolichinus*, vv 133–6, 13, note 2.
57. *Liber maiolichinus*, vv 106–19, 10–11.
58. *Liber maiolichinus*, vv 120–6, 11. See also Heywood, *History of Pisa*, 61–2.
59. *Liber maiolichinus*, vv 184–201, 14.
60. *Liber maiolichinus*, vv 217–41, 15–16. See also Heywood, *History of Pisa*, 63–4.
61. *Liber maiolichinus*, vv 242–63, 16–17 and 'Trattato di alleanza fra il conte di Barcelona e i pisani, 7 settembre 1114, nel Porto di S. Felice', App. I, 137–8. See also Heywood, *History of Pisa*, 64.
62. *Liber maiolichinus*, vv 427–44, 23.
63. *Liber maiolichinus*, vv 377–81, 21. See also Heywood, *History of Pisa*, 65.
64. *Liber maiolichinus*, vv 713, 32.
65. Ibid., vv 730–3, 33.
66. *Liber maiolichinus*, vv 1165–76, 50. See also Heywood, *History of Pisa*, 66.
67. *Liber maiolichinus*, vv 1192–1230, 51–2.
68. Ibid., vv 1510–33, 61–2.
69. *Liber maiolichinus*, vv 2392–9, 92–3. See also Heywood, *History of Pisa*, 67–8.
70. Bernardo Maragone, *Annales Pisani*, 8; *Liber maiolichinus*, vv 3173–504, 119–31.
71. Heywood, *History of Pisa*, 68.
72. Ibid., 69–70.
73. Caffaro, *Annales Ianuenses*, I, 16. See also Heywood, *History of Pisa*, 72–3.
74. Bernardo Maragone, *Annales Pisani*, 8.

75. Ibid., 9.
76. Caffaro, *Annales Ianuenses*, I, 16–17. See also Epstein, *Genoa and the Genoese*, 41; Heywood, *History of Pisa*, 73.
77. Bernardo Maragone, *Annales Pisani*, 9. See also Heywood, *History of Pisa*, 73–4.
78. Epstein, *Genoa and the Genoese*, 41–2; Heywood, *History of Pisa*, 74–5.
79. Caffaro, *Annales Ianuenses*, I, 21–2. See also Manfroni, *Storia della Marina italiana*, I, 176–7.
80. Caffaro, *Annales Ianuenses*, I, 22–3. See also Manfroni, *Storia della Marina italiana*, I, 177.
81. Gentile, ed., *Annales Pisani*, 9, note 5; P. Tronci, *Annali Pisani, rifusi, arricchiti di molti fatti e sequitati fino all'anno 1839* (Pisa, 1868), 61–5. See also Heywood, *History of Pisa*, 78.
82. Caffaro, *Annales Ianuenses*, I, 23. See also Manfroni, *Storia della Marina italiana*, I, 177.
83. Caffaro, *Annales Ianuenses*, I, 26. See also Heywood, *History of Pisa*, 79.
84. *Codice Diplomatico della Repubblica di Genova*, I, docs 64–5, 75–80. See also Heywood, *History of Pisa*, 79–80; Manfroni, *Storia della Marina italiana*, I, 179.
85. Abulafia, *Two Italies*, 62–70.
86. Epstein, *Genoa and the Genoese*, 47–8.
87. Heywood, *History of Pisa*, 90–3, 105–6.
88. Abulafia, *Two Italies*, 124–5.
89. Ibid., 127–9.
90. Caffaro, *Annales Ianuenses*, I, 67–8.
91. Bernardo Maragone, *Annales Pisani*, 27.
92. Caffaro, *Annales Ianuenses*, I, 68–9. See also Epstein, *Genoa and the Genoese*, 78; Heywood, *History of Pisa*, 137–8.
93. Bernardo Maragone, *Annales Pisani*, 27; Caffaro, *Annales Ianuenses*, I, 70–2. See also Heywood, *History of Pisa*, 139–42.
94. Epstein, *Genoa and the Genoese*, 83; Heywood, *History of Pisa*, 147–55; Manfroni, *Storia della Marina italiana*, I, 233–6.
95. Bernardo Maragone, *Annales Pisani*, 35. See also Heywood, *History of Pisa*, 155.
96. Bernardo Maragone, *Annales Pisani*, 36.
97. Oberto Cancelliere, *Annales Ianuenses*, I, 179–80. See also Heywood, *History of Pisa*, 171–2.
98. Bernardo Maragone, *Annales Pisani*, 36–7; Oberto Cancelliere, *Annales Ianuenses*, I, 180–6.
99. Bernardo Maragone, *Annales Pisani*, 37–8; Oberto Cancelliere, *Annales Ianuenses*, I, 186–7. See also Heywood, *History of Pisa*, 172–4.
100. Bernardo Maragone, *Annales Pisani*, 38; Oberto Cancelliere, *Annales Ianuenses*, I, 190–1.
101. Bernardo Maragone, *Annales Pisani*, 39; Oberto Cancelliere, *Annales Ianuenses*, I, 192. See also Heywood, *History of Pisa*, 175–7.
102. Bernardo Maragone, *Annales Pisani*, 46–7; Oberto Cancelliere, *Annales Ianuenses*, I, 209–10. See also Heywood, *History of Pisa*, 188.
103. Bernardo Maragone, *Annales Pisani*, 58; Oberto Cancelliere, *Annales Ianuenses*, I, 254–5. See also Heywood, *History of Pisa*, 203; Manfroni, *Storia della Marina italiana*, I, 249.
104. Bernardo Maragone, *Annales Pisani*, 58–9. See also Heywood, *History of Pisa*, 204.
105. Ottobono Scriba, *Annales Ianuenses*, II, 8–9. See also Heywood, *History of Pisa*, 205–6.
106. Ottobono Scriba, *Annales Ianuenses*, II, 24–6. See also Epstein, *Genoa and the Genoese*, 87; Heywood, *History of Pisa*, 216–17.
107. Ambroise, *History of the Holy War*, II, vv 8177–234, 141–2; *Itinerarium Peregrinorum*, bk 5, ch 10, 291–3.
108. Ottobono Scriba, *Annales Ianuenses*, II, 48–9. See also Epstein, *Genoa and the Genoese*, 89; Heywood, *History of Pisa*, 224–5; Manfroni, *Storia della Marina italiana*, I, 294–5.
109. Manfroni, *Storia della Marina italiana*, I, 302–3; Pryor, 'The Maritime Republics', in *The New Cambridge Medieval History*, V, *c.1198–c.1300*, ed. Abulafia (Cambridge, 1999), 419–46, esp. 424.
110. Ogerio Pane, *Annales Ianuenses*, II, 90–1. See also Epstein, *Genoa and the Genoese*, 103; Pryor, 'Maritime Republics', 424; Manfroni, *Storia della Marina italiana*, I, 303.
111. Ogerio Pane, *Annales Ianuenses*, II, 96–8. See also Epstein, *Genoa and the Genoese*, 103; Manfroni, *Storia della Marina italiana*, I, 303–4.
112. Manfroni, *Storia della Marina italiana*, I, 343–4.

113. Ogerio Pane, *Annales Ianuenses*, II, 103. See also Manfroni, *Storia della Marina italiana*, I, 360.
114. Ogerio Pane, *Annales Ianuenses*, II, 105–6. See also Manfroni, *Storia della Marina italiana*, I, 360–2.
115. Richard of San Germano, *Notarii Chronica*, *anno* 1207, 24. See also Manfroni, *Storia della Marina italiana*, I, 361.
116. Ogerio Pane, *Annales Ianuenses*, II, 109–10. See also Manfroni, *Storia della Marina italiana*, I, 362.
117. Ogerio Pane, *Annales Ianuenses*, II, 113–14. See also Epstein, *Genoa and the Genoese*, 104.
118. Ogerio Pane, *Annales Ianuenses*, II, 142–3. See also Epstein, *Genoa and the Genoese*, 105, 109; Heywood, *History of Pisa*, 204; Manfroni, *Storia della Marina italiana*, I, 364–5.
119. Richard of San Germano, *Notarii Chronica*, *anni* 1227–8, 148–52.
120. Epstein, *Genoa and the Genoese*, 83.
121. Bartolomeo Scriba, *Annales Ianuenses*, III, 59–63. See also Epstein, *Genoa and the Genoese*, 121.
122. Epstein, *Genoa and the Genoese*, 123; Pryor, 'Maritime Republics', 433.
123. Abulafia, *Frederick II*, 311–12; Pryor, 'Maritime Republics', 433–4.
124. Bartolomeo Scriba, *Annales Ianuenses*, III, 104–5. See Manfroni, *Storia della Marina italiana*, I, 395–7.
125. Bartolomeo Scriba, *Annales Ianuenses*, III, 105–7. See also Epstein, *Genoa and the Genoese*, 124.
126. Bartolomeo Scriba, *Annales Ianuenses*, III, 111–12. See also Manfroni, *Storia della Marina italiana*, I, 398.
127. Bartolomeo Scriba, *Annales Ianuenses*, III, 113; 'Rothelin Continuation', ch 37, 60. See also Abulafia, *Frederick II*, 346–7; Manfroni, *Storia della Marina italiana*, I, 398–9; Pryor, 'Maritime Republics', 434.
128. Bartolomeo Scriba, *Annales Ianuenses*, III, 114–62. See also Epstein, *Genoa and the Genoese*, 124–9; Pryor, 'Maritime Republics', 434–5.
129. Bartolomeo Scriba, *Annales Ianuenses*, III, 114–62; 'Rothelin Continuation', ch 79, 115–16. See also J. Dotson, 'Venice, Genoa and Control of the Seas in the Thirteenth and Fourteenth Centuries', in *War at Sea in the Middle Ages*, 119–36, esp. 120–1; Lane, *Venice*, 73–5; Manfroni, *Storia della Marina italiana*, I, 436–9.
130. Epstein, *Genoa and the Genoese*, 150–3; Pryor, 'Maritime Republics', 436.
131. Dotson, 'Venice, Genoa and Control of the Seas', 122–3; Pryor, 'Maritime Republics', 436–7.
132. Pryor, 'Maritime Republics', 437.
133. Epstein, *Genoa and the Genoese*, 156–8.
134. Iacopo Doria, *Annales Ianuenses*, V, 20–3; Templar of Tyre, *The 'Templar of Tyre', Part III of the 'Deeds of the Cypriots'*, trans. P. Crawford (Aldershot, 2003), 87. See also Epstein, *Genoa and the Genoese*, 158.
135. Iacopo Doria, *Annales Ianuenses*, V, 25. See also Epstein, *Genoa and the Genoese*, 158.
136. Iacopo Doria, *Annales Ianuenses*, V, 23–4; Templar of Tyre, *Deeds of the Cypriots*, p. 88. See also Manfroni, *Storia della Marina italiana*, II, 110–11.
137. Iacopo Doria, *Annales Ianuenses*, V, 45. See also Epstein, *Genoa and the Genoese*, 159.
138. Iacopo Doria, *Annales Ianuenses*, V, 30. See also Epstein, *Genoa and the Genoese*, 159.
139. Iacopo Doria, *Annales Ianuenses*, V, 38–40. See also Manfroni, *Storia della Marina italiana*, II, 117–18.
140. Iacopo Doria, *Annales Ianuenses*, V, 51–6; Salimbene de Adam, *The Chronicle of Salimbene de Adam*, eds J. Baird, G. Baglivi and J. Robert Kane (Binghamton, 1986), 542–3; Templar of Tyre, *Deeds of the Cypriots*, 89–91. See also Epstein, *Genoa and the Genoese*, 159; Manfroni, *Storia della Marina italiana*, II, 126–31; Rodgers, *Naval Warfare under Oars*, 130–3.
141. Epstein, *Genoa and the Genoese*, 177; Manfroni, *Storia della Marina italiana*, II, 131–3.
142. Manfroni, *Storia della Marina italiana*, II, 139; Pryor, 'Maritime Republics', 439.
143. Heywood, *History of Pisa*, 72.
144. Iacopo Doria, *Annales Ianuenses*, V, 48–9; Templar of Tyre, *Deeds of the Cypriots*, 88–9. See also Manfroni, *Storia della Marina italiana*, II, 121–2.
145. Iacopo Doria, *Annales Ianuenses*, V, 51. See also Manfroni, *Storia della Marina italiana*, II, 124.
146. Iacopo Doria, *Annales Ianuenses*, V, 52. See also Manfroni, *Storia della Marina italiana*, II, 124; Rodgers, *Naval Warfare under Oars*, 130.

147. Salimbene de Adam, *Chronicle*, 542.
148. Iacopo Doria, *Annales Ianuenses*, V, 52. See also Manfroni, *Storia della Marina italiana*, II, 124.
149. Iacopo Doria, *Annales Ianuenses*, V, 53. See also Manfroni, *Storia della Marina italiana*, II, 125–6.
150. Iacopo Doria, *Annales Ianuenses*, V, 53–4. See also Manfroni, *Storia della Marina italiana*, II, 126; Rodgers, *Naval Warfare under Oars*, 131.
151. S. Busch, *Medieval Mediterranean Ports, Catalan and Tuscan Coasts, 1100 to 1235* (Leiden, 2001), 179–80.
152. Iacopo Doria, *Annales Ianuenses*, V, 54. See also Manfroni, *Storia della Marina italiana*, II, 126–7.
153. Iacopo Doria, *Annales Ianuenses*, V, 55. See also Manfroni, *Storia della Marina italiana*, II, 128; Rodgers, *Naval Warfare under Oars*, 131–2.
154. Templar of Tyre, *Deeds of the Cypriots*, 90.
155. Templar of Tyre, *Deeds of the Cypriots*, 90–1. See also Manfroni, *Storia della Marina italiana*, II, 129; Rodgers, *Naval Warfare under Oars*, 132.
156. Manfroni, *Storia della Marina italiana*, II, 130.
157. Iacopo Doria, *Annales Ianuenses*, V, 55–6.
158. Iacopo Doria, *Annales Ianuenses*, V, 56.
159. Templar of Tyre, *Deeds of the Cypriots*, 91.
160. Salimbene de Adam, *Chronicle*, 543.
161. Heywood, *History of Pisa*, 71–2.
162. Manfroni, *Storia della Marina italiana*, II, 131.
163. Pryor, 'The Maritime Republics', 438–9.
164. Heywood, *History of Pisa*, 72.

Chapter 5. The War of the Sicilian Vespers: Angevin versus Aragonese Sea Power

1. S. Runciman, *The Sicilian Vespers* (Cambridge, 1958), 214–15.
2. Abulafia, *Frederick II*, 406–7.
3. Abulafia, 'The kingdom of Sicily under the Hohenstaufen and Angevins', in *New Cambridge Medieval History*, V, 497–521, esp. 506–7; *The Western Mediterranean Kingdoms, 1200–1500* (London, 1997), 23–5.
4. Runciman, *Sicilian Vespers*, 35.
5. Abulafia, 'Kingdom of Sicily under the Hohenstaufen and Angevins', 508–9; *Western Mediterranean Kingdoms*, 57–8; L. Mott, *Sea Power in the Medieval Mediterranean* (Gainesville, 2003), 10–11.
6. Abulafia, 'Kingdom of Sicily under the Hohenstaufen and Angevins', 509; *Western Mediterranean Kingdoms*, 59; Mott, *Sea Power in the Medieval Mediterranean*, 12.
7. Pryor, 'The naval battles of Roger of Lauria', *Journal of Medieval History*, IX (1983), 179–216, esp. 182.
8. Abulafia, *Frederick II*, 421–2; Mott, *Sea Power in the Medieval Mediterranean*, 13–14.
9. Runciman, *Sicilian Vespers*, 103–4.
10. Ibid., 124–5.
11. Ibid., 125.
12. Abulafia, 'Kingdom of Sicily under the Hohenstaufen and Angevins', 510.
13. Mott, *Sea Power in the Medieval Mediterranean*, 14.
14. Abulafia, 'Kingdom of Sicily under the Hohenstaufen and Angevins', 511.
15. Epstein, *Genoa and the Genoese*, 156–7.
16. Abulafia, *Western Mediterranean Kingdoms*, 65; Mott, *Sea Power in the Medieval Mediterranean*, 15.
17. Abulafia, 'Kingdom of Sicily under the Hohenstaufen and Angevins', 512–3.
18. Abulafia, *Great Sea*, 350; Mott, *Sea Power in the Medieval Mediterranean*, 23; Runciman, *Sicilian Vespers*, 218.
19. Mott, *Sea Power in the Medieval Mediterranean*, 19.
20. Ramon Muntaner, *Chronicle of Muntaner*, trans. Lady Goodenough (2 vols, London, 1921), I, ch 49, 116–8.
21. Muntaner, *Chronicle*, I, ch 48, 112–13, n. 1. See also Abulafia, *Western Mediterranean Kingdoms*, 84–6; Mott, *Sea Power in the Medieval Mediterranean*, 25.

22. Bernat Desclot, *Chronicle of the Reign of King Pedro III of Aragon, A.D. 1276–1285*, trans. F. Critchlow (Princeton, 1928), chs 7–8, 28–33; Muntaner, *Chronicle*, I, chs 49–51, 118–20.
23. Desclot, *Chronicle of King Pedro III*, ch 9, 41–3; Muntaner, *Chronicle*, I, ch 51, 120–3.
24. Desclot, *Chronicle of King Pedro III*, ch 16, 53–5; Muntaner, *Chronicle*, I, ch 57, 133–5. See also Mott, 'Ships of the 13th-century Catalan Navy', *IJNA* , 19.2 (1990), 101–12, esp. 108.
25. Desclot, *Chronicle of King Pedro III*, chs 18–19, 61–6; Muntaner, *Chronicle*, I, ch 60, 136–8. See also Mott, *Sea Power in the Medieval Mediterranean*, 27.
26. Bartolomeo di Neocastro, *Historia Sicula*, in *Cronisti e scrittori sincroni napoletani editi e inediti*, ed. G. del Re (2 vols, Naples, 1868), II, ch 18, 433–4. See also Abulafia, *Frederick II*, 417, 424; *Western Mediterranean Kingdoms*, 76–7.
27. Desclot, *Chronicle of King Pedro III*, ch 10, 40; Neocastro, *Historia Sicula*, ch 32, 445–6. See also Mott, *Sea Power in the Medieval Mediterranean*, 24–5.
28. Muntaner, *Chronicle*, I, ch 62, 139–40.
29. Desclot, *Chronicle of King Pedro III*, ch 8, 28–9. See also Mott, *Sea Power in the Medieval Mediterranean*, 159–62.
30. Muntaner, *Chronicle*, I, ch 134, 338–9.
31. Ibid., I, ch 62, 139–40.
32. Desclot, *Chronicle of King Pedro III*, chs 21–23, 70–6; Muntaner, *Chronicle*, I, ch 64, 141–2. See also Mott, *Sea Power in the Medieval Mediterranean*, 28.
33. Muntaner, *Chronicle*, I, ch 65, 143.
34. Desclot, *Chronicle of King Pedro III*, ch 23, 76–7.
35. Mott, 'The Battle of Malta, 1283: Prelude to a Disaster', in *Circle of War in the Middle Ages*, 145–72.
36. Desclot, *Chronicle of King Pedro III*, ch 26, 81–2; Muntaner, *Chronicle*, I, ch 67, 145–9; Neocastro, *Historia Sicula*, ch 53, 474–5. See also Mott, 'Battle of Malta', 48.
37. Desclot, *Chronicle of King Pedro III*, ch 30, 97–8; Muntaner, *Chronicle*, I, ch 70, 153–6. See also Mott, 'Battle of Malta', 148.
38. Neocastro, *Historia Sicula*, ch 59, 479.
39. Muntaner, *Chronicle*, I, ch 68, 178–9; Neocastro, *Historia Sicula*, ch 73, 491–2. See also Runciman, *Sicilian Vespers*, 235.
40. Desclot, *Chronicle of King Pedro III*, chs 27–28, 89–93; Muntaner, *Chronicle*, I, chs 72–73, 159–64. See also Mott, *Sea Power in the Medieval Mediterranean*, 29–30; Runciman, *Sicilian Vespers*, 236.
41. Mott, *Sea Power in the Medieval Mediterranean*, 30–1, 38.
42. Pryor, 'The Galleys of Charles of Anjou, King of Sicily: ca. 1269–84', *Studies in Medieval and Renaissance History*, XIV (1993), 34–103, esp. 37.
43. Mott, 'Ships of the 13th-century Catalan Navy', 105; Pryor, 'Galleys of Charles of Anjou', 44, 52–6, 64–74.
44. Pryor, 'Galleys of Charles of Anjou', 37.
45. Ibid., 79.
46. *Codice diplomatico dei re aragonesi di Sicilia*, ed. G. La Mantia (2 vols, Palermo, 1919), I, doc. 222, 546–7. See also Manfroni, *Storia della Marina italiana*, II, 89; Mott, *Sea Power in the Medieval Mediterranean*, 92–3.
47. Mott, 'Battle of Malta', 149–51.
48. Desclot, *Chronicle of King Pedro III*, ch 38, 137–8; Muntaner, *Chronicle*, I, ch 81, 185–6. See also Mott, 'Battle of Malta', 155.
49. Mott, 'Battle of Malta', 164–6, 171; Mott, 'Ships of the 13th-century Catalan Navy', 105.
50. Muntaner, *Chronicle*, I, ch 130, 330–1. See also P. Jestice, 'Malta 1283', in *Battles of the Medieval World, 1000–1500*, K. Devries, M. Dougherty, I. Dickie, Jestice and C. Jorgensen (New York, 2006), 108–15, esp. 109; F. Laures, 'The warships of the Kings of Aragón during the 13th and 14th centuries AD', *IJNA*, 16.1 (1987), 19–29, esp. 20; Mott, 'Ships of the 13th-century Catalan Navy', 110–11; Pryor, 'Galleys of Charles of Anjou', 83.
51. Muntaner, *Chronicle*, I, ch 36, 88–90. See Mott, *Sea Power in the Medieval Mediterranean*, 211–12.
52. Muntaner, *Chronicle*, I, ch 76, 173.
53. Ibid., I, ch 130, 330.

54. Ibid., I, ch 83, 192.
55. Jestice, 'Malta 1283', 109; Mott, *Sea Power in the Medieval Mediterranean*, 157.
56. Pryor, 'Naval Battles of Roger of Lauria', 184–9.
57. Muntaner, *Chronicle*, I, ch 83, 192–3.
58. Mott, 'Battle of Malta', 163–4.
59. Mott, *Sea Power in the Medieval Mediterranean*, 33; Pryor, 'Naval Battles of Roger of Lauria', 189–90.
60. Mott, *Sea Power in the Medieval Mediterranean*, 33; Pryor, 'Naval Battles of Roger of Lauria', 190.
61. Desclot, *Chronicle of King Pedro III*, ch 51, 170.
62. Desclot, *Chronicle of King Pedro III*, ch 52, 171–2. See Pryor, 'Naval Battles of Roger of Lauria', 191–2.
63. Desclot, *Chronicle of King Pedro III*, ch 53, 173.
64. Desclot, *Chronicle of King Pedro III*, chs 54–55, 174–7; Muntaner, *Chronicle*, I, ch 113, 278–81; Neocastro, *Historia Sicula*, ch 77, 497–8. See also Mott, *Sea Power in the Medieval Mediterranean*, 34; Pryor, 'Naval Battles of Roger of Lauria', 192–4.
65. Neocastro, *Historia Sicula*, chs 79–80, 501–2. See also Mott, *Sea Power in the Medieval Mediterranean*, 34–6; Runciman, *Sicilian Vespers*, 248–55.
66. Desclot, *Chronicle of King Pedro III*, ch 32, 118, n. 30; Muntaner, *Chronicle*, I, ch 103, 247–9; Neocastro, *Historia Sicula*, ch 73, 491–2. See also Mott, *Sea Power in the Medieval Mediterranean*, 32.
67. Mott, *Sea Power in the Medieval Mediterranean*, 37; Pryor, 'Naval Battles of Roger of Lauria', 195.
68. Muntaner, *Chronicle*, I, ch 127, 319–20. See also Mott, 'Battle of Malta', 167; *Sea Power in the Medieval Mediterranean*, 37–8; Pryor, 'Naval Battles of Roger of Lauria', 195–6.
69. Desclot, *Chronicle of King Pedro III*, ch 86, 315; ch 93, 343. See also Pryor, 'Naval Battles of Roger of Lauria', 196.
70. Desclot, *Chronicle of King Pedro III*, ch 86, 313; Muntaner, *Chronicle*, I, ch 130, 326–9.
71. Muntaner, *Chronicle*, I, ch 130, 329–30.
72. Mott, 'Battle of Malta', 168.
73. Muntaner, *Chronicle*, I, ch 130, 331.
74. Desclot, *Chronicle of King Pedro III*, ch 86, 314–15; Muntaner, *Chronicle*, I, ch 130, 332.
75. Desclot, *Chronicle of King Pedro III*, ch 94, 348–9; Muntaner, *Chronicle*, I, ch 135, 344–6; Neocastro, *Historia Sicula*, chs 94–99, 521–3. See also Pryor, 'Naval Battles of Roger of Lauria', 195–9.
76. Desclot, *Chronicle of King Pedro III*, ch 94, 349.
77. Muntaner, *Chronicle*, I, ch 135, 345.
78. Mott, *Sea Power in the Medieval Mediterranean*, 39; Pryor, 'Naval Battles of Roger of Lauria', 199.
79. Desclot, *Chronicle of King Pedro III*, ch 94, 351.
80. Muntaner, *Chronicle*, I, ch 136, 347.
81. Desclot, *Chronicle of King Pedro III*, ch 94, 353–4.
82. Desclot, *Chronicle of King Pedro III*, ch 95, 357–68; Muntaner, *Chronicle*, I, chs 138–9, 349–56. See also Mott, *Sea Power in the Medieval Mediterranean*, 39–40.
83. Desclot, *Chronicle of King Pedro III*, ch 96, 373–9; Muntaner, *Chronicle*, I, ch 146, 368.
84. Runciman, *Sicilian Vespers*, 259–62.
85. Muntaner, *Chronicle*, II, ch 152, 368–72. See also Mott, *Sea Power in the Medieval Mediterranean*, 41.
86. Runciman, *Sicilian Vespers*, 262–3.
87. Mott, *Sea Power in the Medieval Mediterranean*, 40–2; Pryor, 'Naval Battles of Roger of Lauria', 200.
88. Neocastro, *Historia Sicula*, ch 102, 533–4; ch 104, 535; Muntaner, *Chronicle*, I, ch 109, 266–7; ch 149, 373–5. See also Manfroni, *Storia della Marina italiana*, II, 159–61; Pryor, 'Naval Battles of Roger of Lauria', 200.
89. Neocastro, *Historia Sicula*, ch 110, 540–61. See also Mott, *Sea Power in the Medieval Mediterranean*, 42; Pryor, 'Naval Battles of Roger of Lauria', 200–2.
90. Mott, *Sea Power in the Medieval Mediterranean*, 42; Pryor, 'Naval Battles of Roger of Lauria', 202.

91. Neocastro, *Historia Sicula*, ch 110, 562–3. See also Pryor, 'Naval Battles of Roger of Lauria', 202–3.
92. Muntaner, *Chronicle*, I, ch 105, 252–5; Neocastro, *Historia Sicula*, ch 111, 564–5; Niccolo Speciale, *Rerum Sicularum*, ed. Muratori (RIS, X, Milan, 1727), bk II, ch 11, cols 917–1052, esp. 954–5. See also Pryor, 'Naval Battles of Roger of Lauria', 203.
93. Neocastro, *Historia Sicula*, ch 111, 565. See also Mott, *Sea Power in the Medieval Mediterranean*, 42–3; Pryor, 'Naval Battles of Roger of Lauria', 204.
94. Muntaner, *Chronicle*, II, ch 162, 405–6. See also Runciman, *Sicilian Vespers*, 264–6.
95. Muntaner, *Chronicle*, II, ch 173, 417–20. See also Mott, *Sea Power in the Medieval Mediterranean*, 44–5; Runciman, *Sicilian Vespers*, 267–8.
96. Muntaner, *Chronicle*, II, ch 174, 421–2. See also Runciman, *Sicilian Vespers*, 268.
97. Runciman, *Sicilian Vespers*, 268.
98. Muntaner, *Chronicle*, II, ch 159, 393–4. See also Mott, *Sea Power in the Medieval Mediterranean*, 252–6.
99. Muntaner, *Chronicle*, II, ch 181, 436–8. See also Runciman, *Sicilian Vespers*, 269–70.
100. Muntaner, *Chronicle*, II, ch 185, 445–7. See also Runciman, *Sicilian Vespers*, 271.
101. Mott, *Sea Power in the Medieval Mediterranean*, 46–7.
102. Ibid., Mott, 47.
103. Speciale, *Rerum Sicularum*, bk IV, ch 13, cols 999–1000. See also Pryor, 'Naval Battles of Roger of Lauria', 205.
104. Speciale, *Rerum Sicularum*, bk IV, ch 13, col. 1000. See Pryor, 'Naval Battles of Roger of Lauria', 205–7.
105. Speciale, *Rerum Sicularum*, bk IV, ch 13, cols 1001–6. See also Manfroni, *Storia della Marina italiana*, II, 180–1; Pryor, 'Naval Battles of Roger of Lauria', 207–8.
106. Muntaner, *Chronicle*, II, ch 192, 459–63; Speciale, *Rerum Sicularum*, bk V, ch 10, cols 1015–20. See also Pryor, 'Naval Battles of Roger of Lauria', 208–9; Runciman, *Sicilian Vespers*, 272–3.
107. Pryor, 'Naval Battles of Roger of Lauria', 209.
108. Speciale, *Rerum Sicularum*, bk V, ch 14, col. 1024. See also Manfroni, *Storia della Marina italiana*, II, 183–4; Pryor, 'Naval Battles of Roger of Lauria', 209.
109. Speciale, *Rerum Sicularum*, bk V, ch 14, col. 1025. See also Manfroni, *Storia della Marina italiana*, II, 184–5; Pryor, 'Naval Battles of Roger of Lauria', 209–11.
110. Muntaner, *Chronicle*, II, ch 197, 476.
111. Runciman, *Sicilian Vespers*, 274.
112. Speciale, *Rerum Sicularum*, bk VI, ch 7, col. 1039.
113. Muntaner, *Chronicle*, II, ch 198, 477–9; Speciale, *Rerum Sicularum*, bk VI, ch 10, cols 1040–3. See also Mott, *Sea Power in the Medieval Mediterranean*, 49; Runciman, *Sicilian Vespers*, 275.
114. Pryor, 'Naval Battles of Roger of Lauria', 205, 211.
115. Mott, 'Battle of Malta', 150–3, 164–6.
116. Pryor, 'Naval Battles of Roger of Lauria', 211.
117. Mott, 'Battle of Malta', 155; Pryor, 'Naval Battles of Roger of Lauria', 184.
118. Desclot, *Chronicle of King Pedro III*, chs 38–39, 137–40; Ramon Muntaner, *Chronicle*, I, chs 81–82, 185–8. See also Mott, 'Battle of Malta', 155–6; 'Ships of the 13th-century Catalan Navy', 107–9; Pryor, 'Naval Battles of Roger of Lauria', 183–4.
119. Desclot, *Chronicle of King Pedro III*, chs 40–41, 141–3; Muntaner, I, *Chronicle*, ch 83, 190–1. See also Jestice, 'Malta 1283', 111; Mott, 'Battle of Malta', 156–9; Pryor, 'Naval Battles of Roger of Lauria', 184–5; W. Sayers, 'The Lexicon of Naval Tactics in Ramon Muntaner's *Crònica*', *Catalan Review*, 17 (2003), 177–92.
120. Mott, 'Battle of Malta', 159; Pryor, 'Naval Battles of Roger of Lauria', 185–6.
121. Mott, 'Battle of Malta', 160.
122. Desclot, *Chronicle of King Pedro III*, ch 41, 143–4.
123. Mott, 'Battle of Malta', 166.
124. Desclot, *Chronicle of King Pedro III*, ch 41, 144.
125. Muntaner, *Chronicle*, I, ch 130, 330.
126. Pryor, 'Naval Battles of Roger of Lauria', 188.

127. Muntaner, *Chronicle*, I, ch 83, 192–3.
128. Desclot, *Chronicle of King Pedro III*, ch 41, 144–5.
129. Mott, 'Battle of Malta', 164.
130. Desclot, *Chronicle of King Pedro III*, ch 41, 145. See also Mott, 'Battle of Malta', 162; Pryor, 'Naval Battles of Roger of Lauria', 189.
131. Mott, 'Battle of Malta', 172.

Chapter 6. Venetian-Genoese Competition for Control in the East

1. Dotson, 'Naval Strategy in the First Genoese–Venetian War, 1257–1270', *American Neptune*, 46 (1986), 84–90, esp. 88; 'Fleet Operations in the First Genoese–Venetian War, 1264–1266', *Viator*, 30 (1999), 165–80, esp. 165; 'Foundations of Venetian Naval Strategy from Pietro II Orseolo to the Battle of Zonchio, 1000–1500', *Viator*, 32 (2001), 113–25, esp. 121.
2. Dotson, 'Naval Strategy in the First Genoese–Venetian War', 84–6; Rose, *Medieval Naval Warfare*, 102–3.
3. Tafel and Thomas, *Urkunden der Republik Venedig*, I, no. XXIII, 43–54. See also Dotson, 'Venice, Genoa and Control of the Seas', 119–20; Lane, *Venice*, 28; Rose, *Medieval Naval Warfare*, 100.
4. Epstein, *Genoa and the Genoese*, 84–5; Madden, *Venice*, 84–5.
5. Dotson, 'Foundations of Venetian Naval Strategy', 120–1; Lane, *Venice*, 42–3; Rose, *Medieval Naval Warfare*, 102.
6. Abulafia, 'Henry Count of Malta', 114; Lane, *Venice*, 43; Madden, *Venice*, 148.
7. Abulafia, 'Henry Count of Malta', 115.
8. Abulafia, 'Henry Count of Malta', 115; Madden, *Venice*, 149–50.
9. Dotson, 'Foundations of Venetian Naval Strategy', 120; Lane, *Venice*, 43.
10. Madden, *Venice*, 150.
11. Abulafia, 'Henry Count of Malta', 115–18.
12. *Annalisti Ignoti* ('Unknown Annalists'), *Annales Ianuenses*, IV, 31.
13. '*Eracles* or *Acre* Continuation of William of Tyre', in *Crusader Syria in the Thirteenth Century*, 121–43, esp. bk 34, ch 3, 140.
14. 'Rothelin Continuation', ch 79, 116 and note 2.
15. Manfroni, *Storia della Marina italiana*, I, 433.
16. *Annalisti Ignoti*, *Annales Ianuenses*, IV, 31–2. See also Rose, *Medieval Naval Warfare*, 102.
17. Manfroni, *Storia della Marina italiana*, I, 434.
18. Templar of Tyre, *Deeds of the Cypriots*, 26.
19. 'Rothelin Continuation', ch 79, 117.
20. Manfroni, *Storia della Marina italiana*, I, 436.
21. *Annalisti Ignoti*, *Annales Ianuenses*, IV, 33–4.
22. *Annalisti Ignoti*, *Annales Ianuenses*, IV, 34. See also Manfroni, *Storia della Marina italiana*, I, 437.
23. Dotson, 'Venice, Genoa and Control of the Seas', 121–2; Epstein, *Genoa and the Genoese*, 150–1; Lane, *Venice*, 75–6; Pryor, 'Maritime Republics', 436; Treadgold, *Byzantine State*, 733.
24. *Annalisti Ignoti*, *Annales Ianuenses*, IV, 45–6. See also Dotson, 'Naval Strategy in the First Genoese–Venetian War', 89; Rose, *Medieval Naval Warfare*, 103.
25. *Annalisti Ignoti*, *Annales Ianuenses*, IV, 51–2. See also Dotson, 'Venice, Genoa and Control of the Seas', 122; Pryor, 'Maritime Republics', 436; Rose, *Medieval Naval Warfare*, 103.
26. Lane, *Venice*, 76.
27. *Annalisti Ignoti*, *Annales Ianuenses*, IV, 53.
28. *Annalisti Ignoti*, *Annales Ianuenses*, IV, 53. See also Dotson, 'Naval Strategy in the First Genoese–Venetian War', 89.
29. Dotson, 'Fleet Operations', 171; Rose, *Medieval Naval Warfare*, 101–3.
30. Andrea Dandolo, *Chronica Per Extensum Descripta*, 312. See also Dotson, 'Fleet Operations', 171.
31. *Annalisti Ignoti*, *Annales Ianuenses*, IV, 54. See Dotson, 'Fleet Operations', 168.
32. *Annalisti Ignoti*, *Annales Ianuenses*, IV, 53–6. See also Dotson, 'Fleet Operations', 173; Lane, *Venice*, 77.

33. *Annalisti Ignoti*, *Annales Ianuenses*, IV, 53–5. See also Balard, 'Coastal Shipping and Navigation in the Mediterranean', 135; Dotson, 'Fleet Operations', 173–5; Lane, *Venice*, 77; Pryor, 'Naval Architecture of Crusader Transport Ships', 175–85, 208–9; Rose, *Medieval Naval Warfare*, 103.
34. *Annalisti Ignoti*, *Annales Ianuenses*, IV, 55–6.
35. *Annalisti Ignoti*, *Annales Ianuenses*, IV, 90. See also Dotson, 'Fleet Operations', 176–8.
36. Dotson, 'Fleet Operations', 178.
37. *Annalisti Ignoti*, *Annales Ianuenses*, IV, 90–1.
38. Abulafia, *Great Sea*, 354.
39. Dotson, 'Venice, Genoa and Control of the Seas', 122–4; Lane, *Venice*, 76–7.
40. Templar of Tyre, *Deeds of the Cypriots*, 131. See also Dotson, 'Venice, Genoa and Control of the Seas', 124–5; Lane, *Venice*, 83; Pryor, 'Maritime Republics', 445.
41. Templar of Tyre, *Deeds of the Cypriots*, 132–5. See also Dotson, 'Venice, Genoa and Control of the Seas', 125; Lane, *Venice*, 83; Pryor, 'Maritime Republics', 445.
42. Iacopo da Varagine, *Cronaca di Genova*, ed. G. Monleone (3 vols, Rome, 1941), II, 106.
43. Dotson, 'Foundations of Venetian Naval Strategy', 118.
44. Templar of Tyre, *Deeds of the Cypriots*, 139–40. See also Dotson, 'Venice, Genoa and Control of the Seas', 125–6; Epstein, *Genoa and the Genoese*, 182; Lane, *Venice*, 83; Pryor, 'Maritime Republics', 445.
45. Iacopo da Varagine, *Cronaca*, II, 413–14; Templar of Tyre, *Deeds of the Cypriot*, 139. See also Dotson, 'Venice, Genoa and Control of the Seas', 127; Epstein, *Genoa and the Genoese*, 182–3; Lane, *Venice*, 83.
46. Manfroni, *Storia della Marina italiana*, II, 207.
47. Iacopo da Varagine, *Cronaca*, II, 413–14; Templar of Tyre, *Deeds of the Cypriots*, 139. See also Dotson, 'Venice, Genoa and Control of the Seas', 127; Manfroni, *Storia della Marina italiana*, II, 208.
48. *Anonimo genovese: Poesie*, trans. L. Cocito (Rome, 1970), ch 49, vv 1–220, 281–91; Continuator of Iacopo da Varagine, *Cronaca*, II, 109–11; Templar of Tyre, *Deeds of the Cypriots*, 140. See also Manfroni, *Storia della Marina italiana*, II, 208–9.
49. Manfroni, *Storia della Marina italiana*, II, 209–10.
50. *Anonimo genovese*, ch 49, vv 221–52, 291–3; Continuator of Iacopo da Varagine, *Cronaca*, II, 109–10; Templar of Tyre, *Deeds of the Cypriots*, 140–1. See also Manfroni, *Storia della Marina italiana*, II, 210–11.
51. Templar of Tyre, *Deeds of the Cypriots*, 141. See also Manfroni, *Storia della Marina italiana*, II, 212–13.
52. Templar of Tyre, *Deeds of the Cypriots*, 142.
53. Templar of Tyre, *Deeds of the Cypriots*, 142. See also Dotson, 'Venice, Genoa and Control of the Seas', 127 and note 30; Manfroni, *Storia della Marina italiana*, II, 209.
54. Manfroni, *Storia della Marina italiana*, II, 213, note 4.
55. Ibid., II, 212.
56. *Anonimo genovese*, ch 49, vv 253–372, 293–8; Continuator of Iacopo da Varagine, *Cronaca*, II, 111; Templar of Tyre, *Deeds of the Cypriots*, 142. See also Epstein, *Genoa and the Genoese*, 183.
57. Templar of Tyre, *Deeds of the Cypriots*, 142. See also Manfroni, *Storia della Marina italiana*, II, 213.
58. Manfroni, *Storia della Marina italiana*, II, 214.
59. Templar of Tyre, *Deeds of the Cypriots*, 142. See also Manfroni, *Storia della Marina italiana*, II, 214.
60. Lane, *Venice*, 84; Manfroni, *Storia della Marina italiana*, II, 215; Pryor, 'Maritime Republics', 446.
61. Templar of Tyre, *Deeds of the Cypriots*, 142. See also Lane, *Venice*, 84.
62. Dotson, 'Venice, Genoa and Control of the Seas', 127–8; Lane, *Venice*, 84.
63. Lane, *Venetian Ships*, 129–30.
64. Ibid., 144–5.
65. Ibid., 7–8, Table B on 236.
66. Ibid., 132–3.
67. Ibid., 4–7.
68. Lionel Casson, 'Merchant Galleys', in *Age of the Galley*, 117–26, esp. 123.

69. Marino Sanudo Torsello, *Book of the Secrets*, bk 2, ch 5, 102–3. See also Casson, 'Merchant Galleys', 123–4; Lane, *Venetian Ships*, 9–12.
70. Felix Fabri, *The Book of the Wanderings of Brother Felix Fabri in Palestine and Arabia*, trans. A. Stewart (2 vols, London, 1892), I, 126–7.
71. Lane, *Venetian Ships*, 14.
72. Giovanni Villani, *Cronica*, ed. F. Dragomanni (4 vols, Florence, 1845), II, bk VIII, ch 77, 101. See also I. Friel, 'The Carrack: The Advent of the Full-Rigged Ship', *Cogs*, in *Caravels and Galleons*, 77–90, esp. 78; Hutchinson, *Medieval Ships*, 41–4; Lane, *Venetian Ships*, 36–40; Paine, *Sea and Civilization*, 339–40; Runyan, 'Naval Power and Maritime Technology during the Hundred Years War', in *War at Sea in the Middle Ages*, 53–67, esp. 60–2.
73. Lane, *Venetian Ships*, 14.
74. Abulafia, *Great Sea*, 354–5.
75. Dotson, 'Foundations of Venetian Naval Strategy', 122; 'Venice, Genoa and Control of the Seas', 128.
76. Epstein, *Genoa and the Genoese*, 210–11.
77. Rose, *Medieval Naval Warfare*, 104.
78. Abulafia, *Great Sea*, 367–8; Paine, *Sea and Civilization*, 330.
79. Lane, *Venice*, 175–6.
80. Giorgio Stella, *Annales Genuenses*, ed. Muratori (RIS, XVII, pt. 2, Rome, 1730), col. 1091.
81. Pere III of Catalonia, *Chronicle*, trans. M. Hillgarth (2 vols, Toronto, 1980), II, 454–7.
82. Pere III of Catalonia, *Chronicle*, II, 460. See also Lane, *Venice*, 176.
83. Dotson, 'Venice, Genoa and Control of the Seas', 129; Epstein, *Genoa and the Genoese*, 220.
84. Dotson, 'Venice, Genoa and Control of the Seas', 129; Lane, *Venice*, 178.
85. Pere III of Catalonia, *Chronicle*, II, 457–60. See also Lane, *Venice*, 178.
86. Dotson, 'Venice, Genoa and Control of the Seas', 123–4, 129; Rose, *Medieval Naval Warfare*, 104–5.
87. Lane, *Venice*, 178; Rose, *Medieval Naval Warfare*, 105.
88. Giorgio Stella, *Annales Genuenses*, col. 1091.
89. Dotson, 'Venice, Genoa and Control of the Seas', 129.
90. Lane, *Venice*, 178.
91. Pere III of Catalonia, *Chronicle*, II, 461–2.
92. Giorgio Stella, *Annales Genuenses*, col. 1091.
93. Pere III of Catalonia, *Chronicle*, II, 462.
94. Epstein, *Genoa and the Genoese*, 220.
95. Lane, *Venice*, 178.
96. Pere III of Catalonia, *Chronicle*, II, 468–9. See Dotson, 'Siege and Naval Battle of Alghero', *The Oxford Encyclopedia of Medieval Warfare and Military Technology*, ed. C. Rogers (3 vols, Oxford, 2010), I, 33–4.
97. Matteo Villani, *Cronica*, ed. Dragomanni (2 vols, Florence, 1846), I, bk III, ch 79, 269.
98. Pere III of Catalonia, *Chronicle*, II, 469–70.
99. Matteo Villani, *Cronica*, I, bk III, ch 79, 269.
100. Pere III of Catalonia, *Chronicle*, II, 470.
101. Ibid., II, 470–1.
102. Giorgio Stella, *Annales Genuenses*, col. 1092; Pere III of Catalonia, *Chronicle*, II, 471.
103. Matteo Villani, *Cronica*, I, bk III, ch 79, 271.
104. Pere III of Catalonia, *Chronicle*, II, 471–2. See also Dotson, 'Naval Battle of Alghero', 34.
105. Giorgio Stella, *Annales Genuenses*, col. 1092; Matteo Villani, *Cronica*, I, bk IV, ch 22, 324. See also Epstein, *Genoa and the Genoese*, 220–1.
106. Matteo Villani, *Cronica*, I, bk IV, ch 22, 324.
107. Lane, *Venice*, 178.
108. Giorgio Stella, *Annales Genuenses*, col. 1093; Matteo Villani, *Cronica*, I, bk IV, ch 32, 333.
109. Matteo Villani, *Cronica*, I, bk IV, ch 32, 333. See also Dotson, 'Naval Battle of Porto Longo', in *Oxford Encyclopedia of Medieval Warfare*, III, 138–9; Lane, *Venice*, 179.

110. Giorgio Stella, *Annales Genuenses*, cols 1092–3; Matteo Villani, *Cronica*, I, bk IV, ch 32, 333–5. See also Dotson, 'Naval Battle of Porto Longo', 139.
111. Epstein, *Genoa and the Genoese*, 221; Lane, *Venice*, 179.
112. Epstein, *Genoa and the Genoese*, 221.
113. Lane, *Venice*, 186.
114. Giorgio Stella, *Annales Genuenses*, cols 1106–7. See also Epstein, *Genoa and the Genoese*, 237–8; Madden, *Venice*, 215–19; J. Norwich, *A History of Venice* (New York, 1982), 244–6; Treadgold, *History of the Byzantine State*, 780.
115. Giorgio Stella, *Annales Genuenses*, cols 1103–6. See also Dotson, 'Venice, Genoa and Control of the Seas', 130; Epstein, *Genoa and the Genoese*, 236–7.
116. Giorgio Stella, *Annales Genuenses*, cols 1107–8. See also Dotson, 'Venice, Genoa and Control of the Seas', 130–1; Epstein, *Genoa and the Genoese*, 238.
117. Dotson, 'Venice, Genoa and Control of the Seas', 131; Lane, *Venice*, 191.
118. Giorgio Stella, *Annales Genuenses*, col. 1108.
119. Giorgio Stella, *Annales Genuenses*, col. 1110. See also Lane, *Venice*, 191; Madden, *Venice*, 221; Norwich, *History of Venice*, 248–9; Rose, *Medieval Naval Warfare*, 107.
120. Giorgio Stella, *Annales Genuenses*, cols 1110–11. See also Dotson, 'Venice, Genoa and Control of the Seas', 131; Epstein, *Genoa and the Genoese*, 239; Lane, *Venice*, 191; Madden, *Venice*, 221.
121. Lane, *Venice*, 192.
122. Giorgio Stella, *Annales Genuenses*, col. 1111.
123. Lane, *Venice*, 192; Madden, *Venice*, 221; Norwich, *History of Venice*, 250.
124. Daniele da Chinazzo, *Cronaca della Guerra di Chioggia*, ed. G. Antimaco (Milan, 1864), 48–51; Giorgio Stella, *Annales Genuenses*, cols 1111–12. See also Epstein, *Genoa and the Genoese*, 239; Lane, *Venice*, 191; Madden, *Venice*, 222; Norwich, *History of Venice*, 251.
125. Daniele da Chinazzo, *Cronaca della Guerra di Chioggia*, 52.
126. Daniele da Chinazzo, *Cronaca della Guerra di Chioggia*, 42–3. See also Norwich, *History of Venice*, 250.
127. Lane, *Venice*, 192–3; Madden, *Venice*, 222–4; Norwich, *History of Venice*, 252–3.
128. Lane, *Venice*, 193.
129. Daniele da Chinazzo, *Cronaca della Guerra di Chioggia*, 55–6. See also Norwich, *History of Venice*, 250–3.
130. Lane, *Venice*, 193–4; Madden, *Venice*, 224; Norwich, *History of Venice*, 253.
131. Daniele da Chinazzo, *Cronaca della Guerra di Chioggia*, 76–82; Giorgio Stella, *Annales Genuenses*, cols 1114–15. See also Epstein, *Genoa and the Genoese*, 240; Lane, *Venice*, 194; Madden, *Venice*, 224.
132. Daniele da Chinazzo, *Cronaca della Guerra di Chioggia*, 82–3. See also Epstein, *Genoa and the Genoese*, 240; Lane, *Venice*, 194; Madden, *Venice*, 225; Norwich, *History of Venice*, 254.
133. Daniele da Chinazzo, *Cronaca della Guerra di Chioggia*, 93–6; Giorgio Stella, *Annales Genuenses*, col. 1114. See also Epstein, *Genoa and the Genoese*, 240; Lane, *Venice*, 194.
134. Giorgio Stella, *Annales Genuenses*, col. 1115. See also Epstein, *Genoa and the Genoese*, 240; Lane, *Venice*, 195.
135. Daniele da Chinazzo, *Cronaca della Guerra di Chioggia*, 123–5; Giorgio Stella, *Annales Genuenses*, cols 1116–17. See also Epstein, *Genoa and the Genoese*, 240; Lane, *Venice*, 195; Madden, *Venice*, 225.
136. Dotson, 'Venice, Genoa and Control of the Seas', 133; Epstein, *Genoa and the Genoese*, 241; Lane, *Venice*, 195–6.
137. Lane, *Venice*, 196.
138. Epstein, *Genoa and the Genoese*, 241.
139. Dotson, 'Venice, Genoa and Control of the Seas', 135.
140. *Annalisti Ignoti*, *Annales Ianuenses*, IV, 34. See also Manfroni, *Storia della Marina italiana*, I, 436–7.
141. *Annalisti Ignoti*, *Annales Ianuenses*, IV, 34.
142. Templar of Tyre, *Deeds of the Cypriots*, 28.
143. *Annalisti Ignoti*, *Annales Ianuenses*, IV, 34.

144. Dotson, 'Venice, Genoa and Control of the Seas', 120–1; Epstein, *Genoa and the Genoese*, 46; Lane, *Venice*, 73–5.
145. 'Rothelin Continuation', ch 79, 116 and note 3.
146. Templar of Tyre, *Deeds of the Cypriots*, 25.
147. 'Rothelin Continuation', ch 79, 116–17.
148. Lane, *Venice*, 75.
149. Templar of Tyre, *Deeds of the Cypriots*, 28.
150. *Annalisti Ignoti*, *Annales Ianuenses*, IV, 34.
151. Ibid., IV, 34 and note 2.
152. Manfroni, *Storia della Marina italiana*, I, 438.
153. Templar of Tyre, *Deeds of the Cypriots*, 27.
154. Ibid.
155. Ibid., 28.
156. *Annalisti Ignoti*, *Annales Ianuenses*, IV, 34.
157. *Annalisti Ignoti*, *Annales Ianuenses*, IV, 34–5. See also Manfroni, *Storia della Marina italiana*, I, 438.
158. '*Eracles* Continuation of William of Tyre', bk 34, ch 3, 141.
159. Templar of Tyre, *Deeds of the Cypriots*, 28–9.
160. *Annalisti Ignoti*, *Annales Ianuenses*, IV, 35; '*Eracles* Continuation of William of Tyre', bk 34, ch 3, 141; Templar of Tyre, *Deeds of the Cypriots*, 29. See also Lane, *Venice*, 73–5.

Part II. Northern Europe
(The North Sea, the Baltic Sea and the English Channel)

1. F. Fernández-Armesto, 'Naval Warfare after the Viking Age c.1100–1500', in *Medieval Warfare, A History*, ed. M. Keen (Oxford, 1999), 230–52, esp. 231; Unger, *The Ship in the Medieval Economy, 600–1600* (London, 1980), 55.
2. Bennett et al., *Fighting Techniques of the Medieval World*, 217; Fernández-Armesto, 'Naval Warfare', 234; Hutchinson, *Medieval Ships*, 4; H. Nicholson, *Medieval Warfare* (New York, 2004), 145.
3. Haywood, *Dark Age Naval Power*, 71–2.
4. Ibid., 72–4.
5. Ibid., 93–100.
6. Lewis and Runyan, *European Naval and Maritime History*, 87; Unger, *Ship in Medieval Economy*, 58.
7. Haywood, *Dark Age Naval Power*, 101–3.
8. Ibid., 104–10.
9. Hutchinson, *Medieval Ships*, 5.
10. Hutchinson, *Medieval Ships*, 5–10; Lewis and Runyan, *European Naval and Maritime History*, 89.
11. Hutchinson, *Medieval Ships*, 10–15; Nicholson, *Medieval Warfare*, 147; Rose, *England's Medieval Navy 1066–1509* (Barnsley, 2013), 79; Unger, *Ship in Medieval Economy*, 58–60.
12. Hutchinson, *Medieval Ships*, 15–20; Unger, *Ship in Medieval Economy*, 60–2.
13. Rose, *Medieval Naval Warfare*, 28.
14. Hutchinson, *Medieval Ships*, 50; Nicholson, *Medieval Warfare*, 145.
15. Bennett et al., *Fighting Techniques of the Medieval World*, 217; S. Frere, *Britannia: A History of Roman Britain* (London, 1987), 357.
16. Haywood, *Dark Age Naval Power*, 82–92.
17. Lewis and Runyan, *European Naval and Maritime History*, 86–7; Unger, *Ship in Medieval Economy*, 56.
18. Haywood, *Dark Age Naval Power*, 90, 110–11.
19. Gregory of Tours, *The History of the Franks*, trans. L. Thorpe (London, 1974), bk 3, ch 3, 163–4. See also Haywood, *Dark Age Naval Power*, 114–21; Nicholson, *Medieval Warfare*, 147.
20. Lewis and Runyan, *European Naval and Maritime History*, 89; Unger, *Ship in Medieval Economy*, 61–2.

21. Haywood, *Dark Age Naval Power*, 128–30.
22. Nicholson, *Medieval Warfare*, 146.

Chapter 7. The Viking Onslaught

1. Sawyer, 'Age of the Vikings and Before', in *Oxford Illustrated History of the Vikings*, 1–18, esp. 2.
2. E. Roesdahl, *The Vikings*, trans. S. Margeson and K. Williams (London, 1991), 9.
3. J. Nelson, 'The Frankish Empire', *Oxford History of the Vikings*, 19–47, esp. 36; Roesdahl, *Vikings*, 187–8; Sawyer, 'Age of the Vikings', 3–8.
4. *Anglo-Saxon Chronicles*, trans. M. Swanton (London, 1996), *anno* 793, 54–7.
5. Ibid., *anno* 794, 57.
6. Roesdahl, *Vikings*, 193.
7. J. Bill, 'Ships and Seamanship', *Oxford History of the Vikings*,182–201, esp. 185–8.
8. Viking Ships Museum of Roskilde. See also Bill, 'Ships and Seamanship', 192–3; Roesdahl, *Vikings*, 86–7.
9. R. Simek, 'Vikings', *Oxford Encyclopedia of Medieval Warfare*, III, 407–11, esp. 408–9.
10. Alcuin, *Alcuin of York – his life and letters*, ed. S. Allot (York, 1974), Letter 12, A.D. 793, 18. See also Roesdahl, *Vikings*, 193.
11. Einhard, *Vita Karoli Magni*, in *Charlemagne's Courtier, The Complete Einhard*, trans. P. Dutton (Toronto, 1998), 15–39, esp. ch 14, 24.
12. Haywood, *Dark Age Naval Power*, 64.
13. *Royal Frankish Annals*, in *Carolingian Chronicles*, trans. B. Scholz with B. Rogers (Ann Arbor, 1970), 35–125, esp. *anno* 810, 91–2. See also Haywood, *Dark Age Naval Power*, 167; Nelson, 'Frankish Empire', 21.
14. Haywood, *Dark Age Naval Power*, 165–6.
15. Einhard, *Vita Karoli*, ch 17, 27.
16. Haywood, *Dark Age Naval Power*, 166.
17. *Royal Frankish Annals*, *anno* 820, 107–8. See also Haywood, *Dark Age Naval Power*, 168–9.
18. *Annals of St-Bertin*, trans. Nelson (Manchester, 1991), *anni* 834–7, 30, 33, 35 and 37. See also Nelson, 'Frankish Empire', 23–4; Roesdahl, *Vikings*, 196.
19. *Annals of St-Bertin*, *anni* 835 and 837, 33 and 37. See also Haywood, *Dark Age Naval Power*, 170.
20. *Annals of St-Bertin*, *anno* 841, 51. See also Roesdahl, *Vikings*, 197.
21. *Annals of St-Bertin*, *anno* 841, 50.
22. Ibid., *anni* 842–3, 53–6 and note 2 on 55–6.
23. Nelson, 'The Frankish Kingdoms, 814–898: the West', in *New Cambridge Medieval History*, II, *c.700–c.900*, ed. R. McKitterick (Cambridge, 1995), 110–41, esp. 121–2.
24. *Annals of St-Bertin*, *anno* 843, 56.
25. Nelson, 'Frankish Empire', 26.
26. Nelson, 'Frankish Empire', 26; Roesdahl, *Vikings*, 198.
27. *Annals of St-Bertin*, *anno* 845, 60; *Annals of Fulda*, trans. T. Reuter (Manchester, 1992), *anno* 845, 61. See also Roesdahl, *Vikings*, 198.
28. Bennett and Hooper, *Cambridge Illustrated Atlas*, 20; Nelson, 'Frankish Empire', 30.
29. *Annals of St-Bertin*, *anni* 856–7, 82–5.
30. *Annals of St-Bertin*, *anno* 844, 60. See also G. Jones, *A History of the Vikings* (Oxford, 1984), 213–14.
31. *Annals of St-Bertin*, *anno* 848, 65–6.
32. Ibid., *anno* 849, 68.
33. Ibid., *anno* 859, 90.
34. *Annals of St-Bertin*, *anno* 860, 92–3. See Jones, *History of the Vikings*, 216–18; Roesdahl, *Vikings*, 200.
35. Jones, *History of the Vikings*, 215.
36. Bennett and Hooper, *Cambridge Illustrated Atlas*, 20–1.
37. *Annals of St-Bertin*, *anno* 845, 61; *Annals of Fulda*, *anno* 845, 23. See Jones, *History of the Vikings*, 107.

38. *Annals of St-Bertin*, *anni* 846, 847, 857 and 863, 62, 65, 85 and 104. See also Roesdahl, *Vikings*, 201.
39. *Annals of St-Bertin*, *anno* 858, 86.
40. Ibid., *anno* 858, 87.
41. Ibid., *anno* 861, 95.
42. Ibid., *anno* 862, 98–100.
43. Nelson, 'Frankish Empire', 30; Roesdahl, *Vikings*, 199.
44. Roesdahl, *Vikings*, 210–11.
45. D. Ó Corráin, 'Ireland, Wales, Man, and the Hebrides', in *Oxford History of the Vikings*, 83–109, esp. 85.
46. S. Keynes, 'The Vikings in England, c.790–1016', in *Oxford History of the Vikings*, 48–82, esp. 52; Roesdahl, *Vikings*, 233–4.
47. *Annals of Ulster (to A.D. 1131)*, trans. S. Mac Airt and G. Mac Niocaill (Dublin, 1983), *anno* 794, 250–1.
48. Ibid., *anno* 795, 250–1.
49. Ó Corráin, 'Ireland, Wales, Man, and the Hebrides', 83; Roesdahl, *Vikings*, 212.
50. *Annals of Ulster*, *anno* 798, 252–3.
51. Ibid., 262–3.
52. Ibid., *anno* 821, 276–7.
53. Ó Corráin, 'Ireland, Wales, Man, and the Hebrides', 85.
54. *Annals of Ulster*, *anno* 824, 280–1.
55. Ibid.
56. Ibid., *anno* 832, 288–9.
57. Ibid., 290–1.
58. *Annals of Ulster*, *anno* 834, 292–3. See also Ó Corráin, 'Ireland, Wales, Man, and the Hebrides', 85.
59. Ó Corráin, 'Ireland, Wales, Man, and the Hebrides', 96; Roesdahl, *Vikings*, 212.
60. *Annals of Ulster*, *anno* 837, 294–5.
61. *Annals of Ulster*, *anno* 841, 298–9. See also Ó Corráin, 'Ireland, Wales, Man, and the Hebrides', 88.
62. *Annals of Ulster*, *anno* 845, 302–3. See also Ó Corráin, 'Ireland, Wales, Man, and the Hebrides', 88; Roesdahl, *Vikings*, 224.
63. *Annals of St-Bertin*, *anno* 847, 65.
64. Roesdahl, *Vikings*, 224–8.
65. *Annals of Ulster*, *anno* 839, 298–9. See also Ó Corráin, 'Ireland, Wales, Man, and the Hebrides', 87.
66. Ó Corráin, 'Ireland, Wales, Man, and the Hebrides', 87.
67. Roesdahl, *Vikings*, 213–14.
68. *Anglo-Saxon Chronicles*, *anno* 835, 62–3.
69. Roesdahl, *Vikings*, 234.
70. *Anglo-Saxon Chronicles*, *anno* 836, 62–3.
71. Ibid., *anno* 838, 62–3.
72. Ibid., *anno* 840, 62–3.
73. Ibid., *anno* 841, 62–4.
74. Ibid., *anno* 842, 64–5.
75. Nithard, *Histories*, in *Carolingian Chronicles*, 127–74, esp. bk IV, ch 3, 167.
76. *Anglo-Saxon Chronicles*, *anno* 850, 64–5.
77. *Anglo-Saxon Chronicles*, *anno* 851, 64–5. See also Keynes, 'Vikings in England', 52.
78. *Anglo-Saxon Chronicles*, *anno* 855, 66–7.
79. Ibid., *anno* 865, 68–9.
80. Ibid.
81. Keynes, 'Vikings in England', 55; Roesdahl, *Vikings*, 234.
82. Jones, *History of the Vikings*, 218–19.
83. Bennett and Hooper, *Cambridge Illustrated Atlas*, 22.

84. *Sagas of Ragnar Lodbrok*, trans. B. Waggoner (New Haven, 2009), chs 15–16, 27–32. See also Jones, *History of the Vikings*, 219.
85. *Anglo-Saxon Chronicles*, *anno* 866, 68–9.
86. *Sagas of Ragnar Lodbrok*, ch 17, 35–6. See also Jones, *History of the Vikings*, 219, note 2.
87. *Anglo-Saxon Chronicles*, *anno* 867, 68–70.
88. Ibid., *anni* 869–70, 70–1.
89. Ibid., *anno* 870, 70–3.
90. *Anglo-Saxon Chronicles*, *anni* 870–1, 72–3. See also R. Abels, *Alfred the Great: War, Kingship and Culture in Anglo-Saxon England* (Harlow, 1998), 127–40.
91. *Anglo-Saxon Chronicles*, *anni* 872–3, 72–3. See also Abels, *Alfred the Great*, 141–4.
92. *Anglo-Saxon Chronicles*, *anni* 874–875, 72–5. See also Abels, *Alfred the Great*, 147; Keynes, 'Vikings in England', 55; Roesdahl, *Vikings*, 236.
93. *Anglo-Saxon Chronicles*, *anno* 877, 74–5. See also Jones, *History of the Vikings*, 221.
94. *Anglo-Saxon Chronicles*, *anno* 878, 74–5. See also Abels, *Alfred the Great*, 151–5.
95. *Anglo-Saxon Chronicles*, *anno* 878, 76–7; Asser, *Life of King Alfred*, in *Alfred the Great*, trans. Keynes and M. Lapidge (London, 1983), 65–110, esp. 84–5. See also Abels, *Alfred the Great*, 159–63.
96. *Anglo-Saxon Chronicles*, *anno* 879, 76–7. See also Jones, *History of the Vikings*, 223; Keynes, 'Vikings in England', 57.
97. *Anglo-Saxon Chronicles*, *anni* 878–9, 76–7.
98. Bennett and Hooper, *Cambridge Illustrated Atlas*, 23; Jones, *History of the Vikings*, 224; Roesdahl, *Vikings*, 201.
99. *Anglo-Saxon Chronicles*, *anno* 881, 76–7; *Annals of Fulda*, *anni* 881–2, 90–3; *Annals of St-Bertin*, *anno* 881, 222; Regino of Prüm, *Chronicon*, in *History and Politics in Late Carolingian and Ottonian Europe: The Chronicle of Regino of Prüm and Adalbert of Magdeburg*, trans. S. MacLean (Manchester, 2009), *anni* 881 and 883, 184, 187–8. See also Bennett and Hooper, *Cambridge Illustrated Atlas*, 23–4.
100. Bennett and Hooper, *Cambridge Illustrated Atlas*, 22, map 5.
101. *Annals of Fulda*, *anno* 881, 90; Regino of Prüm, *Chronicon*, *anno* 881, 185.
102. *Annals of St-Bertin*, *anno* 882, 224–6.
103. *Annals of St-Bertin*, *anno* 882, 224, note 11; *Anglo-Saxon Chronicles*, *anni* 882–3, 78–9.
104. *Annals of Fulda*, *anno* 882, 92–3; *Annals of St-Bertin*, *anno* 882, 224–5; Regino of Prüm, *Chronicon*, *anno* 882, 187. See also Jones, *History of the Vikings*, 224.
105. *Annals of Fulda*, *anno* 884, 96–7; Regino of Prüm, *Chronicon*, *anno* 884, 190.
106. *Anglo-Saxon Chronicles*, *anno* 884, 78–9.
107. *Annals of Fulda*, *anno* 884, 96, note 9.
108. Abbo of St-Germain-des-Prés, *Viking Attacks on Paris: Bella parisiacae urbis*, trans. N. Dass (Leuven, 2007), bk I, vv 37–8, 30–1.
109. Abbo of St-Germain-des-Prés, *Bella parisiacae urbis*, bk II, vv 219–20, 74–5.
110. Regino of Prüm, *Chronicon*, *anni* 887–8, 196, 201. See also Bennett and Hooper, *Cambridge Illustrated Atlas*, 24.
111. *Anglo-Saxon Chronicles*, *anno* 890, 82–3; Regino of Prüm, *Chronicon*, *anno* 890, 208–9. See also Sawyer, 'Age of the Vikings', 13.
112. *Annals of Fulda*, *anno* 891, 121–2; Regino of Prüm, *Chronicon*, *anno* 891, 210–12.
113. *Anglo-Saxon Chronicles*, *anno* 892, 84–5. See also Abels, *Alfred the Great*, 287; Jones, *History of the Vikings*, 226.
114. Abels, *Alfred the Great*, 195–204; Bennett and Hooper, *Cambridge Illustrated Atlas*, 23.
115. *Anglo-Saxon Chronicles*, *anno* 893, 84.
116. *Anglo-Saxon Chronicles*, *anno* 896, 90. See also Jones, *History of the Vikings*, 228.
117. Bennett and Hooper, *Cambridge Illustrated Atlas*, 25.
118. Jones, *History of the Vikings*, 226.
119. *Anglo-Saxon Chronicles*, *anno* 893, 85–6. See also Abels, *Alfred the Great*, 294–7.
120. *Anglo-Saxon Chronicles*, *anno* 893, 86. See also Abels, *Alfred the Great*, 297–8.
121. *Anglo-Saxon Chronicles*, *anno* 893, 87–8. See also Abels, *Alfred the Great*, 298–300.

122. *Anglo-Saxon Chronicles*, *anno* 894, 88–9. See also Abels, *Alfred the Great*, 300–1.
123. *Anglo-Saxon Chronicles*, *anno* 895, 89. See also Abels, *Alfred the Great*, 302.
124. *Anglo-Saxon Chronicles*, *anno* 896, 89.
125. Ibid., 90–1.
126. Dudo of St Quentin, *History of the Normans*, trans. E. Christiansen (Woodbridge, 1998), bk 2, chs 15–16, 138–9.
127. D. Douglas, 'Rollo of Normandy', *English Historical Review*, vol. 57 (1942), 414–36, esp. 425.
128. Dudo of St Quentin, *History of the Normans*, bk II, chs 22–9, 43–9. See also Chibnall, *Normans*, 11–12.
129. J. Le Patourel, *The Norman Empire* (Oxford, 1976), 3–5.
130. Chibnall, *Normans*, 14–16.
131. R. Brown, *The Normans* (Woodbridge, 1984), 19, 32–7.
132. *Landnámabók, The Book of Settlements*, trans. H. Pálsson and P. Edwards (Winnipeg, 1972), ch 1, 5. See also S. Rafnsson, 'The Atlantic Islands', in *Oxford History of the Vikings*, 110–33, esp. 110.
133. A. Thorgilsson, *Íslendingabók – Kristni Saga*, trans. S. Grønlie (London, 2006), *Íslendingabók*, ch 1, 3.
134. *Landnámabók*, chs 13–14, 29, 22–3, 27.
135. Snorre Sturlason, *Heimskringla*, 'History of Harald Hairfair', 54–7.
136. Rafnsson, 'Atlantic Islands', 118–19.
137. Viking Ships Museum of Roskilde. See also Bill, 'Ships and Seamanship', 188–90; Roesdahl, *Vikings*, 264.
138. Thorgilsson, *Íslendingabók*, ch 1, 4; *Landnámabók*, ch 9, 21.
139. Thorgilsson, *Íslendingabók*, ch 3, 5.
140. Ibid.
141. Thorgilsson, *Íslendingabók*, ch 5, 6–7. See also Roesdahl, *Vikings*, 268.
142. Thorgilsson, *Íslendingabók*, ch 6, 7.
143. *Landnámabók*, ch 90, 49.
144. 'The Vinland Sagas' ('Saga of the Greenlanders' and 'Erik the Red's Saga'), trans. K. Kunz in *The Sagas of the Icelanders* (New York, 2000), 626–74, esp. 636–42 and 660–1.
145. Roesdahl, *Vikings*, 274.
146. Rafnsson, 'Atlantic Islands', 112–13.
147. T. Noonan, 'Scandinavians in European Russia', in *Oxford Illustrated History of the Vikings*, 134–55, esp. 135; Roesdahl, *Vikings*, 277–8.
148. Jones, *History of the Vikings*, 252; Noonan, 'Scandinavians in European Russia', 141–2.
149. Roesdahl, *Vikings*, 123–5.
150. Jones, *History of the Vikings*, 251–3.
151. *Annals of St-Bertin*, *anno* 839, 44.
152. Jones, *History of the Vikings*, 253.
153. *Russian Primary Chronicle*, trans. S. Cross and O. Sherbowitz-Wetzor (Cambridge, 1953), *anno* 859, 59.
154. *Russian Primary Chronicle*, *anni* 860–2, 59–60.
155. Noonan, 'Scandinavians in European Russia', 134–5; Sawyer, 'Age of the Vikings', 2.
156. *Russian Primary Chronicle*, *anni* 863–6, 60; John Skylitzes, *Synopsis*, 'Michael III and Theodora', 107–8.
157. *Russian Primary Chronicle*, *anni* 870–9, 880–2, 60–1.
158. Noonan, 'Scandinavians in European Russia', 38.
159. *Russian Primary Chronicle*, *anno* 907, 64–5.
160. *Russian Primary Chronicle*, *anno* 912, 65–9. See also Jones, *History of the Vikings*, 259–60; Noonan, 'Scandinavians in European Russia', 148–9.
161. *Russian Primary Chronicle*, *anno* 941, 71–2; John Skylitzes, *Synopsis*, 'Romanos I Lekapenos', 221–2.
162. Liudprand of Cremona, *Antapodosis*, bk V, ch 15, 185–6.
163. Liudprand of Cremona, *Antapodosis*, bk V, ch 15, 185–6; John Skylitzes, *Synopsis*, 'Romanos I Lekapenos', 221. See also Jones, *History of the Vikings*, 260.

164. Liudprand of Cremona, *Antapodosis*, bk V, ch 15, 186.
165. John Skylitzes, *Synopsis*, 'Romanos I Lekapenos', 221.
166. *Russian Primary Chronicle*, *anno* 941, 72.
167. Ibid., *anno* 944, 72–3.
168. Ibid., *anno* 945, 73–8.
169. *Russian Primary Chronicle*, *anno* 948, 82; John Skylitzes, *Synopsis*, 'Constantine VII', 231 and note 31.
170. Jones, *History of the Vikings*, 266.
171. *Russian Primary Chronicle*, *anno* 988, 112–13; John Skylitzes, *Synopsis*, 'Basil II and Constantine VIII', 319, note 100. See also Treadgold, *History of the Byzantine State*, 518.
172. John Skylitzes, *Synopsis*, 'Michael IV', 376 and note 28; Snorre Sturlason, *Heimskringla*, 'History of Harald Hardrade', 506–8. See also Jones, *History of the Vikings*, 266; Noonan, 'Scandinavians in European Russia', 155; Treadgold, *History of the Byzantine State*, 587.
173. Jones, *History of the Vikings*, 355–6; Roesdahl, *Vikings*, 250.
174. *Anglo-Saxon Chronicles*, *anni* 981–2, 124–5.
175. Ibid., *anno* 991, 26–7.
176. Ibid., *anno* 994, 126–9.
177. Jones, *History of the Vikings*, 365.
178. *Anglo-Saxon Chronicles*, *anni* 997–9, 131.
179. Ibid., *anno* 999, 133.
180. Ibid., *anno* 1000, 133.
181. Roesdahl, *Vikings*, 75.
182. Jones, *History of the Vikings*, 135–8.
183. Snorre Sturlason, *Heimskringla*, 'History of Olav Trygvason', 182, 187. See also A. Campbell, 'Additional Notes', in *Encomium Emmae Reginae*, trans. Campbell (London, 1949), App. V, note a, 94–6; Rodgers, *Naval Warfare under Oars*, 75.
184. Snorre Sturlason, *Heimskringla*, 'History of Olav Trygvason', 206–15.
185. *Anglo-Saxon Chronicles*, *anno* 1001, 133.
186. Ibid., *anno* 1002, 133–5.
187. Jones, *History of the Vikings*, 358.
188. *Anglo-Saxon Chronicles*, *anni* 1003–5, 134–6.
189. Ibid., *anni* 1006–7, 136–8.
190. Ibid., *anni* 1008–9, 138–9.
191. Ibid., *anni* 1009–12, 139–43.
192. *Encomium Emmae Reginae*, bk I, chs 3–4, 10–13.
193. Roesdahl, *Vikings*, 252.
194. *Anglo-Saxon Chronicles*, *anno* 1013, 144.
195. Ibid., *anno* 1014, 144–5.
196. *Encomium Emmae Reginae*, bk II, ch 4, 19.
197. *Anglo-Saxon Chronicles*, *anno* 1015, 146.
198. Ibid., *anno* 1016, 146–53.
199. Ibid., *anno* 1017, 154–5.
200. Ibid., *anno* 1018, 154–5.
201. *Anglo-Saxon Chronicles*, *anni* 1027–8, 157. See Jones, *History of the Vikings*, 382; Roesdahl, *Vikings*, 256.
202. Jones, *History of the Vikings*, 382.
203. *English Historical Documents, 500–1042*, ed. D. Whitelock (London, 1979), 'Cnut's letter of 1027', 476–7.
204. Roesdahl, *Vikings*, 295–6.
205. *Anglo-Saxon Chronicles*, *anni* 1035–43, 158–63.
206. Snorre Sturlason, *Heimskringla*, 'History of Magnus the Good', 495–7. See also Rodgers, *Naval Warfare under Oars*, 80.

207. Snorre Sturlason, *Heimskringla*, 'History of Harald Hardrade', 514–25. See also N. Lund, 'The Danish Empire and the End of the Viking Age', in *Oxford History of the Vikings*, 156–81, esp. 175–7.
208. Snorre Sturlason, *Heimskringla*, 'History of Harald Hardrade', 541–2.
209. Ibid., 543–6.
210. Jones, *History of the Vikings*, 408.
211. *Anglo-Saxon Chronicles*, *anno* 1066, 194–9; Snorre Sturlason, *Heimskringla*, 'History of Harald Hardrade', 561–8. See also Jones, *History of the Vikings*, 410–13.
212. Snorre Sturlason, *Heimskringla*, 'History of Harald Hardrade', 566. See also Roesdahl, *Vikings*, 297.
213. Abbo of St-Germain-des-Prés, *Bella parisiacae urbis*, bk I, vv 28–30, 28–9.
214. Ibid., bk I, vv 115, 34–5.
215. Ibid., bk I, vv 114, 34–5.
216. C. Gillmor, 'War on the river, Viking Numbers and Mobility on the Seine and Loire, 841–886', *Viator*, 19 (1988), 79–109, esp. 81–2, 90; Bill, 'Ships and Seamanship'; Viking Ships Museum of Roskilde.
217. Bennett et al., *Fighting Techniques of the Medieval World*, 222; Bennett and Hooper, *Cambridge Illustrated Atlas*, 24.
218. Gillmor, 'War on the river', 86–9; H. Kortüm, 'The Siege of Paris', in *The Oxford Encyclopedia of Medieval Warfare*, III, 105–6.
219. Abbo of St-Germain-des-Prés, *Bella parisiacae urbis*, bk I, vv 36–60, 30–1.
220. Abbo of St-Germain-des-Prés, *Bella parisiacae urbis*, bk I, vv 61–80, 30–3. See also J. Bradbury, *The Medieval Siege* (Woodbridge, 1992), 43–4.
221. Abbo of St-Germain-des-Prés, *Bella parisiacae urbis*, bk I, vv 81–102, 32–3. See also Bradbury, *Medieval Siege*, 44.
222. Abbo of St-Germain-des-Prés, *Bella parisiacae urbis*, bk I, vv 144–8, 36–7 and note 38 on 110.
223. Ibid., bk I, vv 172–80, 36–7.
224. Ibid., bk I, vv 205–10, 38–9.
225. Ibid., bk I, vv 217–19, 38–9.
226. Ibid., bk I, vv 235–6, 40–1.
227. Ibid., bk I, vv 249–54, 40–1.
228. Abbo of St-Germain-des-Prés, *Bella parisiacae urbis*, bk I, vv 301–10, 44–5. See also Bradbury, *Medieval Siege*, 45.
229. Regino of Prüm, *Chronicon*, *anno* 888, 201. See also Gillmor, 'War on the river', 88–90.
230. Abbo of St-Germain-des-Prés, *Bella parisiacae urbis*, bk I, vv 375–80, 48–9.
231. Abbo of St-Germain-des-Prés, *Bella parisiacae urbis*, bk I, vv 415–20, 50–1. See also Gillmor, 'War on the river', 90, note 30.
232. Abbo of St-Germain-des-Prés, *Bella parisiacae urbis*, bk I, vv 504–64, 54–9.
233. Abbo of St-Germain-des-Prés, *Bella parisiacae urbis*, bk I, vv 357–67, 46–7. See also Bradbury, *Medieval Siege*, 45.
234. Abbo of St-Germain-des-Prés, *Bella parisiacae urbis*, bk II, vv 217–18, 74–5; Regino of Prüm, *Chronicon*, *anno* 887, 194–5.
235. Abbo of St-Germain-des-Prés, *Bella parisiacae urbis*, bk II, vv 70–1, 66–7.
236. Ibid., bk II, vv 41–4, 66–7.
237. Ibid., bk II, vv 163–5, 72–3.
238. Ibid., bk II, vv 230–1, 76–7.
239. Ibid., bk II, vv 330–42, 81–3.
240. Bennett and Hooper, *Cambridge Illustrated Atlas*, 24; Bradbury, *Medieval Siege*, 46.

Chapter 8. The Norman Invasion and the Rise of Anglo-French Naval Warfare

1. Brown, *The Normans and the Norman Conquest* (Woodbridge, 1985), 142–50.
2. Wace, *Roman de Rou, The History of the Norman People*, trans. G. Burgess (Woodbridge, 2004), 156–7.
3. Brown, *Norman Conquest*, 104–5.

4. William of Poitiers, *Gesta Guillelmi*, trans. R. Davis and Chibnall (Oxford, 1998), pt II, ch 3, 104–5.
5. William of Malmesbury, *Gesta Regum Anglorum*, trans. R. Mynors, R. Thomson and M. Winterbottom (Oxford, 1998), bk III, 448–9.
6. Wace, *Roman de Rou*, 159.
7. E. Van Houts, 'The Ship List of William the Conqueror', *Anglo-Norman Studies*, 10 (1988), 159–83, esp. App. I–IV, 176–9.
8. Wace, *Roman de Rou*, 163.
9. L. Musset, *The Bayeux Tapestry*, trans. R. Rex (Woodbridge, 2005), scene 38, 200–1; Van Houts, 'Ship List of William the Conqueror', 166 and App. I on 176.
10. William of Jumièges, *Gesta Normannorum Ducum*, trans. Van Houts (2 vols, Oxford, 1995), II, 164–5; William of Poitiers, *Gesta Guillelmi*, pt II, ch 7, 110–11.
11. Brown, *Norman Conquest*, 126; D. Douglas, *William the Conqueror* (London, 1964), 184–5; Musset, *Bayeux Tapestry*, scenes 35 and 36, 182–9.
12. Gillmor, 'Naval Logistics of the Cross-Channel Operation, 1066', *Anglo-Norman Studies*, 7 (1984), 105–31, esp. 117–18.
13. Van Houts, 'Ship List of William the Conqueror', 170.
14. William of Malmesbury, *Gesta Regum Anglorum*, bk V, 728–9. See also Gillmor, 'Naval Logistics of the Cross-Channel Operation', 21–2.
15. Douglas, *William the Conqueror*, 184–92.
16. Gillmor, 'Naval Logistics of the Cross-Channel Operation', 110–15.
17. Bachrach, 'On the Origins of William the Conqueror's Horse Transports', 513–17.
18. Stanton, *Norman Naval Operations*, 44–5.
19. Bachrach, 'William the Conqueror's Horse Transports', 506–8; Bennett, 'Amphibious Operations', 52–3; Gillmor, 'Naval Logistics of the Cross-Channel Operation', 110; Musset, *Bayeux Tapestry*, scene 39, 202–4.
20. Gillmor, 'Naval Logistics of the Cross-Channel Operation', 114.
21. William of Poitiers, *Gesta Guillelmi*, pt II, ch 2, 102–3.
22. Bachrach, 'Some Observations on the Military Administration of the Norman Conquest', *Anglo-Norman Studies*, VIII (1985), 1–25.
23. Orderic Vitalis, *Ecclesiastical History*, trans. Chibnall (6 vols, Oxford, 1969–80), II, bk III, 168–9; William of Poitiers, *Gesta Guillelmi*, pt II, ch 2, 102–3. See also Bachrach, 'Military Administration of the Norman Conquest', 2.
24. Bachrach, 'Military Administration of the Norman Conquest', 2–4.
25. Ibid., 2.
26. Ibid., 11.
27. Ibid., 12.
28. Ibid., 15.
29. William of Poitiers, *Gesta Guillelmi*, pt II, ch 2, 102–3. See also Bachrach, 'Military Administration of the Norman Conquest', 10.
30. N. Hooper, 'Some Observations on the Navy in Late Anglo-Saxon England', in *Anglo-Norman Warfare*, ed. M. Strickland (Woodbridge, 1992), 17–27, esp. 20–3; Rodger, *Safeguard of the Sea*, 23–5.
31. *Anglo-Saxon Chronicles*, *anno* 1066, 194–5.
32. Ibid., *anno* 1066, 196.
33. William of Poitiers, *Gesta Guillelmi*, pt II, ch 2, 102–3. See also Chibnall, *Gesta Guillelmi*, XXIV–XXXV.
34. *Anglo-Saxon Chronicles*, *anno* 1066, 196.
35. Gillmor, 'Naval Logistics of the Cross-Channel Operation', 110–11.
36. Brown, *Norman Conquest*, 132.
37. Jones, *History of the Vikings*, 410.
38. William of Poitiers, *Gesta Guillelmi*, pt II, ch 3, 104–5. See also Brown, *Norman Conquest*, 129.
39. Brown, *Norman Conquest*, 133–6.
40. Guy of Amiens, *Carmen de Hastingae Proelio*, trans. F. Barlow (Oxford, 1999), 8–9.

41. William of Poitiers, *Gesta Guillelmi*, pt II, ch 7, 110–11.
42. Guy of Amiens, *Carmen*, 8–9.
43. William of Poitiers, *Gesta Guillelmi*, pt II, ch 8, 112–13.
44. Guy of Amiens, *Carmen*, 8–11; William of Poitiers, *Gesta Guillelmi*, pt II, ch 2, 114–15.
45. Rodger, *Safeguard of the Sea*, 33.
46. Brown, *Norman Conquest*, 140.
47. William of Poitiers, *Gesta Guillelmi*, pt II, ch 14, 122–5.
48. Brown, *Norman Conquest*, 137.
49. Rodger, *Safeguard of the Sea*, 38–9.
50. *Anglo-Saxon Chronicles*, *anno* 1068, 203.
51. Rodger, *Safeguard of the Sea*, 36.
52. *Anglo-Saxon Chronicles*, *anno* 1069, 202–4; Orderic Vitalis, *Ecclesiastical History*, II, bk IV, 226–7.
53. Brown, *Norman Conquest*, 168–9.
54. *Anglo-Saxon Chronicles*, *anno* 1069, 204.
55. Florence of Worcester, *The Chronicle of Florence of Worcester*, trans. T. Forester (London, 1854), *anno* 1069, 173. See also Brown, *Norman Conquest*, 170.
56. *Anglo-Saxon Chronicles*, *anno* 1070, 206. See also Rodger, *Safeguard of the Sea*, 38.
57. *Anglo-Saxon Chronicles*, *anno* 1075, 211–12.
58. Florence of Worcester, *Chronicle*, *anno* 1085, 184.
59. Lund, 'Naval Power in the Viking Age and in High Medieval Denmark', in *War at Sea in the Middle Ages*, 25–34, esp. 28–33.
60. *Anglo-Saxon Chronicles*, *anno* 1085, 215–16. See also Rodger, *Safeguard of the Sea*, 38.
61. Florence of Worcester, *Chronicle*, *anno* 1071, 177.
62. *Anglo-Saxon Chronicles*, *anni* 1071–2, 206–8. See also S. Morillo, *Warfare under the Anglo-Norman Kings, 1066–1135* (Woodbridge, 1994), 176; Rodger, *Safeguard of the Sea*, 38–9.
63. Florence of Worcester, *Chronicle*, *anno* 1072, 177.
64. *Anglo-Saxon Chronicles*, *anno* 1088, 224; Florence of Worcester, *Chronicle*, *anno* 1088, 188.
65. Henry of Huntingdon, *Historia Anglorum*, ed. trans. D. Greenway (Oxford, 1996), bk VII, ch 1, 414–15. See also Morillo, *Warfare under the Anglo-Norman Kings*, 175–6.
66. Florence of Worcester, *Chronicle*, *anno* 1101, 209.
67. Henry of Huntingdon, *Historia Anglorum*, bk X, ch 4, 708–9. See also Rodger, *Safeguard of the Sea*, 40.
68. Rodger, *Safeguard of the Sea*, 41–3.
69. Dear and Kemp, *Oxford Companion to Ships*, 193; Rodger, *Safeguard of the Sea*, 47; Rose, *Medieval Naval Warfare*, 12.
70. Rodger, *Safeguard of the Sea*, 39.
71. Rose, *England's Medieval Navy*, 35.
72. Rose, *Medieval Naval Warfare*, 26.
73. Rodger, *Safeguard of the Sea*, 49.
74. Guillaume Le Breton, *Philippidos*, in *Oeuvres de Rigord et de Guillaume Le Breton*, ed. H. Delaborde (2 vols, Paris, 1882–5), II, bk VII, vv 173–4, 183. See also Gillingham, 'Richard I, Galley-Warfare and Portsmouth: The Beginnings of a Royal Navy', in *Thirteenth Century England VI* (Woodbridge, 1997), 1–15, esp. 6–7, 12–15; Rodger, *Safeguard of the Sea*, 46.
75. Gillingham, *Richard the Lionheart*, 262–77.
76. Guillaume Le Breton, *Chronique*, in *Oeuvres de Rigord et de Guillaume Le Breton*, I, 168–327, esp. 214; Roger of Wendover, *Flowers of History*, II, 207–8, 213–14. See also F. Brooks, *The English Naval Forces 1199–1272* (London, 1932), 136; Gillingham, 'Beginnings of a Royal Navy', 7; Rodger, *Safeguard of the Sea*, 50–1.
77. Brooks, *English Naval Forces*, 204–6; H. Cannon, 'The Battle of Sandwich and Eustace the Monk', *English Historical Review*, XXVII (1912), 649–70, esp. 651–4; Rodger, *Safeguard of the Sea*, 50–1.
78. Brooks, *English Naval Forces*, 197.
79. Roger of Wendover, *Flowers of History*, II, 263–4.
80. Ibid., II, 261–2.
81. Brooks, *English Naval Forces*, 196.

82. Guillaume Le Breton, *Chronique*, I, 249–50. See also Brooks, *English Naval Forces*, 199–200.
83. Guillaume Le Breton, *Chronique*, I, 251–3; Roger of Wendover, *Flowers of History*, II,272–3. See also Brooks, *English Naval Forces*, 200–3; Paine, *Sea and Civilization*, 335; Rodger, *Safeguard of the Sea*, 54; Rose, *England's Medieval Navy*, 124–5; *Medieval Naval Warfare*, 28–9.
84. Roger of Wendover, *Flowers of History*, II, 298–303. See also Brooks, *English Naval Forces*, 204; France, *Western Warfare in the Age of the Crusades, 1000–1300* (Ithaca, 1999), App. I, 235–41.
85. Roger of Wendover, *Flowers of History*, II, 308–22.
86. Ibid., II, 329, 340–1.
87. Ibid., II, 334–9.
88. Roger of Wendover, *Flowers of History*, II, 357–9. See also Brooks, *English Naval Forces*, 206–9; Rodger, *Safeguard of the Sea*, 54.
89. *Histoire des Ducs de Normandie et des Rois d'Angleterre*, ed. F. Michel (Paris, 1840), 172–7; Roger of Wendover, *Flowers of History*, II, 364, 373–8. See also Brooks, *English Naval Forces*, 210–13; Rose, *England's Medieval Navy*, 125–6.
90. *Histoire des Ducs de Normandie*, 183–5; *History of William Marshal*, trans. A. Holden, S. Gregory, D. Crouch (3 vols, London, 2004), II, vv 15768–871, 290–5. See also Brooks, *English Naval Forces*, 213–14.
91. *Histoire des Ducs de Normandie*, 188–96; *History of William Marshal*, II, vv 17069–84, 355–7; Roger of Wendover, *Flowers of History*, II, 399–403. See also Brooks, *English Naval Forces*, 215–16; Cannon, 'Battle of Sandwich', 656–7; Rose, *England's Medieval Navy*, 127.
92. *Histoire des Ducs de Normandie*, 198–205; *History of William Marshal*, II, vv 17117–696, 358–87; Roger of Wendover, *Flowers of History*, II, 394–9. See also Brooks, *English Naval Forces*, 217–19; Cannon, 'Battle of Sandwich', 658–67; Rodger, *Safeguard of the Sea*, 55; Rose, *England's Medieval Navy*, 128–9.
93. Rodger, *Safeguard of the Sea*, 55–8.
94. Brooks, *English Naval Forces*, 220.
95. Brooks, *English Naval Forces*, 220–3; Rodger, *Safeguard of the Sea*, 59; Rose, *Medieval Naval Warfare*, 31.
96. Rodger, *Safeguard of the Sea*, 75–89; Rose, *England's Medieval Navy*, 10–11; *Medieval Naval Warfare*, 58.
97. Brooks, *English Naval Forces*, 32–5; Rodger, *Safeguard of the Sea*, 39.
98. Brooks, *English Naval Forces*, 86; Rodger, 'The Naval Service of the Cinque Ports', *English Historical Review*, 111 (1996), 636–51, esp. 638–41, 650; Rose, *England's Medieval Navy*, 53–4; 'The Value of the Cinque Ports to the Crown 1200–1500', in *Roles of the Sea in Medieval England*, ed. R. Gorski (Woodbridge, 2012), 41–57, esp. 43–4.
99. Brooks, *English Naval Forces*, 87–8.
100. Brooks, *English Naval Forces*, 132–6; Rodger, *Safeguard of the Sea*, 39–40.
101. Gillingham, 'Beginnings of a Royal Navy', 12–14; Rose, *Medieval Naval Warfare*, 12.
102. Brooks, *English Naval Forces*, 136; Gillingham, 'Beginnings of a Royal Navy', 6–7; Rodger, *Safeguard of the Sea*, 46.
103. Rodger, *Safeguard of the Sea*, 53; Rose, *Medieval Naval Warfare*, 12.
104. Brooks, *English Naval Forces*, 140.
105. Gillingham, 'Beginnings of a Royal Navy', 5; Rodger, *Safeguard of the Sea*, 51; Rose, *England's Medieval Navy*, 44; *Medieval Naval Warfare*, 12.
106. Brooks, *English Naval Forces*, 168–79; Rose, *Medieval Naval Warfare*, 12–13.
107. Brooks, *English Naval Forces*, 182–3; Rodger, 'Naval Service of the Cinque Ports', 644.
108. Brooks, *English Naval Forces*, 183.
109. Brooks, *English Naval Forces*, 192; Rodger, 'Naval Service of the Cinque Ports', 644.
110. Brooks, *English Naval Forces*, 193.
111. Rose, *Medieval Naval Warfare*, 58.
112. Hutchinson, *Medieval Ships*, 89; Paine, *Sea and Civilization*, 336; Rodger, *Safeguard of the Sea*, 78–82.
113. Brooks, *English Naval Forces*, 109.

114. Rodger, 'Naval Service of the Cinque Ports', 651.
115. Rose, *England's Medieval Navy*, 55–7; 'Value of the Cinque Ports', 55.
116. John of Joinville, *Life of Saint Louis*, 197. See Asbridge, *Crusades*, 580–1; Riley-Smith, *Crusades*, 193.
117. Mott, *Sea Power in the Medieval Mediterranean*, 38.
118. Rodger, *Safeguard of the Sea*, 82; Rose, *England's Medieval Navy*, 163; *Medieval Naval Warfare*, 13–14.
119. Rodger, *Safeguard of the Sea*, 82.
120. Hutchinson, *Medieval Ships*, 23; Rodger, *Safeguard of the Sea*, 68, App. II, 474; Rose, *England's Medieval Navy*, 46; *Medieval Naval Warfare*, 62; J. Tinniswood, 'English Galleys, 1272–1377', *Mariner's Mirror*, 35 (1949), 276–315, esp. 276.
121. Rodger, *Safeguard of the Sea*, 82–90.
122. *History of William Marshal*, II, vv 17281–8, 366–7.
123. Matthew Paris, *Historia Anglorum*, II, 217–18. See also Rose, *Medieval Naval Warfare*, 30.
124. *History of William Marshal*, II, vv 17257–61, 364–5.
125. *History of William Marshal*, II, vv 17069–136, 355–9. See also Rodger, *The Safeguard of the Sea*, 54–5.
126. *History of William Marshal*, II, vv 17168–230, 360–5. See also Cannon, 'Battle of Sandwich', 655–7.
127. *Histoire des Ducs de Normandie*, 200; *History of William Marshal*, II, vv 17294, 366–7; Roger of Wendover, *Flowers of History*, II, 399.
128. Cannon, 'Battle of Sandwich', 660.
129. *History of William Marshal*, II, vv 17289–91, 366–7.
130. Brooks, *English Naval Forces*, 204–6; Cannon, 'Battle of Sandwich', 650–4; Rodger, *Safeguard of the Sea*, 50–1.
131. Roger of Wendover, *Flowers of History*, II, 399.
132. *History of William Marshal*, II, vv 17234–9, 364–5; Matthew Paris, *Historia Anglorum*, II, 217–18; Roger of Wendover, *Flowers of History*, II, 400–1, note.
133. Matthew Paris, *Historia Anglorum*, II, 217–18; Roger of Wendover, *Flowers of History*, II, 401, note. See also Cannon, 'Battle of Sandwich', 660.
134. *History of William Marshal*, II, vv 17262–310, 364–9; 17381–4, 370–1.
135. Matthew Paris, *Historia Anglorum*, II, 219; Roger of Wendover, *Flowers of History*, II, 399. See also Rose, *Medieval Naval Warfare*, 30.
136. *History of William Marshal*, II, vv 17365–8, 370–1.
137. *Histoire des Ducs de Normandie*, 201–2. See also Cannon, 'Battle of Sandwich', 659–60.
138. *History of William Marshal*, II, vv 17365–94, 370–3.
139. Rodger, *Safeguard of the Sea*, 55.
140. *History of William Marshal*, II, vv 17354–9, 370–1; Matthew Paris, *Historia Anglorum*, II, 219; Roger of Wendover, *Flowers of History*, II, 401, note. See also Rodger, *Safeguard of the Sea*, 55.
141. *Histoire des Ducs de Normandie*, 201; Roger of Wendover, *Flowers of History*, II, 399. See also Cannon, 'Battle of Sandwich', 663.
142. Guillaume le Breton, *Chronique*, 314. See also Cannon, 'Battle of Sandwich', 663.
143. Matthew Paris, *Historia Anglorum*, II, 219; Roger of Wendover, *Flowers of History*, II, 401, note. See also Brooks, *English Naval Forces*, 218, note 2; Cannon, 'Battle of Sandwich', 663–4.
144. *History of William Marshal*, II, vv 17377–404, 370–3; Matthew Paris, *Historia Anglorum*, II, 219; Roger of Wendover, *Flowers of History*, II, 399–400. See also Cannon, 'Battle of Sandwich', 664.
145. *Histoire des Ducs de Normandie*, 202; *History of William Marshal*, II, vv 17405–33, 17457–62, 372–5; Matthew Paris, *Historia Anglorum*, II, 219; Roger of Wendover, *Flowers of History*, II, 400, note. See also Cannon, 'Battle of Sandwich', 664–5.
146. Matthew Paris, *Historia Anglorum*, II, 219; Roger of Wendover, *Flowers of History*, II, 401, note.
147. *Histoire des Ducs de Normandie*, 202; *History of William Marshal*, II, vv 17434–55, 374–5. See also Cannon, 'Battle of Sandwich', 665.
148. Roger of Wendover, *Flowers of History*, II, 400.

149. *History of William Marshal*, II, vv 17473–94, 376–7.
150. *Histoire des Ducs de Normandie*, 202. See also Cannon, 'Battle of Sandwich', 666.
151. *History of William Marshal*, II, vv 17505–8, 376–7.
152. *History of William Marshal*, II, vv 17510–33, 378–9. See also Brooks, *English Naval Forces*, 219.
153. Roger of Wendover, *Flowers of History*, II, 400. See also Cannon, 'Battle of Sandwich', 666; Rose, *Medieval Naval Warfare*, 30.
154. Brooks, *English Naval Forces*, 219; Rodger, *Safeguard of the Sea*, 55.
155. *Histoire des Ducs de Normandie*, 202. See also Cannon, 'Battle of Sandwich', 667.
156. Matthew Paris, *Historia Anglorum*, II, 221–4; Roger of Wendover, *Flowers of History*, II, 402–3.
157. Cannon, 'Battle of Sandwich', 654.

Chapter 9. The Hundred Years War: Anglo-French Conflict across the Narrow Sea

1. A. Curry, *The Hundred Years' War 1337–1453* (Oxford, 2002), 11.
2. Friel, 'Oars, Sails and Guns: The English and War at Sea, c.1200–c.1500', in *War at Sea in the Middle Ages*, 69–79, esp. 69.
3. Runyan, 'The Cog as Warship', in *Cogs, Caravels and Galleons*, 47–58, esp. 50; 'Naval Power during the Hundred Years War', 59.
4. Rodger, *Safeguard of the Sea*, 91–6; Rose, *Medieval Naval Warfare*, 68–9.
5. Rodger, *Safeguard of the Sea*, 117.
6. Rodger, *Safeguard of the Sea*, 120, 128; Rose, *England's Medieval Navy*, 57–9; Runyan, 'Naval Power during the Hundred Years War', 53.
7. Rodger, *Safeguard of the Sea*, 134–5; Runyan, 'Naval Power during the Hundred Years War', 64.
8. Rodger, *Safeguard of the Sea*, 121.
9. Runyan, 'Naval Power during the Hundred Years War', 54–5.
10. Rodger, *Safeguard of the Sea*, 126–7; Runyan, 'Naval Power during the Hundred Years War', 58–9.
11. Friel, 'English and War at Sea', 75, 79; Rose, *England's Medieval Navy*, 60–1.
12. Curry, *Hundred Years' War*, 56.
13. Rodger, *Safeguard of the Sea*, 65–6, 91–2.
14. Ibid., 114.
15. Ibid.
16. Ibid., 93.
17. Rose, *England's Medieval Navy*, 163–5.
18. Abulafia, *Great Sea*, 360; Rodger, *Safeguard of the Sea*, 93; Rose, *England's Medieval Navy*, 164.
19. Rodger, *Safeguard of the Sea*, 83; Rose, *Medieval Naval Warfare*, 62.
20. Rose, *England's Medieval Navy*, 166.
21. Rodger, *Safeguard of the Sea*, 96; Rose, *Medieval Naval Warfare*, 69.
22. Pryor, 'Galleys of Charles of Anjou', 36–73.
23. Casson, 'Merchant Galleys', 123–4; Dotson, 'Venice, Genoa and Control of the Seas', 124.
24. Friel, 'English and War at Sea', 69.
25. Rodger, *Safeguard of the Sea*, 66.
26. Rose, *England's Medieval Navy*, 69–71; Tinniswood, 'English Galleys, 1272–1377', 283–94.
27. Friel, 'English and War at Sea', 70.
28. Rodger, *Safeguard of the Sea*, 66.
29. Friel, *The Good Ship: Ships, Shipbuilding and Technology in England 1200–1520* (Baltimore, 1995), 147.
30. Rose, *England's Medieval Navy*, 31.
31. Runyan, 'Cog as Warship', 47–9.
32. Rose, *England's Medieval Navy*, 47–9.
33. D. Ellmers, 'The Cog as Cargo Carrier', in *Cogs, Caravels and Galleons*, 29–46, esp. 33–8; Rose, *England's Medieval Navy*, 76–8; Runyan, 'Cog as Warship', 47–54.
34. Friel, 'English and War at Sea', 71.

35. Rose, *Medieval Naval Warfare*, 85.
36. Friel, 'The Carrack: The Advent of the Full Rigged Ship', in *Cogs, Caravels and Galleons*, 77–90, esp. 79–88; 'Henry V's Gracedieu and the wreck in the river Hamble near Burlesdon, Hampshire', *IJNA*, 22 (1993), 3–19; Rose, *England's Medieval Navy*, 50–1, 65, 75–6; *The Navy of the Lancastrian Kings: Accounts and Inventories of William Soper, Keeper of the King's Ships, 1422–1427* (London, 1982), 34–9.
37. Friel, 'English and War at Sea', 72–4; Rose, *England's Medieval Navy*, 120–1.
38. Friel, Carrack', 86–7; Rose, *England's Medieval Navy*, 121.
39. Bennett et al., *Fighting Techniques of the Medieval World*, 232; Runyan, 'Naval Power during the Hundred Years War', 58.
40. Rose, *England's Medieval Navy*, 141–54.
41. Ibid., 139.
42. Rose, *Navy of the Lancastrian Kings*, 48–52.
43. Rodger, *Safeguard of the Sea*, 106–7.
44. *Libelle of Englyshe Polycye*, ed. G. Warner (Oxford, 1926), vv 7, 1. See also Friel, 'Carrack', 88; Rose, *England's Medieval Navy*, 20, 33; Runyan, 'Naval Power during the Hundred Years War', 66.
45. C. Allmand, *The Hundred Years War, England and France at War c.1300–c.1450* (Cambridge, 2001), 9; Curry, *Hundred Years' War*, 12–15.
46. Allmand, *Hundred Years War*, 9–10; Curry, *Hundred Years' War*, 15–18.
47. Curry, *Hundred Years' War*, 27–9.
48. G. Cushway, *Edward III and War at Sea: The English Navy, 1327–1377* (Woodbridge, 2011), 71–2; Rodger, *Safeguard of the Sea*, 96; Rose, *England's Medieval Navy*, 129.
49. Geoffrey le Baker, *Chronicon*, ed. E. Thompson (Oxford, 1889), 61. See also Cushway, *Edward III and War at Sea*, 73; C. Lambert, *Shipping the Medieval Military* (Woodbridge, 2011) figured 403 ships, 118–9.
50. Geoffrey le Baker, *Chronicon*, 62. See also Cushway, *Edward III and War at Sea*, 74; Rodger, *Safeguard of the Sea*, 96; Rose, *England's Medieval Navy*, 131; *Medieval Naval Warfare*, 63–4.
51. Jean Froissart, *Chronicles*, trans. G. Brereton (London, 1968), 60–1.
52. Cushway, *Edward III and War at Sea*, 75.
53. Geoffrey le Baker, *Chronicon*, 63. See also Cushway, *Edward III and War at Sea*, 77.
54. Rodger, *Safeguard of the Sea*, 96.
55. Cushway, *Edward III and War at Sea*, 78.
56. Geoffrey le Baker, *Chronicon*, 63–4. See also Curry, *Hundred Years' War*, 31; Cushway, *Edward III and War at Sea*, 78; Rodger, *Safeguard of the Sea*, 96–7.
57. Cushway, *Edward III and War at Sea*, 78.
58. Geoffrey le Baker, *Chronicon*, 68. See also Cushway, *Edward III and War at Sea*, 78–80; Rodger, *Safeguard of the Sea*, 97–8; Rose, *England's Medieval Navy*, 131.
59. Epstein, *Genoa and the Genoese*, 202–4; Rodger, *Safeguard of the Sea*, 97.
60. Allmand, *Hundred Years War*, 13; Curry, *Hundred Years' War*, 35.
61. Cushway, *Edward III and War at Sea*, 98.
62. Cushway, *Edward III and War at Sea*, 107; Rodger, *Safeguard of the Sea*, 99–100.
63. Allmand, *Hundred Years War*, 13–14; Curry, *Hundred Years' War*, 36.
64. Cushway, *Edward III and War at Sea*, 112; Rodger, *Safeguard of the Sea*, 100–2.
65. Curry, *Hundred Years' War*, 37; Cushway, *Edward III and War at Sea*, 113.
66. Cushway, *Edward III and War at Sea*, 121; Rodger, *Safeguard of the Sea*, 102; Rose, *Medieval Naval Warfare*, 60.
67. Cushway, *Edward III and War at Sea*, 122; Lambert, *Shipping the Medieval Military*, 136–40; Rose, *England's Medieval Navy*, 39.
68. Cushway, *Edward III and War at Sea*, 120–3.
69. Rogers, *War Cruel and Sharp: English Strategy under Edward III, 1327–1360* (Woodbridge, 2000), 217–19.
70. Froissart, *Chronicles*, 70–6. See also Cushway, *Edward III and War at Sea*, 124; Rodger, *Safeguard of the Sea*, 103.

71. Froissart, *Chronicles*, 77–96. See also Rogers, *War Cruel and Sharp*, 238–72.
72. Froissart, *Chronicles*, 68–9. See also Rogers, *War Cruel and Sharp*, 249.
73. Cushway, *Edward III and War at Sea*, 125.
74. Rogers, *War Cruel and Sharp*, 273.
75. Froissart, *Chronicles*, 101.
76. Rogers, *War Cruel and Sharp*, 276.
77. Froissart, *Chronicles*, 97. See also Rogers, *War Cruel and Sharp*, 273.
78. Cushway, *Edward III and War at Sea*, 126.
79. Cushway, *Edward III and War at Sea*, 125–6; Rodger, *Safeguard of the Sea*, 103.
80. Cushway, *Edward III and War at Sea*, 127; Rodger, *Safeguard of the Sea*, 103; Rose, *Medieval Naval Warfare*, 60–1.
81. Allmand, *Hundred Years War*, 16; Curry, *Hundred Years' War*, 41.
82. Cushway, *Edward III and War at Sea*, 128; Rogers, *War Cruel and Sharp*, 278–82.
83. Cushway, *Edward III and War at Sea*, 129; Rogers, *War Cruel and Sharp*, 283.
84. Allmand, *Hundred Years War*, 16; Cushway, *Edward III and War at Sea*, 131.
85. Froissart, *Chronicles*, 111.
86. Curry, *Hundred Years' War*, 41.
87. Cushway, *Edward III and War at Sea*, 134; Rodger, *Safeguard of the Sea*, 103–4.
88. Froissart, *Chronicles*, 113–14; Geoffrey le Baker, *Chronicon*, 109. See also Cushway, *Edward III and War at Sea*, 136–7.
89. Froissart, *Chronicles*, 115.
90. Cushway, *Edward III and War at Sea*, 134.
91. Froissart, *Chronicles*, 115.
92. Ibid., 116.
93. Cushway, *Edward III and War at Sea*, 138.
94. Froissart, *Chronicles*, 116. See also Cushway, *Edward III and War at Sea*, 138–9.
95. Froissart, *Chronicles*, 116.
96. Ibid., 117.
97. Froissart, *Chronicles*, 117–18. See also Cushway, *Edward III and War at Sea*, 139–40; Rose, *England's Medieval Navy*, 134.
98. Cushway, *Edward III and War at Sea*, 140.
99. Geoffrey le Baker, *Chronicon*, 111. See also Rose, *England's Medieval Navy*, 133–4.
100. Rodger, *Safeguard of the Sea*, 104; Rose, *Medieval Naval Warfare*, 66–7.
101. Rodger, *Safeguard of the Sea*, 104.
102. Cushway, *Edward III and War at Sea*, 142.
103. Allmand, *Hundred Years War*, 17; Curry, *Hundred Years' War*, 43.
104. Curry, *Hundred Years' War*, 45.
105. Cushway, *Edward III and War at Sea*, 170–1.
106. Curry, *Hundred Years' War*, 45.
107. Allmand, *Hundred Years War*, 20–1; Curry, *Hundred Years' War*, 45–6; P. Linehan, 'Castile, Navarre and Portugal', in *New Cambridge Medieval History*, VI, *c.1300–c.1415*, ed. M. Jones (Cambridge, 2000), 619–50.
108. Allmand, *Hundred Years War*, 21–2; Curry, *Hundred Years' War*, 46.
109. Allmand, *Hundred Years War*, 23; Cushway, *Edward III and War at Sea*, 186.
110. Cushway, *Edward III and War at Sea*, 186–7.
111. Rose, *England's Medieval Navy*, 166.
112. Rodger, *Safeguard of the Sea*, 109; Linehan, 'Castile, Navarre and Portugal', 640.
113. Curry, *Hundred Years' War*, 46; Cushway, *Edward III and War at Sea*, 192–3; Rodger, *Safeguard of the Sea*, 109.
114. Froissart, *Chronicles*, 181–2. See Allmand, *Hundred Years War*, 22–3; Curry, *Hundred Years' War*, 46–9.
115. Curry, *Hundred Years' War*, 49.
116. J. Sherborne, 'The Battle of La Rochelle and the War at Sea, 1372–5', *Bulletin of the Institute of Historical Research*, 42 (1969), 17–29, esp. 17.

117. Cushway, *Edward III and War at Sea*, 201.
118. Froissart, *Chronicles*, 182–6. See Curry, *Hundred Years' War*, 49; Cushway, *Edward III and War at Sea*, 201–2; Rodger, *Safeguard of the Sea*, 110; Rose, *England's Medieval Navy*, 134–6.
119. Rose, *Medieval Naval Warfare*, 70.
120. Froissart, *Chronicles*, 96–7. See Rodger, *Safeguard of the Sea*, 111; Rose, *England's Medieval Navy*, 166.
121. Rose, *Medieval Naval Warfare*, 70.
122. Rodger, *Safeguard of the Sea*, 112; Rose, *England's Medieval Navy*, 166–7.
123. Froissart, *Chronicles*, 211–30. See Allmand, *Hundred Years War*, 24; Rodger, *Safeguard of the Sea*, 114.
124. Curry, *Hundred Years' War*, 49–50.
125. Allmand, *Hundred Years War*, 25.
126. Ibid., 24.
127. Curry, *Hundred Years' War*, 52.
128. Froissart, *Chronicles*, 243–51. See also Curry, *Hundred Years' War*, 53.
129. Rodger, *Safeguard of the Sea*, 113.
130. Rodger, *Safeguard of the Sea*, 112; Rose, *Medieval Naval Warfare*, 71.
131. Allmand, *Hundred Years War*, 25–6; Curry, *Hundred Years' War*, 53.
132. Allmand, *Hundred Years War*, 23–7; Curry, *Hundred Years' War*, 54–6.
133. Allmand, *Hundred Years War*, 27–8; Curry, *Hundred Years' War*, 56.
134. *Gesta Henrici Quinti*, trans. F. Taylor and J. Roskell (Oxford, 1975), 20–3.
135. Allmand, *Hundred Years War*, 28; Curry, *Hundred Years' War*, 56–9.
136. Rodger, *Safeguard of the Sea*, 143–4; Rose, *England's Medieval Navy*, 137.
137. *Gesta Henrici Quinti*, 146–7.
138. Ibid., 146–9.
139. Ibid., 148–9.
140. *Gesta Henrici Quinti*, 161–7. See Rose, *England's Medieval Navy*, 138–9.
141. Antonio Morosini, *British Naval Documents 1204–1960*, eds Hattendorf, R. Knight, A. Pearsall, Rodger and G. Hill (Aldershot, 1993), no. 19, 30. See also Rodger, *Safeguard of the Sea*, 144; Rose, *England's Medieval Navy*, 138; *Medieval Naval Warfare*, 87.
142. Allmand, *Hundred Years War*, 28–30; Curry, *Hundred Years' War*, 60–6, 86–90; Rose, *Medieval Naval Warfare*, 82.
143. Allmand, *Hundred Years War*, 32–6; Curry, *Hundred Years' War*, 59–60.
144. Rose, *England's Medieval Navy*, 52–3; *Medieval Naval Warfare*, 88.
145. Rodger, *Safeguard of the Sea*, 117, 145.
146. Modern paraphrase of the Middle English quote from the *Libelle of Englyshe Polycye*, vv 7, 1.
147. Jean Froissart, *Chronicles*, 62.
148. Rodger, *Safeguard of the Sea*, 105.
149. Cushway, *Edward III and War at Sea*, 92.
150. Cushway, *Edward III and War at Sea*, 92; Rogers, *War Cruel and Sharp*, 190–2; Rose, *England's Medieval Navy*, 131.
151. Cushway, *Edward III and War at Sea*, 93; Lambert, *Shipping the Medieval Military*, estimated that the English fleet probably numbered 200 to 260 vessels at the time of the battle, 119–126.
152. Rogers, *War Cruel and Sharp*, 196.
153. Cushway, *Edward III and War at Sea*, 94; Rogers, *War Cruel and Sharp*, 193.
154. Cushway, *Edward III and War at Sea*, 94.
155. Froissart, *Chronicles*, 62.
156. Edward III, *British Naval Documents*, no. 14, 22.
157. Rodger, *Safeguard of the Sea*, 99.
158. Rose, *England's Medieval Navy*, 131.
159. *Le grandes chroniques de France*, ed. J. Viard (10 vols, Paris, 1937), IX, 184. See also Cushway, *Edward III and War at Sea*, 94; DeVries, 'God, Leadership, Flemings, and Archery: Contemporary Perceptions of Victory and Defeat at the Battle of Sluys, 1340', *American Neptune*, 55 (1995), 223–42, esp. 232–3; Rogers, *War Cruel and Sharp*, 195.

160. *Chronographia regum Francorum*, ed. H. Moranvillé (2 vols, Paris, 1897), II, 121–2. See English translation of appropriate passage in DeVries, 'God, Leadership, Flemings, and Archery', 232.
161. *Chronographia regum Francorum*, II, 123. See also Rogers, *War Cruel and Sharp*, 194–5.
162. Geoffrey le Baker, *Chronicon*, 68. See also Cushway, *Edward III and War at Sea*, 95.
163. Froissart, *Chronicles*, 62.
164. Ibid., 62–3.
165. Cushway, *Edward III and War at Sea*, 95–6.
166. Rodger, *Safeguard of the Sea*, 99.
167. Cushway, *Edward III and War at Sea*, 96.
168. Edward III, *British Naval Documents*, no. 14, 22.
169. Froissart, *Chronicles*, 63. See also Cushway, *Edward III and War at Sea*, 96–7; Rogers, *War Cruel and Sharp*, 195–6.
170. Geoffrey le Baker, *Chronicon*, 68. See also Runyan, 'Naval Power during the Hundred Years War', 65.
171. Curry, *Hundred Years' War*, 35.
172. Cushway, *Edward III and War at Sea*, 97.
173. Cushway, *Edward III and War at Sea*, 97; Rogers, *War Cruel and Sharp*, 196.
174. Cushway, *Edward III and War at Sea*, 94; Rogers, *War Cruel and Sharp*, 196.
175. R. Neillands, *The Hundred Years War* (London, 1990), 84. See also DeVries, 'God, Leadership, Flemings, and Archery', 224–5.
176. Froissart, *Chronicles*, 63–4; Geoffrey le Baker, *Chronicon*, 68–9. See also Cushway, *Edward III and War at Sea*, 98.
177. Froissart, *Chronicles*, 64.
178. DeVries, 'God, Leadership, Flemings, and Archery', 229; Rogers, *War Cruel and Sharp*, 197.
179. Froissart, *Chronicles*, 64. See also DeVries, 'God, Leadership, Flemings, and Archery', 224–5 (for the second and third redactions of Froissart); Rogers, *War Cruel and Sharp*, 197.
180. Edward III, *British Naval Documents*, no. 14, 22; Geoffrey le Baker, *Chronicon*, 69.
181. Cushway, *Edward III and War at Sea*, 100.
182. Edward III, *British Naval Documents*, no. 14, 22.
183. Geoffrey le Baker, *Chronicon*, 69. See also Rogers, *War Cruel and Sharp*, 97–8 and note 133.
184. Cushway, *Edward III and War at Sea*, 98.
185. Thomas of Burton, *Chronica monasterii de Melsa a fundatione usque ad annum 1396*, ed. E. Bonds (2 vols, Rolls Series, London, 1868), II, 45. See also DeVries, 'God, Leadership, Flemings, and Archery', 226.
186. Cushway, *Edward III and War at Sea*, 98–9.
187. Cushway, *Edward III and War at Sea*, 99; Rogers, *War Cruel and Sharp*, 197–8.
188. Rodger, *Safeguard of the Sea*, 99; Rose, *England's Medieval Navy*, 133.

Chapter 10. The German Hanse: Martial Merchants of the Baltic

1. P. Dollinger, *The German Hansa*, trans. D. Ault and S. Steinberg (Stanford, 1970), xvii; T. Lloyd, *England and the German Hanse, 1157–1611* (Cambridge, 1991), 1, 7.
2. Dollinger, *German Hansa*, xix.
3. *Hansisches Urkundenbuch*, in Dollinger, *German Hansa*, doc. 26, 411–12.
4. Dollinger, *German Hansa*, xx.
5. Ibid., xvii.
6. Ibid., 144.
7. Helmold of Bosau, *Chronica Slavorum*, in Dollinger, *German Hansa*, doc 1, 379–80.
8. Dollinger, *German Hansa*, 19–26; Lloyd, *England and the German Hanse*, 4.
9. Dollinger, *German Hansa*, 28–38; Lloyd, *England and the German Hanse*, 5, 9.
10. Dollinger, *German Hansa*, 8–9, 41–2; Ellmers, 'Cog as Cargo Carrier', 39–40.
11. Ellmers, 'Cog as Cargo Carrier', 37–8; Lloyd, *England and the German Hanse*, 5–6; Paine, *Sea and Civilization*, 332.
12. D. Meier, *Seafarers, Merchants and Pirates in the Middle Ages* (Woodbridge, 2006), 136.

13. Dollinger, *German Hansa*, 39.
14. O. Crumlin-Pedersen, 'The Vikings and the Hanseatic merchants: 900–1450', in *A History of Seafaring based on Underwater Archaeology*, ed. Bass (London, 1972), 181–204, esp. 189.
15. Dollinger, *German Hansa*, 46.
16. Ibid., 46–7.
17. Meier, *Seafarers, Merchants and Pirates*, 119–21.
18. Dollinger, *German Hansa*, 35–42; Rose, *England's Medieval Navy*, 174.
19. Dollinger, *German Hansa*, 64, 101–2.
20. Ibid., xviii.
21. Dollinger, *German Hansa*, 87–8; Lloyd, *England and the German Hanse*, 8.
22. Dollinger, *German Hansa*, 31.
23. Ibid., 63–4.
24. Ibid., 24.
25. Lloyd, *England and the German Hanse*, 4.
26. Dollinger, *German Hansa*, 144.
27. Haywood, *Dark Age Naval Power*, 35–6; P. Marsden, 'Ships of the Roman period and after in Britain', in *History of Seafaring*, 113–32, esp. 122–3; Unger, *Ship in the Medieval Economy*, 60–1.
28. Ellmers, 'Cog as Cargo Carrier', 29–30; Runyan, 'Cog as Warship', 47–50.
29. Crumlin-Pedersen, 'Vikings and the Hanseatic merchants', 199–203; K. Slaski, 'The Hanse Ships', in *Europe of the North Sea and the Baltic: The World of the Hanse*, ed. A. d'Haenens (Antwerp, 1984), 157–71.
30. Ellmers, 'Cog as Cargo Carrier', 40.
31. Ellmers, 'Cog as Cargo Carrier', 35–6; Lloyd, *England and the German Hanse*, 4; Crumlin-Pedersen, 'Vikings and the Hanseatic merchants', 189–90.
32. Runyan, 'Cog as Warship', 47.
33. Ibid.
34. Ibid., 50.
35. Slaski, 'Hanse Ships', 160.
36. Dollinger, *German Hansa*, 141–2; Ellmers, 'Cog as Cargo Carrier', 37–8; Runyan, 'Cog as Warship', 47–8.
37. Ellmers, 'Cog as Cargo Carrier', 38–9; Runyan, 'Cog as Warship', 48.
38. Rose, *England's Medieval Navy*, 174.
39. Crumlin-Pedersen, 'Vikings and the Hanseatic merchants', 190–1; Runyan, 'Cog as Warship', 50.
40. Ellmers, 'Cog as Cargo Carrier', 43–4.
41. Dollinger, *German Hansa*, 143.
42. Ibid., 147.
43. Dollinger, *German Hansa*, 147; Ellmers, 'Cog as Cargo Carrier', 44–5; Slaski, 'Hanse Ships', 162–3.
44. Dollinger, *German Hansa*, 142; Ellmers, 'Cog as Cargo Carrier', 45.
45. B. Bange, 'The Caravel', in *Sailing into the Past*, 87–8; Friel, 'Carrack', 80; *Good Ship*, 177–8; Slaski, 'Hanse Ships', 164.
46. Dollinger, *German Hansa*, 48–9; doc 4, 383.
47. Bill, 'Scandinavian Warships and Naval Power in the Thirteenth and Fourteenth Centuries', in *War at Sea in the Middle Ages*, 35–51, esp. 47; Dollinger, *German Hansa*, 49; Ellmers, 'Cog as Cargo Carrier', 43.
48. Dollinger, *German Hansa*, 38.
49. Ibid., 67.
50. Ibid., 67–8.
51. Ibid., 68–9.
52. 'Confederation of Cologne', in Dollinger, *German Hansa*, doc 7, 385–6.
53. Ibid., doc 7, 386.
54. Dollinger, *German Hansa*, 69–70.
55. Ibid., 70–1.

56. Dollinger, *German Hansa*, 78–9; Meier, *Seafarers, Merchants and Pirates*, 146; M. Pitcaithly, 'Piracy and Anglo-Hanseatic Relations, 1385–1420', in *Roles of the Sea in Medieval England*, 125–45, esp. 129–30; Rose, *England's Medieval Navy*, 175; *Medieval Naval Warfare*, 72–3.
57. Detmar of Lübeck, *Chronicle of Lübeck*, translated by Meier, in *Seafarers, Merchants and Pirates*, 146.
58. Meier, *Seafarers, Merchants and Pirates*, 147; Pitcaithly, 'Piracy and Anglo-Hanseatic Relations', 130.
59. Dollinger, *German Hansa*, 79.
60. Meier, *Seafarers, Merchants and Pirates*, 150.
61. Dollinger, *German Hansa*, 79–80; Meier, *Seafarers, Merchants and Pirates*, 149.
62. Meier, *Seafarers, Merchants and Pirates*, 150–2.
63. Dollinger, *German Hansa*, 80; Meier, *Seafarers, Merchants and Pirates*, 150–2; Pitcaithly, 'Piracy and Anglo-Hanseatic Relations', 130.
64. Meier, *Seafarers, Merchants and Pirates*, 154; Pitcaithly, 'Piracy and Anglo-Hanseatic Relations', 130.
65. Meier, *Seafarers, Merchants and Pirates*, 147.
66. Dollinger, *German Hansa*, 80–1; Meier, *Seafarers, Merchants and Pirates*, 152–3; Pitcaithly, 'Piracy and Anglo-Hanseatic Relations', 130–1; Rose, *England's Medieval Navy*, 175.
67. Meier, *Seafarers, Merchants and Pirates*, 154–7.
68. Ibid., 157–9.
69. Pitcaithly, 'Piracy and Anglo-Hanseatic Relations', 133–4.
70. Lloyd, *England and the German Hanse*, 112–13; Pitcaithly, 'Piracy and Anglo-Hanseatic Relations', 134–5.
71. Dollinger, *German Hansa*, 35, 284, 292–3; Pitcaithly, 'Piracy and Anglo-Hanseatic Relations', 136.
72. Dollinger, *German Hansa*, 257–8.
73. Ibid., 295–6.
74. Dollinger, *German Hansa*, 296; Lloyd, *England and the German Hanse*, 132–3.
75. Dollinger, *German Hansa*, 296.
76. Lloyd, *England and the German Hanse*, 134.
77. Dollinger, *German Hansa*, 296.
78. Lloyd, *England and the German Hanse*, 135.
79. Dollinger, *German Hansa*, 296–7.
80. Ibid., 297–8.
81. Lloyd, *England and the German Hanse*, 174.
82. Dollinger, *German Hansa*, 300.
83. Ibid., 297.
84. Lloyd, *England and the German Hanse*, 174–5.
85. Dollinger, *German Hansa*, 300; Lloyd, *England and the German Hanse*, 175.
86. Rose, *Medieval Naval Warfare*, 93.
87. Lloyd, *England and the German Hanse*, 142–55; Pitcaithly, 'Piracy and Anglo-Hanseatic Relations', 141–2.
88. Robert Wenyngton, *British Naval Documents*, no. 20, 30. See also Rodger, *Safeguard of the Sea*, 150; Rose, *Medieval Naval Warfare*, 94–5.
89. Dollinger, *German Hansa*, 303; Lloyd, *England and the German Hanse*, 180–1.
90. Robert Wenyngton, *British Naval Documents*, no. 20, 30. See also Rose, *Medieval Naval Warfare*, 94–5.
91. Lloyd, *England and the German Hanse*, 181.
92. Dollinger, *German Hansa*, 303; Lloyd, *England and the German Hanse*, 181–2.
93. Lloyd, *England and the German Hanse*,195; Rose, *Medieval Naval Warfare*, 95.
94. Lloyd, *England and the German Hanse*, 139–40.
95. Dollinger, *German Hansa*, 306; J. Fudge, *Cargoes, Embargoes, and Emissaries: The Commercial and Political Interaction of England and the German Hanse, 1450–1510* (Toronto, 1995), 51–5, 60; Lloyd, *England and the German Hanse*, 201–2.

96. Dollinger, *German Hansa*, 306; Fudge, *Cargoes, Embargoes, and Emissaries*, 68; Lloyd, *England and the German Hanse*, 203–4.
97. Dollinger, *German Hansa*, 307; Fudge, *Cargoes, Embargoes, and Emissaries*, 68.
98. Fudge, *Cargoes, Embargoes, and Emissaries*, 69–70.
99. Fudge, *Cargoes, Embargoes, and Emissaries*, 69–70; Lloyd, *England and the German Hanse*, 207.
100. Fudge, *Cargoes, Embargoes, and Emissaries*, 70.
101. Lloyd, *England and the German Hanse*, 207.
102. Caspar Weinreich, *Danzig Chronicle*, in Dollinger, *German Hansa*, doc 12, 393. See also Dollinger, *German Hansa*, 308; Fudge, *Cargoes, Embargoes, and Emissaries*, 71.
103. Dollinger, *German Hansa*, 308; Fudge, *Cargoes, Embargoes, and Emissaries*, 70.
104. Fudge, *Cargoes, Embargoes, and Emissaries*, 71–2; Lloyd, *England and the German Hanse*, 208.
105. Caspar Weinreich, *Danzig Chronicle*, in Dollinger, *German Hansa*, doc 12, 393. See also Dollinger, *German Hansa*, 308; Fudge, *Cargoes, Embargoes, and Emissaries*, 72–3; Rose, *England's Medieval Navy*, 175.
106. Fudge, *Cargoes, Embargoes, and Emissaries*, 73.
107. Dollinger, *German Hansa*, 309; Fudge, *Cargoes, Embargoes, and Emissaries*, 73–6; Lloyd, *England and the German Hanse*, 209–16; Rose, *Medieval Naval Warfare*, 96.
108. Lloyd, 'A Reconsideration of two Anglo-Hanseatic Treaties of the Fifteenth Century', *English Historical Review*, vol. 102, no. 405 (1987), 916–33, esp. 930; Rose, *Medieval Naval Warfare*, 96.
109. Dollinger, *German Hansa*, 331–6, 372–3; Meier, *Seafarers, Merchants and Pirates*, 145.
110. Dollinger, *German Hansa*, 312–15.
111. Ibid., 343.
112. Ibid., 369.
113. Dollinger, *German Hansa*, 346; Meier, *Seafarers, Merchants and Pirates*, 145.
114. Dollinger, *German Hansa*, 351.
115. Ellmers, 'Cog as Cargo Carrier', 46.
116. Dollinger, *German Hansa*, 362–9.
117. Bange, 'The Caravel', 88–90; Dollinger, *German Hansa*, 142, 305; Slaski, 'Hanse Ships', 164.
118. Dollinger, *German Hansa*, 308; Ellmers, 'Cog as Cargo Carrier', 45; Fudge, *Cargoes, Embargoes, and Emissaries*, 71.
119. Fudge, *Cargoes, Embargoes, and Emissaries*, 71.
120. Ibid., 71–3.
121. Dollinger, *German Hansa*, 308.
122. Dollinger, *German Hansa*, 276; Fudge, *Cargoes, Embargoes, and Emissaries*, 73.
123. Caspar Weinreich, *Danzig Chronicle*, in Dollinger, *German Hansa*, doc. 12, 393.
124. Dollinger, *German Hansa*, 308.
125. Fudge, *Cargoes, Embargoes, and Emissaries*, 73.
126. Bange, 'Caravel', 90; Fudge, *Cargoes, Embargoes, and Emissaries*, 73–4; Rose, *Medieval Naval Warfare*, 95–6.

Conclusion: Transition to the Modern Era

1. Doukas, *Decline and Fall of Byzantium to the Ottoman Turks*, trans. Magoulias (Detroit, 1975), 194–9 and notes 233–4 on 304; Michael Kritovoulos, *History of Mehmed, Conqueror*, trans. C. Riggs (Princeton, 1954), 18–22. See also Norwich, *Byzantium, The Decline and Fall* (London, 1995), 414–15; Treadgold, *History of the Byzantine State*, 798–9 and note 10 on 966.
2. Doukas, *Decline and Fall of Byzantium*, 199.
3. Ibid.
4. Doukas, *Decline and Fall of Byzantium*, 200–1. See also Norwich, *Byzantium, Decline and Fall*, 415.
5. Guilmartin, *Gunpowder & Galleys*, 18–20.
6. Doukas, *Decline and Fall of Byzantium*, 200 and note 238 on 305.
7. Kritovoulos, *History of Mehmed the Conqueror*, 43.
8. Doukas, *Decline and Fall of Byzantium*, 201.
9. Ibid., 207.

10. Kedar, 'Prolegomena to a World History of Harbour and river Chains', in *Shipping, Trade and Crusade in the Medieval Mediterranean*, 3–37, esp. 5–6 and fig. 1.1 on 7.
11. Doukas, *Decline and Fall of Byzantium*, 214–15, and notes 271–2 on 311; Kritovoulos, *History of Mehmed the Conqueror*, 55–7. See also Norwich, *Byzantium, Decline and Fall*, 427.
12. Treadgold, *History of the Byzantine State*, 799–800.
13. Dotson, 'Foundations of Venetian Naval Strategy', 124.
14. Haji Khalifeh, *The History of the Maritime Wars of the Turks*, trans. J. Mitchell (London, 1831), 20–1.
15. Guilmartin, *Gunpowder & Galleys*, 102–3.

Selected Bibliography

The following list contains in shortened form those works considered most useful for scholars, students or simply those with an abiding interest who wish to pursue the subject further. It is by no means complete, for such a compilation would fill an entire volume. Many of the noted references, however, provide full bibliographies to facilitate additional research. An unabridged bibliography along with the unedited endnotes for this book is available at: http://www.cantab.net/users/charles.stanton/Charles_Stanton/Charles_D._Stanton.html

Primary Sources

Abbo of St-Germain-des-Prés, *Viking Attacks on Paris: Bella parisiacae urbis*, trans. N. Dass (Leuven, 2007).
Al-Baladhuri, *The Origins of the Islamic State*, trans. P. Hitti (New York, 1916).
Albert of Aachen, *Historia Ierosolimitana*, trans. S. Edgington (Oxford, 2007).
Amari, M., ed., *Biblioteca Arabo-Sicula* (2 vols, Turin, 1880–1).
Amatus of Montecassino, *The History of the Normans*, trans. P. Dunbar (Woodbridge, 2004).
Ambroise, *The History of the Holy War*, trans. M. Ailes and M. Barber (2 vols, Woodbridge, 2003).
Andrea Dandolo, *Chronica Per Extensum Descripta*, ed. E. Pastorello (RIS, vol. XII, Bologna 1938–42).
Anglo-Saxon Chronicles, trans. M. Swanton (London, 1996).
Anna Comnena, *The Alexiad of Anna Comnena*, trans. E. Sewter (London, 1969).
Annals of Ulster (To A.D. 1131), ed. and trans. S. Mac Airt and G. Mac Niocaill (Dublin, 1983).
Ari Thorgilsson, *Íslendingabók – Kristni Saga*, trans. S. Grønlie (London, 2006).
Bernardo Maragone, *Gli annales Pisani di Bernardo Maragone*, ed. M. Gentile (RIS, Bologna, 1936).
Bernat Desclot, *Chronicle of the Reign of King Pedro III of Aragon*, trans. F. Critchlow (Princeton, 1928).
British Naval Documents, 1204–1960, ed. J. Hattendorf et al. (Aldershot, 1993).
Caffaro, *Annales Ianuenses*, eds L. Belgrano and C. Imperiale di Sant'Angelo (5 vols, FSI, Genoa, 1890–1929).
Carolingian Chronicles, trans. B. Scholz (Ann Arbor, 1972).
Constantine VII Porphyrogenitus, *De Administrando Imperio*, ed. G. Moravcsik (Wash. D.C., 1967).
Edbury, P., ed., *The Conquest of Jerusalem and the Third Crusade*, (Aldershot, 1998).
Fulcher of Chartres, *A History of the Expedition to Jerusalem, 1095–1127*, trans. F. Ryan (Knoxville, 1969).
Geoffrey Malaterra, *The Deeds of Count Roger of Calabria and Sicily*, trans. K. Wolf (Ann Arbor, 2005).
Gesta Henrici Quinti: The Deeds of the Henry the Fifth, trans. F. Taylor and J. Roskell (Oxford, 1975).
Haji Khalifeh, *The History of the Maritime Wars of the Turks*, trans. J. Mitchell (London, 1831).
History of William Marshal, trans. A. Holden, S. Gregory, D. Crouch (3 vols, London, 2004).
Ibn al-Athir, *Chronicle of Ibn al-Athir, Crusading Period, Pts I-3*, trans. D. Richards (3 vols, Aldershot, 2006).
Ibn-al-Qalanisi, *The Damascus Chronicle of the Crusades*, trans. H. Gibb (London, 1967).
Ibn Jubayr, *The Travels of Ibn Jubayr (Rihla)*, trans. R. Broadhurst (London, 1952).
Jean Froissart, *Chronicles*, trans. G. Brereton (London, 1968).
John Kinnamos, *Deeds of John and Manuel Comnenus*, trans. C. Brand (New York, 1976).
John Skylitzes, *A Synopsis of Byzantine History 811–1057*, trans. J. Wortley (Cambridge, 2010).
Leo VI, *Taktika*, trans. G. Dennis (Washington, D.C., 2010).
Leo the Deacon, *The History of Leo the Deacon*, trans. A. Talbot and D. Sullivan (Wash. D.C., 2005).

Loud, G., ed., *Roger II and the Creation of the Kingdom of Sicily (Selected Sources)* (Manchester, 2012).
Liudprand of Cremona, *The Works of Liudprand of Cremona*, trans. F. Wright (London, 1930).
Marino Sanudo Torsello, *The Book of the Secrets of the Faithful of the Cross*, trans. P. Lock (Farnham, 2011).
Matthew Paris, *English History: from the year 1235 to 1273*, trans. J. Allen (3 vols, London, 1852–4).
Michael of Rhodes, *Book of Michael of Rhodes*, eds P. Long, D. McGee and A. Stahl (3 vols, Cambridge, 2009).
Nicholson, H., ed., *The Chronicle of the Third Crusade* (Aldershot, 1997).
Nikephoros, Patriarch of Constantinople, *Short History*, trans. C. Mango (Washington, D.C., 1990).
Niketas Choniates, *O City of Byzantium, Annals of Niketas Choniates*, trans. H. Magoulias (Detroit, 1984).
Otto of Freising, *The Deeds of Frederick Barbarossa*, trans. C. Mierow (New York, 1953).
Peters, E., ed., *Christian Society and the Crusades*, 1198–1229 (Philadelphi, 1948).
Procopius, *History of the Wars*, trans. H. Dewing (4 vols, London, 1916).
Ramon Muntaner, *The Chronicle of Muntaner*, trans. Lady Goodenough (2 vols, London, 1920–1).
Raymond of Aguilers, *Historia Francorum*, trans. J. Hill and L. Hill (Philadelphia, 1968).
Robert of Clari, *The Conquest of Constantinople*, trans. E. McNeal (New York, 1936).
Roger of Howden, *The Annals of Roger de Hoveden*, trans. H. Riley (2 vols, London, 1853).
Roger of Wendover, *Flowers of History*, trans. J. Giles (2 vols, London, 1849).
Rose, S., ed., *The Navy of the Lancastrian Kings* (London, 1982).
Russian Primary Chronicle, trans S. Cross and O. Sherbowitz-Wetzor (Cambridge, Mass., 1953).
Sagas of the Icelanders, A Selection, Intro. R. Kellogg, trans. various (New York, 2000).
Sagas of Ragnar Lodbrok, trans. B. Waggoner (New Haven, 2009).
Shaw, M., ed., *Chronicles of the Crusades* (London, 1963).
Shirley, J., ed., *Crusader Syria in the Thirteenth Century*, trans. J. Shirley (Farnham, 1999).
Snorre Sturlason, *Heimskringla*, trans. E. Monsen and A. Smith (Cambridge, 1932).
'Templar of Tyre', *Part III of the 'Deeds of the Cypriots'*, trans. P. Crawford (Farnham, 2003).
Theophanes, *The Chronicle of Theophanes Confessor*, trans. C. Mango and R. Scott (Oxford, 1997).
Vegetius, *Epitome of Military Science*, trans. N. Milner (Liverpool, 1993).
William of Apulia, *La Geste de Robert Guiscard*, trans. M. Mathieu (Palermo, 1961).
William of Tyre, *A History of Deeds Done beyond the Sea*, trans. E. Babcock and A. Krey (2 vols, New York, 1943).

Secondary Sources

Abulafia, D., *The Two Italies* (Cambridge, 1977).
Abulafia, D., *Italy, Sicily and the Mediterranean, 1100–1400* (London, 1987).
Abulafia, D., *The Western Mediterranean Kingdoms 1200–1500* (London, 1997).
Abulafia, D., *The Great Sea: A Human History of the Mediterranean* (London, 2011).
Ahrweiler, H., *Byzance et la mer: la marine de guerre* (Paris, 1966).
Allmand, C., *The Hundred Years War, England and France at War c.1300–c.1450* (Cambridge, 1988).
Asbridge, T., *The Crusades* (New York, 2010).
Bass, G., ed., *History of seafaring based on underwater archaeology* (London, 1972).
Bass, G. and F. van Doorninck, *Yassi Ada: A Seventh-Century Byzantine Shipwreck* (College Station, 1982).
Bass, G. et al., eds, *Serçe Limani: An Eleventh-Century Shipwreck* (College Station, 2004).
Bennett, J., *Sailing into the Past: Learning from Replica Ships* (Annapolis, 2009).
Trim, D. and M. Fissel, eds, *Amphibious Warfare 1000–1700* (Leiden, 2011).
Bennett, M. et al., eds, *Fighting Techniques of the Medieval World, AD 500–AD 1500* (New York, 2005).
Hattendorf, J. and R. Unger, eds, *War at Sea in the Middle Ages and Renaissance* (Woodbridge, 2003).
Brooks, F., *English Naval Forces 1199–1272* (London, 1932).
Brown, R., *The Normans and the Norman Conquest* (2nd edn., Woodbridge, 1985).
Byrne, E., *Genoese Shipping in the Twelfth and Thirteenth Centuries* (Cambridge, 1930).
Casson, L., *Ships and Seamanship in the Ancient World* (Princeton, 1971).
Chalandon, F., *Histoire de la Domination Normande en Italie et en Sicile* (2 vols, Paris, 1907).

Curry, A., *The Hundred Years' War* (Oxford, 2002).
Cushway, G., *Edward III and the War at Sea: The English Navy, 1327–1377* (Woodbridge, 2011).
DeVries, K. and R. Smith, *Medieval Military Technology* (Toronto, 2012).
Dollinger, P., *The German Hansa*, trans. D. Ault and S. Steinberg (Stanford, 1971).
Epstein, S., *Genoa and the Genoese, 958–1528* (Chapel Hill, 1996).
Fahmy, A., *Muslim Sea Power in the Eastern Mediterranean* (London, 1950).
Keen, M., ed., *Medieval Warfare*, (Oxford, 1999).
Flatman, J., *Ships and Shipping in Medieval Manuscripts* (London, 2009).
Friel, I., *The Good Ship: Ships, Shipbuilding and Technology in England 1200–1520* (Baltimore, 1995).
Gabrieli, F., ed., *Arab Historians of the Crusades*, trans. E. Costello (Turin, 1957).
Gardner, R. and R. Unger, eds, *Cogs, Caravels and Galleons: The Sailing Ship 1000–1650* (London, 1994).
Gertwagen, R. and E. Jeffreys, eds, *Shipping, Trade and Crusade* (Farnham, 2012).
Goitein, S.D., *A Mediterranean Society* (6 vols, Berkeley and Los Angeles, 1967–93).
Gorski, R., ed., *Roles of the Sea in Medieval England* (Woodbridge, 2012).
Guilmartin, J., *Gunpowder and Galleys* (Cambridge, 2003).
Kagay, D. and L. Villalon, eds, *The Circle of War in the Middle Ages* (Woodbridge, 1999).
Haldon, J., *Warfare, State and Society in the Byzantine World 565–1204* (Abingdon, 1999).
Hattendorf, J. and R. Unger, eds, *War at Sea in the Middle Ages and the Renaissance* (Woodbridge, 2003).
Haywood, J., *Dark Age Naval Power* (London, 1991).
Heywood, W., *A History of Pisa, Eleventh and Twelfth Centuries* (Cambridge, 1921).
Hitti, P., *History of the Arabs* (New York, 1937, revised 2002).
Hooper, N. and M. Bennett, *Cambridge Illustrated Atlas: Warfare – The Middle Ages* (Cambridge, 1996).
Hutchinson, G., *Medieval Ships and Shipping* (London, 1994).
Jones, G., *A History of the Vikings* (Oxford, 1984).
Lambert, C., *Shipping the Medieval Military* (Woodbridge, 2011).
Lane, F., *Venetian Ships and Shipbuilders of the Renaissance* (Baltimore, 1934).
Lane, F., *Venice, A Maritime Republic* (Baltimore, 1973).
Lewis, A., *Naval power and trade in the Mediterranean, A.D. 500–1100* (Princeton, 1951).
Lewis, A. and T. Runyan, *European Naval and Maritime History, 300–1500* (Bloomington, 1985).
Madden, T., *Venice: A New History* (New York, 2012).
Mahan, A., *The Influence of Sea Power upon History, 1660–1783* (London, 1890).
Manfroni, C., *Storia della Marina italiana* (3 vols, Livorno, 1897–1902).
Meier, D., *Seafarers, Merchants and Pirates in the Middle Ages*, trans. A. McGeoch (Woodbridge, 2006).
Morrison, J., *Greek and Roman Oared Warships 399–30 B.C.* (Oxford, 1996).
Morrison, J., J. Coates and N. Rankov, *The Athenian Trireme* (Cambridge, 2000).
Mott, L., *Sea Power in the Medieval Mediterranean: The War of the Sicilian Vespers* (Gainesville, 2003).
Nicholson, H., *Medieval Warfare: Theory and Practice of War in Europe, 300–1500* (New York, 2004).
Paine, L., *The Sea and Civilization: A Maritime History of the World* (New York, 2013).
Pirenne, H., *Mohammed and Charlemagne*, trans. B. Miall (New York, 1992).
Pitassi, M., *The Navies of Rome* (Woodbridge, 2009).
Pryor, J., *Commerce, Shipping and Naval Warfare in the Medieval Mediterranean* (London, 1987).
Pryor, J., *Geography, technology, and war* (Cambridge, 1988).
Pryor, J., ed., *Logistics of Warfare in the Age of the Crusades* (Aldershot, 2006).
Pryor, J. and E. Jeffreys, *The Age of ΔΡΟΜΩΝ, The Byzantine Navy ca 500–1204* (Leiden, 2006).
Riley-Smith, J., *The Crusades, A History* (New Haven, 2005).
Rodger, N., *The Safeguard of the Sea, A Naval History of Britain 660–1649* (London, 1997).
Roesdahl, E., *The Vikings*, trans. S. Margeson and K. Willliams (2nd edn, London, 1998).
Rogers, C., ed., *Oxford Encyclopedia of Medieval Warfare and Military Technology* (3 vols, Oxford, 2010).
Rodgers, W., *Naval Warfare under Oars, 4th to 16th Centuries* (Annapolis, 1940).
Rose, S., *Medieval Naval Warfare, 1000–1500* (London, 2002).
Rose, S., ed., *Medieval Ships and Warfare* (Aldershot, 2008).

Rose, S., *England's Medieval Navy 1066–1509* (Barnsley, 2013).
Sawyer, P., ed., *The Oxford Illustrated History of the Vikings* (Oxford, 1997).
Stanton, C., *Norman Naval Operations in the Mediterranean* (Woodbridge, 2011).
Treadgold, W., *A History of the Byzantine State and Society* (Stanford, 1997).
Unger, R., *The Ship in the Medieval Economy, 600–1600* (London, 1980).
Verbruggen, J., *The art of Warfare in Western Europe during the Middle Ages* (Amsterdam, 1977).

Index

In that this work covers the entirety of the Middle Ages (500–1500), its index could theoretically be quite large and unwieldy for the topic at hand. Accordingly, it will be limited to maritime-pertinent persons and places as well as ships, shipboard weaponry and sea battles.